Intellectual Property in Common Law and Civil Law

Intellectual Property in Common Law and Civil Law

Edited by

Toshiko Takenaka

University of Washington School of Law, USA

Edward Elgar

Cheltenham, UK • Northampton, MA, USA

Published by
Edward Elgar Publishing Limited
The Lypiatts
15 Lansdown Road
Cheltenham
Glos GL50 2JA
UK

Edward Elgar Publishing, Inc.
William Pratt House
9 Dewey Court
Northampton
Massachusetts 01060
USA

Reprinted 2013

A catalogue record for this book
is available from the British Library

Library of Congress Control Number: 2012943538

This book is available electronically in the ElgarOnline.com
Law Subject Collection, E-ISBN 978 0 85793 437 6

FSC www.fsc.org MIX Paper from responsible sources FSC® C013056

ISBN 978 0 85793 436 9

Typeset by Servis Filmsetting Ltd, Stockport, Cheshire
Printed and bound in Great Britain by T.J. International Ltd, Padstow

Contents

PART IV TRADEMARK AND UNFAIR COMPETITION

PART V ENFORCEMENT AND INFRINGEMENT REMEDIES

PART VI LEGAL ASPECTS COMMON TO ALL BRANCHES OF IP

PART VII APPENDIX

Contributors

Martin J. Adelman, Professor of Law, George Washington University Law School, USA

Theo Bodewig, Professor of Law, Humboldt University, Berlin, Germany

Gail E. Evans, Reader in Intellectual Property Law, Queen Mary University of London, UK

Mario Franzosi, Partner, Avvocati Associati Franzosi Dal Negro Pensato Setti, Italy

Shubha Ghosh, Professor of Law, University of Wisconsin Law School, USA

Sang Jo Jong, Professor of Law, Seoul National University School of Law and Director of the SNU Center for Law & Technology, South Korea

Jan Krauß, Partner, Boehmert & Boehmert, Munich, Germany; Lecturer, University of Washington School of Law, USA

Mary LaFrance, Professor of Law, William S. Boyd School of Law, University of Nevada, Las Vegas, USA

Amy L. Landers, Professor of Law, University of the Pacific McGeorge School of Law, USA

Salil Mehra, Professor of Law, Temple University, Beasley School of Law, USA

Signe H. Naeve, Lecturer, University of Washington School of Law, USA

Frédéric Pollaud-Dulian, Professor of Law, Panthéon-Sorbonne University, France

Christoph Rademacher, Assistant Professor, Waseda Institute for Advanced Study, Japan

Yves Reboul, Professor of Law, University of Strasbourg, France

Brad Sherman, Professor of Law, Law School, Griffith University, Australia

Joseph Straus, Professor of Law, Universities of Munich and Ljubljana, NIPMO-UNISA Chair for Intellectual Property, University of South Africa (UNISA), Pretoria and Emeritus Director, Max Planck Institute for Intellectual Property and Competition Law, Munich, Germany

Mira T. Sundara Rajan, Honorary Member, Magdalen College, Oxford University, UK

Toshiko Takenaka, Professor of Law, University of Washington School of Law, USA

Marketa Trimble, Associate Professor of Law, William S. Boyd School of Law, University of Nevada, Las Vegas, USA

Preface

This book is the result of collaborations between European and Asian scholars who participated in a ten-year project co-sponsored by the Research Center for the Legal System of Intellectual Property (RCLIP) (http://www.21coe-win-cls.org/rclip/e_index.html) at Waseda Law School in Tokyo, Japan and the Center for Advanced Study and Research on Intellectual Property (CASRIP) (http://www.law.washington.edu/Casrip/) at the University of Washington, School of Law (UWLS) in Seattle, Washington, U.S.A. I had the pleasure of working with Professor Ryu Takabayashi, Director of RCLIP, and his colleagues when I taught comparative IP classes at Waseda Law School as a visiting professor from 2004 to 2011. RCLIP received funding from the Japanese government to develop a database on IP cases from major jurisdictions in Asia and Europe (http://www.globalcoe-waseda-law-commerce.org/rclip/db/search_form.php). By making the database publicly accessible free of charge and by sponsoring a number of conferences, RCLIP promoted a comparative law study of IP among not only Japanese scholars but also IP professionals and scholars in other Asian countries and Europe.

CASRIP co-sponsored many such conferences with RCLIP in both Tokyo and Seattle and contributed articles and book chapters for publication based on these conferences. It also translated more than 1500 cases from France, Germany, Italy and Spain and collected approximately 400 cases from India and the U.K. by working with scholars from these countries. These cases have been incorporated into the RCLIP IP case law database. Through discussions with scholars from various countries, I identified many aspects of IP systems that are deeply influenced by common law and civil law traditions. Thus, this book discusses these aspects and examines whether such aspects should remain diverged despite increasing efforts in world harmonization, or whether they should find a common ground for further harmonization.

Many of the contributors in this book are RCLIP database contributors who collected cases from the country of their expertise and/or are speakers for the conferences co-sponsored by CASRIP and RCLIP. Throughout the years, while working on the development of the database, I have formed friendships with the contributors and learned from them about their IP systems. The database project and the CASRIP-RCLIP collaboration will celebrate its tenth anniversary in April 2013. As a memento of the celebration, I asked my friends and colleagues to write an essay on the issues I identified as being influenced by common law and civil law traditions. I am very pleased and proud to share our experiences and research results with the readers of this book.

Before concluding this preface, I would like to thank my colleague, Professor Ryu Takabayashi, for giving me the opportunity to participate in the database project. With his leadership and guidance, the database started as a collection of cases from Asian countries and then expanded to collect cases from Europe. Now, CASRIP is planning to collect cases from Russia, Brazil and South Africa and looks forward to working with scholars in these jurisdictions for the next decade. Moreover, I would like to thank all the contributors and my research assistants, UWLS JD students who edited book chapters, particularly, Mr. Hiroshi Okazawa, Mr. Koji Tauchi and Mr. Yoshinari Oyama, UW IP Law & Policy LL.M. graduates and CASRIP visiting scholars, who oversaw the entire editing process. Finally, I would like to thank my husband, Hisato, for his forbearance and continuous support for my work.

Toshiko Takenaka

PART I

Introduction

1. Towards a history of patent law

Brad Sherman

I. INTRODUCTION

Patent history is a subject that is still largely waiting to be written. Potentially, a history of 'patents' encompasses a number of different factors including patent administration, the professionals that work within the patent system, and the concepts, rules, and procedures that make up and inform patent law. There are also a number of different approaches that could be taken when writing a patent history ranging from comparative examinations and sector specific studies through to more political or theoretically informed histories.

To date, the bulk of the scholarship that has looked at the history of patents has focused on the patent system as an economic tool and on the role that the patent system plays in stimulating (or hindering) research and development. Until recently, most historical accounts have tended to see patents as instruments that are broadly adaptable to economic forces, and whose internal tensions and inconsistencies can be deciphered as effects of conflicts and shifts in economic interests. While this instrumentalist vision has produced some engaging historical accounts of the political and economic effect of patents there has, at least until recently, been much less attention given to the *legal* aspects of patents. It is as if lawyers were embarrassed by their own discipline: that they were more concerned to speak the language of economists, social scientists and policy makers than they were their own. The lack of attention given to the legal history of patents is particularly notable if we contrast existing historical scholarship on patent law with equivalent work in respect to copyright law, which has blossomed over the last 20 or so years into a serious and well developed area of study. The lack of attention that has been given to the legal history of patents is particularly ironic given that many of the rules of patent law are, despite their forward looking aspirations, applied retrospectively: patent law is, in this sense, inherently historical.

To the extent that scholars have looked at the history of patent law, they have been concerned with a number of shared questions and concerns. One of the most pervasive themes that has underpinned historical writing on patent law has been a search for origins. While scholarly accounts about the emergence of patent law have taken a number of forms, typically the legal origins of patents are traced back to one of three sources. In some cases, the patent system is linked back to late mediaeval Venice, where privileges were granted to the inventors or entrepreneurs of useful devices or techniques from the fourteenth century onwards.[1] Because the earliest grants made no real distinction between inventors and entrepreneurs, the tendency is now to shift the point of origin forwards to the fifteenth century, when the newly-acquired prestige of painters and engineers began to rub off on inventors, encouraging their recognition as the creators of technical artifacts.[2] In other instances, (and this is particularly the case in common law countries), patent law is traced back to the 1624 *Statute of Monopolies.* In other instances, patent law is traced back to international treaties, notably the 1883 Paris Convention or in the case of specific aspects of patent law treaties such as the 1977 *Budapest Treaty on the International Recognition of the Deposit of Microorganisms for the Purposes of Patent Procedure.* In addition to these attempts to find the legal or legislative roots of patent law, there have also been attempts to write the history of patent law through the lens of specific organizing principals; whether it be overarching normative principals (often drawn from political philosophy) or more home grown explanations (such as the information function of the patent system).

While there is no denying the heuristic value of these ways of thinking about patent law, particularly when explaining patent law to students or when making policy arguments, in this chapter I wish to revisit the search for origins that dominates the way that we think about the history of patent law. This particular history is based upon two ideas. The first is that it is wrong to see patent law as if it reflects some pre-ordained natural ordering or as if it was governed by a teleology of function. It is also based on the idea that patent law cannot be reduced to simple economic norms, to a specific philosophical positioning, or to a set of higher order principals. In this sense, the chapter is based on the idea that in thinking about the history of patent law, it is important that we should de-naturalize patent law and show that what are often taken as constructs of nature or

---

[1] Frank D. Prager, 'A history of intellectual property from 1545–1787' (1944) 26 Journal of the Patent Office Society 711.

[2] Pamela O. Long, *Invention, Authorship, 'Intellectual Property', and the Origins of Patents: Notes Toward a Conceptual History* (1991) 32 *Technology and Culture* 846.

as timeless inevitable truths are, in fact, the products of a complex and changing alloy of circumstances, practices and habits.

The second idea that underpins this chapter is the belief that when writing a history of patent law as a search for origins it is important to pause and consider: what is meant by 'patent law'? While many histories work on the assumption that patent law is an almost timeless entity that has always existed, albeit in a nascent and emerging form, this chapter is based on the belief that if we suspend our modern preoccupations and let the law speak for itself, a different and somewhat more perplexing picture emerges. If we look at the experience in the United Kingdom, which is the focus of this chapter, an argument can be made that patent law, at least in the sense that we understand it today, did not come into existence until the middle part of the nineteenth century. While there was general acceptance about certain things, such as the possibility of recognizing property rights in intangibles and general agreement about the image of the invention,[3] patent law did not emerge as a separate, discreet and accepted category of law until mid-way through the nineteenth century. Prior to this, there was no law of patents in the sense that we understand and recognize today. Moreover, while it is possible to recognize aspects of patent law in the eighteenth and early nineteenth centuries, these were not given any particular priority. Instead, they were placed alongside and given more or less equal weight to concepts, modes of organization and ways of thinking which, to our modern eyes, are distinctly alien and pre-modern. One of the problems with many of the historical accounts that search for the origins of patent law is that they downplay or ignore these possibilities. By selectively choosing what is read and examined, and by interpreting historical materials in a way that confirms these preoccupations, these histories lose sight of the fact that there were a number of different paths that the law could have followed: the modern patent system that we have inherited was only one of them. Seeing patent law in this way not only opens up new ways of thinking about patent history, it also leads us to question some of the assumptions that underpin the way that we think about patent law. It also enables us to understand some of our contemporary preoccupations and concerns.

---

[3] See Alain Pottage and Brad Sherman, *Figures of Invention* (2011).

II. THE EMERGENCE OF MODERN PATENT LAW

Patent law did not emerge as a discrete and recognizable area of law in the UK until midway through the nineteenth century.[4] Prior to this, there was a sense of openness, fluidity, and uncertainty about the content, shape and nature of the law. Indeed, one of the findings of the 1829 *Select Committee on Patents* was the level of uncertainty and confusion that existed in the law at the time. One area where this was particularly notable was in relation to the type of things that could be patented. Given the important role that subject matter plays in demarcating and defining legal categories, the lack of clarity about what could and could not be patented meant that it was very difficult to define the parameters of the nascent 'patent law' (if it could be called this at the time). These problems were compounded by the fact that patent claims were vague and general (making it difficult to ascertain the scope of what was protected). There was also widespread uncertainty about the purpose and requirements of the patent documentation more generally and the role that this played in demarcating and defining the interests that were protected. These problems were compounded by the haphazard registration system that undermined the faith in issued patents, at least until they were validated by the courts (which was itself a haphazard and uncertain process).

Prior to the emergence of patent law in the middle of the nineteenth century, the law was not only fluid, open and disorganized, there were also competing suggestions as to how the law that granted property rights in scientific and technical inventions should be organized. This was because no one mode of organization, no single way of thinking had yet come to dominate as *the* mode of organization. Instead, there were various competing suggestions as to how the law might (or should) be organized. One example was the proposal to establish a 'law of form', which would have focused on the external appearance and shape of objects (and expressly would have included subject matter now in patents, design and copyright).[5] Another approach was to do away with the now familiar patent-copyright-design style approach and to divide productions of the mind into 'two great classification – works (whatever their intention) addressed to the tastes, passion and existing circumstances of the age, and this adapted to all the fluctuations of society'.[6] Another option proposed

---

4 While this chapter focuses on British patent law, the arguments are directly relevant in many colonies and indirectly relevant in many other countries.

5 T. Turner, *On Copyright in Design* (1849), 12.

6 M. Leverson, *Copyright and Patents: or, Property in Thought* (1854).

that the law should be organized so as 'to contract the limits of utility in form till nothing visible were left'.[7] Yet another approach would have seen that patent law was subsumed within a new area of law to be called the 'Law of Arts and Manufacture'. While these different ways of categorizing the law may now seem somewhat foreign and alien, it is important to keep in mind that at the time these different approaches were treated seriously.

The highly contingent and open nature of the law was also reflected in the way that treatises were organized, committees structured, and reports written. The fluid and open nature of the pre-1850 law was also reflected in the language that was used: commentators regularly spoke of copyright in inventions, patents for art, universal patents for authors, and patents for copyright or patterns. The uncertain and open standing of the law was summed up by the fact that although patents had been granted in one form or another by the Crown for over two centuries, it was said in 1835 that 'there existed no law of patents'.[8]

Despite the uncertain and open nature of the law, by the middle part of the nineteenth century, an important transformation had taken place: there was a much clearer idea as to the nature of patent law, what its main elements were, and where its boundaries were to be drawn. While the process was gradual, haphazard and incomplete, by the 1850s (or thereabouts) patent law had emerged as a separate and distinct area of law replete with its own logic and grammar.[9]

A range of different factors facilitated the emergence of patent law in the UK. In the early part of the nineteenth century, a growing concern with the state of British industry led to calls for reform and improvements in the patent system. In response to the growing calls for reform, in 1829 Thomas Lennard called on Parliament to establish a Select Committee to inquire into the state of patent law.[10] While the Select Committee proved inconclusive, nonetheless it played an important role in bringing about the emergence of modern patent law: it exposed the confused and uncertain nature of the law and also drew together many of the divergent criticisms that existed at the time. More significantly, the evidence of witnesses as to their understandings of the law provided the materials for the processes of reformulation that were to take place over the next two decades.

The first attempt to rectify the many grievances that the Select Committee had identified occurred when Richard Godson, who was

---

7 T. Turner, *On Copyright in Design* (1849), 49–50.

8 Mr Tooke, 'Letters Patent' (13 Aug 1835) 30 *Hansard* col 466.

9 Notably, the invention came to function as the common denominator that ensured that linked the rules of patent law.

10 (9 April 1829) 21 *Hansard* col. 598.

author of one of the earliest treatises on patent law, introduced a Bill to Parliament in 1831.[11] After this Bill was rejected, Godson introduced further Bills that again met with opposition from many of those who advocated reform. As compensation for proposing the postponement of Godson's Bill, Lord Chancellor Brougham promised to 'devote his attention, as early as possible, to the branched of the law to which it related'.[12] While Godson's Bill had directly confronted many of the problems which were identified in the 1829 Select Committee, Lord Brougham's efforts, which culminated in the passage of the 1835 *Act to Amend the Law Touching Letters Patent for Inventions*, were much more modest in scope. Notably, while Lord Brougham had promised to consider 'whole-sale changes', his Act only introduced two significant reforms: to allow for amendment of the patent specification and for extensions of the patent term beyond the fourteen years then permitted.[13]

Given, as the *London Journal of Arts and Sciences* put it, 'excepting numerous technical amendments, Brougham's Bill does not embrace any improvements',[14] it is unsurprising that further efforts were made to reform the law. What is surprising was the way in which the calls for reform of the patent system slowly became subsumed within more radical proposals for the introduction of a general law to promote arts and manufacture in the UK. These suggestions for a law of arts and manufactures (which is similar, in many respects, to the more modern idea of industrial property law), were perpetuated and accentuated by the 1836 *Select Committee on Arts and Manufacturers*, which was set up to inquire into 'the best means of extending the knowledge of the arts and of the principles of design among the people (especially the manufacturing population) of the country'.[15] The clearest example of a general law of arts and manufactures can be seen in the Bills which William Mackinnon and Edward Baines presented to Parliament in 1837,[16] 1837–8[17] and

---

11 R. Godson (9 July 1831) 29 *Hansard* col. 383; 2 PP 177.

12 Quoted in M. Coulter, *Property in Ideas: The Patent Question in Mid-Victorian Britain* (1991), 36.

13 *An Act to Amend the Law Touching Letters Patent for Inventions* 5 & 6 Wm. IV c. 83 (1835) (1835 Lord Brougham's Act). See C. Drewry, *The Patent Law Amendment Act* (1838).

14 J. Schroder, 'Observations on Mr Mackinnon's Bill' (1837) 10 *The London Journal of Arts and Sciences*, 109.

15 1836 *Select Committee on Arts and Manufacturers*.

16 (14 Feb. 1837) 36 *Hansard* col. 554; 1837 *Bill to Amend the Practice relating to Letters Patent for Inventions, and for the Better Encouragement of the Arts and Manufactures* (15 Feb. 1837) 3 PP 315.

17 1837–8 Bill (No. 71) *For the Better Encouragement of the Arts and*

1839.[18] Unlike Godson's Bills, which were primarily seen as patent bills which also proposed amendments to the law in relation to patterns, Mackinnon and Baines' Bills were specifically called *Bills for the Better Encouragement of the Arts and Manufactures*. Moreover, their emphasis was not so much upon patents and designs, as on the promotion of arts and manufacture more generally. As with the various efforts to reform patent law, these failed.

While the various attempts to reform and codify the law that took place in the early part of the nineteenth century and the Select Committees and commentaries that these prompted were unsuccessful, nonetheless they still played an important role in the emergence of patent law. This was because in reforming the law and drafting legislation it was necessary to consider what patent law looked like and ascertain what this abstract category included and excluded. For example, in carving out a separate domain for patent law from the proposed law of arts and manufactures, it was necessary to have an idea of what patent law was, where its boundaries lay, and how it differed from other forms of protection. Moreover, the process of drafting patent bills and legislation had the effect of concretizing ideas, of forcing commentators to determine in more detail the nature of the law.[19] For example, one of the features of the Bill produced by Godson in 1831 was that it set out to clarify the meaning of the word 'manufacture'. When combined with the 1829 *Select Committee on Patents*, where attempts were made to produce statutory formulations of existing judicial practice and to provide rational definitions of what was a 'patentable invention', these efforts played a crucial role in the crystallization of patent law as a separate area of law. Although these processes were presented as if they were reducing the pre-existing law to a codified form, given that patent law did not exist in any recognizable form at the time it is more accurate to say that they were creating rather than finding the law.

One of the notable features of these attempts to outline the nature and limits of this nascent patent law was the positive role that was played by foreign patent systems. While present-day commentators often boast about the insularity of patent law in the UK, it is clear that foreign patent laws played an important role in the crystallization of British patent law. As John Farey, civil engineer and scientific investigator of the pencil,

---

Manufactures, and Securing to Individuals the Benefit of their Inventions for a Limited Time (1837–8) 1 PP 27.

[18] 1839 *Bill for the Better Encouragement of Arts and Manufactures, and Securing to Individuals the Benefit of their Inventions for a Limited Time* (19 Feb. 1839) 4 PP 363.

[19] R. Godson (9 July 1833) 15 *Hansard* col. 976.

said when presenting the patent laws of the United States (which somewhat oddly had been re-translated into English from an official French version), France, Belgium Austria and Spain to the 1829 *Select Committee on Patents*, these laws 'are very superior to our system, and will be useful to study as models', these were 'not to be adopted exactly for this country; but a selection of some articles (with such modifications as our different state of commerce and manufacture require) would serve as guides for us'.[20]

The emergence of patent law as a distinct area of law was also prompted by the growth of design law and the registration of inventions as designs that took place after 1839. This process began when, inspired by French law, a desire developed for British design law to be simplified and consolidated. To this end, the 1839 *Design Legislation* was passed. Unlike previous legislation (such as the 1787 *Calico Printers Act*), which had focused on specific types of designs, the 1839 Act potentially applied to *all* designs. Despite the innovative nature of the 1839 Act, it was quickly replaced by two new acts: the 1842 *Ornamental Designs Act* and the 1843 *Utility Designs Act*. In one sense it was odd that legislation intended to simplify and consolidate the law was divided into the two separate acts. The reason for this was that the new legislation was responding to the (now) familiar problem of the overlap of different rights. This had arisen because as the 1839 *Designs Act* provided protection to *all* articles of manufacture, it potentially protected things that were expected to be protected by patent. This gave rise to a concern that the wrong types of things were being protected under the wrong type of law. The process of abstraction and consolidation which took place under the 1839 Act meant that the law had to draw lines between the subject matter of letters patent and that of design law.[21] At the time, the problems were magnified because there was no clear sense about the shape of the overlapping categories (designs had taken shape, but not yet patents). These problems were compounded by the unsatisfactory state of the patent system and by the fact that patent administration was convoluted, expensive and uncertain.

The technique that was used to differentiate patent and design protection was to identify the nature of the interests that were protected by

---

[20] J. Farey, 1829 *Select Committee on Patents* 132. Numerous references were made in the Report of the Committee to foreign patent laws, to how they differed from and were better than British law. For example see the evidence of W. Wyatt, 119; Millington (on France), 98–9; J. Hawkins (US), 125.

[21] Similar problems occurred with the 1842 *Ornamental Designs Act* in respect of copyright.

each of the areas of law. Drawing on a developing jurisprudence which suggested that patents protected things such as mechanical action, principle, contrivance or application as well as the use, purpose, or result of particular objects, it was agreed that the defining characteristics of patent protection was a concern with the *utility* of inventions. While patent law was said to be concerned with articles of manufacture, the subject of design protection was thought to lie in the external form of the object.[22] In short, the defining characteristic of patent law was thought to be a shared concern with utility, whereas the organizing principle of property in design was with the form that objects took. The utility/form distinction helped to distinguish things that were protected by patents from those protected by designs. Nonetheless, a problem remained unanswered: namely, what was to happen in the case of objects such as paddle wheels or railway sleepers where the utility of the object lay in its form? Ultimately, this problem was resolved bureaucratically: by setting fees in a way that dissuaded 'patents' from being protected as designs, and by placing controls on how applications were drafted. The overlap that occurred as a result of the abstract nature of the 1839 *Design Act* not only led to the crystallization of design law, it also served to focus attention on the ambit of the subject matter protected by patent law. Moreover, as with the examples offered by foreign patent laws, the formation of design law also provided a point of reference from which patent law could be contrasted.

As with other areas of intellectual property law, the appearance of specialist treatises which set out to explain the law (as distinct from the earlier more polemical tracts and pamphlets) also played an important role in shaping patent law. This was because the production of a text required the law to be reduced to writing and in so doing to a particular format. Indeed, as Collier said in his *Essay on the Law of Patents* (1803), he aimed to arrange the subject of enquiry with accuracy and to detail the leading principles applicable to them in the respective divisions where they were proposed.[23] While the treatises which were produced at the time, which do not differ that much from contemporary textbooks, were presented as if they were finding the law or reducing it to a coherent set of principles, they played a much more creative role than is often recognized.

While the growing importance of treatises, the various efforts to reform the law, along with the public debates, Select Committees and Reports

---

22 This was revisited in the US with design patents and oddly, plant patents in the late nineteenth and early twentieth centuries.

23 J. Collier, *An Essay on the Law of Patents* (1803), vi–vii.

that these spawned all played their part in the emergence of patent law, nonetheless the most important role was played by the judiciary.[24] Prompted by changing attitudes towards technology and science, which were influenced by the growing professionalization of the scientific community, the courts helped to clarify the scope and meaning of the subject matter protected. More specifically, building upon earlier decisions such as *Boulton and Watt v Bull*,[25] *R v Arkwright*[26] and *Hornblower v Bull*,[27] the courts clarified the extent to which principles as well as improvements or patents of addition could be patented. Perhaps the most important judicial intervention of the period came with the 1842 decision of *Crane v Price* which settled the question as to whether a method or process as distinct from the thing produced could be the valid subject matter of a patent.[28] Hindmarch went so far as to suggest that it was not until *Crane v Price* was handed down that patentees were fairly sure of what the courts meant by a manner of new manufacture: the definition of the subject matter for which the grant of patents was permitted by the 1624 *Statute of Monopolies*.[29]

The upshot of these decisions, which were reported and discussed in the growing number of treatises and specialist periodicals on patent law and reinforced by the rise of specialist patent agents who understood both the requirements of the courts and the subject matter protected, was that the nature of patent law came to be defined more clearly. Webster captured this situation when he said of his first work on patents written in 1839 that 'it was of a smaller size and character than perhaps would have been advisable'. As he said, this was because 'I found the state of the law, on many points, in so much uncertainty that I thought it would not be prudent to do much more than to present the practical forms with notes, and a very general review and outline of principles.' While in his earlier work he found the law uncertain and ambiguous, in 1849 Webster was able to say 'that the law has from the number of fresh cases latterly become a good deal more settled . . . I think that the principles of the law are pretty well

---

24 W. Carpmael, 'Introductory Observations of the Law of Patents for Inventions' (1835), 70; E. Hulme, 'Privy Council Law and Practice of Letters Patent for Inventions from the Restoration to 1794' (1917) 33 *LQR* 180.

25 (1795) 126 ER 651.

26 (1785) 1 *Web Pat Cas* 64; *Dav Pat Cas* 61.

27 (1799) 101 *ER* 1285.

28 (1842) 134 *ER* 239. See also *Hill v Thompson* (1818) 129 *ER* 427; *Morgan v Seaward* (1836) 150 *ER* 874.

29 W. Hindmarch, *Law and Practice of Letters Patent for Inventions* (1848), 84; *An Act Concerning Monopolies and Dispensations with Penal Laws and Forfeitures Thereof* 21 Jac. I c. 3 (1624).

settled now'[30] – a point which was reiterated by a number of other commentators at the time.

While the close relationship between the patent system and the royal prerogative made reform of patent law a slow and complicated process, nonetheless it was clear by the 1850s that modern patent law began to be perceived and presented as a separate and defined area of law. Importantly, the law that took shape at the time carried with it a number of traits that shaped and continue to shape patent law. Although numerous examples could be given, I wish to focus here on those characteristics that played a role not only in moulding patent law but also in demarcating patent law from the other categories of intellectual property law.

One characteristic that helped to differentiate patents from the other forms of protection was the subject matter that patent law protected, or more accurately the image that developed as to what patent law ought to protect. While it was acknowledged that patent law extended to include a range of inventions (from the trivial to the more important) it was asserted that patent protection should be reserved for what were taken to be the more deserving inventions. This meant that so-called trivial inventions such as weighing machines and kaleidoscopes did not belong in patent law but instead deserved their own form of protection: namely, utility design protection.

Hand-in-hand with the growing perception that patents ought to be reserved for more important inventions was the belief that patents were intended to promote the introduction of new trades and manufactures. For example, speaking of the statutory basis of the patent monopoly it was said that it may be 'fairly inferred that it is not the manufacture, but the manufacturing, which appears to be contemplated. It is the opening of a new channel of industry, the establishment of a new trade, the beneficial employment of capital and labour in a new direction, that is intended to be promoted.'[31] While patents were granted for the creation or production of products per se, designs presupposed and required the existence of manufactured products: they were in this sense both derivative and secondary. This not only reinforced the separation of patents from designs, it also led to design law being subjugated to what was taken to be the more important and superior patent law. The prioritization of patents over design, which matured into the false belief that patent law preceded and shaped

---

30 1849 *Report of the Committee Appointed by the Lords of the Treasure on the Signet and Privy Seal Office* 34 (Q. 720).

31 W. Spence, 'Patents as Channels of Industry' (1868) *TNAPSS* 256.

design law, was reinforced by an evolutionary view of history, which a number of commentators used to explain the law.

There are a myriad of other things that contributed to the emergence of modern patent law: the evolution of textual form of the patent specification and other figures of invention, the construction of bureaucratic archives and associated examination procedures, the development of technologies for the reproduction and communication of textual descriptions, and, more generally, a new quality of governmental attention to 'things'. It also depended on the development of a situation where technical ideas were able to be abstracted, visualized and reified as agents in their own right, as things that circulate independently of (human) bodies and without reference to the social status of their bearers or sponsors. As this particular way of organizing the law was utilized in textbooks, legislation, libraries and elsewhere it was entrenched and further reinforced. Once the shape and form of the law came to be accepted, it was quickly adopted as the only possible mode of organization.

The emergence of modern British patent law that occurred gradually and haphazardly across the middle part of the nineteenth century brought with it many changes. One change initiated by the emergence of patent law, that is particularly relevant here, is that it allowed commentators to begin to write histories of the law. Ignoring the openness and uncertainty that had characterized the law for so long, commentators began to search for the origins of the modern law (which was typically found in the 1624 *Statute of Monopolies* or in mediaeval Venice). Hand-in-hand with this search for origins, the formation of British patent law also saw the beginnings of the idea of the isolation and insularity of British law (and by inference common law based systems). This led to the familiar 'common law' 'civil law' caricatures, which tend to ignore the important points of connection and the sharing of concepts and ideas that occurred between common law and civil law countries.

Another change initiated by the emergence of patent law in the nineteenth century was in terms of the approach that was taken to the law. While one of the defining traits of pre-modern and early modern 'patent' law was a concern with self-styled metaphysical questions,[32] this way of thinking gradually disappeared over the course of the nineteenth century, where it was replaced by the language of political economy, utilitarianism and, over time, more modern variants. In so doing there was a shift away

[32] See *Folsom v Marsh* (1841) 9 F Cas 342, 344; M. Renouard, *Traite des brevets d'invention*, cited in Thomas Webster, *The Law and Practice for Letters Patent for Inventions* (1841).

from *a priori* discussions about things such as the nature of invention to a more consequentialist mode of thinking. Rather being concerned, for example, about questions such as 'what does it mean to invent a chemical invention?' or 'when is an invention reduced to practice?', discussions tended to shift to concerns about the impact that the grant of a chemical patent might have on industry. This way of thinking has also influenced the approach taken to patent history. At the same time, with the categories agreed upon, the role of the treatise writer was now relegated to one of filling the gaps, of placing new decisions and new technologies into pre-existing and accepted categories. While the sub-categories have changed, the more general categories have remained largely unchanged. While these particular ways of thinking about patent law and history have dominated for over a 150 years, there has been a recent return to something similar to the earlier style of thinking about patent history.[33] Although these new histories have already made important contributions to our knowledge of patent law, there is so much more that can and should be written about. Once we place the search for the origins of patent law in an historical context and accept that it too is the product of a specific set of circumstances, we open up a range of different possibilities. Whatever topic is chosen, if these recent studies are anything to go by, patent history has a promising future.

---

[33] See M. Biaglio, 'Patent Republic: Specifying Inventions, Constructing Authors and Rights' (2006) 73 *Social Research* 1129; 'From Print to Patents: Living on Instruments in Early Modern Europe, 1500–1800' (2006) 44 *History of Science* 139; O. Bracha, *Owning Ideas: A History of Anglo-American Intellectual Property* (S.J.D. Dissertation, Harvard Law School, 2005); M. Biaglio, P. Jaszi and M. Woodmansee (eds), *Making and Unmaking Intellectual Property* (2011).

PART II

Patents

2. *Ordre public* and morality issues in patent eligibility

Joseph Straus*

I. INTRODUCTION

Patents, as other intellectual property rights, are generally understood as an instrument of economic policy providing incentives for and rewarding a broad range of useful human activity. Despite this prevailing economic rationale, the roots of, the justification for, and some limitations of exploitation are reasoned ethically. Traditionally, ethical aspects in intellectual property rights have been discussed in the broad context of justification of these rights. Lockean theory of natural rights to the fruits of own's labour, the doctrine of intellectual property, as well as Hegel's personality justification, suggesting that the best way of progressing science and arts is to protect scientists and artists from theft, so as to become the basis for learning by others, are such examples.[1] Modern critics of intellectual property rights also put emphasis on ethical aspects when, for instance, claiming that increasing scope of patentable subject matter or legislatively creating new forms of abstract objects, such as plant variety rights, effectively constitutes the creation of capital, which has the danger that it can act as an enormous power resource for a select few.[2] Furthermore, a global protectionist scheme for intellectual property would help to promote the

* Dr. jur. Dres. h.c., Professor of Law (Universities of Munich and Ljubljana), NIPMO-UNISA Chair for Intellectual Property, University of South Africa (UNISA), Pretoria, Marshall B. Coyne Visiting Professor of International and Comparative Law, George Washington University Law School, Washington D.C., Emeritus Director at the Max Planck Institute for Intellectual Property and Competition Law, Munich.

[1] Cf. Straus, Joseph (2001), Intellectual Property Rights: Ethical Aspects, in Smelser, Neil J. and Paul B. Baltes (eds), International Encyclopaedia of the Social & Behavioural Sciences, Amsterdam-Paris-New York-Oxford-Shannon-Singapore-Tokyo, p. 7621.

[2] Drahos, Peter (1996), A Philosophy of Intellectual Property, Dartmouth, Aldershot, UK, p. 158.

formation of global faction, resulting in the danger of global rent seeking and perhaps providing temptation to multinational elites to increase their profits through the simple stratagem persuading a supranational body to elevate levels of protection for abstract objects already in existence.[3]

As the title of this contribution suggests, its task is a more limited one. It is primarily focussed on the impact of *ordre public* and morality on the eligibility of (certain) subject matter for patenting. However, it should be emphasized from the outset, that also in this narrower context, in which especially patent law is primarily understood and accepted as an instrument of technical and economic policy, it firmly forms part of the legal order. Consequently, patent law, as other laws, are subject to barriers inherent in the legal system, set by the Constitution, by public policy and by morals. These barriers exist in most countries, in legal orders of regional organizations of states, such as the European Union,[4] and international regional multinational treaties, such as the 1973 adopted Convention on the Grant of European Patents (European Patent Convention – EPC). As an example, Article 53 (a) of the EPC excludes from patentability inventions the commercial exploitation of which would be contrary to *ordre public* or morality.[5] These two general clauses were understood to constitute the necessary gates of entry for overriding social and ethical considerations into the patent law system, which is otherwise neutral in its judgement and entirely devoted to the technological appreciation of inventions.[6] Apart from the rules of Article 4^{quater} of the Paris Convention for the Protection of Industrial Property of 1883 (PC), which prevented the Member States of the Paris Union to exclude from patentability inventions whose commercialization was prohibited by law or administrative regulations,[7] prior to the adoption of the International Agreement on Trade Related Aspects of Intellectual Property Rights (TRIPS) in 1994, states and regional organizations of states were, in principle, free, whether and if and under which conditions and which subject matter and for what reasons would they exclude from patentability. The TRIPS Agreement with its mandatory patentability standards has introduced some impor-

---

[3] Drahos, Peter at p. 192.

[4] Cf. *infra* under Chapter III 'The European Situation'.

[5] Until the 2000 revision of the EPC, Article 53 (a) had excluded from the patentability generally 'inventions the publication or exploitation of which would be contrary to *ordre public* or morality'.'

[6] Cf. Beier, Friedrich-Karl and Joseph Straus (1986), Genetic Engineering and Industrial Property, Industrial Property 447 *et. seq* (at 448).

[7] Cf. Bodenhausen, G.H.C. (1967), Guide to the Application of the Paris Convention for the Protection of Industrial Property, Geneva, p. 65 *et seq.*

tant limitations in this respect in general, but also as far as conflicts with *ordre public* or morality are at hand.

II. THE TRIPS AGREEMENT AND ITS '*ORDRE PUBLIC*' AND 'MORALITY' CLAUSES

(i) General

Under Article 27 (2) of the TRIPS Agreement

> Members may exclude from patentability inventions, the prevention within their territory of the commercial exploitation of which is necessary to protect *ordre public* or morality, including to protect human, animal or plant life or health or to avoid serious prejudice to the environment, provided that such exclusion is not made merely because the exploitation is prohibited by their law.

Article 27 (2) TRIPS, thus, makes it clear that the Agreement itself does not impose the exclusion from patentability of inventions the commercial exploitation of which would contradict *ordre public* or morality, but only permits WTO Member States to provide for such exclusions in their national or regional legal instruments. However, the TRIPS Agreement makes such exclusions dependent on certain conditions. Consequently, the possibility of WTO Member States to exclude certain subject matter from patentability based on considerations of *ordre public* or morality has been limited and Article 27 (2) TRIPS now being the controlling mandatory international test standard.[8]

(ii) *Ordre Public*

As observed by *Pires de Carvalho*,[9] the TRIPS Agreement borrowed the term: '*ordre public* or morality', upon a proposal by the European Community,[10] from the text of the EPC. By adopting the notion of *ordre public* instead of 'public order' or 'public interest', the TRIPS Agreement

---

8 Cf. Rogge, Rüdiger (1998), Patente auf genetische Informationen im Lichte der öffentlichen Ordnung und der guten Sitten, 1998 GRUR 303 *et seq.* (at 303).

9 The TRIPS Regime of Patents Rights, 3rd ed., The Hague 2010, p. 297.

10 Supported also by Japan and developing countries (cf. Correa, Carlos M. (2007), Trade Related Aspects of Intellectual Property Rights – A Commentary on the TRIPS Agreement, Oxford, p. 287).

adopted a more narrow standard,[11] which the EPC modelled on Article 2 (a) of the Strasbourg Convention on the Unification of Certain Points of Substantive Law on Patents for Invention of 1963.[12] Thereunder the notion of *ordre public* comprises only the 'major principles of the legal order', such as the inviolability of human dignity and the right to life, physical integrity, and personal freedom, as for instance laid down in Article 2 (2) of the Basic Law (Constitution) of the Federal Republic of Germany.[13] Such principles are not necessarily infringed solely because exploitation of the invention is prohibited by law or administrative regulations. The European patent law harmonizers decided in favour of this narrow standard because it was not necessarily in the general interest to deny patentability in all cases where the exploitation of the invention concerned was prohibited, for instance under a foodstuff law allowing certain additives. The inventor of a new additive with possibly less harmful effects should indeed have the possibility of obtaining a patent since it is possible that the prohibition of exploitation may subsequently be removed.[14] Or

---

[11] Cf. Gervais, Daniel (2003), The TRIPS Agreement: Drafting History and Analysis, 2nd ed., London, p. 222.

[12] For the background to this provision and interpretation of the French term '*ordre public*' contained therein, cf. Pfanner, Klaus (1962), Vereinheitlichung des materiellen Patentrechts im Rahmen des Europarates, 1962 GRUR Int. 545 *et seq.* (at 547); and the same author, the same title, 1964 GRUR Int. 247 *et seq.* (at 248 and 249); further Rogge Rüdiger (1998), 1998 GRUR 303.

[13] Cf. German Federal Supreme Court (BGH), 18 October 1967, 48 BGHZ 327 (at 330); In its referral to the Court of Justice of the European Union of 17 December 2009 – *Neurale Vorläuferzellen*, the German BGH with reference to the established German case law and doctrine emphasizes that the fundamental principles of the legal order ('tragende Grundsätze der Rechtsordnung') are composed of the basics of the state, social and economic life in the Federal Republic of Germany and the essential constitutional principles, which make up the 'set in stone' ('unverrückbar') basis of the state and social life (2010 GRUR Int. 236, at 239); cf. also Moufang, Rainer (1991), in: Europäisches Patentübereinkommen – Münchner Gemeinschaftskommentar, 15th issue, Köln-Berlin-Bonn-München, Art. 53 EPC, marginal notes 30–31, who emphasizes that also the fundamental principles of international treaties by which the Contracting States to the EPC are bound, such as the European Convention on Human Rights (ECHR), are to be viewed as *ordre public*; see also Kraßer, Rudolf (2009), Patentrecht, 6th ed., Munich, pp. 252–3; Gervais, Daniel, op. cit., at p. 222, observes in this context: 'While public order may be defined as the maintenance of public safety, *ordre public* concerns the fundamentals from which one cannot derogate without endangering the institutions of a given society.'

[14] When the German law maker was implementing the Article 2 (a) rule of the Strasbourg Convention into the German Patent Act, the Statement of reasons of the Federal Government (Federal Government Publication 220/75 at p. 7), reflected exactly these arguments.

in more modern terms, even if the somatic cell gene therapy, or the use of human embryonic stem cells for curing Parkinson's disease may be prohibited for safety considerations today, which could be cleared by further scientific achievements and developments related to transfer vectors, etc., in for instance two or three or possibly only in five years, resulting in subsequent removal of those prohibitions, why should an inventor of suitable stem cells, or gene constructs respectively, not be granted a patent, but left empty handed and others allowed to use his/her invention for free after the removal of the ban. It would not only be unfair but also counterproductive in terms of providing incentives for the necessary investment into innovation. In the chosen construct, account is taken of the fundamental consideration that a patent does not afford its owner a positive right to use, but solely a right to prohibit.[15] It also should be added in this context that, for instance, in the respective German case law, the legality or morality of an invention has always been judged in respect of the *normally intended use* of the patented product or process and not on the simple possibility of misuse. Where a given product, for instance a toxic chemical substance, can be legally used as a pesticide, the fact that the same substance can also be used in warfare against human beings, and is indeed prohibited by international law, does not mean that it is excluded from patentability.[16]

Despite considerable consensus of states on what constitutes the fundamentals of a given society, thus its *ordre public*, the TRIPS Agreement has, for the first time in the history introduced some mandatory standards, that is imposing on WTO members that laws which

> protect human, animal or plant life or health or to avoid serious prejudice to the environment,

in principle form part of *ordre public*.

The wording of Article 27 (2) of the TRIPS Agreement, however, makes it also clear that WTO Members may invoke the exclusion of patentability on grounds of *ordre public* or morality only under certain conditions.

Firstly, and most importantly, exclusion from patentability of a specific invention is only allowed, if the commercial exploitation of that invention is prohibited in the territory of the respective Member.[17] As *Correa* has

---

[15] Cf. also Beier, Friedrich-Karl and Joseph Straus (1986), Industrial Property 449.

[16] Cf. German Federal Supreme Court (BGH) Judgement of 19 October 1971, 1972 GRUR 704 (707) – *Wasser-Aufbereitung*; cf. also the referral of BGH of 17 December 2009, 2010 GRUR Int. 236 (239) – *Neurale Vorläuferzellen*.

[17] Cf. Correa, Carlos M. at p. 291; Pires de Carvalho, Nuño at p. 298

observed, 'The obvious purpose of this condition is to prevent a situation in which an invention is declared non-patentable but its commercialization is permitted.'[18] As further observed by *Pires de Carvalho*, the phrase 'necessary to protect *ordre public* or morality' requires that a causal connection exists between the measure taken (exclusion from patentability) and the effect sought (protection of *ordre public* or morality).[19] According to *Pires de Carvalho*,[20] the application of Article 27 (2) TRIPS requires a two-step test based on two criteria available in the legal system of the WTO. As regards the *necessity* of excluding an invention from *commercial exploitation*, WTO Members must observe Article 2 (2) of the WTO Agreement on the Application of Sanitary or Phytosanitary Measures (the 'SPS' Agreement), which sets forth that:

> Members shall ensure that any sanitary or phytosanitary measure is applied only to the extent necessary to protect human, animal or plant, is based on scientific principles and is not maintained without sufficient scientific evidence.[21]

Only after that had been established, and evidence found that the exclusion of an invention from commercial exploitation *contributes* indeed to the protection of *ordre public* or morality, the second test has to be undertaken, namely whether *the necessity* exists to exclude an invention from patentability in order to prevent its commercial exploitation. For this second step, the yardstick, according to *Pires de Carvalho* is Article 2 of the WTO Agreement on Technical Barriers,[22] which requires that

> Members shall ensure that technical regulations are not prepared, adopted or applied with a view to or with the effect of creating unnecessary obsta-

('Exclusion from patentability must be preceded by exclusion from commercial exploitation, where exclusion from commercial exploitation is necessary to protect *ordre public* and morality.'); Straus, Joseph, Implications of the TRIPS Agreement in the Field of Patent Law, in: Beier, Friedrich-Karl and Gerhard Schricker (eds) (1996), From GATT to TRIPS – The Agreement on Trade Related Aspects of Intellectual Property Rights, Weinheim and New York, pp. 160 *et seq.* (at p. 182); Schatz, Ulrich and Dieter Stauder in: Singer, Margarete and Dieter Stauder (eds) (2010), Europäisches Patentübereinkommen, Kommentar, 5th ed. Cologne, Article 53, marginal note 43 (p. 175) and marginal note 55 (p. 177); implicitly also Gervais, Daniel at p. 223.

18 Id. at p. 291.

19 Pires de Carvalho, Nuño at p. 289.

20 Id. at pp. 209–10.

21 Annex 1A to the Marrakesh Agreement establishing the World Trade Organization.

22 Id.

> cles to international trade. For this purpose, technical regulations shall not be more trade-restrictive than necessary to fulfil a legitimate objective . . . (paragraph 2),

and that

> Technical regulations shall not be maintained if the [. . .] objectives can be addressed in a less trade-restrictive manner. (paragraph 3).

From the above *Pires de Carvalho* summarizes:

> In other words, if the objective of excluding the commercial exploitation of inventions in a certain field of technology can be achieved in a way that does not require excluding inventions from patentability, then that way should always be preferred.[23]

Finally, the last part of Article 27 (2) TRIPS, which reads:

> . . . provided that such exclusion[24] is not made merely because the exploitation is prohibited by domestic law.

requires that a Member may not base the exclusion from patentability on legal prohibitions unrelated to *ordre public* or morality.[25] In other words, whereas the prohibition of commercial exploitation is a basic precondition for the exclusion, it in itself is not sufficient, if it is not based on reasons routed in *ordre public* or morality.[26] This reflects the genuine understanding, derived already from Article 2 (a) of the Strasbourg Convention and similarly implemented in the second half-sentence of Article 53 (a) EPC,[27] of the European[28] and now also the global international law maker, that inventors may not be deprived of their rights if the exploitation of the invention at issue is prohibited by laws or regulations, which do not form part of the *ordre public*, that is, 'major principles of the legal order'. He or she, the inventor, should enjoy the fruits of their creative efforts if the prohibition of exploitation of the invention is subsequently removed, for

---

23 Id. at p. 210.

24 From patentability [J.S.].

25 Cf. also Correa, Carlos at p. 291; Gervais, Daniel at p. 223.

26 Cf. Gervais, Daniel at p. 223.

27 Which reads: '. . . such exploitation shall not be deemed to be so contrary merely because it is prohibited by law or regulation in some or all of the Contracting States'.

28 Cf. specifically Rogge, Rüdiger (1998), 1998 GRUR 303.

example as a result of new scientific findings, etc.[29] *Pires de Carvalho*, therefore, draws from Article 27 (2) TRIPS the practical consequence for the work of patent examiners, namely that they have, first, to check whether the law prohibits the commercialization of the claimed invention. If that is not the case, the usual patentability requirements are to be examined and the decision taken according to the results reached.[30] Arguing that the exploitation of an invention could be contrary to *ordre public* or morality even if such exploitation were allowed by specific laws,[31] implies the assertion that the laws at stake must be unconstitutional and/or immoral.[32]

(iii) Morality

Article 27 (2) TRIPS enumerates *ordre public* or morality as two seemingly independent standards for values, the protection of which allows, under the conditions discussed above, WTO Members to exclude from patentability inventions the commercial exploitation of which would violate either or both of them. The leading commentaries on TRIPS are quite short as regards the notion of morality. *Gervais* observes that morality is a different concept as compared with *ordre public* and that 'it seems to correspond to the French concept of '*bonnes mœurs*', further that 'it naturally depends to a certain degree on particular culture of a country or region'.[33] *Correa*, after having observed that there is no internationally accepted interpretation of the morality concept,[34] states that

---

29 See also Straus, Joseph (1995), Patenting Human Genes in Europe – Past Developments and Prospective for the Future, 26 IIC 920 *et seq.* (at 930–31).

30 Cf. Pires de Carvalho, Nuño at p. 300; and Straus, Joseph (1995), 26 IIC 933.

31 As argued by the Technical Board of Appeal of the European Patent Office (EPO) in a decision of 21 February 1995 (1995 OJ EPO 545 – *Plant Cells/Plant Genetic Systems*).

32 Cf. Straus, Joseph (1995), 26 IIC 931; and the critics of Rogge, Rüdiger (1998), 1998 GRUR 303; and Schatz, Ulrich, and Stauder, Dieter, op. cit., Article 53, marginal note 56 (p. 177).

33 Id. at p. 223.

34 Referring to the decision T 356/93 of the Board of Appeal of the EPO of 21 February 1995 (1995 OJ EPO 545 – *Plant Cells/Plant Genetic Systems*), and observing that the principles developed therein on the morality notion were not to be viewed as internationally accepted (op. cit., p. 288). In the referred decision, the Technical Board of Appeal held: 'The concept of *morality* is related to the belief that some behaviour is right and acceptable whereas other behaviour is wrong, this belief being founded on the totality of the accepted norms which are deeply rooted in a particular culture. For the purposes of the EPC, the culture in question is the culture inherent in European society and civilisation. Accordingly, under

> Morality judgements depend on the values prevailing in a particular society at particular time. Such values are not the same in different cultures and countries and change over time. Like '*ordre public*', morality is a vague and evolutive concept,[35] and their content will be dependent on national perception by patent offices or judges.[36]

In the German legal doctrine, the former Presiding Judge of the Federal Supreme Court *Rüdiger Rogge* emphasizes that the reference to the notion of morality was necessary to directionally regulate specifically not foreseeable variety of factual constellations. However, *Rogge* also points to the danger of such provisions being applied in a very subjective, eventually discretionary manner resulting in a disproportional loss of legal certainty.[37] It is, therefore, following *Rogge*, necessary to narrow down this provision according to its purpose and context. The notion of morality, which in German translation reads as 'gute Sitten', that is 'bonnes mœurs', refers, on the one hand to extra-legal ('außerrechtliche') principles, but on the other hand forms part of the legal order. Consequently, what is at hand, is to put in effect in a specific case the value standards ('Wertmaßstäbe'), which are anchored in the general legal order. A potential violation of the morality standard must be of such weight that it would justify an exception of the fundamentally existing claim or right to a patent. Prohibitions which are not anchored in statutory provisions, therefore, have to be essentially generally recognized as obligatory and have to be limited to elementary rules.[38]

III. EUROPEAN UNION

(i) General

As observed above,[39] Article 27 (2) of the TRIPS Agreement has been modelled on Article 53 (a) EPC. However, with the very essential difference that it does not exclude from patentability certain inventions based

---

Article 53(a) EPC, inventions the exploitation of which is not in conformity with the conventionally accepted standards of conduct pertaining to this culture are to be excluded from patentability as being contrary to morality.' (1995 OJ EPO 557).

35 In this context Correa refers to F. Pollaud-Dulian, La Brevabilité des Invention, Etude Comparative de Jurisprudence, France-OEB (1997: Paris, Le Droit des Affaires, No. 16), p. 166.

36 Correa, Carlos at p. 288.

37 1998 GRUR 304.

38 Rogge, Rüdiger (1998), 1998 GRUR 305; cf. also Kraßer, Rudolf at p. 256 with further references.

39 II. (ii).

on reasons of *ordre public* or morality, but only allows WTO Member States for such exclusions under certain conditions in national laws.

Article 53 (a) EPC, which reads in full

> European patents shall not be granted in respect of:
> (a) inventions the commercial exploitation of which would be contrary to '*ordre public*' or morality; such exploitation shall not be deemed to be so contrary merely because it is prohibited by law or regulation in some or all of the Contracting States.

has served also as point of departure when the Directive 98/44/EC of the European Parliament and of the Council of July 6, 1998 on the Legal Protection of Biotechnological Inventions (Directive)[40] was adopted. Prior to addressing the specific provisions of the Directive, which are directly linked to exclusions of inventions from patentability based on reasons of *ordre public* or morality, it should be emphasized that Article 27 (2) TRIPS is binding for the European Union as well as its Member States. Article 1 (2) of the Directive sets forth that the Directive shall be without prejudice to the obligations of the Member States pursuant to international agreements, and in particular the TRIPS Agreement[41] and the Convention on Biological Diversity. However, not only the EU Member States' obligations under the TRIPS Agreement are not affected by the Directive, this equally applies to the obligations of the European Union itself. In its judgement of October 18, 2011[42] the Court of Justice of the European Union (CJEU), under the heading 'Agreements Binding the European Union and/or the Member States', explicitly recited Article 27 (1) and (2) TRIPS in full.[43] This means that the Directive itself as well as its application and interpretation must comply with Article 27 (2) of the TRIPS Agreement.

Whereas in the text of the Directive only Article 6 is directly addressing exclusions from patentability related to *ordre public* or morality, altogether ten Recitals directly or indirectly refer to *ordre public* or morality as the yardstick for eligibility of inventions for patentability. Recital 16, in a very broad way emphasizes that the patent law must be applied so as to respect the fundamental principles safeguarding the dignity and integrity of the person, and that the human body, at any stage in its formation

---

[40] OJ 1998 No. L212 at p. 13.

[41] In Recital 36 of the Directive, Article 27 (2) of TRIPS is literally reproduced.

[42] Judgement of Grand Chamber in case C-34/10 – *Oliver Brüstle v. Greenpeace e.V.*

[43] No. 3 – 'Legal Context'.

or development including germ cells, cannot be patented. After another general statement that the Directive must stress that inventions must be excluded from patentability, where their commercial exploitation offends against *ordre public* or morality,[44] a further Recital emphasizes the need for the Directive to also include an illustrative list of inventions excluded from patentability

> so as to provide national courts and patent offices with a general guide to interpreting the reference to *ordre public* and morality,[45]

which cannot be presumed to be exhaustive. However, it at the same time points out that processes, the use of which offend against human dignity, such as processes to produce chimeras from germ cells or totipotent cells of humans and animals, were obviously also excluded from patentability.[46]

The Recitals further refer to the exclusion under the aspect of *ordre public* or morality, of processes for modifying the germ line genetic identity of human beings and processes for cloning human beings,[47] of uses of human embryos for industrial or commercial purposes,[48] and also processes for modifying the genetic identity of animals, which potentially cause them to suffer, without any substantial benefit for medical research, prevention, diagnoses or therapy to man or animal.[49]

As regards the Recitals of the Directive, it also has to be mentioned that Recital 39 emphasizes that *ordre public* and morality correspond in particular to ethical or moral principles recognized in a Member State, and that such ethical or moral principles supplement the standard legal examinations under patent law regardless of the technical field of the invention.[50] Moreover, Recital 43 refers to Article F (2) of the Treaty on European Union, pursuant to which the European Union is to respect fundamental rights, as guaranteed by the European Convention for the Protection of Human Rights and Fundamental Freedoms signed in Rome

---

44 Recital 37 of the Directive.

45 Recital 38 of the Directive.

46 Recital 38, second half sentence of the Directive.

47 Recital 40 of the Directive.

48 Recital 42 of the Directive, which, however, at the same time emphasizes that this exclusion 'does not affect inventions for therapeutic or diagnostic purposes which are applied to the human body and are useful to it'.

49 Recital 45 of the Directive.

50 Under Article 7 of the Directive a European group on ethics in science and new technologies has been established to evaluate all ethical aspects of biotechnology. As is clarified by Recital 44 of the Directive, this group may only be consulted at the level of basic ethical principles.

on 4 November 1950 and as they result from the constitutional traditions common to the Member States, as general principles of Community Law.

The wording of the Directive itself reflects the considerations proclaimed in the Recitals, in two articles. First, Article 5 (1) states that

> The human body, at the various stages of its formation and development and the simple discovery of one of its elements, including the sequence or partial sequences of a gene, cannot constitute patentable inventions.

Whereas the exclusion from patentability of the 'simple discovery' of elements of the human body, including the gene sequences, addresses the delimitation between non-patentable discoveries, as such, and inventions,[51] the exclusion of the 'human body, at various stages of its formation and development', is clearly aimed at guaranteeing human dignity and integrity.[52]

Directly addressed are *ordre public* and morality in Article 6 of the Directive. Its first paragraph sets forth that

> Inventions shall be considered unpatentable where their commercial exploitation would be contrary to *ordre public* or morality; however, exploitation shall not be deemed to be so contrary merely because it is prohibited by law or regulation.

This provision according to the established case law of the ECJ (now Court of the European Union – CJEU) allows the administrative authori-

---

[51] Article 5 (1) of the Directive is in this respect complemented by Article 5 (2), which requires that an element isolated from the human body or otherwise produced by means of a technical process, may constitute a patentable invention, even if the structure of that element is identical to that of a natural element. Under this provision the envisaged protection covers only the result of inventive scientific or technical work, and extends to biological data existing in their natural state in human beings only where necessary for the achievement and exploration of a particular industrial application (European Court of Justice – ECJ judgement of 9 October 2001, in Case C-377/98 – *Kingdom of the Netherlands, supported by Italian Republic and by Kingdom of Norway v. European Parliament and Council of the European Union, supported by Commission of the European Communities* [2001] ECR I – 7079, ¶75; Judgement of 16 July 2005 – in Case C-456/03 – *Commission of the European Community v. Italian Republic*, [2005] ECR I-5335 at ¶69). Only inventions which combine a natural element with a technical process enabling it to be isolated or produced for an industrial application can be the subject of a patent application. Consequently, an element of the human body may be part of a product which is patentable but it may not, in its natural environment be appropriated (ECJ Judgement in case C-377/98 at ¶ 72 and 73; and ECJ in Case C-456/03 at ¶ 67).

[52] ECJ Judgment in Case C-377/98 at ¶ 70.

ties and courts of the Member States a wide discretion in applying the exclusion from patentability of inventions, which is necessary to take account of the particular difficulties to which the use of certain patents may give rise in the social and cultural context of each Member State, a context which the national legislative, administrative and court authorities are better placed to understand than are the Community authorities.[53] However, as it is explicitly pointed out in the second paragraph of Article 6, no such discretion exists for the Member States as regards the patentability of four specifically identified categories of inventions.[54] Article 6 (2) reads as follows:

> On the basis of paragraph 1, the following, in particular, shall be considered unpatentable:
> (a) processes for cloning human beings;
> (b) processes for modifying the germ line genetic identity of human beings;
> (c) uses of human embryos for industrial or commercial purposes;
> (d) processes for modifying the genetic identity of animals which are likely to cause them suffering without any substantial medical benefit to man or animal, and also animals resulting from such processes.

(ii) The *Brüstle v. Greenpeace* Case

Based on a referral of the German Federal Supreme Court (BGH) of 17 December 2009[55] in which the Court of the European Union was asked, *inter alia*, to ascertain whether the human embryonic stem cells which served as base material for the process patented in the case at issue, constitute 'embryos' within the meaning of Article 6 (2) (c) of the Directive and whether the organisms of which those human embryonic stem cells can be obtained constitute 'human embryos' within the meaning of that article, although they are not all totipotent cells, but only pluripotent cells obtained from embryos at the blastocyst stage, the CJEU, for the first time, had to interpret Article 6 (2) of the Directive.[56] Specifically, the German Federal Supreme Court asked (1) what is meant by the term 'human embryos' in Article 6 (2) (c),[57] (2) what is meant by the expression

---

53 ECJ in Case C-377/98 at ¶ 37 and 38.

54 ECJ in Case C-456/03 at ¶ 78.

55 2010 GRUR Int. 236 – *Neurale Vorläuferzellen.*

56 Judgment of the Court (Grand Chamber) of 18 October 2011 in the Case C-34/10 – *Oliver Brüstle v. Greenpeace e. V.*

57 (a) Does it include all stages of the development of human life, beginning with the fertilization of the ovum, or must further requirements, such as the attainment of a certain stage of development, be satisfied?

'use of human embryos for industrial or commercial purposes'? Does it include also use for the purposes of scientific research?, and (3) is technical teaching to be considered unpatentable pursuant to Article 6 (2) (c) of the Directive even if the use of human embryos does not form part of the technical teaching claimed with the patent, but is a necessary precondition for the application of that teaching, either because the patent concerns a product whose production necessitates the prior destruction of human embryos, or because the patent concerns a process for which such a product is needed as base material.[58]

In addition to these explicit questions, the German Federal Supreme Court drew attention to the fact that a prohibition of patentability, which also covers acts of exploitation, which according to the laws of some Member States were allowed, could be incompatible with Article 27 (2) of the TRIPS Agreement. The Court pointed out that according to the latter rule, which is mentioned in Recital 36 of the Directive and whose second paragraph corresponds with Article 6 (1) of the Directive, inventions can be excluded from patentability only when the prevention of their industrial exploitation is necessary to protect *ordre public* or morality. An interpretation which would force Member States to deny patent protection despite the fact that the exploitation of the invention at hand, according to the national legal order, would not be contrary to morality or *ordre public*, may contradict also Article 1 (2) of the Directive, emphasizing that the Directive 'shall be without prejudice to the obligations of the Member States' in particular under the TRIPS Agreement.[59]

Since the CJEU in the *Brüstle v. Greenpeace* case limited itself to replying to questions raised by the German Federal Supreme Court and saw no necessity to interpret either the notion of '*ordre public*' or that of 'morality' anew in an European context beyond its former case law, it should suffice also to focus here only on some aspects of this much discussed judgment.[60]

(b) Are the following organisms also included:
- fertilized human ova into which a cell nucleus from a mature human cell has been transplanted;
- fertilized human ova whose division and further development have been stimulated by parthenogenesis?

(c) Are stem cells obtained from human embryos at the blastocyst stage also included (reproduced in Brüstle at ¶ 23).

[58] Id.

[59] Cf. *Neurale Vorläuferzelle*, 2010 GRUR Int. at ¶ 62 (cf. Straus, Joseph, Comment, 2011 GRUR Int. 1048 *et seq.*).

[60] Cf., for instance, Rigby, Barbara (2011), A Ban on Stem Cell Patents in Europe?, 12 World Intellectual Property Report BNA 50 *et seq.*; Hübel, Andreas (2011), Patentability of Pluripotent Stem Cells Unlikely Although they are not

The Court justified its narrow approach by the fact that under Article 6 (2) of the Directive, by the decision of the legislator, the 'use of human embryos for industrial or commercial purposes' is by all means contrary to *ordre public* or morality. As regards the notion of 'human embryo', which the Directive does not define and for which no European consensus exists, the CJEU, contrary to the European Court of Human Rights (ECHR),[61] found it necessary to, for the purposes of the application of the Directive, in this regard designate an autonomous concept of European Union law which must be interpreted in a uniform manner throughout the territory of the Union.[62] The Court went on by stating that the lack of a uniform definition of the concept of human embryo would create a risk of the authors of certain biotechnological inventions being tempted to seek their patentability in the Member States which have the narrowest concept of human embryo and are accordingly the most liberal as regards possible patentability, because those inventions would not be patentable in the other Member States. Such a situation, according to the Court, would

---

Considered as Embryo, Mitteilungen der deutschen Patentanwälte 494 *et seq.*; Moran, Nuala (2011), European Court Bans Embryonic Stem Cell Patents, 29 Nature Biotechnology 1057 *et seq.*; Taupitz, Jochen (2012), Menschenwürde von Embryonen – europäisch-patentrechtlich betrachtet, GRUR 1 *et seq.*; Straus, Joseph (2011), Comment, GRUR Int. 1048 *et seq.*; Plomer, Aurora (2011), EU Ban on Stem Cell Patents is a Threat Both to Science and the Rule of Law, The Guardian (http://www.guardian.co.uk/science/blog/2011/dec/12/eu-ban-stem-cell-patents (last visited 15 December 2011); Paton, Mark and Alex Denoon (2011), The Ramifications of the Advocate General's Opinion in the *Oliver Brüstle* case, E.I.P.R. 590 *et seq.*

61 In the case *Evans v. United Kingdom*, ECHR explicitly found: '. . . in the absence of any European consensus on the scientific and legal definition of the beginning of life, the issue of when the right to life begins comes within the margin of appreciation which the Court generally considers that States should enjoy in this sphere. Under English law . . . an embryo does not have independent rights or interests and cannot claim – or have claimed in its behalf – a right to life under article 2' (Judgement of 7 March 2006, application No. 6339/05, confirmed by decision of the Grand Chamber of 10 April 2007 (No. 46). Cf. Plomer, Aurora (2009), Human Dignity, Human Rights and Article 6 (1) of the EU Directive on Biotechnological Inventions, in Plomer, Aurora and Paul LC Torremans (eds), Embryonic Stem Cell Patents – European Law and Ethics, Oxford, pp. 203 *et seq.* (pp. 222–3).

62 *Brüstle* at ¶ 26. The Court emphasized that, 'Although, the definition of human embryo is a very sensitive social issue in many Member States, marked by their multiple traditions and value system, the Court is not called upon, by the present order for reference, to broach question of a medical or ethical nature, but must restrict itself to a legal interpretation of the relevant provisions of the Directive.' (*Brüstle* at ¶ 30).

adversely affect the smooth functioning of the internal market which was the aim of the Directive.[63] Without examining the drafting history of the Directive, which suggests a different understanding of Article 6 (2) (c) of the Directive,[64] the Court deduced from the Recitals in connection with Article 5 (1) of the Directive that the context and aim of the Directive thus show that the European Union legislature intended to exclude any possibility of patentability where respect for human dignity could thereby be affected. Therefore the concept of 'human embryo' within the meaning of Article 6 (2) (c) of the Directive must be understood in a wide sense, namely as any human ovum, as soon as fertilized, if that fertilization is such as to commence the process of development of a human body.[65] Moreover, the Court added, that this classification must also apply to a non-fertilized human ovum into which the cell nucleus from a mature human cell has been transplanted and a non-fertilized human ovum whose division and further development have been stimulated by parthenogenesis. The Court reasoned that latter qualification by the capability of those cells 'of commencing the process of development of a human being just as an embryo created by fertilization of an ovum can do so'.[66]

As regards the second question, the Court simply held that although the aim of scientific research must be distinguished from industrial or commercial purposes, the use of human embryos for the purpose of research which constitutes the subject-matter of a patent application cannot be separated from the patent itself and the rights attaching to it.[67] Consequently, according to the holding of the Court, the exclusion from patentability

---

63 *Brüstle* at ¶ 18.

64 Mr Willy Rothley, Member of the European Parliament and the competent reporter for the Directive in the European Parliament, stated in the context of interest: 'In relation to the use of embryos, the Council has set some limitations: They are not to be used for industrial or commercial purposes. But I would only ask you to remember that this was done with the United Kingdom in mind. We cannot as European legislators decree that something which does not contravene the underlying legal principles of all Member States is in contravention of public order, and we cannot brand something that we do not jointly regard as abhorrent as a contravention of common decency. That is not acceptable! It is only exemplary and in any case, that is to say, other ways of using embryos may be investigated with the proviso that they do not contravene public order and common decency for other reasons.' Quoted from Porter, Gerard (2009), The Drafting History of the European Biotechnology Directive, in Plomer, Aurora and Paul LC Torremans (eds), Embryonic Stem Cell Patents – European Law and Ethics, Oxford, pp. 3 *et seq.* (at p. 22).

65 *Brüstle* at ¶ 34 and 35.

66 Id. at ¶ 36.

67 Id. at ¶ 43.

concerning the use of human embryos for industrial or commercial purposes in Article 6 (2) (c) of the Directive also covers the use for purposes of scientific research.[68]

Finally, the Court of the European Union declared also an invention as unpatentable, even if the claims of the patent do not concern the use of human embryos, where the implementation of the invention requires the destruction of human embryos. In this context the Court emphasized that also in such a case, there is use of human embryos within the meaning of Article 6 (2) (c) of the Directive and that the fact that destruction may occur at a stage long before implementation of the invention, as in the case of the production of embryonic stem cells from a lineage of stem cells the mere production of which implied the destruction of human embryos, were irrelevant.[69] The Court reasoned this interpretation by stating that 'not to include in the scope of the exclusion from patentability' set out in Article 6 (2) (c) of the Directive technical teaching claimed, as the ground that it does not refer to the use, implying their prior destruction of human embryos would make the provision concerned redundant by allowing a patent applicant to avoid its application by skilful drafting of the claim.[70]

In the context of this contribution there is neither space nor necessity for arguing about the definition of the notion 'human embryo' as laid down by the Court of Justice of the European Union, nor about its holding that the use of human embryos for scientific research is also covered by Article 6 (2) (c) of the Directive, thus, equating research in human embryonic pluripotent stem cells, which were legally, meaning in accordance with the competent law in force, generated from (supernumerary) embryos, with 'use of human embryos for industrial or commercial purposes'. However, the necessity exists to specifically observe, on the one hand, that the CJEU by declaring the destruction of human embryos from which, like in the *Brüstle* case, the human pluripotent embryonic stem cells were (legally) generated as part of the technical teaching at hand in the application, although it has neither been claimed, nor described, nor is it necessary for performing/implementing the invention as claimed, has obviously adopted a very contestable approach, actually not in line with its former case law.[71] On the other hand, the Court remained entirely silent, and by

68 Id. at ¶ 46.
69 Id. at ¶ 49.
70 Id. at ¶ 50.
71 In the Case C-377/98, ECJ explicitly emphasized: 'Reliance on this fundamental right [human integrity – J.S.] is, however, clearly misplaced as against a directive which concerns only the grant of patents and whose scope does not

doing so, fully ignoring the consideration of the German Federal Supreme Court that such an interpretation could contradict the binding standard of Article 27 (2) of the TRIPS Agreement and at the same time disregard the rule of Article 1 (2) of the Directive, how the fact is to be judged that a number of Member States allow commercial exploitation of products generated from human embryonic stem cells in their national laws. In fact, not only national laws of a number of Member States, but also the Directive 2004/23/EC of the European Parliament and of the Council of 31 March 2004 on setting standards of quality and safety for the donation, procurement, testing, processing, preservation, storage and distribution of human tissues and cells,[72] according to its Recital 7 applies to 'tissues and cells including hematopoietic peripheral blood, umbilical-cord (blood) and bone-marrow stem cells, reproductive cells (eggs, sperm), foetal tissues and adult and *embryonic stem cells*'.[73] Moreover, according to Article 1 (1) of this Directive, it applies to donations, procurement, testing, processing, preservation, storage and distribution of human tissues and cells intended for human applications and of manufactured products derived from human tissues and cells intended for human applications. Thus, also to products manufactured from human embryonic pluripotent stem cells. Finally, mention should also be made, in the context at hand, of the Regulation (EC) No. 1394/2007 of the European Parliament and of the Council of 13 November 2007 on advanced therapy medical products and amending Directive 2001/83/EC and Regulation (EC) No. 726/2004.[74] As pointed out in Recital 7, this regulation of advanced therapy medical products at Community level should not interfere with decisions made by Member States on whether to allow the use of any specific type of human cells, such as *embryonic stem cells*,[75] or animal cells. It should also not affect the application of national legislation prohibiting or restricting the sale, supply or use of medicinal products, containing, consisting of or derived from these cells. In other words, at the European Union's level, the commercial exploitation of, for instance, medical products derived from human embryonic stem cells, which were generated from destructed human embryos, is, in principle, allowed.[76]

---

therefore extend to activities before and after that grant, whether they involve research or the use of the patented product.' (¶ 79).

[72] OJ 2004 No. L 102, p. 48 of 7 April 2004.

[73] Emphasis added [J.S.].

[74] OJ 2007 No. L 324, p. 121 of 10 December 2007.

[75] Emphasis added [J.S.].

[76] Cf. for more Plomer, Aurora (2009), Towards Systemic Legal Conflicts: Article 6 (2) (c) of the EU Directive on Biotechnological Inventions, in Plomer,

In fact, products derived from human embryonic stem cell lines are in the meantime traded in the markets of the Member States of the European Union. As an example the 'Product Selection Guide' of the US company Millipor advertises so-called ENStem-A™ Human Neural Progenitor Cells derived from NIH-approved H 9 Human Embryonic Stem Cells (hESCs), for research use only.[77] Under the given legal order of the European Union, in principle, allowing the commercial exploitation of human embryonic pluripotent stem cells, meaning stem cells the base material of which, to use the language of the CJEU, obtained by destruction of human embryos,[78] but at the same time excluding such products from patent protection, based on the consideration that such exclusion is necessary to prevent their commercial exploitation which would be contrary to *ordre public* or morality, is certainly not covered by Article 27 (2) TRIPS. The German Federal Supreme Court correctly made that point, although still 'veiled' in a question. Should the CJEU *Brüstle v. Greenpeace* holdings endure, the EU legislator will either have to prohibit all commercialization of any products originating in human embryonic stem cells, meaning generated from destructed human embryos, or undertake changes in the EU Biotech Directive, which will make an interpretation impossible according to which the notion of an invention, meaning of a technical teaching how to solve a problem by technical means, is entirely independent of the claims and even of the description, but covers not only

---

Aurora and Paul LC Torremans (eds), Embryonic Stem Cell Patents – European Law and Ethics, Oxford, pp. 173 *et seq.* Aurora Plomer observes in this context: 'In general, hESC-based products may be made on an industrial scale and commercialized in Europe, irrespective of whether the activities involved destruction of human embryos. A broad exclusionary construction, if correct, would therefore lead to the paradox contradiction that applicants engaging in activities which are lawful and morally permissible in EU Member States are denied patent protection on the related invention on the basis that the practice of invention is deemed immoral from within patent law.' (at p. 180).

77 Millipor catalogue No. SCR055-ENStem-A™ Human Neural Progenitor Expansion Kit. The kit components are *inter alia*, 1. > 1×10^6 viable ENStem-A™ Human Neural Progenitor Cells (Part. No. SCC003) derived from NIH approved H9 human embryonic stem cells, cryopreserved. Stored in liquid nitrogen. Characterization of cells: each lot of ENStem-A™ Human Neural Progenitor Cells has been validated for high levels of expression of Nestin and Sox II, and low level expression of Oct-4. The ability of ENStem-A™ Cells to differentiate into multiple neuronal phenotypes and maintain a normal caryotype after multiple passages has been verified . . . The cells have been confirmed to be negative for microplasms (cf. Millipor Product Selection Guide – Neuroscience, Antibodies, Proteins, Kits and other reagents (12/12/2007/SCC03/VC/LR/CP)).

78 Cf. *Brüstle*, ¶ 48.

the base material, but also its generation, no matter how legal that generation may have been. If neither changes will be undertaken, the European Union and its Member States allowing the respective commercialization could well brought before the Dispute Settlement Body of WTO, for not complying with Article 27 (2) TRIPS.[79]

IV. EUROPEAN PATENT CONVENTION

(i) General

As it has been pointed out, Article 53 (a) EPC, according to which European patents shall not be granted in respect of inventions the commercial exploitation of which[80] would be contrary to *ordre public* or morality, provided that such exploitation shall not be deemed to be so contrary merely because it is prohibited by law or regulation in some or all of the contracting states, had served as model for Article 27 (2) TRIPS, and as starting point for the respective provisions of the EU Directive, in particular its Article 6 (1). However, since the adoption of the Directive its rules have had decisive impact on the subsequent development of the European Patent Convention. The Administrative Council of the European Patent Organization, as its legislative body, by a decision of 16 June 1999, inserted a new Chapter VI (now V) entitled 'Biotechnological Inventions' into Part II of the EPC Implementing Regulations.[81] These new provisions entered into force on 1 September 1999 and transposed the Directive into the European Patent law. Rule 26 (1) (formerly 23b (1)) EPC expressly provides that the relevant provisions of the Convention shall be applied to European patent applications and patents concerning biotechnological inventions in accordance with the provisions of this new chapter, and that the Directive shall be used as a supplementary means of interpretation. Rule 28 (formerly 23d) EPC on 'Exceptions to Patentability' expressly refers to Article 53 (a) EPC. As a consequence of these amendments of the Implementing Regulations to the EPC, Rule 28 in literae (a), (b), (c) and (d) EPC corresponds to Article 6 (2) of the Directive. The introductory paragraph of Rule 28 EPC, however, differs from that of Article 6 (1) of the Directive, by directly linking Article 53 (a) EPC to the new Rule. It

79 See also the comment of Straus, Joseph (2011), 2011 GRUR Int. 1049.

80 Cf. also fn. 5 *supra*.

81 Decision of the Administrative Council of 16 June 1999 amending the Implementing Regulations to the European Patent Convention, 1999 OJ EPO 437.

specifically indicates that under Article 53 (a), European patents shall not be granted in respect of biotechnological inventions which, in particular concern the same processes and uses as enumerated in Article 6 (2) of the Directive. In a Notice of 1 July 1999 concerning the amendment of the Implementing Regulations to the European Patent Convention,[82] in which the reasons for implementing the EU Directive into the Implementing Regulations were given, it has also been pointed out that under Article 164 (1) EPC the Implementing Regulations are an integral part of the Convention and hence are binding on the EPO's boards of appeal (Article 23 (3) EPC) and on national courts. Consequently, for practical application of the EPC, only the interpretation of its provisions laid down in the Implementing Regulations is binding. A different interpretation of the Convention would be possible only if it is specifically demonstrated that a particular rule of interpretation is inconsistent with the Convention itself.[83] Despite this close link between the Directive and the EPC, and the practically identical wording of provisions dealing with patent eligibility of inventions in the light of *ordre public* or morality, no link exists between the two as regards the final application and interpretation of the respective provisions. Whereas the Court of Justice of the European Union is the last instance for interpreting the Directive, as it has to be applied by national patent offices and courts of the Member States of the EU, the final competence to interpret the EPC, including its implementing regulations, lies with the Enlarged Board of Appeal of the EPO.[84]

(ii) The *Onco-mouse/HARVARD* Case

In view of these historical developments and having regard to the advances in the area of biotechnology as well as of the accompanying sensitivities of the public at large, it should not come as a surprise that the EPO had to address patentability issues under Article 53 (a) EPC well ahead of the adoption of the Directive. A great deal of attention has attracted a decision of 3 October 1990 of the Board of Appeal in which the patent eligibility of an invention of genetic manipulation of animals involving the insertion of an activated onco-gene had to be tested under Article 53

---

82 1999 OJ EPO 573.

83 No. 11 of the Notice (id. at p. 575).

84 In its Decision of 25 November 2008 (2009 OJ EPO 306) – *Use of Embryos/WARF*, the Enlarged Board of Appeal of the EPO concluded that it has no power to ask ECJ for a preliminary ruling under the existing provisions of the EPC (No. 11 at p. 321).

(a) EPC.[85] Contrary to the Examining Division which argued that patent law were not the right legislative tool for regulating problems arising in connection with genetic manipulation of animals, the Board considered that in a case of that kind there were compelling reasons to consider the implications of Article 53 (a) EPC in relation to the question of patentability. The Board specifically referred to the suffering of animals due to the insertion of activated onco-genes making them prone to develop tumours which necessarily cause suffering. It also addressed the danger which genetically manipulated animals could cause, if released into the environment. Eventually, the Board held that in the light of Article 53 (a) EPC the patentability of the invention at hand would 'seem to depend mainly on a careful weighing up of the suffering of animals and possible risks to the environment on the one hand, and the invention's usefulness to mankind on the other'.[86] The case, therefore, was remanded to the first instance to perform the ordered test.

When the Opposition Division of the EPO performed the 'weighing up' test ordered by the Board of Appeal, it first emphasized that following accepted case law of the EPO, Article 53 (a) EPC can only apply in exceptional cases. It then pointed out that for the purposes of Article 53 (a) EPC '*ordre public*' and morality were to be assessed primarily by looking at laws or regulations which are common to most of the European countries because these laws and regulations were the best indicator about what is considered right or wrong in European society. In so far as such laws or regulations exist, it appears neither necessary nor appropriate to rely on other possible means of assessment such as public opinion polls, as requested by a number of opponents. The Opposition Division subsequently observed that statutory law regulating the use of test animals in medical research, thus animals of the kind at issue in the patent in suit, was highly indicative because it shows whether the exploitation of the invention is *de facto* prohibited or not. The Opposition Division then found that the use of animals for experimental or other scientific purposes is allowed under certain conditions in most if not all states parties to the EPC, as well as by the EU Directive 86/609/EC. The Opposition Division therefore concluded in this regard:

> . . . that patenting of those animals of the present invention being it useful as test animals in the sense of this Directive complies with the principle requirement of morality because the exploitation of the invention is explicitly allowed.[87]

---

85 EPO T 19/90, 1990 OJ EPO 476 – *Onco-Mouse/HARVARD*.

86 No. 5 of the Reasons (id. p. 490).

87 Decision of 7 November 2001, 2003 OJ EPO 473 – *Onco-Mouse/HARVARD* (Nos. 9.3–9.4, at pp. 501–2).

In view of the order to also provide for the 'weighing up' test, that is, take into consideration animal suffering, which was not put into question, on the one hand, and substantial medical benefit, on the other, the Opposition Division derived from the wording 'which are likely to cause them suffering' in Rule 28 (d) (formerly Rule 23 d (d)) EPC (i.e. corresponding to Article 6 (2) (d) of the Directive) that it hints on a future event and contains an element of probability.[88] The Opposition Division followed from this that for the purposes of Rule 23 d (d) (now 28 (d)) EPC the – undisputed – likelihood for suffering of the test animals is to be balanced against the *bona fide* belief of the inventor in a substantial medical benefit at the effective date of the patent. Since it could not be denied that the animals of the invention were made for good cause, namely progress in cancer research, there were *bona fide* reasons at effective date to expect a substantial medical benefit. Consequently, Rule 28 (d) EPC were no bar to patentability in the case at hand. Thus, the patent was upheld.[89]

The *Onco-Mouse/HARVARD* case, eventually, ended on a second appeal with a decision of the Board of Appeal of the EPO of 6 July 2004.[90] The patent was upheld again and the Board also confirmed the 'weighing up' test, as ordered by the Board in T 19/90, as the right test under Article 53 (a) EPC in cases like that at hand.[91] However, the Board also laid down some more general rules for interpreting Article 53 (a) EPC in the light of Rule 23 d (now Rule 28) EPC. Before briefly referring to these rules, it seems appropriate to mention that the Board seemingly did not share the view of the Opposition Division, namely to use statutes and regulations of state parties to the EPC regulating, in case at issue animal testing, as an indicator for judging the patentability under Article 53 (a) EPC. In any way, the Board remained silent on this. As regards the relationship between Article 53 (a) and Rule 23 d (now Rule 28) EPC, the Board stated that if a case falls within one of the four categories of exceptions set out in Rule 23 d (now Rule 28) EPC, then it must *ipso facto* be denied a patent under Article 53 (a) EPC. However, cases not falling within those limited exclusions, specifically enumerated, must be considered under Article 53 (a) EPC,[92] with the consequence that even an invention which relates to, for instance transgenic animals and which does not cause them to suffer

---

88 No. 9.5, second ¶ (id. at p. 503).
89 No. 9.5 (id. at pp. 503–4).
90 EPO T 315/03, 2006 OJ EPO 15 – *Transgenic Animals/HARVARD*.
91 No. 10.5 *et seq.* of the Reasons (id. at pp. 53 *et seq.*)
92 No. 10.1 of the Reasons (id. at p. 51).

at all, may still be excluded from patentability under Article 53 (a) EPC if, for instance it could constitute a threat to evolution.[93]

As to Article 53 (a) EPC, the T 350/03 Board of Appeal emphasized that the Decision T 356/93[94] supplied working definitions of the concept of morality and *ordre public* for the purposes of Article 53 (a) EPC. The Board literally reproduced those definitions. Since the definition offered by that Board for the notion of morality has already been reproduced in this contribution,[95] only that of *ordre public* should be quoted here as follows:

> 5. It is generally accepted that the concept of '*ordre public*' covers the protection of public security and the physical integrity of individuals as part of society. This concept encompasses also the protection of the environment. Accordingly, under Article 53 (a) EPC, inventions the exploitation of which is likely to breach public peace or social order (for example, through acts of terrorism) or to seriously prejudice the environment are to be excluded from patentability as being contrary to '*ordre public*'.[96]

The Board, eventually, summarized its overall approach to application of Article 53 (a) and Rule 23 d (now Rule 28) EPC as follows:

> 10.10 To summarize the assessment of a 'real' Article 53 (a) EPC objection, decision T 356/93 supplies working definitions of morality and '*ordre public*'. The many bases (economic, religious, etc.) for definitions of morality suggested by the appellants are of no assistance since no single such basis represents an accepted standard in European culture. Opinion poll evidence is of very limited value for the reasons given in T 356/93. In animal manipulation cases, the test in T 19/90 is appropriate. This differs in several respects from the test in Rule 23 d (d) EPC,[97] most importantly by allowing for matters other than animal suffering and medical benefit to be taken into account. Since the T 19/90 test is 'mainly' the basis of assessment, other arguments as to the appropriate standard of morality or '*ordre public*' can additionally be considered but, like any other argument, must be supported by evidence. Assessment of a 'real' Article 53 (a) EPC objection is made as of the filing or priority date, evidence arising after that date may be taken into account provided it is directed to the position at the effective date.[98]

---

[93] Cf. No. 10.7 of the Reasons (id. at p. 54).

[94] Decision of 21 February 1995, 1995 OJ EPO 545 – *Plant Cells/Plant Genetic Systems*.

[95] See fn. 34 *supra*.

[96] Reproduced in No. 10.2 of the Reasons (2006 OJ EPO 51–2).

[97] Thus, now Rule 28 (d) EPC [J.S.].

[98] Id. at pp. 55–6.

(iii) The *Use of Embryos/WARF* Case[99]

In this, last to be briefly discussed case, the Enlarged Board of Appeal of the EPO (EBA) had to apply Article 53 (a) EPC and Rule 23 d (c) (now Rule 28 (c)) EPC, corresponding to Article 6 (2) (c) of the Directive, to an application which claimed a cell culture which comprised primate embryonic stem cells,[100] and which was refused by the Examining Division on the grounds of the named provisions. The Examining Division, first, pointed out that in the application as originally filed for the generation of human embryonic stem cell cultures the use of human embryos as starting material was described as being indispensible. It then followed that the use of a human embryo as starting material for the generation of a product of industrial application (i.e. the claimed embryonic stem cell cultures) meant a use thereof for industrial purposes within the meaning of Rule 23 d (c) (now 28 (c)) EPC and was thus excluded from patenting under the said provision in conjunction with Article 53 (a) EPC 1973. The Opposition Division emphasized that the provisions of Rule 23 d (c) (now 28 (c)) EPC in conjunction with Article 53 (a) EPC 1973 were not directed exclusively to the claimed subject matter but rather concerned inventions, thus including all aspects that made the claimed subject matter available to the public. The description provided only one source of starting cells, namely a pre-implantation embryo. It was therefore irrelevant that the claimed subject-matter related to cell cultures and not to a method of production of said cultures.[101]

Although the referral to the Enlarged Board of Appeal contained altogether four questions, here only one should be dealt with in some detail. The reasons being that the holdings of the Enlarged Board of Appeal of the EPO are well reflected in the *Brüstle v. Greenpeace* Judgment of the CJEU, were the Court of Justice of the European Union explicitly referred to it and concurred with the Enlarged Board of Appeal in a number of aspects.[102] The referring Board of Appeal asked, *inter alia*, whether the

---

99 *Use of Embryos/WARF, supra.*

100 Claim 1 of this application reads as follows: '1. A cell culture comprising primate embryonic stem cells which (i) are capable of proliferation *in vitro* [sic] culture for over one year, (ii) maintain a karyotype in which all chromosomes normally characteristic of the primate species are present and are not noticeably altered through culture for over one year, (iii) maintain the potential to differentiate to derivatives of endoderm, mesoderm, and ectoderm tissues throughout the culture, and (iv) are prevented from differentiating when cultured on a fibroblast feeder layer.'

101 III of the Decision (id. pp. 309–10).

102 Cf. also III. (ii).

Rule 23 d (c) (now 28 (c)) EPC forbids the patenting of claims directed to products (here: human embryonic stem cell cultures) which, as described in the application – at the filing date could be prepared exclusively by a method which necessarily involved the destruction of the human embryos from which the said products are derived, if the said method is not part of the claims?[103]

As regards the general characterization/interpretation of Article 6 (2) (c) of the Directive, and consequently also of Rule 28 (c) (formerly Rule 23 (d) (c)) EPC, the EBA characterized it as being 'straight forward and prohibits the patenting if a human embryo is used for industrial or commercial purposes'.[104] The EBA opined that such a reading were also in line with the concern of the legislator to prevent a misuse in the sense of a commodification of human embryos[105] and with one of the essential objectives of the whole Directive to protect human dignity. The Board also emphasized that this concern was also evidenced by the selective policy of the Community in funding stem cell research.[106] In line with that broad approach was also the approach of the EBA, eventually also accepted by the CJEU, as regards the definition of the term 'embryo'. The fact that neither the EU legislator nor the EPC legislator has chosen to define the term 'embryo', as used in the Directive and in Rule 28 EPC, although they must presumably have been aware of the definitions used in national laws, the Board interpreted in the sense that given the purpose of the Directive to protect human dignity and prevent the commercialization of embryos, this can only lead to the presumption 'that 'embryo' was not to be given any restrictive meaning in Rule 28 (formerly Rule 23 (d)) EPC as to do so would undermine the intention of the legislator, and that what is an embryo is a question of fact in the context of any particular patent application'.[107]

The EBA, like later on the CJEU, also has chosen to apply a very broad definition of invention to which the application at hand related. Starting from the observation that Rule 28 (c) EPC, as well as the corresponding provision of the Directive, does not mention claims, but refers to "inven-

---

[103] Question No. 2 (id. p. 308).

[104] No. 18 of the Reasons (id. p. 324).

[105] On this latter aspect, the EBA referred to a decision of the German Federal Patent Court (Bundespatentgericht – BpatG) of 5 December 2006 (No. IV 2.2 *et seq.*), i.e. the *Brüstle v. Greenpeace* decision from which Brüstle appealed to the BGH (2007 GRUR Int. 752 – *Humane embryonale Stammzellen*, with critical comment by Sattler de Sousa e Brito, Clara).

[106] Id.

[107] No. 20 of the Reasons (id. at p. 325).

tion' in the context of its exploitation' not just the explicit wording of the claims needs to be looked up 'but the technical teaching of the application as a whole as to how the invention is to be performed'. The Board then went on by arguing that since in the case at hand the only teaching of how to perform the invention to make human embryonic stem cell culture was the use (involving their destruction) of human embryos, this invention falls under the prohibition of Rule 28 (c) (formerly Rule 23 d (c)) EPC. In other words, and explicitly emphasized by the Board, claims actually do not matter, since that would have the undesirable consequence of making avoidance of the patenting prohibition merely a matter of clever and skilful drafting of such claims.[108]

The EBA further argued that a claimed new and inventive product must first be made before it could be used. Such making according to EBA was the ordinary way commercially to exploit the claimed invention and falls within the monopoly granted, because someone having a patent directed to this product had the right to exclude others from making or using such product. Consequently, the EBA held, that 'making the claimed product remains commercial or industrial application of the invention even where there is an intention to use that product for further research'.[109]

Finally, the EBA rejected the complaint that by adopting Rule 28 (formerly Rule 23 d)) EPC the legislator acted *ultra vires*, meaning beyond the scope of Article 53 (a) EPC. Instead, the EBA held that Rule 28 EPC remained within the scope of Article 53 (a) EPC and of the TRIPS Agreement and that therefore 'it is not necessary nor indeed appropriate to discuss whether the standard of *ordre public* or morality should be European one or not, whether it matters if research in certain European countries involving destruction of human embryos to obtain stem cells is permitted, whether the benefit of the invention for humanity should be balanced against the prejudice to the embryo, or what the point in time is to assess *ordre public* or morality under Article 53 (a) EPC. The legislators have decided, remaining within the ambit of Article 53 (a) EPC, and there is no room to manoeuvre.'[110] This decision has been widely criticized in the legal doctrine, *inter alia* also because the EBA entirely ignored the fact that the products it excluded from patentability may be commercialized in a number of states party to the EPC.[111]

---

108 No. 22 of the Reasons (id. at p. 326).

109 No. 25 of the Reasons (id. at p. 327).

110 No. 31 of the Reasons (id. at pp. 329–30).

111 For criticism of this decision reference is made in particular to the contributions in Plomer, Aurora and Paul LC Torremans (eds) (2009), Embryonic Stem Cell Patents – European Law and Ethics, Oxford/New York; Bostyn, Sven

V. UNITED STATES OF AMERICA

In contrast to the rules laid down in the EU Directive and the EPC, the US Patent Law (35 U.S.C.) does not dispose of any provision which would link the patentability issue of an invention to any specific considerations of ethics or morals. Title 35 U.S.C. § 101 provides for the issuance of a patent to a person who invents or discovers 'any' new and useful 'manufacture' or 'composition of matter'. As emphasized by the US Supreme Court in its famous *Diamond v. Chakrabarty* decision of 17 March 1980,[112] the Congress, choosing such extensive terms as 'manufacture' and 'composition of matter', modified by the comprehensive 'any', contemplated that the patent laws should be given wide scope, and that the relevant legislative history also supported a broad construction. While laws of nature, physical phenomena, and abstract ideas were not patentable, a claim to a hitherto unknown natural phenomenon, thus to a non-naturally occurring manufacture or composition of matter – a product of human ingenuity 'having a distinctive name, character and use' and were, therefore patentable.[113]

With regard to arguments brought forward by the petitioner, supported by *amici*, namely to grave risks that may be generated by research endeavours such as that of the respondent *Chakrabarty*, that is a human-made, genetically engineered bacterium, capable of breaking down multiple components of crude oil,[114] suggesting that genetic research may pose a serious threat to the human race, or at the very least, that dangers are far too substantial to permit such research to proceed apace at this time, the US Supreme Court reacted as follows:

> We are told that genetic research and related technological developments may spread pollution and disease, that it may result in a loss of genetic diversity, and that its practice may tend to depreciate the value of human life. These arguments are forcefully, even passionately, presented; they remind us that, at times,

---

(2009), Patenting Human Embryonic Stem Cells in Peril: The Decision of the Enlarged Board of Appeal in G 2/06, BSLR 13 *et seq.*; Straus, Joseph (2010), Zur Patentierung humaner embryonaler Stammzellen in Europa – Verwendet die Stammzellforschung menschliche Embryonen für industrielle oder kommerzielle Zwecke?, GRUR Int. 911 *et seq.* with further references.

112 *Diamond v. Chakrabarty*, 447 US 303, 100 S. Ct. 2204 (1980).

113 Id. at 308–10.

114 Claim 36 of the 1972 filed application of General Electric as Assignee of Chakrabarty, related to invention of 'A bacterium from the genus pseudonoms containing therein at least two stable energy-generating plasmid, each of said plasmids providing a separate hydrocarbon degradative pathway.'

> human ingenuity seems unable to control fully the forces it creates – that, with Hamlet, it is sometimes better 'to bear those ills we have than fly to others that we know not of.
>
> It is argued that this Court should weigh these potential hazards in considering whether respondent's invention is patentable subject matter under 101. We disagree. The grant or denial of patents on micro-organisms is not likely to put an end to genetic research or to its attendant risks. The large amount of research that has already occurred when no researcher had sure knowledge that patent protection would be available suggests that legislative or judicial fiat as to patentability will not deter the scientific mind from probing into the unknown any more than Canute could command the tides. Whether respondent's claims are patentable may determine whether research efforts are accelerated by the hope of reward or slowed by want of incentives, but that is all.
>
> What is more important is that we are without competence to entertain these arguments – either to brush them aside as fantasies generated by fear of the unknown, or to act on them. The choice we are urged to make is a matter of high policy for resolution within the legislative process after the kind of investigation, examination, and study that legislative bodies can provide and courts cannot. That process involves the balancing of competing values and interests, which in our democratic system is the business of elected representatives. Whatever their validity, the contentions now pressed on us should be addressed to the political branches of the Government, the Congress and the Executive, and not to the courts.[115]

During the last 30 years, the US Congress and the US Executive have resisted all contentions to introduce into the statute any exclusionary provisions along the lines of those adopted in Europe. Of contentions, opposing patents in the area of modern biotechnology and claiming that exceptions should be introduced into the law, only the so-called 'Blue Mountain Declaration' of 2 June 1995, which was orchestrated by Jeremy Riffkin's 'Foundation for Economic Trends', together with the 'General Board of Church and Society', and which was signed by a large number of religious leaders, should be mentioned here. It contained, *inter alia*, the following passages:

> The humans, animals, micro-organisms and plants comprising life on earth are part of the natural world into which we were all born. The conversion of these life-forms, their molecules or parts into corporate property through patent monopolies is counter to the interests of the peoples of the world.
>
> No individual institution or corporation should be able to claim ownership over species or varieties of living organisms. Nor should they be able to hold patents on organs, cells, genes or proteins, whether naturally occurring, genetically altered or otherwise modified.[116]

---

115 *Diamond*, 447 U.S. at 316–17 (1980).

116 Cf. Stone, Richard (1995), Religious Leaders Oppose Patenting Genes and

Mention should also be made of the fact that a part of the US-Academic IP Community has also raised objections against patenting in the area of biotechnology and pointed to issues of ethics and morals.[117] However, it seems to be fair to observe that the US courts, despite the lack of any statutory exclusionary provisions of patentability based on reasons of ethics or morals, have provided for a stable and adequate application of patent law to new technologies. This stability has undoubtedly contributed to the impressive growth in innovative commerce and technology in the USA.[118]

VI. CONCLUSIONS

Linking patent eligibility of inventions to *ordre public* and/or morality implies a complicate and tense relationship. Although to a different degree, both, *ordre public* and morality are subject to unpredictable, or at least difficult to predict evolutionary changes, as a consequence of scientific and technological developments as well as changes of public acceptance. Granting of patents, which do not confer on their owners any positive licence to exploit the patented invention, but only an exclusive right to use it in compliance with regulatory provisions and rights of third parties, and whose main macro-economic aim is to provide sufficient incentives for investment into risky research and development, hopefully leading to

---

Animals, Science, Vol. 268, p. 1126. However, those views were not shared by all theological institutions; they were, e.g. explicitly opposed by the Head of the Center for Theology and Natural Sciences (CTNS), Berkeley, Professor Peters. Cf. for more Straus, Joseph (1996), Intellectual Property in Human Genome Research Results, OECD STI – Science Technology Industry Review No. 19, pp. 45 *et seq.* (at 52 *et seq.*).

117 Cf. for instance Boyle, James (2003), Enclosing the Genome: What Squabbles over Genetic Patents Could Teach Us, in Kieff, F. Scott (ed), Perspectives on Properties of the Human Genome Project, Amsterdam-Boston-Heidelberg-London-New York-Oxford-Paris-San Diego-San Francisco-Singapore-Sydney-Tokyo, pp. 97–122.

118 Cf. Newman, Pauline (2003), Commentary on the Panel Presentations, in Kieff, F. Scott, op. cit. pp. 355 *et seq.* (at p. 359). As the last in the long row of US court decisions providing for stability as regards patentability standards in new technologies, the decisions of the Court of Appeals for the Federal Circuit of 29 July 2011 and of 16 August 2012 in *The Ass'n for Molecular Pathology v. U.S. Patent and Trademark Office and Myriad Genetics Inc.*, 653 F.3d 1329, 99 U.S.P.Q.2d 1398 (2011) and 2012 U.S. App. Lexis 17679 in which the Court upheld Myriad's patents on two isolated human genes (BRCA 1 and BRCA 2). However, the US Supreme Court on November 30, 2012, granted a writ of certiorary in this case (Order List: 568 U.S., Docket 12-398).

badly needed innovation and, via market success, to reward of inventors and innovators, should not be made dependent on rules and principles, which are more or less short lived, more or less broadly accepted by the public at large and, by all means, nearly without exception, subject to unpredictable evolutionary changes. Developments of science, technology and industry in the USA and in Europe reveal the higher efficiency of the US approach over that adopted in Europe. This is true not only in terms of scientific, technological and economic achievements, as demonstrated in the area of biotechnology, but even in terms of ethics and morals and last but not least, in terms of compliance with the mandatory international standard anchored in Article 27 (2) of the TRIPS Agreement. This is best demonstrated by the deplorable, actually not acceptable consequences of the Judgment of the Court of Justice of the European Union in the *Brüstle v. Greenpeace* case, namely that under the pretext to protect human dignity, the *Brüstle* invention remained unprotected, but at the same time stem cell lines of the type used by *Brüstle* for his invention, can in a great number of the EU Member States be legally generated from supernumerary human embryos, the products of the *Brüstle* type invention can be commercialized in most of the EU Member States, and the *Brüstle* invention can be freely copied EU-wide. This does not appear to be either in line with ethics and morals, or with the basic mission of the patent system, or with Article 27 (2) of the TRIPS Agreement. It certainly does not serve the rightly understood macro-economic interests of the European Union and its citizens.

3. First-inventor-to-file under the America Invents Act: A view of first-to-file lawyer and a view of first-to-invent lawyer

Toshiko Takenaka* with Martin J. Adelman

I. INTRODUCTION

On September 16, 2011, President Obama signed the America Invents Act ('AIA') into law and ended the long patent law debate over the *first-to-file v. first-to-invent* priority.[1] After the Philippines' switch to the first-to-file in 1998, the U.S. has been the only country to follow the first-to-invent priority.[2] The United States (U.S.) first-to-invent priority finds root in the Statute of Monopoly where any letters of patent were granted to the true and first inventor.[3] Because these terms are copied in the first U.S. patent statute and some patent systems in common law countries which are based on the Statute of Monopoly, such as Canada and the Philippines, used to

---

* Professor of Law, Washington Research Foundation/W. Hunter Simpson Professor of Technology Law, Director, Center for Advanced Study and Research on Intellectual Property (CASRIP), University of Washington School of Law. This paper is based on research that the author conducted in Germany at the Max Planck Institute for Intellectual Property and Competition Law in Munich with a generous scholarship from the institute. The author is particularly grateful to Prof. Joseph Straus, Prof. Martin Adelman and Prof. Rochelle Dreyfuss for their invaluable comments and her research assistants, Ms. Kris Lee and Ms. Lori Tonnes-Priddy.

1 America Invents Act, Pub. L. No. 112–29, 125 Stat. 284 (Sept. 16, 2011). For the priority debates, see George E. Frost, *The 1967 Patent Law Debate – First-to-Invent v. First-to-File,* 5 Duke L.J. 923 (1967); Vito J. DeBari, *International Harmonization of Patent Law: A Solution To The United States' First-To-File Debate*, 16 Fordham Intell. Prop. Media & Ent. L.J. 687 (1992).

2 Gerald J. Mossinfhoff and Vivian S. Kuo, *World Patent System Circa 20XX, A.D.*, 38 IDEA 529, 548 (1998).

3 Martin J. Adelman et al., Cases and Materials on Patent Law 249 (2nd ed. 2003).

follow the first-to-invent priority,[4] scholars in civil law countries may view the first-to-invent priority as a tradition in common law countries.[5] On the other hand, some U.S. scholars view the first-to-invent as a tradition unique to the U.S. and fiercely protect the tradition, arguing that a patent grant to a first to-file who is not a first-to-invent is unconstitutional.[6]

The enactment of AIA has ended the long debate between the *first-to-invent v. the first-to-file* by adopting the first-inventor-to-file ('FITF') priority. AIA's legislative history makes clear the superiority of the first-to-file over the first-to-invent and adopts FITF by bringing together the best aspects of both systems. American legal scholars claim that the U.S. will adopt a first-to-file system for the first time, bringing a sweeping change to the definition of prior art and priority.[7] A leading U.S. patent scholar, Prof. Adelman, also celebrates the abandonment of first-to-invent in his article which accompanies this article to express a first-to-invent lawyer's view. However, will AIA in fact bring a sweeping change as the U.S. legal community claims? Will FITF bring the benefits that Congress aims to bring by adopting the best aspects of a first-to-file system? A first-to-file lawyer such as this author, may view FITF differently from Prof. Adelman and other U.S. lawyers.

Thus, this article will analyze the extent of changes on patent procurement FITF will bring to the priority rule in the U.S. patent system and examine how much AIA contributes to the harmonization of patent systems. First, to understand the extent the filing date is relevant to patentability under the Pre-AIA U.S. Patent Act ('Pre-AIA Patent Act'), it will examine the grace period and the first-to-invent priority rule.[8] It will

---

[4] Robin Coster, *From First-To-Invent to First-To-File: The Canadian Experience,* AMERICAN INTELLECTUAL PROPERTY ASSOCIATION, April 2002 (http://www.torys.com/Publications/Documents/Publication%20PDFs/ARTech-19T.pdf); David S. Abrams and R. Polk Wagner, *Poisoning the Next Apple: How the America Invents Act Harms Inventors,* 65 STANDFORD L.REV. (2012) (http://papers.ssrn.com/sol3/papers.cfm?abstract_id=1883821).

[5] Although Japan is a civil law country, Japan originally adopted a first-to-invent priority because Japan modeled U.S. patent system for its first patent law.

[6] Michael A. Glenn and Peter J. Nagle, *Article 1 and the First Inventor To File: Patent Reform or Doublespeak*, 50 IDEA 441, 446 (2010).

[7] *See, e.g., Patent Office – 'First to File' Bill (2011)*, N.Y. TIMES, Sept. 9, 2011, http://topics.nytimes.com/top/news/science/topics/inventions_and_patents/index.html); Cynthia Hsu, *America Invents Act: Patents Now Awarded to First to File*, FINDLAW, Sept. 26, 2011, http://blogs.findlaw.com/in_house/2011/09/america-invents-act-patents-now-awarded-to-first-to-file.html); Dan L. Burk, *From 'First to Invent' to 'First to File' – Changing Lanes in U.S. Patent Procedure?*, 42 IIC 2011 627 (2011).

[8] 35 U.S.C.

discuss the different roles played by the grace period between the Pre-AIA U.S. patent system and the first-to-file patent system, particularly the European Patent Convention ('EPC')[9] and the Japanese Patent Act ('JPA')[10], which represents a typical first-to-file system in Asia.

This article will then examine a prevailing view in the U.S. legal community that interprets the grace period provision under AIA to allow a disclosure to give rise to a priority right ('the first-to-disclose priority'). The grace period under the first-to-disclose priority functions in exactly the same manner as under the first-to-invent priority, by allowing inventors to establish the first-to-invent by evidence of disclosure, instead of conception and reduction to practice as under the Pre-AIA priority rule. This article will argue that this first-to-disclose priority prevents AIA from taking advantage of benefits that a first-to-file system will bring by relying on a determinative date—the first disclosure date—to examine patentability. Accordingly, this article will propose an interpretation leading to the best practice that Congress aimed to adopt, by bringing benefits from both first-to-file and first-to-invent systems.

Second, this article will compare the definitions of prior art under AIA and under EPC and JPA in contrast to the old definitions under Pre-AIA Patent Act to examine the extent that AIA will harmonize the U.S. system with the rest of the world. It will also discuss ambiguity resulting from an adoption of the definitions from the Pre-AIA Patent Act. U.S. courts interpreted the Pre-AIA Patent Act definitions reflecting policies unique to the first-to-invent priority but it is not clear whether they will change their interpretations reflecting the new policy under AIA.

II. PRE-AIA FIRST-TO-INVENT SYSTEM

(i) Prior Art and Grace Period under Pre-AIA Patent Act

The U.S. has been known as the only country to still follow the first-to-invent system. The Pre-AIA Patent Act provides the definition of prior art under §102(a), which is comparable to EPC Article 54(2) and JPA Article 29(1).[11] It provides the definition of prior rights under §102(e), which is

---

[9] Convention on the Grant of European Patents, art. 54, Oct. 5, 1973, 1065 U.N.T.S. 255 (entered into force on October 7, 1977).

[10] Japanese Patent Act, Law No. 121 of 1959.

[11] 35 U.S.C. § 102(a)

(a) the invention was known or used by others in this country, or patented or described in a printed publication in this or a foreign country, before

comparable to EPC Article 54(3) and JPA Article 29-2.[12] Because these definitions were adopted to determine whether a person who seeks to patent his invention is the first-to-invent, these provisions apply to those other than that person. Further a prior invention gives rise to the prior art even if the invention is kept secret and thus has never been disclosed prior to the invention made by another who seeks to patent the same or obvious invention.[13] This is a stark contrast to the definition of the prior art under a first-to-file system.

On its face, these definitions make clear that novelty and priority follow the first-to-invent system by defining the prior art and prior rights as of the date of invention.[14] Contrary to such well accepted perceptions, if the U.S. first-to-invent is analyzed by focusing on the function of the statutory bar provisions, the priority rule and the examination practice at USPTO, the Pre-AIA Patent Act in fact has already followed the first-to-file system with a limited exception for an opportunity to establish the first-to-invent.[15]

Under the Pre-AIA Patent Act, statutory bar provisions define the prior art as of the date one year prior to the date of application ('critical date').[16]

---

the invention thereof by the applicant for patent. (underline added by the author)

12 35 U.S.C. § 102(e)

(e) the invention was described in – (1) an application for patent, published under section 122(b)· by another filed in the United States before the invention by the applicant for patent or (2) a patent granted on an application for patent by another filed in the United States before the invention by the applicant for patent, except that an international application filed under the treaty defined in section 351(a) shall have the effects for the purposes of this subsection of an application filed in the United States only if the international application designated the United States and was published under Article 21(2) of such treaty in the English language. (underline added by the author)

(Available at: http://www.uspto.gov/web/offices/pac/mpep/documents/appxl_35_U_S_C_102.htm)·

13 35 U.S.C. § 102(g)

14 *See supra* notes 11–12 (the underlines are added by the author).

15 Toshiko Takenaka, *Rethinking the United States First-to-Invent Principle from a Comparative Law Perspective: A Proposal to Restructure § 102 Novelty and Priority Provisions*, 39 HOUS. L. REV. 621 (2002) [hereinafter Takenaka, *Rethinking*]; Toshiko Takenaka, *The Novelty and Priority Provision under the United States First-To-File Principle: A Comparative Law Perspective,* in PATENT LAW AND THEORY: A HANDBOOK OF CONTEMPORARY RESEARCH 383 (Toshiko Takenaka ed., 2008).

16 35 U.S.C. § 102(b)

(b) the invention was patented or described . . ., more than one year prior to the date of the application for patent in the United States;

The statutory bar events characterize prior art not only for novelty but also for non-obviousness.[17] The substance of the condition provided in § 102(b) in removing from the prior art pre-filing disclosures during a specific period of one year from the filing date, seems to fit the definition of the grace period under a first-to-file system.[18] However, the significance of a grace period is very different between the first-to-invent and first-to-file systems. Under a true first-to-invent system, a grace period is not an exception, but a principle, because the novelty is determined as of the date of invention.[19] A true first-to-invent system requires that a patent office grant a patent on subject matter that was published and has become old prior to the date of application, as long as the subject matter is new and non-obvious as of the invention date. Under such a system, the subject matter's condition on the date of filing has nothing to do with its patentability.

However, Pre-AIA Patent Act does not follow the true first-to-invent system because it has an exception to the first-to-invent principle: statutory bars which prevent inventors from obtaining a patent after the expiration of a grace period once inventors engage in one of the activities listed in § 102(b), (c), and (d). The U.S. Supreme Court adopted this concept of statutory bars in *Pennock* (1829).[20] Thus, under the Pre-AIA U.S. first-

---

Id. § 102(d)

(d) the invention was first patented or caused to be patented, . . . more than one year before the filing of the application in the United States. (the underlines are added by the author)

[17] *Application of Foster*, 343 F.2d 980 (C.C.P.A. 1965).

[18] A commentator of a first-to-file country defines grace period as 'a specific period of time prior to the filing of a patent application by the inventor or his or her successor in title, during which time disclosures of an invention do not forfeit a right to patent the invention'. *See* Joseph Straus, *Grace Period and the European and International Patent Law: Analysis of Key Legal and Socio-Economic Aspects*, 20 IIC Studies, 3 (2001). U.S. legal scholars also view the similarity between § 102(b) and first-to-file novelty provisions. *See* Martin J. Adelman et al., Cases and Materials on Patent Law 206 (1998) (recognizing that § 102(b) statutory bars appear similar to the novelty provisions inherent in a first-to-file system).

[19] Canadian patent law long followed this true type of first-to-invent system until it was revised to adopt a first-to-file system. *Christiana v. Rice*, [1931] A.C. 770, 777–9, 782–3 (Can.) (appeal taken from Can.) (interpreting the Canadian Patent Act of 1923 to hold that the right to a Canadian patent goes to the first inventor regardless of where that invention occurred, even if the first inventor had not made his invention accessible to the public in any way). *See generally* Adelman, *supra* note 18, at 318 (explaining the evolution of Canadian patent law).

[20] *Pennock v. Dialogue*, 27 U.S. 1, 23–4 (1829) (clarifying the inventor's rights with respect to his invention by positing the principle that an inventor loses the right to a patent if he puts his invention into public use before filing a patent

to-invent system, granting a patent on subject matter disclosed prior to the date of application, is a principle, and denying a patent on subject matter disclosed prior to the grace period because of a statutory bar, is an exception. Moreover, during the grace period, inventors' rights to patent are protected from any disclosure or filing, by both their own acts and acts of third parties who have independently completed a patentably indistinguishable invention.[21] This follows that the two competing inventors should contest the first-to-invent priority either at the patent office or in a court, where disclosures and filing are used as evidence to establish a conception and reduction to practice under the priority rule.[22]

This is a stark contrast to the grace period under a first-to-file rule where a third party's independent disclosure or filing will destroy the novelty and priority with respect to the invention.[23] In the first-to-file world, determining the priority on the basis of the filing date is principle and a disclosure has nothing to do with the first-to-file priority. Although the grace period provides an exception to this rule to encourage inventors to disclose their inventions early, the exception should apply only to the extent to accomplish this goal, which is achieved as long as the exception protects inventors' rights for patent from disclosures deriving from their own acts.

As a result, the first-to-invent conditions for taking advantage of the grace period under § 102(b) are much more generous than the conditions under the first-to-file system. There are no restrictions on the types of disclosures that can benefit from the grace period and be automatically removed from the prior art for examination of both novelty and non-obviousness as long as § 102 is concerned.[24] It is not necessary to take any additional steps at the time of the patent application to remove the prior art during the grace period.[25] USTPO examiners do not consider

---

application). Although the concept of a grace period did not yet exist in American patent law at the time of *Pennock*, the Court established that, despite the emphasis on the first-to-invent principle, the first inventor's rights are not without boundary.

[21] However, courts distinguish the inventor's own act and a third party's act. In *W.L. Gore & Assocs. v. Garlock, Inc.*, 721 F.2d 1540, 1549–50 (Fed. Cir. 1983), the CAFC refused to find 'public use' with respect to subject matter that a third party used secretly.

[22] For a general discussion of the priority context, *see* Donald S. Chisum, Chisum on Patents § 10.09 (1978, Supp. 2011) [hereinafter Chisum on Patents]. As will be discussed below, under the Pre-AIA Patent Act, inventors can also rely on their secret acts to establish their conception and reduction to practice.

[23] *See, e.g.*, EPC Article 55; JPA Article 30; Draft SPLT Article 9.

[24] 35 U.S.C. § 102(b).

[25] *Id. compare* EPC Article 55(2), *with* JPA Article 30 Paragraph 4 (both

any disclosure in a patent or printed publication, on sale or in public use, for examining the patentability of an invention as long as such activities occurred during the grace period, except for the first-to-invent priority.

Despite these differences, the statutory bar provisions require USPTO to examine U.S. patent applications under the first-to-file rule with respect to the prior art which has become available prior to the grace period, that is, the critical date. In other words, contrary to a well-established perception, the Pre-AIA Patent Act has been following a first-to-file rule since the filing date is most relevant to determine patentability for § 102 prior art since the 1829 *Pennock* case, while also preserving an opportunity for inventors to establish a first-to-invent priority during the grace period.

(ii) Priority under Pre-AIA Patent Act

The § 102 (b) statutory bar provision extensively limits the opportunity to establish a first-to-invent priority between two inventors who invented identical and obvious inventions independently. An inventor is deprived of an opportunity to establish a first-to-invent priority with respect to his claimed invention under examination, if he fails to file an application within the grace period of one year from a disclosure by a third party inventor who invented a patentably indistinguishable invention.[26] In other words, a first-to-file priority rule applies to third party independent inventors who disclosed their inventions prior to the critical date.

A first-to-invent priority rule applies only to a third party inventor who kept his invention secret at least before the critical date. An inventor of a claimed invention under examination is given an opportunity to establish a first-to-invent priority prior to the critical date if both the inventor and third party inventor kept their inventions secret until the filing date.[27] However, the first-to-invent rule for secret prior inventions prevents inventors from establishing the priority far beyond the grace period. Under the Pre-AIA priority rule, if an inventor attempts to rely on the date of conception of his invention, he must continue to be diligent to reduce the invention to practice during the period between the competing inventor's conception date and the inventor's date of reducing his invention to

---

systems require applicants to file evidence of a pre-filing disclosure and a petition to apply an exception under the grace period provision).

[26] 37 C.F.R. § 1.131 (2001); Manual for Patent Examining Procedure ('MPEP') § 715 (8th ed. 2001, Rev. 2010).

[27] An inventor's confidential commercial use of his invention may give rise to a public use and thus § 102(b). For more discussion, *see infra* note 50.

practice.[28] A lack of activity on the invention prevents him from relying on the date of conception.[29] Likewise, if an inventor attempts to rely on the date of constructing and testing an embodiment of a claimed invention for establishing reduction to practice, he must file a patent application without delay.[30] An unreasonable delay in filing a patent application gives rise to abandonment, suppression or concealment, which prevents the inventor from relying on the date of reduction to practice.[31] The requirements of continuous diligence for completing an invention and filing a patent application make it difficult for inventors to bring the priority back far beyond the grace period. Because these requirements are not clear from the definition of secret prior invention under the Pre-AIA Patent Act,[32] U.S. inventors could readily lose their priority by failing to continue to work on their inventions.

Finally, Pre-AIA USPTO examination practice follows the first-to-file examination practice by making the filing date most relevant to determining the first-to-invent priority between multiple inventors who kept their inventions secret before the critical date. Under U.S. case law, the filing date of a U.S. patent application with an adequate disclosure of the invention is presumed to be the invention date.[33] Relying on this assumption, USPTO examiners give applicants a chance to eliminate a prior art reference only if the examiner finds a reference which was published earlier than the inventor's filing date but during the grace period. The Pre-AIA Patent Act offers two procedures to eliminate a reference with evidence of the first-to-invent. If a reference is a U.S. patent or patent application pending at USPTO claiming the same or obvious subject matter, the first-to-invent priority is contested between two inventors through inter partes proceedings called interference.[34] If a reference is any other reference than the above U.S. patent or pending patent application, the priority is resolved through ex-parte proceedings called swearing back practice.[35]

---

[28] 35 U.S.C. § 102(g); *Keizer v. Bradley*, 270 F.2d 396, 399–400 (C.C.P.A. 1959).

[29] *Griffith v. Kanamaru*, 231 U.S.P.Q. 892, 893 (B.P.A.I 1986).

[30] This date is called an actual reduction date. For a discussion on actual reduction to practice, *see* Chisum on Patents, *supra* note 22, § 10.06.

[31] 35 U.S.C. § 102(g). *Paulik v. Rizkalla,* 760 F.2d 1270, (Fed. Cir. 1985), *appeal after remand,* 796 F.2d 456 (Fed. Cir. 1986).

[32] 35 U.S.C. § 102(g).

[33] This date is called a constructive reduction date. For a discussion of constructive reduction to practice, *see* Chisum on Patents, *supra* note 22, § 10.05.

[34] 35 U.S.C. § 135.

[35] 37 C.F.R. § 1.131 (2001). Further, an inventor can eliminate a prior art reference by showing that the reference is his own work under 37 CFR §1.132.

In interference proceedings, USPTO follows a first-to-file rule by imposing on second-to-file inventors the ultimate burden of showing the priority over the first-to-file inventor.[36] Due to the difficulty in meeting the burden, the U.S. priority rule grants the priority to first-to-file inventors far more frequently than to second-to-file inventors.[37] In addition, the high cost associated with interference proceedings discourages second-to-file inventors from taking advantage of the first-to-invent priority system.[38] As a result, only a very small portion of U.S. applications, less than 0.1%, engage in the priority contest in interference proceedings.[39]

In ex-parte proceedings, an applicant files an affidavit swearing the date of invention with corroborative evidence of conception and reduction to practice.[40] If an examiner finds the evidence sufficient to support the date prior to the effective date of reference, the examiner removes the reference from his consideration of patentability and withdraws a rejection.

However, unsophisticated inventors such as individual inventors and small and mid-size enterprises often fail to take advantage of the first-to-invent priority opportunity because they do not keep records of the activities which resulted in the invention and cannot show an earlier inven-

---

[36] 37 C.F.R. § 1.657 (2001).

[37] *See* Charles R.B. Macedo, *First-to-File: Is American Adoption of the International Standard in Patent Law Worth the Price?*, 18 AIPLA Q.J. 193, 217 (1990) (observing that senior parties win 75% of the interferences). *Edwards v. Strazzabosco,* 58 U.S.P.Q.2d 1836 (B.P.A.I. 2001) (a panel of the trial section at the USPTO Board noted a 75% success rate for senior parties over junior parties.); Gerald J. Mossinghoff, *The U.S. First-To-Invent System Has Provided No Advantage to Small Entities,* 84 J. PAT. & TRADEMARK OFF. SOC'Y 425 (2002) (during the period between 1983 and 2000, of the total of 2,858 interference cases, 1917 were favorable to the first-to-file inventors). *But see* Charles L. Cholz, *A Critique of Recent Opinions in Patent Interferences*, 84 J. PAT. & TRADEMARK OFF. SOC'Y 163, 181 (2002) (the author points out a conflict between the assessment of the Edwards panel and the last interference statistics published by the USPTO); Mark Lemley and Colleen Chien, *Are the U.S. Priority Rules Really Necessary?* Hastings Law Journal, Vol. 54, p. 1299 (2003) (the authors' survey indicates that 43% of junior parties won in the cases that are litigated to judgment and actually resolved on priority grounds).

[38] *See, e.g.*, Macedo, *supra* note 37, at 218–19 (estimating that conducting interferences costs patent applicants approximately $15,000,000 per year). According to a survey conducted by American Intellectual Property Association (AIPLA) in 2010, the median of the estimated cost which inclusive all costs in a two party interference is $338,000. AIPLA, Report of Economic Survey 2011, 30 (2011).

[39] Mossinghoff, *supra* note 37, at 427.

[40] 37 C.F.R. § 1.131 (2001). Further, an inventor can eliminate a prior art reference by showing that the reference is his own work under 37 CFR §1.132.

tion with corroborative evidence.[41] Even for sophisticated inventors at multinational firms, it is very likely that a practice of maintaining records on continuous work is more expensive than the practice of filing an application early. Accordingly, labeling the Pre-AIA U.S. patent system as a first-to-invent system is misleading,[42] because the Pre-AIA first-to-invent system frequently does not award patents to first-to-invent inventors due to the complex rules and cost of maintaining proof of invention.[43] The filing date is most relevant to patentability for an overwhelming majority of patent applications. In addition, secret inventions, which allow inventors to establish the first-to-invent priority beyond the grace period, introduce a lot of uncertainty in patent validity because USPTO cannot examine patentability with respect to secret prior art.

III. FIRST-INVENTOR-TO-FILE UNDER AIA

(i) Purposes and Goals of AIA

The FITF system was introduced as a system drawn on the best aspects of the first-to-invent and first-to-file systems, to contribute to the purpose of AIA to provide a more efficient and streamlined patent system that will improve patent quality and limit unnecessary and counterproductive litigation costs.[44] To achieve this goal, AIA redefines the prior art to capture the efficiency of the first-to-file system, by making the filing date most relevant in determining whether an application is patentable, while maintaining the one year grace period for inventors.[45] AIA also aims to eliminate the current costly and complex interference proceedings for determining the first-to-invent priority, by relying on the date of the first application and establishing a simpler and more effective administrative proceeding called a derivation proceeding to make sure that a patent

---

41 *See, e.g.*, *Gould v. Schawlow*, 363 F.2d 908, 920 (C.C.P.A. 1966) (finding the inventor failed to establish his diligence because of a lack of corroborative evidence to support his activity).

42 Takenaka, *Rethinking*, *supra* note 15, at 624, 646.

43 Statement of Steven W. Miller Vice President and General Counsel, Intellectual Property The Procter & Gamble Company, America Invents Act, Committee on House Judiciary, Subcommittee on Intellectual Property, Competition and Internet Subcommittee (March 30, 2011) (http://judiciary.house.gov/hearings/pdf/Miller03302011.pdf).

44 112th Congress, 1st Session, Report on America Invents Act ('AIA Report'), 41–2.

45 *Id.* at 42.

is granted to a true inventor.[46] However, as will be discussed below, whether AIA can eliminate a complex administrative procedure for a priority contest depends on how USPTO and courts interpret the FITF provision.

(ii) Prior Art under AIA

Reflecting on these goals, the Pre-AIA novelty and priority provisions are revised to make clear that the prior art and prior rights are measured from the filing date of the application. New § 102(a) provides the definition of prior art, which is comparable to EPC Article 54(2) and JPA 29(1).[47] This definition makes clear that the prior art is measured from the filing date.[48] The prior art definition under AIA is different from the definition under EPC Article 54(2) in listing not only a broad definition of such invention, an invention which is available to the public as provided in EPC Article 54(2), but also includes in examples of the prior art inventions, an invention being patented, described in a printed publication, in public use or on sale.[49] At the House judicial committee, a deletion of public use and on sale was discussed and included in a manager's amendment.[50] However, that part of the amendment failed to pass the committee.[51] Thus the final bill which passed into law includes these examples.

These examples may introduce a lot of ambiguity in the scope of the prior art under AIA because U.S. courts interpreted these examples reflecting the first-to-invent policy and have given a meaning which departs from the ordinary meaning.[52] For example, 'public use' includes

---

[46] *Id.*

[47] AIA Section 3, §102(a)(1) the claimed invention was patented, described in a printed publication, or in public use, on sale, or otherwise available to the public <u>before the effective filing date of the claimed invention</u>.

[48] *Id.* (the underline is added by the author).

[49] AIA Section 3, §102(a)(1). JPA Article 29(1) lists three examples of the prior art, publicly known inventions, publicly used inventions and inventions described in a printed publication. However, Japanese courts interpret these examples in the same manner as the prior art under EPC Article 54(2) in requiring inventions made available to the public.

[50] Harold C. Wegner, *Chairman Lamar Smith Restores Grace Period in America Invents Act,* http://www.patents4life.com/wp-content/uploads/2011/04/GracePeriodRestored.pdf.

[51] Dennis Crouch, Patent Reform 2011, PATENTLYO (Apr. 15, 2011), (http://www.patentlyo.com/patent/2011/04/patent-reform-2011.html).

[52] For a discussion of US case law for interpreting these examples, *see* Takenaka, *Rethinking*, *supra* note 15, at 634.

an inventor's own secret but commercial use[53] yet excludes experimental public use.[54] U.S. courts adopted this meaning, departing from the ordinary meaning of 'public use', reflecting policies unique to the first-to-invent priority rule for forcing inventors to file a patent application early while guaranteeing sufficient time to complete inventions.[55] Inventions 'being patented' and 'being described in a printed publication' are listed separately, but case law does not make clear the distinction between two prior art inventions, in requiring both inventions becoming available to the public in a minimum way to constitute part of the prior art.[56] Legal commentators argue that it is likely that U.S. courts would interpret the definition of the state of art under AIA differently from that of EPC Article 54 because U.S. courts usually retain their interpretation of a term through their case law unless the interpretation is expressly repealed by Congress.[57]

---

[53] *Metallizing Eng'g Co. v. Kenyon Bearing & Auto Parts Co.*, 153 F.2d 516, 517–18 (2d Cir. 1946).

[54] *City of Elizabeth v. Am. Nicholson Pavement Co.*, 97 U.S. 126, 134–5 (1877)

[55] Takenaka, *Rethinking*, *supra* note 15, at 634. Under a first-to-invent system, all prior inventions constitute the prior art regardless of whether they are publicly accessible or kept secret. A first-to-invent system under the Pre-1989 Canadian Patent Law also included secret prior art. *Christiani v. Rice,* [1930] S.C.R. 443 (Can.).

[56] For an analysis of 'being patented,' *see Duplan Corp. v. Deering Milliken, Inc.*, 353 F. Supp. 826, 832–3 (D.C.S.C. 1973), which explains the difference between patents issued on the date the patent is granted as opposed to the date of publication. *See also* CHISUM ON PATENTS, *supra* note 22, § 3.06[4]. For an analysis of 'described in a printed publication', *see In re Hall*, 781 F.2d 897, 899–900 (Fed. Cir. 1986), which held that a doctoral thesis was prior art because it was a printed publication that was available to the public even though the thesis was in a single catalogue index in a single library. *See also* CHISUM ON PATENTS, *supra* note 22, § 3.04[2].

[57] E.g., John Duffy & Robert Merges, *Leathy-Smith America Invents Act*, (https://docs.google.com/leaf?id=0B1P2D6tikiwFMDliMzhhNWMtNGM3ZC00MDYxLTlmMjEtMjE2YjVkMDUwN2Y1&hl=3n US); Brad Pendersen, *Taking the Leahy-Smith America Invents Act for a Test Drive*, Practicing Law Institute (Sept. 26, 2011); Paul Janicke, *A Commentary on the New Patent Law of the United States*, GRUR Int'l 2011, 887.

However, a leading patent practitioner, who was involved in legislating AIA supports a view that Congress repealed the pre-AIA case law interpretation by including the term 'otherwise available to the public' in new §102(a). See Robert A. Armitage, 'Understanding the America Invents Act and Its Implications for Patenting', 40 *AIPLA Quarterly Journal* 1 (2012), http://www.uspto.gov/aia_implementation/armitage_pdf.pdf. USPTO adopted this view in its proposed examination guidelines, 77 Fed. Reg. 43742, 43759 (July 26, 2012) (http://www.uspto.gov/aia_implementation/first-inventor-to-file_proposed_rules.pdf.)

With respect to the geographical scope, AIA will bring the prior art under AIA into harmony with EPC and JPA. The Pre-AIA Patent Act excludes foreign activities which give rise to on sale or public use from the prior art and thus do not trigger the grace period.[58] This geographical limitation functions against U.S. inventors because it gives foreign applicants more time to exploit the invention prior to filing for a U.S. patent in their own countries.[59] AIA will eliminate this discrimination by making clear that public use or on sale constitutes the prior art regardless of the place where the act takes place.

New § 102(a) also provides prior rights, which are comparable to prior rights under EPC Article 54(3) and JPA 29-2, for inventions described in a patent or patent application pending at USPTO.[60] This definition makes clear that the prior rights are also measured by the filing date.[61] This prior right provision functions to give an inventor a priority right on the basis of her filing date instead of the invention date. Because this prior right provision does not apply to an application filed on the same filing date of the claimed invention under examination, multiple patents may issue to the same or obvious inventions if more than one application is filed by different inventors who independently invented the inventions.[62]

AIA eliminated the provision for including secret prior inventions in the prior art.[63] Although the concept of conception under the first-to-invent priority may play an important role for deciding whether a third party invention is derived from the invention under examination, other concepts for determining the first-to-invent will fade away as patents examined under the first-to-invent system expire.

AIA harmonized the patent defeating effective date of prior rights with that of EPC and JPA prior rights by repealing the *Hilmer* doctrine. Under the Pre-AIA Patent Act, the Court of Claims and Patent Appeals

---

58 35 U.S.C. §§ 102(a), (b) (1994).

59 *See* William LaMarca, *Reevaluating the Geographical Limitation of 35 U.S.C. § 102(B); Policies Considered*, 22 U. Dayton L. Rev. 25, 36–7 (1996).

60 AIA § 102(a)(2) the claimed invention was described in a patent issued under section 151, or in an application for patent published or deemed published under section 122(b), in which the patent or application, as the case may be, names another inventor and was effectively filed <u>before the effective filing date of the claimed invention</u>.

61 *Id.* (the underline is added by the author).

62 This practice is the same as EPC but different from JPA. JPA Article 39 requires applicants to engage a discussion to select one applicant who receives a patent for the invention. If applicants are unable to reach an agreement, none of applicants can obtain a patent.

63 35 U.S.C. § 102(g).

interpreted the Paris Convention Article 4B,[64] which does not give rise to an obligation only with respect to a defensive patent-defeating effect in *Hilmer.*[65] Accordingly, under the *Hilmer* doctrine, U.S. courts give the priority only with respect to claimed subject matter, while refusing to give the same effect to disclosed but unclaimed subject matter if the subject matter is included in the prior right reference. In contrast, to avoid this complexity, most first-to-file countries give the effect of priority under the Paris Convention to both claimed and unclaimed subject matter.[66] U.S. commentators extensively criticized the illogical problems caused by the *Hilmer* doctrine.[67] U.S. trade partners also criticized the *Hilmer* doctrine as a violation of the priority right provision under the Paris Convention, as well as, the non-discrimination policy provision regarding the place of invention under WTO-TRIPS.[68] In response to these criticisms, the prior right provision was revised to give the patent defeating effect on the international patent application under the Patent Cooperation Treaty (PCT),[69] which has the filing date on and after November 29, 2000 if the application is published in English.[70] This revision introduced a lot of complexity in determining patentability.[71]

---

[64] The Convention on international exhibitions signed at Paris on November 22, 1928 and last revised on November 30, 1972.

[65] *Application of Hilmer*, 359 F.2d 859 (C.C.P.A. 1966). This interpretation is supported by some U.S. scholars. ADELMAN, *supra* note 18, at 824 (advancing that 'the Paris Convention patentee is given a patent-defeating right retroactive to the priority date for what is claimed in the patent', but noting most countries 'employ a whole continents' patent-defeating effect that covers everything disclosed in the priority document that is carried forward into the patent application').

[66] Reinhard Wieczorek, *Convention Applications as Patent-Defeating Prior Rights*, 6 IIC 135, 156–65 (1975).

[67] *See* DONALD S. CHISUM, ELEMENTS OF UNITED STATES PATENT LAW, 104 (2000) [hereinafter CHISUM ELEMENTS]; Kevin L. Leffel, Comment, *Hilmer Doctrine and Patent System Harmonization: What Does A Foreign Inventor Have At Stake?*, 26 AKRON L. REV. 355 (1992); Harold C. Wegner, *TRIPS Boomerang–Obligations for Domestic Reform,* 29 VAND. J. TRANSNAT'L L. 535 (1996).

[68] Agreement on Trade-Related Aspects of Intellectual Property Rights, Apr. 15, 1994, Marrakesh Agreement Establishing the World Trade Organization. Professor Chisum also pointed out this problem, *see* CHISUM ELEMENTS, *supra* note 67, at 104.

[69] Patent Cooperation Treaty, June 19, 1970, 28. U.S.T. 7645, 1160 U.N.T.S. 231, *amended* Sept. 28, 1979, *modified,* Feb. 3, 1984 and Oct. 3, 2001.

[70] 35 U.S.C. § 102(e) amended by the American Inventors Protection Act of 1999 (AIPA) (Pub. L. 106–113, 113 Stat. 1501 (1999)) and as further amended by the Intellectual Property and High Technology Technical Amendments Act of 2002 (Pub. L. 107–273, 116 Stat. 1758 (2002)).

[71] Because of this complexity, USPTO has a Q&A website to determine

AIA removed this complexity by repealing the *Hilmer* doctrine and moved the U.S. system in line with EPC and JPA as well as other patent systems. New § 102(a) makes clear that a prior right reference will become effective as of the effective filing date.[72] Because AIA defines the effective filing date to include the earliest application entitled to a right of priority under the Paris Convention and PCT,[73] it will give the patent defeating effect to the entire disclosure of the pending patent application, as of the priority date under the Paris Convention and the international filing date under PCT.

However, some discrepancy between AIA and EPC remains with respect to the scope of grounds for citing prior right references. AIA is different from EPC and JPA because a prior right reference is available for rejecting a claim not only for lack of novelty but also for obviousness.[74] A prior right reference is available for rejecting claims only for lack of novelty under EPC and JPA.[75] AIA also differs from EPC in excluding applications which name the same inventor(s), are owned by the same person or are subject to obligation of assignment to the same person from application of a prior right reference.[76] However, AIA's exclusions are in line with JPA.[77]

(iii) Grace Period

Although the definition of the prior art under AIA moved the U.S. patent system more in line with the rest of world, whether AIA in fact follows a first-to-file without a first-to-invent exception depends on how U.S. courts will interpret the definition of the disclosures that are not prejudicial to patentability during the grace period under new §102(b). The prevailing view in interpreting the definition is to give the priority and grant a patent to one who discloses the invention first, while denying a patent with respect to another inventor who independently invented the same invention and

---

patentability with respect to the prior right reference under35 U.S.C. § 102(e). (http://www.uspto.gov/patents/law/aipa/18month/102efaq.jsp)

72 AIA §122(a)(2).

73 AIA Section 3(i)(2).

74 *Hazeltine Corp. v. United States,* 820 F.2d 1190, 1196 (Fed. Cir. 1987).

75 EPC Article 56, JPA Article 29(2).

76 AIA Section 3, §§ 102(a)(2), 102(b)(2)(C).

77 The scope of exclusion for prior right references is the same as the scope under JPA. JPA prevents JPO from citing a prior right to reject a claim for lack of inventive step but JPO uses the substantial identity standard to reject claims obvious from a prior right reference. For a discussion of the prior effect of prior rights under JPA, *see* Toshiko Takenaka, *The Substantial Identity Rule under the Japanese Novelty Standard,* 9 UCLA PACIFIC BASIN LAW JOURNAL 220 (1991).

filed first, as long as the first-to-disclose inventor files a patent application within one year from the disclosure.[78] In other words, an inventor can eliminate a §102(a)(1) prior art reference as well as a §102(a)(2) prior right reference by showing an early date of disclosure during the one year grace period from her effective filing date. If U.S. courts uphold this interpretation, FITF is in fact a revised version of a first-to-invent with minor modifications and needs an administrative proceeding similar to the current interference proceeding to determine a first-to-disclose priority.

On its face, new § 102(b) is comparable to EPC Article 55 in defining disclosures of an invention which are removed from the state of art.[79] One obvious difference between AIA and EPC is the length of the grace period. The grace period under AIA is one year, or twelve months,[80] and thus twice as long as the six-month grace period under EPC and JPA.[81]

A more significant difference is the scope of disclosures. AIA copied some terms from the definition of disclosures from the grace period provision under Article 9 of the Draft Substantive Patent Law Treaty (Draft SPLT)[82] by listing disclosures by an inventor and a third party who obtained the information directly or indirectly from the inventor.[83] AIA however also takes account of an invention made by multiple inventors and includes disclosures by a joint inventor.[84] Further, AIA lists disclosures of the inventor and a third party deriving from the inventor,

---

78 Duffy & Merges, *supra* note 57, at 25–47; Pendersen, *supra* note 57, at 6; Janicke, *supra* note 57, at 893.

79 AIA Section 3, § 102(b) Exceptions–

(1) DISCLOSURES MADE 1 YEAR OR LESS BEFORE THE EFFECTIVE FILING DATE OF THE CLAIMED INVENTION– A disclosure made <u>1 year or less</u> before the effective filing date of a claimed invention shall not be prior art to the claimed invention under subsection (a)(1) if . . . [a list of groups of disclosures].

80 *Id.* (the underline is added by the author).

81 EPC Article 55(1), JPA Article 30(1)–(3). For more discussions, see Joseph Straus, Priority Right and Period of 'Grace' – The Separate Issues under the European Patent Law, Gert Dannemann and Tereza Wolf (eds.), GLOBAL PERSPECTIVES OF CONTEMPORARY INTELLECTUAL PROPERTY ISSUES, 351 (1999).

82 World Intellectual Property Organization, *Draft Substantive Patent Law Treaty Article 9 (1)(i) & (iii)* (http://www.wipo.int/edocs/mdocs/scp/en/scp_10/scp_10_4.pdf). For a discussion of Draft SPLT, *see* Toshiko Takenaka, *The Best Patent Practice or Mere Compromise? A Review of the Current Draft of the Substantive Patent Law Treaty and a Proposal for a 'First-To-Invent' Exception for Domestic Applicants*, 11 TEX. INTELL. PROP. L.J. 259 (2003).

83 AIA Section 3, § 102(b)(1)(A) the disclosure was made by the inventor or joint inventor or by another who obtained the subject matter disclosed directly or indirectly from the inventor or a joint inventor.

84 *Id.*

together as one group, in contrast to the Draft SPLT, which lists the inventor and a third party as two different groups.[85]

AIA lists the definition of another group, which reads: 'the subject matter disclosed had, before such disclosure, been publicly disclosed by the inventor, a joint inventor or another who obtained the subject matter disclosed directly or indirectly from the inventor or a joint inventor.'[86]

This definition is different from the definition of the third group of disclosures under the Draft SPLT, which still limits the scope of disclosures to those derived from the inventor:

> by an Office and the information was contained
>
> (a) in another application filed by the inventor [and should not have been made available to the public by the Office], or
> (b) in an application filed without the knowledge or consent of the inventor by a third party which obtained the information directly or indirectly from the inventor.[87]

Unlike the Draft SPLT, the AIA §102(b)(1)(B) definition does not limit the actor of the second group disclosure, which should occur after the first disclosure defined in §102(b)(1)(A). Like AIA, the Pre-AIA Patent Act grace period provision does not specify an actor of statutory bar events (disclosures) and applies the exception to the inventor's own act as well as an act of a third party who does not derive the invention from the inventor.[88] Accordingly, U.S. academics and lawyers read the AIA definition as they read the Pre-AIA grace period provision, in removing any disclosure by anyone from the state of art for determining the patentability, regardless of whether the disclosure resulted from an act of the inventor or co-inventor.[89] This interpretation is supported by some discussions in

---

[85] *Id.*

[86] AIA Section 3, § 102(b)(1)(B).

[87] SPLT Article 9. This provision is essentially the same as the grace periods provision under Article 12 of the 'Basic Proposal' for the Treaty Supplementing the Paris Convention. For more discussion, see Straus, *supra* note 18, at 13. Many first-to-file countries adopted the grace period provision of the Basic Proposal. See Straus, *supra* note 18, at 30.

[88] 35 U.S.C. § 102(b). For a discussion of a third party bar event, *see supra* note 21.

[89] Duffy & Merges, *supra* note 57 at 25–47; Pendersen, *supra* note 57, at 6; Janicke, *supra* note 57 at 893; Armitage, *supra* note 57 at 74. USPTO proposed examination guidelines also supports this view. The guidelines require strict identity between subject matter under the examination and subject matter of pre-filing disclosure. See the guidelines, *supra* note 57, at 43767; 43769.

Congress where a sponsor of the AIA bill emphasized the protection of an inventor by giving the priority based on his or her disclosure.[90]

AIA also lists these two groups of disclosures as exceptions to prior rights.[91] U.S. academics and lawyers read the application of the second group disclosure exception to prior right references in the same manner as the prior art under new §102(b)(1)(B).[92] Such exception protects the first-to-disclose inventor by preventing any other inventors from establishing a prior right after her disclosure. Accordingly, this interpretation guarantees the first-to-disclose inventor not only a patent defeating effect but also a priority right to obtain a patent based on the date of first disclosure. This view is foreign to the first-to-file world where a disclosure gives rise only to patent defeating effect. However, U.S. lawyers who are trained in the first-to-invent world view the disclosure during the grace period as evidence of invention, which gives rise to the priority for obtaining a patent as well as the patent defeating effect.[93]

This interpretation will bring some changes to the Pre-AIA first-to-invent priority rule by limiting the evidence for the first-to-invent priority to a disclosure. However, the effect of these changes is very marginal.[94]

---

90 *See, e.g.*, June 22, 2011, H4420–4452 (http://thomas.loc.gov/cgi-bin/query/R?r112:FLD001:H04421), H4429–31: Discussion of Mr. SMITH of Texas. ('Additionally, subsection 102(b)(1)(B) is designed to make a very strong grace period for inventors that have made a disclosure that satisfies 102(b). Inventors who have made such disclosures are protected during the grace period not only from their own disclosure but from other prior art from anyone that follows their disclosure. This is an important protection we offer in our bill.') H4480–4505 (http://thomas.loc.gov/cgi-bin/query/R?r112:FLD001:H04481) ('The grace period protects the ability of an inventor to discuss or write about their ideas for a patent up to 1 year before they file for patent protection. These simple requirements create a priority date that is fixed and public so that everyone in the world can measure the patent against competing applications and patents and relevant prior art.') *See also* Janicke, *supra* note 57 at 893.

91 AIA Section 3, §§ 102(b)(2)(A), 102(b)(2)(B). These subjections also list a third class to exclude a disclosure in the application owned by the same person or subject to an obligation of assignment to the same person.

92 Duffy & Merges, *supra* note 57 at 25–47; Pendersen, *supra* note 57 at 6; Janicke, *supra* note 57, at 893.

93 Toshiko Takenaka, *Harmony with the Rest of the World?; America Invents Act*, 7 Oxford Intellectual Property Law & Practice Journal, 4 (forthcoming 2012). See also, Armitage, *supra* note 57 at 78.

94 This author once proposed a revision of § 102 priority similar to the new § 102 priority under AIA in limiting the first-to-invent priority within the one year grace period by eliminating § 102(g) secret prior art. However, this option of revision is the most modest because the impact of this revision is marginal. For more discussion, *see* Takenaka, *Rethinking*, *supra* note 15, at 661.

The Pre-AIA Patent Act follows a first-to-file rule with respect to a third party independent inventor who disclosed his invention before the critical date. A first-to-invent rule continues to apply under AIA with respect to a third party independent inventor who kept the invention secret up to the critical date, although the evidence to establish a first-to-invent priority is limited to a disclosure under AIA. A change brought by AIA is to apply a first-to-file rule to a third party inventor who did not disclose his invention during the one year grace period, because the inventor can no longer rely on secret conception or reduction to practice. A first-to-invent by a disclosure also effectively eliminates an inventor from establishing a priority beyond the grace period. However, even under the Pre-AIA Patent Act, the first-to-invent priority rule prevents inventors from establishing a priority far beyond the grace period of the invention of the claimed invention under examination. As a result, although AIA further limited the narrow exception of opportunity to establish a first-to-invent under the Pre-AIA, a first-to-invent rule remains as long as a third party independent inventor discloses or files a patent application during the grace period for the claimed invention under examination.[95]

The structure of new §102(b) also supports the view that AIA follows a first-to-invent system. Although the subtitle of new §102(b) makes clear that disclosures removed from the prior art are exceptions,[96] the condition for taking advantage of the grace period remains generous by not limiting the type of disclosures. AIA does not require any additional process to claim the exceptions. This suggests that new §102(b) under AIA continues to follow a first-to-invent principle by granting a patent to a first-to-invent inventor during the grace period regardless of the confidential status of the invention on the filing date. Thus USPTO will automatically eliminate a disclosure during the grace period under new §102(b).

The view that AIA follows a first-to-invent system is reinforced by the prior user provision.[97] Mitigating the belief that AIA will adopt a first-

---

[95] With respect to a third party inventor who discloses his invention during the grace period of a claimed invention, the inventor also must file a patent application within one year from the disclosure. AIA Section 3, § 102(b)(1)(B).

[96] AIA Section 3, § 102(b).

[97] AIA Section 5, § 273. Defense to infringement based on prior commercial use

(a) In General– A person shall be entitled to a defense under section 282(b) with respect to subject matter consisting of a process, or consisting of a machine, manufacture, or composition of matter used in a manufacturing or other commercial process, that would otherwise infringe a claimed invention being asserted against the person if –

(1) such person, acting in good faith, commercially used the subject matter in the United States, either in connection with an internal commercial use

to-file system and will be disadvantageous to inventors who are first-to-invent but failed to file a patent application, AIA will expand the scope of inventions for which a defense of infringement based on a prior use of an invention is applicable. Under the Pre-AIA Patent Act, a defense based on a prior use is available only with respect to a method of doing or conducting business.[98] Under AIA, the defense will be available for a process, machine, manufacture or composition of matter used in a manufacturing or other commercial process, regardless of the field of technology.[99] Unlike prior user rights in the first-to-file world, AIA makes not only the filing date but also the first disclosure date most relevant to securing a prior user right, in requiring a substantial commercial use of the invention being made at least one year before the first disclosure of invention claimed in the patent, against which a defense is asserted if the inventor made a disclosure before filing a patent application.[100] This requirement supports the view that AIA follows a first-to-invent rule because a first-to-invent date evidenced by the first disclosure functions in the same manner as the effective filing date, in giving rise to a priority right which prevents any third party right for the invention disclosed or claimed during the prescribed one year period.[101] This function is a stark contrast to the function of a disclosure in a first-to-file system where a disclosure only gives rise to a patent defeating effect.

IV. ANALYSIS

The adoption of the new definition of the prior art contributes to worldwide patent harmonization through the removal of the geographical limitation and repeal of the *Hilmer* doctrine. This will facilitate USPTO's collaboration with other patent offices by exchanging examination results through the patent prosecution highway.[102]

---

or an actual arm's length sale or other arm's length commercial transfer of a useful end result of such commercial use; and '
(2) such commercial use occurred at least 1 year before the earlier of either –
(A) the effective filing date of the claimed invention; or
(B) the date on which the claimed invention was disclosed to the public in a manner that qualified for the exception from prior art under section 102(b).

98 35 USC §273(a)(3).

99 AIA Section 5, §273(a).

100 AIA Section 5, §273(a)(1)(B).

101 *Id.*

102 The Patent Prosecution Highway is a collaborative effort among patent

Unfortunately, the scope of the prior art under the new definition is unclear because the examples of the prior art under the Pre-AIA Patent Act remain in the new definition under AIA. These examples may be interpreted by U.S. courts to include acts conflicting with the broad definition of the prior art, which requires public accessibility. Such interpretation conflicts with the first-to-file novelty policy which rewards a person who discloses subject matter which was not publicly accessible at the filing date. This policy is a stark contrast to the first-to-invent policy for rewarding patents to first-to-invent inventors regardless of disclosure of the subject matter. Such conflicting interpretation will mislead inventors who are not well informed of U.S. case law and could lead to forfeitures of their rights for a patent.[103] U.S. courts should interpret the new definition in light of the first-to-file novelty policy and exclude subject matter which was not publicly accessible at the filing date. They should read the definition to include any publicly accessible subject matter regardless of the inventor's intent to use subject matter for experimentation.

A serious problem in the Pre-AIA Patent Act is the discrepancy between the statutory language and the examination practice at USPTO.[104] AIA will make the U.S. patent system more user-friendly by moving the definition of the prior art more in line with the examination practice. The new definition makes clear that patentability is measured by the filing date and protects U.S. inventors by giving a notice to file a patent application within a grace period.

In addition, the new definition of prior rights contributes substantially to the goal of AIA to provide an efficient patent system by eliminating secret prior inventions from the prior art. This elimination will also improve patent quality because USPTO cannot examine secret prior inventions. It will also protect inventors from misunderstanding the complex rule of priority, which in fact follows a first-to-file rule.

In contrast, the complex and unclear terms used to define disclosures under the AIA grace period protection present a serious problem. If U.S. courts adopt the prevailing view of U.S. lawyers and academics, FITF will bring only minor change to the current first-to-invent rule under the Pre-AIA Patent Act. Because FITF makes the date of disclosure most relevant to patentability with respect to the priority between the inventor of a claimed invention under the examination and a third party independent

---

offices to accelerate examination by sharing information and examination results (http://www.uspto.gov/patents/init_events/pph/pphbrochure.jsp).

103 Takenaka, *Rethinking*, *supra* note 15 at 656–7.

104 Takenaka, *Rethinking*, *supra* note 15 at 645.

inventor who disclosed or filed his invention during the grace period of the claimed invention, AIA will need an administrative proceeding to determine the priority between the two inventors. In this proceeding, inventors need to establish a first-to-invent priority by the evidence of disclosure.

Because AIA does not require applicants to identify a pre-filing disclosure at the time of filing, it is likely that USPTO will maintain the current examination practice to give an opportunity to establish an earlier disclosure date only when an examiner finds a prior art reference during the grace period. If a reference is a U.S. patent or patent application claiming an invention identical or obvious from the claimed invention under examination, examiners will need to start an inter-partes administrative proceeding between two inventors in which the inventors will contest the priority by their disclosures.

It is likely that this proceeding is as costly and complex as the current interference proceeding, which will lead to a direct conflict with an important goal of FITF to eliminate a complex and costly administrative procedure to determine the priority between multiple inventors who independently invented patentably indistinguishable inventions.[105] The legislative history puts emphasis on the benefit of the first-to-file file system of eliminating the uncertainty resulting from the invention date, which is the determinative date in contrast to the filing date, which is the objective date.[106] Unfortunately, the disclosure date is also the determinative date which should be established. Under AIA, the disclosure date must be established with evidence, which is publicly accessible in contrast to corroborative evidence with which the actual invention date is determined under the Pre-AIA Patent Act. The only difference between the AIA and Pre-AIA priority is the requirement of public accessibility with respect to evidence for establishing the priority. However, the difference might be marginal if a disclosure is interpreted broadly to include any non-confidential communication. Extensive discovery may be necessary to find out what is disclosed through such communication. Moreover, inventors must continue to maintain extensive recording and documents in case they are required to prove the date of disclosure for establishing the priority. As a result, the first-to-disclose interpretation will prevent AIA from fully taking advantage of the first-to-file benefits.

Because U.S. Congress acknowledges the first-to-file benefits, U.S. courts should interpret the AIA grace period provision in light of the first-to-file policy for making only the filing date relevant to patentability. If

105 AIA Report, *supra* note 44, at 42.

106 *Id.* at 41.

U.S. courts interpret the AIA grace period provision in the same manner as the grace period provisions under EPC Article 55, JPA Article 30 or SPLT Article 9, FITF will not require a complex and expensive priority contest proceeding. This first-to-file grace period interpretation removes disclosures from the state of art or prior rights only if the disclosures are made by the inventor, a joint inventor or a third party who directly or indirectly obtained the invention from the inventor of a joint inventor.[107] This limitation allows a third party disclosure or filing, preventing an inventor who published his invention during the grace period from obtaining a patent. Because the inventor's disclosure destroys the third party invention's novelty, neither party can obtain a patent.

This first-to-file interpretation is supported by the judicial committee's report introduced to Congress on June 1, 2011.[108] If the exception applies to disclosures deriving from the inventor of the claimed invention, a proceeding for determining the priority between two inventors is not necessary. Thus, the report makes clear that AIA aims to eliminate the current interference proceeding and replace it with a new derivative proceeding.[109] Through the Senate and House debates, the scope of disclosure is described as a first-to-disclose priority although the language of the definition for disclosures under § 102(b) remains the same as originally reported by the judicial committee.[110] Because the debates did not pay much attention to the priority content on multiple independent inventors, the bill was passed into law without clarifying how the priority is determined.

If the first-to-disclose interpretation is adopted, FITF is even worse than the Pre-AIA first-to-invent with respect to protection of American inventors in encouraging inventors' pre-filing disclosures, which will destroy inventors' rights for patent outside the U.S.. As acknowledged in AIA's legislative history, it is common for American inventors to file

---

107 Denise L. Loring and Diana G. Santos, *Statutory Patent Reform and Its effect on Patent Infringement Litigation,* 1061 PLI/PAT 305 (Sept.-Nov. 2011); D. Christopher Ohly, *The America Invents Act of 2011,* 23 NO. 6 INTELL. PROP. & TECH. L.J. 3 (June 2011).

108 AIA Report, *supra* note 44, at 42 (the Act maintains a 1-year grace period for U.S. applicants. Applicants' own publication or disclosure that occurs within 1 year prior to filing will not act as prior art against their applications. Similarly, disclosure by others during that time based on information obtained (directly or indirectly) from the inventor will not constitute prior art).

109 AIA Section 3, §135.

110 For a detailed discussion on legislative history on the grace period provision, *see* HAROLD C. WEGNER, THE 2011 PATENT LAW: LAW & PRACTICE, 4TH ED. 133–48 (2011) (http://www.grayonclaims.com/storage/PatentLaw2011FourthEditionOct26REV.pdf).

for patent protection in several countries at the same time.[111] Even if an inventor files a patent application within the prescribed grace period, very likely six months, the scope of non-prejudicial disclosures under EPC and any other first-to-file countries is much narrower than that of AIA.[112] Because of the narrow scope of non-prejudicial disclosures under EPC, a pre-filing disclosure results in forfeiture of rights for patents in Europe. Although the exception of the first-to-disclose priority is very narrow, the discrepancy of the grace period may still present a hurdle for USPTO to collaborate with EPO, JPO and other offices to examine applications filed with multiple patent offices.[113] A pre-filing disclosure also results in forfeiture of rights for patents in Asian countries, except for Japan where JPA's grace period provision was revised to cover any disclosure as long as such disclosure derived from an act of the inventor and a patent application is filed within six months from the disclosure.[114]

To protect inventors, the U.S. may ask the rest of the world to adopt a one year grace period covering any disclosure. However, first-to-file countries will face a serious dilemma because the adoption of such a generous grace period may encourage a first-to-disclose priority race in the U.S. This will expose inventors of these countries to the risk of an expensive priority contest with American inventors who try to establish priority based on their pre-filing disclosure. This will also increase the need for priority contests which will lead to increased examination costs in addition to increased costs resulting from new multiple post-grant review proceedings.

Moreover, a pre-filing disclosure may also result in a forfeiture of a right for a U.S. patent if the disclosure does not meet the enablement requirement.[115] It is likely that a disclosure violates the written description requirement if it violates the enablement requirement.[116] Such disclosure may not establish a prior right for a claimed invention but may constitute a prior art reference for obviousness.[117]

---

111 AIA Report, *supra* note 44, at 41.

112 EPC Article 55.

113 To protect American inventors from forfeiture of rights for foreign patents and facilitating USPTO's collaboration with other offices, the author once proposed to limit the opportunity to applicants who file only with USPTO. For more discussions, *see* Takenaka, *Rethinking*, *supra* note 15, at 663.

114 2011 JPA Revision, Article 55. Law of Revising Part of Japanese Patent Act, June 8, 2011 Law No. 63 (the revision will become effective on April 1, 2012).

115 35 USC§123¶1.

116 *Ariad Pharm., Inc. v. Eli Lilly & Co.*, 598 F.3d 1336, 1352 (Fed. Cir. 2010) (en banc).

117 *Symbol Tech., Inc. v. Opticon, Inc.*, 935 F.2d 1569 (Fed. Cir. 1991).

V. CONCLUSION

A first-to-invent system dies hard in the U.S.. Even if the terms of Patent Act are revised to clarify that patentability must be measured from the filing date, U.S. lawyers and courts may interpret the terms from the first-to-invent perspective and try to determine patentability from the invention date. AIA made the U.S. patent system more efficient by removing the complexity of examination and eliminating misleading definitions of the prior art. It also harmonized the U.S. system with EPC and the rest of the world by eliminating secret prior inventions from the prior art and further limiting the opportunity for inventors to establish the first-to-invent priority.

As Congress acknowledged in AIA's legislative history, the first-to-file priority is the better practice than the first-to-invent priority. The serious drawback of the first-to-invent priority resulted from the invention date which is determinative through priority contest proceedings. Because the disclosure date is also determinative, FITF will not be able to take advantage of the best aspect of a first-to-file system if the grace period provision is interpreted to give a priority right based on a pre-filing disclosure. FITF incompletely brings together the best aspects of both the first-to-file and the first-to-invent systems as long as it keeps the exception that establishes the first-to-invent priority with a pre-filing disclosure. Unless U.S. courts and lawyers interpret FITF from the first-to-file perspective, a further revision is necessary for FITF to become the best practice for determining patent priority.

Appendix

The America Invents Act, its unique first-to-file system and its transfer of power from juries to the United States Patent and Trademark Office

Martin J Adelman

Theodore and James Pedas Family Professor of Intellectual Property and Technology Law, George Washington University Law School, USA

The signing of the Leahy-Smith America Invents Act (AIA) by President Obama on 16 September 2011 is a landmark event in the history of American patent law. It has already been the subject of numerous articles on the web and in the law reviews as well as in the popular press. I have no intention here of going into all the details of the AIA, I just want to leave the reader with a sense for its eventual impact on American patent law. All the details are to be found in its 37 sections whose titles give the reader a good sense of the scope of the AIA. In one sense Section 1 says it all. It reads:

> (a) Short Title.— This Act may be cited as the 'Leahy-Smith America Invents Act'.
> (b) Table of Contents.— The table of contents for this Act is as follows:
> Sec. 1. Short title; table of contents.
> Sec. 2. Definitions.
> Sec. 3. First inventor to file.
> Sec. 4. Inventor's oath or declaration.
> Sec. 5. Defense to infringement based on prior commercial use.
> Sec. 6. Post-grant review proceedings.
> Sec. 7. Patent Trial and Appeal Board.
> Sec. 8. Preissuance submissions by third parties.
> Sec. 9. Venue.
> Sec. 10. Fee setting authority.
> Sec. 11. Fees for patent services.

Sec. 12. Supplemental examination.
Sec. 13. Funding agreements.
Sec. 14. Tax strategies deemed within the prior art.
Sec. 15. Best mode requirement.
Sec. 16. Marking.
Sec. 17. Advice of counsel.
Sec. 18. Transitional program for covered business method patents.
Sec. 19. Jurisdiction and procedural matters.
Sec. 20. Technical amendments.
Sec. 21. Travel expenses and payment of administrative judges.
Sec. 22. Patent and Trademark Office funding.
Sec. 23. Satellite offices.
Sec. 24. Designation of Detroit satellite office.
Sec. 25. Priority examination for important technologies.
Sec. 26. Study on implementation.
Sec. 27. Study on genetic testing.
Sec. 28. Patent Ombudsman Program for small business concerns.
Sec. 29. Establishment of methods for studying the diversity of applicants.
Sec. 30. Sense of Congress.
Sec. 31. USPTO study on international patent protections for small businesses.
Sec. 32. Pro bono program.
Sec. 33. Limitation on issuance of patents.
Sec. 34. Study of patent litigation.
Sec. 35. Effective date.
Sec. 36. Budgetary effects.
Sec. 37. Calculation of 60-day period for application of patent term extension.

The changes brought about by these 37 sections reach deeply into both substantive patent law and its administration by the United States Patent and Trademark Office (USPTO) and the courts. Specifically the AIA will change American patent law's current mixture of first-to-file and first-to-invent principles into a fully fledged first-to-file system modified only by the creation of a unique one-year grace period, having the unusual feature of effectively creating a conclusive presumption that any third party disclosure made before filing by the inventor but after an inventor's or joint inventor's public disclosure, was derived from the inventor or joint inventor. Furthermore, in the numerous other substantive changes brought about or to be brought about by the AIA, most of which seem designed to reduce the number of litigation issues, is the effective elimination of the best mode requirement. In addition, the AIA also eliminates numerous current provisions that require various acts to have been 'without deceptive intent'. Finally the AIA is more trade secret friendly, primarily by creating a full throated prior user right. This brings me to changes in the role of the USPTO itself.

CHANGES IN THE ROLE OF THE USPTO OWING TO THE AIA RESULTING IN A DIMINISHING ROLE FOR JURIES

The most important change contained in Section 6 is the creation of an opposition like post-grant review available for the first nine months after grant which permits the opposer to raise all patent invalidity issues. However, in contrast to oppositions in the EPO, this opposition, with its strict deadlines, is handled directly by a newly created Patent Trial and Appeal Board (Section 7), with a direct appeal to the Federal Circuit. Section 7 also restructures inter partes reexamination, now inter partes review, and provides for a new supplemental examination procedure to give the patentee the opportunity to cure certain failures to provide prior art during the original reexamination. These provisions in total will create a massive shift in patent disputes from the courts and juries to the USPTO, since administrative decisions are not subject to the Seventh Amendment to the American constitution dating from 1791, 'the right to trial by jury at common law shall be preserved'. Thus the issues decided under the proceedings of Section 6, not being decided at common law, are outside the command of the Seventh Amendment, falling solely into the hands of the USPTO and Federal judges. It is my view, and I believe the view of most knowledgeable observers around the world, that patent law issues should not be put in the hands of juries. No Congressional enactment authorizes the use of juries for any patent issues in the United States. Of course there will be questions outside the jurisdiction of the USPTO that remain for juries, such as damages, equivalents under the doctrine of equivalents, and willfulness. All of this is for the future, which will show how much American patent litigation work will actually be shifted out of the courts to the USPTO by the AIA.

THE AIA'S FIRST-TO-FILE SYSTEM WITH ITS UNIQUE GRACE PERIOD

Turning away from procedure, I believe nearly all would agree that the most important substantive patent law change brought about by the AIA is the abandonment of America's highly modified first-to-invent patent system and replacing it with a first-to-file system incorporating a unique one-year grace period. The basic idea of a first-to-invent system is that prior art is everything invented before the inventor's invention date. Of course rules have to be developed to determine when an invention is completed and whether the prior inventions may be made anywhere or are geographically limited. The purest form of first-to-invent patent law existed in Canada as construed by the Privy Council in the famous case of *Rice v Christiani*.[1] In *Rice* the Privy Council held that under Canadian law a second inventor could not obtain a patent even though the first inventor made and maintained his invention as a trade secret in a county other than Canada. In contrast to Canada, at least as of 1931, the United States over the years made many modifications to its first-to-invent system, including limiting the inventions which counted as prior art to those made in America. More significantly, the United States developed a second theory for creating prior art, one that owes nothing to first-to-invent theory, but rather looks like a provision from a first-to-file system. It simply says (§ 102(b)) that, at least after 1965, when the landmark case of *In re Foster*[2] was decided, any technical teaching 'patented or described in a printed publication in this or a foreign country or in public use or on sale in this country' more than one year before the actual filing date, not the Paris Convention date, in the USPTO is prior art for all purposes. Further, it is often said that § 102(b) creates a one-year grace period, but technically of course it does not. A first-to-invent patent system needs no grace period as the inventor needs no protection from her early disclosure, since any teaching stemming from the work of the inventor cannot be prior art. Only inventions made before the inventor made her invention are prior art. For this reason, however, a first-to-invent prior art system does not encourage early filing. Indeed, it rewards delay. To deal with the need to encourage early filing, American patent law developed the complex jurisprudence of § 102(b), and it is § 102(b) that makes the American patent system function effectively because it allows one to look at a publication or the sale of a product or a public use and determine whether it is prior art, completely aside from the complexities of who invented what, and when and where did she do it.

Unfortunately for those who have to learn American patent law, 'public use' in some circumstances (use by the applicant only, but not third party use) has been interpreted to mean secret commercial use, and 'on sale' includes offers for sale where such offers can be secret so long as the invention is ready for patenting. These provisions have led to an extensive jurisprudence that is frankly unnecessary and costly. Unfortunately the new first-to-file prior art prior provision of AIA in Section 3 states that prior art is created 'where the claimed invention was patented, described

---

1 1931 A.C. 770 (Privy Council) (available in the UK-RPTS-ALL database on Westlaw).

2 343 F.2d 980 (C.C.P.A. 1965).

in a printed publication, or in public use, on sale, or otherwise available to the public before the effective filing date of the claimed invention'. This section is ambiguous since 'public use' and 'on sale' may be given their ordinary meeting when ultimately interpreted by the courts, an interpretation that would fit with the words 'otherwise available to the public', words that could be viewed as meaning other ways of putting information in the hands of the public besides those described by 'public use' and 'on sale'. However, what is most likely is that 'public use' and 'on sale' will be given the meaning they currently have in American patent law. While this question will be the subject of future litigation, anyone advising a client should make the conservative assumption that the words have their current and not their ordinary meaning,

To preserve most of the results under the current American patent law, it is necessary to specifically provide for a grace period, which Section 3 of the AIA defines as follows:

> A disclosure made 1 year or less before the effective filing date of a claimed invention shall not be prior art to the claimed invention under subsection (a) (1) if—
> the disclosure was made by the inventor or joint inventor or by another who obtained the subject matter disclosed directly or indirectly from the inventor or a joint inventor; or
> the subject matter disclosed had, before such disclosure, been publicly disclosed by the inventor or a joint inventor or another who obtained the subject matter disclosed directly or indirectly from the inventor or a joint inventor.[/quotation]

Section (A) is unremarkable except for the question of whether all activities defined by the AIA as prior art that are not derived from the inventor or a joint inventor are covered by the word 'disclosure'. Thus would, for example, an inventor's secret use of a process to make an unpatented product be considered disclosed so as to qualify for the benefit of a grace period? I strongly suspect that the answer is yes, particularly because section (B) does not speak of 'disclosure', but of 'public disclosure', suggesting of course that not all disclosures make the information available to the public.

Section (B), however, covers where a second inventor who has not derived from the first inventor publishes an article after the inventor's publication, but before the first inventor files for his patent. Ordinarily in first-to-file systems with grace periods, if there is no derivation, such a publication would remain prior art against the first filer. However, section (B) makes it clear a public disclosure creates what is, in effect, a conclusive presumption that anyone who makes a public disclosure after the first inventor's disclosure is not an independent inventor. There is some logic in the approach as it removes any ambiguity with regard to subsequent publications, but it sharply deviates from all other first-to-file systems containing grace periods.

This brings me to the provision that all first-to-file systems must have, a provision making unpublished patent applications prior art as of their filing date if they issue or are published before abandonment. This is covered by (a)(2) which reads:

> (2) the claimed invention was described in a patent issued under section 151, or in an application for patent published or deemed published under section 122(b), in which the patent or application, as the case may be, names another inventor and was effectively filed before the effective filing date of the claimed invention.

This is a standard first-to-file provision using the whole contents approach. However, current American law departs from the whole contents approach of conventional first-to-file systems by using unpublished applications as prior art for all purposes, not just for novelty, at least since 1965 owing to *Hazeltine Research, Inc. v Brenner*,[3] a feature maintained by the AIA. Moreover, as one would expect, if the filing date was after an inventor or a joint inventor made a public disclosure of the invention, it is excluded just as if it were a publication. This follows from the following: '(B) the subject matter disclosed had, before such subject matter was effectively filed under subsection (a)(2), been publicly disclosed by the inventor or a joint inventor or another who obtained the subject matter disclosed directly or indirectly from the inventor or a joint inventor'.

So there we have it. American patent law has been reworked in a significant way. It has joined fully the first-to-file world, attempted to reduce the number of issues litigated in the courts and massively shifted power away from juries to the USPTO.

---

3 382 U.S. 252 (1965).

4. The inventive step and cooperative harmonization

Amy L. Landers*

I. INTRODUCTION

The legal concept of invention has deep historic and political roots. The principle that patents should be reserved for genuine contributions has been traced back as early as the 16th century.[1] Although there are central consistencies among current systems, today the inventive step[2] is marked by distinctions that arise from patent systems based on diverse doctrines, approaches, and economic policies.

There is worldwide support for the inventive step's existence. Unlike more controversial doctrines in intellectual property, there is a virtually uniform understanding that utility patents should not be granted for trivial advances. Currently, over one hundred nations and regions have implemented an inventive step requirement.[3] As additional evidence of its

* Professor of Law, University of the Pacific McGeorge School of Law.

1 *See* Franklin D. Prager, *Standards of Patentable Invention from 1474 to 1952*, 20 U. Chi. L. Rev. 69, 71–2 (1952). Some research suggests that the concept of invention derives earlier, from the Venetian Patent Act of 1474, which described that a patent could be granted for an 'ingenious' invention—i.e., 'a requirement of inventive merit,' which finds that 'the invention must not be a trifling, all too obvious application of a known technology'. Guilio Mandich, *Venetian Patents (1450–1550)*, 30 J. Pat. Off. Soc'y 166, 177 (1948).

2 Herein, the term 'inventive step' is inclusive of the nonobviousness doctrine consistent with the definition in Article 27 of the Agreement on Trade-Related Aspects of Intellectual Property Rights, Apr. 15, 1994, Marrakesh Agreement Establishing the World Trade Organization, Annex 1C, Legal Instruments–Results of the Uruguay Round,1869 U.N.T.S. 299, 33 I.L.M. 1197 (1994) [hereinafter TRIPS].

3 *See* Standing Comm. on the Law of Patents, World Intellectual Prop. Org. Revised Annex II, Certain Aspects of National/Regional Patent Law, in Report On the International Patent System, SCP/12/3 Rev.2 (2009) *available at* http://www.wipo.int/edocs/mdocs/scp/en/scp_12/scp_12_3_rev_2-annex2.pdf (surveying over one hundred countries and regions).

acceptance, participants of the World Intellectual Property Organization's (WIPO) efforts toward a worldwide Substantive Patent Law Treaty (SPLT), have achieved broad consensus in principle that an inventive step requirement warrants inclusion in the draft.[4]

Relevant to deep level harmonization, currently there is considerable variation in the requirement's application. This lack of uniformity has a notable impact on those engaged in global commerce. Incentive systems thrive on stability. Those engaged in research seek certainty. Understanding the potential for patentability in key geographic markets is important to rights holders, and for those who wish to avoid infringing patent rights. International variation creates a patchwork of rules in a world where goods and services flow easily between geographic boundaries. National incentive systems are endangered if patenting in one jurisdiction is easily circumvented by copies readily obtainable from others. A single benchmarked standard would allow global work sharing arrangements to reduce application backlogs. Comprehensive solutions to these problems would appear to demand deep level harmonization.

Yet uniformity has significant costs. As Professors Reichman and Dreyfuss argue, a single standard may be premature in light of the burdens on developing countries created by the World Trade Organization's (WTO) Agreement on Trade-Related Aspects of Intellectual Property Rights (TRIPS Agreement).[5] There is much to be said for a measured approach. Of all of the patentability requirements, inventive step permits implementation of policy goals in a manner that can be finely tuned to increase overall welfare, inventive activity, and economic growth.[6] Obtaining consensus among nations with vastly different experiences and needs may be implausible.

Those involved in the global effort for the SPLT may have reached the same conclusion. According to one account, '[c]ountries are showing

---

4 World Intellectual Property Organization, Standing Committee on the Law of Patents, Report on the International Patent System, SCP/12/3 Rev. 2, 48 (2/3/09) (recognizing that 'discussions have produced agreement in principle on a number of points (such as the right to a patent, prior art, sufficiency of disclosure or the requirements of novelty and inventive step') *available at* http://www.wipo.int/edocs/mdocs/scp/en/scp_12/scp_12_3_rev_2.pdf (last visited 7/17/11).

5 Jerome H. Reichman and Rochelle Cooper Dreyfuss, *Harmonization Without Consensus: Critical Reflections On Drafting A Substantive Patent Law Treaty*, 57 Duke L.J. 85, 98 (2007).

6 *Id.* at 120 (noting that differences arise in intellectual property because 'each society values its own specific kinds of creativity and prioritizes its technological requirements in its own way').

signs of giving up on the WTO'.[7] The potential for worldwide adoption of any SPLT is presently unclear. In an era of financial instability, nations have increasingly prioritized pressing internal economic concerns, such as bolstering currency value and addressing unemployment. Although once focused on opening international borders, nations now place a higher premium on security. One critical question is whether the harmonization efforts of the 1990s were merely part of a 'globalization mega-trend' or whether interest in establishing worldwide uniformity remains.[8]

Recently, harmonization appears to have shifted in both scale and focus. Currently, the most promising efforts appear to be incremental. In part, this work stems from imperatives that place pressure on the largest volume examining agencies. These demands include a global application backlog, high patentee costs, and public pressure for higher patent quality. As some examples, The Five IP Offices (IP5) and the Patent Prosecution Highway (PPH), have provided opportunities for agencies to discuss deep harmonization as one of their goals. These efforts are outside the phenomenon that Peter Yu has identified as the 'international intellectual property regime complex'.[9] Rather, these are tightly coordinated efforts built around issues of common administrative concerns. This 'cooperative harmonization' does not purport to sweep globally, but rather is limited to particular nations and only as far as necessary to serve the participants' national interests.

It is not clear that the reach of these partial harmonization efforts will extend to the inventive step. That standard is currently splintered even among developed nations. Even if successful on a small scale, harmonizing the inventive step may never translate to the global stage. It is evident that nations have distinct past experiences with the patent system and hold strong opinions about intellectual property rights. At its most fundamental level, the inventive step is freighted with assumptions about how scientific advance occurs, the level of risk inherent in technological investigations, and the type of advance that warrants the grant of a governmental right. Harmonizing those beliefs is a challenging endeavour.

One significant open issue is the extent to which current cooperative efforts, motivated by administrative concerns, will engage with the larger

---

[7] Graeme B. Dinwoodie and Rochelle C. Dreyfuss, *Designing a Global Intellectual Property System Responsive to Change: The WTO, WIPO, and Beyond*, 46 Hous. L. Rev. 1187, 1194 (2009).

[8] European Patent Office, Scenarios for the Future 54 (2007), *available at* http://www.epo.org/news-issues/issues/scenarios.html.

[9] Peter K. Yu, *International Enclosure, the Regime Complex, and Intellectual Property Schizophrenia*, 2007 Mich. St. L. Rev. 1, 16 (2007).

policy objectives of the patent system as part of their charge. Doing so requires careful attention to the substantive standards adopted and the appropriate benchmark level. A review of existing standards shows the perspectives across the world are subject to considerable diversity. Attempting to harmonize these viewpoints into a single inventive step standard seems far from resolution. Until then, variation is both inevitable and, to a large extent, desirable.

II. AN INTERNATIONAL HISTORIC FRAMEWORK

It is an oversimplification to suppose that the inventive step requirement was created in the courts when a particular society reached a state of technological maturity. This circumstance seems to most closely match the US experience[10] and perhaps that of the United Kingdom. Industrial growth may have been the reason that prompted the doctrine's earliest roots in opinions from the English courts during the sixteenth century.[11] By 1890, during a later era of industrialization, its courts expressly embraced the doctrine.[12]

The experiences of other nations were somewhat different. Although a civil law nation, the German Patent Office is said to have created the requirement despite a lack of any textual support in the initial 1877 patent code.[13] Rather, the examining agency developed the doctrine as a protection against a flood of trivial applications.[14] Germany's early patent system did not precisely parallel the US or British systems. Instead, Germany added a technical progress requirement that asked the patentee to include 'a teaching causing an enrichment of the state of the art'.[15]

---

[10] *See* John F. Duffy, *Inventing Invention: A Case Study of Legal Innovation*, 86 TEX. L. REV. 1, 2–3 (2007) (describing the US development of the doctrine, noting that 'the nonobviousness requirement did not develop until the rapid technological and social changes of the nineteenth century demanded it').

[11] JUSTINE PILA, THE REQUIREMENT FOR AN INVENTION IN PATENT LAW, 21–4 (Oxford 2010); Friedrick-Karl Beier, *The Inventive Step in Its Historical Development*, 17 INT'L REV. INDUS. PROP. & COPYRIGHT L. (IIC) 301, 309–12 (1986).

[12] *See* Duffy, *supra* note 10 at 53; Beier, *supra* note 11 at 310–11.

[13] *Id.* at 317–18.

[14] *Id.* at 317.

[15] Wolfgang G. Fasse, *Basic Patentability Requirements in the United States and Germany*, 44 J. PAT. OFF. SOC'Y 27, 32 (1962); Yi-Chen Su, *What About Know-How: Heightened Obviousness and Lowered Disclosure is Not a Panacea to the American Patent System for Biotechnology Medication and Pharmaceutical*

This piece was eliminated when Germany harmonized its laws with the European Patent Convention.[16]

France had a patent system for nearly two hundred years before formally adopting the inventive step into its statutes in 1968. Any court decisions that imposed an inventive step requirement were quickly overruled on the grounds that such efforts were inconsistent with the code in effect at the time.[17] France's decision to implement the inventive step was ultimately prompted by an external event, specifically, the adoption of the 1963 Convention on the Unification of Certain Points of Substantive Law (Strasbourg Convention), an agreement that sought to set unified patent standards among major European nations.[18]

The history of China's patent system evidences the influence of its political history. Adopting a modern patent system did not occur until 1984, although the country had instituted alternative reward systems since ancient times.[19] China's former systems included a rarely-used dual track of privately owned patents and inventor certificates.[20] According to one source, during the later years of the Cultural Revolution, '[a]ll legal rules, including intellectual property regulations, became completely meaningless'.[21] The adoption of the current law during the 1980s included an inventive step requirement.[22] Like the former German standard, China's current inventive step requirement is bifurcated.[23] This includes a require-

---

Inventions in a Post-KSR Era, 14 MARQ. INTELL. PROP. L. REV. 321, 326 (2010) (describing Germany's former technical progress requirement as a heightened nonobviousness requirement).

[16] Beier, *supra* note 11 at 323.

[17] *Id.* at 315–16 (quoting *Cour d'appel de Paris* decisions of March 21 and of May 31, 1957, 1957: GRUPR Int. 435 *Coq életrique*).

[18] *See* FRÉDÉRIC POLLAURD-DULIAN, PROPRIÉTÉ INTELLECTUELLE-LA PROPRIÉTÉ INDUSTRIELLE, 98 (2011); Georges Vianès, *The New French Patent Law*, 11 INT'L REV. INDUS. PROP. & COPYRIGHT L. (IIC) 131, 133–4 (1980); Christopher Wadlow, *Strasbourg, The Forgotten Patent Convention, and the Origins of the European Patents Jurisdiction,* 41(2) INT'L REV. INDUS. PROP. & COPYRIGHT L. (IIC) 123 (2010).

[19] *See* David Ben Kay, *The Patent Law of the People's Republic of China in Perspective*, 33 UCLA L. REV. 331, 332 (1985) (stating, 'The government's decision to adopt a patent system represents an ambitious step in its effort to reform the domestic economic structure.'); Peter Ganea, *Patents, Utility Models and Design*, in PETER GANEA AND THOMAS PATTLOCH, INTELLECTUAL PROPERTY LAW IN CHINA 1–2 (Christopher Heath, ed. 2005).

[20] *Id.* at 3 (observing that 'between 1950 and 1963, only four patents and six inventor certificates were granted').

[21] *Id.* at 3.

[22] *Id.* at 362.

[23] STATE INTELLECTUAL PROPERTY OFFICE OF THE PEOPLE'S REPUBLIC OF

ment that the invention includes 'prominent substantive features' and represents 'notable progress' in the art.[24] According to this standard, solutions must have an advantageous effect, and not be merely technologically distinct from the existing state of the art.[25]

India's first patent system derived from its colonial years, when the British East India Company first introduced patent laws there.[26] During this period, foreign patent holders outnumbered Indian patentees by a rate of nine to one,[27] which in addition to other factors constrained local technological development. After gaining independence, the Indian government began to develop policies to foster domestic economic activity.[28] As part of this effort, India passed patent laws in 1970 that precluded protection for chemical products. Relieved from the major concerns about patent infringement within that field, India began developing a pharmaceutical industry that eventually became known as the 'pharmacy for the developing world'.[29] India grew its manufacturing capability by creating low-cost drugs and reformulating combinations to simplify treatment for regions that lacked sufficient medical facilities.

Most recently, India reformed its patent system to comply with the TRIPS' mandate that patents be granted for all inventions, including

---

China, Guidelines for Patent Examination, ch. 4, § 3.2.2, *available at* http://www.sipo.gov.cn/zlsqzn/sczn2010eng.pdf; see *also* Ganea and Pattlock, *supra* note 19 at 17.

24 Patent Law of the People's Republic of China, ch. 2, art. 22 (2000).

25 *See* Heather Lin et al., *China: The Patentability Criterion of Inventive Step/Nonobviousness*, AIPPI Question Q217, ¶¶ 16–20 (4/21/11). The extent to which the notable progress standard is applied during the examination stage is uncertain. *See* Gong Jianhau, *Bewilderment in Judging Inventiveness*, China Intellectual Property Magazine, April 2007, *available at* http://www.chinaipmagazine.com/en/journal-show.asp?id=336, (suggesting that examiners may not rigorously apply the notable progress requirement).

26 *See* Sriividhya Ragavan, *Of Inequals of the Uruguay Round,* 10 Marq. Intell. Prop. L. Rev. 273 (2006).

27 N. Rajogapala Ayyangar, Report on the Revision of the Patents Law, 12 (1959).

28 *See* Sudip Chaudhuri, The WTO and India's Pharmaceuticals Industry 36–7 (Oxford 2005).

29 Janice M. Mueller, '*The Tiger Awakens: The Tumultuous Transformation of India's Patent System and the Rise of Indian Pharmaceutical Innovations,*' 68 U. Pitt. L. Rev. 491, 514 (2006); Medicins Sans Frontiers – Doctors Without Borders, Ideas & Opinions; Prognosis: Short-Term Relief, Long-Term Pain: The Future of Generic Medicines Made in India (April 21, 2005), *available at* http://www.doctorswithoutborders.org/publications/article.cfm?id=1504&cat=ideas-opinions.

product claims for pharmaceuticals.[30] Yet the present system appears to bear the imprint of India's past policies relating to chemical inventions. Today, India imposes an additional patentability requirement that certain types of chemical substances deliver efficacy.[31] In effect, this rule prevents incumbent pharmaceutical patentees from 'ever-greening' existing patents by imposing the requirement that an invention demonstrate a sufficient medical benefit. Recently, India's patent office relied on this requirement to invalidate a Novartis patent for the cancer treatment Glivec, despite the fact the drug is protected by patents in 35 other countries.[32] Although it is not entirely clear whether this efficacy requirement is distinct from the inventive step, as a practical matter, India may be benchmarking pharmaceutical claims at a higher level than other regions. In one recent example, the Indian Patent Office invalidated a pharmaceutical patent that had been filed in over sixty other jurisdictions, granted in fifty, and deemed nonobvious by a US District Court.[33]

This overview demonstrates that individual nations have vastly different histories and experiences with inventive step. Certainly, history does not dictate the future. However, these examples illustrate that the landscape of the inventive step is far from even.

III. DIVERSE APPROACHES TO THE INVENTIVE STEP

Current implementations of the inventive step demonstrate significantly diverse approaches. First, there are doctrinal differences across jurisdictions. Second, it is not clear whether the inventive step is uniformly

---

30 TRIPS, *supra* note 2 at Art. 29.

31 Patents Act, No. 39 of 1970, India Code, § 3(d) updated by The Patents (Amendment) Act of 2005, No. 15, Act of Parliament 2005 (India), *available at* http://indiacode.nic.in (providing that an invention does not include 'the mere discovery of a new form of a known substance which does not result in the enhancement of the known efficacy of that substance. . .').

32 Novartis Ag v. Union Of India, (2007) 4 MLJ 1153; see Janice M. Meuller, *Taking TRIPS to India—Novartis, Patent Law, and Access to Medicines*, 356 N. Engl. J. Med. 541 (2007) (noting that Novartis had patented the drug in 35 other countries).

33 *Compare* Hoffmann-La Roche AG v. Ranbaxy Laboratories Ltd., (India Patent Office, Apr. 30, 2010), *available at* http://www.ip-watch.org/weblog/wp-content/uploads/2010/05/valgancyclovir_decision_final.pdf *with* Roche Palo Alto LLC v. Ranbaxy Laboratories, Ltd., CIVA 06-2003, 2009 WL 3261252 (D.N.J. Sept. 30, 2009).

benchmarked. Harmonization on either front would require each region to re-tool in anticipation of the accompanying impact at a local level.

(i) Defining the Prior Art

The scope of the art relevant to the inventive step varies by jurisdiction. Temporally, the European Patent Convention (EPC), which has a first-to-file system, defines prior art to include existing knowledge at the time of an application's filing date. This is an absolute standard that includes 'everything made available to the public by means of a written or oral description, by use, or in any other way, before the date of filing of the European patent application'.[34] Japan's patent law, which is also a first-to-file system, includes a six-month grace period for inventors.[35]

In the US, the prior art was long based on a first to invent system and defined through the filter of section 102 of the Patent Act.[36] This section had a complex set of rules relating to geographic restrictions, grace periods and a definition of prior art that included items not available to the public.[37] Currently, the US system has moved toward a first-to-file system that defines prior art to include nearly all publicly available information existent at the time of filing. Similar to the Japanese system, the newly adopted US statute retains a grace period for disclosures made by an inventor for one year.

Systems differ in their definition of analogous art. Currently, the US system is commonly regarded as implementing the broadest test, allowing a reference if either: (1) from the same field of endeavor, regardless of the

---

[34] Convention on the Grant of European Patents, art. 54(2), *opened for signature* Oct. 5, 1973, 13 I.L.M. 270, [hereinafter European Patent Convention]; European Patent Office, Guidelines for Examination in the European Patent Office, Pt. C, Ch. IV, §11.2 (2010), [hereinafter European Patent Office Guidelines], http://documents.epo.org/projects/babylon/eponet.nsf/0/7ffc755ad943703dc12576f00054cacc/$FILE/guidelines_2010_complete_en.pdf.

[35] Japan Patent Law, Ch. II §§ 29, 30.

[36] *See, e.g.,* Proctor & Gamble Co. v. Teva Pharmaceuticals, 566 F.3d 989, 998–9 (Fed. Cir. 2009) (examining whether an asserted patent could serve as 'prior art' based on the date of invention); In re Omeprazole Patent Litigation, 536 F.3d 1361, 1381 (Fed. Cir. 2008) (acknowledging that two references were excluded because they did not qualify as 'prior publications' under section 102); Eli Lilly and Co. v. Sicor Pharmaceuticals, Inc., 705 F.Supp.2d 971, 998 (S.D. Ind. 2010).

[37] See Toshiko Takenaka, *The Best Patent Practice or Mere Compromise? A Review of the Current Draft of the Substantive Patent Law Treaty and a Proposal for a 'First to Invent' Exception for Domestic Applicants*, 11 TEX. INTELL. PROP. L.J. 259, 275–83 (2003) (detailing several distinctions between US law and that adopted by the EPO and Japan).

problem addressed, or (2) reasonably pertinent to the particular problem with which the inventor is involved.[38] This includes information within the relevant technical field, as well as from unrelated fields, if the art solves the same type of problem that is the subject of the claim.[39]

By comparison, the analogous arts test of the European Patent Office ('EPO') is narrower, limiting consideration to the relevant technological field.[40] This approach does allow consideration of general common knowledge and information from related fields.[41] For claims that span more than one discipline, the work from corresponding fields can be included through the use of the hypothetical 'team of scientists' construct from other scientific domains, instead of the singular person of ordinary skill used for inventions that arise from a single scientific or technical domain.[42]

(ii) Identifying the Invention: Technical Character

The U.S. nonobviousness standard separates the inventive aspects of the claim from the prior art by comparing the claim as a whole to prior art references.[43] In contrast, the EPO's analysis excludes consideration of features of a claim that make no contribution to the technical character of the invention.[44] This may arise where a claim's distinguishing feature directly derives from a field excluded from patentability under the EPC.[45]

---

[38] Innovention Toys, LLC v. MGA Entertainment, Inc., 637 F.3d 1314, 1321 (Fed. Cir. 2011); In re Clay, 966 F.2d 656, 658–9 (Fed. Cir. 1992).

[39] In re Paulsen, 30 F.3d 1475 (Fed. Cir. 1994).

[40] Stephen G. Kunin and Philippe J.C. Signore, *A Comparative Analysis of the Inventive Step Standard in the European and Japanese Patent Offices from a U.S. Perspective,* IP LITIGATOR 15, 17 (Jan./Feb. 2008); European Patent Office Guidelines, *supra* note 34, § 11.2; Ricoh Co./Order Management, ¶ 10, T 0172/03 2003 E.P.O.R. 11 (Technical Bd. App. 2000).

[41] *See* European Patent Office Guidelines, *supra* note 34, Pt. C, Ch. IV, § 11.3; Ex-Cell-O/Laminated paperboard container, T80/88, 1991 E.P.O.R. 596, 601 (Technical Bd. App. 1990).

[42] *See* Rockwater v. Technip France SA [2004] EWCA (Civ) 381 (Eng.); Sandoz GmbH v. Roche Diagnostics GmbH, [2004] EWHC (Ch) 1313 (Eng.). European Patent Office Examination Guidelines, *supra* note 34 at Pt. C, Ch. IV, § 11.2.

[43] KSR Intern. Co. v. Teleflex Inc., 550 U.S. 398, 399 (2007); Graham v. John Deere Co. of Kansas City, 383 U.S. 1, 17 (1966) ('differences between the prior art and the claims at issue are to be ascertained').

[44] *See* Programs for computers, (G 3/08), 2010 E.P.O.R. 36 ¶ 82 (Enlarged Bd. App. 2010); PBS Partnership/ Controlling Pension Benefit Systems, T 931/95, 2002 E.P.O.R. 52 (Technical Bd. App. 2000).

[45] Duns Licensing Assoc./Estimating sales activity, T 154/04, 2007 E.P.O.R. 38, ¶ 48 (Technical Bd. App. 2006).

(iii) Structure of the Inventive Step Test

The EPO's primary test for the inventive step is the problem solution approach, based on the concept that every invention must be a solution to a technical problem. The problem solution analysis is undertaken in three steps. First, one must determine the closest prior art, which is identified as the most promising starting point that would lead to the development of the claim. Typically, the closest prior art is a reference aimed at the same objective or purpose as the claim and with the most relevant technical features in common.

Second, one formulates the technical problem to be solved. This is done by isolating the distinguishing features between the closest prior art and the claim to define the technical effect derived from the distinguishing features.[46] This technical problem may vary from the statement of the objective of the invention stated in the application.[47] Third, one answers whether the person of ordinary skill would (and not simply could) have modified the closest prior art to create the claimed invention to solve the technical problem or obtain an advantage. This step asks whether the person of ordinary skill would have solved the identified problem given the current state of the art.

Although the EPO's framework is structured, the ultimate determination of inventive step is undertaken in the last portion of the test and relies on a flexible analysis. As in some examples, the inventive step may be met where there is a new and surprising technical advantage, a combination of features with a synergistic effect, or where there is a new insight into a cause of a phenomenon that is applied to solve a known problem.[48]

Although employed by one of the most influential patent agencies in the world, the problem solution approach has been subject to criticism.[49]

---

46 European Patent Office Guidelines, *supra* note 34 at Pt. C, Ch. IV, § 11.5.2.

47 *See* G.S.A. Szabo, *The Problem and Solution Approach to the Inventive Step*, 8(10) Eur. Intell. Prop. Rev. 293 (1986).

48 European Patent Office Guidelines, *supra* note 34 at Pt. C, Ch. IV, §§ 11.7–11.9.

49 *See* Alcan/Aluminum alloys, T 465/92, 1995 E.P.O.R. 501 ¶ 9.5 (Technical Bd. App. 1994) (recognizing limitations of the test and formulating an alternative analysis); Steven Crespi, *Recombinant Patents in Litigation-A Comparative Study of Some EPO and UK National Court Decisions*, 28 Int'l Rev. Indus. Prop. & Copyright L. (IIC) 603, 614–15 (1997) (stating that formulating a problem for claims to recombinant DNA seems 'sometimes seems rather artificial' because the claims are not phrased as a solution to a problem); Takenaka, *supra* note 37, at 343–4.

For example, the test is difficult to apply for certain types of inventions or where there is no close prior art.[50] Further, the test is said to introduce subjectivity in the formulation of the problem.[51]

Some EPC members, including the UK, have declined to use the problem solution approach in the national courts.[52] Instead, the UK applies a multifactor analysis.[53] First, the test requires the identification of one of ordinary skill and the available common general knowledge of such a person.[54] Second, the inventive concept is identified. This is done by construing and then summarizing the claim—'[o]ne is trying to identify the essence of the claim in this exercise'.[55] Third, one identifies the differences between the prior art and the claim.[56] During this last step, the final determination is based on whether the invention would have been obvious to one of skill in the art.

(iv) Technology-specific Rules

Some jurisdictions, including China and Japan, supplement the analytic methods for assessing the inventive step with technology specific rules set forth in examination guidelines.[57] As one example, China's guidelines include the following section for chemical claims:

---

[50] *See Actavis*, [2010] EWCA (Civ) 82 at ¶ 35; Alcan, 1995 E.P.O.R. 501 at ¶ 9.5 (recognizing that the problem-solution approach does not work well when any close prior art is lacking).

[51] Actavis, [2010] EWCA (Civ.) 82 at ¶ 32.

[52] *See* European Patent Convention, *supra* note 34 at art. 56; *see* Alfred Keukenschrijver, *European Patents with Effect for Germany in Light of Recent Federal Supreme Court Decisions*, 34(7) INT'L REV. INDUS. PROP. & COPYRIGHT L. IIC 711, 715 (2003) (noting that problem-solution approach 'is not applied in the precedents of the [German] Federal Supreme Court'); Actavis UK Ltd v. Novartis AG, [2010] EWCA (Civ) 82 (Eng.) (observing that the UK does not apply the problem-solution approach).

[53] *See* KSR Intern. Co. v. Teleflex Inc., 550 U.S. 398 (2007); Graham v. John Deere Co., 383 U.S. 1 (1966).

[54] *See* Pozzoli SPA v. BDMO SA, [2007] EWCA (Civ.) 588, ¶¶ 16–17 (Eng.) (describing test).

[55] *Id.* at ¶ 17.

[56] *Id.* at ¶ 22–3.

[57] State Intellectual Property Office of the Peoples' Republic of China, Guidelines for Patent Examination – 2010, *supra* note 23, at Pt. 2, Chs. 9 and 10; Japan Patent Office Examination Guidelines, Part VII: Examination Guidelines for Inventions in Specific Fields (2010), *available at* http://www.jpo.go.jp/tetuzuki_e/t_tokkyo_e/1312-002_e.htm.

> When a compound is novel, not similar in structure to a known compound, and has a certain use and effect, the examiner may deem it to involve an inventive step without requiring that it shall have an unexpected use or effect.[58]

These rules ease the administrative burden of examination and provide clarity to patent applicants. Further, they establish a set analytic method for the inventive step that differs from the more traditional, open-ended tests.

(v) The Inventive Step as a Benchmark

The most significant issue for the inventive step is the benchmark, the level of advance that satisfies the standard. Research concerning the benchmark for the inventive step has yielded inconclusive results. In 2008, the USPTO, the EPO, and the Japan Patent Office ('JPO') conducted a joint assessment of six actual and hypothetical cases.[59] Of these, the offices came to the same conclusion on five cases and differed on one. Although the study provides some fascinating insights into the application of the different analytic methods, generalizations based on this limited exercise cannot be made.

Beyond the inventive step, one comparative study has concluded that significant variation exists for patent issuance standards.[60] Specifically, this work considered outcomes from the USPTO, the JPO, and the EPO for applications from patent families with priority years dating from 1990 to 1995.[61] The study's main conclusion was there is a 'substantial amount

---

[58] State Intellectual Property Office of the Peoples' Republic of China, Guidelines for Patent Examination – 2010, *supra* note 23, at Pt. 2, Ch. 10, § 6.1(1).

[59] European Patent Office, Japan Patent Office & United States Patent & Trademark Office, Comparative Study on Hypothetical/Real Cases: Inventive Step/Non-obviousness (2008), *available at* http://www.trilateral.net/projects/worksharing/study/cases2.pdf.

[60] Paul H. Jensen, Alfons Palangkaraya and Elizabeth Webster, *Disharmony in International Patent Office Decisions*, 15 The Fed. Cir. B.J. 679 (2005). This study has been criticized in Ron D. Katznelson, *Bad Science in Search of 'Bad' Patents*, 17 Fed. Circuit B.J. 1 (2007).

[61] Jensen, *supra* note 60; see *also* Elizabeth Webster, Alfons Palangkaraya and Paul H. Jensen, *Characteristics of International Patent Examination Outcomes*, 95 Econ. Letters 95 (2007) (studying patents for later years); *cf.* Mark A. Lemley, Mark A. and Bhaven N. Sampat, *Examiner Characteristics and the Patent Grant Rate*, 19–20 (Stanford Law and Economics Olin, Working Paper No. 369, 19–20, 2009) *available at* http://ssrn.com/abstract=1329091 (comparing grant rates between the U.S. PTO and the EPO).

of disharmony' across the three offices.[62] However, the extent to which this variation is based on the inventive step is not clear.[63]

Going forward, perhaps the single most important question is the optimal level of the inventive step as a potential global benchmark. All nations seem to have a common interest in maximizing knowledge creation in the aggregate. There is uniform agreement that withholding patent protection for trivial advances is a necessary part of that goal. However, there is considerable debate about the proper balance between granting patents as an incentive, the need for technological access to create follow-on invention, and the role for protection relating to essential products such as food and medicine.

A single answer is not likely a correct one. The inventive step serves a unique function among the patentability requirements. Its flexibility has the potential to reflect meaningful judgments about the desirability of certain types of inventive activity. These decisions can incorporate aspects of science, law, economics, and public policy. Crystallizing the standard across all nations will prevent regional variation, and is not likely to serve the economic policies of any particular nation well. This circumstance is compounded if the benchmark must be static over time. Because it controls the balance between patent protection and the public domain, a benchmark will undoubtedly be the most controversial barrier to true deep level harmonization.

IV. A STATUS REPORT: MAJOR EFFORTS AT PATENT HARMONIZATION

At present, deep harmonization through the use of an international treaty does not appear imminent. The TRIPS Agreement has a multi-faceted purpose that does not endeavor to accomplish deep substantive coordination.[64] Although the Agreement provides that patent systems must have an inventive step limitation, the document leaves the term open.[65] TRIPS

---

62 *Id.* at 692.

63 *See* Webster, et. al., *supra* note 61 at 368 (suggesting that the differences may be partially explained by the strategic behavior of patentees).

64 *See* TRIPS, *supra* note 2 at Art. 7, 8 and 30. *See generally* Peter K. Yu, *The Objectives and Principles of the TRIPS Agreement*, 46 Hous. L. Rev. 979, 1024 (2009) (describing flexibilities that were negotiated and included into the TRIPS Agreement, which are important to preserve its legitimacy).

65 TRIPS, *supra* note 2 at Art. 27 ('patents shall be available for any inventions . . . provided that they are new, involve an inventive step and are capable of industrial application').

is implemented by members who 'have the distinctive characteristics of having wide internal divergences in their socioeconomic conditions and technological capabilities'.[66] Key provisions recognize that the Agreement must be implemented to maximize social and economic welfare, and the protection of the public interest.[67] As Professor Peter Yu writes, these provisions are important to 'confirm that the Agreement was a bargain struck between developed and less-developed countries over a multiyear negotiation process'.[68] TRIPS was designed to allow for national and regional variation.

Certainly, WIPO's efforts toward the SPLT are not near completion. In 2004, the US, Japan, and the EPO developed a partial draft agreement that included common definitions of the prior art, grace periods, the inventive step, and novelty. Unlike the TRIPS Agreement, which did not include a substantive standard for the inventive step, the 2004 draft SPLT does.[69] In 2006, the SPLT discussions reached an impasse when several developing countries expressed concern that an incremental agreement would result in a failure to incorporate necessary protections and limitations in the SPLT, including issues relating to the 'public interest, flexibility on existing intellectual property laws, transfer of technology, curbing of anti-competitive practices and disclosure of the origin of genetic resources in patent applications for developing countries'.[70] Since that time, WIPO's Standing Committee on the Law of Patents has continued work. Nonetheless, the potential success of these efforts is in doubt. In expressing her frustration with stalled efforts to reinvigorate the SPLT, the former President of the EPO stated, '[t]here are times when I think all these harmonization initiatives are merely an excuse to travel'.[71] International harmonization of the

---

[66] Graeme B. Dinwoodie and Rochelle C. Dreyfuss, *Designing a Global Intellectual Property System Responsive to Change: The WTO, WIPO and Beyond*, 46 Hous. L. Rev. 1187 (2009).

[67] TRIPS, *supra* note 2, art. 7 and 8.

[68] Yu, *supra* note 64 at 1023.

[69] WIPO Standing Committee on the Law of Patents, Report on the International Patent System, 10th Session, Geneva, May 10 – 14, 2004, Draft Substantive Patent Law Treaty, Art. 12(3), *available at* http://www.wipo.int/edocs/mdocs/scp/en/scp_10/scp_10_2.pdf.

[70] WIPO Standing Committee on the Law of Patents, Report on the International Patent System, 12th Sess., June 23–27, 2008, SCP/12/3 Rev.2, ¶ 172, at 50 (Feb. 3, 2009) (report prepared by the Secretariat, summarizing events of the May 10–14, 2004 meeting) *available at* http://www.wipo.int/edocs/mdocs/scp/en/scp_12/scp_12_3_rev_2.pdf.

[71] *Cf.* Alison Brimelow, Not Seeing the Woods for the Trees: Is the Patent System Still Fit for Purpose? Second Annual Francis Gurry Intellectual Property Lecture, Univ. of Melbourne, Melbourne, Aus. (March 1, 2010) (expressing doubt

detailed substantive requirements of the inventive step through the SPLT has slowed its pace considerably, and any conclusion appears to be years away.

V. CURRENT DEVELOPMENTS: COOPERATIVE HARMONIZATION OR SPLINTERS?

The WTO and WIPO have been engaged in a global effort. Yet harmonization can occur on an incremental basis. How successful and how far these efforts will reach is unclear.

Presently, some groups have begun deep harmonization efforts on a reduced scale based on commonly shared concerns. This work proceeds in a manner that bears some resemblance to the European Union's ('EU') Enhanced Cooperation procedure, albeit on a far less structured basis. As background, the EU allows for enhanced cooperation for less than all member states to move forward on areas of common concern where unanimity cannot be obtained.[72] The process is subject to formalities, including approval by the Council of the European Union.[73] Further, the EU's enhanced cooperation procedure is subject to several requirements, including that such efforts 'further the objectives of the Union' and 'reinforce its integration process'.[74]

One example of the formal process of enhanced cooperation is the current effort to create a community patent. During discussions, two of the twenty-nine EU members objected to the patent translation requirements that were part of the proposed system. Under a more rigid regime, this disagreement would have completely halted discussions. Instead, the Council of the European Union formally authorized the use of the enhanced cooperation procedure for twenty-seven of the twenty-nine nations that were in accord.[75] Both the enhanced cooperation and

---

that harmonization efforts will be successful due to participant's unwillingness to change).

[72] *See* Consolidated Version of the Treaty of the European Union, tit. IV, art. 20 (March 30, 2010), 2010 O.J. (C 83) (hereinafter, TEU); Consolidated Version of the Treaty on the Functioning of the European Union, tit. III, May 9, 2008, 2010 O.J. (C 83) (hereinafter TFEU).

[73] *Id.*, art. 329.

[74] TEU, *supra* note 72, at art. 20, para. 1.

[75] Press Release 7506/11, Council of the European Union, Council Authorizes Enhanced Cooperation on the Creation of a Unitary Patent System (March 10, 2011), *available at* http://europa.eu/rapid/pressReleasesAction.do?reference=PRES/11/54&format=HTML&aged=0&language=EN&guiLanguage=en.

the unitary patent system (once created) are open to all EU members, including those nations that had originally objected.[76]

Incremental patent harmonization efforts are not subject to the formalities of the EU's enhanced cooperation. Nonetheless, such informal methods appear to be making some progress by moving forward without the cooperation of all nations. This includes efforts undertaken by the IP5. This organization is comprised of representatives of examining agencies that are the largest volume offices in the world, the EPO, the JPO, the Korean Intellectual Property Office (KIPO), the State Intellectual Property Office of the People's Republic of China (SIPO), and the United States Patent and Trademark Office (USPTO). The group was formed by the lead decision makers of each agency, and together they are responsible for examining over 80 percent of the world's patent applications.

The IP5 was created from a desire to reduce agency application backlog by engaging in work sharing.[77] The goals of the IP5 include both procedural and substantive harmonization of the law without limiting each country's freedom to grant or deny patents.[78] Currently, the organization is moving toward sharing search information, examination results, and best practices. This can be viewed as a favorable development that might allow the agencies to free resources that can be shifted to address patent quality. Furthermore, the IP5 sends an important signal about the gains possibly obtained from incremental harmonization efforts. This organization provides a forum for the world's high volume patent offices to discuss areas of common agreement and to identify issues that might be harmonized in the future.

Another mechanism arises from the pilot Patent Prosecution Highway Project ('PPHP'). Over a dozen international patent examination offices have undertaken this program, which can build from the work performed under the Patent Cooperation Treaty. The PPHP allows an applicant who receives approval of at least one claim from an Office of First Filing to request fast track examination from a participating Office of Second Filing for similar claims in corresponding applications. Certainly, this would not obligate the Office of Second Filing to grant the application.

---

[76] *Id.*; see *also* TEU, *supra* note 72, tit. IV, art. 20, para. 1; TFEU, *supra* note 72, tit. III, art. 328, para. 1.

[77] The goals listed on the IP5's website are '[t]he elimination of unnecessary duplication of work among the offices, enhancement of patent examination efficiency and quality, and guarantee of the stability of patent right'. The Five IP Offices, Objectives (http://www.fiveipoffices.org/obj.html) (last visited 6/26/11).

[78] Press Release, The Five IP Offices, IP Heads Meeting in Tokyo, Japan (June 2011) *available at* http://www.fiveipoffices.org/index/PressStatement.pdf.

However, an examiner in the Office of Second Filing is likely to learn about, and at least consider, substantive input from the earlier grant. As a practical matter, information about the benchmark level of inventiveness may stabilize as examiners begin sharing results and opinions on a high volume basis.

The EU's effort to create a community patent system can be viewed as another incremental harmonization effort. Once in place, applications will be examined by a single agency and litigated in a single court system dedicated to patent disputes. Given that one of the purposes of the EU is the free flow of trade throughout the community, the desirability of uniform protection within the entire geographic region is evident.

It is less clear whether all of these coordinating efforts can reach the full scope of the inventive step. For example, the USPTO does not have the substantive rulemaking authority to modify the national standard for the inventive step. Certainly, an inability to substantively modify the law limits the uniformity that agency coordination can achieve.

Even if these efforts lead to harmonization, the coordinators are primarily developed nations. It is not clear whether developing nations will adopt any result that might be achieved. Although developing nations may find work-sharing attractive to minimize the resources needed for patent examination, it cannot be expected that they will necessarily agree with standards set by developed nations. If this becomes a goal, developed nations might gear standards that might carry persuasive force on a worldwide basis.

VI. CONCLUSION: THE INVENTIVE STEP IN CONTEXT

The former director of the American Intellectual Property Law Association was quoted as saying, '[t]he World Patent is something my grandchildren will not see, but it is the ultimate patent system: search once, examine once, and grant a patent that is recognized around the world'.[79] This skepticism reflected in that comment appears sound. Of all of the patentability requirements, the inventive step is the most likely to manifest jurisdictional variation. Each patent system has currently established precedent that was created without any unified global vision. These distinct histories, politics and policies cannot be easily erased.

---

79 European Patent Office, *supra* note 8, at 39 (quoting Michael Kirk, then-Executive Director of the American Intellectual Property Law Association).

A failure to fully achieve deep harmonization of the inventive step should not be viewed as a failure of the patent system. Rather, the inventive step's value is its ability to be used as a tool to draw a reasoned line between the patentable and the public domain. Considered in this context, countries may view competing goals at the national level as far more pressing than international harmonization.

Currently, small, cooperative groups are working together to determine their own harmonization course. If their chosen standards carry worldwide persuasive force, they are likely to lead to de facto harmonization that need not be part of any formal treaty. Nonetheless, given the present state of the inventive step, such a shift may be quite difficult to achieve.

5. Equitable doctrines in international patent laws

Jan Krauß*

I. INTRODUCTION

This chapter first briefly introduces the different systems of patent-related equitable doctrines and then specifically addresses the doctrine of inequitable conduct of several jurisdictions including the United States, the United Kingdom, Germany, and the Rules as present in the European Patent Convention ('EPC'). Based on the recent decision of the Court of Appeals for the Federal Circuit ('CAFC'), *Therasense*,[1] this chapter will then seek to provide a comparative analysis of the current status of the '*duty of candor and good faith*' in the U.S. and international equitable doctrines.

II. WHAT ARE 'EQUITABLE DOCTRINES'?

Equitable doctrines are a set of legal principles that supplement the written explicit rules of law. Equity is commonly said to 'mitigate the rigor of common law' allowing courts to use their discretion and apply justice in accordance with Roman and natural laws.[2] While historically equity was merely based on general ethical concepts, today in both the English and American systems equity has become a body of rules or principles. Furthermore, for equity analysis, precedent (i.e. case-law) is now taken

* Dr. Jan Krauß, Patent Attorney, Boehmert & Boehmert, Munich, Germany.

1 *Therasense, Inc. v. Becton, Dickinson & Co.*, 649 F.3d 1276 (Fed. Cir. 2011).

2 Mary Ann Glendon et al., *Comparative Legal Traditions in a Nutshell* 142–3 (3rd ed. 2008); Martin Josef Schermaier, *Bona fides in Roman contract law, in Good Faith in European Contract Law* 63 (Reinhard Zimmermann and Simon Whittaker eds., 2000); W.T. Tête, *Tort Roots and Ramifications of the Obligations Revision* 32 Loy. L. Rev. 47 (1986); Saul Litvinoff, *Good Faith* 71 Tulsa L. Rev. 1645, 1651–3 (1997).

into account as well and over time some equitable doctrines have found their way into the legal codes.[3]

Similar to common law systems, civil law systems (i.e. German law)[4] address equity, particularly in the form of 'general clauses' which allow similar leeway in applying the law.

Several equitable doctrines can be identified in the patent system, such as the defenses of prosecution laches[5] and patent misuse.[6] Also important are estoppels (*venire contra factum proprium*), such as prosecution history estoppels ('PHE'[7]) by a patent applicant, and – last but not least – the equitable doctrine of unclean hands with its sub-element of inequitable conduct.[8] All of these doctrines play a role during the prosecution (i.e. before the patent office) and the enforcement (i.e. before the court) of patents. A violation of the rules can lead to unenforceability of the patent and even to invalidation of the whole patent. This is why some of these rules, particularly the inequitable conduct doctrine, have gained such popularity as a defense in U.S. patent litigation cases. Today some courts (such as the CAFC) even speak of such defenses as a 'plague.'[9]

III. THE DUTY OF CANDOR UNDER U.S. PATENT LAW

In general, U.S. patent attorneys as well as anyone else involved in U.S. patent prosecution, are required by their professional code of conduct to provide only true statements to courts and to the U.S. Patent and Trademark Office ('USPTO') thus complying with their duty of candor and good faith.[10] The same duty of candor holds true for actions during the pendency of a patent application whereby '*each individual associated with the filing and prosecution of a patent application*' is required to

---

[3] For example, Section 138 para. 1 of the German Civil Code (BGB) states that 'a legal transaction that offends good morals (*die guten Sitten*) is void'.

[4] In the form of 'billigem Ermessen' (equitable discretion) and 'Treu und Glauben' (good faith).

[5] *Symbol Techs., Inc. v. Lemelson Med.*, 277 F.3d 1361, 1366 (Fed. Cir. 2002).

[6] *Morton Salt Co. v. G. S. Suppiger Co.*, 314 U.S. 488, 52 USPQ 30 (1942).

[7] *Warner-Jenkinson Co., Inc. v. Hilton Davis Chemical Co.*, 520 U.S. 17 (1997); *Festo Corp. v. Shoketsu Kinzoku Kogyo Kabushiki Co., Ltd.*, 535 U.S. 722 (2002).

[8] *Therasense*, 649 F.3d 1276.

[9] *Burlington Indus., Inc. v. Dayco Corp.*, 849 F.2d 1418, 1422 (Fed. Cir. 1988); *Kimberly-Clark Corp. v. Johnson & Johnson*, 745 F.2d 1437, 1454 (Fed. Cir. 1984).

[10] For a general discussion of duty of candor, *see* Donald S. Chisum, *Chisum on Patents, § 11.03[4]*.

disclose any information to the USPTO which a '*reasonable*' examiner would most likely consider relevant during a decision regarding patentability.[11] A violation of the duty of candor, also designated as '*inequitable conduct*,' can be punished as a violation of the professional code of conduct.[12]

The USPTO doctrine of inequitable conduct is codified in 37 CFR 1.56 (commonly referred to as 'Rule 56').[13] Unfortunately, the scope of Rule 56 is not clearly defined. The duty does however apply to *absolutely everyone* who is somehow associated with the patent application. Therefore the duty applies to a very large group of individuals including the inventors, the attorneys or patent agents involved in the preparation or prosecution of the patent, and anyone else 'substantially involved' in the preparation or prosecution of the application and associated with the inventor or assignee.[14] For example, in the case of university tech transfer institutions, the group of individuals subject to the duty of candor would likely include the technology manager involved in the prosecution of a particular patent application. Even non-inventor scientists who were involved in interviews at the USPTO would be subject to the duty.

It is therefore required that each of these individuals actually know about the requirements of the duty of candor and act in agreement with them, since respective mistakes ('errors' or 'omissions') until recently could never be retroactively 'repaired'.[15]

Usually the required information is provided to the USPTO in an information disclosure statement ('IDS') in the form of a publication of the state of the art. The required information is not limited to publications but indeed relates to *any* material relevant to patentability. In practice this

---

11 37 C.F.R. § 1.56 (1992). In *Therasense*, the CAFC rejected the 'reasonable examiner-standard'. *Therasense*, 99 U.S.P.Q.2d 1065.

12 Article 4 of the Rules of professional conduct as adopted by the Administrative Council of the European Patent Organisation reads: 1. A professional representative who fails to comply with the Rules of professional conduct may incur one of the following penalties: a) a warning, b) a reprimand, c) a fine not exceeding EUR 10.000, d) deletion from the list of professional representatives for not more than six months, or e) deletion from the list of professional representatives for an indefinite period.

13 37 C.F.R. § 1.56 (1992).

14 Chisum, *supra* note 10, §11.03[c].

15 Reissue or any procedure has not been available to cure or otherwise purge inequitable conduct in obtaining a patent. The America Invents Act introduced a supplemental examination procedure, which can be used to cure inequitable conduct. Leahy-Smith America Invents Act of 2011, H.R. 1249, 112th Cong. § 7 (2011).

latter kind of information often is much more difficult to evaluate and thus 'more dangerous,' as indicated from the case-law discussed below. Information is *material to patentability* if (1) it is not identical ('*cumulative*') to information already present in the prosecution file of the application, and (2) either by itself or in combination with other information causes a *prima facie* case of a lack of patentability of a claim; or rebuts or is inconsistent with a position which was put forward by the applicant in the context of either (1) a rebuttal against an argument of a lack of patentability by the office, or (2) an argument put forward in support of patentability.

A failure to file the required information can lead to inequitable conduct if the information is *both* (1) relevant for the patentability, and (2) the information was withheld from the Patent Office with deceptive intent.[16] Once both elements are found, inequitable conduct leads to unenforceability of the complete patent in court and is thus punished severely. Additionally, the Court can even order a refund of attorney's fees to the opposing party,[17] an otherwise rather unusual event.

In view of the decision in *Therasense* as discussed below, the USPTO in the meantime has proposed to change Rule 56.[18] The USPTO proposes to harmonize the standard for materiality under §§ 1.56 and 1.555 with the standard for materiality required to establish inequitable conduct according to *Therasense*, namely the 'but-for-plus' standard (see below). Harmonizing the materiality standard should reduce incentives to submit information of marginal relevance. Therefore the USPTO proposed to amend Rule 56 (b) (and similarly Rule 1.555) as follows:

> *(b) Information is material to patentability if it is material under the standard set forth in Therasense.*[19] *Information is material to patentability under Therasense if:*
>
> *(1) The Office would not allow a claim if it were aware of the information, applying the preponderance of the evidence standard and giving the claim its broadest reasonable construction; or*
>
> *(2) The applicant engages in affirmative egregious misconduct before the Office as to the information.*

---

16 *Kingsdown Med. Consultants, Ltd. v. Hollister, Inc.*, 863 F.2d 867 (1988).

17 According to 35 U.S.C. § 285, the court in exceptional cases may award reasonable attorney fees to the prevailing party.

18 The proposed rule changes are *available at* http://www.patentspostgrant.com/wp-content/uploads/2011/07/TherasenseRules.pdf.

19 *Therasense*, 649 F.3d 1276.

IV. THE DUTY OF CANDOR IN EUROPE

Although not identical to the U.S., and despite differences between the common law system of the U.K. and the codified law systems as present in continental Europe, there are European rules that are similar to the duty of candor in the U.S. These rules are also based on the principles of natural law and have even found their way into the patent laws and/or the Codes of Conduct for the national attorneys. However, as explained below, the European rules have only very limited effects on the validity and/or enforceability of a patent.

In the U.K., Section 14 of the Code of Conduct for patent attorneys states that a regulated person must not knowingly deceive or mislead a court or tribunal.[20] In the case of a breach of the code, a number of sanctions can be applied ranging from a warning or reprimand to a fine or even temporary or permanent removal from the Register.

Section 124 of the German Patentgesetz ('PatG') requires that parties involved in proceedings at the German Patent and Trademark Office ('GPTO'), the Federal Patent Court, and the Supreme Court provide complete and true statements with respect to factual circumstances.[21] Nevertheless during examination the applicant is only required to indicate the relevant state of the art if explicitly ordered to do so by the GPTO (§ 34 PatG). Therefore failure by the applicant to mention the state of the art in the application (or elsewhere) does not constitute a violation of § 124 PatG. In other words, the duty of candor does not require applicants to present all relevant state of the art.

In the German case law some litigation defendants have attempted to raise the defense of fraud ('Patenterschleichung' (fraudulent acquisition of a patent)).[22] This defense is based on an alleged violation of § 124 PatG (as mentioned above) and thus alleges that the patentee failed to present certain state of the art at the GPTO, evidence that ultimately would have made a grant impossible.

In Germany (where most of the European patent litigation cases are currently filed), infringement proceedings and parallel validity challenges are handled separately in two independent courts ('bifurcated system').

---

20 *Code of Conduct*, Intellectual Property Regulation Board, http://www.ipreg.org.uk/information/code_conduct.php (last visited Dec. 21, 2011).

21 § 124 of the Patentgesetz in the version as published on December 16, 1980 (BGBl. 1981 I p. 1), last amended by Article 1 of the law of July 31, 2009 (BGBl. I p. 2521).

22 For a summary, *see* Georg Benkard, *Patentgesetz*, § 9 PatG, marginal number 70 (10th ed. 2006).

In this system the infringement court (Landgericht, similar in its function to the U.S. District Court) is generally bound by the validity of the patent as granted and the invalidity argument usually does not interest the infringement court judges. Notably, quite a number of other jurisdictions similarly presume the validity of a granted patent. Despite potential 'timing problems' that can arise because of the separate validity challenges and infringement proceedings (i.e. situations where remedies granted in infringement proceedings must be retroactively 'erased' upon a finding of invalidity) the bifurcated system normally results in rather streamlined infringement case scenarios that are relatively fast (and thus less costly). The bifurcated system also allows for a qualified analysis of the validity of the patent in suit by technically skilled judges. Recently Germany has amended the patent law in order to further streamline the nullity proceedings.[23]

In view of the above it is not surprising that German courts, in addition to rejecting the allegations of a violation of §124 PatG, regard a defense based on an alleged fraudulent acquisition of a patent in the infringement proceedings as inadmissible. The courts reason that any state of the art that had not been considered during the lifetime of a patent (and in some cases even after patent expiration) could be properly raised as a ground for invalidity in a parallel nullity procedure.[24]

Similar to the national rules, the European Patent Attorney ('professional representative') disciplinary rules of conduct in Article 1 require that a professional representative shall not knowingly make any false or misleading statement. In the case of a breach of this obligation sanctions can be applied.[25]

Nevertheless the EPC does not contain rules with respect to a duty of candor for applicants of European Patents. Article 124 of the recently amended EPC stipulates that the European Patent Office ('EPO') may invite applicants to provide information on prior art taken into consideration in national or regional patent proceedings concerning an invention to which the European patent application relates. Rule 141 EPC specifically mentions a copy of the results of any search carried out by the authority with which a previous (priority) application was filed. If the applicant fails to reply in due time to an invitation, the European patent

---

23 'Gesetz zur Vereinfachung und Modernisierung des Patentrechts' of July 31, 2009, Bundesgesetzblatt 2009 Part I No. 50.

24 *See, e.g.*, LG Düsseldorf, Decision of 17. November 2005, 4b O 218/04, and OLG Düsseldorf, Decision of 14. June 2007, 2 U 135/05 – Bodenlauf, and OLG Düsseldorf, Decision of 26. June 2008, 2 U 130/06 – Farbrad.

25 *See supra* text accompanying note 12.

application is deemed to be withdrawn. Practitioners have nicknamed this rule 'European IDS' although Article 124 EPC has no effect on granted European Patents.

Due to the absence of an EU Patent in Europe, European Patents must still be litigated on a country-by-country basis. Nevertheless on March 10, 2011, the Council of the European Union agreed that there will be an EU Patent. Despite quite a few recent political obstacles, for the last missing piece in the system, the Unified Patent Court regulation, signature is planned in 'the second half of 2012', and entry into force is planned in 1 January 2014.[26] Normally the prosecution history of the underlying European Patent is not taken into account by national courts.[27] There are very few examples in the case law where the 'background' of a patent grant was actually taken into account during infringement proceedings. Further, each of these examples involve *venire contra factum proprium* issues.[28] Here are some examples from EU member states:

> U.K.:
> '*Had it been necessary for the judge to take account of the letter [in the file wrapper] in order to resolve the issue of construction, I consider that he would have been entitled to do so.*'[29]
>
> The Netherlands:
> '*If, after consideration of the description and the drawings, reasonable doubt exists as to the interpretation of the claims, a notion similar to a 'File wrapper estoppel' only applies when it appears from the public record that the patentee had good cause to relinquish part of the scope of protection.*'[30]
>
> Germany:
> '*Statements during the examination proceedings have no general relevance for the interpretation of the claims, nevertheless, such statements can be of help for the interpretation of claims*' and '*Statements of the applicant in the opposition procedure can support an objection based on good faith in favor of a third party*

---

[26] http://www.european-council.europa.ec/home-page/highlights/eu-unitary-patent-%E2%80%93-a-historical-breakthrough?lang=en

[27] For Germany, *e.g.*, BGH GRUR 1992, 40 – 'Beheizbarer Atemluftschlauch'; BGH GRUR 2002, 511 – 'Kunststoffrohrteil.', and BGH GRUR 2011, 701 – Okklusionsvorrichtung.

[28] BGH, GRUR 2001, 323, 'Temperaturwächter'; further examples for patent right laches can be found in T. Steinke, Die Verwirkung im Immaterialgüterrecht: Eine rechtsvergleichende Betrachtung zum deutschen, schweizerischen und österreichischen Recht mit europarechtlichen Bezügen, Göttingen 2006, 144, Footnote 737.

[29] Royal Courts of Justice Strand, [2001] EWCA Civ 1589.

[30] Dutch Supreme Court, Van Bentum v. Kool; Ciba-Geigy AG v. Ote Oprics BV.

> *involved in patent infringement proceedings against a respective claim only under particular circumstances. If the applicant in the opposition proceedings in view of already approaching infringement proceedings agrees to discuss a concrete embodiment as raised as a defense by the opponent, and then, in order to increase his chances to be able to defend the patent, declares in a binding manner that this embodiment would not be covered by the scope as desired, he is bound by this declaration.*'[31]

As discussed above, the '*duty of candor*' could also be influenced by acts performed outside of the U.S. and thus include, for example, European and German patent attorneys who have an essential function in the prosecution of a U.S. patent even if the prosecution is primarily handled by U.S. patent attorneys. In practice however, while most of the non-U.S. applicants for a patent and their representatives are more or less familiar with the requirements for filing an IDS, nearly no one is aware of the actual scope of the information requirement in the context of the '*duty of candor*' and the resulting drastic consequences for the validity/enforceability of a U.S. patent. The same holds true for the interaction between statements and acts made during prosecution and their effects on subsequent infringement proceedings.

Finally, despite the introduction of the 'Enforcement-Directive'[32] by the European Union, in many European countries there are still only quite limited mechanisms for discovery and production of documents from opponents. Additionally, rather strong rights protecting privacy and confidential documents exist, particularly with respect to attorneys' work products and the attorney-client privilege.[33] This leads to remarkably different approaches between the U.S. and Europe.

---

[31] BGH – X ZR 105/ 04 – Luftabscheider für Milchsammelanlage, GRUR 2006, 923; BGH Weichvorrichtung I (GRUR 1993, 886); BGH Weichvorrichtung II (Mitt. 1997, 364).

[32] Directive 2004/48/EC of the European Parliament and of the Council of 29 April 2004 on the enforcement of intellectual property rights.

[33] In fact, there is no general principle recognizing legal privilege under German law. However, attorney-client communications are protected by several seizure prohibitions that are connected to an individual's right to refuse testimony and are the source of an external attorney's obligation of secrecy, unless the secrecy is waived by the client. Thus, it is generally understood that German procedural laws give privilege to communications between company employees or managers and external attorneys. In addition, §203 of the German Criminal Law (StGB) punishes a breach of confidentiality as a criminal offence.

V. CASE LAW IN THE US REGARDING '*INEQUITABLE CONDUCT*'

Three Supreme Court cases form the basis for the inequitable conduct doctrine in the U.S.: *Keystone Driller Co. v. General Excavator Co*,[34] *Hazel-Atlas Glass Co. v. Hartford-Empire Co.*,[35] and *Precision Instrument Mfg. Co. v. Automotive Maintenance Machinery Co.*[36] Each of these cases dealt with particularly severe instances of unclean hands including perjury, the manufacture of false evidence, and the suppression of evidence. They also involved deliberately planned and carefully executed schemes to defraud not only the USPTO but also the courts.[37] Thus the remedy for each was dismissal of the case and the preclusion of the patentee from obtaining relief from the court due to unclean hands.

Today the inequitable conduct doctrine includes a broader scope of misconduct, including not only egregious affirmative acts of misconduct intended to deceive both the USPTO and the courts, but also mere nondisclosure of information to the USPTO. Further, the remedy invoked also changed from dismissal of the lawsuit to 'unenforceability of the entire patent' involved in the lawsuit. Along with this, a showing of both materiality and intent came to be required as defined in *Star Scientific Inc. v. R.J. Reynolds Tobacco Co.*[38] In *Star Scientific*, the applicant misrepresented or omitted information that was *both* (1) material for the patentability ('first element'), and (2) withheld with the specific intent to deceive the USPTO ('second element'). The level of proof required for establishing intent and materiality must meet the clear and convincing evidence standard. Before deciding, the court must weigh the equities to determine whether the entire patent becomes unenforceable.

Over time the case law put more and more importance on the first element, as in *Am. Hoist & Derrick Co. v. Sowa & Sons, Inc.*[39] (employing 'a broad view of materiality' and further applying a 'reasonable examiner' standard based on 37 C.F.R. § 1.56 (1977)), and lowered the standard

---

34 *Keystone Driller Co. v. General Excavator Co.*, 290 U.S. 240 (1933).

35 *Hazel-Atlas Glass Co. v. Hartford-Empire Co.*, 322 U.S. 238, 250–51 (1944).

36 *Precision Instrument Mfg. Co. v. Auto. Maint. Mach. Co.*, 324 U.S. 806 (1945).

37 *Therasense*, 649 F.3d 1276.

38 *Star Scientific, Inc. v. R.J. Reynolds Tobacco Co.*, 537 F.3d 1357 (Fed. Cir. 2008).

39 *Am. Hoist & Derrick Co. v. Sowa & Sons, Inc.*, 725 F.2d 1350, 1362 (Fed. Cir. 1984).

for the second element, as in *Driscoll v. Cebalo*[40] (establishing a 'knew or should have known' standard) and *Orthopedic Equip. Co., Inc. v. All Orthopedic Appliances, Inc.*[41] (finding gross negligence sufficient to establish intent to deceive). The analysis shifted even further with the use of a 'sliding scale' that permitted a finding of inequitable conduct 'based on a reduced showing of intent if the record contained a strong showing of materiality, and vice versa'.

Initially the concept of expanding the scope of inequitable conduct was partially intended to ensure full disclosure to the USPTO. However as already briefly mentioned above, this change created numerous unintended negative consequences both for the USPTO and beyond including increased costs, reduced likelihood of settlement, burdened courts, strained USPTO resources (patent prosecutors regularly bury USPTO examiners with a deluge of prior art references, most of which have marginal value and create a 'tidal wave of disclosure [that] makes identifying the most relevant prior art more difficult'[42]), and increased USPTO backlog. Also, inequitable conduct allegations are used strategically to expand discovery into corporate practices that took place before patent filing, and to disqualify the prosecuting attorney from the litigation.

Furthermore, the patentee in turn has no real effective measures with which to defend himself since inequitable conduct cannot be cured by reissue, and the respective 'taint' can spread from a single unenforceable patent to render unenforceable other related patents and applications in the same technology family.[43] Also, inequitable conduct may lead to remedies based on antitrust and unfair competition, may invoke the 'exceptional case' provisions of 35 USC § 285 regarding attorney's fees, and may be used to pierce the attorney-client privilege under the crime-fraud exception.

The CAFC in an *en banc* decision in *Kingsdown Medical Consultants v. Hollister Inc.*[44] tried to steer against the devaluation in order to prevent further abuse of the inequitable conduct-defense by the accused infringer. In this case the court found that negligence, gross negligence, or the application of a 'should have known' standard does not satisfy the intent

---

[40] *Driscoll v. Cebalo*, 731 F.2d 878, 885 (Fed. Cir. 1984).

[41] *Orthopedic Equip. Co., Inc. v. All Orthopedic Appliances, Inc.*, 707 F.2d 1376, 1383–4 (Fed. Cir. 1983).

[42] *Therasense*, 649 F.3d at 1289 (reference to the Brief for the United States as Amicus Curiae).

[43] *Consol. Aluminum Corp. v. Foseco Int'l Ltd.*, 910 F.2d 804, 808–12 (Fed. Cir. 1990).

[44] *Kingsdown*, 863 F.2d at 876.

requirement. Rather there must be clear and convincing evidence that an applicant *made a deliberate decision* to withhold a *known* material reference.[45]

Despite the efforts of the CAFC (in particular the efforts of Chief Judge Rader), in practice courts nearly always found inequitable conduct whenever (and sometimes even wherever) information was identified as material for patentability but had not been presented to the USPTO.

The following two cases are discussed in more detail representing extreme examples of the pre-*Therasense* trend in CAFC case law. The dissenting opinions of these cases highlight the divided views among CAFC judges leading to *Therasense's en banc* review of materiality and intent, analyzing the two separate elements required for establishing inequitable conduct.

(i) *Aventis Pharma S.A. v. Amphastar Pharmaceuticals, Inc.*[46]

Aventis was the owner of U.S. patent No. 5,389,618 ("618 patent') and a *reissue*-patent thereof, U.S. patent No. RE 38,743 ("743 patent'), relating to a composition of heparin-polysaccharides with low molecular weight for the prevention and treatment of thrombosis by inhibiting blood clotting and simultaneously minimizing the possibility of bleeding, particularly during high-risk surgery.

The initial claim for the '618 patent was rejected for lacking novelty/inventive step according to 35 U.S.C. §§ 102(b) and 103 in view of the relevant state of the art, which included European patent 40,144 ('EP '144'). Aventis amended the claim and argued against the novelty rejection according to 35 U.S.C. § 102(b), presenting differences between the physical properties of the compound as claimed and 'EP '144'. For this Aventis filed data by Dr. Uzan regarding the half-lives of the compounds in plasma in order to show that the half-lives of the '618 compound, when compared to the EP '144 compound, were longer at 40 mg. Dr. Uzan was a chemist for Aventis yet not an inventor for the '618 patent. Aventis objected to the lack of an inventive step according to 35 U.S.C. § 103 by stating that the properties of the compound as claimed were not shown by EP '144, and thus EP '144 could not render this property of the compound as obvious to the person of ordinary skill in the art. The examiner was unconvinced by the argument and again rejected the claims. Aventis

---

45 *Molins PLC v. Textron, Inc.*, 48 F.3d 1172 (Fed. Cir. 1995).

46 *Aventis Pharma S.A. v. Amphastar Pharms., Inc.*, 525 F.3d 1334 (Fed. Cir. 2008).

replied by filing a second declaration by Dr. Uzan that contained results showing a statistically significant difference between a 40 mg dosage of the composition as claimed and an *undisclosed* dosage of the composition of the state of the art (thus, Aventis did not disclose the dosage difference to the examiner). In response to the second declaration the examiner granted the '618 patent.

In the context of filing for market approval for a generic version of Aventis' composition, the defendants, Amphastar Pharmaceuticals, Inc. and Teva Pharmaceuticals USA, Inc., each filed an 'Abbreviated New Drug Application' (ANDA) with the Food and Drug Administration ('FDA'). Aventis responded by filing an infringement suit against both companies in the District Court for the Central District of California. The District Court held that the patents were unenforceable on the grounds of inequitable conduct since Aventis' statement that the composition as claimed would have a better half-life than the composition of the state of the art was material for the patentability. Furthermore a *clear* intent to deceive could be identified since 'no reasonable explanation for the comparison of half-lives at different dosages could be found and comparisons at the same dosages showed small differences in the half-lives'. On appeal the CAFC confirmed the decision of the District Court and upheld the analysis of the materiality of the dosages with respect to comparing the half-lives, and the analysis of Aventis' intent to deceive with respect to omitting the disclosure of the dosages to the USPTO. The CAFC further identified different levels of relevance for the statements comparing the half-lives when arguing in favor of an inventive step versus novelty.

In his dissenting opinion Judge Rader criticized the decisional trend of exclusively focusing on the materiality of the information as withheld, in order to construe therefrom the separate element of intent to deceive. Judge Rader explained:

> *More recently, however, the judicial process has too often emphasized materiality almost to the exclusion of any analysis of the lofty intent requirement for inequitable conduct. Merging intent and materiality at levels far below the Kingsdown*[47] *rule has revived the inequitable conduct tactic. . . . Surely if Dr. Uzan had intended to deceive the USPTO, he would not have made this omission so conspicuous. . . . Most important, Dr. Uzan himself revealed the error. This candor is inconsistent with deceptive intent. . . . Thus, both materiality and intent seem suspect on this record. In sum, . . . I would reverse the district court's determination of inequitable conduct.*[48]

47 *See supra* text accompanying note 15.
48 *Aventis*, 525 F.3d at 1350–53.

(ii) *Monsanto Co. v. Bayer Bioscience N.V.*[49]

The relevant claims in U.S. patent No. 5,545,565 ('the '565 patent') related to genetically engineered corn plants that had been transformed with an expression construct encoding a protein containing the amino-terminal part of an insecticidal toxin from *Bacillus thuringiensis* ('bt-toxin'). In this case the patentee (Bayer) did not file with the USPTO a hand-written internal memo relating to one of the references that was filed with the USPTO. The reference was an abstract of a poster presentation at a scientific meeting. A Bayer researcher, Dr. Mariani, attended the meeting and took notes on the poster in form of a memo that contained much more information than the corresponding abstract (the 'Barnes-abstract'). She circulated the memo among the Bayer researchers and the in-house patent attorney in Germany, Dr. Meulemanns, who was responsible for the prosecution of the patent at stake. Dr. Meulemanns then provided statements with respect to the patented invention, which stood in contrast to the information contained in the internal memo. Although Dr. Meulemanns declared in court that he spoke with Dr. Mariani about the Barnes-poster, he said that she would have been unable to remember 'anything' about the poster. However, in view of Dr. Mariani's clear recollection during a deposition regarding the notes and the poster, the District Court did not find Dr. Meulemanns' statements credible. The District Court found the notes highly relevant to patentability under the 'reasonable examiner' test (see above) especially since they would create a '*prima facie case of unpatentability*'. The court also found an intent to deceive the USPTO on behalf of Bayer.

The District Court found an intent to deceive based on the in-house patent attorney's actions in Germany (*outside* of the US), constituting a breach of the duty of candor for a U.S. application. Furthermore the court found that the applicant (Bayer) *should have known* that the withheld information would have been material for the USPTO analysis regarding patentability (this requires knowledge regarding the standard of the patentability requirements in the U.S.). The decision reads:

> *We do not suggest that all internal documents of potential relevance must be submitted to the PTO as a matter of course. Rather, it is the particular circumstances that render the internal documents material in this case.*[50]

After the court found materiality for the withheld information, with regard to intent the court merely relied on purely *circumstantial evidence* to

[49] *Monsanto Co. v. Bayer Bioscience N.V.*, 514 F.3d 1229 (Fed. Cir. 2008).
[50] *Id.* at 1240.

shift the burden of proof to the patentee, forcing him to present a credible explanation as to why the information was not submitted to the USPTO.

As the court explained:

> *To prove intent, 'the involved conduct, viewed in light of all the evidence, including evidence of good faith, must indicate sufficient culpability to require a finding of intent to deceive.' Direct evidence of intent to deceive is not necessary, but may be inferred from the surrounding circumstances. We have held that absent a credible reason for withholding the information, '[i]ntent may be inferred where a patent applicant knew, or should have known, that withheld information would be material to the PTO's consideration of the patent application.' . . . absent a credible reason for Meulemanns to have not understood the content of Mariani's notes after having discussed them with Mariani, the district court did not clearly err in inferring the requisite intent. Intent is easily inferred when, as here, an applicant makes arguments to the PTO that it knows, or obviously should have known, are false in light of information not before the examiner, and the applicant knowingly withholds that additional information.*[51]

(iii) *Therasense, Inc. (Abbott) v. Becton, Dickinson and Co.*[52]

As explained above, in *Therasense*, the *en banc* CAFC attempted to cure the 'plague' of inequitable conduct allegations by raising the standards for proving that the alleged bad act was material to patentability and that the patentee undertook the alleged bad act with the intent to deceive the USPTO.

At the outset of the case a panel CAFC extended the scope of the duty of candor for U.S. applications even further. Even contradicting declarations or statements in other (even technically different) applications (including applications outside of the U.S.) could be used in order to establish inequitable conduct.

Following proceedings without a jury, Judge Alsup in the Northern District of California found Abbott's (formerly Therasense's) patent No. 5,820,551 ("551 patent') unenforceable due to *inequitable conduct* during the prosecution thereof.[53] On appeal the CAFC panel affirmed the decision.[54]

The invention related to an electric-strip glucose-measuring device without a separation membrane layer – wherein the lack of a membrane became a decisive feature in the discussion. During prosecution the

---

51 *Id.* at 1240–41.

52 *Therasense*, 649 F.3d 1276.

53 *Therasense, Inc. v. Becton, Dickinson & Co.*, 565 F. Supp. 2d 1088 (N.D. Cal., 2008).

54 *Therasense, Inc. v. Becton, Dickinson & Co.*, 593 F.3d 1289 (Fed. Cir. 2010).

application for the '551 patent was rejected due to another Abbott patent (the '382 patent of another family). In response, Abbott's research director filed a declaration stating that a person of ordinary skill in the art would not consider the other patent in the context of the invention of the '551 patent. Thus the '551 patent was granted.

During the course of a concurrent EPO oral hearing for the '382 patent family, Abbott declared that the membrane was merely a '*safety measure*' and '*preferred*' and explicitly stated: '*It is submitted that this disclosure is unequivocally clear. The protective membrane is optional, however, it is preferred when used on live blood.*'

The court regarded the EPO statements as material to the U.S. proceedings and held:

> *To deprive an examiner of the EPO statements-statements directly contrary to Abbott's representations to the PTO-on the grounds that they were not material would be to eviscerate the duty of disclosure. Moreover, if this could be regarded as a close case, which it is not, we have repeatedly emphasized that the duty of disclosure requires that the material in question be submitted to the examiner rather than withheld by the applicant.*[55]

In order to first mitigate the surprise for all parties involved the court offered a fig leaf by explaining that such results should be 'rare'. Despite this the court confirmed the presence of inequitable conduct. The court relied on earlier case law where – exclusively in U.S. cases – it was explicitly found that statements made during the prosecution of other applications should not be regarded as material when they are presented in form of '*mere attorney-arguments*' since an applicant himself should not be limited by his attorney in his analysis of the state of the art.[56] However, for affidavits and declarations increased standards apply.[57] Thus incorrect statements by the patentee in affidavits or declarations, as opposed to attorney arguments, were regarded as inherently material.

Furthermore, 37 C.F.R. § 1.56(b)(2)[58] establishes that prior statements by an applicant are automatically material to the USPTO if these

---

55 *Therasense*, 593 F.3d at 1304–5.

56 *See, e.g.*, *Innogenetics, N.V v. Abbott Labs.*, 512 F.3d 1363 (2007), *discussing Life Techs., Inc. v. Clontech Labs., Inc.*, 224 F.3d 1320, 1326 (Fed. Cir. 2000).

57 *See, e.g.*, *eSpeed, Inc. v. BrokerTec USA, L.L.C.*, 480 F.3d 1129, 1136 (Fed. Cir. 2007).

58 Which (shortened) reads: '*information is material to patentability when it is not cumulative to information already of record or being made of record in the application, and . . . [i]t refutes, or is inconsistent with, a position the applicant takes in . . . [o]pposing an argument of unpatentability relied on by the Office . . .*'

statements directly contradict statements made by the same applicant in other pending proceedings before the USPTO.

Since the Abbott statements were not pure attorney arguments and were filed as affidavits the court found that the EPO statements were '*highly material to the prosecution of the '551 patent*' and decided that Abbott '*intended to deceive the PTO by withholding those submissions*'.[59] Thus the court found inequitable conduct.

In his dissenting opinion Judge Linn posed that Abbott had presented a sufficient explanation for why the EPO statements were not submitted.[60] This was not adequately considered by the court. While it would not be sufficient to examine whether the information would be *objectively* irrelevant, instead it would be decisive if the parties involved *subjectively* believed that the reference would be immaterial at the time of withholding it.

For the reasons set out above the CAFC granted Abbott's petition for rehearing *en banc* and vacated the judgment of the panel.[61] The *en banc* court in a 6–1–4 decision first established that the accused infringer must prove by clear and convincing evidence that the applicant knew of the reference, knew that it was material, and made a deliberate decision to withhold it. The court further stressed that intent and materiality are separate requirements and therefore a district court should not use a 'sliding scale' whereby a weak showing of intent may be deemed sufficient because of a strong showing of materiality and vice versa. Instead a court must weigh the evidence of intent to deceive independently of its analysis of materiality. Proving that an applicant knew of a reference, should have known of its materiality, and decided not to submit it to the USPTO does not prove specific intent to deceive.

Regarding evidence of intent to deceive, because direct evidence of deceptive intent is rare, a district court may infer intent from indirect and circumstantial evidence. The specific intent to deceive must be 'the single most reasonable inference able to be drawn from the evidence'.

Since a higher intent standard standing alone may not reduce the number of inequitable conduct cases before the courts and may not cure the problem of overdisclosure of marginally relevant prior art to the USPTO, the court also 'adjusted' the standard for materiality. In doing so the court rejected the definition of materiality in USPTO Rule 56. Since Rule 56 sets a low bar for materiality, the standard results in the practice

---

[59] *Therasense*, 593 F.3d at 1308.

[60] *Therasense*, 593 F.3d at 1312 (Linn, J., dissenting).

[61] *Therasense*, 649 F.3d 1276.

by patent prosecutors of disclosing too much prior art of marginal relevance and by patent litigators of continuing to charge inequitable conduct in nearly every case as a litigation strategy.

Accordingly, the court adjusted the materiality standard by applying the 'but-for materiality' approach as established in the Supreme Court case *Corona Cord Tire Co. v. Dovan Chemical Corp.*[62] Thus when an applicant fails to disclose prior art to the USPTO the prior art is deemed but-for material if the USPTO would not have allowed a claim had it been aware of the undisclosed prior art. Hence in assessing the materiality of a withheld reference courts must now determine whether the USPTO would have allowed the claim had it been aware of the undisclosed reference. In making this patentability determination courts should apply the preponderance of the evidence standard and give claims their broadest reasonable construction.

While but-for materiality generally must be proved to satisfy the materiality prong of inequitable conduct, the CAFC recognized an exception for cases of affirmative egregious misconduct. In other words, if the applicant clearly 'deliberately planned and carefully executed scheme[s]' to defraud the USPTO and the courts, the conduct (understandably) is material irrespective of but-for materiality.

Importantly for patentees in litigation, the court also rejected 'automatic' unenforceability of the patent in suit even when materiality and intent are proven. The court held that a patent should only be rendered unenforceable by inequitable conduct 'where the patentee's misconduct resulted in the unfair benefit of receiving an unwarranted claim'. This requirement substantially limits the discretion of district courts.

On June 1, 2011, Becton Dickinson filed a motion with the Federal Circuit to stay the issuance of the mandate in the *Therasense* case pending the filing of a petition for *writ of certiorari* to the Supreme Court.

VI. BRIEF CRITIQUE OF *THERASENSE*

There are two factual issues in *Therasense* that I would like to critique. They both relate to the materiality and intent requirements as analyzed in the case, in particular by the District Court and the CAFC panel.

Regarding intent, here the applicant commented on the state of the art in the form of statements. Thus no actual 'technical' state of the art was withheld but there were two statements (applicants' opinions) filed that

---

62 *Corona Cord Tire Co. v. Dovan Chemical Corp.*, 276 U.S. 358, 373–4 (1928).

were subsequently compared by the court(s). These statements were given by the applicant in two different jurisdictions in quite different contexts (although they both related to inventive step/obviousness questions). The applicant was certainly aware of this situation. In Europe the EPO decides on the question of inventive step in an 'objective' analysis after hearing the applicant as a technical expert (see below). This – according to my understanding – leads to the interesting effect that here it was *impossible* for the applicant to have any intent to deceive the EPO. Nevertheless the courts in the U.S. treated the statements equally with regard to intent. In other words, the courts did not decide whether the the U.S. statement or the European statement was incorrect.

Regarding materiality, again differences between the U.S. and European proceedings must be considered. There is no problem-solution approach at the USPTO. The comments in Europe were related to an analysis that requires the identification of a single 'closest state-of-the-art' document. Thus the discussion in Europe concerned the presence or absence of a semipermeable membrane versus a different (protective) membrane *in view of this state of the art*. It was not discussed (and this was not required) whether a membrane at all would be a mandatory requirement. From reading the decision of the court it seems that this argument was merely regarded as some 'lame excuse' ('flatly inconsistent'[63]) by the applicant. Nevertheless the argument makes sense, particularly from a European point of view.

(i) *Therasense* and Europe

How would *Therasense* have been decided in Europe, for example by a German Landgericht? As mentioned above there is no equivalent to Rule 56 in the German PatG and there is no effect of inequitable conduct on a granted patent. Section 124 PatG does not provide consequences of a violation thereof and therefore general considerations regarding bad faith must be applied (see below). Of note if the applicant fails to fully disclose state of the art known to him during the prosecution (after the German examiner has requested him to do so based on § 34 para. 7 PatG) the application will be rejected. If such a request has not been issued by the examiner, the examination of the patent is then exclusively based on the relevant state of the art presented by the Patent Office.

It must be kept in mind that in Europe (including Germany) the patentability of an invention is based exclusively on an *objective* analysis of

---

63 *Therasense*, 649 F.3d 1276.

the state of the art by the person of ordinary skill in the art. Therefore, although the German Supreme Court often relies on expert opinions, the final analysis of the invention is 'detached' and thus independent from any opinion of the applicant. Consequently, despite the fact that the analysis of an inventive step includes a 'humanized' evaluation, statements or affidavits filed in the proceedings cannot establish patentability and are (usually) taken into account as technical expert opinions.

In summary, the validity of the patent as granted cannot be affected by false statements and/or by withholding relevant state of the art. If during litigation, state of the art is found that is relevant for the validity of the patent in suit the defendant must use this state of the art in a parallel nullity procedure. If the state of the art is *prima facie* relevant, infringement proceedings may be stayed by the Landgericht.

Since the principles of equity also apply under German law, the enforcement of a patent by the patentee must reside within the boundaries of good faith.[64] Otherwise the defendant is entitled to raise a defense based on bad faith, particularly in the case of an estoppel by the patentee (*venire contra factum proprium*, see above). Nevertheless estoppels are rare and usually only exist *inter partes*. Further, the patent in suit does not become completely unenforceable.

The Patent Office and the courts are entitled to ignore false statements made by the patentee. Additionally, the courts are allowed to generally cast doubts on statements made by a party who has earlier provided a false statement, possibly resulting in changes regarding the burden of proof. Further, as with the provisions of 35 USC § 285, the court may take into account bad faith when deciding on the costs of the proceedings. It is currently in dispute whether a patent obtained by fraud to the Patent Office could still be regarded as null and void (in particular by a litigation court). The current German case law seems at least to exclude situations where relevant state of the art was withheld.[65] However, a willful false statement may also have consequences outside of the patent laws, such as requiring compensation for damages (according to § 826 of German Civil Law; BGB). Such statements based on fraud could be punished as a criminal offence (§ 263 of German Criminal Law; StGB).

In *Therasense*, the CAFC panel found the patent unenforceable since material information in the form of the EPO statements was not made available to the USPTO. In fact the applicant provided a contradicting statement regarding an inventive step. Thus actually no state of the art

---

64 Benkard, *supra* note 22, § 9 PatG, marginal number 69.

65 *See supra* note 44.

was withheld from the USPTO. Irrespective of whether the statements in Europe or the U.S. were true or false, in Germany these types of statements are merely regarded as expert opinions and could not render the patent in suit unenforceable. As mentioned above, the defendant would be required to raise the argument in a parallel nullity proceeding. Further it seems unlikely that the infringement court would have even stayed the proceedings.

The situation may be different (but only slightly) in the above-mentioned *Monsanto* scenario where actual state of the art (the content of the Barnes-poster) was not considered during examination. Since the analysis of the state of the art is objective Dr. Mariani's notes may have indicated that the state of the art presented in the poster could be interpreted more broadly than the state of the art presented in the abstract. Again this would not render the patent unenforceable but perhaps a European court would stay the infringement proceedings if a respective nullity suit was filed based on new and highly relevant state of the art (allegedly) identified in the poster.

(ii) The Effects of U.S. Case Law on the Practice in Europe

For the European practitioner *Therasense* did not change the general policy whereby the U.S. duty of candor and good faith can still extend both to individuals and to acts in Europe (and elsewhere). However because of changes to both the intent and materiality requirements, *Therasense* has for everyone certainly reduced the danger of losing a U.S. patent on the grounds of inequitable conduct.

Some commentaries on the *Therasense* decision claim that the 'but-for materiality' standard will lead to a drastic reduction in the volume of state of the art filed at the PTO and that this will lead to an increased burden on the PTOs.[66] This seems to be unlikely (particularly with respect to Europe where this practice has taken place for decades) since Rule 56 still applies irrespectively of whether the practitioner is located in the U.S. or not. Thus relevant state of the art still must be presented. Further the relevant individuals must be identified who are involved in the filing and the prosecution of a U.S. patent application. Once such a group is identified certainly the best defense against upcoming problems is tight communication within the group, which should prevent errors and harmonize state-

66 Jason Rantanen and and Lee Petherbridge, *Therasense v. Becton Dickinson: A First Impression*, Loyola-LA Legal Studies Paper, http://ssrn.com/abstract=1859764 (last visited Dec. 22, 2011).

ments regarding the possible impact and importance of state of the art. Furthermore this ensures that all relevant/material information can be identified and submitted. Of course the fact that this may 'cross borders' in patent families that may be prosecuted on an international basis does not make it any easier. Still problems occur particularly for small companies and U.S.-inexperienced applicants as well as for large companies with a large number of subsidiaries, companies represented by several external law firms, and universities with a large number of publications by the inventors. It also must be kept in mind that the case-law seems to distinguish between in-house and external counsel in case of 'attorney arguments.'

VII. HARMONIZATION BETWEEN EUROPE AND THE U.S.?

Despite the changes, *Therasense* did not lead to a complete harmonization of the legal situation between Europe and the U.S. Of course this is not 'the fault' of *Therasense* as the structures of the laws in this field are fundamentally different; namely the difference between permanent unenforceability of the patent (partially or fully) in the U.S. and no effect on the patent in Europe.

The 'but-for materiality' standard made the practical situation in the U.S. more similar to the situation in Europe particularly where the applicant has been requested to file the relevant state of the art with the office based on Art. 124 EPC as described above. As these rules only apply before grant the European IDS may be seen as an attempt to harmonize with U.S. law. However it seems that these measures currently focus more on avoiding double work for the PTOs. For example, an effective implementation of the Patent Prosecution Highway ('PPH')[67] seems to suffer from the differences.

In order to achieve greater harmonization more general legal changes need to be implemented. Some changes to the system may be forthcoming from the very recently established America Invents Act ('AIA'),[68] which passed the U.S. Senate with a solid (89–9) vote and went into force on September 16, 2011. As mentioned earlier, regarding inequitable conduct,

---

[67] *See e.g.*, *Patent Prosecution Highway (PPH) – Fast Track Examination of Applications*, The United States Patent and Trademark Office, http://www.uspto.gov/patents/init_events/pph/index.jsp (last visited Dec. 22, 2011).

[68] Leahy-Smith America Invents Act of 2011, H.R. 1249, 112th Cong. (2011)

the AIA established the 'supplemental examination,' an *ex parte* procedure for the patent owner to remedy problems in order to eliminate the possibility of an inequitable conduct allegation in patent litigation. According to the procedure the owner may request supplemental examination of a patent to consider, reconsider, or correct any 'information believed to be relevant to the patent'. There are no limitations on the nature of the 'information' to be considered or corrected and the information may include state-of-the-art issues, the accuracy of prior declarations, statements regarding inventorship, and printed publications and patents. However, there are some exclusions to the 'repair' of unclean hands, such as material fraud on the USPTO, and requests will not have a retroactive effect on inequitable conduct issues already raised. The procedure will become effective one year from the date of enactment (September 16, 2012) and will apply to any patent issued before, on, or after the effective date.

As one of the first statements regarding the effects of this procedure the Generic Pharmaceutical Association ('GPhA') has acknowledged that this provision could significantly reduce the availability of inequitable conduct as a defense for generic challengers under the Hatch-Waxman Act. GPhA also believes that this provision could negatively impact the market for affordable generic medicines by increasing brand companies' 'incentive[s] to be dishonest and cheat'. After all 'this legislation offers a free ride for those looking to mislead and misrepresent the PTO . . . while proponents may try to argue that the mechanism provided in the bill merely allows patent holders to correct inadvertent mistakes, what we are talking about here is purposeful lying and any claims to the contrary are simply disingenuous'.[69]

[69] *GPhA Urges the House to Send 'The America Invents Act' Back to the Drawing Board*, Generic Pharmaceutical Association, http://www.gphaonline.org/media/press-releases/2011/gpha-urges-house-send-'-america-invents-act'-back-drawing-board (last visited Dec. 22, 2011).

PART III

Copyright

6. Tradition and change: The past and future of authors' moral rights

Mira T. Sundara Rajan

> There is today what Mr. Justice Holmes might have called a far reaching free trade in legal ideas. — Otto Kahn-Freund[1]

Authorship is the foundation of copyright law—and this statement is one that seems to hold true, as few assertions do, virtually always and everywhere. Without the concept of authorship, copyright law cannot exist. Copyright originates in the desire to protect, and to reward, the work of the author. Every other element of copyright law grows out of this fundamental objective—this deep-laid legal foundation.

An important manifestation of authorship in copyright laws is the recognition of the non-commercial rights associated with creative works. These rights, generally known by the term 'moral rights,'[2] are, quite simply, rights of authorship. They include the fundamental interests of attribution—the right to be named as the author of one's own work—and integrity—the right to protect one's work from harm.[3] Different legal systems respond differently to the evolution of authorship. These diverse, sometimes divergent reactions are often based on underlying differences in the orientation of national laws towards authorship, as reflected, at a fundamental level, in their attitudes to authors' moral rights. The presence and form of moral rights bring distinctiveness and cultural color to the ways in which copyright adapts to technology in different jurisdictions. In some instances, countries continue to emphasize the importance of authorship

---

1 *See* Otto Kahn-Freund, *On Uses and Misuses of Comparative Law,* 37 Mod. L. Rev. 1, 10 (1974) (referring to the dissent of Justice Oliver Wendell Holmes in *Abrams v. U.S.*, 250 U.S. 616, 630 (1919)).

2 The term is an awkward translation from the French *droit moral;* in other jurisdictions, they are known by other names—of which, the German *persönlichkeitsrecht,* or personality right, is perhaps the most practical. *See* Mira T. Sundara Rajan, *Moral Rights: Principles, Practice and New Technology* 7–17, 53 (2011) (discussing moral rights versus *droit moral).*

3 Sundara Rajan, *supra* note 2, at 11, 33–5.

in a technological context, recognizing moral rights for the contributors to a film[4] or the makers of software;[5] while, in other ways, they attempt to limit the reach of moral rights in a technological environment.[6]

As copyright works increasingly move across borders, and as the international community itself is increasingly aware of its own diversity, moral rights are a growing presence. In much of the world, and particularly in common-law countries, not enough is known about them. In fact, an awareness of moral rights is of crucial importance for copyright industries, whether technology- or culture-related; their future ultimately lies in international markets.[7] An American filmmaker who wants to make movies in Europe needs to know about moral rights; so too, does a software developer who wants to hire engineers in India, or a record label that wants to distribute music in Russia.[8] Moral rights are relevant to large-scale undertakings—to what is, in a way, the most massive of them all—Google's Books project.[9] At the international level, national influences affect the

---

[4] *See, e.g.*, the French copyright provisions on film: art. L113–7, L121–5 and L121–6 of the French Intellectual Property Code, *Loi N° 92–597 du 1er juillet 1992 relative au code de la propriété intellectuelle (partie législative)*, *Journal officiel de la République française du 8 février 1994* (as am.); *Légifrance: Le service public de la diffusion du droit, available at* http://www.legifrance.gouv.fr/affichCode.do?cidTexte=LEGITEXT000006069414&dateTexte=20100412 [hereinafter French Intellectual Property Code].

[5] *Id.* art. L121–7.

[6] For example, France recognizes rights in the creation of software, but it imposes limits on them that are not enforced for other types of copyright works: *see id.* (though it is also worth noting that these provisions precisely reflect the language of the Berne Convention, and could therefore not be considered restrictive by international standards). India has recognized moral rights in creative works, including technological works such as software; but it has scaled back its general scheme for the protection of moral rights in dramatic ways and its current law reflects a strong difference of opinion dividing government from the courts. *See* Sundara Rajan, *supra* note 2, at 164–81. The case of India is discussed in some detail *infra*.

[7] This point was noted in relation to Google, in private conversation, by William Patry, Senior Copyright Counsel for Google, August 2011.

[8] The general difficulty of law enforcement in countries like India and Russia—for different reasons in each case—should be duly noted. However, Western companies and organizations wishing to operate in these parts of the world should adhere to lawful practices; and, indeed, it is the duty of legal counsel to advise them on legal conduct, internationally and within the specific jurisdictions of interest. Of course, they also need to understand the landscape of legality in these countries, and the context in which their operations will be interpreted.

[9] The issues involving moral rights and Google books are considered in Mira T. Sundara Rajan, *Creative Commons: America's Moral Rights?*, 21 Fordham Intell. Prop. Media & Ent. L.J. 905, 905–8, 952–65 (2011).

patterns of harmonization. The growing presence and influence of emerging jurisdictions is likely to move the international treatment of moral rights in dramatically new directions.

There is a certain poignancy to moral rights. Despite their long history in civil law countries, and widespread acceptance for them in the developing and post-socialist world, the dominant trend of copyright practice today seems to place little emphasis on authorship. In the common-law countries, in particular, the focus is on ownership. Somewhat paradoxically, the advent of new technologies has heightened this shift. Technology is intensely dependent on 'content'—and therefore, authorship—for the realization of value; and yet, the novel conception of creative work as 'content' has simultaneously reduced the activity of authorship to the mere provision of goods for consumption in the virtual marketplace. Authorship is at once more important than ever before and increasingly inconsequential. This is not to suggest that there is anything inevitable about any of these attitudes, or that technology *per se* is responsible: our reactions to technology are, after all, matters of our own choosing. But it is an interesting time to consider the place of authorship in copyright law, to identify the movements in the traditionally diverse countries of common-law and civil law heritage, and to explore some possible paths to greater mutual understanding in a future where cultural concerns may be brought to our attention by voices that were largely inaudible in the past.

I. RIGHTS OF AUTHORSHIP: THE COMMON-LAW AND CIVIL-LAW TRADITIONS

When it comes to authorship, it is widely accepted that the common-law countries and the civil-law countries hold opposing views. The crux of the matter is represented by the moral rights of authors—rights of authorship that hold a prominent place in the copyright laws of Continental European countries but, until recently, and with the lone exception of Canada,[10] were never recognized in the laws of common-law countries.[11]

---

[10] Canada enacted moral rights in its copyright legislation of 1931, just three years after they were adopted in the Berne Convention. *See* Mira T. Sundara Rajan, *Culture Matters: Why Canada's Proposed Amendments to its Copyright Law Should Revisit Moral Rights, in From 'Radical Extremism' to 'Balanced Copyright': Canadian Copyright and the Digital Agenda* 486–9 (Michael Geist ed. 2010), *available at* http://www.irwinlaw.com/content/assets/content-commons/666/CCDA%2016%20Sundara%20Rajan.pdf [Hereinafter *Culture Matters*]. The growth of technological protection measures that operate to restrict online

Nevertheless, it is worth remembering that this divergence of ways is largely a reflection of developments over time. The origin of both common-law and civil-law copyright systems lies in the basic concept that rights should flow from authorship. Creative work is not understood as a form of common property, nor is the creative domain properly free

---

activities within the territory of a given country or region is a factor to consider. For example, Canada's pending reform to its copyright legislation has met with strong criticism because of a catch-all provision that would make any circumvention of a digital lock an infringement of copyright law. *See* Bill C-11, §§ 41.1–41.21, *available at* http://www.parl.gc.ca/HousePublications/Publication.aspx?Docid=5144516&file=4. The Bill was originally introduced as Bill C-31 in 2010, and was subject to a nationwide consultation process–although the impact of this process on the content of the Bill remains questionable. The legislation was re-introduced, largely intact, by the re-elected Conservative government on Sept. 29, 2011.

[11] It should be noted that India, too, may be considered an exception to this rule, as it adopted comprehensive moral rights provisions in 1957 – second to Canada's 1931 provisions, but long before the enactment of moral rights in the British Copyright, Designs and Patents Act of 1988. Under current Indian law, '[a]ny modification' can lead to a violation of the right of integrity, but, in keeping with the language of the Berne Convention, the author must show 'damage to his honour or reputation': *see Indian Copyright Act 1957*, Act 14 of 1957, § 57, *available at* http://copyright.gov.in/Documents/CopyrightRules1957.pdf [hereinafter Indian Copyright Act]. Prior to the amendments of 1994, the Indian law did not include this requirement of proof; the old version of § 57 can still be found on the website of the Commonwealth Legal Information Institute, *available at* http://www.liiofindia.org/cgi-bin/disp.pl/in/legis/cen/num_act/ca1957133/ca1957133.html?query=copyright%20law. India's copyright system is based on common law principles, developed under British Imperial rule of the country, although it is spiced with civil law flavors from France and Portugal, European countries with a significant Indian presence. Indeed, the French administered the Indian territory of Pondicherry, on India's southeast coast, *during* the period of British rule; it was home to an important community of nationalist exiles involved in India's agitation for independence, early in the twentieth century. However, the context of development, and India's rich and unique indigenous legal history, are significant influences in Indian law, and to call India a common law country is a somewhat imperfect application of that term. The origins of Indian law are examined briefly in Mira T. Sundara Rajan, *Moral Rights in Developing Countries: The Example of India, Part I,* 8 *Journal of Intellectual Property Rights* 357, 360–64 (2003) [hereinafter *Moral Rights*], *available at* http://nopr.niscair.res.in/bitstream/123456789/4907/1/JIPR%208(5)%20357-374.pdf (National Institute of Science, Communication and Information Resources, Council for Scientific and Industrial Research, Government of India). For an updated version of this article, see Mira T. Sudara Rajan, Moral Rights and Protection of Cultural Property: Amar Nath Sehgal v. Union of India, The Quarterly Review of Corporation Law and Society (No. 17) 134 (Noriyuki Shiga trans., 2009) available at: http://www.globalcoe-waseda-law-commerce.org/activity/pdf/17/06.pdf

of all claims—a Wild West open to whoever wills and can enforce that will. Rights should exist; and those rights belong with the creator of the work. This is true, not only of the Statute of Anne, the first modern copyright law and a classic legislative statement of common-law copyright principles;[12] but also, of the copyright system of the United States, where it is perhaps not sufficiently emphasized that the idea of copyright as a limited monopoly, enshrined in the U.S. Constitution, is nevertheless a monopoly to which *only creators* are fundamentally entitled.[13]

A look at common-law history is significant, because it suggests that the obstacles to harmonizing copyright concepts across legal systems may not be as intimidating as they seem at first glance. Indeed, the greater emphasis on rights of authorship in modern civil-law systems is not beyond the comprehension of common-law jurisdictions. On the contrary, British courts explored what was meant by rights of authorship long before moral rights were as much as a gleam in the eye of French or German jurists. When British judges ultimately expressed reservations about them, their objections arose out of concern for the protection of free speech, still fragile in the eighteenth-century kingdom. For the common law and civil law traditions, achieving perspectives in unison is a historical possibility. The dual pressures of technology and the emergence of new copyright jurisdictions from the former developing and socialist worlds, with their own, unique perspectives on authorship rights, may lend both reasons and methods to the pursuit of this achievement.

(i) Authorship Rights and the Common-Law: Queen Anne and her Spiritual Heirs[14]

The Statute of Anne of 1710 was the first common-law copyright law to recognize an author's right in his or her own work.[15] Prior to this Statute, printing was regulated by a 'privilege' granted directly to the printer by the Sovereign. Printing privileges were the sole province of the Stationers'

---

[12] 8 Anne, c. 19 (1710) [hereinafter Statute of Anne], *available at* http://avalon.law.yale.edu/18th_century/anne_1710.asp. A facsimile copy of the act may also be viewed online, *available at* http://www.copyrighthistory.com/anne.html.

[13] *See* U.S. Const. art. I, § 1, cl. 8, *available at* http://www.law.cornell.edu/constitution/ (granting Congress the power '[t]o promote the progress of science and useful arts, by securing for limited times *to authors and inventors* the exclusive right to their respective writings and discoveries'. [italics mine]).

[14] A detailed version of this discussion may be found in Sundara Rajan, *supra* note 2, at 88–100.

[15] Statute of Anne, *supra* note 12.

Company, a group of printers who enjoyed the exclusive right to print works. Through the tightly-controlled membership of the Stationers' group, it was the Sovereign who effectively acquired the power to supervise all publications appearing in the realm. The Stationers' monopoly made it easy for the monarch to monitor printed literature; the result was censorship.

The recognition of rights based on authorship was a true breakthrough in concepts which was made possible only by the influence of writers and activists advocating for free speech. Notably, John Locke's labour theory of property was easily transferred to literary creation, and John Milton's arguments for freedom of the press were based on his understanding of the relationship between a work and the personality of its creator.[16] Indeed, paragraphs of Milton's famous pamphlet on free speech, '*Areopagitica*,' read like an exposition of moral rights philosophy:

> For books are not absolutely dead things, but do contain a potency of life in them to be as active as that soul whose progeny they are; nay, they do preserve as in a vial the purest efficacy and extraction of that living intellect that bred them.[17]

The Statute represented a political breakthrough in another sense: it broke the economic monopoly enjoyed by the Stationers and, in particular, by the printers' oligopoly, known as the Conger, which had come to dominate eighteenth-century printing.[18] Prior to the Statute, the Stationers acquired the right to print a work from its author, and continued to exercise it without practical limitations in time. Moreover, as Lyman Ray Patterson points out in his seminal work, an entire industry had grown up around the printing of classics, whose authors were deceased, and in rela-

---

16 Milton's *Areopagitica* is a manifesto of the movement for a free press: *see* John Milton, *Areopagitica,* (1971), with a commentary by Sir Richard C. Jebb, and with supplementary material. The text is posted on the website of the St Lawrence Institute, *available at* http://www.stlawrenceinstitute.org/vol14mit.html.

17 *Id.*

18 *See* Lyman Ray Patterson, *Copyright in Historical Perspective* 151 (1968) [hereinafter Patterson]. Discussing the position of the publishers–and presumably with reference to the expiry of the Statute's grandfather clause applying to already-published works, which functioned as a transitional provision in the Statute–Patterson comments: 'In 1710, copyright was the right of a publisher to the exclusive publication of a work, and functioned to prevent literary piracy; by 1774, copyright had come to be the right of an author, and still functioned to protect the exclusive right of publication.' The language of the Statute of Anne recognizes an *author's* copyright, and it came to do so as a result of the lobbying by authors over the preceding half-century, famously including Milton and Locke.

tion to which, the question of the author's consent was irrelevant.[19] The Stationers recognized each others' prerogatives, and the printing right of each was in effect the exercise of a 'copyright' that fellow members of the oligopoly would respect.

The Statute of Anne destroyed this system. Under the terms of the new law, the right to print was no longer a right of the Stationers; it was a right of the author, to be allotted to the printer for a fourteen-year period, after which time, it would return to the author.[20] At the same time, the Stationers themselves could no longer benefit from the exclusive right to print. Instead, printing was thrown open to the world at large, and the Stationers had to compete in an open market. Finally, the Stationers would no longer have exclusive rights—*de facto* privileges—in classic works. On this last issue, the Statute relented slightly, including a transitional provision for the continued protection of Stationers' printing rights in classic works for 21 years. But under this 'grandfather' clause, too, privileges would expire. After 21 years, the works would fall into the public domain, and then could be printed by anyone.

How could the Stationers and their collaborators consent to the passing of their lucrative monopoly without a struggle? The issue came to a head in two celebrated cases, *Millar v. Taylor,* decided in 1769, and *Donaldson v. Beckett,* which settled the issue finally in 1774.[21] Both cases involved rights to print a long poem by James Thomson, 'The Seasons,' and the struggle arose between the booksellers of London, who wanted to hold on to their monopoly, and Scottish booksellers, represented by Alexander Donaldson of Edinburgh, who began to print inexpensive editions of classic works, arguing that the expiry of the grandfather clause in the Statute of Anne opened these works to public exploitation in 1731. In their struggle to hold on to power, the Stationers did something that was to be precedent-setting on a grand scale: in a strategy that is weirdly familiar in the Digital Age, the booksellers donned the mask of the author to argue for the promotion of their own interests.[22] The rejection of their suit by the English courts dealt

---

[19] *See id.* at 151–2; *see also* Lawrence Lessig, *Free Culture: How Big Media Uses Technology and the Law to Lock Down Culture and Control Creativity* ch. 6 (2004). This history also receives a detailed re-consideration in Ronan Deazley, *Re-Reading Donaldson (1774) in the Twenty-First Century and Why it Matters*, 25 (6) Eur. Intell. Prop. Rev. 270 (2003) [hereinafter Deazley].

[20] Statute of Anne, *supra* note 12, ¶ II.

[21] *Millar v. Taylor,* 4 Burr 2303, (1769) [hereinafter *Millar*] and *Donaldson v. Beckett*, Brown's Parl Cases 129 (1774).

[22] In this regard, Patterson notes: '. . . [C]opyright did not come into existence until the printing press facilitated the reproduction and widespread distribution of books. To protect the right to exclusive distribution, publishers created copyright.

a death-blow to the monopoly that they had enjoyed. In this process, the courts also ended by dismissing the possibility that others could be entitled to rights, by virtue of their authorship alone, beyond the rights granted explicitly by the Statute of Anne. The possibility of legal recognition for the natural, non-commercial, or 'moral' interests of authors—based, not in legislation, but in authorship alone—was definitively eliminated from English law.[23]

In *Millar v. Taylor,*[24] the court, led by Lord Mansfield, explored and supported the theory of natural rights of authorship, concluding that those rights could extend beyond the rights specified by the Statute of Anne. Fearful of the consequences of this ruling, a more cautious court in *Donaldson v. Beckett*[25] overturned the earlier decision, choosing, instead, to impose strict limits on authorship rights according to the words of the Statute.[26] Because the idea that authors' moral rights were never recognized in English law has been so prevalent, it is worth quoting at some length from Lord Mansfield's comments—to show, in fact, that his comprehension of the author's moral right was thorough and comprehensive, and utterly complete in prefiguring the reach of French and German legislation.

In Lord Mansfield's eyes, the author's right originated in principles of 'just[ice]'. A failure to recognize the enduring nature of this right would lead to the following ill effects:

> He is no more master of the use of his own name. He has no control over the correctness of his own work. He can not prevent additions. He can not retract errors. He can not amend; or cancel a faulty edition. Any one may print, pirate, and perpetuate the imperfections, to the disgrace and against the will of the author; may propagate sentiments under his name, which he disapproves,

---

From this protection the author who created the work gained at best a reward secondary to that of the publisher. Copyright, therefore, originally functioned to encourage not creation, but distribution. In this regard, copyright's function is essentially the same today.' (footnotes omitted) *See* Lyman Ray Patterson, Free Speech, Copyright and Fair Use, 40 Vand. L. Rev. 1 (1987).

23 Moral rights provisions were finally adopted as Chapter IV of the Copyright, Designs and Patents Act of 1988, § 48, *available at* http://www.opsi.gov.uk/acts/acts1988/ukpga_19880048_en_1.htm.

24 Statute of Anne, *supra* note 12, ¶ II.

25 *Id.*

26 The reasons behind the *Donaldson* ruling and the perceived implications of authors' moral rights as recognized by Lord Mansfield are discussed in detail in Sundara Rajan, *supra* note 2, at 92–100. This history is told in detail by Lyman Ray Patterson in his pioneering work; *see* Patterson, *supra* note 18; *see also* Deazley, *supra* note 19.

> repents and is ashamed of. He can exercise no discretion as to the manner in which, or the persons by whom his work shall be published.[27]

This paragraph could not be a clearer statement of what is meant by moral rights. Lord Mansfield recognizes every moral right later described by French and German writers: the right of attribution ('use of his own name'), the right of integrity (references to 'correctness,' 'additions,' 'errors'), and even, a right of withdrawal. On this last count, he objects to the 'perpetuation' of the work in circumstances where the author 'repents' or feels 'ashamed' and, in doing so, he gives voice to a principle that is now well established in Continental European law, but remains one of the most controversial aspects of moral rights in the common-law view. The principle of disclosure occupies a central position in Mansfield's understanding of authors' rights: he defines it as the author's 'discretion as to the manner in which, or the persons by whom his work shall be published'.

Nothing in the wording of the Statute of Anne suggested a moral right. The most that could be said was that the Statute established an author's personal right to control the publication of his own work—a kind of implicit recognition of the principle of disclosure, which is, quite simply, the right to decide upon the publication of one's own, unpublished manuscripts. Disclosure could be said to be the primordial right underlying all copyright protection, whether economic or moral in nature. The right to 'authorize' the publication of one's work, with its economic connotations, is the right to disclose it; the right to decide whether it should be published or not, and by whom, is the moral right of disclosure.

The Statute of Anne explicitly 'vest[ed] the Copies of Printed Books in the Authors or Purchasers of such Copies'.[28] As far as 'Purchasers,' or publishers, were concerned, the right was purely a transitional right; the focus of the new system was to give to authors a right to control publication of their own unpublished manuscripts.

The policy rationales behind the right of disclosure are apparent in the preface of the Statute, which stated:

> Whereas Printers, Booksellers, and other Persons, have of late frequently taken the Liberty of Printing, Reprinting, and Publishing, or causing to be Printed, Reprinted, and Published Books, and other Writings, *without the Consent of the Authors or Proprietors* of such Books and Writings, to their very great *Detriment*, and too often to the *Ruin of them and their Families*: For Preventing

---

27 *Millar, supra* note 21, at 2398; this passage is also quoted by Mark Rose, *Authors and Owners: The Invention of Copyright* 80 (1993).

28 These are the opening words of the Statute of Anne, *supra* note 12.

> therefore such Practices for the future, and for the *Encouragement of Learned Men to Compose and Write useful Books*; [italics mine] . . .

The Statute clearly articulates three policy rationales: the importance of consent from the author or owner of a copyright before re-printing of the work can be lawful; the financial difficulty suffered by authors—and owners!—and their families, and the availability of legal action against unauthorized re-printing in order to correct it; and, finally, the provision of an incentive to 'encourage' the creation of 'useful Books'.

In the light of *Millar v. Taylor*, it is difficult to agree to the proposition that moral rights are alien to English law. However, overwhelming practical concerns about the expansion of copyright through the common law, including the possibility of renewed restrictions through the Stationers, demanded to be addressed. In this environment, the court in *Donaldson* clarified that there could be no place for moral rights, or indeed, for any common-law right beyond the Statute of Anne.

(ii) Moral Rights in the Civil Law Countries: Inalienability and Perpetual Protection

The trajectory of authors' rights in the civil law countries has been far more straightforward. As in the common law countries, authors in civil-law countries were recognized as having rights flowing from their engagement in a creative activity. In the common law example, these individual rights led directly to an entitlement to legislative protection, embodied in the Statute of Anne—and vigorously protected in principle by the British courts in early litigation under the new Act. However, these rights, which were essentially natural rights, were subject to interpretation and limitation in practice by the very terms of their legislative recognition: an author's copyright was, and was only, what was granted by the Statute of Anne.

Historically, the civil law countries were much more open to accepting a natural rights basis for copyright law. France has what may be the most comprehensive system of recognition for rights of authorship in the world. In the French case, the notion of individual rights of authorship acquired tremendous potency against the background of the French Revolution.[29] The initial recognition of authorship, as Carla Hesse points out, allowed the French administration, at least formally, to 'encourag[e] . . . and empower [. . .] both the individual author and the public at large at the

---

[29] This history is examined in detail in Sundara Rajan, *supra* note 2, at 51–9.

expense of . . . corporate monopoly'.[30] The concept of authors' rights in the French context gave rise to not one, but two concepts of copyright—individual rights of authorship and literary property. She comments:

> Contrary to Foucault's Diderotist interpretation, the revolutionary legislation actually reflected not one but both sides of the Enlightenment debate, effecting an epistemologically impure and unstable legal synthesis that combined an instrumentalist notion of the public good with a theory of authorship based upon natural rights. Precisely because of this legal instability, the regime by which the public exchange of ideas was regulated would be challenged and renegotiated repeatedly over the course of the revolutionary period. The legal history of French authorship thus suggests that Foucault's essay requires a historical revision: the central mechanism of the modern regime of knowledge, as it emerged from the epistemology of the French Enlightenment, was unstable from its very beginnings.[31]

The emergence of natural rights of authorship was subject to slow practical development and theorizing over more than a century; France formally enacted moral rights only in its copyright legislation of 1957. The character of French law, as it gradually gathered force over the decades of the 19th century and eventually found expression in statute, was an emphatic adherence to the individual rights basis of authorship. It did not, of course, neglect the property aspects of copyright; rather, it comprehensively included its non-property aspects, and imposed an obligation on all those dealing with copyright works to balance proprietary manipulation against authorial prerogatives. Indeed, the exceptionally strong drive towards individual rights found expression, in large measure, in the near-sacrosanct treatment of moral rights.[32]

---

[30] *See* Carla Hesse, *Enlightenment Epistemology and the Law of Authorship in Revolutionary France, 1777–1793,* 30 Representations 109, 113 (1990). But she goes on to comment, at 114: 'The creation of the author by the absolutist state was the product of a political initiative within the royal administration rather than a result of commercial protest, and it had the explicit purpose of consolidating state control over the form, content, and means of disseminating knowledge by removing the publisher as intermediary between the state and the author. Now the author would be directly accountable to the Crown and its laws for the publication of knowledge.'

[31] *Id.* at 130.

[32] Note, for example, the comments of French scholar Henri Desbois, on the expansive nature of the author's moral right of integrity under French law; *see* Henri Desbois, *Le Droit d'auteur en France* 538–9, ¶ 449 (3rd ed. 1978) [hereinafter Desbois]. Desbois emphasizes the 'individualist conception [that] animates the law in its entirety and particularly the fundamental provisions of a general kind, such as Article 1 which specifies that the author enjoys a right of intangible

As a result, the French copyright law may be said to be rather absolutist in its treatment of authorship. Notably, it includes two profound limitations on the ability to challenge an author's moral rights: an absolute prohibition on waivers, and the assurance of perpetual protection for an author's moral rights in his or her work.[33]

The potential impracticality of the position on waivers has generated some angry commentary from French scholars, such as Pierre Recht's seminal work of 1969.[34] And, importantly, French practice in copyright-related areas and industries has not achieved a perfectly harmonious interaction with its own legislation. The example of ghostwriting, where an author writes a text to be published under someone else's name, illustrates the French quandary. Ghostwriting is widespread in France, and it appears to be a clear practical illustration of how and why rights of authorship, and the moral right of attribution in particular, might be waived or, indeed, forfeited. But the French jurist cannot allow moral rights to be waived; this would compromise the absolute priority given by French law to the author's individual rights. Accordingly, the ghostwriter is not actually considered to waive attribution; rather, he asserts his right to remain anonymous, or to write under a pseudonym, both of which are considered to be implicitly protected by French legislation.[35] Michel Vivant and Jean-Michel Bruguière recognize this possibility;[36] but prefer

property, exclusive and opposable against the world, from the simple fact of [. . .] creation . . . [It] is sufficient for the author . . . to have impressed his personality upon the work, that, in other words, he has created, in order that protection be due to him. His work calls for respect as it is, as he intends for it to be, because, by way of the creation, it is the personality of the creator which receives help and protection.' ['La conception individualiste anime la loi tout entière et singulièrement les dispositions fondamentales, d'ordre général, telles que l'article 1er qui précise que l'auteur jouit d'un droit de propriété incorporelle, exclusif et opposable à tous, *du seul fait de sa création* . . . [I]l suffit que l'auteur ait imprimé le cachet de sa personnalité à l'oeuvre, *qu'en d'autres termes il l'ait crée,* pour que protection lui soit due. Son oeuvre appelle le respect telle qu'elle est, telle qu'il a voulu qu'elle soit, car, à travers la création, c'est la personnalité du créateur qui reçoit aide et protection.']

33 *See* French Intellectual Property Code, *supra* note 4, at art. L-121–1, which provides that the author's moral rights are 'perpetual, inalienable, and imprescriptible'.

34 *See* Pierre Recht, *Le Droit d'Auteur, une nouvelle forme de propriété: histoire et théorie* 274–5 (Gembloux: Librairie Générale de Droit et de Jurisprudence, Editions Duculot, 1969).

35 Canadian law explicitly protects these aspects of attribution. *See* Canadian Copyright Act, R.S., 1985, c. C-42, ¶ 14.1 (1), *available at* http://laws-lois.justice.gc.ca/eng/acts/C-42/page-8.html [hereinafter Canadian Copyright Act].

36 *See* Michel Vivant and Jean-Michel Bruiguière, *Le Droit d'Auteur*, ¶¶ 464–6

to interpret French jurisprudence on this issue as supporting the idea that the right of attribution may be temporarily 'suspended'. In theory, this leaves open the possibility that the author may choose to come forward and claim attribution at any time. However, French law also requires that the agreement for 'ghostwriting' be entered into in good faith, and any attempt to claim attribution must not have been pre-meditated. These points of legal interpretation seem tortuous, and on this issue, Vivant and Bruguière refer to a '*jurisprudence tourmentée*'.[37] Indeed, they ultimately suggest that the practice of ghostwriting simply amounts to 'usages contra legem'.[38]

The German approach to rights of authorship is somewhat more practical in both respects, potentially allowing moral rights to be waived,[39] and limiting the duration of protection to the same term as authors' economic rights in their work—currently, the lifetime of the author and 70 years after his or her death.[40] These provisions seem to represent a spirit of pragmatism in German law which does not, however, compromise the principle of recognition for authors' prerogatives. German law is defined by its efforts to balance authorship against the realities of a commercial marketplace, and its innovations include detailed rules on the allowability of waivers,[41] and a separate law on maintaining the balance of power between authors and industry in contractual relationships.[42]

(2009); they also cite A. and H.J. Lucas, who note the difficulty of distinguishing between the abdication of the right and the assertion of anonymity (¶ 465).

37 *Id.* at ¶ 465.

38 *Id.*

39 *See* Urheberrechtsgesetz, 9.9.1965, *Bundesgesetzblatt*, Teil I [BGBl. I] at 1273, last amended by Gesetz, 10.8.2004, BGBl. I at 1774 § 13, *available at* http://www.iuscomp.org/gla/statutes/UrhG.htm [hereinafter German Copyright Law]; it should be noted that this English translation of the law is only up to date until 1998. In fact, this law does not mention waiver in relation to the moral rights; but it includes specific *prohibitions* on waivers in the context of exploitation of the work. So, for example, an author's right to revoke his or her work because of 'changed conviction' could not be waived (art. 42), and it is also not possible to waive an artist's right to a resale royalty (art. 26).

40 *Id.* at art. 64.

41 *See, e.g.*, *id.* at arts. 40–42.

42 *See* Gesetz zur Stärkung der vertraglichen Stellung von Urhebern und ausübenden Künstlern vom 22. März 2002, BGBl. I S. 1155, *available at* http://www.bgblportal.de/BGBL/bgbl1f/BGBl102021s1155.pdf. [Law to Strengthen the Contractual Position of Authors and Performing Artists of March 22, 2002, amending the Copyright Law of September 9, 1965, as last amended by Article 16 of the Law of December 13, 2001.] The law is discussed by Jens Schovsbo, *Integrating Consumer Rights into Copyright Law: From a European Perspective*, 31 J. Consum. Policy 393 (2008).

The fundamental importance given to authorship in the German tradition is also reflected in a rather unique way: not only does German legislation feature moral rights prominently, but it also provides that copyright, as a whole, can never actually be acquired by purchase.[43] Rather, copyright is always vested in the author; the right to use works is acquired through licensing. This situation, which might appear dangerous to common-law eyes, is made workable by a rigorous system of checks and balances built into the German scheme. It would be extremely difficult for an author to abuse the copyright law by, for example, entering into licensing arrangements in bad faith and using litigation as a means of self-promotion. The rigour and detail of the German law would not allow it.[44]

(iii) The Spirit of Compromise: Common-Law Countries and the Berne Convention

This cursory survey of moral rights in the common law and civil law systems allows us to identify the fundamental attitudes of each towards authorship. The British common law tradition developed from two fundamental characteristics. The first of these was the establishment of the first modern copyright system on the basis, indeed, of an authorship right—a precedent that was later followed in every modern legal system. Accordingly, the right to 'authorize' the printing of a work belonged to the author alone; without the author's consent, no commercialization of the work was permissible.[45] But, the extent of this right of authorship had absolute limits, as determined by the words of the copyright statute. In this sense, the attitude of British law towards natural rights of authorship *beyond* those granted by statute was clearly one of suspicion, if not outright hostility.

Copyright was therefore a limited right, derived from authorship, but defined by the words of the copyright statute. This legal attitude was exported by Britain to all of its colonies, resulting in near-universal reservations about moral rights in all countries of common-law heritage. Canada, the only possible exception to this rule, was the first common law country to enact moral rights its copyright law, in 1931; but the enactment

---

[43] German Copyright Law, *supra* note 39, art. 29.

[44] This attitude is illustrated by the provision on alteration of the work by the person exploiting it; generally, alteration is not allowed, but, at the same time, alterations to which the author cannot 'reasonably refuse' his or her consent are permitted. *Id.* art. 39(2).

[45] Provision in the Statute of Anne for the continuance of publishers' rights in works that they already controlled was, once again, a transitional provision and not the crux of the statute: *see* Statute of Anne, *supra* note 12, ¶ II.

appears to have had little practical impact on Canadian publishing.[46] In the United States, the rejection went still deeper, with the American preference for a registration-based system of copyright and near-total refusal to recognize moral rights, keeping the country aloof from the international copyright system for most of its history.

In recent years, the landscape of moral rights has shifted dramatically where the common-law countries are concerned, with Britain adopting its first-ever statutory provisions on moral rights in 1988—albeit in extremely restrictive form[47]—and the adoption of comprehensive new provisions in Australia.[48] The United States joined the Berne Convention in 1988,[49] but it has yet to enact general protection for moral rights. Rather, it has created a limited moral rights scheme in its Visual Artists Rights Act of 1990.[50] These changes have gone some way towards bridging the distance

---

[46] To date, there has only been one successful case on moral rights in Canadian law: *Snow v. The Eaton Centre Ltd*, 70 C.P.R. (2d) 105 (1982); this case was decided under the pre-1988 provisions of the Canadian Copyright Act, § 12 (7) dealing with moral rights. Interestingly, the Canadian Supreme Court had recognized 'a species of personal or moral right in the product of his brain' as early as 1911: *see Morang & Co. v. LeSueur,* 45 S.C.R. 95, 98 (1911), *available at* http://csc.lexum.org/en/1911/0scr45-95/0scr45-95.html. For a history of the Canadian provisions, *see* Sundara Rajan, *supra* note 2, at 122–7.

[47] Some aspects of this approach are mirrored in New Zealand; for example, as in the UK, authors must have asserted their attribution right in order to claim it. *See* Copyright Act 1994, No. 143 (as at Oct. 7, 2011), Public Act, § 96 [hereinafter New Zealand Copyright Act]. The Irish adoption of moral rights illuminates the concept of 'honor' from its formulation of the integrity right: *see Irish Copyright and Related Rights Act 2000, § 109 (1)*. Elizabeth Adeney finds this change significant, and negative: *see, generally,* Elizabeth Adeney, *The Moral Right of Integrity: The Past and Future of 'Honour'*, 2 I.P.Q. 111 (2005); *but see* the examination of this question in Sundara Rajan, *supra* note 2, at 184.

[48] Copyright Act 1968 (Cth), Part IX, *available at* http://www.austlii.edu.au/au/legis/cth/consol_act/ca1968133/ [hereinafter Australian Copyright Act]; the moral rights provisions were enacted by the Copyright Amendment (Moral Rights) Act 2000, *available at* http://www.comlaw.gov.au/ComLaw/Legislation/Act1.nsf/0/D25408DC39D0C132CA257434001EEDAE/$file/1592000.pdf. The moral rights provisions entered into force from Dec. 21, 2000.

[49] The United States officially became a member of the Berne Convention on Nov 17, 1988. *See* Berne Notification No. 121–Accession by the United States of America, *available at* http://www.wipo.int/treaties/en/html.jsp?file=/redocs/notdocs/en/berne/treaty_berne_121.html.

[50] Visual Artists Rights Act, 17 U.S.C. § 106A (1990). Moral rights and related interests also enjoy some protection in state-level legislation; for a helpful overview, Mikaela Sturrock, *U.S. Copyright Law and Traditional Expressions* at 10–11, *available at* http://tlc.usm.maine.edu/documents/Sturrock.pdf (last visited Nov. 9, 2011).

between common law and civil law countries where rights of authorship are concerned.

The international copyright arena has played a critical role in bringing moral rights to the common-law world. Without the Berne Convention, it seems unlikely that common-law countries would have attempted to codify moral rights at all. At the same time, it is worth remembering the peculiar character of Berne's Article *6bis*. It is an experiment in compromise; and the compromise, in its turn, is an expression of the peculiar relations between civil and common-law jurisdictions where rights of authorship are concerned. These points of interpretation are important. The Berne approach differs from French, and even German, law; Berne principles have brought a degree of openness and flexibility to both the substance of moral rights and to the methods for their implementation. In this environment, further compromise is possible, expansion is realistic, and, for better or for worse, evolution of the theory of moral rights seems likely on the international stage.

Berne introduced the protection of moral rights in 1928, more than forty years after the initial adoption of the Convention.[51] As described by Elizabeth Adeney in her detailed study of the negotiations surrounding the Berne Convention, the idea of bringing moral rights into Berne had been in circulation for some time.[52] Clearly, the interest in setting an international baseline standard for moral rights protection was chiefly of interest to the civil law countries, who saw it as a basic element of copyright protection. However, the terms on which moral rights were recognized were so general that, as Adeney observes, common law countries may well have thought, or hoped, that they were agreeing to something that they could at least argue they already had. Indeed, a review of British copyright law in 1952 concluded that the law satisfied the requirements of Berne where moral rights were concerned.[53] Yet a review of the same provisions in 1977 reached the opposite conclusion![54]

---

[51] International Convention for the Protection of Literary and Artistic Works Signed at Berne on September 9th, 1886, revised at Berlin on November 13th, 1908, and revised at Rome on June 2nd, 1928, Article 6*bis* [hereinafter Rome Act, 1928]. The current text of Berne, as amended, is *available at* http://www.wipo.int/treaties/en/ip/berne/trtdocs_wo001.html.

[52] *See* Elizabeth Adeney, *The Moral Rights of Authors and Performers: An International and Comparative Analysis* ¶¶ 6.01–6.69 (2006).

[53] *See* The Gregory Committee, *Report of the Copyright Committee*, Cmnd. 8662 (1952).

[54] *See Whitford Committee Report,* Cmnd. 6732 (1977). *See also* the analysis of the Whitford Committee Report in Patricia M. Leopold, *The Whitford Committee's Report on Copyright and Designs Law*, Modern L. Rev. 685, 689, 690

The Berne provisions on moral rights, as adopted in 1928, stated as follows:

> Independently of the author's copyright, and even after transfer of the said copyright, the author shall have the right to claim authorship of the work, as well as the right to object to any distortion, mutilation or other modification of the said work which would be prejudicial to his honour or reputation.[55]

Two basic rights received protection—attribution, the right to be recognized as the author one's own work; and integrity, the right to protect one's work from harm. But the spirit of compromise is evident in the requirement, where the right of integrity is concerned, that an author must be able to show 'prejudic[e] . . . to his honor or reputation' before a violation of the integrity right can be found. This idea of balance represents an infusion of common-law views; it was largely unknown to France, and Germany's version of balance was more author-oriented than Berne.[56] Nevertheless, it has since become a defining feature of the integrity right as it is known in the international community.

Subsequent amendment of the Berne provisions deepened the compromise, rather than attenuating it. In 1948, a specific duration for

---

(1977) (on *droit de suite*). She notes: 'In 1952 the Gregory Committee suggested that these matters were in general best regulated by contract between the parties concerned. Now, however, specific legislation is necessary if the United Kingdom is to ratify the 1971 Paris revision of the Berne Convention. Accordingly, *Whitford* supports the introduction of moral rights on the lines of recent legislation in the Netherlands, since this limits the right of an author to object modification of the work where it would be unreasonable to do so. This, it is thought, would prevent an author's heirs from holding filmmakers and broadcasters to ransom until they were 'bought off'–apparently quite a popular technique.' (But note that Leopold does not provide any examples of this last assertion.)

[55] Rome Act, 1928, *supra* note 51, Article 6*bis* (1). Article 6*bis* (2) deals with the practical exercise of the rights, and in 1928, it provided: 'The determination of the conditions under which these rights shall be exercised is reserved for the national legislation of the countries of the Union. The means of redress for safeguarding these rights shall be regulated by the legislation of the country where protection is claimed.'

[56] *See,* for example, the comments of Desbois, *supra* note 32, at 538–9, on French law. The German approach is not quite as open-ended as the French in its treatment of the integrity right, requiring that authors establish 'jeopard[y]' to their 'legitimate intellectual or personal interests in the work'. *See* German Copyright Law, *supra* note 39, art. 14 on 'Distortion of the Work,' which provides: 'The author shall have the right to prohibit any distortion or any other mutilation of his work which would jeopardize his legitimate intellectual or personal interests in the work.'

moral rights protection was introduced; the term of protection granted was equivalent to the term for economic rights, and probably reflects an increasing commercial orientation in the post-World War II world. In an earlier analysis, I commented:

> In a sense, the new formulation improved upon the old by establishing a definite minimum duration for the protection of moral rights. Under the Brussels Act, the rights had to be protected until the expiration of copyright. But the reach of the Article was severely limited by the proviso that this minimum duration of protection would only apply '[i]n so far as the legislation of the countries of the Union permits.' The new provision was not so much an improvement in protection as a paring down, whittling, or shaping of the loose and open-ended language of 1928 in Article 6bis (2) of the Berne Convention.[57]

Changes in 1967 further re-shaped the provision to accommodate the common-law countries, essentially allowing tort law to substitute legislative protection for moral rights for at least 'some' if not 'all' non-commercial rights of authorship.[58] In a way, with this latest amendment to Berne, the common law of copyright had come full circle: authorship rights are not supposed to exist beyond statute, yet tort law must now provide for what the statute cannot protect. Interestingly, even as measured by this standard, the common-law countries uniformly appear to have decided that some level of statutory protection for moral rights must exist. As noted above, all of them, with the notable exception of the United States, have enacted moral rights for authors in their copyright laws.[59] However, in this regard, it is important to draw closer to the laws themselves, and consider their shape. An interesting observation can be made: the enactment of moral rights in the common law countries is generally far from straightforward, and the common law countries have chosen to implement moral rights in a great diversity of different forms. This is the case in spite

---

57 Mira T. Sundara Rajan, *supra* note 2, at 245.

58 *See* Rome Act, 1928, *supra* note 51, Article 6*bis* (2), which concludes: '. . . However, those countries whose legislation, at the moment of their ratification of or accession to this Act, does not provide for the protection after the death of the author of *all* the rights set out in the preceding paragraph may provide that *some* of these rights may, after his death, cease to be maintained.' [itals.mine]

59 Significantly, the latest ruling of the U.S. Supreme Court on the application of alternate means of protection to authors' moral rights–in this, § 43 (1) (a) of the Lanham Act–seems to limit, and possibly eliminate, the use of false advertising measures to protect attribution. See the insightful analysis in Graeme W. Austin, *The Berne Convention as a Canon of Construction: Moral Rights after Dastar*, 61 N.Y.U. Ann. Surv. Am. L. 111, 118 (2005); *see also* the detailed discussion of the current U.S. position in Sundara Rajan, *supra* note 2, at 144–8.

of the fact that all of them have taken Article 6*bis* of the Berne Convention as their model provision.

For example, the British treatment of authorship rights, as adopted in its copyright reforms of 1988, was highly restrictive.[60] It included the unprecedented requirement that authors must assert the right of attribution before they can benefit from protection under the British legislation.[61] This restrictive approach to attribution is more generally characteristic of British moral rights, which are among the most complex, difficult, and limited provisions in British copyright legislation.

On the other hand, Australian law takes a comprehensive approach to moral rights.[62] Not only does Australia make no demand that authorship be asserted; the Australian law also adopts a detailed and nuanced approach to the integrity right. Interestingly, Australia does not go so far as to abandon the requirement that authors must show damage to their honor or reputation, as the open-ended integrity right does under French law;[63] but Australian law does recognize and resolve certain truly contentious issues, such as establishing that destruction of an artwork should be prohibited by the integrity right,[64] and providing that the conditions in which art is displayed may lead to integrity violations.[65]

These trends suggest three interesting conclusions. First, while the Berne Convention has clearly provided the impetus for common-law countries to think about moral rights, these countries do not feel called upon to emulate Berne precisely in their own legislation. They feel a sense of flexibility in implementation. A flexible approach is clearly facilitated by the language of Article 6*bis* of the Berne convention. Interestingly, in his 1994 study, Gerald Dworkin felt that the flexibility allowed by Berne

---

60 *See* Copyright, Designs and Patents Act 1988 (c 48), c. IV (§§ 77–89), Office of Public Sector Information, *available at* http://www.opsi.gov.uk/acts/acts1988/UKpga_19880048_en_1.htm.

61 *Id.* at § 78; *see also* New Zealand Copyright Act, *supra* note 47, at § 96.

62 *See* Australian Copyright Act, *supra* note 48.

63 The Australian provision on damage to honor or reputation appears in a detailed breakdown of the integrity right in the legislation; it is somewhat unusually presented, with specific sections addressing the treatment of different categories of copyright works. *See id.* at §§ 195AJ–195AL.

64 *Id.* at § 195AK(a). Section 195AT provides for safeguards, where the destruction of a work will not be considered a violation of the right of integrity, including situations where the author cannot be located, or where the author has been given an opportunity to remove the work. Attempts made in good faith to restore the work will also not lead to a violation of the right of integrity; *see also* Canada's similar provision in the Canadian Copyright Act, *supra* note 35, § 28.2 (3) (b).

65 Australian Copyright Act, *supra* note 48, at § 195AK (b).

was inadequate, and he argued that '[t]he potential clashes between personality and economic interests exist everywhere and are likely to increase significantly' with 'further multimedia technological developments. . . . From this perspective, then, the fault may not lie with the common law countries, but rather with Article 6bis. The time is ripe, surely, for a major study of Article 6bis, to be undertaken with a view to replacing it with a more flexible system.'[66]

Secondly, the common-law countries have now become so diversified in their approaches to moral rights that it may no longer be possible to talk of a single 'common-law perspective' at all. This branching out from a common origin suggests that further diversity—and, indeed, the expansion of the rights—is possible. Notably, the psychological limits that existed in the past, whether for economic or cultural reasons, may be growing less important.

Finally, the exploration of moral rights in the common law world brings credibility to the implementation of moral rights in new ways, and on new terms. In this regard, the experience of common law countries deserves to be compared to what is happening to moral rights in emerging jurisdictions. In fact, moral rights have long been accepted in developing and socialist, or post-socialist, countries. Some of these jurisdictions have developed a serious interest in moral rights, and have found themselves involved in the interesting enterprise of reshaping this legal doctrine to deal with complex social realities—the pressures of development and technological change. Their experience suggests that moral rights have acquired definite global relevance, and that the significance of these rights is only likely to increase in the technological environment.

(iv) An Experiment in Authorship: Emerging Jurisdictions and the Indian Example

Emerging jurisdictions have played a curious role in the evolution of authorship rights. India offers a fascinating example of a broader trend, which can be observed tracing a parallel pattern, whether on a smaller or a greater scale, in much of the developing world.

Modern India made its entrance onto the international stage as a common-law country, firmly ensconced in the tradition of British imperial law. In reality, this common law heritage could only represent the surface, perhaps merely the façade, of India's legal tradition. Prior to British rule,

---

66 Gerald Dworkin, *The Moral Right of the Author: Moral Rights and the Common Law Countries,* 19 Colum.-VLA J.L. & Arts 229, 265–6 (1995).

and even alongside it, India had its own legal systems—its ancient Sanskrit law codes, its social rules and hierarchies, and its vast store of custom and culture.[67] It was also touched by the influence of Continental Europe, with the Portuguese and the French finding their way onto Indian soil.[68]

In the initial period of Indian independence after 1947, India gradually found a voice on national and international copyright matters. The country adopted its first comprehensive law on copyright in 1957.[69] With India's growing prowess in technology, including the copyright-intertwined world of software development, India's voice has become more prominent, and it stands to become more influential.

It is a striking fact of Indian law that, in spite of its common-law heritage, India has chosen to adopt rights of authorship as an integral part of its copyright law. India has placed great emphasis on the recognition of authors' moral rights. In the Indian Copyright Act of 1957, India adopted comprehensive provisions on moral rights that emphasized their inalienable quality and left open the possibility of perpetual protection.[70] Only France could have been said to offer stronger protection to moral rights.

However, India's initial empowerment of authors took an unexpected twist. In the early 1990s, apparently when the Indian government realized that it could become responsible for moral rights violations in relation to cultural works in its own possession, it moved to modify the law of 1957 and restore it to more conventional bounds—specifically, the confines of the Berne Convention.[71] The shift was firmly rejected by a powerful and independent judiciary which holds itself responsible for protecting Indian culture, even safeguarding it, where necessary, from India's political leadership. In the landmark 2005 case of *Amar Nath Sehgal v. Union of India,* the Delhi High Court ultimately turned to the international community for support, invoking international agreements on cultural property to trump legislative amendments to the Indian Copyright Act that it perceived as ill-advised.[72]

In a remarkable judgment, the Delhi High court specified that Indian law on moral rights could not be amended at will; rather, the amendments would have to be in harmony with India's commitments to international

---

[67] *See Moral Rights*, *supra* note 11.

[68] *See supra* text accompanying note 11.

[69] Indian Copyright Act, *supra* note 11.

[70] *Id.; see* discussion of term of protection in the pre-1994 Indian provisions in Sundara Rajan, *supra* note 2, 169–71.

[71] *See* Sundara Rajan, *supra* note 2, at 176–8.

[72] *See Amar Nath Sehgal v. Union of India,* 30 P.T.C. 253 (Delhi High Court) (2005).

treaties. The approach essentially drew its power from the broad and comprehensive protection offered to culture through cultural property legislation. The Court observed:

> [T]he various declarations by the international community in the conventions [on cultural property] noted above, lift the moral rights in works of Art if the same acquire the status of cultural heritage of a nation. India is a signatory to the conventions and it would be the obligation of the State to honour its [. . .] declarations.[73]

This statement formally draws upon the existence of cultural property conventions, but the fundamental idea is one of natural rights and prerogatives—not in terms of authorship *per se,* but directly in relation to cultural works themselves. Not only is it a pioneering guide to the interpretation of moral rights law in India—and, potentially, elsewhere—but it also points to the relevance of moral rights for the protection of cultural property and other elements of the public domain.[74]

II. CONCLUSION: THE FUTURE OF AUTHORSHIP RIGHTS

These examples, drawn from the common law, developing, and civil law worlds, offer some sense of the many possibilities for implementing and interpreting moral rights in new ways. In particular, the pressures exerted by both common-law exploration and legal innovation in emerging jurisdictions have developed many variations on the original themes of moral rights doctrine. Key issues, where the fluidity of law and doctrine is apparent, include the admissibility of waiver, widely considered across common-law and developing jurisdictions; the relationship between cultural and intellectual property laws, as explored in India, but also hinted

---

[73] *Id.*at ¶ 55. Under the terms of this ruling, it may still be possible to argue that a work is not culturally important, and would therefore not qualify for protection from destruction. The likelihood of success with this argument seems rather slight, for two reasons: the Indian judge's emphasis on the concept of 'creative corpus,' or body of work as a whole, could be an attenuating factor; and, as a practical matter, the persistence that would be required of an artist to pursue a claim, financially and otherwise, suggests that only recognized artists can come forward.

[74] For a discussion of moral rights and public domain works, particularly in the Indian context, *see* Mira T. Sundara Rajan, *Moral Rights in the Public Domain: Copyright Matters in the Poetical Works of Indian National Poet C. Subramania Bharati,* Singapore J. Leg. Stud. 161 (2001).

at in provisions such as Russia's assertion that 'any interested party' may exercise moral rights in an artwork;[75] and the variability of duration of protection for moral rights, first observed in the split between the 'dualist' theory of France, which mandates perpetual protection, and 'monist' Germany which largely unifies the protection of moral and economic rights.[76]

A relatively new area of interest, brought to the fore by the greater inclusiveness of the international dialogue on copyright law, involves the potential of moral rights for the protection of indigenous peoples and cultures—a source of great excitement.[77] Interestingly, one possible

---

[75] *See* Part IV of the Russian Civil Code on intellectual property: Grazhdanski Kodeks Rossiiskoi Federatsi, Chast' Chetvërtaya [Civil Code of the Russian Federation, Part IV], Federal Law No. 230-FZ of December 18, 2006, Rossijskaja Gazeta No. 289 (4255) of Dec. 22, 2006 = Sobranie zakonodatel'stva RF (SZ RF) No. 52 (Part I) of Dec. 25, 2006, Item 5496, at 14803, art. 1267 (2) [2008 Civil Code]. The new Part IV is not yet available in English; it may be found in the original Russian on the website of *Rospatent*, the federal agency of the Russian Federation responsible for intellectual property matters at http://www1.fips.ru/wps/wcm/connect/content_ru/ru/documents/russian_laws/codeks_rf/gkrf_ch4 (last visited Nov. 9, 2011). *See also* Sundara Rajan, *supra* note 2, at 328.

[76] The 'dualist' and 'monist' and theories of moral rights, associated, respectively, with France and Germany, are discussed in Sundara Rajan, *supra* note 2, at 67–9, 75–82. These classifications are no longer water-tight–if they ever were–and the example of Canada illustrates the case of an ostensibly 'dualistic' country which has sought to restrain moral rights from further expansion: *see id* at 131–4; *see also Culture Matters, supra* note 10, at 494–7.

[77] WIPO is currently exploring the possibility of establishing basic treaties for the protection of traditional cultures, including an agreement specifically on 'traditional cultural expressions'. The proposed draft makes mention, not of moral rights, but of moral interests; Article 2 states: 'The economic and moral interests of the beneficiaries of traditional cultural expressions, as defined in Articles 1 and 2, [should] [shall] be safeguarded in a reasonable and balanced manner. As regards the moral interests, the beneficiaries should have the right to be acknowledged to be the source of the traditional cultural expression unless this turns out to be impossible / except where omission is dictated by the manner of the use and to object to any distortion, mutilation or other modification of, or other derogatory action in relation to, the said traditional cultural expression, which would be prejudicial to the reputation or integrity of the traditional cultural expression.' The document is on the WIPO website, *available at* http://www.wipo.int/edocs/mdocs/tk/en/wipo_grtkf_ic_19/wipo_grtkf_ic_19_4.pdf (last visited Nov. 9, 2011). Independently of WIPO, Australia had previously proposed an amendment to enact 'indigenous communal moral rights' in 2003, a pioneering initiative in the international community. However, the Bill was unsatisfactory to all concerned, and was rejected pending re-examination of the issue. *See Copyright Amendment (Indigenous Communal Moral Rights) Bill* 2003 (Cth) (Austl.); details are examined in Sundara Rajan, *supra* note 2, at 151–7.

answer to the intellectual property conundrum presented by the traditional knowledge of indigenous peoples may lie in the near-heretical concept of moral rights granted to corporations, uniquely recognized in the laws of Japan and Korea.[78] The doctrine of moral rights has traditionally allowed protection only of the personal rights of an individual author; are these corporate moral rights representative of a culture of greater corporate responsibility, or—historically, at least—closer and more continuous involvement of individuals in the lives of corporations? Regardless, the recognition of a moral right to be claimed by a group would undoubtedly advance the cause of indigenous peoples, whose efforts to remain linked to their own cultural expressions has often foundered on the rock of individual authorship.

Many of these new legal developments are clearly linked to technological change. Technology has transformed culture throughout the industrialized world, and, by a pleasing irony, brought emphasis to new aspects of that most ancient of human phenomena, authorship. If the Romantics emphasized individual authorship, our age seems to be one where the varieties of authorship are continually growing. The reality of multiple authorship is apparent in software, film, music, and the visual arts; the direct intervention of technology brings a world of new possibilities to the materials, methods, and means of communicating copyright works. The world of moral rights in the twenty-first century is necessarily one of great diversity, but it is diversity with a common goal: the continued recognition of authorship in all its forms. The evolution of the doctrine of moral rights suggests that it has become an increasingly flexible and subtle instrument for the protection of authorship. Moral rights will continue to evolve in the new technological era, but the future points towards a kind of harmonization that does not mean uniformity of the law. Above all, moral rights show no sign of becoming obsolete in the world of technology. On the contrary, they will be with us for some time to come—and may ultimately outlast that priority of the past, the economic rights in copyright works.

---

78 India also appears to allow a corporation to hold moral rights in the case of a film production company: *see* Sundara Rajan, *supra* note 2, at 392.

7. Japan's copyright law revisions, disruptive innovation and user-generated content

Salil Mehra[1]

I. INTRODUCTION

In January 2010, several revisions to Japan's Copyright Law became effective. In particular, knowingly downloading infringing copies of several varieties of copyrighted files was removed from an existing safe harbor for private copying. (Uploading infringing material had already been carved out.) Although specific penalties for the newly prohibited conduct were not set forth in the revisions, the change effectively sets down a marker concerning permissible conduct, and the government and copyright industry have publicized the effects of this change.[2]

The Copyright Law revisions, by their terms, did not move solely in the direction of stronger protection for copyright holders. Specifically, in the same set of revisions, data storage copies of others' copyrighted works made in the context of computer processing, including by Internet search and indexing sites (such as Google, Yahoo! and Bing) were granted an explicit safe harbor from infringement actions.

On balance, these sets of changes have the clear impact of favoring copyright industry controlled distribution channels. And in particular, user-generated content and its distribution are likely to face increased hurdles to compete with the new special favorites of the law. The result

---

[1] James E. Beasley Professor of Law, Temple University, Beasley School of Law, Philadelphia, PA. Abe Fellow, Japan Foundation/Center for Global Partnerships, 2010–2011.

[2] *See, e.g.*, Government of Japan Cabinet Office, *Ihou? Gouhou? Daunroodo ni gochuui – seifu intaanetto bideo* [Illegal? Legal? Be careful downloading – government internet video], http://nettv.gov-online.go.jp/prg/prg2824.html (last visited Aug. 1, 2011) (Japanese government public service announcement stressing that, as of January 2010, not only the uploading of infringing content, but also the knowing download of infringing content, will be illegal).

may be a tendency to ossify the current structure of the Internet as experienced by Japanese users.[3] The costs to a deeply wired nation's evolving relationship with the Internet are ultimately unknowable, but may well be considerable.

This chapter continues with an overview of the specific statutory changes at issue. It then continues to discuss the nature of user-generated content and its interaction with the statutory changes. It further proceeds to explain the negative implications for user-generated content by highlighting several cases of Copyright Law application in Japan over the past decade.

II. USERS AND THE COPYRIGHT LAW

Japan does not have a generalized fair use doctrine such as the United States.[4] However, it is the United States, and not Japan, which is anomalous. The American four-factor test focuses on the purpose and the relationship of the copy to the original work. Japan's Copyright Law instead provides specific purposes for which copying will be allowed, including library, news or education use.[5] It may be at first assumed that, like other civil law countries, Japan has taken the approach of enacting specific exemption provisions. While that may be true, the Japanese approach also resembles that of some common law countries, including the fair dealing approach of Australia, Canada and the United

---

3 Indeed, Youtube, plus the innovative Niconico Douga site, both famous for their user uploaded and downloaded video, have licensed content from JASRAC, Japan's copyright collection clearing house, in exchange for a 2 percent royalty payment. *See* IT media, Inc., *Nikoniko douga to Youtube, JASRAC ni chosakukenryo shiharai e* [Niconico douga and Youtube to pay copyright fees to JASRAC] (Oct. 30, 2007), http://www.itmedia.co.jp/news/articles/0710/30/news065.html (last visited Aug. 20, 2011). Given the two online video giants' license deals with the incumbent copyright holders, the extent to which revisions, such as Article 47–8 discussed *infra*, seem to restrict copyright and favor large-scale data processing and storage needs of, for example, video streaming websites looks less anomalous, and more a part of the revisions' fabric of favoring not only the incumbent copyright industry, but also mainstream, existing Internet channels that have come to settled terms with the copyright industry.

4 *See* 17 U.S.C. § 107 (listing four-factor test including, not specific reasons for permitted use, but rather the 'character of the use,' the 'nature of the work,' 'the amount . . . of the portion used,' and 'the effect of the use upon the potential market for or value of the copyrighted work').

5 *See* Copyright Act, Law No. 65 of 2010, art. 32–42 (Japan) (listing, among other purposes, news reporting and library use).

Kingdom.[6] And indeed, Japanese courts have shown some evolutionary flexibility in applying these exemptions.[7]

In addition to the specifically enumerated purposes for which copies of protected works may be permitted, Article 30 of the Copyright Law specifically allows copies to be made for private use. The right to make copies for private use allows citizens to copy protected works extends beyond their individual enjoyment; the private use right extends to allow the circulation of these copies within a limited circle.

III. BACKGROUND

By way of background, Article 30 has been amended and supplemented over the years due to changes in technology and the willingness of Japanese lawmakers to continually revisit the balance between copyright industries and users. For example, prior to 1971 the right to make copies for private use did not extend to copies made 'by means of mechanical or chemical techniques'.[8] However, the dawn of electromagnetic audiotape led lawmakers to eliminate this restriction on the private copying right.[9] This change thus allowed consumers to make copies of record albums onto reel-to-reel and cassette tapes – and allowed producers to build an industry selling such recording equipment to consumers.

But the evolution of Article 30 did not stop there. The emergence of digital audio formats and private digital audio recording capabilities, such as digital audio tape, led Japanese lawmakers to supplement the private use right with a private recording levy starting in 1993.[10] This scheme,

---

[6] *See* Giuseppina D'Agostino, *Healing Fair Dealing? A Comparative Copyright Analysis of Canadian Fair Dealing to UK Fair Dealing and US Fair Use*, 53 McGill L.J. 309 (2008).

[7] *See, e.g.*, Supreme Court, Mar. 28, 1980, Case No. 923(O) of 1976, 967 Hanrei Jiho 45 (Japan) (extending right to make quotations for criticism or parody to photomontage adding additional image apparently mocking original photographer's work).

[8] Masaakira Katsumoto, *The New Japanese Copyright Law* 137 (1975). *See also* Teruo Doi, *Japanese Copyright Law in the 21st Century* 217, 278 (2001) (Copyright Act, Law No. 39 of 1899, art. 30) ('[It] shall not be regarded as an infringement [to]: (i) Reproduc[e] without the intention of publishing and not by mechanical or chemical means . . . .').

[9] *Id.*

[10] *See* Salil K. Mehra, *The iPod Tax: Why the Digital Copyright System of American Law Professors' Dreams Failed in Japan*, 79 U. Colo. L. Rev. 421 (2008) [hereinafter Mehra, *The iPod Tax*] (describing the rise and fall of this system).

which covered recording formats including recordable digital audiotape (DAT), minidiscs (MD), and blank compact discs (CDs), authorized a clearinghouse (JASRAC) to distribute the proceeds of this levy to copyright holders.[11]

However, the emergence of the Internet and new computer memory formats complicated this bargain between copyright holders, electronics and hardware manufacturers, users, and government. The Internet lowered transaction costs making it easier for users to communicate and transfer files among each other; such peer-to-peer (P2P) communication also enabled the unauthorized transfer and copying of copyrighted recorded music and other content. New computer memory formats, including hard disk and flash memory had two significant effects. First, they dramatically lowered the cost of storing large quantities of data, including digitized musical recordings. Second, the statutory coverage of the digital recording levy did not, by its terms, extend to these new formats.

These challenges required a revisit of the bargain represented by Article 30 and the digital copyright levy scheme. At the turn of the 21st century, attempts to use digital rights management (DRM) technologies and bolster them with anticircumvention prohibitions[12] failed to prevent the emergence of large-scale unauthorized sharing of copyrighted music files.[13] Subsequent negotiations aimed at broadening the coverage of the existing digital copying levy to include computer storage, including that used by MP3 players, iPods and smart phones, also failed to come to a resolution.[14]

IV. THE REVISIONS

(i) Article 30 – Narrowing Japan's Private Copying Safe Harbor

As a result, the recent Copyright Law revisions of Article 30 took place amidst a troubled background. Japanese users continue to lack an analogue to fair use and instead look to safe harbors based on private use or

---

[11] Additional clearinghouses were established for video recording; this discussion focuses on music because it was concerning music that the primary challenges to the system arose.

[12] The Copyright Law was amended to prohibit anticircumvention as part of Japan's implementation of its commitments under the Trade in Intellectual Property and Services (TRIPS) agreement.

[13] *See* Mehra, *The iPod Tax, supra* note 10.

[14] *Id.*

the specific enumerated purposes for copying without authorization under Articles 32 to 42. Copyright holders face the same technological challenges to the enforceability of their rights that have concerned music and other industries worldwide. And hardware, electronics and computer manufacturers seek to avoid regulations that would inhibit their businesses.

By its terms, the revision of Article 30 took the form of adding a subsection 3 limiting the private right to makes copies of protected work as follows (addition italicized):

> Article 30 (Copying for private use)
>
> 1 Concerning works protected by copyright (hereinafter to be referred to simply as 'protected works'), for the purpose of private, household or corresponding use within a limited circle (hereinafter referred to as 'private use'), save for the following listed cases, persons making such use may make copies [of protected works].
>
> . . . .
>
> (3) *Knowingly receiving digital forms of music or audio/videorecordings via automated public transmission infringing the rights of copyright holders. . . .*[15]

It had already been prohibited to electronically distribute, or upload, files infringing the rights of copyright holders. The effect of the amendment was to similarly prohibit the knowing reception, or downloading, of such transmissions. Because a far larger number of users generally download infringing files than upload them, the result was to broaden the potential impact.

Such broadening can have two separate impacts. First, there is the potential to set down limits showing what appropriate online conduct is. Those users who respect such limits as a matter of habit or principle may conform their behavior accordingly. Second, some users may avoid downloading – including not merely knowing infringement but also other downloading – for fear of punishment. The revisions to Article 30 or other sections of the Copyright Law do not set forth any explicit punishment for knowing downloading of infringing content. However, as discussed *infra*, users might well be concerned about the latitude police and prosecutors may have to construe this new prohibition.

---

[15] Satoshi Ikemura, *Chosakukenhou Komentaaru* 11 (Keiso Shobo 2010) 11 (reprint of new statutory provision Article 30 of the Copyright Law) (translated by Salil Mehra) (jurisdictional parenthetical omitted; italics indicates new added provision).

(ii) Article 47–8 – creating a new safe harbor for cloud computing?

The revisions to the Copyright Law are also relevant to the balance between users, the copyright industry and, lastly, the proprietors of hardware, networks and platforms. In particular, Article 47–8 provides a potential safe harbor that is relevant to hardware devices, search engines, social networks and, potentially, cloud computing (also sometimes more narrowly referred to as 'software as a service'):

> *Article 47–8 (copies in accordance with the use of [copyright] protected works on computers)*
> *In cases where applicable copies of protected works are made for use on computers [or similar devices] or in cases in which applicable dissemination of copyrighted works are received [thereon] via wireless or wired transmission (such cases being limited to where the use or the utilization of the copies concerned does not harm the rights of copyright holders), for the range of information processing in accordance with the purpose of these applicable computer uses, to the degree that it is required for smooth and efficient data processing, appropriate copies of the protected works concerned may be made on computer memory media [or storage media].*[16]

The language of this revision by its terms would appear to cover ephemeral data-processing copies on computer hard drives, RAM or flash memory. In the normal course of activity, computers constantly make copies of the files they work on; to the extent that users utilize computers to view or listen to protected works, including through Internet browsers, copies are made constantly without explicit authorization. In this light, the new Article 47–8 may simply appear to be codification of the common-sense view that such data-processing copies should not automatically be viewed as infringing the copyright of the protected work.[17]

However, there is also a notable forward-looking interpretation of

---

16 *Id.* at 122 (reprint of new statutory provision Article 47–8 of the Copyright Law) (translated by Salil Mehra) (italics indicates that the entire section is new).

17 *See* Shinto Teramoto, *Kaisetsu kaisei chosakukenhou* [Explanation of Copyright Law Revisions] 69–70 (Koubundou 2010) (explaining reading of new Article 47–8 as a safe harbor for computer RAM copies created, for example, during the viewing of a movie DVD or in transmitting copyright-protected data collections). The view that common-law doctrine should also reflect this digital-age common sense has similarly gained traction abroad. *See, e.g.*, Matthew Sag, *Copyright and Copy-Reliant Technology*, 103 Nw. U. L. Rev. 1607 (2009) (arguing that acts that do not reproduce the author's original expression, including automated copying by technology, should not as a default rule be deemed infringement).

Article 47–8. Today, many kinds of business are conducted via computer, especially over the Internet. In addition to the hard disk, RAM or flash memory copies that current uses generate, future uses will also likely generate copies of protected works on computer memory or storage devices. Based on the deliberations of the advisory council (*shingikai*) involved in its drafting,[18] Article 47–8 can also be interpreted to provide comfort to providers of incipient business models, including education over the Internet, software as a service, and cloud computing, that the automated copies they create of protected work will not reasonably be deemed infringement.[19]

The inclination to preserve space for new business models to grow online is critical for future innovation, and there are certainly those within Japan who recognize the importance of developing copyright provisions that avoid ossification of the current state of the Internet and its existing business models.[20] However, Article 47–8 contains the important caveat that such copies are allowed to the extent that they do not harm the rights of the copyright holders. While it is important to protect existing rights holders, this does provide an avenue by which the comfort provided is subject to future challenge – a possibility that may be particularly important for upstarts and insurgents in the Internet sphere. Meanwhile, strong incumbents, such as Google (via Youtube) and Yahoo!, who have already heavily invested in cloud computing and have already licensed some content and agreed on royalty payment, represent the rights' holders who could potentially hold up new innovative business models. As a result, the potential for rights holder objections may serve to raise the costs of upstart rivals to these incumbents.

V. CONCERNS BASED ON APPLICATION

The ultimate test as to whether the recent revisions to the Copyright Law will chill user generated content will depend on how these provisions are

---

[18] Agency for Cultural Affairs, *Bunkashingikai chosakuken bunkakai houkokusho* [Report of the subcommittee meeting of the copyright culture deliberative council], 1 (Jan. 2006), http://www.bunka.go.jp/1tyosaku/pdf/singi_houkokusho_1801.pdf [hereinafter *Bunkashingikai*].

[19] Teramoto, *supra* note17 (setting forth this interpretation based on *Bunkashingikai*, *supra* note 18).

[20] *See, e.g.*, Yuko Noguchi, *Digitaru jidai no chosakuken* [Copyright for the digital age] (Chikuma 2010) 254–7 (explaining the importance of maintaining an approach that permits the development of new business models).

applied in practice. Interpretation and application are particularly important in the Japanese context due to the fairly significant use of arrest and prosecution to deal with purportedly infringing use. The lessons to be drawn from past experience are not heartening. While these cases do not specifically deal with the intimate contours of copyright infringement or private copying, they do illustrate the risk that individuals may face if they take innovative actions that upset the status quo. And more to the point, they demonstrate the latitude that police and prosecutors have, and the willingness to use that latitude to arrest independent software developers.

Two examples may be particularly chilling. First, in *Japan v. Kaneko*, a staff member of Tokyo University's computer science department was prosecuted for creating and distributing a software program that others used to commit copyright infringement by transferring music files. The researcher, Isamu Kaneko, was arrested for making available the software program, *Winny*, which fostered anonymous P2P file sharing.[21] While there was no finding that Kaneko committed a direct infringement, he posted a series of statements, some seemingly contradictory, ranging from rants against the existing copyright industry, to plans to develop a revenue collection and distribution function within *Winny* to ensure that artists and composers received payment. Though convicted at the trial court level, he was acquitted on appeal – five years after his initial arrest.[22]

The Kaneko case in some ways represents a failure of Japanese policy, at least from the standpoint of fostering Internet innovation. According to some experts, *Winny* was actually superior in speed and efficiency relative to contemporary P2P file sharing software developed in the United States.[23] Perhaps even more important than its substantive benefits, *Winny* was an early, and arguably successful, example of user-generated innovation. Kaneko directly distributed the program over an anonymous Internet discussion forum and solicited improvements from the users. As

---

[21] *See* Salil Mehra, *Keep America Exceptional! Against Adopting Japanese and European-Style Contributory Copyright Infringement*, 13 Vand. J. of Ent. & Tech. L. 811, 816–20 (2011) (describing the arrest, trial opinion and appeal).

[22] *Id.*

[23] Interview with Jun Murai, Dean of Keio University's Faculty of Environment and Information Studies (May 26, 2011) [hereinafter Interview with Murai] (sometimes described as 'the father of Japan's Internet' due to his leadership of several Internet backbone projects over the past few decades, and his graduate students).

a result, Kaneko's prosecution did not stifle him alone – it discouraged a mode of independent software development.[24]

In a second, more recent case, a software developer in Aichi prefecture was arrested for unauthorized access to a library's computer system.[25] While that may not sound very threatening, the case itself suggests that risks of independent software development, given the fairly tough stance that authorities take. The developer, an avid borrower of library books, was apparently frustrated with the poor search interface of the library's website. Being a computer engineer, he developed a small software program, or script, that would repeatedly call up data on the library's webpage. Unfortunately, the script was designed in such a way that over a two-week span in April 2010, it effectively registered 33,000 visits from the developer's computer to the library homepage. Given the resemblance of this activity to a denial-of-service attack, he was arrested on May 25, 2010; nearly three months later the prosecution was dropped due to 'inability to find a strong intent to harm operations'.[26]

These stories would be amusing were they not also pointed lessons for Japanese small-scale innovators. Challenges to the copyright industry, and annoying mistakes, can apparently be punishable by arrest. The message that some developers have drawn is that it is safer to work within established organizations, and to avoid significantly disruptive innovation.[27] Because the greatest innovations are often also the most disruptive, this situation is potentially a silent hazard for Japanese innovators.

VI. DISRUPTIVE INNOVATION, USER-GENERATED CONTENT AND COPYRIGHT IN JAPAN

The recent revisions to the Copyright Law could be construed narrowly by their terms – recent examples of police and prosecution activity do not

---

[24] *Id.*

[25] *See* Asahi Shimbun Company, *Toshokan HP etsuran funou, saibaa kougeki no yogisha taiho* [Bumbling library homepage search – cyber attack suspect arrested], http://www.asahi.com/national/update/0820/NGY201008200021.html (last visited Aug. 20, 2011) [hereinafter *Toshokan*]; Yahoo Japan Corporation, *Okazaki shiritsu chuo toshokan saibaa jiken matome* [Conclusion to the Okazaki central municipal library cyber incident], http://r25.yahoo.co.jp/fushigi/jikenbo_detail/?id=20100625-00002724-r25 (last visited Aug. 15, 2011).

[26] *See Toshokan*, *supra* note 25.

[27] *See Interview with Murai*, *supra* note 23.

give comfort, however. As observers have noted, *everything* on the Web is downloaded.[28] At least one interpretation is that '[s]ince it is impossible to know beforehand whether downloaded content is legal or not, any page view' would potentially 'place the user at risk of violating copyright law'.[29]

Such a view might seem extreme and an example of fear mongering. However, it is worth considering the balance of costs from the user perspective. Downloading from an iffy source now carries a (perhaps minor) degree of risk of future penalties. However, downloading from a safe established source presumably carries virtually no risk of penalties – not only have Niconico Douga or Youtube explicitly licensed content from Japan's copyright industries, users may conclude that there is safety in numbers, since it is quite hard to imagine arrests of all the users who might download content over, for example, Mixi, one of Japan's leading social networking sites.

This impact of the new Copyright Law revisions may be an intended feature of the drafters, rather than an accident. Professor Yoshiyuki Tamura has criticized both the revisions and the process and policy dynamics that produced them.[30] At a general level, he points to copyright law's lack of connection to tangible products, thus leaving no natural limit to its expansion. Combined with the relative strength of the copyright industry in the political process, and the relative weakness of users, he argues that Copyright Law in Japan will have a built-in tendency to reflect a crude political bargain based on interest group lobbying.[31] The end result, in this view, would be a one-way ratchet leading unavoidably to weaker user rights, and entrenched incumbents stalling progress as they expand the scope of their protection.

VII. CONCLUSION

What are the options going forward to protect disruptive innovation and user rights? This is a question of import beyond simply the Japanese context. One possibility is to move away from a copyright system based on specific rules that can be amended via the lobbying process, and that

---

[28] Chris Salzberg, *Japan Toughens Up Internet Regulation, The Japan Times*, Jan. 16, 2008 (describing the potential huge impact of the new statutory language in Article 30).

[29] *Id.*

[30] *See* Yoshiyuki Tamura, *Rethinking Copyright Institutions for the Digital Age*, 1 W.I.P.O.J. 63–74 (2009).

[31] *Id.*

are subject to application by enforcement agents with little interest in user rights or broader concerns about innovation. A move towards more difficult to manipulate, more general standards, enforced by judges insulated from the political process, may help keep copyright law from becoming an incumbent industry protection system.[32]

Such a step sounds specifically like American-style fair use doctrine. And American fair use does have its attraction to Japanese scholars and lawyers.[33] However, there may be real difficulty in trying not only to import a concept such as fair use, but to change a regime over from specific rules – such as the Japanese Copyright Law's emphasis on enumerated exceptions and cases – to broader standards. Another alternative may be to seek specific rules protecting users and insurgent innovators to safeguard them from overzealous police and prosecutors. The virtue of such an approach is that it may fit more simply into the existing framework.

Whatever steps are taken, the recent revisions to Japan's Copyright Law pose a potential threat to disruptive innovation and user-generated content. Both by their terms and by the mode of interest-group controlled lawmaking they represent, the revisions present a future risk. Given past experience, the possibility of expansive interpretation by police and prosecutors worsens this risk. For Japan to attain its ambition as a 'nation built on intellectual property,'[34] it cannot let its Copyright Law become, ironically, a barrier rather than a bridge.

---

[32] *Id.* at 70–72.

[33] *See, e.g.*, Noguchi, *supra* note 20 at 215–16 (explaining the merits of fair use by showing how it could simplify strained Japanese judicial opinions that try to allow reasonable de minimis uses of protected works, such as extremely small copies of images to be used in catalogs).

[34] This was the goal set out somewhat famously a decade ago by Japan's Strategic Council on Intellectual Property. *See* Strategic Council on Intellectual Property, *Intellectual Property Outline*, July 3, 2002, http://www.kantei.go.jp/foreign/policy/titeki/kettei/020703taikou_e.html#0-2 (last visited Aug. 15, 2011).

8. The dragon and the white whale: Three steps test and fair use

Frédéric Pollaud-Dulian

When it comes to limitations of intellectual property rights, all national or international regulations contain more or less precise lists of exceptions, but many of the regulations complete their list with a moderative tool. This tool may be used to reinforce authors' rights or to favor the interests of users or the public good. The three steps test and the principle of narrow interpretation on one side, and the American fair use provision of §107 of the Copyright Act of 1976 on the other side, illustrate these two different objectives and highlight an essential opposition between American copyright and authors' rights countries, most notably the European Union. Professor Goldstein compared fair use with Moby Dick, the great white whale.[1] If we have to refer to mythological animals, the triple test would be more akin to a benevolent dragon protecting the authors' treasure from looting. We would like to show how different three steps test and fair use still remain in spite of the important effort to get them closer to what the international treaties amount to. These differences are not superficial ones. They are rooted in the very grounds of two conceptions of intellectual property. We will study the complex and conflicting relationship between American fair use and the three steps test as an interesting example of this persistent opposition. Our purpose here is not to criticize one system and to praise the other, but to rather look at two different ways to deal with the scope of exceptions to intellectual property rights. First, Section I will compare formally and fundamentally the two legal mechanisms and thereafter, it will be necessary for Section II to study their compatibility.

---

[1] Paul Goldstein, *Fair Use in Context*, 31 COLUM. J.L. & ARTS 433 (2008) ('Fair use is the *great white whale* of American Copyright Law. Enthralling, enigmatic, protean, it endlessly fascinates us even as it defeats our every attempt to subdue it.') (emphasis added).

I. RELATIONSHIP BETWEEN FAIR USE AND THE THREE STEPS TEST

The two juridical mechanisms are rooted in two different conceptions of intellectual property (i), and though they may resemble each other in some aspects, they are deeply dissimilar (ii).

(i) The Consequences of Two Different Approaches to Exceptions

Exceptions and limitations to intellectual property rights are primarily implemented in two ways depending on the grounds for and aims of such legislation. These two different and somewhat opposite approaches take root in different legal traditions.[2] On one hand, civil law countries emphasize the defense of individual property and the natural rights of the creative individuals. On the other hand, many common law countries, particularly the USA, center their approach on the idea that copyright protection is justified and consequently limited by public good considerations, as the US Constitution (Article I, §8) clearly states. In this context, promoting 'the Progress of Science and useful Arts' follows an utilitarian conception of intellectual property by which the interests of society, education, the freedoms of users and economic considerations (and so on) are broadly taken into account to balance the exclusive rights. Such an utilitarian conception is absolutely strange to civil law authors' rights legislation. This fundamental difference does not prevent the use of many exceptions, which may be found within US legislation and case law, including within the fair use doctrine, to be similarly implemented in legislation in authors' rights countries. But on one hand, legislation that enumerates precisely and restrictively each and every exception prevents the judge from enlarging this exhaustive list or from giving a broader meaning to an exception. On the other hand, while US copyright law contains a list of legal exceptions, there is also the fair use doctrine, which is an open and flexible exception that allows courts to create new limitations. Thus, in countries with authors' rights legislation, the courts are bound by a principle of strict or narrow interpretation of exceptions, while US courts have substantial latitude, not even being bound by the four factors of §107.

Other states like Great Britain or Australia have an intermediate approach since their copyright laws refer to the concept of 'fair dealing'.

---

[2] Sam Ricketson, Limitations and Exceptions of Copyright and Related Rights in the Digital Environment (April 5, 2003), WIPO Doc. SCCR/9/7, *available at* http://www.wipo.int/edocs/mdocs/copyright/en/sccr_9/sccr_9_7.pdf.

At first sight, fair use and fair dealing may appear very similar, and it is true that the concepts probably share a similar philosophical background. But fair dealing works differently because it is not an autonomous exception, but rather one factor among others that is included in the regulation of one definite and special exception. So there is no general provision of fair dealing as an independent moderative tool like in US copyright law, and the list of the numerous exceptions is exhaustive.

The general force behind fair use is not easy to discern because both scholars and courts have refered to many ideas and principles that tend to shift over time.[3] However, implicit consent, incentive to create, free competition, the First Amendment and market failure theory may contribute to the justifications ('a posteriori') for the various fair use decisions, but the justifications cannot be transposed to authors' right legislation. In such a system, the legislator choses to build the frontiers of exclusive rights and takes into account other interests, including education and freedom of expression. But the essence of the system remains to protect the author's interests because he is the source of the creation, regardless of any other interest. In other words, civil law countries consider exceptions very cautiously, if not with reluctance, and view them as a 'necessary evil,' while the American approach considers fair use a necessary tool to counterbalance an otherwise overprotective legal system for authors.[4]

Every copyright legislation has to take into account the need for safeguards against too large of exceptions or compulsory licences, which otherwise would deprive exclusive rights of their substance. But this need is more strongly taken into account when the author and his work (and other rights owners) are put at the core of the protection, rather than in the law where public good or various external interests come first, or at least are balanced with the authors' interests. In every system, neither exclusive rights nor exceptions are limitless. The necessity of preventing excessive broad exceptions and compulsory licenses is a constant concern of international conventions on intellectual properties. This concern is obvious in the Berne Convention, where one could find a list of particular exceptions and a general safeguard rule, the three steps test. This approach to exceptions resembles American law, albeit in the opposite direction. The Berne Convention's moderative clause is intended to limit the scope of exceptions, while in US copyright law, the fair use clause tends to moder-

---

3 Pamela Samuelson, *Unbundling Fair Uses*, 77 FORDHAM LAW REVIEW 2537, 2615–17 (2009).

4 *Id.* at 2618.

ate the exclusive right by broadening limitations. However, it is impossible to achieve a satisfactory level of international protection of works and harmonization if States are left free to adopt or extend any limitations to exclusive rights and so deprive foreign works or authors of substantial protection.

In the European Union, exceptions are enumerated exhaustively in national laws (Member States of the Union having been compelled to chose their exceptions among those listed by the EU Directive 2001/29), and the interpretation of these legally defined exceptions is restrictive. In a very important *Infopaq* decision,[5] the EU Court of Justice provided four criteria which must necessarily be used by national and European courts. The *Infopaq* case concerned only one particular exception of article 5, §1 of 2001/29 Directive, but it is clear that these criteria have to be applied to the other exceptions in article 5. First, the legal conditions of each exception in the EU Directive are cumulative in the sense that non-compliance with any one exception will prevent the act from being exempted. Second, as for the interpretation of each of those conditions in particular, one should keep in mind that the provisions of a directive which deviate from a general principle established by that directive must be interpreted strictly. In other words, the general principle to interpret European directives fits with the traditional author's right principle. This is not surprising since in civil law systems (like the French system), any exception rule in any legal field has to be narrowly interpreted by the courts. This holds true for the exemptions provided for in article 5 of 2001/29 Directive, which are derogations from the general principle established by this directive, requiring an authorization from the rightholder for any reproduction or communication of a protected work. Third, the exemption must be interpreted in the light of article 5, §5 of 2001/29 Directive, under which each exemption is to be applied only in certain cases that do not conflict with a normal exploitation of the work and do not unreasonably prejudice the legitimate interests of the rightholder. This is the three steps test clause. Fourth, the European Union Court of Justice has added a very interesting criterium that had not been expressed before in French or EU case law or legislation: 'in accordance with recitals 4, 6 and 21 in the preamble to 2001/29 Directive, the conditions laid down in article 5(1) thereof must also be interpreted in the light of the need for legal certainty for authors with regard to the protection of their works'. This puts the main concern of the European legislator throughout the 2001/29 Directive in deep contrast

---

[5] Case C-5/08EU, Infopaq International A/S v. Danske Dagblades Forening, 2009 E.C.R. I-06569, at 55–9.

with the American approach of the exceptions, specially with the fair use rationale.

(ii) A Comparison between Fair Use and The Three Steps Test

Fair use was initiated and developed by US courts mid-nineteenth century but was not introduced to copyright law until 1976. The three steps test originates from the Berne Convention, an international treaty first introduced in 1971, and became an internal law in Europe only through the implementation of EU 2001/29 Directive by Member States during the years following its adoption in May 2001. Fair use played an important part in the construction of American jurisprudence. The three steps test is just beginning to prove its own importance and usefulness in practice. For both mechanisms, recent history is full of controversies, but for opposite reasons. Both are praised for their flexibility as tools that are able to adapt copyright law to new challenges and to specific cases. Both are criticized for their uncertainty and their alleged inadequacy to solve contemporary problems. While fair use is occasionally described as being threatened by international conventions, however, the three steps test has distinctly been strengthened by the TRIPS Agreement and, in the European Union, by EU 2001/29 Directive. Since the Directive allows courts to apply the three steps test in particular cases, this rule has simultaneously gained a new momentum and a new meaning. Despite American jurisprudence attachment to fair use, US copyright remains isolated on an international level: nowhere else has this rule really taken root.[6] Even countries where social interest is supposed to be the final aim of intellectual property law and in countries that are open to the so-called 'balance of interests' (Germany for example), did not implement any comparable rule to the contrary. Even 'fair dealing' that may be found in many common law countries' copyright laws cannot be assimilated to American fair use. In contrast, three major international treaties on copyright have adopted the three steps test, as well as the 27 States of the European Union.

According to §107, fair use depends on four factors, while the three steps test relies on three factors. Theoretically, all of the factors have to be fulfilled in both cases. As far as the three steps test is concerned, it is clear. The three steps test, as the name itself indicates, must be conducted in the

---

[6] Marshall A. LEAFFER, UNDERSTANDING COPYRIGHT LAW 529, § 10.18 (5th ed. 2010); Marshall Leaffer, *The Uncertain Future of Fair Use in a Global Information Marketplace*, 62 OHIO ST. L.J. 849, 865 ('As for fair use, the United States presently stands alone in the world of intellectual property community.').

predefined order and if only one step is missed, the exception does not comply with the test and must be put aside. The failure of any single step is enough to neutralize the limitation under discussion. Because the three steps are exhaustive, Judges cannot disclose another step, even by pretending that it was an implicit condition in the law. In contrast, the four legal factors of §107, while always analyzed together, are reviewed on a case-by-case basis. It can be assumed that some of the criteria may be decisive in one case and not in another, and that one single factor may indeed be sufficient in some occasions to convince the court, regardless of the others. Moreover, the four legal factors are not exhaustive: the list given by §107 is an open-ended one. Courts may discover other criteria in some cases if necessary (good faith, industry custom, etc.).

If one looks at the various legal factors, there is an obvious affinity between the fourth factor of §107 ('the effect of the use upon the potential market for or value of the copyrighted work') and the second step (requiring that the exceptions or limitations 'do not conflict with normal exploitation' of the work). It can be added that the WIPO dispute settlement panel as well as the French *Cour de Cassation* have included the consideration of actual and potential types of exploitation in the appreciation of this second step. But the first step – 'certain special cases' – is clearly related to the requirement of specific provisions and to the principle of restrictive interpretation of exceptions, which is fundamental in civil law countries.

When it comes to discerning the advantages of the two mechanisms, the usual answer in both cases can always be summed up in one word: flexibility.[7] This characteristic is not surprising since they both work as equitable rules of reason or moderating instruments. The counterpart of this supposed advantage[8] is that they may both be deemed as more or less lacking precision and security, generating unpredicable results and uncertainty. Maybe these criticisms are stronger against fair use. Concerning the three steps test, uncertainty arises more from the application of the second and third steps than from the first one, which in our opinion does not give rise to any hesitation. Also, the three steps test in Europe has a different scope than in US copyright. Traditionally, since its introduction in the Berne Convention (article 9, §2) by the 1967 revision and later in WIPO Copyright Treaty 1996 (article 10) and the TRIPS Agreement (article 13), the three steps test is fundamentally an international law regulation,

---

7 P. Samuelson, *supra* note 4, at 2537.

8 M. Leaffer, *supra* note 7, at 849 ('In the abstract, there is much to be said for the vaunted flexibility of the US Doctrine. In reality, though, one can hardly characterize recent fair use case law as manifesting that flexibility.').

intended to forbid the Member States of the Berne Union to adopt too large exceptions or compulsory licenses. But since the implementation of the 2001/29 UE Directive of May 22, 2001 'on the harmonization of certain aspects of copyright and related rights in the information society' (article 5.5), the three steps test has also become an internal rule that allows a court to decide not to enforce a legal exception in a particular case where its legal requirements are not fulfilled. In other words, the application of this exception in this case would violate one of the three steps (and, more precisely, would 'conflict with a normal exploitation of the work' or 'unreasonably prejudice the legitimate interests of the rightholder'). This rule is, for example, now enforced through article L.122-5[9] of the French *Code de la Propriété intellectuelle*.

Until now, article L.122-5 has been seldom and cautiously applied by French courts. The most important decision to be quoted is a very interesting and, in the author's opinion, excellent 1996 decision of the *Cour de cassation* that refers to the three steps test in the context of the copyright's owners using technical devices to prevent unauthorized copying of videos.[10] According to many scholars, the flexibility advantage of fair use is counterbalanced by its drawbacks, which are imprecision and unpredict-

---

[9] Article L.122–5, ¶ 2 Intellectual Property Code (France) ('Les exceptions énumérées par le présent article ne peuvent porter atteinte à l'exploitation normale de l'œuvre ni causer un préjudice injustifié aux intérêts légitimes de l'auteur.'). The lack of reference to 'special cases' is explained by the legislature's conviction that it was unnecessary to mention it in this place because the exhaustive list of precisely determined legal exceptions in article L.122–5 and the restrictive interpretation principle were sufficient to fulfil this requirement.

[10] Cass., lère ch. civile, 28 février 2006 ('Vu les articles L. 122–5 et L. 211–3 du Code de la propriété intellectuelle, interprétés à la lumière des dispositions de la directive n° 2001/29/CE du 22 mai 2001 (. . .), ensemble l'article 9.2 de la Convention de Berne; attendu, selon l'article 9.2 de la Convention de Berne, que la reproduction des œuvres littéraires et artistiques protégées par le droit d'auteur peut être autorisée, dans certains cas spéciaux, pourvu qu'une telle reproduction ne porte pas atteinte à l'exploitation normale de l'œuvre ni ne cause un préjudice injustifié aux intérêts légitimes de l'auteur; que l'exception de copie privée prévue aux articles L. 122–5 et L. 211–3 du Code de la propriété intellectuelle, tels qu'ils doivent être interprétés à la lumière de la directive européenne susvisée, ne peut faire obstacle à l'insertion dans les supports sur lesquels est reproduite une œuvre protégée, de mesures techniques de protection destinées à en empêcher la copie, lorsque celle-ci aurait pour effet de porter atteinte à l'exploitation normale de l'œuvre, laquelle doit s'apprécier en tenant compte de l'incidence économique qu'une telle copie peut avoir dans le contexte de l'environnement numérique.') Bull. civ. I n°126 p.115, JCP.-G. 2006-II-10084, comment by A. Lucas, RIDA Juillet 2006, p.269, RTDcom. 2006 p.370, comment by F. Pollaud-Dulian.

ability.[11] However, it is true that this uncertainty has been, if not doubted, at least minimized by other scholars who defend the fair use as a means to counterbalance 'what would otherwise be an unreasonably broad grant of rights to the authors and an unduly narrow set of negotiated exceptions and limitations'.[12] The three steps test may also be criticized for its uncertainty. Yet, if the three factors also seem very complicated and somewhat vague, the first factor is quite precise and clear, and the problem of interpretation arises essentially with the other two factors, which occasionally may be difficult to apply. This is inherent in a case by case rule. Besides, the WTO panel decision has broadly highlighted the significance of the three steps test and is usually well received by French jurisprudence. Finally, one can imagine that the European Union Court of Justice[13] will adopt a unifying definition of the three steps that will not significantly depart from what the panel said. Every court in the European Union will have to respect the interpretation chosen by the Court of Justice so that the feared uncertainty will either vanish or become quite limited.

However, the uncertainty problem in both systems is linked with the juridical technique itself: the two somewhat opposite rules are using similar reasoning. Appearing as rules of reason and balancing tests, they are moderative mechanisms that are more familiar to common law systems, but rather strange in civil law countries.[14] They both intend to balance the interests of copyright owners and those of the public or other users and they allow judges to avoid the application of a legal rule when the rule is considered to lead to excess or abuse. Although similiar in this regard, the mechanisms have different aims: while fair use tends to avoid a misuse of exclusive rights and preserve the users' interests or freedom or the society's interest in some free uses of works, the three steps test, is intended to protect the authors' exclusive rights when they are threatened

---

11 Marshall Leaffer, *supra* note 7, at 849 ('The truth is that in American law the ambit of fair use has receded; its contours ever more uncertain. Determining what constitutes a fair use of a copyrighted work in a given situation is a hazardous undertaking. Providing guidance on fair use is the last thing that a practicing lawyer, even one versed in copyright, would prefer to do.').

12 Pamela Samuelson, *supra* note 4, at 2618.

13 *See e.g.*, case C-462/09, *Stiching de Thuiskopie v. Opus and Van Der Lee*, 2011 still unpublished in E.C.R. ; see in this case RTDCom. 2012 p. 551, comment by F. Pollaud-Dulian; Case 145/10, *Eva-Maria Painer v. StandardsVerlag*, 2011, still unpublished, RTDCom. 2012 p. 118, comment by F. Pollaud-Dulian.

14 André Lucas, *Pour une interprétation raisonnable du triple test ou pourquoi il faut éviter d'ajouter le flou au flou*, Auteurs & Media 2009/3, at 239; Jane C. Ginsburg, *Toward supranational copyright law? The WTO panel decision and the three steps test for copyright exceptions*, RIDA January 2001, at 57.

by the will of the legislator who may adopt a law that excessively extends legal limitations or that enables abnormal uses of legal exceptions.

Both of these rules aim to set aside the application of a legal rule when it conflicts with the fundamental purposes of author's right or copyright. But since copyright and continental authors' rights have different foundations and purposes, it is not surprising that fair use and the three steps test appear as opposite techniques since they are thought to achieve opposite goals.

Moreover, it is difficult to rely on the four factors of the fair use defense.[15] Besides the definition of the factors, uncertainty remains in the meaning of fair use itself and in the purposes other than those which are given as examples in §107. In addition, the role of each of these factors and the respective importance of each of them in the courts' decisions are not clear.

II. INCOMPATIBILITY BETWEEN FAIR USE AND THE THREE STEPS TEST

The compatibility or incompatibility between fair use and the triple test is fiercely debated. This controversy indeed has two different aspects: could one use the three steps test to introduce a type of fair use in Europe (i) and is there any compatibility between American fair use and the three steps test (ii)?

(i) A Minor Controversy about the Three Steps Test's Significance in Europe

A few – minority but activist – European scholars[16] propose to import fair use into EU law through a distorted interpretation of the three steps

---

[15] David Nimmer, *'Fairest of Them All' and Other Fairy Tales of Fair Use*, 66 Law & Contemporary Problems 263 (Winter/Spring 2003) ('In the end, reliance on the four statutory factors to reach fair use decisions often seems naught but a fairy tale.').

[16] Martin Senftleben, *Bridging the Differences Between Copyright's Legal Traditions – The Emerging EC Fair Use Doctrine*, 57 Journal of the Copyright Society of the USA 521 (2010) (hereinafter *Bridging the Differences*); Martin Senftleben, *Fair Use in the Netherlands – A Renaissance? Tidjschrift voor auteurs, media en informatierecht* Vol. 33, No. 1 pp. 1–7 (2009), *available at* http://ssrn.com/abstract=1563986; Martin Senfleben, *The International Three-Steps Test : A Model Provision for EC Fair Use Legislation*, 1 J. of Intell. Prop., Information Tech. & E-Commerce L. 67 (2010); Christophe Geiger, Jonathan Griffiths and Reto M. Hilty, *Towards a Balanced Interpretation of the 'Three-step test' in Copyright*

test, which is supposed to be 'balanced' and 'holistic' according to EU Directive n°2001/29. The scholars argue that adopting a European 'fair use' clause would not only bring European author's right regulations and US copyright law closer together, but would also fulfill the need for more flexibility in Europe and put an end to what Professor Senftleben described – wrongly – as the 'lamentable state' of the EU system of copyright limitations.[17] If the EU Directive should deserve any critique about its exceptions regulation, it should be aimed at the excessive amount of exceptions that it contains in article 5 and at the choice left to Members States of the Union. However, this does not justify such a severe description of the state of law and, as one can easily understand, this defect is contrary to M. Senftleben's approach because it is grounded on the wish to introduce more limitations through fair use doctrine.

This proposal to introduce a European 'fair use' clause relies on ideological grounds, which differ fundamentally from the continental conception of authors' rights and more closely resemble US copyright law. It puts aside the traditional central position of the author's concern in authors' rights and replaces it with a preference for social goals and underlying lobbies and economic interests (for example, the call by some consumers associations for free access to works). The European approach of a narrow exhaustive list of exceptions combined with a restrictive interpretation principle is accused of harming freedoms of expression and even freedom of competition. It ignores deliberately the fact that freedom of expression or creation is not limited by copyright law, since on one hand, ideas (as well as themes, styles, theories, facts, historical, scientific informations, etc.) are not protected by copyright nor by authors' law and, on the other hand, some of the legal exceptions in authors' right laws are meant to facilitate the exercise of various freedoms (freedom to criticize, to create, to teach, etc.),[18] for example the short quotation exception. Informations are not monopolized through author's rights because informations are not considered to be works, but rather considered parts of what authors' right calls 'ideas'. Reciprocally, works are not to be treated as informations. It is not sufficient to say that the Information Age and

---

Law, *EIPR* 2008, at 489; – ' Le rôle du test des trois étapes dans l'adaptation du droit d'auteur à la société de l'information': *e-Bulletin du droit d'auteur* janvier-mars 2007 (also available in English); Christophe Geiger, Jonathan Griffiths and Reto M. Hilty, *Declaration on a Balanced Interpretation of the Three Steps Test in Copyright Law*, 39 I.I.C. 707 (2008).

[17] *Bridging the Differences*, *supra* note 17.

[18] See Council Directive 2001/29, article 5, § 3, 2001 O.J. (L 122–5) (EC); *see also* Art. L3, 4, 7, 9 Intellectual Property Code (France).

technological developments require a 'changing of paradigm' and more exceptions or more flexibility in exceptions, both of which imply an unsaid but necessary weakening of the exclusive rights. One has to justify these assertions by something other than merely criticizing the state of the right and assumptions.

Each legal system has its own idiosyncrasies and what may be good and accepted in a given country is not necessarily good to import into a different country with different sociocultural backgrounds, as well as different legal system and history. Some may find it interesting that the European scholars who are so fond of American copyright as a tool to enlarge exceptions to authors' rights,[19] are very reluctant to accept the American model when it is proposed to lengthen the duration of rights.[20] This gives the impression that their aim is more to reduce intellectual property rights than to bring European legislation up to date or even closer to the American legal experience. It is also doubtful that American copyright law and European authors' rights law have become closer in 'a remarkable convergence' thanks to an international harmonization.[21] Obviously, the fair use doctrine finds its roots in the utilitarian conception of the American copyright and is in perfect accordance with principles expressed by the US Constitution. In this way, copyright is not only grounded in the social, educational and economic interests (i.e. bound to the interest of the society), but is also fundamentally limited by these interests. Works and their authors are more a means than the core of the legislation. Conversely, in European civil law countries, authors' rights are grounded in the interests of the creators because they have created a work and, especially in the French system, the interests of the society or those of the audience are secondary. It explains that the exclusive rights are broadly conceived while the exceptions are limited and subject to a restrictive interpretation rule that forbids the judges from enlarging the exceptions or from creating new exceptions by analogy.

Whatever opinion one has of the opportunity to import fair use into Europe, using the three steps test for this purpose would imply a reverse reading of the legal provisions. To be transformed into a fair use *à l'européenne* provision, the three steps test in the 2001/29 EU Directive would warrant the exact opposite meaning and goal than those attributed to it by the European legislator. The three steps test has never been con-

---

19 *Bridging the Differences*, *supra* note 17, at 541.

20 Christophe Geiger, *Vers une propriété intellectuelle éternelle? La contestable extension de durée de protection du droit d'auteur et des droits voisins*, Recueil Dalloz 2008 p. 2880.

21 *Bridging the Differences*, *supra* note 17, at 522.

ceived as a way to give the judges a means to create or enlarge exceptions. Section 5 of the EU Directive provides a closed, exhaustive list of exceptions and adds the three steps mechanism to allow judges to moderate the undesirable and harmful effects of an exception in particular situations. Specifically, the mechanism allows flexibility in cases where applying the legal exception would conflict with a normal exploitation of the work or would unreasonably prejudice the legitimate interests of the rightholder. The *Infopaq* decision of the European Union Court of Justice is unambiguous on this matter. The same analysis can be applied to article 13 of the TRIPS Agreement. As Professor Cohen Jehoram[22] wrote: 'The three steps test of article 13 is not an independent exception but rather an *extra* requirement for all exceptions which already exist under the Berne Convention, and as such represents an enhancement of author's rights. It is not a *Berne-minus* but a *Berne-plus* provision.'

(ii) The Major Question of the Compatibility of US Fair Use Doctrine and the Three Steps Test

Does fair use comply with Berne Convention and other international conventions on copyright? Factors put forth in favor of compliance include the fact that no objection was raised when the US joined Berne Convention, that fair use under §107 would be secure enough through precedent and the four factors, that American courts actually apply fair use in accordance with the three steps, and that article 9, §2 of Berne Convention was adopted in 1971 (Paris Revision Act) and would no longer fit with the modern technological environment.[23]

Professor H. Cohen-Jehoram deduced from both the reading of article 13 of the TRIP's Agreement and the decision of the dispute settlement panel of the WTO of July 27, 2000, that §107 of the US copyright Act does not respect TRIP's article 13: 'the American fair use doctrine leads to an open case-by-case analysis, and as such undermines all legal certainty'.

---

[22] Herman Cohen Jehoram, *Some Principles of Exceptions to Copyright*, in : Festschrift für Adolf Dietz, Beck Verlag publishing 2005 at 384 ; Herman Cohen Jehoram, *Restrictions on Copyright and their Abuse*, 27 E.I.P.R. 359 (2005); Herman Cohen Jehoram, *The Evolution of Copyright Exceptions*, in : Perspektiven des geistigen Eigentums und wettbewerbsrechts. Festschrift für G. Schricker, Beck Verlag publishing 2005 at 249.

[23] M. Leaffer, *supra* note 7, at 502 ('After all, article 9 (2) was adopted 25 years ago, a response to the media, marketing conditions, and technological challenges of the day.'); *cf. id.* ('Despite these vast technological changes, the doctrine of fair use has changed little from its first judicial recognition in the nineteenth century.').

The same conclusion arises from article 10 of the 1996 WIPO Treaty. Cohen-Jehoram's opinion is shared by many other scholars, including prominent scholars such as Professor Paul Goldstein,[24] Professor André Lucas[25] and Professor Sam Ricketson.[26] [27] Opposite to most countries and especially to European ones, the American system of fair use allows judges to enlarge or even create some exceptions through analogical reasoning. This is not in compliance with Berne Convention, which gives a precise and exhaustive list of exceptions.[28] It is true that article 9, §2 is interpreted as giving the option to maintain or even create other specific limitations to the reproduction right beyond those stated in the Convention. But this is applicable only in 'certain special cases' and only if the case meets the two other triple test criteria. Moreover, it is admitted that under the TRIP's Agreement (unlike under the Berne Convention),[29] every exception of the Berne Convention can be subjected to the three steps test.[30] This analysis was confirmed by the WTO panel. It is very dubious, in the author's opinion, that a general 'fair use' provision might be considered

---

24 P. Goldstein, *supra* note 1, at 442.

25 A. Lucas, *supra* note 15, at 233 ('L'enjeu concerne surtout le *fair use* Américain dont la conformité au test, sur ce point, est très douteuse. On pourra déployer toutes les ressources de la dialectique, il sera tout de même difficile de plaider qu'un système d'exceptions se présentant expressément comme ouvert ne fait céder le droit exclusif que dans des *cas spéciaux* (. . .)').

26 S. Ricketson, *supra* note 2, at 68–9 ('The question remains, however, whether 'fairness' itself is a criterion that is sufficiently defined and narrow in scope and reach for the purposes of the first part of the three-step test.'). Samuel Ricketson goes on to state: 'At first blush, the answer to this question would appear to be 'no': 'fairness' is an insufficiently clear criterion to meet the first part of the three-step test. Against this it can be argued that a use will never be 'fair' in isolation; its fairness will only be established if it is tied to some identified purpose that then meets the guidelines contained in both provisions. The more general and less defined the purpose, the less likely is it to be a fair one. The only difficulty will be knowing in advance what purposes, other than those specifically mentioned, will meet this requirement, and, in this regard, it might be argued that the rationale behind the first part of the three-step is precisely to avoid this indeterminacy, so that it is clear in advance what purpose a particular exception is to serve . . .' *Id.*

27 *Contra* Tyler G. Newby, *What's Fair Here Is Not Fair Everywhere: Does the American Fair Use Doctrine Violate International Copyright Law?*, 51 Stan. L. Rev. 1633 (1999).

28 Art. 2bis, 10; 10bis; 11 bis; 11ter, 13 & 14.

29 SAM RICKETSON, THE BERNE CONVENTION FOR THE PROTECTION OF LITERARY AND ARTISTIC WORKS: 1886–1986 482, §9.6 (1987).

30 D. Gervais, L'accord sur les ADPIC, Larcier publishing, Bruxelles 2010, p.255 ; Mihály Ficsor, *How Much of What? The Three Steps Test and its Application in Two Recent WTO Dispute Settlement Cases*, RIDA April 2002 at 111.

as a 'certain special case' within the meaning of the Berne Convention,[31] as well as within the meaning of the TRIP's Agreement. According to the WTO dispute settlement panel, 'in the case at hand, in order to determine whether an exception is confined to 'certain special cases,' one has first to examine whether the exception has been 'clearly defined'; second, to ascertain whether the exemption is 'narrow in scope, inter alia, with respect to its reach'.

The panel tried to define the two parts of the criterium. First it said that: 'the ordinary meaning of 'certain' is 'known and particularized, but not explicitly identified,' 'determined, fixed, not variable; definitive, precise, exact'. In other words, it means that, under the first condition, an exception or limitation in national legislation must be clearly defined. However, there is no need to identify explicitly each and every possible situation to which the exception could apply, provided that the scope of the exception is known and particularized. This guarantees a sufficient degree of 'legal certainty.' Concerning the significance of the 'special case' requirement, the panel considered that:

> This term means that more is needed than a clear definition in order to meet the standard of the first condition. In addition, an exception or limitation must be limited in its field of application or exceptional in its scope. In other words, an exception or limitation should be narrow in quantitative as well as a qualitative sense. This suggests a narrow scope as well as an exceptional or distinctive objective. To put this aspect of the first condition into the context of the second condition ('no conflict with a normal exploitation'), an exception or limitation should be the opposite of a non-special, that is, normal case. The ordinary meaning of the term 'case' refers to an 'occurrence,' 'circumstance' or 'event' or 'fact.'[32]

How could one seriously pretend that fair use is 'definitive, precise, clearly defined' (meaning 'certain') and corresponds to a quite well defined field ('special case')? The definition of fair use that may be applied in 'any particular case' is broad and vague; its four criteria are uncertain, and it is very difficult and sometimes impossible to predict if a particular use is or is not a fair one. Moreover, courts can build new hypotheses of fair use with new criteria. This does not comply with article 9, §2 of the Berne Convention, as interpreted by Prof. S. Ricketson:

> [T]he words embody a general criterion, and this can be seen as possessing two distinctive aspects. First, the use must be for a quite specific purpose: a broad

---

[31] H. Cohen-Jehoram, *supra* note 23, at 387.

[32] Dispute Settlement Reports 2000, Volume 8 By World Trade Organization, p. 3810

> kind of exemption would not be justified. Secondly, there must be something *special* about this purpose, *special* here meaning that it is justified by some clear reason of public policy or some other exceptional circumstance.[33]

The second aspect – requirement of a public policy reason – wrongfully has not been endorsed by the WTO panel,[34] according to M. Ficsor.[35] It is true that the panel also specified,

> In other words, ('certain') means that, under the first condition, an exception or limitation in national legislation must be clearly defined. However, there is no need to identify explicitly each and every possible situation to which the exception could apply, provided that the scope of the exception is known and particularized. This guarantees a sufficient degree of legal certainty.

---

[33] Ricketson, *supra* note 32, at 482.

[34] '(6.111) (. . .) we believe that the term 'certain special cases' should not lightly be equated with 'special purpose'. It is difficult to reconcile the wording of Article 13 with the proposition that an exception or limitation must be justified in terms of a legitimate public policy purpose in order to fulfill the first condition of the Article. We also recall in this respect that in interpreting other WTO rules, such as the national treatment clauses of the GATT and the GATS, the Appellate Body has rejected interpretative tests which were based on the subjective aim or objective pursued by national legislation. In our view, the first condition of Article 13 requires that a limitation or exception in national legislation should be clearly defined and should be narrow in its scope and reach. On the other hand, a limitation or exception may be compatible with the first condition even if it pursues a special purpose whose underlying legitimacy in a normative sense cannot be discerned. The wording of Article 13's first condition does not imply passing a judgment on the legitimacy of the exceptions in dispute. However, public policy purposes stated by law-makers when enacting a limitation or exception may be useful from a factual perspective for making inferences about the scope of a limitation or exception or the clarity of its definition.' See A. Lucas, who criticizes this part of the panel report, 'Le triple test de l'article 13 de l'Accord ADPIC à la lumière du rapport du Groupe spécial de l'OMC Etats-Unis/article 110.5 de la loi sur le droit d'auteur', *in* : Festschrift für Adolf Dietz, Beck Verlag 2001, p.429; *Cf.* Jane C. Ginsburg, *Toward Supranational Copyright Law? The WTO Panel Decision and the Three Steps Test for Copyright Exceptions*, RIDA January 2001, at 39, *available at* http://ssrn.com/abstract=253867 or doi:10.2139/ssrn.253867 (who approves).

[35] Ficsor, *supra* note 33, at 223–9. M. Ficsor concludes 'It does not seem to be compatible with the TRIPS Agreement (and equally the WCT and the WPPT) – and, in respect of the right of reproduction, with the Berne Convention – to allow the introduction of exceptions and limitations with the only condition that they should be somehow limited, without the obligation to offer sound and valid special legal-political justifications. The proliferation of exceptions and limitations based on such an uncontrolled practice might lead to the undermining of the value of economic rights.' *Id.* at 244.

Can one deduce from the last two phrases that 'fair use' is complying with the 'certain special case' requirement? I do not think so, first, because American scholars themselves usually do not consider that the qualification of 'fair use' is certain and predictable and, second, because the very wording of §107 leaves the possibility to modify and enlarge or restrain the scope of the fair use so that there does not seem to exist a sufficient degree of certainty except maybe for the traditional cases that the legislator incorporated into the law in 1976.[36] Even the four factors are uncertain in practice. Their meaning and their respective weight in appreciating each case[37] are less than secure. This has been pointed out clearly on many occasions by American scholars. For example, Professor P. Goldstein, who is not convinced by the use of the four factors nor by the building of a general theory of fair use, which he calls 'the great whale of grand theory,' prefers to rely on the research of the category of uses in which one particular use falls and the study of various decisions of the courts about this category. He thinks that this approach, while being uneasy in determining the category and the category's equities, offers more predictability than the statute's four factors ('context first, factors second').[38] Furthermore, Professor David Nimmer makes the point:[39] 'How do the factors work out in practice? The literature reveals that judges, treatise writers and other commentators offer a host of different explanations for how fair use cases actually are decided, apart from the four factors.' Examining sixty cases and elaborating with statistics, Professor Nimmer concludes:

---

[36] *Contra* : *Briding the Differences*, *supra* note 17, at 547.

[37] M. Leaffer, *supra* note 7, at 494 ('Practical application of §107's four factors has not led to predictable results. In a given case, one may find majority and dissenting opinions disagreeing completely on the application of each factor. This is hardly surprising. The factors are boadly stated, overlapping and vague, and the legislative history provides little insight as to their meaning, what weight to give to them, or how they interrelate.'); *cf.* Samuelson, *supra* note 4, at 2615 ('In Internet access cases, it should further be relevant whether the plaintiff made its work available on open sites on the Internet and/or declined to opt out of the information-access tool. The commerciality of the defendant's purpose should be given little weight because developing useful information access tools is sufficiently expensive that the defendant would most likely need to recoup its expenses. Similarly, the nature of the work – whether informational or creative – should generally be given less weight in information-access cases because improving access to the plaintiff's work is socially valuable regardless of its creative status (. . .) Lastly, courts should recognize that iterative copying is often required in order to make a useful information-access tool (. . .)').

[38] P. Goldstein, *supra* note 1, at 433.

[39] D. Nimmer, « *Fairest of them all* and other fairy tales of fair use », at 267, 280.

> In the ultimate analysis, my review of the cases convinces me that the high correspondence in judicial opinions between the individual fair use factors and court's ultimate disposition, as opposed to the absence of any meaningful correspondence in the chart, reflects an important insight into how judges actually resolve fair use cases: Courts tend first to make a judgement that the ultimate disposition is fair use or unfair use, and then align the four factors to fit that result as best they can. At base, the four factors fail to drive the analysis, but rather serve as convenient pegs on which to hang antecedent conclusions.[40]

This is not surprising because legislative history indicates that in 1976, the American legislature intended to restate the judicial precedents in §107 without restraining the judge's ability to use additional different criteria and to enlarge fair use applications.[41] In conclusion, it seems certain that the American fair use doctrine does violate Berne Convention, the TRIPS Agreement and the 1996 WIPO Treaty, at least as far as works that were not first published in the US are concerned (see more precisely article 5 of the Berne Convention).

The 'certain special case' requirement may not be the only step that §107 does not comply with. As Professor Ricketson points out, §107 may not comply with the third step either because this step implies that the courts take into account not only the author's economic interests, but also their non-pecuniary interests (moral, artistic, intellectual, etc.). To summarize,

> In this regard, the reference to unpublished works in the last sentence of §107 indicates that one important concern of authors – with respect to the unauthorized dissemination or disclosure of their works – may be disregarded if the other factors listed in the Section are satisfied. In addition, there is no express reference in the Section to the need to ensure that detriment to author, whether economic or non-economic, is proportionate or within reason, although possibly the first factor may relate to such matters.

---

[40] *Id.* at 281–2 ('The clash of the nine justices themselves in Harper & Row demonstrate that jurists up to the Supreme Court level feel the need to align the factors unanimously in favor of the desired result, perceiving that any deviation could be a fatal chink in the armor.').

[41] House Report Rep. N° 94–1476 (1976) p. 66 ('Beyond a very broad statutory explanation of what fair use is and some of the criteria applicable to it, the courts must be free to adapt the doctrine particular situations on a case-by-case basis. Section 107 is intended to restate the present judicial doctrine of fair use, not to change, narrow or enlarge it in any way.'); *see also* M. Leaffer, *supra* note 7, at 494.

III. CONCLUSION

Could the three steps test become some kind of *Captain Achab* for the fair use *big white whale*? It would certainly not be fair to compare the doctrine to Captain Achab's insane obsession with his unique target. The three steps test is not specifically and exclusively aimed at the fair use *white whale*. However, is fair use obsolete? The answer has to be balanced. If one sticks to the American juridical tradition or to the very spirit of copyright, fair use is still firm and lively. If one takes into account the international evolution in the field of intellectual property, its future is less predictable.[42] Fair use does not comply with article 9 of Berne Convention, but after all, the US joined this Convention without implementing in any way its article 6bis. As Professor Goldstein states:

> Of course Berne leaves American courts free to treat American authors as shabbily as they please, but this means only that what was originally a legal question has become a moral one : is it right to give a nation's authors a level of protection that falls below the international norm? American exceptionalism is not always a good thing.[43]

But today there is a major difference, because the TRIPS Agreement imposes the three steps test and contains an efficient dispute settlement system. However, the question may never arise, and status quo may go on. After all, do dragons ever meet whales? In the author's opinion, the essential issue is to decide what has to be groundly predominating in intellectual property regulation: authors' interests, creation, individual property or collective interest, consumers' demands, economics? Is intellectual property intended to protect authors because they create works or is it intended as a tool to serve various collective interests?

---

42 M. Leaffer, *supra* note 7.
43 P. Goldstein, *supra* note 1, at 442.

9. Fair use: A tale of two cities

Sang Jo Jong[1]

I. INTRODUCTION

On February 7, 2007, Stephanie Lenz ('Lenz') videotaped her young children dancing in her family's kitchen. The song '*Let's Go Crazy*' by *the artist professionally known as Prince* played in the background.[2] Lenz uploaded the video to *YouTube*. As the copyright owner to '*Let's Go Crazy*,' Universal Music Corporation sent *YouTube* a takedown notice. *YouTube* removed the video the following day. Lenz sent *YouTube* a DMCA counter-notification asserting that her video constituted fair use of '*Let's Go Crazy*' and demanded the video be re-posted. Lenz also filed suit in the Northern District of California against Universal alleging misrepresentation pursuant to 17 U.S.C. § 512(f).[3]

About two years later, the plight of an internet user like Lenz was also heard in a court in Seoul, Korea. On February 2, 2009, an internet user named 'Yang'[4] uploaded a video file in the form of User Generated Content ('UGC'), in which his five-year-old daughter was dancing on a chair and singing a copyrighted song titled '*Must Have Been Crazy*'. The video, and a posting including the chorus of the song lyrics, was uploaded to his blog on the NAVER portal site, the most popular internet portal

---

[1] Professor of Law, Seoul National University School of Law and Director of the SNU Center for Law & Technology. The author expresses his gratitude to Professor John Leitner, Seoul National University School of Law, for his wonderful views and comments on this essay, to Ms. Lisa Ellingson, an LL.M. candidate at Seoul National University School of Law for her help and to Mr. Jinchul Hong, a J.D. candidate at the University of Washington School of Law, for his help in translation of a substantial part of this essay.

[2] The video is 29 seconds in length, and '*Let's Go Crazy*' can be heard for approximately 20 seconds, albeit with difficulty given the poor sound quality of the video.

[3] *Lenz v. Universal Music Corp.*, 572 F. Supp. 2d 1150, 88 U.S.P.Q.2d 1629 (N.D. Cal. 2008).

[4] This user name was associated with the blog where the video in the case was uploaded, http://blog.naver.com/yang456/140062293006.

site in Korea.[5] The copyright to the song was assigned to the Korea Music Copyright Association ('KOMCA'), which sent NAVER a takedown notice. NAVER removed the video file immediately. Although Yang asserted his video constituted fair use and requested NAVER to repost the video, NAVER rejected the request by asserting the period for a request to repost specified in the Enforcement Decree of the Copyright Act elapsed and, Yang did not submit relevant documents to justify any legitimate right to his video. Eventually, Yang filed a suit in the Central District of Seoul, Korea.[6]

The above episodes in San Jose and Seoul are reminiscent of '*A Tale of Two Cities*' written by Charles Dickens.[7] As the novel depicts the plight of the French peasantry and compares and contrasts life in Paris and London in the years leading up to the French Revolution, the above episodes clearly demonstrate the plight and entry barriers internet users have faced during the course of the internet revolution in San Jose and Seoul. It is worth comparing the tales of these two cities, particularly in the US and Korea, who are facing the internet revolution and noting how the interests of copyright owners, internet service providers, and internet users are influenced by what are termed 'takedown' and 'put back' policies. Tracing the tale of two cities regarding the adjudication and resolution of these internet disputes reveals a substantial difference in the American and Korean 'fair use doctrines' and their underlying philosophies. A comparative analysis of fair use in the US and Korea will be presented in Part II. Takedown policies and their impact on fair use in each country will be reviewed in Part III.

II. COMPARATIVE FAIR USE

(i) The Fair Use Doctrine

1. The function of fair use

The doctrine of fair use developed over the years as courts tried to balance the rights of copyright owners with society's interest in making copies or adaptations. From the inception of copyright law, the courts have excused

---

[5] The video file took approximately 53 seconds. The URL of the video file on the plaintiff's blog is http://blog.naver.com/yang456/140062293006.

[6] Seoul High Court [Seoul High Ct.], 2010Na35260, Oct. 13, 2010 (S.Kor.).

[7] Charles Dickens, A TALE OF TWO CITIES: A STORY OF THE FRENCH REVOLUTION, http://www.gutenberg.org/files/98/98-h/98-h.htm (last visited April 28, 2012).

some uses of copyrighted works either on the basis of implied consent by copyright owners facing insurmountable transaction costs or because the social benefit of the use outweighs the loss to the copyright owner.[8] The fair use doctrine has been codified in Section 107 of the U.S. Copyright Act of 1976: 'The fair use of a copyrighted work . . . for purposes such as criticism, comment, news reporting, teaching . . ., scholarship, or research, is not an infringement of copyright.'[9]

Empirical studies have been made to quantify the economic contribution of copyright-protected industries; and thus, to demonstrate the quantifiable value of copyright law.[10] An empirical study has also shown that the fair use doctrine has contributed to innovation and economic growth. In 2007, the Computer and Communications Industry Association (CCIA) released a report, which showed the fair use exception to copyright contributed to more than $4.4 trillion dollars in annual revenue for the United States economy, representing one-sixth of the total US gross domestic product. The CCIA updated its report in 2010 and found, notwithstanding this recessionary environment, the fair use economy remained steady while the remainder of the US economy contracted.[11] The beneficiaries of fair use encompass a broad range of companies,[12] particularly those whose business activities involve the internet. Actually, for the past decade or so, most judicial decisions relating to fair use have dealt with internet activities.[13]

---

[8] Paul Goldstein, Copyright, §§10:4–10:8 (Little, Brown and Co., 1996).

[9] 17 U.S.C. § 107 (1976).

[10] World Intellectual Property Organization, Economic Contribution & Mapping, http://www.wipo.int/ip-development/en/creative_industry/economic_contribution.html.

[11] Thomas Rogers, Andrew Szamosszegi, Capital Trade, Inc., Fair Use in the U.S. Economy, at 6, http://www.ccianet.org/CCIA/files/ccLibraryFiles/Filename/000000000526/CCIA-FairUseintheUSEconomy-2011.pdf.

[12] Among others, this includes photographic and photocopying equipment manufacturing, computer and peripheral equipment manufacturing, audio and video equipment manufacturing, semiconductors and related devices manufacturing, manufacturing and reproducing magnetic and optical media, electronic shopping, electronic auctions, newspaper publishers, directory mailing list and other publishers, software publishers, other publishers, motion picture and video industries, sound recording industries, data processing, hosting, and related services, other information services, video tape and disc rental, legal services, graphic design services, education services, performing arts companies, independent artists, writers and performers, computer and office machine repair and maintenance.

[13] Religious Technology Center v. Lerma, 908 F. Supp. 1353 (E.D. Va. 1995); UMG Recordings v. MP3.com, 92 F.Supp.2d 349 (S.D.N.Y. 2000); A & M

2. Limitations on copyright in Korea

Although the internet revolution has been taking place in Korea as well, the fair use doctrine is unable to meet the demands there. While some opportunity for fair use of copyrighted materials is believed necessary to fulfill the policy goal of copyright law in the US,[14] such a flexible and broad concept of fair use does not exist in Korea. Rather similar to the German and Japanese approaches, the Copyright Act of Korea simply specifies a number of exceptions to copyright.[15] Lack of an explicit fair use concept in Korea is thought to have originated in the philosophical backgrounds of its copyright law. Copyright is regarded as a natural right granted to an author for his/her labor. Since limitations on copyright are merely exceptions to a natural right, those limitations are only allowed when there is no unreasonable prejudice against the legitimate interests of an author, and to the extent they are not in conflict with the author's moral rights.[16] However, despite detailed statutory provisions on limitations, it is impossible in reality to enumerate all the possible exceptions necessary to reflect technological developments. Legislative responses to technological developments in Korea have thus failed to balance the interests of copyright owners and users/consumers. Since its inception in 1957, the Copyright Act of Korea has been amended several times to strengthen the author's rights and neighboring rights without paying appropriate attention to relevant exceptions.[17] For the past two decades,

---

Records v. Napster, 239 F. 3d 1004 (9th Cir. 2001); Video Pipeline Inc. v. Buena Vista Home Entertainment, 342 F.3d 191 (3rd Cir. 2003); Kelly v. Arriba Soft Corp., 336 F.3d 811 (9th Cir. 2003); Kelly v. Arriba Soft Corp., 336 F.3d 811 (9th Cir. 2003); Field v. Google Inc., 412 F. Supp. 2d 1106 (D. Nev. 2006).

[14] Joseph M. Miller, Fair Use through the Lenz of § 512(c) of the DMCA: A Preemptive Defense to a Premature Remedy?, 95 Iowa L. Rev. 1697 (2010), at 1711.

[15] Jeo jak gwon beop [Copyright Act], art. 23–38 (S.Kor.) For the English version, visit http://en.wikisource.org/wiki/Copyright_Act_of_South_Korea.

[16] The limitations are categorized as 'limitations on an author's property rights,' which are interpreted as not applicable to the moral rights of the author: Jeo jak gwon beop [Copyright Act], art. 38 (Relationship with Author's Moral Rights) (S.Kor.).

[17] In 1986, the Act was wholly amended to introduce internationally-recognized standards. In 1994, the term of the neighboring right was extended from 20 years to 50 years, and the criminal sanctions against copyright infringement were upwardly adjusted. In 2000, the transmission right was added to the author's property right. In 2003, a *sui generis* right was granted for databases and the take-down procedure for copyright owners was introduced. In 2004, stage performers and record producers were granted the transmission right. In 2009, the Minister of Culture, Sports and Tourism was granted the power to order three strike penalties.

proposals[18] have been made in vain to introduce a statutory provision on fair use.[19] This strengthened copyright system eventually led to the abuse of criminal procedure and the suicide of a young student who was alleged to have infringed copyright.[20]

Under the current Copyright Act of Korea, exceptions are available for political speeches, current news reporting, or school education.[21] It does not constitute infringement of copyright to reproduce copyrighted works of current news articles and editorials or for the purpose of judicial proceedings, for private use, for examination questions, for visually impaired persons, or in libraries in certain circumstances.[22] Limitations are also imposed on copyright in cases of exhibition or reproduction of works of art, public performance and broadcasting for non-profit purposes, ephemeral sound or visual recordings by broadcasting organizations,[23] and most frequently, quotations from publicly available works.[24]

(ii) Key Factors

Under the US copyright law, when determining whether the use made of a work in any particular case is a fair use, four non-exclusive factors are analyzed: (1) the purpose and character of the use, (2) the nature of the copyrighted work, (3) the amount and substantiality of the portion used, and (4) the effect of the use upon the potential market.

1. Purpose and character of the use

The first factor, 'purpose and character of the use,' is designed to determine whether the use in question is consistent with the policy goal of copyright law to help stimulate the creation of original expressions. As is often the case in criticism, comment, news reporting, research, nonprofit education uses, and parody, the most common form of fair use is found

---

In 2011, the term of copyright protection was extended from the author's life plus 50 years to the author's life plus 70 years.

18 http://likms.assembly.go.kr/bill/jsp/BillDetail.jsp?bill_id=ARC_D0H8F1W0G1I0N1Z7L3I4V0J2D8N5T6.

19 http://clt.re.kr/pressdata/journal.php?pageNo=3&kind=schedule.

20 http://www.dt.co.kr/contents.html?article_no=2009120802010351699001.

21 Jeo jak gwon beop [Copyright Act], art. 24–26 (S.Kor.).

22 Jeo jak gwon beop [Copyright Act], art. 23, 27, 30–33 (S.Kor.).

23 Jeo jak gwon beop [Copyright Act], art. 28, 29, 34, 35 (S.Kor.).

24 As will be seen below, the quotation exception under Article 28 of the Copyright Act of Korea is frequently relied upon as an equivalent defense by internet users.

when the alleged infringer's work is 'transformative' and does not merely supersede the copyrighted work.

There have been several court decisions dealing with fair use on the internet. In the most distinctive case, *Kelly v. Arriba Soft Corp.*, where a visual search engine displayed search results as 'thumbnail' images, the Ninth Circuit held that the use of thumbnail images was transformative since it benefited the public by enhancing internet information gathering techniques.[25] The decision was also followed in *Perfect 10 v. Amazon. com*[26]. By contrast, the reproduction of an audio CD into MP3 format was equivalent to verbatim copying and did not 'transform' the work.[27] Likewise, sampling, space-shifting, and peer-to-peer distribution of MP3 files on the internet was regarded as transformative use.[28]

2. Nature of the copyrighted work

The second factor, 'nature of the copyrighted work,' generally focuses on whether the copyrighted work is a creative work as opposed to factual and whether it is unpublished or published. The fact that a work is creative and/or unpublished will weigh against a finding of fair use,[29] and yet will not in itself bar a finding of fair use, depending upon consideration of the other factors.

3. Amount and substantiality

The third factor, 'amount and substantiality of the portion used,' is often less important than the other factors, especially the first, because the extent of copying allowed depends on the purpose and character of the use. For example, posting three brief quotations on the internet was held to be fair use mainly because those quotations were for the purpose of news commentary.[30] In addition, displaying thumbnail images as a whole in search engine results was a fair use because those images were used for the transformative purpose of facilitating efficient searches.[31]

---

[25] 336 F.3d 811, at 818 (9th Cir. 2003).

[26] 508 F.3d 1146 (9th Cir. 2007).

[27] UMG Recordings v. MP3.com, 92 F.Supp.2d 349 (S.D.N.Y. 2000).

[28] A & M Records v. Napster, 239 F. 3d 1004 (9th Cir. 2001).

[29] In Harper & Row, Publishers, Inc. v. Nation Enterprises, 471 U.S. 539 (1985), the US Supreme Court held it was not fair use for the defendant to copy approximately 300 words from plaintiff's copyrighted but unpublished memoirs.

[30] Religious Technology Center v. Pagliarina, 908 F. Supp. 1353 (E.D. Va. 1995).

[31] Kelly v. Arriba Soft Corp., 336 F.3d 811 (9th Cir. 2003).

4. Effect on the potential market

The fourth factor, 'the effect of the use upon the potential market,' which is the most important consideration in the fair use analysis, is an inquiry into the degree to which the use prejudices the sale, diminishes the profits, or supersedes the objects, of the original work. The effect on the market has often been subject to hot debates when the use takes place on the internet. For example, in *A & M Records v. Napster*,[32] the file-sharing service Napster claimed its users were not infringing copyrights because they were simply engaged in sampling and space-shifting. However, the Ninth Circuit found that sampling and space-shifting by Napster users had adverse effects on the sale of the recordings on audio CD, and on the developing digital download market. The potential harm to the recording and digital download markets was the key factor in denying the fair use defense. In *Perfect 10 v. Amazon.com*, however, where Perfect 10's commercial interest in selling low-resolution images to the market of mobile device users was found merely as 'hypothetical,' the court was more impressed by the transformative character of *Google's* use of thumbnailed images than its effect on a more speculative and as-yet unrealized market.[33] Is the frequency of downloading images or other digital files important in assessing the effect on the potential market? It seems extremely difficult under the current copyright law to evaluate, however, in one way or another, the effect of non-commercial user-generated contents upon the relevant market is present. This difficulty explains why the dispute between Lenz and Universal Music went to court.[34]

(iii) Limitations on Copyright in Korea

1. Private reproduction

A *de minimis* effect on the market may be a good basis for an exception to copyright in Korea, through what is termed a 'private reproduction'.[35] Under the Copyright Act of Korea, a person who uses a copyrighted work already made public for the non-profit purpose of personal, family, or other similar uses within a limited scope, is permitted to reproduce the

---

32 A & M Records v. Napster, 239 F. 3d 1004 (9th Cir. 2001).

33 Perfect 10 v. Amazon.com, 508 F.3d 1146 (9th Cir. 2007).

34 In Lenz v. Universal Music Corp., 572 F. Supp. 2d 1150, 88 U.S.P.Q.2d 1629 (N.D. Cal. 2008), Universal contended that copyright owners cannot be required to evaluate the question of fair use prior to sending a takedown notice because fair use is merely a judicially determined excused infringement of a copyright rather than a use authorized by the copyright owner or by law.

35 Jeo jak gwon beop [Copyright Act], art. 30 (S.Kor.).

work or software. The private reproduction is permitted as an exception to infringement of copyright, not only because of its *de minimis* effect on the market, but also because such a personal activity is difficult to detect. This is the case when a consumer makes an MP3 file from his/her CD and stores it in his/her MP3 player[36] or records a movie broadcast on TV at night to watch it at a more convenient time.[37]

During the last two decades or so of the internet revolution, the concept of 'private' reproduction faced a lot of legal and economic challenges. When an MP3 file is downloaded by an internet user, the digital copy may be available to other unspecified users through a P2P network. Due to the availability of a copy to others, downloading the copy through a P2P network might not be regarded as 'the use for the non-profit purpose of his family or other similar uses within a limited scope' encompassed under the Copyright Act of Korea.[38] There are a variety of internet activities, which may be situated between downloading digital copies to MP3 players and sharing them through a P2P network. For example, it is still unclear, what will happen if one stores a digital copy in their own cloud or on a closed blog, where the copy is shared by a limited number of friends.[39]

2. Quotation Utilization

Works already made public can be quoted within a reasonable limit in accordance with the general practice for the purposes of reporting, criticism, education, research, etc.[40] Unlike fair use in the US, the exceptions of private reproduction and quotation are available only with regard to works already made public. The exceptions may not be interpreted to affect the protection of the author's moral rights, including the author's right to publish in whatever way and whenever he/she wants.[41] Accordingly, unpublished memoirs[42] or examination questions that are

---

[36] Space-shifting has been interpreted as a fair use in Ass'n of Am. v. Diamond Multimedia Sys., Inc., 180 F.3d 1072, 1079 (9th Cir.1999). Likewise, space-shifting will be regarded as a private use under the Copyright Act of Korea.

[37] Time shifting is interpreted as a fair use in Sony Corp. v. Universal City Studios, Inc., 464 U.S. 417, 449–50, 104 S.Ct. 774, 78 L.Ed.2d 574 (1984). Likewise, time shifting will be regarded as a private use under the Copyright Act of Korea.

[38] Seoul High Court [Seoul High Ct.], 2003Na21140, Jan. 12, 2005, and Seoul High Court [Seoul High Ct.], 2003Na80798, Jan. 25, 2005 (S.Kor.).

[39] Korea Internet Security Agency, A Brief Introduction to the Amendment Proposal for the Enforcement Decree of the Internet Communication Business Act, National Parliament.

[40] Jeo jak gwon beop [Copyright Act], art. 28 (S.Kor.).

[41] Jeo jak gwon beop [Copyright Act], art. 38 (S.Kor.).

[42] Harper & Row v. Nation Enterprises, 471 U.S. 539 (1985).

not available to the general public are not subject to the exception of legitimate quotation.[43]

The legitimate quotation of a work already made public is permissible only within a reasonable limit so the interest of the copyright owner is not harmed unfairly. Whether the quotation falls within the reasonable limit is determined by considering the totality of the circumstances, including the purpose of the quotation, the nature of the quoted work, the content and amount of the quotation, the interactive relationship between the quoted work and the quoting work, the general notion of the readers, and the replacement of the market demand for the original work. Although the dictionary definition of quotation is different from, and actually much narrower than, fair use in the US, it is interesting to note that the concept of quotation has expanded to cover not only literary expression but also pictures, songs, videos, software, and other copyright-protected works. The influence of the fair use doctrine on the quotation exception in Korea is also found in the key factors to consider when determining the quotation exception as expressed below.

If quotation of an entire work is permitted, there is a danger it will replace the demand for the original work and seriously undermine the interest of the copyright owner; thus, legitimate quotation is generally construed to be limited to only part of existing works.[44] However, there may be some legitimate cases to quote an entire work. In fact, quoting an entire work may be inevitable when partial quotation of works from, for example, photographic or art works is meaningless. Especially, as is the case of *Kelly v. Arriba Soft Corp.*,[45] in which low-resolution thumbnail images appearing on internet search sites were regarded as inevitable reproduction under the Copyright Act of Korea and thus, considered legitimate quotation that does not seriously harm the economic interests of the copyright owner.[46] It is worth noting that the Korean Court's interpretation of the quotation exception is extremely flexible in its accommodation of internet technology, especially in comparison with a German interpretation that held *Google* liable for reproducing thumbnail images.[47]

---

43 Seoul High Court [Seoul High Ct.], 93Na47372, May 5, 1995 (S.Kor.).

44 When pornographic pictures were reproduced with some introductory remarks in a pulpy magazine, reproduction of the pictures in their entire size was designed to attract consumers and, thus, interpreted as not qualifying as legitimate quotation: Supreme Court [S.Ct.], 90DaKa8845, Oct. 23, 1990 (S.Kor.).

45 336 F.3d 811 (9th Cir. 2003).

46 Supreme Court [S.Ct.], 2005Do7793, Feb. 9, 2006 (S.Kor.).

47 Adi Robertson, *Google* Image Search Thumbnails 'Infringement' Under

As legitimate quotation is allowed for the purpose of reporting, criticism, education and research, etc., a user's work (the quoting work) must clearly distinguish itself from the other's work (the quoted work), and the quoted work must be in a status of a means to meet the ends of supplementation, elaboration, illustration, or reference. In other words, the relation of the means and ends is equivalent to a master-servant relationship where the quoting work has the status of a master while the quoted work is the servant. In *Yang*, for example, where the video uploaded to an internet portal site in the form of a UGC was a master work including the dance moves of a five-year-old girl with the so-called 'chair dance,' the original song in the background was simply a servant work in the video.[48] Particularly, the *Yang* Court took notice of the creativity of the video, importance of freedom of expression, and the cultural contribution of the UGC on the one hand, and the small portion of the original work used in the video on the other.

3. Fair Use Facing the Internet Revolution

From 1997 to June 2009, worldwide Internet user levels rose from 2 percent to 24 percent of the population.[49] The internet revolution has increasingly allowed internet users not only to consume copyrighted works, but also to create their own versions of works and post those works on the internet.[50] In working out an appropriate boundary of fair use or legitimate quotation, a balance must be struck between conflicting interests of original works and user-generated contents. However, the boundary of fair use or legitimate quotation in the US and Korea is still unclear. This ambiguity or unclear boundary substantially increases the costs of internet service providers and, also pushes internet users to face many legal risks. The *Lenz* and *Yang* cases are just the tip of a huge iceberg sitting on many more potential disputes. Just as the poor are brutalized in France and England in '*A Tale of Two Cities*,' so too are internet users in the US and Korea, who are all victimized by the ambiguity of fair use.

German Ruling, PUBLIC KNOWLEDGE (Oct. 17, 2008), http:// www.publicknowledge.org/node/1803.

[48] Seoul High Court [Seoul High Ct.], 2010Na35260, Oct. 13, 2010 (S.Kor.).

[49] http://www.internetworldstats.com/stats.htm.

[50] W. Ron Gard and Elizabeth Townsend Gard, The Present (User-Generated Crisis) is the Past (1909 Copyright Act): An Essay Theorizing the 'Traditional Contours of Copyright' Language, 28 Cardozo Arts & Ent. L.J. 455 (2011), at 463; David E. Ashley, The Public as Creator and Infringer: Copyright Law Applied to the Creators of User-Generated Video Content, 20 Fordham Intell. Prop. Media & Ent. L.J. 563 (2010), at 572.

In comparing the copyright laws of the two jurisdictions, it appears the limitations on copyright under the Copyright Act of Korea apply in limited circumstances and, leave more ambiguous areas unresolved than the US copyright law. Many public uses like UGC or internet links on portal news sites require license agreements if the public user or the portal site is to avoid infringement in Korea. However, in France, the limits of the quotation exception emerged clearly as there is no general fair use provision. When several French publishers and authors brought a lawsuit against *Google* for its *Google* Book service, a French Court held that *Google's* provision of 'snippets' of the scanned books did not meet the quotation exception under French Law.[51]

III. TAKEDOWN POLICY AND FAIR USE

(i) Takedown Policy

1. Digital Millennium Copyright Act

The Digital Millennium Copyright Act (DMCA) was enacted to both preserve copyright enforcement on the internet and provide a 'safe harbor' to internet service providers from copyright infringement liability for passive or automatic actions.[52] Internet service providers may qualify for immunity from copyright liability stemming from (a) transitory network communications, (b) system caching, (c) online storage, or (d) linking to/of infringing materials when they satisfy the statutory requirements.[53] When a copyright owner finds infringing material over the internet and requests its internet service provider to takedown the material, then the internet service provider must expeditiously remove, or disable access to, the material. In addition, the internet service provider may terminate its service to 'repeat infringers'.[54] In reality, during the

---

[51] Tribunal de grande instance [TGI] [ordinary court of original jurisdiction] Paris, 3e ch., Dec. 18, 2009, 09/00540, available at http:// www.juriscom.net/ documents/tgiparis20091218.pdf: Seagull Haiyan Song, Reevaluating Fair Use In China—A Comparative Copyright Analysis of Chinese Fair Use Legislation, the U.S. Fair Use Doctrine, and the European Fair Dealing Model, 51 IDEA 453 (2011), at 478; Jane C. Ginsburg, International Issues: Which Country's Law Applies When Works Are Made Available over the Internet?, 34 Colum. J.L. & Arts 49 (2010).

[52] Perfect 10, Inc. v. CCBill, LLC, 340 F.Supp.2d 1077, 71 U.S.P.Q.2d 1568 (C.D.Cal.2004).

[53] 17 U.S.C.A. § 512 (a) through (d).

[54] 17 U.S.C.A. § 512 (i).

course of the takedown procedure, internet service providers usually give a warning message to the alleged infringers that any repeated incidents of copyright infringement could lead to the deletion of their account and all their files.[55] It is beyond doubt that the practice of warning against repeat infringers appears to be a serious threat to internet users. More harmful to the society as a whole is the abuse of takedown notices made by copyright owners targeting competitors, which hurts legitimate end-users[56] or chills free speech.[57]

In response to the notification of 'takedown,' however, the internet users may send a counter-notification requesting restoration of the removed material. Then, the internet service provider replaces the removed material and ceases disabling access to it in not less than 10 or more than 14 business days following receipt of the counter notice.[58] In addition to the possibility of replacement, as was the case in *Lenz*, the internet user may claim damages against any person who 'knowingly materially' misrepresents that the material is indeed infringing.[59] It is not clear yet when a person is regarded as having 'knowingly materially' misrepresented a claim of infringement and whether the copyright owner must have a good faith belief about that.

2. Statutory amendments in Korea

The internet revolution forced not only the US but also Korea to make amendments to their Copyright Acts. Modeled after the DMCA, the Copyright Act of Korea was amended in 2003 to provide a 'safe harbor' to internet service providers.[60] The liability of an internet service provider for infringement by other persons on copyrights or neighboring rights may be reduced or waived in those cases where such internet service provider removes or disables infringing reproduction or transmission when made

---

[55] Lenz v. Universal Music Corp., 572 F. Supp. 2d 1150 (N.D. Cal. 2008) at 1152.

[56] *Google* reported that nearly 40% of the claims were invalid: Keith Black, Technical Knockout: How Mixed Martial Arts will Change Copyright Enforcement on the Web, 21 Fordham Intell. Prop. Media & Ent. L.J. 739 (2011), at 768.

[57] For example, just weeks before the general election, several videos were removed from the McCain campaign's *YouTube* channel: Wendy Seltzer, Free Speech unmoored in Copyright's Safe Harbor: Chilling Effects of the DMCA on the First Amendment, 24 Harv. J.L. & Tech. 171 (2010), at 172.

[58] 17 U.S.C.A. § 512 (g).

[59] 17 U.S.C.A. § 512 (f).

[60] The Copyright Act of Korea was amended on May 27th 2003 by Law No. 6881.

aware of such infringement.[61] The Copyright Act was amended again in 2011[62] to provide detailed requirements for each separate category of internet service providers, such as (a) transitory network communications, (b) system caching, (c) online storage, or (d) linking to/of infringing materials, when they satisfy the statutory requirements.[63]

The Copyright Act also provides a takedown procedure for copyright owners who find infringing materials over the internet. In addition to a takedown procedure, the Copyright Act has adopted a graduated response to what is called the 'three-strikes' mechanism. According to the three-strikes mechanism under the Copyright Act of Korea, the Minister of the Ministry of Culture, Sports and Tourism may request an internet service provider to give a warning notice to an alleged infringer or takedown infringing materials, and further request the internet service provider to suspend or terminate the alleged infringer's internet account after more than three warning notices on their bulletin board after three requests for takedown.[64] As was the case in the French and British legislation for three-strikes,[65] use of the three-strikes approach heightened concerns as to its possible impact on internet users' fundamental rights of free speech and due process.[66]

Regarding the counter-notification, the Copyright Act of Korea allows internet users to request replacement of the removed material. For the purpose of requesting replacement, however, an internet user should prove that his/her reproduction or transmission is based on legitimate rights.[67] Unlike *YouTube* in the *Lenz* case, where *YouTube* re-posted the video approximately six weeks later from the counter-notification by Lenz, the Korean portal site operator NAVER rejected the internet user Yang's request for replacement on the grounds that Yang did not prove any legitimate right to his video file.[68] Actually, Yang could not submit any relevant document to prove his right, but simply claimed that uploading his video file on his blog was a fair use. It is fair to conclude that, because of strict provisions of the Copyright Act of Korea, its internet

---

[61] Article 77 of the Copyright Act of Korea amended on May 27th 2003.

[62] The Copyright Act was amended on June 30th 2011 by Law No. 10807.

[63] Article 102 of the Copyright Act of Korea amended on May 27th 2011.

[64] Jeo jak gwon beop [Copyright Act], art. 133 ¶2 (S.Kor.).

[65] David W. Quist, Three Strikes and You're Out: A Survey of Foreign Approaches to Preventing Copyright Infringement on the Internet, 66 Bus. Law. 261 (2010).

[66] http://www.ipleft.or.kr/node/2552.

[67] Jeo jak gwon beop [Copyright Act], art. 103 ¶3 (S.Kor.).

[68] Seoul High Court [Seoul High Ct.], 2010Na35260, Oct. 13, 2010 (S.Kor.).

users are more vulnerable to the problem of abusive takedown notices than those in the US.

Any person, who requests the reproduction or transmission of works be stopped or replaced without any legitimate rights, shall thereby provide compensation for any damages incurred.[69] Given the statutory provision that copyright owners should prove infringement in order to request takedown, the court in *Yang* interpreted 'those without legitimate rights' as including copyright owners who did not prove infringement. When uploading user-generated content constitutes a fair use of a copyrighted work, the copyright owner does not have any legitimate right to request takedown. Since compensation for damages incurred by takedown or put-back is a type of tort liability, there must be an intention or negligence for recovery. The court in *Yang* found that the defendant, KOMCA, sent to internet portal sites takedown notices against 332,992 video files without any diligent or reasonable review. Accordingly, it was held in *Yang* that the plaintiff copyright owner should pay damages for Yang's mental anguish, which was caused by the defendant's negligent takedown notice.[70]

(ii) The Impact of Fair Use

How does the fair use doctrine affect the takedown mechanism? Are copyright owners expected to engage in a fair use analysis prior to issuing a takedown notice? There have been a variety of views on this issue. Some commentators argue that requiring copyright owners to engage in a fair use analysis creates an improper burden on copyright owners and such a requirement is inconsistent with the overall structure and purpose of the DMCA.[71] By contrast, many more commentators have pointed out the importance of fair use and free speech on the internet and, thus, were in favor of imposing good faith obligation upon copyright owners.[72]

---

[69] Jeo jak gwon beop [Copyright Act], art. 103 ¶6 (S.Kor.).

[70] Seoul High Court [Seoul High Ct.], 2010Na35260, Oct. 13, 2010 (S.Kor.).

[71] Mareasa M. Fortunato, Let's not Go Crazy: Why Lenz v. Universal Music Corp. undermines the Notice and Takedown Process of the Digital Millennium Copyright Act, 17 J. Intell. Prop. L. 147 (2009).

[72] Cattleya M. Concepcion, Beyond the Lens of Lenz: Looking to Protect Fair Use during the Safe Harbor Process under the DMCA, 18 Geo. Mason L. Rev. 219 (2010); Ian Chuang, Be Wary of Adding Your Own Soundtrack: *Lenz v. Universal* and How the Fair Use Policy Should Be Applied to User Generated Content, 29 Loy. L.A. Ent. L. Rev. 163 (2009); Steven D. Jamar, Crafting Copyright Law to Encourage and Protect User-Generated Content in the Internet Social Networking Context, 19 Widener L.J. 843 (2010); Charles W. Hazelwood,

Some of those issues were well reflected in *Lenz v. Universal Music Corp.*[73] Universal emphasized that Section 512(c)(3)(A) of the DMCA does not mention fair use, let alone require a good faith belief that a given use of copyrighted material is not fair use. Universal also contended that even if a copyright owner were required by the DMCA to evaluate fair use with respect to allegedly infringing material, any such duty would arise only after a copyright owner receives a counter-notice and considers filing suit.[74] However, the *Lenz* Court concluded that the fair use of a copyrighted work is not an infringement of copyright, thus, the copyright owner must evaluate whether the allegedly infringing material makes fair use of the copyright before they issue a takedown notice.

The uncertain and uncomfortable situation regarding fair use analysis turned up during the course of takedown procedures in Korea as well. When a person sends a takedown notice without any legitimate rights, they will thereby be liable for any damages incurred under the Act.[75] Although the defendant argued that copyright itself is a legitimate right for a takedown notice, the *Yang* Court held that 'a takedown notice sent without any legitimate rights' includes a case where there is no infringement or, at least, excused infringement.[76]

Despite the court decisions in *Lenz* and *Yang*, it is not clear whether an internet service provider will have to follow a takedown notice if the copyright owner and internet user have conflicting views on fair use. There are a substantial number of debates about whether remix and other UGC constitute fair use.[77] When the copyright owner sends a takedown notice with some fair use analysis and a good faith belief that use of the material in the manner complained of is not authorized, does the internet service provider take down the material even if there is a strong case for fair use? With its relatively subjective standard of reasonableness, the *Lenz* court did not go far enough to eliminate abusive practices on the part of copyright owners.[78] Internet service providers are not obliged to put the mate-

---

Jr., Fair Use and the Takedown/Put Back Provisions of the Digital Millennium Copyright Act, 50 IDEA 307 (2010).

[73] 572 F. Supp. 2d 1150 (N.D. Cal. 2008).

[74] Lenz v. Universal Music Corp., 572 F. Supp. 2d 1150, 1154 (N.D. Cal. 2008) at 1154.

[75] Jeo jak gwon beop [Copyright Act], art. 103 ¶6 (S.Kor.).

[76] Seoul High Court [Seoul High Ct.], 2010Na35260, Oct. 13, 2010 (S.Kor.).

[77] Steven Hetcher, The Kids are Alright: Applying a Fault Liability Standard to Amateur Digital Remix, 62 Fla. L. Rev. 1275 (2010).

[78] Joseph M. Miller, Fair Use through the Lenz of § 512(c) of the DMCA: A Preemptive Defense to a Premature Remedy?, 95 Iowa L. Rev. 1697 (2010), at 1723.

rials back on the internet, unless they receive any proof the materials are not infringing on the copyright under the Copyright Act of Korea.[79] It is not clear, however, to what extent and in what way the internet users have to prove their use constitutes legitimate quotation. Thus, it is inevitable that copyright owners launch a massive campaign of infringement suits against internet users.[80] Facing the abusive practice of takedown notices, the internet service providers and internet users found themselves in an important position.[81]

Regarding the amount of damages, although the court held that fees and costs associated with responding to a takedown notice are recoverable, it is not clear whether lost profits or any other costs resulting from a wrongful takedown notice would be recoverable.[82] As in the case in Korea, if the court awards a nominal amount of damages like $200 for mental stress in *Yang*,[83] the compensation does not really prevent copyright owners and internet service providers from negligent/abusive takedowns. The uncertain and ambiguous fair use doctrine does not really help internet users especially where time-sensitive or controversial subjects are involved.[84]

---

79 Article 103 (3) of the Copyright Act of Korea provides that, 'in those cases where a reproducer/interactive transmitter . . . requests resumption of the reproduction or interactive transmission of works etc. by proving that his reproduction or interactive transmission is based on legitimate rights, an online service provider shall promptly notify the relevant claimant of such request for resumption and a scheduled date of resumption, and resume the reproduction or interactive transmission on such scheduled date'.

80 Christopher M. Swartout, Toward a Regulatory Model of Internet Intermediary Liability: File-Sharing and Copyright Enforcement, 31 Nw. J. Int'l L. & Bus. 499, 508–10 (2011).

81 *Google* reported that more than half of the takedown notices had been from copyright owners targeting competitors; of those, nearly 40% of the claims were invalid: Keith Black, Technical Knockout: How Mixed Martial Arts Will Change Copyright Enforcement on the Web, 21 Fordham Intell. Prop. Media & Ent. L.J. 739 (2011), at 768.

82 Ian Rubenstrunk, The Throw Down over Takedowns: An Analysis of the Lenz Interpretation of 17 U.S.C. § 521(F), 10 J. Marshall Rev. Intell. Prop. L. 792 (2011), at 801.

83 Seoul High Court held that, although damages to property and person are all subject to compensation, evidence indicates nothing more than damages caused by mental stress, that is $200: Seoul High Court [Seoul High Ct.], 2010Na35260, Oct. 13, 2010 (S.Kor.).

84 Charles W. Hazelwood, Jr., Fair Use and the Takedown/Put Back Provisions of the Digital Millennium Copyright Act, 50 IDEA 307 (2010), at 329.

IV. CONCLUSION

Statutory provisions on fair use in the US and Korea are different from each other. Especially in Korea, natural rights theory has had some influence on its fair use provisions. Copyright, as a natural right of an author, should be protected fully, unless specific conditions of private production or quotation are met. Despite the difference in their statutes, the courts apparently share a relatively common goal of balancing conflicting interests of copyright owners and internet users. It is worth noting that the courts in Korea have expanded the quotation exception to accommodate rapid changes in the internet revolution. It is clear, however, that the quotation exception is still uncertain, ambiguous, and limited in its application. Unless some new business models or new technological solutions are worked out,[85] the current copyright law with the quotation exception, as it is, will simply produce an increasing number of young criminals.[86]

The copyright tale of 'two cities' above has demonstrated the plight of internet users facing the internet revolution in the twenty-first century. Due to the ambiguity of fair use or the quotation exception, copyright owners may still send takedown notices in many instances even after fair use analysis. Once a copy is taken down from the internet, internet users may request internet service providers to put it back on, through the basis of fair use in the US. However, internet users in Korea are required to provide appropriate evidence for their legitimate rights like the quotation exception, which is almost impossible to prove.[87] In reality, finding themselves in a David-versus-Goliath battle against copyright conglomerates,[88] most internet users are reluctant to bear the cost and time to fight to the end. Much worse is the threat of the three-strikes rule. Because of its chilling effect, the three-strike rule does not allow sufficient breathing room for the fair use defense.[89]

---

[85] Lauren G. Gallo, The (IM) Possibility of 'Standard Technical Measures' for UGC Websites, 34 Colum. J.L. & Arts 283 (2011).

[86] The number of students who were charged with copyright infringement was 611 in 2006, 2,832 in 2007, and 23,000 in 2008. The number of students who were indicted with copyright infringement was 31 in 2006, 76 in 2007, and 207 in 2008.

[87] Jeo jak gwon beop [Copyright Act], art. 103 ¶3 (S.Kor.).

[88] David E. Ashley, The Public as Creator and Infringer: Copyright Law Applied to the Creators of User-Generated Video Content, 20 Fordham Intell. Prop. Media & Ent. L.J. 563 (2010), at 588.

[89] Eldar Haber, The French Revolution 2.0: Copyright and the Three Strikes Policy, 2 Harv. J. Sports & Ent. L. 297 (2011), at 322.

PART IV

Trademark and Unfair Competition

10. Passing off and unfair competition regimes compared

Mary LaFrance[1]

I. INTRODUCTION

With respect to both registered and unregistered trademarks, there is a distinct cultural difference between legal regimes that give primary importance to the policy of preventing consumer deception, and those that treat this goal as subsumed within the larger goal of regulating competition. For the most part, the narrower goal of consumer protection predominates in the common law countries, while civil law countries have embraced the broader concept of unfair competition.[2] However, approaches to competition are more nuanced than this, and such a two-part classification oversimplifies the cultural conflict. Within the common law and civil law sectors, there are a variety of approaches, and some common law jurisdictions have interpreted the common law doctrine of passing off more broadly than others, although stopping short of a full-fledged law of unfair competition.

In general, the approach of civil law countries elevates the goal of

---

[1] This chapter is based on an article that was originally published in 2011 Mich. St. L. Rev. 1413, and which was awarded the 2012 Ladas Memorial Award in the Professional Category by the International Trademark Association (INTA). The author benefited from the comments of participants in the *Conference on Law and Multi-Agential Governance: The Impact of Law on Market, Competition and/or Innovation,* at the Hokkaido University School of Law, Sapporo, Japan, on Aug. 18–20, 2011, especially Professors Yoshiyuki Tamura, Branislav Hazucha, Adi Ayal, Antonina Bakardjieva Engelbrekt, Shuya Hayashi, Ryu Kojima, Matias Leistner, Ryoko Oki, Masabumi Suzuki, and Noriyuki Yanagawa. The author also thanks Professor Marketa Trimble for her assistance with German materials, and Professor David Vaver for his observations on English case law.

[2] As used here, the term 'unfair competition' refers to the broad civil law doctrine which restricts competitive activities even in the absence of consumer confusion. In the US, however, 'unfair competition' is typically used as a synonym for passing off.

fairness above that of competition and has thus been criticized as anti-competitive. The common law approach tends to make competition the primary goal, treating fairness as a consideration only when a competitor's conduct is particularly extreme. Such extreme conduct may be found, for example, where the competitor's actions are likely to mislead or confuse consumers about the origin or nature of the goods on offer.

While both approaches consider the interests of both consumers and competitors, under the common law approach the interests of consumers have generally been considered to be of primary importance. In contrast, discussions of unfair competition in the civil law countries tend to focus less on consumers and more on generalized, and typically ill-defined, notions of 'fair and honest' behavior by market competitors. In some instances, broad interpretations of unfair competition law display such a reverence for trademarks as to imbue them with something approaching moral rights.

Judge Jacob of the United Kingdom (UK) recognized the tension between the common law tort of passing off and the broader doctrine of unfair competition in *Hodgkinson & Corby Ltd. v. Wards Mobility Services Ltd.*:

> Never has the tort shown even a slight tendency to stray beyond cases of deception. Were it to do so it would enter the field of honest competition, declared unlawful for some reason other than deceptiveness. Why there should be any such reason I cannot imagine. It would serve only to stifle competition.[3]

The culture clash between passing off and unfair competition has come to a head most recently in a series of cases involving comparative advertising, but it can also be seen in the laws pertaining to character and personality merchandising. A similar conflict appears to be emerging in the context of keyword advertising. The divergent approaches to passing off and unfair competition law illustrated by these examples must be taken into account by all trademark owners, in the United States (US) and elsewhere that hope to engage in cross-border marketing of their goods or services.

While significant differences between the passing off and unfair competition regimes remain, the gap has been narrowing. In a piecemeal fashion, case law in common law countries has broadened the concept of passing off to apply to an ever-broadening group of activities.[4] Within

---

[3] [1994] 1 WLR 1564, [1995] FSR 169.

[4] Hazel Carty, *Character Merchandising and the Limits of Passing Off*, 13 Legal Stud. 289, 290 (1993).

the European Union (EU), the conflict between these doctrines has been highlighted; and their convergence hastened, by decisions of the European Court of Justice (ECJ), which has interpreted several harmonization directives in a manner consistent with a broad concept of unfair competition, thus creating pressure on the UK to interpret 'passing off' in a manner far removed from its original meaning. In common law countries that are not bound by EU policy, trademark owners have used their influence over lawmakers to steadily broaden the scope of trademark protection (for both registered and unregistered marks) to avoid the consumer deception requirement for traditional passing off claims, leading in some cases to legislative recognition of dilution[5] and cybersquatting[6] claims. Even where such specific legislation does not apply, trademark owners have often succeeded in persuading courts to give ever-broader scope to the concept of passing off. If this trend continues, many of the differences between the passing off and unfair competition regimes may eventually disappear.

II. TRADITIONAL AND EXPANDED CONCEPTS OF PASSING OFF

The concept of passing off lies at the heart of the system of trademark protection in the common law countries. It is rooted in the common law action for deceit. Although intent to deceive was originally an element of the action, it is no longer required as the focus of the tort has shifted to the effect of the deceit on consumers. While the tort has expanded considerably over time, causing observers to remark on its 'protean qualities,'[7] it still does not approach the broad concept of unfair competition law as recognized in continental Europe, because it is not a general action for misappropriation of the intangible value of a mark.[8]

The essential elements of a traditional passing off claim (often called the 'classic trinity') are: (1) goodwill (an ill-defined term that refers to the consumer's desire to purchase goods because of their association with a mark), (2) misrepresentation as to source, and (3) a likelihood of damage to goodwill as a result of the misrepresentation.[9] In its classic

---

[5] *See* 15 U.S.C. § 1125(c); *see infra* notes 140–42 and accompanying text.

[6] *See id.* § 1125(d).

[7] Carty, *supra* note 4, at 289.

[8] Lionel Bently and Brad Sherman, Intellectual Property Law 711 (3d ed. 2009).

[9] *See* Erven Warnink BV v. J Townend & Sons (Hull) Ltd, [1979] AC 731,

form, passing off occurs when a merchant places a competitor's trademark on goods or services in order to deceive or confuse the rival's customers into purchasing the mislabeled goods. However, different common law jurisdictions have expanded the traditional tort of passing off in a variety of ways. While these expanded versions still fall short of a general law of unfair competition, in some cases they appear to be influenced by similar principles, such as unjust enrichment or 'free riding'.

In the UK, the concept of 'extended form passing off' applies to misrepresentations about the qualities or characteristics of goods.[10] It expands the passing off concept beyond protecting the goods of a particular merchant, instead protecting all merchants who produce a particular category of goods, if the defendant has made a misleading use of the word or phrase that identifies the category. Thus, a likelihood of confusion is still required. However, the goodwill in question is not attached to a trademark and does not belong to a single trader; it belongs collectively to all of the traders who offer goods possessing the qualities characteristic of the category. While only a small number of cases have addressed this form of passing off, plaintiffs have succeeded in claims arising from the misleading use of such terms as 'advocaat,'[11] 'champagne,'[12] 'sherry,'[13] 'Scotch whisky,'[14] 'Harris tweed,'[15] and 'Swiss chocolate'.[16] Recently, a maker of vodka succeeded in bringing such a claim against the manufacturer of VODKAT, an alcoholic beverage which did not meet the legal requirements to be marketed as 'vodka' under European law.[17] The term VODKAT did not resemble the trademark used on any particular brand of vodka, and thus could not be challenged under a traditional passing off theory. Nonetheless, it was actionable under the broader theory because

742 (HL); Reckitt & Colman Ltd. v. Borden, Inc., [1990] RPC 341; BMW Canada, Inc. v. Nissan Canada, Inc., [2007] FCJ No. 991, ¶ 30.

[10] This concept has gained a foothold in Canada as well. *See* John McKeown, *Vodka, Champagne and Passing Off, http://www.casselsbrock.com/Doc/Vodka__Champagne_and_Passing_Off.*

[11] Erven Warnink BV v. J Townsend & Sons, (Hull) Ltd, [1979] AC 731, 742 (HL).

[12] *See* Bollinger v. Costa Brava Wine, [1960] RPC 16 (defendant could not call its sparkling wine 'Spanish champagne' because it would mislead consumers into believing that it came from the Champagne region of France).

[13] Vine Prods. Ltd v. Mackenzie & Co., Ltd., [1969] RPC 1.

[14] John Walker & Sons v. Douglas McGibbon, [1972] SLT 128.

[15] Argyllshire Weavers Ltd v. A Macaulay Tweeds Ltd, [1965] SLT 21.

[16] Chocosuisse Union des Fabricants Suisses de Chocolat v. Cadbury Ltd., [1998] RPC 117, *aff'd,* [1999] RPC 826.

[17] Diageo North America Inc. v. Intercontinental Brands (IBC) Ltd, [2010] EWCA Civ. 920, [2010} EWHC 17 (30 July 2010).

it implicitly misrepresented the nature of the product. The VODKAT case is particularly notable because it was the first to hold that 'extended form passing off' is not limited to prestige or luxury products. Even a generic term such as vodka, in the court's view, has a reputation sufficient to give rise to goodwill. In a separate opinion, Lord Justice Rix expressed concern that by applying the concept of extended form passing off to a generic product such as vodka the court had improperly broadened the doctrine, which had previously been applied only to prestige products (champagne), highly specialized products (advocaat), or products with specific geographic origins (champagne and Swiss chocolate).[18] In Rix's view, passing off should not 'by dint of extensions upon extensions trespass beyond the legitimate area of protection of goodwill into an illegitimate area of anti-competitiveness'.[19] Lord Justice Rix's concerns echo the concerns that have been voiced by other UK judges who perceive a cultural shift in the English law of passing off, away from the traditional focus on protecting marks as source indicators, and toward embracing a general law of unfair competition.

Extended form passing off is not recognized in the US. Instead, the Lanham Act provision on 'false advertising' provides a federal remedy for merchants who are injured by a competitor's false statements about the nature of *either* the competitor's goods *or* the goods of the complaining merchant.[20] However, a false advertising claim under the Lanham Act can succeed only if the competitor's statements are literally false or likely to deceive or confuse consumers;[21] if the claim is not literally false, the plaintiff must prove that consumers were actually misled.[22] Thus, false advertising does not apply to the sale of sparkling wine from California as 'champagne' (which consumers in the US perceive as a generic term), although it would apply if the merchant explicitly claimed, or strongly implied, that the wine was made in France. Similarly, it is unlikely that the VODKAT mark would be actionable as false advertising, unless evidence shows that the name leads a substantial number of consumers to believe that the product is 100 percent vodka.

Another branch of passing off – known as 'false endorsement' – has been recognized in the US, the UK, and Australia. Whereas traditional passing off occurs when the defendant's unauthorized use of an origin

---

[18] *Diageo*, [2010] EWCA Civ. 920, at ¶ 76.

[19] *Id.*

[20] 15 U.S.C. § 1125(a)(1)(B).

[21] Lipton v. Nature Co., 71 F.3d 464, 474 (2d Cir. 1995).

[22] Clorox Co. v. Procter & Gamble Comm. Co., 228 F.3d 24 (1st Cir. 2000); United Indus. Corp. v. Clorox Co., 140 F.3d 1175, 1182 (8th Cir. 1998).

indicator makes consumers likely to believe that the plaintiff is the source of the goods or services offered by the defendants, false endorsement may be found where consumers are likely to believe that the plaintiff endorses, approves, or is somehow affiliated with the defendant's goods or services. In the UK, false endorsement has allowed some celebrities to prevent the unauthorized commercial use of their names or likenesses,[23] in spite of the UK's refusal to recognize a true right of publicity as is recognized in the US. In the US false endorsement claims may be combined with right of publicity claims; however, they can also be used to prevent unauthorized merchandising activities using origin indicators other than names and likenesses, for example, unregistered trademarks. One problem with the false endorsement concept is that courts have had difficulty defining the exact nature of the connection which consumers must perceive between the defendant and the plaintiff.[24] In the UK, for example, Sir Michael Kerr suggested that it was sufficient if the public perceived the plaintiff as somehow 'mixed up' in the defendant's business.[25] In contrast, Lord Justice Millett has suggested that the public must perceive the plaintiff as responsible for the quality of the defendant's goods; a perception of financial support was not enough.[26] The Australian courts struggled with the same question, without finding a clear resolution, in *Hogan v. Koala Dundee* and subsequent cases.[27] It is clear, however, that false endorsement can be found even if the goods or services are dissimilar.[28] Increasingly, courts rely on the public's familiarity with merchandising practices to bolster a finding that false endorsement confusion is likely. For example, in 1991 a UK court found passing off where a defendant used images of the Teenage Mutant Ninja Turtles on clothing without a license; the court reasoned that a substantial portion of the public knows that reproducing characters on goods generally involves a license, thus making it likely that the public would believe the defendant's goods to be licensed.[29]

Passing off has also been extended to misrepresentations regarding the quality of a plaintiff's goods. For example, a UK court found passing off where the defendants sold merchandise that the plaintiff manufacturer

23 Irvine v. Talksport, Ltd., [2002] FSR 60, *aff'd,* [2003] EWCA Civ. 423.

24 Hazel Carty, An Analysis of the Economic Torts 194 (2001).

25 Ewing v. Buttercup Margarine, 34 RPC 232, 237 (1917); Carty, supra note 24, at 194.

26 Harrods v. Harrodian School, 1996 RPC 697; Carty, *supra* note 24, at 194.

27 12 IPR 508 (1988); *see infra* notes 104–13 and accompanying text.

28 Carty, *supra* note 24, at 195.

29 Mirage Studios v. Counter-Feat Clothing Co., Ltd., [1991] FSR 145.

had discarded as substandard, while representing that it was the plaintiff's new, improved product.[30] While the defendants were truthful in representing the plaintiff as the source of the goods, their representation was misleading because it failed to disclose that the goods were not of first quality. This application is also widely accepted in the US,[31] where it is also used to prevent importation of grey market goods.[32]

Another expansion of traditional passing off recognized in several common law jurisdictions is a concept known as 'reverse,' 'inverse,' or 'upside down' passing off, which applies when the defendant offers the plaintiff's goods to the public while falsely identifying them as the defendant's own goods, or where the defendant falsely attributes to its own goods qualities that are present in the plaintiff's goods, for example, by using photographs or samples of the plaintiff's goods or by quoting testimonials from customers referring to the plaintiff's goods.[33] The UK courts have only reluctantly embraced this tort;[34] it has been more frequently invoked in the US.[35]

In both the UK and the US, however, the most common application does not involve the actual sale of the plaintiff's goods under the defendant's name; rather, it involves a type of false advertising which misrepresents the quality of the defendant's goods. This activity does not utilize the plaintiff's goodwill, because it does not mention the plaintiff's trademark or trade name. Arguably, it is not passing off at all.[36] The concept of reverse passing off seems much closer to an unfair competition claim, because what is being appropriated is not the plaintiff's goodwill (since the defendant does not even refer to the plaintiff as the source of the goods), but the plaintiff's creativity and effort in creating a quality product. This

---

30 Spalding v. Gamage, (1915) RPC 273 (HL); Carty, *supra* note 24, at 191.

31 *See, e.g.,* Davidoff & Cie, S.A. v. PLD Int'l Corp., 263 F.3d 1297, 1301–02 (11th Cir. 2001).

32 *See, e.g.,* Societe des Produits Nestle, S.A. v. Casa Helvetia, Inc., 982 F.2d 633, 644 (1st Cir. 1992).

33 Carty, *supra* note 24, at 195–6.

34 Carty, *supra* note 24, at 196; *see* Matthew Gloag & Son Ltd. v. Welsh Distilleries Ltd., [1998] FSR 718, 724; John Roberts Powers School v. Tessensohn, [1995] FSR 947; Bristol Conservatories Ltd. v. Conservatories Custom Built Ltd, [1989] RPC 455.

35 A larger number of courts in the US have purported to apply it, but on closer inspection these cases have actually involved false advertising. *See* Mary LaFrance, *When You Wish Upon Dastar: Creative Provenance and the Lanham Act,* 23 Cardozo Arts & Ent. L. Rev. 197, 207–09 (2005).

36 Lionel Bently and Brad Sherman, Intellectual Property Law 755 (2009).

amounts to a claim of misappropriation,[37] which common law regimes have generally been reluctant to recognize. On the other hand, reverse passing off fits within the overall purpose of passing off law, which is to prevent consumer deception.

III. UNFAIR COMPETITION

Article 10bis of the Paris Convention for the Protection of Industrial Property requires signatories to provide protection against unfair competition, which is defined as 'any act of competition contrary to honest practices in industrial or commercial matters'.[38] The only acts expressly proscribed by Art. 10bis are those that create confusion with the business of a competitor, those which falsely discredit a competitor's business, and those which mislead the public as to the characteristics of the goods being offered. All three of these activities involve deception,[39] which is the basis for the doctrine of passing off as recognized in common law jurisdictions. Yet most civil law jurisdictions interpret unfair competition to include many practices that do not involve deception. According to the ECJ, the requirement of 'honest practices in industrial or commercial matters,' as reproduced in Article 6(1) of the EC Trademarks Directive,[40] implies a 'duty to act fairly in relation to the legitimate interests of the trademark owner,'[41] language which leaves much room for interpretation, and which has been criticized as 'circular'.[42] The ECJ has identified as 'unfair' not only those uses that misleadingly suggest a commercial connection between two parties, but also those which take 'unfair advantage of [the] distinctive character or repute' of a mark, those which discredit or denigrate a mark, and those which present a product as 'an imitation or replica' of the trademark owner's product.[43]

The term 'free riding' has been used to describe the kinds of non-deceptive activities that may constitute unfair competition. The World

---

[37] In the US, the misappropriation tort has largely been limited to 'hot news,'based on the facts of International News Service v. Associated Press, 248 U.S. 215 (1918).

[38] Art. 10bis(1)–(2).

[39] *See* Tom Alkin, *Should There Be a Tort of 'Unfair Competition' in English Law?,* 3 J. Intell. Prop. L. & Prac. 48 (2008).

[40] First Council Directive 89/104/EEC (Dec. 21, 1988).

[41] Gillette Co. v. L-A Laboratories Oy, [2005] FSR 37, 2005 ECJ EUR-Lex LEXIS 41;2005 ECR I-02337 (Mar. 17, 2005).

[42] Alkin, *supra* note 39, at 49.

[43] *Gillette,* [2005] FSR at 37.

Intellectual Property Organization (WIPO) has defined 'free riding' as 'any act that a competitor or another market participant undertakes with the intention of directly exploiting another person's industrial or commercial achievement for his own business purposes without substantially departing from the original achievement'.[44]

Civil law jurisdictions have used difference mechanisms to develop their unfair competition doctrines. Some countries have developed their unfair competition law through judicial interpretation of a general provision in the civil code (*e.g.*, France, Italy, and the Netherlands).[45] In other countries, unfair competition doctrines are based on specific legislation (*e.g.*, Austria, Belgium, Denmark, Finland, Germany, Japan, Luxembourg, Peru, Korea, Spain, Sweden, and Switzerland) or specific provisions within broader legislation (*e.g.*, Bolivia, Brazil, Bulgaria, Canada, Colombia, Hungary, Mexico, Peru, Rumania, and Venezuela).[46]

In France, unfair competition law derives from a general tort liability statute, Art. 1382 of the French Civil Code. Two categories of unfair competition have been recognized: (1) concurrence deloyale (interference with competition), and (2) concurrence parasitaire (free riding). Concurrence deloyale generally requires confusion, but it does not require competition.[47] Concurrence parasitaire does not even require confusion.[48] For example, a French court found concurrence parasitaire when a candy company began marketing its candy bars in 3-packs of 300g bars, which was the same configuration already in use by the plaintiff, its more established competitor, which held a 42 percent market share. Without finding any confusing similarity in the brand names or trade dress, the court relied on the principle of unjust enrichment to hold that the defendant was unfairly 'profiteering from the success' of the plaintiff.[49]

As the French decision illustrates, deception and confusion are not required in order to establish a claim of unfair competition in most civil

---

44 WIPO, Protection Against Unfair Competition 55 (1994) (WIPO Pub. No. 725(E)).

45 Anselm Kamperman Sanders, Unfair Competition Law 23 (1997).

46 *Id.* In France, the law is Art. 1382 of the Civil Code. In Italy, it is Art. 2598 of the 1942 Civil Code.

47 Sanders, *supra note* 45, at 24–7.

48 Judgment of October 20, 1993, Cour d'appel, Versailles, [1994] R.J.D.A., No. 751, *discussed in* 1–9 Doing Business in France § 9.04[3].

49 Societe Mars Alimentaire v. Societe Aegean Trade Cy and Istanbul Gida Dis Ticaret As, Paris 17.5.1993, [1993] PIBD no. 550 III–522; [1993] EIPR D-282. This case is discussed in A.W.J. Kamperman Sanders, Unjust Enrichment, The New Paradigm for Unfair Competition Law? 15–18 (The Intellectual Property Institute 1996).

law regimes. Indeed, some civil law jurisdictions treat 'slavish imitation' of product features as actionable unfair competition, regardless of whether those features are protected by intellectual property laws or whether the imitation leads to consumer confusion.[50] For example, German unfair competition laws have protected fashion designs even though they are not eligible for protection under more specific intellectual property laws.[51] The application of unfair competition laws to otherwise-lawful imitations seems to be based on the notion that the imitator is improperly appropriating (usually with minimal cost or effort) the benefits of another party's creative investment.[52] In Spain, imitation is unlawful if it is 'systematic' and designed to impede a competitor to a degree beyond 'a normal market response'.[53] Not surprisingly, the line between lawful and unlawful imitation has often been difficult to draw.[54]

IV. CONFLICT AND CONVERGENCE: THREE CASE STUDIES

Within the EU, the culture clash between the narrower common law concept of passing off and the broader scheme of regulation under unfair competition law has led Lord Justice Jacob of the UK to lament that 'European trademark law is in danger of becoming a forest of case law where everyone loses their way.'[55] As discussed below, three areas of litigation provide useful case studies of the conflicts and convergence between passing-off regimes and unfair competition regimes – (1) copycat products and comparative advertising, (2) merchandising, and (3) keyword advertising.

(i) Copycat Products and Comparative Advertising

The application of trademark law to 'copycat' products and comparative advertising illuminates the divide between the Anglo-American approach

---

50 Sanders, *supra* note 45, at 27, 39, 49; Christopher Heath, The Law of Unfair Competition in Japan 120–40 (2001) (comparing approaches to slavish imitation in Europe and Japan).

51 Heath, *supra* note 50, at 122–3.

52 *Id.* at 122–3.

53 *Id.* at 123 (citing § 11 of Spain⊠s Unfair Competition Act 3/1991).

54 *Id.* at 128–9, 136–40.

55 O2 Holdings Ltd. v. Hutchison 3G UK Ltd., [2006] EWCA Civ 1656, [2007] RPC 407, ¶ 35 (Jacob, L.J.).

to unfair competition and the approach that predominates in civil law countries. Passing-off regimes tend to encourage relatively unbridled comparative advertising, except where it is misleading. They also impose no restrictions on products which imitate other products, provided that the imitation does not mislead (for example, by imitating a competitor's trade dress in a way that misleads consumers as to the origin of the goods), and does not infringe rights protected by copyright and patent laws.

In the US, comparative advertising is a highly valued type of commercial speech. The only requirement is that it be truthful – or at least not demonstrably false in its assertions of fact. There is a high tolerance for 'puffery,' which refers to vague claims that one product is superior to others, without any specific factual assertions to support those claims. For the most part it is permissible to disparage a competitor's products, again provided that there are no demonstrably false assertions of fact.[56] In truthful comparative advertising, it is acceptable to identify competitors by their trademarks. This policy applies regardless of whether the advertising claims that the products are similar, or claims that one party's product is superior to the other's. It is also acceptable to ridicule or disparage a competitor's products, so long as there is no factual misrepresentation. For example, in television ads aired during Super Bowl broadcasts, rivals Coke and Pepsi, and Miller and Anheuser-Busch, have frequently ridiculed their competitors' products (and sometimes their competitors' customers); in a popular and long-running series of television ads, Apple Computer has stereotyped Microsoft products (and implicitly their loyal customers) as stodgy, overweight, conventional, and bland.

Copycat products are permissible in the US as long as they do not violate intellectual property rights (patents, copyrights, trade dress, or trade secrets). Where a vendor offers a non-infringing product that is identical to the product of a famous brand, it is lawful to advertise it as such, and to identify the famous brand by its trademark. Thus, for example, generic or 'house brand' medications which contain the same active ingredient as the products offered by brand-name competitors may

---

[56] The case of Deere & Co. v. MTD Products, 41 F.3d 39 (2d Cir. 1994) is the exception that arguably proves the rule. In that case, the Second Circuit found actionable dilution where the defendant's ad portrayed the plaintiff's 'running deer' trademark in a disparaging way (presenting the deer as fearful and intimidated by the competitor's product). The court's finding of liability was based on a dilution theory rather than a passing-off or general unfair competition theory. The decision has been roundly criticized, and does not represent mainstream thinking under prevailing dilution theory in the US.

be advertised as such. This policy applies equally to 'copycat' perfumes.[57] Thus, it is lawful to sell a copycat perfume and to identify, in advertising or any other promotional materials or labels, the famous perfume which it imitates. The comparative advertising right is, however, limited by the passing off concept that underlies the law of trademark infringement, that is, the famous maker's trademark must not be used in a way that would confuse consumers about the origin of the copycat product. Thus, if the famous 'Chanel No.5' trademark were featured too prominently on the label of the copycat perfume bottle, this could lead some consumers to believe that the copycat product and genuine Chanel No.5 are offered by the same maker. This would be a classic case of passing off.

Civil law regimes have historically taken a highly restrictive approach to comparative advertising, sometimes prohibiting it altogether.[58] For example, Germany traditionally took the view that 'practically all forms of comparative advertising, even if true, [are] unfair competition – the notion was that the newcomer should not 'piggyback' on the established reputation of another'.[59] In France, truthful comparative advertising is permitted only if it objectively compares essential, pertinent, verifiable, and representative characteristics of the products;[60] a claim of unfair competition will arise if the defendant's advertising, even if truthful, makes derogatory or personal attacks against the plaintiff.[61]

The recent trend in the EU, however, has been toward liberalization.[62] This trend culminated in the 1997 Comparative Advertising Directive (CAD), which instructs member states to permit comparative advertising under specified conditions.[63] Several of these conditions are directed toward the narrow goal of preventing consumer confusion as to the origin or qualities of goods and services, and thus are entirely consistent with the approach of passing-off regimes.[64] Others, however, go well beyond

---

57 Smith v. Chanel, 402 F.2d 562, 566 (9th Cir. 1968).

58 *See* 2–31 The Law of Advertising § 31.04 (2011).

59 O2 Holdings Ltd. v. Hutchison 3G UK Ltd., [2006] EWCA Civ 1656, [2007] RPC 407, ¶ 41 (Jacob, L.J.).

60 Consumer Code Art. L. 121–8.

61 Judgment of March 23, 1999, Cass. Com. No 96-22.334; Judgment of May 31, 1996, TGI Paris, Europe 1 Telecompagnie v. NR, *discussed in* 1–9 Doing Business in France § 9.04[4] (2010).

62 2–31 The Law of Advertising § 31.04 (2011).

63 Directive 97/55/EC (amending Directive 84/450/EEC). The 1997 Directive was replaced in 2006 with Directive 2006/114/EC (hereinafter CAD). The comparative advertising restrictions discussed in the text are retained in the 2006 version.

64 CAD, Art. 4(a), (h).

this goal and reflect the values of unfair competition law. Most notably, Article 4 of the CAD permits comparative advertising provided that:

> (c) it objectively compares one or more material, relevant, verifiable and representative features of those goods and services;
> (d) it does not discredit or denigrate the trademarks, trade names, other distinguishing marks, goods, services, activities or circumstances of a competitor;
> . . .
> (f) it does not take unfair advantage of the reputation of a trademark, trade name, or other distinguishing marks of a competitor or of the designation of origin of competing products; [and]
> (g) it does not present goods or services as imitations or replicas of goods or services bearing a protected trademark or trade name.[65]

Until recently, the UK approached comparative advertising in the same way as the US, encouraging such advertising as fundamentally pro-competitive. That was before the case of *L'Oreal SA v. Bellure NV*. At issue here was the question whether the makers of copycat perfumes could name the famous perfumes they imitated on comparison lists that disclosed to consumers which of the defendants' products corresponded to each of the famous perfumes. The Court of Appeal of England and Wales referred several questions to the ECJ concerning the precise relationship between the EC trademarks directive (which grants broad protection to trademarks against those who would denigrate or take 'unfair advantage' of their reputations) and the CAD.[66] There was no question of consumer confusion, and thus no passing off.[67]

The ECJ ruled that the prohibition against using a competitor's trademark in comparative advertising applied not only in the case of counterfeit goods but also in the case of 'any imitation or replica,' that such use was prohibited even if the advertisement was not misleading or likely to confuse consumers, and that such use, by its very nature, took 'unfair advantage' of the competitor's trademark.[68] The court noted that the policy of EU trademark law was to protect all of the functions of a trademark, not only its function as an origin indicator and a guarantee of product quality, but also the functions of 'communication, investment or advertising'.[69]

---

65 *Id.* Art. 4(c), (d), (f), (g).

66 *L'Oreal SA v. Bellure NV*, [2007] EWCA Civ. 968, ¶ 164 (Oct. 10, 2007).

67 'Consumers are not stupid. They will not see the cheap copy as being the same in quality as the original. They will see it for what it is and no more.' *Id.* at ¶ 63. (Jacob, L.J.).

68 L'Oreal SA v. Bellure NV, C-487/07 (June 18, 2009), ¶¶ 73–4, 79.

69 *Id.* at ¶58.

This ruling was not well-received in the UK, where Lord Justice Jacob declared that the ECJ had placed a 'muzzle' on lawful competitive activity, infringing the defendants' rights of free speech, and impairing the consumer's right to receive information about competing products.[70] He also labeled the ECJ's policy anticompetitive.[71] In particular, he suggested that 'countries with a healthy attitude to competition law, such as the US, would not keep a perfectly lawful product off the market by the use of trademark law to suppress truthful advertising'.[72] He accused the ECJ of failing to define what constitutes 'unfair' advantage, and allowing its disapproval of the defendants' business to influence its decision:

> I regret that the ECJ in this case has not addressed the competition aspects of what it calls 'riding on the coattails'. The trouble with deprecatory metaphorical expressions such as this ('free-riding' is another), containing as they do clear disapproval of the defendants' trade as such, is that they do not provide clear rules by which a trader can know clearly what he can and cannot do.[73]

Finally, he questioned the ECJ's assertion that the law should protect the 'communication, investment or advertising' functions of a mark, as distinct from its function as an origin indicator; Jacob saw no basis in the legislation for protecting these functions, and found them 'vague and ill-defined'.[74] He also saw 'no rational basis' for the ECJ's holding that lawful imitations should be treated the same as counterfeits under the comparative advertising directive.[75]

The ECJ's ruling was promptly criticized by researchers at the Max Planck Institute, who noted, with respect to the court's restriction of truthful commercial speech, that '[w]hereas French courts would not have blinked at the suggestion, English judges are harder to convince'.[76] One Max Planck researcher called for repeal of Art. 4(g) of the CAD.[77]

---

70 *L'Oreal SA v. Bellure NV*, [2010] EWCA Civ. 535, [2010] RPC 23 (May 21, 2010) ¶¶ 7–15.

71 *Id.* at ¶ 16–19.

72 *Id.* at ¶20.

73 *Id.* at ¶17.

74 *Id.* at ¶¶ 29–30.

75 *Id.* at ¶39.

76 Annette Kur, Lionel A.F. Bently, Ansgar Ohly, *Sweet Smells and a Sour Taste – The ECJ's L'Oreal Decision,* Max Planck Institute for Intellectual Property, Competition & Tax Law Research Paper No. 09-12, University of Cambridge Faculty of Law Research Paper No. 10/01 (Aug. 17, 2009).

77 Annette Kur, The Future of the Advertising Function (Max Planck Institute Mar. 23, 2011).

As Lord Justice Jacob pointed out with evident satisfaction, the ECJ's opinion has been roundly criticized in other quarters as well.[78]

(ii) Merchandising Rights

In the analysis of disputes over unauthorized merchandising, a similar tension exists between the narrow approach of passing off and the broader concept of unfair competition. However, the concept of passing off in some common law jurisdictions has expanded to more closely resemble unfair competition law.

Generally speaking, the concept of merchandising involves using a mark on goods not specifically to identify their origin, but to capitalize on consumers' affection for the mark. Merchandising often involves placing a popular mark on goods that are different from the goods for which the mark is famous, for example, placing the Ferrari mark on a T-shirt. A merchandising right may be asserted with respect to a registered mark or a wide variety of unregistered marks, for example, the titles of films, television shows, or videogames; the names or likenesses of athletes, entertainers, or other celebrities; and the names or likenesses of fictional characters. In some instances, unauthorized merchandising involves the use of copyrighted images (for example, where the use involves the image of a fictional character, such as Mickey Mouse), in which case the complaint would probably include both copyright and trademark claims. This discussion, however, focuses solely on trademark claims (registered or unregistered) that arise from unauthorized merchandising.

Under the approach of the civil law countries in the EU, the unauthorized use of a trademark, a fictional character, or a celebrity's name or likeness will often be actionable even if consumers would not believe that there was any endorsement or licensing arrangement, because under the law of unfair competition this is a type of 'free riding' on the reputation of the celebrity or the owner of the mark. In France, even if there is no competitive link between the parties' goods, unauthorized merchandising would be addressed under the doctrine of 'agissements parasitaires'.[79] In Germany, both registered and unregistered marks that have prestige value

---

[78] *See, e.g.,* Darren Meale and Joel Smith, *Enforcing a Trademark When Nobody's Confused: Where the Law Stands after L'Oreal and Intel,* 5 Journal of Intellectual Property Law & Practice 96, 103 (2010); Dev Gangjee and Robert Burrell, *Because You're Worth It: L'Oreal and the Prohibition on Free Riding*, 73(2) Modern Law Review 282 (2010).

[79] Patrick Martowicz, *France,* in Heijo Ruisenaars, Character Merchandising in Europe 121 (2003).

are protected against actions which exploit their reputation.[80] Unfair competition remedies for unauthorized merchandising have been especially strong in Austria. When the emblem of an English football club was used on merchandise without the club's consent, the Austrian Supreme Court held the defendant liable for parasitic exploitation of the club's image and reputation, emphasizing that the reason the emblem was attractive to consumers was because it signified the club's achievements, which were the result of the club's efforts and expenditures.[81] The Court has consistently applied the same rationale (effort/expense/achievement) in later cases involving noncompeting goods and services.[82]

Nonetheless, there are exceptions, even in countries where the civil law ordinarily provides strong protection for the reputations of well-stablished marks. In 2010, Germany's highest court refused to find either a likelihood of confusion or the taking of 'unfair advantage' where a defendant sold remote-controlled scale-model replicas of the Opel Astra which featured the Opel logo (a registered trademark) affixed to the grille.[83] Even though Opel had registered this mark both for motor vehicles and toys, the Bundesgerichtshof (BGH) considered the fact that the replica car market in Germany had existed since the late 19th century, and concluded that German consumers would perceive the presence of the mark simply as one of the details necessary to making an accurate replica of the Opel Astra. A European commentator notes, however, that in other civil law jurisdictions the same facts might lead to a different conclusion, 'taking into account "local" customs and views relating to (toy) cars'.[84]

In some civil law regimes, unfair competition laws do not encompass every instance of unauthorized merchandising, because the laws impose a secondary meaning requirement or require a competitive relationship between the parties.[85] The International Association for the Protection of Industrial Property (AIPPI) has urged these countries to expand their unfair competition laws in order to eliminate these restrictions.[86]

---

[80] Christian Schertz and Susanne Bergmann, *Germany,* in Ruisenaars, *supra* note 79, at 136–7.

[81] Reinhard Schanda, *Austria,* in Ruisenaars, *supra* note 79, at 23 (discussing OGH 17.9.1996 – Football Association – OBl 1997, 83).

[82] *Id.* at 23–4 (collecting cases).

[83] Adam Opel AG v. Autec AG, Case 48/05, 2007 ECJ EUR-Lex LEXIS 1972;2007 ECR I-01017 (Jan. 25, 2007); Opel-Blitz II, Case 1 ZR 88/08, Bundesgerichtshof (Jan. 14, 2010).

[84] Birgit Clark, *Bundesgerichtshof decides in the Opel/Autec car case,* 5 J. Intell. Prop. L. & Prac. 213–14 (2010).

[85] Ruijsenaars, *supra* note 79, at 8.

[86] *Id.* at 9.

Under the traditional English law of passing off, a mark is not infringed unless it is used to misrepresent the origin of goods or services. A series of cases in the 1970s established that unauthorized merchandising was not passing off because the mark appealed to consumers without indicating the origin of the goods; passing off would occur only if consumers would infer that quality control was being exercised by the party authorized to license the mark.[87] Unlike the US, the UK does not recognize a right of publicity; thus, English courts generally do not recognize a cause of action for unauthorized commercial appropriation of a celebrity's name or likeness, even where the plaintiff disguises the claim as one of 'false endorsement.' For example, members of the musical group *Abba* could not prevent the use of their images on T-shirts and other products,[88] and the *Spice Girls* could not win a passing off claim against a defendant that made stickers featuring their likenesses.[89] However, a well-known racing car driver had a passing off claim when a radio station used his likeness in an ad that implied that he endorsed the radio station; the court used the false endorsement branch of passing off, concluding that consumers might actually believe that the driver endorsed the station.[90] And while the traditional English approach to passing off allowed a football club's insignia to be used on clothing as a "badge of allegiance" when there was no likelihood of confusion as to source, under the expanded approach to passing off this conclusion was no longer tenable.[91] As these cases illustrate, the line between false endorsement and 'mere' commercial appropriation is difficult to discern. As recently as 1999, however, English courts continued to reject the claim of a merchandising right in a celebrity's identity.[92]

---

[87] Taverner Rutledge v. Trexpalm, [1977] RPC 275; Lyngstad v. Anabas, [1977] FSR 62; Wombles Ltd. v. Sombles Skips Ltd., [1977] RPC 99.

[88] Lyngstad v. Anabas Prods., Ltd., [1977] RPC 275.

[89] *See* Halliwell v. Panini (Lightman, J.) (June 6, 1997) (unreported); BBC Worldwide Ltd. v. Pally Screen Printing , [1998] FSR 665 (failure to label stickers as 'not authorized' was not implicit misrepresentation that they were authorized).

[90] Irvine v. Talksport, Ltd., [2002] FSR 60, *aff'd,* [2003] EWCA Civ. 423; *see* M. Learmouth, *Eddie, Are You OK? Product Endorsement and Passing Off,* [2002] IPQ 306.

[91] Arsenal Football Club Plc v. Reed, [2003] EWCA Civ. 696 , *rev'g* [2001] RPC 46; *see also BBC Worldwide,* [1998] FSR at 674 (finding it possible that buyers of T-shirts with Teletubbies images would not perceive this as an indication of source or endorsement).

[92] Elvis Presley Enters., Inc. v. Sid Shaw Elvisly Yours, [1999] RPC 567, 597–8. A court in Hong Kong followed a similar rule in Lau Tak Andy v. Hang Seng Bank Ltd., [2000] 1 HKC 280, which refused to enjoin the use of a celebrity's image on credit cards because this did not represent to the public that the celebrity endorsed or licensed the cards.

In general, the UK courts have been reluctant to expand the passing off doctrine to create a merchandising right in fictional characters.[93] While the use of a celebrity's name or likeness might in some cases imply endorsement of a product, it is more difficult to make that argument with respect to the names or images of fictional characters, since their fictional existence makes it impossible that such a character would literally 'endorse' a product.[94] For many years, English courts rejected character merchandising claims on the ground that the plaintiff and the defendant were not engaged in a 'common field of activity'.[95] More recently, English courts have relied less on the 'common field of activity' restriction, but have still declined to find misrepresentation unless the defendant affirmatively represents that the use of the character is authorized, for example, by claiming that the merchandise is 'official'.[96] Even this may be changing, however. In the 1991 case of *Mirage Studios v. Counter-Feat Clothing Co., Ltd.*, an English court found that the unlicensed use of the Teenage Mutant Ninja Turtles on clothing constituted passing off; the court reasoned that a substantial portion of the public is aware that reproducing characters on goods generally involves a license, thus making it likely that the public would believe the defendant's goods to be licensed, even though the owner of the characters did not at that time license them in the UK.[97] Commentators have noted that it is difficult to distinguish between use of a character as a source indicator and use of the character as mere product decoration.[98] This is almost the same distinction as the elusive one, noted earlier, between false endorsement and mere appropriation of a celebrity's likeness.[99]

---

[93] Among the many cases refusing to find passing off are: McCulloch v. May (1948) 65 RPC 58 (radio character); Conan Doyle v. London Mystery Magazine, Ltd (1949) 66 RPC 312 (Sherlock Holmes); Wombles v. Womble Skip [1977] RPC 99 (Wombles of Wimbledon); Lygnstad v. Anabas, [1977] FSR 62 (ABBA group); BBC Worldwide v. Pally Screen Printing, [1998] FSR 665 (Teletubbies).

[94] *See* Carty, *supra* note 4, at 291.

[95] *See id.* at 294–5 (collecting cases).

[96] Elvis Presley Trademarks, [1997] RPC 543, 558 (Laddie, J.) ; Wilkie v. McCulloch, (1823) 2 S. 413; Arsenal FC plc v. Reed, [2001] RPC 922 (Laddie, J.) (no passing off because defendant made clear that his goods were not official Arsenal merchandise); *see* Hector MacQueen, Charlotte Waelde, Graeme Laurie, Contemporary Intellectual Property: Law and Policy 779 (2011).

[97] Mirage Studios v. Counter-Feat Clothing Co., Ltd., [1991] FSR 145.

[98] Carty, *supra* note 4, at 293.

[99] It has been predicted that the UK will have to broaden its protection for merchandising rights in order to comply with § 5(2) of the EU Trademark Directive, which provides that member states may forbid the use of registered marks, even on dissimilar goods, when (1) the mark has a reputation, and (2) the

Under the more liberal approach to passing off embraced in the US, unauthorized merchandising activity is typically actionable under a false endorsement theory even if consumers would be unlikely to believe that the trademark owner (or celebrity) is the actual *source* of the defendant's goods. One of the broadest endorsements of this application of passing off came from the Fifth Circuit, in a case that upheld a university's right to prevent the use of its distinctive colors and insignia on unauthorized merchandise. While acknowledging that consumers might not care whether the merchandise they purchased was officially licensed by the university, the court held that they would in fact believe that this merchandise was licensed. The court's reference to 'free riding' suggests that its broad notion of passing off is strongly influenced by unfair competition concepts:

> [Defendant's] use of the Universities' colors and indicia is designed to create the illusion of affiliation with the Universities and essentially obtain a 'free ride' by profiting from confusion among the fans of the Universities' football teams who desire to show support for and affiliation with those teams. This creation of a link in the consumer's mind between the T-shirts and the Universities and the intent to directly profit therefrom results in 'an unmistakable aura of deception' and likelihood of confusion.[100]

However, there is some conflict even among the federal courts. While many courts are willing to infer some likelihood of confusion in these cases,[101] others have held that no infringement exists when the consumer is likely to perceive the mark simply as ornamentation or as a badge of

---

use of the mark 'takes unfair advantage of, or is detrimental to, the distinctive character or the repute of the trademark.' Carty, *supra* note 4, at 292. It should be noted, however, that this language is permissive rather than mandatory, and it applies only to registered marks.

[100] Louisiana State Univ. v. Smack Apparel, 550 F.3d 465, 484–5 (5th Cir. 2008). This language echoes a passage from the same court's prior decision in Boston Professional Hockey Ass'n v. Dallas Cap & Emblem Mfg., 510 F.2d 1004 (5th Cir. 1975), which held that the sale of patches bearing another's trademark could infringe even if the patches were not already attached to other merchandise. The court held that the patches themselves were the infringing goods, and that it was 'irrelevant' whether or not the consumers were confused about the source of the patches: 'The argument that confusion must be as to the source of the manufacture of the emblem itself is unpersuasive, where the trademark, originated by the team, is the triggering mechanism for the sale of the emblem.' *Smack Apparel,* 510 F.2d at 1012; *accord,* Boston Athletic Ass'n v. Sullivan, 867 F.2d 22 (1st Cir. 1989).

[101] *Smack Apparel,* 550 F.3d at 484–5; Boston Athletic Ass'n v. Sullivan, 867 F.2d 22 (1st Cir. 1989); University of Georgia Athletic Ass'n v. Laite, 756 F.2d 1535 (11th Cir. 1985); Boston Professional Hockey Ass'n v. Dallas Cap & Emblem Mfg., 510 F.2d 1004 (5th Cir. 1975).

allegiance. Some courts have reached this result by applying an exception for the 'functional' use of a mark,[102] or by finding that there is no likelihood of confusion as to source or sponsorship.[103]

Australia has yet to choose between the stricter and more liberal interpretations of passing off. There is conflicting case law on unauthorized merchandising, with some courts adopting an approach close to that of the civil law countries, under which the owner of the mark can recover if consumers make some sort of association between the defendant's goods and the owner of the mark, even if they do not believe there is a commercial arrangement.[104]

However, the Australian courts have not reached a consensus on the nature of the association which consumers must perceive. In the 1960 case of *Henderson v. Radio Corp. Pty. Ltd.*,[105] the New South Wales Supreme Court held that the unauthorized use of two dancers' images on a record sleeve constituted passing off because consumers would believe that the dancers endorsed or approved the recording. However, the court also advanced a second ground for its decision – that the dancers' reputation

---

[102] *See, e.g.,* International Organization of Job's Daughters v. Lindenburg and Co., 633 F.2d 912, 917–19 (9th Cir. 1980); University of Pittsburgh v. Champion Prods., Inc., 566 F.Supp. 711, 720–21 (C.D. Pa. 1983). The Ninth Circuit initially applied the *Job's Daughters* analysis to reject a merchandising claim involving the 'Betty Boop' character in Fleischer Studios, Inc. v. A.V.E.L.A., Inc., 636 F.3d 1115 (9th Cir. 2011), but it later withdrew this part of the opinion without explanation, Fleischer Studios, Inc. v. A.V.E.L.A., Inc., 2011 U.S. App. LEXIS 17220 (Aug. 19, 2011). The withdrawn opinion in *Fleischer Studios* also cautioned that extending trademark protection to the merchandising of public domain character images would allow an end-run around the limited term of copyright protection. *Fleischer Studios*, 636 F.3d at 1124.

[103] Board of Governors of Univ. of North Carolina v. Helpingstine, 714 F.Supp. 167, 173 (M.D.N.C. 1989); University of Pittsburgh v. Champion Prods., Inc., 566 F.Supp. 711, 719–20 (C.D. Pa. 1983). Scholarly commentary on merchandising rights is also divided. *See, e.g.,* Irene Calboli, *The Case for a Limited Protection of Trademark Merchandising,* 11 U.Ill. L.Rev. 865 (2011); Stacey L. Dogan and Mark A. Lemley, *The Merchandising Right: Fragile Theory or Fait Accompli?,* 54 Emory L.J. 461 (2005); Robert C. Denicola, *Institutional Publicity Rights: An Analysis of the Merchandising of Famous Trade Symbols,* 62 N.C.L. Rev. 603 (1984).

[104] *See* Hogan v. Koala Dundee, 12 IPR 508 (1988) (finding false endorsement where store's trade dress imitated items closely associated with Paul Hogan's character in 'Crocodile Dundee' film); Pacific Dunlop v. Hogan, 87 ALR 14 (1987) (ad which imitated scene from Crocodile Dundee constituted misrepresentation of commercial origin); Henderson v. Radio Corp. Pty., Ltd, [1960] SR (NSW) 576 (finding false endorsement where dancers' likenesses appeared on record sleeve).

[105] [1960] SR (NSW) 576 (rejecting 'common field of activity' requirement).

had been wrongfully appropriated. This 'wrongful appropriation rationale' is comparable to the right of publicity recognized in the US, and also suggests a 'free riding' or 'unjust enrichment' rationale characteristic of unfair competition regimes. Later case law, however, utilized the narrower false endorsement rationale, finding that unauthorized merchandising of character images or distinctive elements of a motion picture may lead consumers to believe there is a licensing arrangement.[106] In a 1988 decision involving merchandising rights in the film *Crocodile Dundee*, the Federal Court of Australia criticized the false endorsement rationale as 'artificial,' and as overly dependent on the public's perceptions (or misperceptions) as to the state of the law on merchandising.[107] Instead, the court invoked the broader misappropriation rationale:

> The essence of the wrong done in the [character and celebrity merchandising] cases . . . is not in truth a misrepresentation that there is a licensing or sponsoring agreement between the applicant and the respondent; it is in the second ground taken in the *Henderson* case, namely wrongful appropriation of a reputation or, more widely, wrongful association of goods with an image properly belonging to the applicant.[108]

Emphasizing that 'association' could refer to 'a connection other than one relating to 'quality or endorsement,''[109] the court enjoined the respondent from using any names or images 'calculated to induce the public to believe that the first respondent or goods sold by it is associated with the film "Crocodile Dundee" or the character portrayed by the applicant Paul Hogan in the film'.[110] Only one year later, the same court was deeply divided on a decision to uphold a passing off claim arising from a television ad that imitated the famous knife scene from *Crocodile Dundee.* Judge

---

106 *See, e.g.,* Children's Television Workshop Inc. v. Woolworths (NSW) Ltd [1981] 1 NSWLR 273 (unauthorized use of 'Sesame Street' characters on toys likely to mislead consumers into believing there is a licensing arrangement); *see also* Moorgate Tobacco Co. Ltd. v. Philip Morris Ltd., 156 CLR 414 (1984) (rejection of general tort of unfair competition has not prevented adaptation of passing off tort to unauthorized use of indicia suggesting 'association, quality or endorsement' of goods).

107 Hogan v. Koala Dundee Pty Ltd, 83 ALR 187 (Federal Court of Australia 1988). Christopher Wadlow has described the state of Australian merchandising law as follows: 'Misrepresentation must still be shown, and the misrepresentation can be found in the public supposing there to be some sort of commercial arrangement of an unspecified kind between the plaintiff and the defendant.' Christopher Wadlow, The Law of Passing Off 298–9 (2d ed. 1995).

108 *Hogan,* 83 ALR 187.

109 *Id.* (citing *Moorgate Tobacco,* 156 CLR 414).

110 *Id.*

Sheppard, dissenting, found the passing off claim untenable, because viewers 'could not reasonably conclude that Mr. Hogan had consented to or authorized the advertisement'.[111] The other two judges upheld the trial court's finding of passing off, but applied different rationales. Judge Beaumont believed that the lower court was reasonable to conclude that a significant number of viewers would believe 'that a commercial arrangement had been concluded between the first respondent and the appellant under which the first respondent agreed to the advertising'.[112] In contrast, Judge Burchett adopted a broader rationale, closer to unfair competition. He noted that 'the question becomes whether the vagueness of the message prevents the application of the principles of passing off'. In his view, passing off could be found regardless of whether viewers believed that the parties had a commercial licensing arrangement:

> In my opinion, the vagueness of the suggestion conveyed in this case is not sufficient to save it. That vagueness is not incompatible with great effectiveness. It would be unfortunate if the law merely prevented a trader using the primitive club of direct misrepresentation, while leaving him free to employ the more sophisticated rapier of suggestion, which may deceive more completely. In my opinion, the deployment in circumstances of the present kind of techniques of persuasion, designed to influence prospective customers in favour of a trader or his products upon the basis of some underlying assumption which is false, may be held to be misleading or deceptive or to be likely to mislead or deceive within the meaning of s 52, and may also be held to constitute passing off.[113]

These cases suggest that Australia may be edging toward a more liberal application of passing off theory to protect merchandising rights, comparable to that which has developed in the US, thus blurring the traditional boundaries between deception-based protection and the anti-free-riding concept embraced by unfair competition regimes.

(iii) The Latest Battleground: Keyword Advertising

The disharmony between the passing off and unfair competition regimes in Europe is being highlighted once again in the context of keyword advertising. The lower courts in France have (with one exception) held advertisers and *Google* liable for the unauthorized use of trademarks as keywords ('adwords').[114] In one such case, the Court of Strasbourg found

---

[111] Hogan v. Pacific Dunlop Ltd., 14 IPR 398 (Federal Court of Australia 1989).

[112] *Id.*

[113] *Id.*

[114] *See* AdWords Lawsuits in France – Trademarks as Keywords Illegal?,

no trademark infringement, but held that the use of adwords constituted unfair competition under section 1382 of the French Civil Code.[115]

In contrast, in a declaratory judgment action the BGH in Germany rejected both trademark and unfair competition claims arising from an advertiser's use of a competitor's company name as an adword.[116] The trademark claim failed because the court found no likelihood of confusion as to source. The unfair competition claim was based on two assertions: (1) that the advertiser was taking unfair advantage of the reputation of the mark, and (2) that the advertiser's use of the mark would enable it to attract the trademark owner's customers. The BGH rejected both of these assertions, finding that (1) it was improbable that an internet user would transfer the perceived qualities associated with the adword to the advertiser's offer, and (2) the trademark owner had no protectable right to retain its customer base. Although another case involving adwords was referred to the ECJ, that case involved only trademark infringement and not unfair competition.[117]

In March of 2010 the ECJ issued three opinions holding that the use of adwords by advertisers is trademark use (and thus potential infringement if the use is likely to cause confusion), but that the use of adwords by *Google* is not.[118] However, the questions referred to the ECJ in these cases (referred by France, Austria, and Germany) did not address the question of unfair competition. In a fourth case referred to the ECJ, the

---

http://www.linksandlaw.com/adwords-google-keyword-lawsuit-France.htm (collecting cases); Google's Ad Words Lawsuits Worldwide, http://www.linksandlaw.com/adwords-pendinglawsuits.htm.

[115] Atrya v. Google and K par K/Techni Feneres (Trib. de Grand Instance de Strasbourg, 1ere Ch. Civile, July 20, 2007).

[116] The Beta Layout case, Bundesgerichtshof, Case 1 ZR 30/07 (Jan. 22, 2009).

[117] Eis.de GmbH v. BBY Vertriebsgesellschaft mbH (the 'Bananabay' case), Bundesgerichtshof, Case 1 ZR 125/07 (Jan. 22, 2009).

[118] Google Fr. SARL v. Louis Vuitton Malletier SA (23 March 2010), http://eurlex.europa.eu/Lex UriServ/LexUri Serv.do?uri=CELEX:62008J0236:EN:HTML, 2010 ECJ EUR-Lex LEXIS 119 (joined cases C-236/08 to C-238/08) (referred by the French Court of Cassation); Die BergSpechte Outdoor Reisen und Alpinschule Edi Koblmüller GmbH v. Günter Guni (25 March 2010), Case C-278/08, http://eurlex.europa.eu/LexUriServ/LexUriServ.do?uri=CELEX:62008J0278:EN:HTML, 2010 ECJ EUR-Lex LEXIS 124 (referred by Austria's Oberster Gerichtshof); Eis.de GmbH v. BBY Vertriebsgesellschaft mbH (26 March 2010), Case C-91/09, http://eur-lex.europa.eu/LexUriServ/LexUriServ.do?uri=CELEX:62009O00091:FR:HTM,. 2010 ECJ EUR-Lex LEXIS 490 (referred by German BGH). For a detailed discussion of these rulings, see Tyson Smith, *Googling a Trademark: A Comparative Look at Keyword Use in Internet Advertising*, 46 Texas Int.L.J. 232, 238–42 (2010).

Hoge Raad of the Netherlands asked for a preliminary ruling on the question whether states may prohibit keyword advertising that 'takes unfair advantage of, or is detrimental to, the distinctive character or the repute of the trademark'.[119] However, the ECJ's ruling in this case, issued in July of 2010, found it unnecessary to reach this question in light of its disposition on the other questions presented.

The question whether the unauthorized use of trademarks in keyword advertising constitutes unfair competition arose again in *Interflora, Inc. v. Marks & Spencer*, an English case that was referred to the ECJ in 2009.[120] Since May 2008, search engine *Google* had adopted a more aggressive policy on keyword advertising in the UK and Ireland than in continental Europe, apparently based on the difference between the approaches to trademark protection in the common law and civil law regimes. The Advocate General of the EU issued a preliminary opinion in 2011, stating that, in the adwords context, if the sponsored link mentions the trademark, then the question of free riding 'depends on whether we are faced with legitimate comparative advertising, or on the contrary, with riding on the coat-tails of the trademark proprietor'.[121] Under this approach, the trademark owner is entitled to prevent the use of its mark in sponsored links when (1) the mark is used as a generic term for the goods or services, or (2) the advertiser attempts 'to benefit from [the mark's] power of attraction, its reputation or its prestige, and to exploit the marketing effort expended by the proprietor of that mark'.[122]

In September of 2011, the ECJ issued its opinion in *Interflora*.[123] For the first time, the court considered not only the trademark claims arising from keyword advertising, but also the unfair competition claims. The court's analysis largely tracks the opinion of the Advocate General.

In addressing the trademark claims, the court emphasized that Marks & Spencer's use of Interflora's mark presented a case of 'double identity,' because Marks & Spencer was using an identical mark in connection with identical goods or services.[124] Under these circumstances, Interflora's

---

119 Portakabin Ltd. v. Primakabin (8 July 2010), http://curia.europa.eu/jurisp/cgi-bin/gettext.pl? lang=en&num=79899291C19080558&doc=T&ouvert=T&seance=ARRET.

120 Interflora, Inc. v. Marks & Spencer PLC Flowers Direct Online Limited, [2009] EWHC 1095 (Ch).

121 Case C-323/09, Opinion of Advocate General Jaaskinen (Mar. 24, 2011).

122 *Id.*

123 Case C-323/09, Interflora, Inc. v. Marks & Spencer PLC Flowers Direct Online Ltd., 22 September 2011.

124 *Id.* ¶ 33.

mark was entitled to 'absolute' protection,[125] meaning that Marks & Spencer would be liable if its use of Interflora's mark was likely to have an 'adverse effect on one of the functions of the trademark, irrespective of whether the function concerned is the essential function of indicating the origin of the product or service covered by the trademark or one of the other functions of the mark, such as that of guaranteeing the quality of that product or service or that of communication, investment or advertising'.[126] In contrast, if Marks & Spencer were not offering identical goods or services, then it would be liable only if its use of the Interflora mark gave rise to a likelihood of confusion as to origin[127] – the same rule that would apply in a passing off regime.

Because the two parties in this case offered identical services, Marks & Spencer's keyword advertising was actionable if it affected the communication, investment, or advertising functions of the Interflora mark, even if consumers were not likely to be confused about the origin of Marks & Spencer's services. The ECJ concluded that, in this case, keyword advertising did not impair the advertising function of the mark,[128] but left it to the English courts to determine whether the defendant's activity impaired the investment function of the mark – that is, whether it jeopardized Interflora's ability to maintain a reputation capable of attracting consumers and retaining their loyalty.[129] The ECJ also left it to the English courts to determine whether Marks & Spencer's use of the Interflora mark undermined the distinctiveness of that mark to such a degree that consumers might come to perceive the mark as a generic term for flower delivery services.[130]

In contrast to previous keyword advertising cases, the ECJ in *Interflora* also considered whether the unauthorized use of Interflora's mark constituted unfair competition – specifically, whether such a use 'without due cause . . . takes unfair advantage of the distinctive character or repute of the trade-mark,' thus constituting unlawful 'free riding'.[131] The court had no difficulty concluding that keyword advertising is designed to capitalize on the distinctive character and repute of a mark, and that the advertiser

---

125 *Id.* ¶ 36.
126 *Id.* ¶ 38.
127 *Id.* ¶ 36.
128 *Id.* ¶¶ 57, 59.
129 *Id.* ¶¶ 62, 65.
130 *Id.* ¶¶ 76–83. The court referred to this process as 'dilution'. Id. ¶ 76–7.
131 *Id.* ¶ 92. This standard is drawn from the unfair competition provision of the 2008 Trademark Directive, Council Directive 2008/95/EC, Article 5(2), which carries over from Article 5(2) of its predecessor, Council Directive 89/104/EC.

derives an advantage from its unauthorized use of the mark to attract the attention of consumers who may then decide to purchase the advertiser's goods or services.[132] The remaining question was whether this advantage was unfair. Here, the court drew directly from its analysis in the *L'Oreal* case, holding that the use of another party's mark in keyword advertising can, in the absence of 'due cause,'

> be construed as a use whereby the advertiser rides on the coat-tails of a trademark with a reputation in order to benefit from its power of attraction, its reputation and its prestige, and to exploit, without paying any financial compensation and without being required to make efforts of its own in that regard, the marketing effort expended by the proprietor of that mark in order to create and maintain the image of that mark. If that is the case, the advantage thus obtained by the third party must be considered to be unfair.[133]

Although the ECJ left it to the English courts to apply this standard to the facts, the court observed that unfairness was 'particularly likely to be the conclusion' where the keyword advertiser is offering goods which are 'imitations' of the goods or services offered by the trademark owner.[134] In contrast, if the advertiser merely offers an 'alternative' to the trademark owner's goods or services, then the keyword advertising should be considered fair, because offering consumers an alternative constitutes 'due cause' for referencing a competitor's trademark:

> By contrast, where the advertisement displayed on the internet on the basis of a keyword corresponding to a trademark with a reputation puts forward – without offering a mere imitation of the goods or services of the proprietor of that trademark, without causing dilution or tarnishment and without, moreover, adversely affecting the functions of the trademark concerned – an alternative to the goods or services of the proprietor of the trademark with a reputation, it must be concluded that such use falls, as a rule, within the ambit of fair competition in the sector for the goods or services concerned and is thus not without "due cause" . . .[135]

Thus, for purposes of unfair competition, *Interflora* tells us that it is crucial to determine whether the advertiser's goods or services are 'imitations' or 'alternatives'. But what is the difference? Unfortunately, the ECJ did not address this question. In a context such as flower delivery services, it is difficult to see what would distinguish an 'imitation' service

---

132 *Id.* ¶¶ 86–7.
133 *Id.* ¶ 89 (citing *L'Oreal*, ¶ 49).
134 *Id.* ¶ 90.
135 *Id.* ¶ 91 (citing Article 5(2) of Directive 89/104/EC). *See also id.* ¶ 95.

from an 'alternative' service. The Advocate General's opinion suggested that Marks and Spencer's service was an alternative, and not an imitation, but offered no explanation for this conclusion.[136] The ECJ opinion leaves the ultimate application of this principle to the domestic courts. In light of their hostility to *L'Oreal*, it seems likely that the English courts will perceive *Interflora* as a thorny bouquet. Whether or not the imitation/alternative distinction proves viable will have a significant impact on the outcome of future adwords cases throughout the EU.

In the US, the application of passing off doctrine to keyword advertising remains unsettled. The federal courts have yet to reach a consensus on whether keyword advertising constitutes 'trademark use' at all.[137] The answer may depend on whether the trademark is used simply to trigger the ad, or whether it is actually displayed in the resulting ad.[138] Even if trademark use is found, the question whether that use is likely to cause confusion turns on a fact-intensive multi-factor analysis.[139] It is safe to say, however, that, in determining whether keyword advertising is infringement, American courts will not concern themselves with the question whether the competitor's goods are 'imitations' or 'alternatives'.

V. CONCLUSION

The common law regime that has come under the greatest pressure to abandon the deception-based concept of passing off in favor of a broader unfair competition law is the UK. However, courts in that jurisdiction have expressed deep reservations about whole-heartedly embracing the broad notion of unfair competition law that prevails in the civil law regimes of continental Europe, in particular because the quest for

---

136 Case 323/09, Opinion of Advocate General Jaaskinen ¶¶ 104–05 (Mar. 24, 2011).

137 *See* Rosetta Stone Ltd. v. Google, Inc., 676 F.3d 144, 152-53 & n.4 (4th Cir. 2012) (assuming, without deciding, that keyword advertising is trademark use). The trend, however, is toward recognizing this as a trademark use. *See* Network Automation, Inc. v. Advanced System Concepts, 638 F.3d 1137, 1145 (9th Cir. 2011); Rescuecom Corp. v. Google, Inc., 562 F.3d 123, 128–9 (2d Cir. 2009).

138 *See* Hamzik v. Zale Corp./Delaware, 2007 U.S. Dist. LEXIS 28981, at *3 (N.D.N.Y. Apr. 19, 2007) (suggesting that display of mark may be trademark use even if sponsored linking is not); *see also* Tiffany, Inc. v. eBay, Inc., 576 F.Supp.2d 463 (S.D.N.Y. 2008) (implying agreement with *Hamzik*).

139 *See Rosetta Stone,* 676 F.3d at 153–60 (finding triable issues of fact under likelihood of confusion factors); *Network Automation*, 638 F.3d at 1149–54 (finding district court's multi-factor analysis inadequate).

'fairness' threatens to undermine the goals of 'competition'. It remains to be seen whether their concerns will influence the rest of the EU.

Free from these pressures to conform to EU policy, the US continues to favor free competition over highly regulated markets and abstract notions of fairness and 'free riding,' and is therefore likely to continue to favor the passing off regime. Even in the US, however, aggressive litigation by trademark owners has led to considerable expansion of the passing off doctrine, with respect to both registered and unregistered marks, and today the concept of 'false endorsement' has been interpreted so broadly as to approximate misappropriation. Australia seems to be following a similar path.

In some common law countries, legislative actions have also eroded the traditional requirement of deception or confusion in trademark law. In this regard, the most significant legislative development is the recognition of trademark dilution, which dispenses with the requirement of confusion in certain circumstances. In the US, the dilution provisions in section 43(c) of the Lanham Act protect only 'famous' marks against two types of non-confusion-related harms, blurring and tarnishment.[140] In Canada, the dilution statute prohibits any use of a registered mark that will 'depreciate the value of the goodwill attaching thereto'.[141] Dilution statutes afford trademark owners a significant degree of control over non-confusing uses of their marks; even though they apply only to a subset of marks, these laws clearly have the effect of introducing broader unfair competition concepts into common law regimes. In the US and Canada, however, dilution claims generally require some evidence of harm (or potential harm) to the goodwill or reputation of the mark; thus, pure 'free riding' is typically not sufficient – at least, not yet. [142]

---

[140] 15 U.S.C. § 1125(c).

[141] *See* Trademarks Act, § 22. In Canada, unlike the US, dilution protection is limited to registered trademarks. In addition, the Canadian Supreme Court has interpreted § 22 narrowly. *See* Veuve Clicquot Ponsardin, Maison Fondee en 1772 v. Boutiques Cliquot Ltee, [2006] 1 RCS 824, 2006 CSC 23.

[142] *See* Robert G. Howell, *Depreciation of Goodwill: A 'Green Light' for Dilution from the Supreme Court of Canada in an Accommodating Infrastructure,* 17 Transnat'l Law & Contemp. Probs. 689, 706–10 (2008); Darren Meale and Joel Smith, *Enforcing a* Trademark *When Nobody's Confused: Where the Law Stands After L'Oreal and Intel,* 5 J. Intell. L. & Prac. 101–2 (2010); Mary LaFrance and Gail H. Cline, *Identical Cousins? On the Road with Dilution and the Right of Publicity,* 24 Santa Clara Computer & High Tech L.J. 669–71 (2007–08)(discussing Canada's dilution statute). For a debate on the role of free-riding in American dilution law, compare David J. Franklyn, *Debunking Dilution Doctrine: Toward a Coherent Theory of the Anti-Free-Rider Principle in American Trademark Law,* 56

In the common law regimes, passing off has increasingly become disconnected from its moorings in the law of deceit. Countries that place a high value on vigorous competition have resisted this trend with varying degrees of success. In the context of copycat products and comparative advertising, their resistance has been especially strong; the UK, however, cannot maintain its position unless it persuades the rest of the EU to tolerate a less-regulated competitive environment. While the seemingly unstoppable growth of the merchandising right in the US contrasts sharply with the UK's continued refusal to recognize such a right, cracks in the latter's resistance have emerged, even without pressure from the EU, as the line between false endorsement and 'free riding' has become less distinct. This blurring has also become evident in Australia. Although the different approaches to trademark protection continue to reflect the strong cultural difference between legal regimes which prioritize the protection of brand owners' investments and those which prioritize consumer protection, the pressures toward doctrinal convergence will intensify as trademark owners seek to aggressively expand their brand identities without regard to national borders.

Hastings L.J. 117 (2004) with Mark A. Lemley, *Property, Intellectual Property, and Free Riding*, 83 Tex. L. Rev. 1031 (2005).

11. Trade dress

Signe H. Naeve

I. INTRODUCTION

When I teach trade dress to my students, I ask them to picture a small robin's egg blue colored box with a white satin ribbon. Generally, the description evokes a smile from the female students while many of the male students look a little bit baffled. The color and configuration of the packaging I described from Tiffany & Co. creates a specific association and expectation in the minds of the students just as it does with its recipients. Imagine the recipient's disappointment to receive such a box, only to discover something other than Tiffany's jewelry inside. Thus, in the same way that trademarks (like 'Tiffany's') can acquire goodwill and serve to signify the source of a good or service to consumers, trade dress (like the blue box with a white ribbon) can serve this same function.

Trade dress is much more than the packaging from Tiffany's, however. Trade dress can include the shape and distinctive features of a bottle or even colorful restaurant décor. This chapter will explore all of these facets of trade dress while comparing the common law system of the United States with the primarily civil law traditions of the European Union. It will first examine the relevant trade dress provisions from international instruments. Next, it will compare the registration systems and other respective means of protecting trade dress in the US and the EU. This will be followed by an exploration of specific elements of trade dress protection, namely distinctiveness and functionality. The chapter will then explore *sui generis* design protection in the US and the EU, with a focus on the EU Design Protection Directive and Regulation. The chapter will end by highlighting areas of harmonization and divergence.

II. DEFINITIONS AND INTERNATIONAL STANDARDS

None of the international intellectual property conventions mention the term 'trade dress' per se, hence we must cull the most relevant portions from treaties pertaining to trademark and design to establish the framework for international protection. Of these, the Paris Convention, the Agreement on Trade-Related Aspects of Intellectual Property (TRIPS), the Madrid Protocol, and the Hague Convention are the most relevant. In some instances applied art protection under copyright laws will also apply, but this avenue is beyond the scope of discussion in this chapter.

(i) Paris Convention

The 1883 Paris Convention, with its subsequent amendments, created a harmonized and substantive approach to trademark protection, leaving the procedural aspects to its members. The relevant provisions establish basic protection for trademark and industrial property. Article 1 sets the scope of industrial property protection to include: 'patents, utility models, industrial designs, trademarks, service marks, trade names, indications of source or appellations of origin, and the repression of unfair competition'. Article 5*quinquies* incorporates protection for industrial design within the ambit of industrial property, simply stating: 'Industrial designs shall be protected in all the countries of the Union.' While Article 5 mandates protection of industrial design, that protection could come from a combination of existing IP regimes such as copyright and trademark. Article 5 does not require that a member enact *sui generis* design legislation.

Article 6, meanwhile, establishes some basic conditions for registration:

> (1) The conditions for the filing and registration of trademarks shall be determined in each country of the Union by its domestic legislation.
> (2) However, an application for the registration of a mark filed by a national of a country of the Union in any country of the Union may not be refused, nor may a registration be invalidated, on the ground that filing, registration, or renewal, has not been effected in the country of origin.
> (3) A mark duly registered in a country of the Union shall be regarded as independent of marks registered in the other countries of the Union, including the country of origin.

This article of the Paris Convention maintains the territoriality principle in international law confirming that trademark is territorial in scope. According to this principle just because a trademark is valid (or invalid) in one country does not mean that it must be registered (or denied registration) in a subsequent country.

Article 6 *quinquies*, meanwhile, introduces the important concept of distinctiveness:

> Trademarks covered by this Article may be neither denied registration nor invalidated except in the following cases:
> (i) when they are of such a nature as to infringe rights acquired by third parties in the country where protection is claimed;
> (ii) when they are devoid of any distinctive character, or consist exclusively of signs or indications which may serve, in trade, to designate the kind, quality, quantity, intended purpose, value, place of origin, of the goods, or the time of production, or have become customary in the current language or in the bona fide and established practices of the trade of the country where protection is claimed;
> (iii) when they are contrary to morality or public order and, in particular, of such a nature as to deceive the public. It is understood that a mark may not be considered contrary to public order for the sole reason that it does not conform to a provision of the legislation on marks, except if such provision itself relates to public order.

Significantly, under this Article, a mark can be denied registration or invalidated if it is 'devoid of any distinctive character,' which will be discussed in greater depth later in this chapter.

(ii) TRIPS

More than 100 years after the signing of the Paris Convention, the Treaty on Trade-Related Aspects of Intellectual Property (TRIPS) linked intellectual property protection to trade. TRIPS mandates compliance with the substantive obligations regarding trademarks from the Paris Convention and adds some key provisions expanding trademark protection. Namely, TRIPS adds an expanded definition of the scope of protected material in Article 15:

> Any sign, or any combination of signs, capable of distinguishing the goods or services of one undertaking from those of other undertakings, shall be capable of constituting a trademark. Such signs, in particular words including personal names, letters, numerals, figurative elements and combinations of colours as well as any combination of such signs, shall be eligible for registration as trademarks. Where signs are not inherently capable of distinguishing the relevant goods or services, Members may make registrability depend on distinctiveness acquired through use. Members may require, as a condition of registration, that signs be visually perceptible.

While the Paris Convention protects 'utility models, industrial designs, trademarks, service marks, trade names, indications of source or appellations of origin, and the repression of unfair competition,' TRIPS defines trademarks as '[a]ny sign, or any combination of signs, capable of distinguishing the goods or services of one undertaking from those of other undertakings'. The Paris Convention states the broad category of IP, a utility model, industrial design, trademark or service mark; but TRIPS describes the protection from the standpoint of the function that the IP serves. Thus, a trademark is more than just a word or logo, but 'any sign ... capable of distinguishing the goods or services'. This could include sound marks, scent marks, and trade dress. The TRIPs agreement makes this expansion even more clear in Article 15(1) which states that, 'figurative elements and combinations of colours as well as any combination of such signs, shall be eligible for registration as trademarks'. It is this expansion that applies specifically to trade dress.

Similar to the Paris Convention, TRIPS also incorporates protection for industrial designs. Article 25 provides:

> 1. Members shall provide for the protection of independently created industrial designs that are new or original. Members may provide that designs are not new or original if they do not significantly differ from known designs or combinations of known design features. Members may provide that such protection shall not extend to designs dictated essentially by technical or functional considerations.
> 2. Each Member shall ensure that requirements for securing protection for textile designs, in particular in regard to any cost, examination or publication, do not unreasonably impair the opportunity to seek and obtain such protection. Members shall be free to meet this obligation through industrial design law or through copyright law.

Key to this provision is the allowance for 'new or original' material. This definition lays the foundation for criteria that differ from patent or copyright novelty and nonobviousness standards. This section also provides for the exclusion of some 'functional' material, which will be discussed in greater depth later in the chapter.

Article 26 of TRIPS establishes the exclusive rights for the owner of industrial designs and provides that the protection shall last for at least 10 years:

> 1. The owner of a protected industrial design shall have the right to prevent third parties not having the owner's consent from making, selling or importing articles bearing or embodying a design which is a copy, or substantially a copy, of the protected design, when such acts are undertaken for commercial purposes.
> 2. Members may provide limited exceptions to the protection of industrial designs, provided that such exceptions do not unreasonably conflict with the normal exploitation of protected industrial designs and do not unreasonably prejudice the legitimate interests of the owner of the protected design, taking account of the legitimate interests of third parties.
> 3. The duration of protection available shall amount to at least 10 years.

To round out these international instruments, trademarks can be registered through the international registration process created under the Madrid Protocol and industrial design can be registered in accordance with the Agreement of the Hague Concerning Industrial Design.

III. PROCUREMENT OF TRADE DRESS PROTECTION

(i) United States

Moving from international treaties to domestic legislation, trade dress in the United States is protected at both the state and federal levels. Federal protection through the federal trademark statute, the Lanham Act, will primarily be discussed in this chapter because it is the broadest means of protection. The United States defines trade dress to include, 'the design of a product (i.e., the product shape or configuration), the packaging in which the product is sold (i.e., the "dressing" of a product), the color of the product or of the packaging in which the product is sold, and the flavor of the product.' See US Trademark of Examining Procedure (TMEP) § 1202.02 (citing *Wal-Mart Stores, Inc. v. Samara Brothers, Inc.*, 529 US 205 (2000) (seersucker children's clothing); *Two Pesos, Inc. v. Taco Cabana, Inc.*, 505 US 763 (1992) (bright pink restaurant décor); *Qualitex Co v. Jacobson Products Co., Inc.*, 514 US 159 (1995) (green-gold dry cleaning press pads); *In re N.V. Organon*, 79 USPQ2d 1639 (TTAB 2006) (orange flavored medicine)). The United States Patent and Trademark Office (USPTO) has recognized, however, that this list is not exhaustive and "almost anything at all that is capable of carrying meaning" may be used as a "symbol" or "'device" and constitute trade dress that identifies the source of origin of a product.' TMEP 1202.02 (citing *Qualitex*, 514 US at 162). This broad definition ties trade dress back to the same purpose of trademark as a source indicator.

Not surprisingly then, the US treats trade dress primarily as a subset of trademark. Consistent with trademark protection in the United States, protecting trade dress derives from both registration and common law protection. An applicant can file an application to protect trade dress through the same registration system as word marks and design marks. The examiner will evaluate the application under the same limitations. There is no separate 'registry' for trade dress as opposed to more traditional trademarks. The scope of the protection is only limited in as much as it has not acquired distinctiveness or violates functionality doctrines.

Also consistent with trademark protection in the US, trade dress can be protected without registration under common law. This means that without registering trade dress, it will be protected within the geographic scope where it is being used. Due to some of the difficulties in obtaining registration for trade dress, many owners may still opt to follow this route of protection. This approach is not unlike the policies supporting unregistered design protection in the EU, which has attempted to provide some scope of protection outside of what can prove to be lengthy and expensive registration procedures.

Although trade dress is protected under the same 'systems' as trademark, trade dress is only explicitly mentioned in one place in the Lanham Act. In 1998 the Trade Dress Protection Act was introduced in Congress, which would have explicitly incorporated trade dress into the Lanham Act. However, it was not enacted. Only more recently were the words 'trade dress' even added to the Lanham Act, and then only in the context of civil actions under the Trademark Dilution Revision Act. The lack of an explicit reference, however, does not exclude trade dress from registration or protection in the United States.

(ii) Europe

Trademark law in the EU, in comparison, is governed both by a Trademark Directive that sets forth standards for each country to follow when adopting and modifying their respective national trademark laws, as well as a Community Trademark Regulation that establishes one unified trademark standard for Community Trademark applications. The language of both intentionally mirrors each other to create the same legal standards for national and community trademarks. A trademark applicant can thus elect to file a trademark application in individual countries, file a Community Trademark (CTM) application through the Office of Harmonization for the Internal Market (OHIM) in Alicante, Spain, or both. Whether filing in an individual country or a CTM application, the Directive and the Regulation have explicit requirements for distinctiveness and non-functionality.

IV. TRADE DRESS ELEMENTS – DISTINCTIVENESS

(i) United States

To protect trade dress in both the US and the EU, it must be distinctive and non-functional. The distinctiveness requirement traces back to the same requirement that is placed upon trademark protection and reflects the international instruments previously discussed. To acquire trademark protection in the US, the mark must be either inherently distinctive or have acquired distinctiveness. The Lanham Act states that, with some specific exclusions such as functionality, 'nothing in [the Lanham Act] shall prevent the registration of a mark used by the applicant which has become distinctive of the applicant's goods in commerce'. 15 U.S.C. § 1052(f).

To understand distinctiveness, it will help to understand that some trademarks are stronger than others. Trademarks are viewed on a spectrum of relative strength, as articulated in *Abercrombie & Fitch Co. v. Hunting World, Inc.*, 537 F.2d 4 (2d Cir. 1976). On this spectrum, the strongest marks are those that are either fanciful or arbitrary. A fanciful mark is a word that is simply 'made up' and is not part of the existing English lexicon. Examples are 'Exxon' or 'Kotex.' An arbitrary mark, meanwhile, takes a known word, but applies it in an unexpected way, such as 'Apple' for computers. These marks are viewed as being very strong. Proof of use and an adequate specimen are needed to register them, but they do not require additional proof that the consuming public recognizes their source.

Further down the spectrum are marks that are suggestive. These marks are also considered inherently distinctive because additional proof is not required to show that they identify a unique source to the consuming public. A suggestive mark is one that requires the consumer to pause for a moment to make a connection between the mark and the product. It is not arbitrary like applying 'Apple' to computer, but neither is it descriptive of the product nor generic. An example is 'Chicken of the Sea,' which is not chicken at all, but rather canned tuna (as made famous by Jessica Simpson on the American television show *Newly Weds: Nick and Jessica*, http://www.mtv.com/shows/newlyweds-nick_and_jessica/series.jhtml).

The spectrum gets more complicated when we reach descriptive marks. These are words that describe a quality of the good or service, like 'Seattle's Best Coffee' or 'hula hoop'. For First Amendment and other policy considerations, the US will only allow a monopoly on descriptive words once they have acquired secondary meaning in the minds of the consuming public. This means that when someone sees a 'Seattle's Best Coffee' logo, a singular source of coffee must come to mind. Prior to proof of this connection, the mark is not inherently distinctive and cannot get trademark protection. At the very end of the spectrum are generic marks, which describe the genus, rather than the species of a good or service. These marks will never be inherently distinctive and can never attain trademark protection.

These classifications are important to understand because courts have struggled with where to place trade dress on this spectrum, and indeed, whether it fits on this spectrum at all. One of the main questions that courts have had to address is whether trade dress can ever be inherently distinctive. After two landmark trade dress decisions, the answer to this question is maybe. These cases created a dichotomy between trade dress packaging and trade dress design, drawing a similar line as the descriptive and suggestive marks on the *Abercrombie* scale. According to these cases, product 'packaging' can be inherently distinctive and no proof of secondary meaning is required, whereas product 'design' is not inherently distinctive and secondary meaning is required.

This packaging/design distinction comes from the landmark Supreme Court decisions, *Two Pesos v. Taco Cabana*, 505 U.S. 763 (1992) and *Wal-Mart v. Samara Brothers*, 529 U.S. 205 (2000). *Taco Cabana* involved restaurant décor for a Mexican restaurant in Texas, described as, '[A] festive eating atmosphere having interior dining and patio areas decorated with artifacts, bright colors, paintings and murals. The patio includes interior and exterior areas with the interior patio capable of being sealed off from the outside patio by overhead garage doors. The stepped exterior of the building has a festive and vivid color scheme using top border paint and neon stripes together with bright awnings and umbrellas.' *Taco Cabana*, 932 F. 2d at 1117. Two Pesos, a competitor, copied the décor and argued to the court that the decor was not protectable. The trade dress had not acquired secondary meaning in the relevant market, so the Supreme Court was asked to determine whether the décor could be inherently distinctive or whether Taco Cabana would be required to show secondary meaning prior to obtaining protection. The Court held that it was possible for the restaurant décor, later described as trade dress packaging, to be inherently distinctive, and hence no showing of secondary meaning would be required for protection.

This guidance lasted until 2000 when the Supreme Court was presented with another trade dress case, this one involving seer-sucker patterned children's clothing. At first glance the Court seemed to overrule the *Taco Cabana* decision when it held that the trade dress protection sought for the clothing could not be inherently distinctive. What *Samara Brothers* did, however, was to create a separate category for trade dress 'design,' as distinct from trade dress 'packaging'. According to the Court, trade dress design, in contrast to trade dress packaging, could not be inherently distinctive. The Court also created a third category for trade dress that fell somewhere between the two categories. The Court cautioned that if in doubt, err should be toward identifying trade dress as product design and requiring secondary meaning prior to protection. Although somewhat confusing, the packaging/design distinction is consistent with the concern in the US for protecting functional attributes through trademark. More than packaging, design, by its nature, is subject to functional considerations and concerns. Although distinctiveness analysis is independent from functionality analysis, given the higher concern that design creates over packaging, it is not surprising that it is more difficult to protect design.

Simply because trade dress is *possible* of being inherently distinctive, according to *Taco Cabana*, doesn't necessarily mean that it *is*. Thus, the USPTO has identified additional criteria, also from case law, that it will consider when assessing inherent distinctiveness. The USPTO will consider several factors from a 1977 case, *Seabrook Foods, Inc. v. Bar-Well Foods, Ltd.*, 568 F.2d 1342, 1344 (C.C.P.A. 1977), involving the outer packaging for frozen foods. The examiner is instructed to ask whether the trade dress is:

(1) a 'common' basic shape or design;
(2) unique or unusual in the field in which it is used;
(3) a mere refinement of a commonly adopted and well-known form of ornamentation for a particular class of goods viewed by the public as a dress or ornamentation for the goods;
(4) capable of creating a commercial impression distinct from the accompanying words?

TMEP 12.02(b)(ii).

Some of the examples cited by the USPTO in its manual of examining procedure help to illustrate the application of the *Seabrook* factors. First it cites the First Circuit's decision in *Yankee Candle Co. v. Bridgewater Candle Co., LLC*, 259 F.3d 25, where the trade dress for the common elements of candle labels were held to be nondistinctive product packaging lacking sufficient evidence of acquired distinctiveness. Next it cites *In re Hudson News Co.*, 39 USPQ2d 1915 TTAB 1996), *aff'd per curium*, 114 F.3d 1207 (Fed. Cir. 1997), where the Board reasoned that for the 'blue motif' of a retail store to be registered without showing secondary meaning, the trade dress 'would have to be immediately recognizable as a distinctive way of identifying the source of the store services'. Third, it cites *In re Brouwerij Bosteels,* __ USPQ2d ___, Ser. No. 77357895 (TTAB August 26, 2010) where the product packaging trade dress for a beer glass and stand with wording and scrollwork would be viewed as a 'mere refinement' rather than an inherently distinctive source indicator. Fourth, it cites *In re File*, 48 USPQ2d 1363 (TTAB 1998) where the tubular lights used in a bowling alley would be perceived as 'simply a refinement of the commonplace decorative or ornamental lighting . . . and would not be inherently regarded as a source indicator'. Fifth, it cites *In re J. Kinderman & Sons Inc.*, 46 USPQ2d 1253 (TTAB 1998) where the packaging for Christmas tree lights were not inherently distinctive, even though no one else was using the same design.

(ii) Europe

In comparison to the US, in the EU, Article 2 of the Trademark Directive and Article 4 of the Community Trademark Regulation define a trademark as 'any signs capable of being represented graphically, particularly words, including personal names, designs, letters, numerals, the shape of goods or of their packaging, provided that such signs are capable of distinguishing the goods or services of one undertaking from those of other undertakings'. It is this latter half of the definition that pertains to trade dress: 'the shape of goods or of their packaging'. The key is the final part of the definition, that the trade dress must distinguish the provider of the goods or services from another provider. Thus the question may be asked, 'Is the sign [trade dress] perceived as an indication of trade origin?' The answer must be yes for trademark or trade dress protection.

Related to this question is the question of distinctiveness. Under Article 3 of the Directive and Article 7 of the Regulation, trademarks can be refused registration or declared invalid if they are 'devoid of any distinctive character'. As discussed in the section on distinctiveness of trade dress in the US, the US recognizes a distinction between trade dress packaging and design. It is possible for packaging to be inherently distinctive, while design requires a showing of secondary meaning. Trade dress that is 'packaging' could be registered whereas trade dress that is 'design' would require additional proof before it could be registered. This is consistent in approach to the *Abercrombie* sliding scale for the strength of different marks, ranging from arbitrary and fanciful to suggestive to descriptive to generic.

A sliding scale has also been recognized by courts in Europe as well. The scale represents the public's perception of signs in relation to their ability to identify the source of a good or service. The stronger the relationship between the public's ability to perceive the sign as an indicator of source, the stronger the mark, similar to the US *Abercrombie* scale. At one end of the spectrum in the EU are invented words and fancy devices. Similar to fanciful and arbitrary marks in the US, these are the most distinctive. Next along the scale are semi-descriptive words and devices. Toward the end are shapes of containers and at the very end is the shape of goods.

These last two categories on the scale are similar to the trade dress packaging/design separation in the US. 'Shapes of containers' are like product packaging, whereas 'shape of goods' is like product design. Similar to the US, product packaging is treated as being more distinctive than product design. Placing the 'shape of containers' ahead of 'shape of goods' on the spectrum shows that the EU treats containers, or packaging, as being inherently more distinctive than the shape of goods or design.

But, what does it mean for a sign to be 'devoid of any distinctive character'? Regarding trade dress, this will generally mean that the shape is largely dictated by the shape of the product. In the EU, '[t]he closer the shape for which registration is sought resembles the shape most likely to be taken by the product in question, the greater the likelihood of the shape being devoid of any distinctive character'. Tritton, *Intellectual Property in Europe*, pg. 280 (citing C-136/02 *Mag Instrument v. OHIM* [2004] E.C.R. I-9165; [2005] E.T.M.R. 46, ECJ). A key case for trade dress involves the shape of liquid detergent packaging and noted:

> . . . a simple departure from the norm or customs of the sector is not sufficient to render inapplicable the ground for refusal given in Art.3(1)(b) of the Directive. In contrast, a trade mark which departs significantly from the norm or customs of *[sic]* sector and *thereby* fulfills its essential function of indicating origin is not devoid of any distinctive character.

Case C-218/01 *Henkel KgAA v. OHIM* [2004] E.C.R. I-1715; [2005] E.T.M.R. 45, ECJ. Thus, the shape varies significantly from the norm or custom, then it might be distinctive; if it is dictated by the shape or design, then it may not be distinctive. However, simply because the merits of a product's shape or design have been recognized does not make it distinctive.

Three cases illustrate these principles. A 3D shape of a candy wrapper and a figurative representation of a candy wrapper might not be registrable where the shape of the packaging is largely dictated by the shape of the product itself. *See* Case C-25/05P *August Storck KG v. OHIM*, judgment June 22, 2006. A tall bottle with a narrow top, integral handle, small pouring aperture, and two level stopper would only be registrable if the packaging 'significantly departs from the norm or customs of the sector'. *See* Case C-218/01 *Henkel KGAA v. Deutsche Patent-und Markenamt* [2005] E.T.M.R. 45, ECJ. Drinking pouches, meanwhile, could be unregistrable if they would monopolize the standard form of a stand-up pouch. *See* Joined cases T-146/02 and C-153/02, Deutsche SiSI-Werke GmbH & Co Betriebs KG v. OHIM [2004] E.C.R. II-447; [2004] E.T.M.R. 72, CFI.

Ultimately, distinctiveness will be determined in the EU from the perspective of 'average consumers of the goods or services in question who are reasonably well informed and reasonably observant and circumspect'. Tritton, *Intellectual Property in Europe*, p. 280 (citing Case C-363/99 *Koninklijke v. Benelux-Merkenbureau (Postkantoor)* [2004] E.C.R. I-1619; [2004] E.T.M.R. 57, ECJ). The trademark applicant can submit studies, which must be considered by the examining body. This evidence can be relevant in light of Article 3(3) of the Directive and Article 7(3) of the Regulation, which provide room for acquired distinctiveness:

> A trademark shall not be refused registration or be declared invalid in accordance with paragraph 1(b), (c) or (d) if, before the date of application for registration and following the use which has been made of it, it has acquired a distinctive character. Any Member State may in addition provide that this provision shall also apply where the distinctive character was acquired after the date of application for registration or after the date of registration.

Even acquired distinctiveness, however, cannot overcome a rejection due to functionality.

V. TRADE DRESS ELEMENTS – NON-FUNCTIONALITY AND AESTHETIC FUNCTIONALITY

(i) United States

In the US and the EU, trade dress must be both distinctive (either inherently distinctive or through acquired distinctiveness) and it must be non-functional. The concept of functionality with regard to trade dress developed initially from common law and was not codified until 1998 with the 'Technical Corrections to Trademark Act of 1946'. The changes to the Lanham Act in 1998 prohibited the registration of 'matter that, as a whole, is functional'. 15 U.S.C. § 1052(e)(5). 'Matter that, as a whole, is functional' cannot be registered on either the Primary or Supplemental register, even with a showing of distinctiveness. Furthermore, functionality is a ground for cancellation and a defense to infringement in a case involving incontestable registration.

The supporting principles behind the development of the functionality doctrine in both the US and the EU were pro-competitive in nature, seeking to limit monopoly control over a shape of a product, particularly if it limited the creation and sale of suitable alternatives. In the US, in particular, the judiciary sought to draw a distinction between trademark and patent laws as evidenced by leading functionality cases such as *Qualitex Co. v. Jacobson Prods. Co., Inc.*, 514 U.S. 159 (1995) and *TrafFix Devices, Inc. v. Marketing Displays, Inc.*, 532 U.S. 23 (2001). In *Qualitex*, the Supreme Court considered whether color (for gold-green dry cleaning press pads) was unprotectable per se as a trademark. The Court addressed depletion and scarcity arguments, which arguably are still accepted in the EU, and dismissed them because it reasoned that functionality would step in to stop the monopoly control of colors that were necessary to compete in the marketplace. The Court held that it was possible for color to serve a trademark function. In *TrafFix*, meanwhile, the Court considered the viability of trademark protection for the dual-spring on a traffic sign, which had previously warranted a utility patent. In part, for policy reasons, the Court denied to issue a ruling that would extend the protection from an expired patent through trademark.

A product feature is functional if 'it is essential to the use or purpose of the product or affects its cost or quality' regardless of alternatives. *TrafFix*, 532 U.S. at 33. Another way to describe functionality is 'if exclusive use of [the] feature would put competitors at a significant non-reputation-related disadvantage.' Qualitex, 514 U.S. 165 (citing *Inwood Labs., Inc. v. Ives Labs., Inc.*, 456 U.S. 844, 850, n. 10 (1982)). This second definition is sometimes linked directly to aesthetic functionality. Traditionally, functional features are elements which have one or both purposes: 'to insure "practical operation of the article," or to "promote efficiency for the purpose to which it is devoted", or to secure the "excellence" or "functional perfection" of the product; and/or (2) for the sake of economy, for example, to reduce the cost of manufacture'. Altman, Louis and Malla Pollack (2010), *Callmann on Unfair Competition, Trademarks and Monopolies*, 3, US: Thomson Reuters.

When assessing functionality, the USPTO harkens back to a 1982 case, *In re Morton-Norwich Products, Inc.*, 671 F.2d 1332, 1340–41 (C.C.P.A. 1982). According to the Trademark Manual of Examining Procedure, examiners should consider one or more of the *Morton-Norwich* factors:

> (1) the existence of a utility patent that discloses the utilitarian advantages of the design sought to be registered;
> (2) advertising by the applicant that touts the utilitarian advantages of the design;
> (3) facts pertaining to the availability of alternative designs; and
> (4) facts pertaining to whether the design results from a comparatively simple or inexpensive method of manufacture.

TMEP 1202(a)(v) (citing *Morton-Norwich*, 671 F.2d at 1340–41).

These factors highlight the policy concern of extending patent protection through trademark. If a utility patent for the features exists, then this weighs against permitting trade dress protection. If the advertising highlights the 'useful' features, then this too can weigh against trade dress protection. Even though the availability of alternative designs is not dispositive, similar to the EU, it is relevant to protect pro-competitive policies. If alternatives are available, then there may be several useful ways to design the same product. Finally, and also to support pro-competitive policies, the *Morton-Norwich* factors consider whether the design is inexpensive to manufacture. If it is, then a competitor should not be forced to create a more expensive design just to differentiate the products.

As a companion to utilitarian functionality, a common law principle for protection against aesthetic functionality has developed. Arguably more ambiguous, aesthetic functionality is also rooted in pro-competitive principles. Aesthetic functionality permits competitors to use the same aesthetic features of a product, as separate from the useful features, when those features are necessary for competition.

One of the first cases to introduce aesthetic functionality in the US involved the floral pattern on china. The Ninth Circuit reasoned in *Pagliero v. Wallace China Co.*, 198 F.2d 339 (9th Cir. 1952) that the floral pattern 'was originally intended primarily to beautify the china and not to identify the manufacturer'. Although the design later came to identify the manufacturer, this result was subsequent to the primary intent of beautifying the product. Thus, even though the features resulted in selling more plates, they did not serve a trademark function, they served an aesthetic function. Accordingly, the concept of aesthetic functionality provides an additional limitation on trade dress protection where the attractive features sell the product, but do not serve as a trademark.

(ii) Europe

The EU was influenced in many instances by the functionality case law in the United States, both more classic utilitarian functionality, such as in the *TrafFix* case, as well as aesthetic functionality principles, such as in the *Pagliero* case. In the EU, specific sections relevant to functionality were included in the Directive and the Regulation, while case law interpretation still provides important guidance for their application.

The Directive and Regulation deny registration or approve invalidation for: 'Signs which consist exclusively of: (i) the shape which results from the nature of the goods themselves; (ii) the shape of goods which is necessary to obtain a technical result; (iii) the shape which gives substantial value to the goods.' Dir. Art. 3(1)(e). Reg. Art. 7(1)(3). Although this language sounds like the same guidance for determining distinctiveness, these sections actually refer to functionality limitations. Recall that the closer the shape is to the actual product, the less likely that it will be found to be distinctive. If the shape results from the nature of the goods themselves or if the shape of the goods is necessary to obtain a technical result, then it may be functional as well. Accordingly, trade dress can be denied protection either for a lack of distinctiveness or because it is functional. Said another way, a finding of non-functionality will not overcome a lack of distinctiveness, just as a finding of distinctiveness or acquired distinctiveness will not overcome functionality. Under either scenario, protection would be denied.

To understand the application of Articles 3 and 7, it is helpful to examine two key decisions from the European Court of Justice (ECJ). The first is the *Philips* case, [Case C-299/99 *Koninklijke Philips Electronics NV v. Remington Consumer Products Ltd*, 2002 E.T.M.R. 81 (E.C.J. 2002)] and the second is the *Lego* case, [Case C-48/09, Lego Juris A/S v. Office for Harmonisation in the Internal Market, 2010 ECR ____ (ECJ Advocate-General, January 26, 2010) (EU)]. First, in *Philips*, Philips developed a three-headed rotary electric shaver and nearly 20 years later successfully registered a trademark for the shape and configuration of three circular heads with rotating blades in the shape of a triangle. Later, Philips' competitor, Remington, began selling a similarly shaped electric razor. Philips sued Remington for infringement and Remington countersued for revocation of the trademark. After the case wound through the lower courts, the Appellate Court referred a number of questions to the ECJ, including:

> (a) Can the restriction imposed by the words 'if it consists exclusively of the shape of goods which is necessary to achieve a technical result' appearing in Article 3(1)(e)(ii) be overcome by establishing that there are other shapes which can obtain the same technical result, or (b) is the shape unregistrable by virtue thereof if it is shown that the essential features of the shape are attributable only to the technical result, or (c) is some other and, if so, what test appropriate for determining whether the restriction applies?

The Court considered the policies underlying the trademark restrictions: promoting competition, limiting monopolies, and avoiding creating barriers for competitors from incorporating technical solutions or functional characteristics into a product because they are owned as a trademark by someone else. Supporting those policies, the Court held that if the trademark is determined by the functional shape then trademark protection is not applicable, whether or not alternatives are available.

This holding was expanded in the *Lego* case to create several steps when addressing the functionality provisions of the Directive and the Regulation. In *Lego*, the ECJ acknowledged the anti-monopoly policy behind the trademark regulations as well as the importance of the 'essential characteristics' of a trademark in assessing functionality. However, it expanded these starting points into a three-level analysis. The Court said that the first step in the analysis is to identify the most important elements of the trademark, the 'essential characteristics,' and then to analyze each feature. Also within this first step, the relationship between the feature and the technical result should be compared. Finally, within this first step, will be a determination of the functionality of each essential characteristic, wherein patents could be considered. If all of the essential features are functional, then the analysis is complete. If they are not, then the court said to proceed to the second step.

In the second step, according to the Court, we will have identified and narrowed the essential characteristics, some of which will be functional and some of which will not. An important policy consideration at this point is the significant non-reputation related disadvantage that a competitor could encounter if not allowed to use the shape. This language sounds similar to the definition of functionality in the US at this stage. According to the Court, it *is* appropriate to consider alternatives. Only if we pass through steps one and two, will we then consider distinctiveness. The Court indicated that the overall impression and the consumer are now important at this stage. Thus, the Court moved the objective analysis prior to any subjective determinations. This multi-step analysis thus incorporates both distinctiveness and functionality assessments.

Furthermore, while the first two subsections of the Directive and the Regulation pertain to more of a utilitarian functionality, subsection (iii), 'the shape which gives substantial value to the goods,' has been interpreted to provide aesthetic functionality limitations. In the EU, the concept of aesthetic functionality can also be drawn from the 1950s US Ninth Circuit case, *Pagliero* and its progeny. Although rarely invoked in the EU because it is such a strong limitation, there has been one leading ECJ decision involving fashion.

In 2007, the ECJ decided *Benetton v. G-Star*. G-Star made jeans and it registered two shape marks for, 'sloping stitching from hip height to the crotch seam, kneepads, yoke on the seat of the trousers, horizontal stitching at knee height at the rear, band of a contrasting colour or of another material at the bottom of the trousers at the rear, all on one garment' and 'seams, stitching and cuts on the kneepad of the trousers, slightly baggy kneepad'. G-Star sued Benetton in Amsterdam District Court seeking to enjoin Benetton from making similar jeans and Benetton sought annulment of the marks claiming that 'the shapes at issue determined the market value of the goods to a great extent as a result of their beauty or original character'.

The first instance court dismissed G-Star's claims and Benetton's counterclaim. The Amsterdam Regional Court of Appeal allowed G-Star's appeal and dismissed Benetton's application. The Regional Court agreed with the lower court that,

> [T]he Elwood trousers were a great commercial success, that G-Star had conducted intensive advertising campaigns to give those trousers, which have specific characteristics, recognition as a G-Star product, and that, as a result, the reputation of the Elwood trousers was largely attributable not to the aesthetic attractiveness of the shape but to the attractiveness resulting from recognition of the trade mark.

Benetton appealed to the Supreme Court of the Netherlands, which stayed the proceedings and referred the following question to the ECJ:

> (1) Must Article 3(1)(e), third indent, be interpreted as meaning that the prohibition contained therein permanently precludes the registration of a shape as a trade mark where the nature of the product is such that its appearance and shaping determine its market value entirely or substantially as a result of their beauty or original character, or does the prohibition not apply where, prior to the application for registration, the attractiveness of the relevant shape to the public has been determined predominantly by the recognition of it as a distinctive sign? (2) if the answer to Question 1 is to the latter effect, to what extent must this attractiveness have prevailed for the prohibition no longer to apply?

The ECJ interpreted the question literally and, applying *Philips*, held that 'the shape of a product which gives substantial value to that product cannot constitute a trademark under Article 3(3) of that directive where, prior to the application for registration, it acquired distinctiveness as a result of its recognition as a distinctive sign following advertising campaigns presenting the specific characteristics of the product in question'. Dinwoodie and Janis, *Trade Dress and Design Law* at 184. Thus, G-Star's specific features in its jeans had acquired distinctiveness prior to registration due to their aesthetic quality, as highlighted in G-Star's advertising. That aesthetic quality, made the sign functional under Article 3(3), and removed it from trademark-eligible material. It is noteworthy; however, that G-Star was later successful in Milan, Italy with the same jean pattern under a theory of 'slavish imitation' even though it no longer had a registered trademark.

VI. DESIGN PROTECTION

It is impossible to discuss trade dress protection in the international context without also discussing *sui generis* design protection regulations. Indeed, design protection provides a notable complement to trade dress protection in the EU, without a direct comprehensive counterpart in the US. The US has enacted piecemeal industry-focused protection under the Copyright Act. The US also issues design patents, but neither copyright nor patent compare to the comprehensive coverage for both registered and unregistered designs available in the EU.

There are three levels of protection for design in the EU. First, there is the registered Community design right. Second, there is the unregistered Community design right. Third, there is the national-level registered design right. In 1998, the EU enacted a Directive on the Legal Protection of Design. The Directive mandated that each member state enact a law providing for a national *registered* design right in that country. Three years later, the Council enacted a parallel Regulation covering community-wide *registered* and *unregistered* design rights. As a result, there is national registered design right protection as well as Community-level protection for both registered and unregistered designs.

Both the Directive and the Regulation define design as 'the appearance of the whole or a part of a product resulting from the features of, in particular, the lines, contours, colours, shape, texture and/or materials of the product itself and/or its ornamentation'. Dir. Art. 1(a), Reg. Art. 3(a). The unregistered design right runs for three years from the date that the design is first made available to the public. The owner of the right then has one year to file an application for a registered design right, similar to statutory bars in patent. The unregistered right only permits the owner to prevent unauthorized reproduction; accordingly independent creation would be a defense to copying. Not surprisingly, registered rights are broader in scope and longer in duration than unregistered rights; the registered design right can last for 25 years from the date of filing. Significant to both is that neither instrument references or distinguishes between the aesthetic or functional nature of the design.

To obtain protection, the design must be 'new' and have 'individual character'. 'New' is not an absolute novelty standard like in patent. There are some limitations on the novelty requirement, although prior art can be considered from a different marketing sector than the design seeking protection. *See Green Lane Prods. Ltd. v. PMS Int'l Group Plc* [2008] EWCA Civ. 358. Individual character, meanwhile, is found when 'the overall impression [the design] produces on the informed user differs from the overall impression produced on such a user by any design which has [previously] been made available to the public'. Dir. Art. 5, Reg. Art. 6. The informed user is a designer with general knowledge of the design category, not necessarily an informed consumer. *See Procter & Gamble Co. v. Reckitt Benckiser (UK) Ltd.* [2007] EWCA Civ. 936. These standards place the tests for obtaining design protection somewhere between the more stringent requirements for patent protection and the less stringent requirements for copyright protection.

Design protection in the EU is significant because it fills several gaps left unprotected by trademark, copyright or design patent. This coverage also has a direct impact on certain industries, such as the fashion industry, where a trend might be fleeting or the design might contain both aesthetic and functional elements. Without clearly delineated design protection, there might be either no protection or overprotection. For example, if there were functional elements or aesthetic functionality, then there might be no protection for a design. If there were no novelty, or the design were an incremental improvement, then it might be nonobvious and not qualify for design patent protection. If there were nonseparable (either physically or conceptually) functional elements, then the design might be a useful article and not qualify for copyright protection. Conversely, if the design were to qualify for trademark protection as trade dress with some functional elements, then the monopoly on the design would perpetuate as long as the trade dress indicated a source of origin and maintained its goodwill. Likewise, the term of copyright protection is now so long, that protection would potentially survive for several generations.

In contrast to the EU's comprehensive approach, the US has attempted a *sui generis* approach to design protection, but it has been industry-focused and has only had limited success. The US has incorporated into the Copyright Act *sui generis* protection for boat hull designs and mask works. The addition of boat hull protection was a direct response to the *Bonito Boats* case, 489 U.S. 141 (1989), where a Florida statute that would have protected boat hulls was ruled pre-empted by the Supreme Court. Several congressional attempts have been made to enact similar protection following these models for fashion design, but none have been successful thus far. As a result, the fashion industry, like many other industries that produce goods incorporating both form and function, has only limited protection for discrete elements in the overall design, such as the incorporation of a trademark in a pattern or an ornamental aspect or feature that is not a useful article under copyright law.

VII. HARMONIZATION AND DIVERGENCE

Some scholars have looked to the EU Design Directive and Regulation as a model that the US could follow for design protection as a complement to trade dress protection. Indeed, design protection in the EU fills some of the gaps left open by trade dress and other areas of IP, specifically for packaging and designs that incorporate both form and function. The design protection, furthermore, is important for industries, such as the fashion industry, where some designs are original and have market value but are fleeting in nature. The broad *sui generis* protection for design in the EU, in contrast to the more limited *sui generis* protection under US copyright law, is ultimately the biggest difference between the EU and the US with regard to trade dress protection.

Some of the other differences are more nuanced in nature. For example, while both the US and the EU require distinctiveness and non-functionality for trade dress protection, there are some slight variations.

Both the US and the EU have recognized sliding scales in trademark and trade dress valuing more distinctive source indicators at one end and less distinctive source indicators at the other end. Both the US and the EU place product design lower on the scale than product packaging, however the US has drawn a line between packaging and design that is similar to the line between descriptive and suggestive trademarks. Because design packaging is capable of being inherently distinctive, no showing of secondary meaning is required in the US, whereas a showing is required for product design.

Regarding functionality, both the US and the EU have established absolute bars against registration and both will allow arguments for invalidation of trade dress that is functional. Similar anti-competitive policies support this result; however, the EU has developed a more complex multi-step process than the US with regard to assessing functionality, while the US has several factors that it will consider. On paper, the EU seems slightly more tolerant of functional attributes in its approach by identifying the essential elements in the first step of the analysis, but then moving on to the second step even if there are some functional attributes. The US, in comparison, will consider several factors such as the existence of a utility patent, advertising touting the useful features, the availability of alternatives, and the manufacturing expense. The US seems to focus more on the marketing and public disclosures than the actual attributes of the trade dress. The EU will also consider utility patents and the availability of alternatives, but the latter only comes later in its multi-step analysis.

Furthermore, there is potentially a difference in the timing for determining functionality, especially with aesthetic functionality. While the aesthetic functionality doctrines are similar, the EU leans more toward determining aesthetic functionality at the time of the application for registration, whereas aesthetic functionality can develop at any time in the US. US courts also seem more willing to apply aesthetic functionality, whereas the EU arguably views aesthetic functionality as a harsh penalty and is seemingly less willing to apply it.

The respective starting points for protection in the US and the EU also necessarily color the ways and means that trade dress is protected. The US approach is not unlike the way it protects geographical indicators (GIs) as a subset of trademark, primarily under certification and collective marks, while the European Union treats GIs as existing parallel to trademarks with their own certification system. In both scenarios, trade dress and GIs, the US strives to fit trade dress protection within the existing trademark skein. The EU uses trademark, but it has also created an independent system for design protection to address what they recognized as the unique challenges of the genre.

In broad strokes, the US seems to value the efficiency and consistency of applying an existing system with some modifications, even if it has large gaps in protection, while the EU has taken a multi-faceted approach by enacting *sui generis* design right protection. The US applies more of an inside out approach, starting with the system and then fitting the element within the system; while the EU, broadly speaking, starts with the element in need of protection and then determines the appropriate system. Interestingly, these respective approaches vary in theory from the traditional inductive approach of common law countries where individual cases combine to develop a broader rule, which is then applied to a specific case, compared to the deductive approach of civil law countries using a broader rule and then applying it in individual cases.

Regardless of these observations, it is indisputable that in both the US and the EU, trade dress has developed primarily from common law traditions, has continued to evolve with case law, and that both jurisdictions will continue to learn from the other's respective decisions.

BIBLIOGRAPHY

International Treaties

Agreement on Trade-Related Aspects of Intellectual Property, http://www.wto.org/english/docs_e/legal_e/27-trips.pdf

Hague Agreement Concerning the International Registration of Industrial Designs, http://www.wipo.int/treaties/en/registration/hague/

Paris Convention for Protection of Industrial Property, http://www.wipo.int/treaties/en/ip/paris/trtdocs_wo020.html

Protocol Relating to the Madrid Agreement Concerning the International Registration of Marks, http://www.wipo.int/treaties/en/registration/madrid_protocol/

Regulations and Directives (EU)

Commission Regulation (EC) No 1041/2005 of 29 June 2005 amending Regulation (EC) No 2868/95 implementing Council Regulation (EC) No 40/94 on the Community trade mark

Commission Regulation (EC) No 2245/2002 of 21 October 2002 implementing Council Regulation (EC) No 6/2002 on Community designs

Council Regulation (EC) No 207/2009 of 26 February 2009 on the Community trade mark.

Council Regulation 6/2002/EC of December 2001, O.J. L. 3 (Jan. 5, 2002)

Directive 89/104/EEC to approximate the laws of the Member States relating to trade marks

Directive 2008/95/EC of the European Parliament and of the Council of 22 October 2008 to approximate the laws of the Member States relating to trade marks

Directive 98/71/EC of the European Parliament and of the Council of 13 October 1998 on The Legal Protection of Design

Statutes (US)

Lanham Act, 15 U.S.C. § 1052(e)(5)

Lanham Act, 15 U.S.C. § 1052(f)

Lanham Act, 15 U.S.C. § 1064(3), § 1115(b)(8)

Lanham Act, 15 U.S.C. § 1091(c)

Administrative Regulations and Manuals

U.S. Trademark Manual of Examining Procedure 2010, Chapter 1200, Section 1202, 'Registration of Trade Dress', http://tess2.uspto.gov/tmdb/tmep/1200.htm#_T120202, access 16 August 2011

Cases (US)

Abercrombie & Fitch Co. v. Hunting World, Inc., 537 F.2d 4 (2d Cir. 1976)

Bonito Boats, Inc. v. Thunder Craft Boats, Inc., 489 U.S. 141 (1989)

Fleischer Studios, Inc. v. A.V.E.L.A., Inc., 636 F.3d 1115 (9th Cir. 2011)

In re Brouwerji Bosteels, ___ USPQ2d __, Ser. No. 77357895 (TTAB August 26, 2010)

In re File, 48 USPQ2d 1363 (TTAB 1998)

In re J. Kinderman & Sons Inc., 46 USPQ2d 1253 (TTAB 1998)

In re Morton-Norwich Prods., Inc., 671 F.2d 1332 (C.C.P.A. 1982)

Inwood Labs., Inc. v. Ives Labs., Inc., 456 U.S. 844 (1982)

Pagliero v. Wallace China Co., 198 F.2d 339 (9th Cir. 1952)

Qualitex Co. v. Jacobson Prods. Co., Inc., 514 U.S. 159 (1995)

Rosetta Stone Ltd. v. Google Inc., 730 F.Supp.2d 531 (E.D. Va. 2010)

Seabrook Foods, Inc. v. Bar-Well Foods, Ltd., 568 F.2d 1342 (C.C.P.A. 1977)

TrafFix Devices, Inc. v. Mktg. Displays, Inc., 532 U.S. 23 (2001)

Taco Cabana Int'l Inc. v. Two Pesos, Inc., 932 F. 2d 1113 (5th Cir. 1991)

Two Pesos, Inc. v. Taco Cabana, Inc., 505 U.S. 763 (1992)

Wal-Mart Stores, Inc. v. Samara Bros., Inc., 529 U.S. 205 (2000)

Yankee Candle Co. v. Bridgewater Candle Co., LLC, 259 F.3d 25 (1st Cir. 2001)

Cases (EU)

Case *Benetton Group Spa v. G-Star Int'l BV* [2007] E.C.R. I-07709 (E.C.J. 2007)

Case C-363/99 *Koninklijke v. Benelux-Merkenbureau (Postkantoor)* [2004] E.C.R. I-1619; [2004] E.T.M.R. 57, ECJ)

Case C-299/99 *Koninklijke Philips Electronics NV v. Remington Consumer Products Ltd*, 2002 E.T.M.R. 81 (E.C.J. 2002)

Case C-48/09, *Lego Juris A/S v. Office for Harmonisation in the Internal Market*, 2010 ECR ____ (ECJ Advocate-General, January 26, 2010)
Case C-25/05P *August Storck KG v. OHIM*, judgment June 22, 2006
Case C-218/01 *Henkel KgAA v. OHIM* [2004] E.C.R. I-1715; [2005] E.T.M.R. 45, ECJ
Case C-218/01 *Henkel KGAA v. Deutsche Patent-und Markenamt* [2005] E.T.M.R. 45, ECJ
Combine Cases T-146/02 and C-153/02, *Deutsche SiSI-Werke GmbH & Co Betriebs KG v. OHIM* [2004] E.C.R. II-447; [2004] E.T.M.R. 72, CFI
Green Lane Prods. Ltd. v. PMS Int'l Group Plc [2008] EWCA Civ. 358
Procter & Gamble Co. v. Reckitt Benckiser (UK) Ltd. [2007] EWCA Civ. 936

Books, Chapters, Articles and other Secondary Sources

Altman, Louis and Malla Pollack (2010), *Callmann on Unfair Competition, Trademarks and Monopolies*, 3, US: Thomson Reuters
Dinwoodie, Graeme B. and Mark D. Janis (2010), *Trade Dress and Design Law*, US: Wolters Kluwer
Dinwoodie, Graeme B. and William O. Hennessey, Shira Perlmutter, Graeme W. Austin (2008), *International Intellectual Property Law and Policy*, 2d ed., US: LexisNexis
Dinwoodie, Graeme B. (1999), 'Essay: The Integration of International and Domestic Intellectual Property Lawmaking', *Columbia-VLA Journal of Law & the Arts*, 23, US: 307–15
Dinwoodie, Graeme B. (1996), 'Federalized Functionalism: The Future of Design Protection in the European Union', *AIPLA Quarterly Journal*, 24 (2, 3, 4), US: 611–723
Harrison, Roslyn S. (1997), 'Trade Dress Law in the United States, Western Europe, and Pacific Rim Countries', *Practicing Law Institute Patents, Copyrights, Trademarks, and Literary Property Course Handbook Series*, US: 461–564
Hilliard, David C., Joseph Nye Welch II, and Uli Widmaier (2008), *Trademarks and Unfair Competition*, 7th ed., US, LexisNexis
Kieff, F. Scott and Ralph Nack (2010–11), *International, United States and European Intellectual Property Selected Source Materials*, US: Wolters Kluwer
Kur, Annette (2009), 'Too pretty to protect? Trade mark law and the enigma of aesthetic functionality', in Josef Drexl, Reto M. Hilty, Laurence Boy, Christine Godt, Bernard Remiche (eds.), *Technology and Competition Contributions in Honor of Hanns Ullrich*, Belgium: Larcier 139–59Kur, Annette (1996), 'TRIPS and Design Protection', in Friedrich-Karl Beier and Gerhard Schricker (eds.), *From GATT to TRIPS: The Agreement on Trade-Related Aspects of Intellectual Property Rights*, US: Wienheim 141–56
Machnicka, Agnieszka (2009), 'Fashion design – The European Union and the United States compared: The role of fashion creations and their legal recognition', in Josef Drexl, Reto M. Hilty, Laurence Boy, Christine Godt, and Bernard Remiche (eds.), *Technology and Competition Contributions in Honor of Hanns Ullrich*, Belgium: Larcier 199–220
Rigney, David E. (originally published in 1988), 'Application of secondary

meaning test in action for trade dress infringement under § 43(a) of Lanham Act (15 U.S.C.A. § 1125(a))', *American Law Reports Federal*, 87, US: 15 *et seq.*
Tritton, Guy and Richard Davis, Michael Edenborough, James Graham, Simon Malynicz, and Ashley Roughton (2008), *Intellectual Property in Europe*, (3d ed.), UK: Thomson Sweet & Maxwell

12. A comparative analysis of the protection of geographical indications in the European Union and the United States under *sui generis* and trademark systems

Gail E. Evans

I. INTRODUCTION

As a form of intellectual property the geographical indication (GI) is distinguished by its variety of form and complex character, being so embedded in the legal cultures of civil and common law systems, that continued international harmonization is proving an exceptionally difficult task.[1] The definition within the Agreement on Trade-Related Aspects of Intellectual Property Rights (TRIPS) of 1994 remains the most successful attempt yet to harmonize the variety of definitions which represent the various ways in which GIs are protected under national laws.[2] Significant among these

[1] Further on the history of international harmonization, see, World Intellectual Property Organization (Marcus Höpperger, WIPO), 'Introduction to Geographical Indications and Recent Developments in the World Intellectual Property Organization', San Francisco, California, 2003, WIPO/GEO/SFO/03/1 at p. 4.

[2] Geographical indications are defined in TRIPS Article 22 as 'indications which identify a good as originating in the territory of a Member, or a region or locality in that territory, where a given quality, reputation or other characteristic of the good is essentially attributable to its geographical origin': TRIPS, Annex 1C of the Marrakesh Agreement Establishing the World Trade Organization, signed in Marrakesh, Morocco on 15 April 1994: http://www.wto.org/english/tratop_e/trips_e/t_agm0_e.htm. The Paris Convention for the Protection of Industrial Property (1883, as amended 1979) identifies geographical indications (both appellations of origin and indications of source: Art. 1(2)) as a distinct intellectual property right, but does not include an express definition. Article 1(1) of the Madrid Agreement for the Repression of False or Deceptive Indications of Source on Goods of 1891, while containing no definition as such, refers to the term

is the *sui generis*[3] system of the EU on the one hand; and the trademark system of the US on the other. The well-known designations 'Feta' cheese and 'Washington' apples are but two examples of geographical indications utilized by producers from the EU and the United States to differentiate agricultural commodities based on a linkage of origin with quality.

In the EU, foundational Regulation 2081 of 1992 on the Protection of Geographical Indications and Designations for Agricultural Products and Foodstuffs,[4] (GI Regulation) owes much of its heritage to the civil law systems for the registration of appellations of origin in particular France, Italy, Portugal and Spain.[5] The GI Regulation defines two types of registrable names, namely 'protected geographical indications (PGIs) and 'protected designations of origin' (PDOs).[6] The differences between the PGI and the PDO are marked by the character and extent of the linkage of production to the defined geographical area. While the PDO and the PGI

'indications of source' (which is understood to include appellations of origin) as 'all goods bearing a false or deceptive indication by which one of the countries to which this Agreement applies, or a place situated therein, is directly or indirectly indicated as being the country or place of origin shall be seized on importation into any of the said countries'. Article 2(1) of the Lisbon Agreement for the Protection of Appellations of Origin and their International Registration, 1958 ('Lisbon Agreement') defines the narrower term 'appellation of origin' as 'the geographical name of a country, region, or locality, which serves to designate a product originating therein, the quality and characteristics of which are due exclusively or essentially to the geographical environment, including natural and human factors'.

3 *Sui generis*, a Latin expression meaning 'of its own kind', is a term used to identify a legal classification that exists independently because of the specific creation of an entitlement or obligation.

4 Entered into force on 25 July 1993: its fifth recital states in the relevant part: 'the labeling of agricultural products and foodstuffs is subject to the general rules laid down in Council Directive 79/112 of 18 December 1978 . . . in view of their specific nature, additional special provisions should be adopted for agricultural products and foodstuffs from a specified geographical area'. That system does not apply to wines and spirits, which are covered by separate European regulations.

5 For a brief description of national laws for the protection of appellations of origin in France and Italy see, Bernard O'Connor, *Law of Geographical Indications* (London: Cameron & May 2004) at pp. 165–190 and; Lucatelli S. 'Appellations of Origin and Geographical Indications in OECD Member Countries: Economic and Legal Implications.' OECD, Directorate for Food, Agriculture and Fisheries, Trade Directorate, (2000) COM/AGR/APM/TD/WP(2000)15/FINAL at pp. 57–65.

6 Council Regulation (EC) No. 510/2006 (adopted on 20 March) on the Protection of Geographical Indications and Designations of Origin for Agricultural Products and Foodstuffs (replacing former Council Regulation (EEC) No. 2081/92: OJL 208, 24.7.1992), <http://eur-lex.europa.eu/LexUriServ/LexUriServ.do?uri=CELEX:31992R2081:EN:HTML>.

each bear a distinctive relationship to the place of production, each differs in the character of that relationship.[7]

By contrast, in the US with its predominantly common law tradition,[8] we find the registration of geographical indications embodied in statutory trademark law. As a general rule, a geographical indication cannot be registered as a trademark,[9] but it can be registered as a certification mark. Certification may apply to materials, methods of manufacture, quality, or geographical origin.[10] As with the specification that accompanies an application for a GI, registration entails submission to the US Patent and Trademark Office (USPTO) of the standards for the certification program. As defined in the statute, the owner of a certification mark is not the end-user of the certification mark.[11] Instead, the owner is that party responsible for the certification or approval that is communicated to consumers by the mark.

The deep division between common and civil law countries regarding the regulation of GIs is manifest in the low number of signatories to the Lisbon Agreement for the Protection of Appellations of Origin.[12] Additionally, within the framework of World Trade Organization (WTO) negotiations, the continued disagreement over increased protection, including the character of a multilateral register for GIs, is further

---

[7] Further see, G.E. Evans, 'The Comparative Advantages of Geographical Indications and Community Trade Marks for the Marketing of Agricultural Products in the European Union', International Review of Intellectual Property and Competition Law (IIC), 2010, 41(6), 647–652.

[8] The Trademark Act (Lanham Act) is found in Title 15 of the US Code. Note: this act does not exclusively govern US trademark law, since both common law and state statutes also control some aspects of trademark protection. Cf. England, the home of the common law, which originated in the early Middle Ages in the King's Court (Curia Regis), from the latter 20th century, has been in the singular position of having to implement Community regulations on the protection of designations of origin, which are, in conception, a transplantation of French civil law: further see J.H. Baker, *An Introduction to English Legal History* (4th ed. Butterworths, London, 2002) at pp. 2–3.

[9] The presumption that a geographic term is inherently weak does not attach to geographic terms that are used to certify regional origin. Generally, geographically descriptive terms are regarded as inherently weak, without evidence of acquired distinctiveness. However, 15 U.S.C.§1052(e)(2) (Trademark Act), provides a specific exception for marks used to certify indications of regional origin under Section 4 of the Act. See Tea Board of India v. The Republic of Tea, Inc., 80 USPQ2d 1881 (TTAB 2006) pp. 50–51.

[10] See 15 USC § 1127 respecting the definition of a certification mark.

[11] See 37 CFR Rules of Practice, § 2.45(a).

[12] There are 27 contracting parties to the Lisbon Agreement: http://www.wipo.int/lisbon/en/legal_texts/.

symptomatic of the enduring differences in the regulation of GIs between common and civil law systems. We may well ask whether the mandate to protect GIs under the TRIPS Agreement has after all, had relatively little impact on the character of national law and legal tradition?

On the contrary, where previously more prescriptive treaties failed, TRIPS has succeeded in effecting a compromise between civil and common law systems, arguably by providing no more than minimum standards of protection, and allowing Members the freedom to choose the legal means of protection.[13] For the United States, as a common law jurisdiction, this meant the freedom to protect GIs as part of the trademark system.[14] On the other hand, consistent with the civil law tradition, the EU has continued to protect GIs as a distinct form of intellectual property, under a *sui generis* system of registration and protection that is independent of the trademark system.[15]

Two questions remain: first, as to the direct impact of Articles 22 to 24 of the TRIPS Agreement on national systems for the protection of GIs and; secondly, as to their indirect impact on the interrelationship of the

---

[13] TRIPS Art. 22(2) relies on the historic success of the Paris Convention by mandating that WTO Member States 'provide the legal means for interested parties to prevent any use which constitutes an act of unfair competition within the meaning of Article 10bis of the Paris Convention (1967). For a comparison of the common law tort of passing off and the unfair competition laws of civil law countries see: World Intellectual Property Organization (Marcus Höpperger, WIPO), 'Introduction to Geographical Indications and Recent Developments in the World Intellectual Property Organization', San Francisco, California, 2003, WIPO/GEO/SFO/03/1 at pp. 5–6.

[14] On the protection of GIs under the American system of certification and collective marks see Justin Hughes, 'Champagne, Feta, and Bourbon – the Spirited Debate About Geographical Indications', Hastings Law Journal, Vol. 58, p. 299, 2006, at pp. 308–311.

[15] Note: the regulation of GIs in the EU is currently undergoing codification and amendment with a view to simplifying the registration process and improving product certification: See Proposal for a Regulation on Agricultural Product Quality Schemes, COM (2010) 733 Final, Brussels, 10.12.2010, 2010/0353 (COD) ('Commission text') and; the Proposal for a Regulation on Agricultural Product Quality Schemes, Presidency compromise text, 23 February 2011: Committee on Agriculture and Rural Development, Report tabled for plenary sitting 12.09.2012 (first reading 12.7.2011) on the Proposal for a Regulation on Agricultural Product Quality Schemes (COM (2010) 0733 – C7-0423/2010 – 2010/0353 (COD)): http://www.europarl.europa.eu/oeil/popups/ficheprocedure.do?lang=en&reference=2010/0353(COD). See further, G.E. Evans, 'The Simplification of European Legislation for the Protection of Geographical Indications: The Proposed Regulation on Agricultural Product Quality Schemes', EIPR, Issue 11, 2012, pp. 30–46.

US trademark system with that of the EU's *sui generis* system of protection. Paradoxically, the reception of the GI Regulation within the law of the United Kingdom suggests that given the distinctive adaptability of the common law, the wholesale transplantation of the *sui generis* model is a feasible proposition.[16] The success of that transplantation and the rapid adoption of GIs as a means of protecting local products throughout the UK, attests to the potential for the assimilation of the *sui generis* model within the common law system, at least within a highly integrated regional polity with a mixed system of laws.[17]

While the TRIPS obligations have served to strengthen the registration of GIs throughout the EU, what of their impact on the Community Regulation as mediated by a third country, notably the US and its trade mark system? In 2005, the difficulty in registering US-based GIs under the EU's *sui generis* system prompted the US to bring a complaint before the WTO. The US case was chiefly based on the discriminatory nature of the European GI Regulation in so far as, contrary to TRIPS' obligations, it required third countries to adopt 'EU-style' protection; and failed to enforce earlier US trademarks giving priority to European GIs. On the one hand, in compliance with the WTO ruling, the GI Regulation was amended in 2006 in order to simplify applications for registration from third countries. However, in the matter of priority, US concerns remain over the way in which earlier trademarks containing a geographical name may be obliged to coexist with later registered geographical indications to the detriment of their distinctiveness.[18] The seemingly irresolvable dispute

---

[16] In principle however, in the case of the US, as Kenneth Port reminds us, civil law notions of trademark ownership may be inconsistent with the commerce clause of the Constitution, which governs the power to make federal trademark law: see further 'The Congressional Expansion of American Trademark law: A Civil Law System in the Making' 35 Wake Forest L. Rev. (2000) 827, at pp. 835–46, in respect of the intention to use provision (15 U.S.C. 1051(b)).

[17] On the sources of UK and EU law see: W. Cornish, D. Llewelyn, T. Aplin, *Intellectual Property: Patents, Copyrights, Trade Marks And Allied Rights* (7th ed. Sweet and Maxwell, 2010) at pp. 21–7.

[18] Office of the United States Trade Representative, 2007 at 4, 15–16: 'Special 301 Report': http://www.ustr.gov/sites/default/files/asset_upload_file230_11122.pdf. The issue is whether, allowing a GI to coexist will in time have an adverse impact on the mark's distinctiveness. In Consorzio del Prosciutto di Parma v. Parma Sausage Products, the TTAB recognized that it was 'only as a result of petitioner's publicity efforts in the United States, undertaken almost 20 years after the issuance of respondent's registration, that the cloud of geographic deceptiveness has been raised over respondent's mark': 23 USPQ 2d 1894 (1992 TTAB). Further see Dev Gangjee, 'Quibbling Siblings: Conflicts Between Trade Marks And Geographical Indications', Chicago-Kent Law Review, (2007) 82 (3). pp. 1253–91.

between American brewer Anheuser-Busch and Czech rival Budějovický Budvar for respective rights in the name 'Budweiser' as both trademark and geographical indication continues to engage trademark offices and courts throughout the EU.[19]

Likewise, given the strong demand by producers in the EU for the protection of their GIs in the lucrative US market, should we query the impact of the *sui generis* model of registration on the common law jurisdiction of the United States? In sum, to what extent are calls by EU and US governments for the reciprocal protection of marks and geographical indications giving rise to an involuntary harmonization of the two systems?[20] By examining recent case law, this chapter aims to assess the extent to which the EU *sui generis* and the US trademark models for the protection of GIs are undergoing change triggered by the TRIPS Agreement and sustained by calls for continued reform within the WTO and the World Intellectual Property Organization (WIPO). As a result of the TRIPS Agreement it is argued, the EU and the US systems for the registration of GIs are engaged in a regulatory competition that is gradually transforming significant aspects of each system, whether in statutory provision or the manner of its interpretation. It is an assessment that is limited to the most significant issues touching GIs for agricultural products other than wines and spirits; and one that has yet to take account of the impact of bilateral and regional trade agreements between the EU, US and their respective trading partners.

---

[19] The battle over the right to the name 'Budweiser' has pitted the world's largest brewer, Anheuser-Busch of the United States, against the 'boutique' Czech brewer Budejovicky Budvar. The latter, based in the Czech town of Ceske Budejovice (also known as Budweis), claims it has been brewing a beer under the name since the 13th century, although the American beer has gained broader international reputation in recent years. Further see G.E. Evans, 'Substantive Trademark Law Harmonization: On the Emerging Coherence between the Jurisprudence of the WTO Appellate Body and the European Court of Justice' in G. Dinwoodie and M. Janis eds., *Trademark Law and Theory: A Handbook of Contemporary Research*, ch. 7, Edward Elgar, 2009, 177–203.

[20] A term used by Kenneth Port with respect to the impact of civilian trademark law on that of the US: see 'The Congressional Expansion of American Trademark law: A Civil Law System in the Making' 35 Wake Forest L. Rev. (2000) 827, at p. 830. Also commenting on the influence of civilian law on US trademark law as a result of the TRIPS Agreement, see Marshall Leaffer, 'Appellations of Origin and Geographic Indications in US Law after NAFTA and GATT', in International Intellectual Property Law And Policy, Vol. 2 (1998) at pp. 45–1 – 45–18.

II. THE EU GI REGULATION

The EU Regulation of GIs for food and agricultural products follows a *sui generis* model of protection that comprises a unique system for the registration of GIs that is independent of the trademark system.[21] The formation of the European Community enabled the European Commission to make the protection for geographical indications an integral part of Common Market agricultural policy. Council Regulation 2081/92 on the Protection of Geographical Indications and Designations for Agricultural Products and Foodstuffs states in its seventh recital that in view of the 'diversity in the national practices for implementing registered designations of origin and geographical indications . . . a Community approach should be envisaged . . . a framework of Community rules on protection will permit the development of geographical indications and designations of origin since, by providing a more uniform approach, such a framework will ensure fair competition between the producers of products bearing such indications and enhance the credibility of the products in the consumers' eyes'.

Regulation 510 of 2006 on the Protection of Geographical Indications defines two types of registrable names, namely 'Protected Designations of Origin' (PDOs) and 'Protected Geographical Indications' (PGIs).[22] The PDO is the more narrowly defined. To qualify for a PDO, the product must be produced within the specified geographical area, and the product's quality or characteristics must be 'essentially due to that area'. The requirements for a PDO are more stringent in so far as the product must not only originate in the place but its quality also must be exclusively due to a particular geographical environment with its inherent natural as well

---

[21] For a description of Regulation 510/2006 see G.E. Evans, 'The Comparative Advantages Of Geographical Indications And Community Trade Marks for the Marketing Of Agricultural Products in the European Union, *International Review of Intellectual Property and Competition Law* (IIC), 2010, 41(6), 645, at 649–55 and; on the proposed amendments see G.E. Evans, 'The Simplification of European Legislation for the Protection of Geographical Indications: The Proposed Regulation on Agricultural Product Quality Schemes', EIPR, Issue 11, 2012, pp. 30–46.

[22] See Arts. 2(1)(a) and 2(1)(b) for the respective definitions of PDO and PGI; to the same effect see Arts. 2(2)(a) and 2(2)(b) of foundational Regulation (EEC) No. 2081/92. Further on amendments to the definitions see, G.E. Evans, 'The Simplification of European Legislation for the Protection of Geographical Indications: The Proposed Regulation on Agricultural Product Quality Schemes', EIPR, Issue 11, 2012, pp. 30–46.

as human factors.[23] For example, the reputation of 'feta'[24] as a PDO is held to be 'essentially due' to a particular geographical environment, in so far as the specification narrates that there are natural and human factors which give this cheese its particular characteristics, including the amount of sunshine, temperature changes, the practice of transhumance, extensive grazing and vegetation.[25] In addition, the production, processing and preparation of the product must take place within a defined geographical area.

By comparison, the PGI[26] is defined broadly enough for most locally based products to take advantage of its protection. The PGI requires the product be produced, processed or prepared in the geographical area, and the quality, reputation or other characteristics to be generally 'attributable' rather than 'essentially due' to that area. At its most attenuated point the definition of a PGI simply requires a link between the product and the reputation of the place.[27] The product need not originate entirely from the

---

[23] Protected designation of origin is defined as 'the name of a region, a specific place or, in exceptional cases, a country, used to describe an agricultural product or a foodstuff: originating in that region, specific place or country, and the quality or characteristics of which are essentially or exclusively due to a particular geographical environment with its inherent natural and human factors, and the production, processing and preparation of which take place in the defined geographical area': Art. 2(1) (a) of Regulation 510/2006.

[24] Note that the name 'Feta' (for a soft white cheese) is a traditional non-geographical name: Art. 2(2) of Regulation 510/2006 states that traditional non-geographical names designating an agricultural product or a foodstuff which fulfil the conditions referred to in para. 1 shall also be considered as designations of origin or geographical indications within the meaning of Art. 2(2).

[25] Commission Regulation (EC) No. 1829/2002 of 14 October 2002 amending the Annex to Regulation (EC) No. 1107/96 with regard to the name 'Feta', Recitals 35 and 36. Further, documentary evidence submitted by the Greek government refers to 'the development of small native breeds of sheep and goats . . . fitted for survival in an environment that . . . in terms of quality, is endowed with an extremely diversified flora, thus giving the finished product its own specific aroma and flavour'. Joined Cases C-465/02 and C-466/02 *Germany and Denmark v. Commission* [2005] ECR I-9115 (henceforth '*Feta*'), para. 51ff.

[26] Protected geographical indication is defined as 'the name of a region, a specific place or, in exceptional cases, a country, used to describe an agricultural product or a foodstuff: originating in that region, specific place or country, and which possesses a specific quality, reputation or other characteristics attributable to that geographical origin and the production and/or processing and/or preparation of which take place in the defined geographical area': Art. 2(1)(b) of Regulation 510/2006.

[27] The Green Paper and the Impact Assessment question whether such scope risks weakening the intensity of the link between product and place. Specifically, it inquires whether the criteria for PGIs as distinct from PDOs should be made

defined area and need only have one particular quality, rather than the majority of the food's characteristics, that is attributable to the geographical area. The difference between PDO and PGI therefore, will turn on the proximity of the relationship of the product and its qualities with the place of production.

When considering the scope of protection, the PDO is capable of providing the stronger rights as it normally includes all elements of production and processing in the specification.[28] On the other hand, in the case of the PGI, the product need not originate entirely from within the designated region and need only have one particular quality that is attributable, rather than exclusively due to, the geographical area. In the case of *Spreewälder Gurken*[29] the CJEU ruled that a foodstuff may be treated as originating from the geographical area concerned if it is processed or produced in that area, even if the raw materials are sourced from outside the defined area.[30]

As the PGI requires only that production or processing should take place in the defined geographical area, all the raw materials may be sourced from outside. On the one hand, the possibility of sourcing all raw materials from outside the defined geographical area makes the PGI a very flexible form of protection. There would be few producers groups, having the capacity collectively to mobilize production that would not be able to take advantage of the marketing exclusivity offered by the GI system. Both protected geographical indications and protected designations of

---

stricter to strengthen the link between the product and the geographical area: see European Commission, 'Green Paper on agricultural product quality: product standards, farming requirements and quality schemes,' Brussels, 2008, pp. 13–14; and European Commission of Agricultural Product Quality Policy: Impact Assessment Agricultural Product Quality Policy: Impact Assessment, Part B, Geographical Indications, p. 122.

[28] A limited exception remains in the amended Regulation of 2006 for the sourcing of materials from outside the defined area. Art. 2(3) states: 'Notwithstanding paragraph 1(a), certain geographical designations shall be treated as designations of origin where the raw materials for the products concerned come from a geographical area larger than, or different from, the processing area, provided that: (a) the production area of the raw materials is defined; (b) special conditions for the production of the raw materials exist; and (c) there are inspection arrangements to ensure that the conditions referred to in point are adhered to. The designations in question must have been recognized as designations of origin in the country of origin before 1 May 2004.'

[29] Case C-269/99 *Carl Kühne GmbH & Co. KG and Others v. Jütro Konservenfabrik GmbH & Co. KG*, Judgment of the Court (2001) on a reference for a preliminary ruling from the *Landgericht* Hamburg.

[30] *Carl Kühne*, Note 41, para. 61.

origin are of indefinite duration, so long as the conditions of the product specification continue to be met.[31]

Consistent with the *sui generis* nature of the EU system for the registration of GIs, there is an independent filing procedure.[32] Groups of producers from Member States apply directly to their national authorities, who subsequently forward applications to the European Commission for further scrutiny.[33] Following the amendment of the Regulation in 2006,[34] the procedure for third country applicants has been simplified so that they also benefit from a one-step process, either filing applications online or sending them to the Commission for examination via their national authorities.[35] In the case of third-country applicants, the GI must be protected in its country of origin.[36] Since the amendment, the number of

---

31 To be eligible for a PDO or a PGI, applicants must complete a product specification which contains standards and conditions for quality control and inspection: see Art. 4, Regulation 510/2006. See also Art. 12 regarding cancellation of registered names in the event the conditions of the specification are no longer ensured.

32 The procedure for filing an application for a PGI or a PDO with the European Commission is set out in Arts 5, 6, 7, 12 and 15 of Regulation 510/2006. Note that the European Community is not a Contracting Party to the Lisbon Agreement, a system which enables the international protection for appellations of origin in those countries that are parties to the Agreement: <http://www.wipo.int/lisbon/en/members/>.

33 See, e.g. in the United Kingdom applications are administered by the Department for Environment, Food and Rural Affairs (DEFRA), <http://www.defra.gov.uk/foodfarm/food/industry/regional/foodname/apply.htm>. Third country producers or those outside the EU can complete an application online using the database DOOR or send it directly to the European Commission via their national authority. See GI Regulation, Recital 11 and Arts 5 and 6.

34 Regulation (EEC) No. 2081/92 was repealed and replaced with Regulation (EC) No. 510/2006 (adopted on 20 March) on the Protection of Geographical Indications and Designations of Origin for Agricultural Products and Foodstuffs.

35 In *EC – Geographical Indications* the United States and Australia successfully challenged the former Regulation (EEC) No. 2081/92 on the protection of geographical indications for agricultural products as discriminatory of foreign rightholders. In the result, the amended EC Regulation (EC) No. 510/2006 has facilitated the process for the registration of GIs from third countries: see G.E. Evans, 'The Protection of Geographical Indications after Doha: *Quo Vadis*?' *Journal of International Economic Law*, Volume 9, Number 3, pp. 575–614 (2006) (with M. Blakeney).

36 *See* Recital 13, Reg. 510/2006: stating that protection should be open to GIs of third countries that are protected in their country of origin. In *EC–Geographical Indications* (DS174) the WTO Panel concluded that former Regulation 2081/92 was in breach of national treatment under Art. 3.1 of the TRIPS Agreement, in so far as GIs located in the territory of a WTO Member outside the EU could only

applications has gradually increased, so that, with the economy of a single application, third country producers may obtain protection throughout the twenty-seven Member States of the European Union.[37]

III. US GEOGRAPHICAL CERTIFICATION MARKS

While TRIPS recognizes geographical indications as a discrete form of intellectual property, the US Trademark Act (Lanham Act) does not specifically refer to 'geographical indications'. In contrast to the civil law system, the concept of geographical indications as a separate form of intellectual property is historically unknown to US jurisprudence.[38] Instead, the United States protects geographical indications as a sub-set of the trademark system, normally as certification marks,[39] less frequently as collective marks.[40]

In so far as the provisions for the registration of certification marks

---

be registered under the Regulation if that Member satisfied the conditions in Art. 12(1), which required it to adopt a system for GI protection that was equivalent to that in the European Communities and provide reciprocal protection to products from the European Communities: paras. 7.140, 7.204 and 8.1.

[37] E.g. China has eight registered PDOs and PGIs: http://ec.europa.eu/agriculture/quality/door/list.html.

[38] See Marshall Leaffer regarding the amendment to the Lanham Act that explicitly recognizes for the first time the protection of appellations of origin (Uruguay Round Agreements Act of 1994, Pub. L. No. 103–465, § 522, 108 Stat. 4982, 15 U.S.C. § 1052(a) (1994) (amending Lanham Trademark Act of 1946, Pub. L. No. 489, ch. 540, 60 Stat. 427 (codified in 15 U.S.C. § 1052 (1976))); and the amendment prohibiting registration of geographical indications where the goods do not come from the region indicated (NAFTA Implementation Act of 1993, Pub. L. No. 103–182, § 333(a), 107 Stat. 2114, 15 U.S.C. § 1052(e), (f) (1993) (amending 15 U.S.C. § 1052 (1976)): 'Appellations of Origin and Geographic Indications in US Law after NAFTA and GATT', in International Intellectual Property Law And Policy, Vol. 2 (1998) at pp. 45–1 – 45–18.

[39] A certification mark protects a geographical indication when it is used to 'certify regional . . . origin' in respect of goods or services: 15 U.S.C. § 1127. Examples of PDOs and PGIs registered in the US as certification marks include: PARMIGIANO-REGGIANO and; STILTON cheeses. Notable US geographical certification marks include WASHINGTON for apples and; FLORIDA SUNSHINE TREE for citrus fruit. Further see Justin Hughes, 'Champagne, Feta, and Bourbon – the Spirited Debate About Geographical Indications', *Hastings Law Journal*, Vol. 58, p. 299, 2006, at p. 308.

[40] A collective mark indicates the commercial origin of goods or services in the members of a group: 15 U.S.C. § 1127. See, e.g. 'Frankfurter Apfelwein', owned by Verband Der Deutschen Fruchtwein-Und Schaumwein-Industrie EV is protected in the US as a collective mark.

most nearly approximate the European regulation of GIs, throughout this chapter our focus will be the US certification mark. Under the Lanham Act a geographical certification mark is a 'mark used upon or in connection with the products . . . of one or more persons other than the owner of the mark to certify regional or other origin . . .'[41] A certification mark protects a geographical indication when it is used to certify that the product originates in a specific geographic region, as exemplified by term ROQUEFORT for cheese,[42] but unlike the PDO and PGI, there is no statutory requirement that its use should be demarcated by a defined geographic area.

Nevertheless, both certification mark and GI share a common purpose in so far as they serve to inform consumers that the product meets the specified standards. Like the geographical indication, the certification mark may only be used by persons other than the proprietor. The certification mark is applied by producers, to the product, with the authorization of the owner of the mark. It may be registered in the name of any person, nation, state, or municipality, even though the applicant does not possess an industrial or commercial establishment.[43] Both are characterized by certifiable production standards. In the case of the PDO or a PGI, the role of the producer group is to monitor use and have in place an inspection system, to ensure that the product conforms with the standards for quality control provided in the specification.[44] The Lanham Act stipulates that the certification mark owner must set the relevant certified standards for quality, safety, purity, or other desirable characteristics, and then exercise control over the use of the mark by certified parties.[45]

With respect to the ease of, and criteria for registration, geographical certification marks are registrable under the Trademark Act 'in the same manner and with the same effect as are trademarks'.[46] In seeking to

---

41 15 U.S.C. § 1127.

42 For a certain sheep's milk cheese, coming from the caves of Roquefort, France: see Community of Roquefort v. William Fehndrich, Inc., 303 F.2d 494, 133 U.S.P.Q.633 (2d Cir. 1962).

43 15 USC § 1054. Cf. Paris Convention for the Protection of Industrial Property, Article 6ter, which prevents the use of state emblems and is applicable to geographical indications, but only if the indication is the same as a state emblem, e.g., a flag.

44 Applicants must complete a product specification which contains standards and conditions for quality control and inspection: see Art. 4, Reg. 510/2006.

45 To satisfy this requirement, the applicant must submit a copy of the standards for the certification program to the US Patent and Trademark Office (USPTO): 37 CFR Rules of Practice, § 2.45(a).

46 15 USC § 1054 provides that certification marks are 'subject to the

incorporate geographical terms within trade mark law, the requirement that the mark should be distinctive of the goods formerly presented a major obstacle to their registrability. In the case of individual marks, in the absence of acquired distinctiveness, the law considers geographical names as prima facie descriptive and therefore unregistrable. However, certification marks are now subject to a statutory derogation from the prohibition on the registration of signs that serve to designate geographical origin. The Act stipulates that a geographical name may be protected as a certification mark 'even though it is primarily geographically descriptive'.[47] Therefore, to be eligible for registration, a geographically descriptive term does not need proof of secondary meaning.[48]

Although a private owner and private entity may perform verification of compliance with the required standards of production, in the case of both trademark and GI, ownership and certification are frequently undertaken by government or governmental agency.[49] For example, in the case of Parma Ham, the authority which oversees producers' compliance with the required standards of manufacture is an association of producer representatives, by Italian law, the Consorzio del Prosciutto di Parma. The 'Consorzio' or association that manages the PDO is responsible for ensuring the quality of their product by monitoring the use of the name in trade and, if necessary, informing the authorities of unauthorized use or practice. Currently, the responsibility for establishing and maintaining systems for inspection and compliance rests with national authorities. They are obliged to have in place inspection systems, which are able to provide the monitoring and compliance structures necessary to ensure that the product conforms to the specification.[50] Proposed measures to reform

---

provisions relating to the registration of trademarks, so far as they are applicable. . .'. Further see §1052(e)(2): primarily geographically deceptively misdescriptive marks: a geographically misdescriptive mark is not registrable even if it is not deceptive (meaning that consumers would not consider the geographic term to be a source indicator) as in the term 'Swiss Army Knife'.

47 15 USC § 1052(e)(2) prohibits registration of names primarily geographically descriptive, but specifically excepts 'indications of regional origin' registrable under section 1054. To the same effect see Schedule II UK Trade Marks Act, 1994, s. 50 concerning certification marks.

48 An application for a geographical certification mark may even be filed on the basis of an intention to use: see 15 U.S.C. 1051(b).

49 15 USC § 1054. See, e.g. Idaho Potato Commission, Idaho Code, Title 22, Chapter 12, 22–1207; Florida Citrus Commission enabling statute: Title XXXV Chapter 601 Section 04, 2012, 601.101regarding certification mark ownership.

50 Regulation No 510/2006: Art. 11 concerning the verification of compliance with specifications; Art. 10 regarding official controls; Recital 16; and Art. 4.1 stating that to be eligible to use a PGI or PDO a product must comply with

the GI Regulation seek to specify in some detail the role and responsibility of producer groups and Member States, especially with regard to taking appropriate administrative and judicial action to prevent the unlawful use of the PDO or PGI.[51] By comparison, the Idaho Potato Commission's duties are specific but considerably less prescriptive of the steps in the production process, being more closely related to those of a trademark licensor.[52] The Commission, a self-governing agency of the State of Idaho, according to its governing statute, is responsible for the advertising, promotion, labelling and packaging of the product, as well as the licensing and enforcement of the mark.[53]

Generally speaking, the functions of PGIs, PDOs and trademarks are similar. Consider the designation, *Prosciutto di Parma*. As either PDO or trademark, the name is capable of indicating in short form valuable information about the origin of the product. Generally speaking, a GI describes an agricultural product that originates in a specific place from which its reputation is derived.[54] For its part, a trademark identifies the source of the product as originating from a particular undertaking. Both the GI and

---

the specification. The task of establishing controls is, in line with Regulation No 882/2004 on official feed and food controls, to be undertaken in the first place under the responsibility of national competent authorities.

[51] On reform see Proposal for a Regulation on Agricultural Product Quality Schemes, COM (2010) 733 Final, Brussels, 10.12.2010, 2010/0353 (COD) Articles 13(3); 33–35 and 42: http://www.europarl.europa.eu/oeil/popups/ficheprocedure.do?lang=en&reference=2010/0353(COD). See further, G.E. Evans, 'The Simplification of European Legislation for the Protection of Geographical Indications: The Proposed Regulation on Agricultural Product Quality Schemes', EIPR, Issue 11, 2012, pp. 30–46.

[52] Idaho Potato Commission, Idaho Code, Title 22, Chapter 12.

[53] See powers and duties of commission: Idaho Potato Commission, Idaho Code, Title 22, Chapter 12, 22–1207. Proprietor of: US Trademark Registration No. 2,403,069 (filed Mar. 17, 1997) 'Famous Idaho Potatoes Famous Potatoes Grown In Idaho' certification mark owned by Idaho Potato Commission; US Trademark Registration No. 1,735,559 (filed July 21, 1991) 'Grown In Idaho Idaho Potatoes' certification mark owned by State of Idaho Potato Commission; US Trademark Registration No. 943,815 (filed June 7, 1971) 'Premium Packed Idaho Potatoes' certification mark owned by State of Idaho. Idaho Potato Commission v. M & M Produce Farm & Sales, 335 F.3d 130, 132 (2d Cir. 2003).

[54] Art. 22 of the TRIPS Agreement defines the GI as identifying a good as 'originating in the territory of a Member . . . where a given quality, reputation or other characteristic of the good is essentially attributable to its geographical origin'. See also Reg. 510/2006. Art. 2(1)(a) and (b) respecting the definitions of PDO and PGI.

the trademark enable consumers to predict the quality of the products they purchase, thereby saving search costs.[55]

Nevertheless, their functional similarity does not mean that the two forms of protection are comparable in scope or that their enforcement results in equal outcomes. Unlike an individual mark, a geographical certification mark does not indicate origin in a single commercial source.[56] The term is used by all persons in the region, as a certification mark indicating regional origin.[57] The placing of the mark on goods constitutes a certification by a competent authority independent of producers, that the prescribed characteristics of the certifier and mark owner have been met.[58]

The application for a geographical certification mark may describe the regional origin which the mark certifies, especially in cases where the term in question does not clearly indicate the intended region. However, it is not an essential feature of its statutory definition. Of course, this does not exclude the possibility that the applicant for a certification mark may include, within the certification standards of the product, the existence of a special link between the characteristics of the product and its geographical origin.[59] When seen as no more than technical obstacles, it is possible

---

[55] See Recital 4, GI Regulation; Recital 8, CTM Regulation. See also William M. Landes and Richard A. Posner, *The Economic Structure of Intellectual Property Law* (2003) pp. 166–8; and William Cornish and David Llewelyn, *Intellectual Property: Patents, Copyright, Trade Marks and Allied Rights* (6th edn, Sweet & Maxwell, 2007) pp. 620–3.

[56] 15 USC § 1127 and; TRIPS Art. 15 respecting the definition of a certification mark and a trademark.

[57] See, e.g. Registration No. 1160492 (issued on July 7, 1981) to the Republic of Colombia, provides the 'certification standards and conditions for Colombian coffee, including soluble coffee ('Certified Product'), authorized and certified by the Republic of Colombia,' and goes on to specify the type of beans, region of Colombia, and characteristics of the coffee certified.

[58] The owner must preserve its objectivity by declaring that it will not engage in the production or marketing of any goods or services to which the certification mark is applied: see the conditions for cancellation in 15 USC § 1064.

[59] The owner must set the relevant certified standards for quality, safety, purity, or other desirable characteristics, and then exercise control over the use of the mark by certified parties: see *Information on the System for Protection of Geographical Indications in the United States of America*, World Trade Organization, Council for Trade-Related Aspects of Intellectual Property Rights: Communication of the Permanent Mission of the United States (IP/C/W/76/Add.10), September 19, 1997. See also OECD, Appellations of Origin and Geographical Indications in OECD Member Countries: Economic and Legal Implications, Working Party on Agricultural Policies and Markets of the Committee for Agriculture Joint Working Party of the Committee for Agriculture and the Trade Committee, COM/AGR/APM/TD/WP(2000)15/FINAL (2000: Paris, OECD), p. 10.

to accommodate the varying criteria for the registration, but to do so does not address the differing economic and social perspectives underpinning the definition of certification marks and geographical indications.

In short, even though marks and geographical indications have features in common that serve to differentiate products, further international harmonization is rendered particularly difficult given that each form of intellectual property possesses certain elements that characterize its distinct legal tradition and agricultural heritage. On the one hand, as an indicator of regional origin, the certification mark remains more closely associated with a competitive, industrial model of agriculture. Like an individual mark, the certification mark is renewable at ten-year intervals indefinitely so long as the mark continues in use. In contrast, the GI is more absolute in nature, in so far as the rights the EU accords protected geographical indications (PGIs) and protected designations of origin (PDOs) are of indefinite duration, provided the conditions of the product specification continue to be met.[60] In the case of the PDO and PGI, use is connected with the characteristics and reputation of a specific place, to the extent that if a particular landholding disappears for commercial or environmental reasons, then so will the form of protection.[61] The nature and extent of these differences will be explored in the following parts of the chapter, first in relation to signs that have allegedly become generic and subsequently with respect to signs that due to their identity or similarity conflict, either prior to, or following registration.

IV. REGISTRABILITY AND GENERIC INDICATIONS

During the twentieth century, increased international trade, giving rise to the notion of a global marketplace and sophisticated marketing techniques based on geographical 'branding' rendered the historical adoption of Old World names by New World immigrants an ever more contentious issue of agricultural competition. In the United States, parmesan cheese is an example of a geographical name that became generic for aged, hard

---

[60] See Reg. 510/2006, Art. 12 regarding cancellation of registered names in the event the conditions of the specification are no longer ensured.

[61] See, e.g. when in 2004 Scottish and Newcastle Brewery closed the Tyne Brewery and moved the production of Newcastle brown ale from Newcastle to neighbouring Gateshead, PGI 'Newcastle Brown Ale' was cancelled: see Commission Regulation 952/2007 of 9 August 2007: pursuant to Art. 12(2) and Art. 17(2) of Reg. 510/2006.

cheese. However, in the EU 'Parmigiano Reggiano' is a protected designation of origin (PDO), used exclusively to identify a specific cheese produced in Parma, Italy, under specific conditions.[62] Differences in approach to the eligibility of generic geographic terms for registration in civil and common law jurisdictions has formerly put an end to attempts at international harmonization or at best resulted in an agreement that fails to bridge the legal and cultural divide.

In an attempt to preserve GIs from usurpation, the Madrid Agreement for the Repression of False or Deceptive Indications of Source on Goods[63] prohibits members from allowing geographical indicators to become generic without a decision by a national court. The Madrid Agreement likewise prohibits the false or deceptive use of indicators which suggest that a good originated in the territory of a member state. However, by way of compromise, it grants national courts the capacity to determine whether a designation has become generic, except in the case of wines.

The Lisbon Agreement for the Protection of Appellations of Origin and their International Registration[64] represents a further attempt to protect designations of origin and to counter their use abroad as generic names. The key feature of the Agreement is that members' appellations of origin are protected as such in the country of origin and registered by the International Bureau of WIPO.[65] According to the Lisbon Agreement,

---

[62] Note that the standard and label of the Codex Alimentarius would make Parmesan a generic term, meaning that a cheese from the US could legally use a Parmesan label in international trade. See further Marsha A Echols, *Geographical Indications for Food Products: International Legal and Regulatory Perspectives*, Kluwer Law International, The Netherlands, 2008 at pp. 188–190.

[63] The Madrid Agreement for the Repression of False or Deceptive Indications of Source on Goods, April 14, 1891, as amended July 14, 1967, 21 U.S.T. 1583, 828 U.N.T.S. 389 proscribing the false or deceptive use of indicators which suggest that a good originated in the territory of a member state, and granting national courts the discretion to determine whether an indicator has degenerated into genericism, except in the case of wines, available at http://www.wipo.int/treaties/en/ip/madrid/trtdocs_wo032.html [Accessed January 4, 2013].

[64] The Lisbon Agreement for the Protection of Appellations of Origin and their International Registration (hereinafter referred to as 'the Lisbon Agreement') was adopted in 1958 and revised at Stockholm in 1967. It entered into force on September 25, 1966, and is administered by the International Bureau of the World Intellectual Property Organization (WIPO). The object of the Lisbon Agreement concerns appellations of origin, as defined in Article 2(1) as indications in which the quality and characteristics are 'exclusively or essentially due to the geographical environment, including natural and human factors'.

[65] Members may adopt any form of procedure to register geographical indications, be it by judicial or administrative determination: Article 5. Once registered, an AO is protected in other contracting states 'in accordance with this

appellations of origin (AOs) cannot be deemed generic by any of the members of the Lisbon Union as long as they are protected in their respective countries of origin.[66] As a result even when AOs become generic in a foreign contracting state, that state would still be required to protect them. Moreover, irrespective of the kind of product, contracting states to the Lisbon Agreement are required to ensure that any kind of usurpation or imitation is prohibited under their laws, even if the true origin of the product is indicated or if the appellation is used in translated form or accompanied by terms such as 'kind,' 'type,' 'make,' 'imitation', or the like.[67]

Given its strict protection and lack of flexibility towards requirements for the registration and protection of GIs, the US is neither signatory to the Madrid or the Lisbon Agreement.[68] In contrast, France and Italy, reflecting both their long legal tradition and strength of support for the protection to appellations of origin have been members of the both Madrid and Lisbon Agreements and have been signatories of the Lisbon Agreement for over fifty years.[69] What might be loosely characterized as an attempt to 'export' the civil law approach to the protection of GIs, has met with little multilateral success to date,[70] in view of the small number of signatories to the Lisbon Agreement. Three further attempts by WIPO to reach multilateral agreement during the latter decades of the 20th century,

---

agreement': Article 1: http://www.wipo.int/export/sites/www/lisbon/en/legal_texts/lisbon_agreement.pdf.

66 See Article 6 respecting the presumption that a protected appellation cannot become generic.

67 Article 3, Lisbon Agreement.

68 INTA, brief issue, 'Lisbon Agreement for the Protection of Appellations of Origin, Violation of the. TRIPS Agreement', June 2000 arguing that Lisbon Art. 5(6) is contrary to, and superceded by TRIPS Art. 24(5) in its privileging of AO over prior trademarks containing the geographical name: at p.11. See also Roland Roland Knaak, 'The Protection of Geographical Indications According to the TRIPS Agreement' in Friedrich-Karl Beier and Gerhard Schricker, eds, From GATT to TRIPS: the Agreement on Trade-Related Aspects of Intellectual Property Rights (Weinheim, New York: VCH, 1996) 117 at 119. See also Albrecht Conrad, 'Protection of Geographical Indications in the TRIPs Agreement, *The Trademark Reporter*, Vol. 86, Issue 1 (1996), pp. 11–46 at 30. Membership of the Lisbon Agreement stands at 27: http://www.wipo.int/lisbon/en/legal_texts.

69 The contracting parties to the Madrid Agreement number 35: see http://www.wipo.int/treaties/en/ShowResults.jsp?country_id=ALL&start_year=ANY&end_year=ANY&search_what=C&treaty_id=3 3 [Accessed January 4, 2013]

70 See Norma Dawson, 'Locating Geographical Indications – Perspectives from English Law', The Trademark Reporter, Vol. 90, Issue 4 (July–August 2000), p. 590 at 591–2.

most notably in the Draft Treaty on the Protection of Geographical Indications, likewise met with little success.[71]

Similarly, the two tiered form of protection incorporated in the TRIPS Agreement reveals the continued division between the common and civil law approaches to the regulation of GIs. Article 24 contains a number of exceptions to the general obligations to protect GIs in Article 22, notably an exception permitting the continued use of names which have become generic in a member state. Subsequently, attempts by the WTO to reach agreement on the form and legal consequences of a multilateral register of GIs have divided the EU and US according to their traditional models of protection with regard to provisions for generic names.[72]

Given the constitutional limitations on 'quality monopolies' and the corresponding limitations on trademarks,[73] the US has questioned the extent to which Members would be able to invoke the exception in Article 24.6 of the TRIPS Agreement concerning designations that have become generic after the 18-month period stipulated in the EC Proposal for the lodging of reservations.[74] Under Article 24.6, Members may decide not to protect a geographical indication belonging to a third party because in their territory the name is considered generic. Consequently, as the law stands, a WTO Member need not extend protection to a foreign GI if it is 'customary in common language as the common name for such goods', without regard to the situation in the territory of export.[75] Under the EU proposal, if a WTO Member State is unwilling or unable to examine a GI notification and lodge a reservation or challenge its registration within 18 months, it would no longer be able to claim that that particular name

---

[71] WIPO Draft Treaty on the Protection of Geographical Indications (which unlike the Lisbon Agreement did not require signatories to have domestic laws for the protection of appellations of origin: 25.8.1975, TAO/II/2; WIPO, Draft of the Model Law for Developing Countries on Appellations of Origin and Indications of Source: 30.10.1974, TAO/I/INF.1; WIPO, 'The Need for a New Treaty and its Possible Contents', 9.4.1990, WIPO doc., GEO/CE/1/2.

[72] G.E. Evans, 'The Multilateral Register for Geographical Indications and The Doha Mandate': Anuario Andino De Derechos Intelectuales (Andean Yearbook of Intellectual Property Rights) 2008, Palestra, Lima, 397–419.

[73] See Kenneth Port 'The Congressional Expansion of American Trademark law: A Civil Law System in the Making' 35 Wake Forest L. Rev. (2000) 827, at pp. 835–46.

[74] WTO Council for Trade-Related Aspects of Intellectual Property Rights Special Session, Minutes Of Meeting, 12–13 June 2006, TN/IP/M/17 at pp. 5–10.

[75] In addition, in the case of GIs which have become generic in their country of origin, Article 24(9)(d) provides that there is no obligation under the TRIPS Agreement to protect GIs 'which are not or cease to be protected in their country of origin, or which have fallen into disuse in that country'.

was generic.[76] The GI would be entered on the multilateral register and henceforth protected against unauthorized use.

Contrary to the US position, the notion underpinning the EU proposal for a multilateral register is one which reflects civilian regulation of AOs that nation states not only have sovereignty over their territory but also over the associated place names where those names are capable of product differentiation by virtue of a reputational or quality link with that territory. The effect of the presumption of registrability in EU Proposal would be to reverse the burden of proof thereby substantively altering the balance of rights and obligations under the TRIPS Agreement. Thus, in the event the EU notified 'Feta' as a geographical indication, there would be a presumption of eligibility for protection in all the WTO Members. The proposal would thus oblige all those Members where the term 'Feta' was generic to defend such a determination against the presumption that would flow from the register. Once entered on the multilateral register, though a designation might be altered, or even lost, as a result of changes in technology or processing techniques, it could not be lost as a result of changes in understanding or usage of the protected name. In effect, this would be similar to the position under the Lisbon Agreement, which protects an appellation that has been granted protection in one of the countries of the Special Union from becoming generic, as long as it is protected as an appellation of origin in its country of origin.

The issue becomes urgent for competitors because, in contrast to trademark law, registration renders the geographical indication immune from further attack on grounds of descriptiveness or customary usage. As we shall see in the following part, European disputes that have arisen over names long considered generic by some EU Member States demonstrate the additional risk that producers in third countries incur when they trademark products based on geographical names.

V. GENERICNESS AND THE EUROPEAN REGULATION OF GIS

Like trademark law, the GI Regulation prohibits the registration of names that have become generic.[77] EC Regulation, Article 3(1), defines a

---

[76] In the event a Member failed to place a reservation and found out subsequently that some of its local producers were using a GI for a wine or spirit, it would have to rely upon the exception in Article 24.4 of the Agreement.

[77] Art. 3(1).

'name that has become generic' as the name of an agricultural product or a foodstuff which, although it relates to the place or the region where this product or foodstuff was originally produced or marketed, has become the common name of an agricultural product or a foodstuff. However, unlike trademark law, once registered a PDO or PGI is protected from becoming generic.[78] Consequently, although a designation may be altered, or even lost, as a result of changes in technology or processing techniques, it cannot be lost as a result of changes in understanding or usage of the protected name. The Court of Justice of the EU (CJEU), having been asked several times to rule on the interpretation of 'generic', has developed a set of factors to be applied to its assessment in such cases. Notwithstanding, the statutory prohibition, the court's jurisprudence shows that names which face objection based on their genericness, are likely to face comparatively fewer legal obstacles than they would be subject to, if the assessment were to be made under trademark law.

(i) Method of Assessment

The text of Article 3(1) of Regulation 510/2006 states that if the evidence indicates that the name in question has a principal significance as a generic term denoting a type of product, registration will be refused. Notwithstanding, the CJEU has ruled that terms such as *Feta*, *Parmesan* and *Bayerisches Bier*, long considered to have become generic, are protected under the GI Regulation.[79] In the case of *Feta*, despite the European Commission having granted the name PDO status in 2002, the decision was appealed by Germany, Denmark, France and the UK who applied for annulment of the registration of 'feta' as a PDO, on the basis that the name had become generic. However, in 2005, the CJEU dismissed their action, finding their claim unfounded.[80]

---

[78] To this end Article 13(2) states that 'protected names may not become generic'.

[79] The Regulation 510/2006 allows the CJEU final decision as to whether a GI has become generic of the product among consumers in Europe. Cf. Madrid Agreement for the Repression of False or Deceptive Indications of Source on Goods, 14 April 1891, as amended 14 July 11967, 21 UST 1583, 828 UNTS 389, proscribing the false or deceptive use of indicators which suggest that a good originated in the territory of a Member State, and granting national courts the discretion to determine whether an indicator has degenerated into genericism, except in the case of wine: <http://www.wipo.int/treaties/en/ip/madrid/trtdocs_wo032.html>.

[80] *Feta*, paras. 107–10.

Similarly, in the case of *Parmesan*,[81] Germany unsuccessfully argued that although the term 'parmesan' had historical roots in the region of Parma, it had become a generic name for hard cheeses of diverse origins, grated or intended to be grated, as distinct from the PDO 'Parmigiano Reggiano'.[82] The Grand Chamber of the CJEU took a broad view of the protection accorded such compound designations, rejecting the contention that they are infringed only when used in the exact form in which they are registered.[83] Again, in the case of the PGI 'Bayerisches Bier',[84] the defendant, a Dutch beer producer, failed to convince the court that the term 'Bayerisches' or translations of it had become generic for beer produced in accordance with 'the Bavarian method' of production.[85]

The remainder of Part IV considers the criteria adopted by the CJEU in finding that these names retained a direct link between the reputation of the product and its geographical origin. In establishing whether or not a name has become generic, Art. 3(1) of the Regulation directs the court to take account of all factors, in particular:

(a) The existing situation in the Member States and in areas of consumption; and
(b) The relevant national or Community laws.

The CJEU has elaborated these factors at length, finding that, when determining the status of a name, it is necessary to consider the following criteria:

i. Supply, that is, the places of production of the product concerned both inside and outside the Member State;
ii. Persistence of geographic connotation;
iii. Demand, that is, the consumption of that product inside and outside that Member State;

---

[81] Case C-132/05, *Commission of the European Communities v. Germany*, CJEU, Grand Chamber, 2008 (henceforth *Parmesan*).

[82] Under Art. 13(1) (d) of Regulation (EC) No. 510/2006 (and former GI Regulation (EEC) No. 2081/92), 'where a registered name contains within it the name of an agricultural product or foodstuff, which is considered generic, the use of that generic name on the appropriate agricultural product or foodstuff shall not be considered to be contrary to points (a) or (b) in the first subparagraph'.

[83] *Parmesan*, para. 31.

[84] Case C-343/07 Bavaria N.V. and Bavaria Italia Srl v. Bayerischer Brauerbund, CJEU, 2009 (henceforth Bavaria).

[85] Concerning the history of the Bavarian bottom-fermentation brewing method see Case C-343/07 Bavaria Italia at para. 96.

iv. It is perceived by consumers inside and outside the Member State concerned; and
v. The existence of national legislation specifically relating to that product, and the way in which the name has been used in Community law.[86]

1. Place of Production

Consistent with the definitional requirements for PDOs and PGIs, the first inquiry the court makes is to ascertain the degree of historic connection, if any, between a specific place and the origin of the product in question. In *Bayerische Bier* the CJEU found that the name is generic only if the direct link between the geographical origin of the product and its reputation or a specific quality of that product has disappeared, so that the name does no more than describe a style or type of product.[87] To this end, it is important to provide evidence that that the product in question is still made using traditional methods. In *Feta*, for example, Denmark claimed that even in Greece, until the late 1980s, 'feta' type cheese was not only produced in Greece to methods other than the traditional Greek methods, but that such cheese was also imported under the name 'feta'.[88] On the other hand, a product which fails to comply with the specification or with traditional methods, provided it is made exclusively for export, is not considered relevant to the determination.[89]

2. Product Status under National Law

Evidence that, prior to the application date, traditional methods were not continuously maintained or that some product was imported will not be necessarily fatal where the national government has acted to preserve the traditional methods of production. For example, the exclusivity attaching to the name 'feta' was saved from loss by the Greek government's enactment of legislation in 1988 to protect the name and to establish a specific geographical area of production, based on locally sourced raw materials

---

[86] *Parmesan*, paras 53 and 101; see also Joined Cases C-465/02 and C-466/02 *Germany and Denmark v. Commission* [2005] ECR I-9115 ('*Feta*'), paras 76–99.

[87] Case C-343/07 *Bavaria NV, Bavaria Italia Srl v. Bayerischer Brauerbund eV*, CJEU, 2009, para. 107.

[88] *Feta*, para. 77. The production of *Feta* commenced in 1972 in Germany, in the 1930s in France and Denmark: *Feta*, para. 81.

[89] In *Parmesan* it was not considered relevant to the determination that cheese which failed to comply with the specification for the PDO 'Parmigiano Reggiano,' was produced in Italy, because the cheese in question was exclusively intended for export to countries where the term 'Parmesan' did not enjoy protection: para. 38.

and traditional practices.[90] In addition, evidence of collective marks and bilateral agreements to reserve the name in question, will be persuasive in demonstrating that the name is not generic.[91]

3. The Character of the Market

The court will consider the character of the market and market share for the product in question. In *Feta* the size of the domestic market was persuasive. The Court noted that the consumption of 'feta' was concentrated in Greece, having been persuaded by the fact that more than 85 percent of Community consumption of 'feta', per capita, per year, took place in Greece.[92]

4. Production and Consumption

The court will consider evidence as to the pattern and duration of production and consumption throughout the EU. The chief inquiry involves ascertaining whether the substantial proportion of production takes place within a defined area of the Member State in question. In *Feta*, it was found that while Denmark and Germany had produced substantial quantities for some considerable time, Greece still had the largest production, indicating that the production of 'feta' had remained concentrated in Greece.[93]

---

[90] Ministerial Order No. 2109/88, 1988, based the definition of the geographical area of production on traditional practices; and Ministerial Order No. 313025, 1994, codified the rules applicable to feta cheese: see *Feta*, paras 76 and 78. Similarly see Case T-291/03 *Consorzio per la Tutela del Formaggio Grana Padano v. OHIM, Biraghi SpA*, CFI, 2007: the term 'Grana' was held not to be generic, based on Italian legislation respecting the name 'grana padano' dating back to 1938: paras 73–8. See also, Case C-446/07 *Grandi Salumifici Italiani SpA v. Regione Emilia-Romagna*, 2009, Opinion of A-G Sharpston, concluding that there could be no finding that a name can be found to be generic while it is subject to an application for PGI or PDO registration: para. 36; followed by the CJEU, 2009, para. 49.

[91] In 1972, the name 'Feta' was protected by bilateral agreement between the Austria and Greece and since then the use of the name in Austria has been reserved exclusively for Greek products: *Feta*, paras 93–4. Again, between 1960 and 1970 the existence of the collective marks 'Bayrisch Bier' and 'Bayrisches Bier', as well as five different bilateral agreements relating to the protection of the name 'Bayerisches Bier' as a geographical name, was said to show that that name was not generic: *Bavaria*, para. 109.

[92] The Court noted that although other EU Member States produced a substantial proportion of feta, the bulk of European production, at about 85 percent, remained in Greece: para. 85.

[93] The Commission acknowledged that feta was produced in Member States other than the Hellenic Republic, in particular, Denmark, Germany and France:

5. Consumer Perception

The court noted that the majority of consumers in Greece considered that the name 'feta' carried a geographical and not a generic connotation. The court also considered evidence of how the name was perceived by consumers elsewhere in the EU.[94] Significantly, it noted that in other Member States, 'feta' was commonly marketed with labels referring to Greek cultural traditions and civilization. The fact that the majority of consumers in Denmark believed that the name was generic was not considered conclusive.

6. Evaluation

Consistent with the civilian tradition, in determining whether the name had lost its geographical connotation, the court framed its analysis in terms of production and marketing, placing particular emphasis on the agricultural heritage, historical roots and collectively shared know-how involved in the linkage of product and place.[95] In Feta, the court found a persistence of geographical connotation based on the fact that, the majority of cheeses bearing the name 'feta' produced in Member States other than Greece, make explicit or implicit reference to Greek territory, culture or tradition. By inference therefore, the court determined that consumers in those Member States perceived 'feta' as a cheese associated with Greece, even if in reality it had been produced in another Member State.[96]

(ii) Restrictive Interpretation of Genericness

The court's restrictive interpretation of genericness means that producers established within the EU, stand a good chance of recovering exclusive rights to a name. To all intents, the law only requires an unspecified pro-

---

para. 87. In the years 1985–1998, Greece produced 115,000 tonnes of feta annually, whereas 27,640 tonnes were produced in Denmark; and production in France varied between 7,960 and 19,964 tonnes; and in Germany it varied between 19,757 and 39,201 tonnes: *Feta*, paras 80–3. Further, see 'UK Dismay as Greeks Win Feta Cheese Rights', *Financial Times*, 25 October 2005, <http://www.ft.com/cms/s/a01bdebe-4571-11da-981b-00000e2511c8.html>.

[94] *Feta*, para. 89; see also *Parmesan*, para. 54. Note that evidence as to consumer perceptions from all Member States of the EU was not considered necessary: *Feta*, para. 86.

[95] Feta, paras 85 and 88; and Parmesan para. 56. See also Laurence Bérard and Philippe Marchenay, *From Localized Products to Geographical Indications*, CNRS Ressources des terroirs, 2008 at pp. 10 and 18:http://www.ethno-terroirs.cnrs.fr/textes/Localized_Products_to_GI.pdf

[96] *Feta*, para 87.

portion of producers to use the name in an evocative sense for the reputation of the product to be found still linked to a geographical place. Thus, having rejected claims that 'feta' is generic, the CJEU ruling gave exclusive rights in the name to producers in mainland Greece and the department of Lesbos to market the product throughout the EU.[97]

While both the GI and trademark systems prohibit the registration of geographical names that have become generic, the foregoing analysis indicates that there are fewer obstacles to recovering exclusive use of a name under the GI system. Case law of the CJEU in *Feta*, *Parmesan* and *Bayerisches Bier* highlights the way in which the court has succeeded in giving a restrictive interpretation to the exclusion of generic names in Article 3 of the Regulation, to the effect that, if the name retains the ability to evoke the place of production, it will likely be allowed to proceed to registration. While those producers in the defined geographical areas benefit from the increased marketing exclusivity, the immediate economic impact on the interests of competitors, particularly existing trademark owners, who must go to the expense of re-branding and re-labelling, is relatively discounted.[98] In the case of Feta, the restitution of goodwill in the geographic name to the country of origin has been achieved at the cost of considerable litigation and expense for competitors inside and outside the EU. An awareness of the controversial nature of such wealth transfers may have prompted the amendment in the proposed Regulation on Agricultural Product Quality Schemes[99] empowering the Commission, to

---

[97] *Feta*, paras. 21, 53, 54, 89 and 109. Compare the finding of the German Federal Patent Court in February 2009, which overturned a decision of the German Patent and Trade Mark Office (DPMA) and decided that the Bavarian sausage speciality 'Münchner Weißwurst' did not fulfil the requirements to qualify as a PGI. The Federal Patent Court left open whether the terms 'original' or 'genuine' 'Münchner Weißwurst' would qualify as PGIs. See further Dev Gangjee, 'A Sharper Image of Generic Use through the Lens of Feta', *European Intellectual Property Review*, 2007, 29(5), pp. 172–9.

[98] See INTA letter to the Office of the United States Trade Representative (USTR) concerning EC Council Regulation 2081/92 and amending Regulation 510/2006: www.inta.org/Advocacy/Documents/March262004.pdf

[99] Art. 38, Proposed Article 51(1)(b): Proposal for a Regulation on Agricultural Product Quality Schemes, Presidency compromise text, 23 February 2011: Committee on Agriculture and Rural Development, Report tabled for plenary sitting 12.09.2012 (first reading 12.7.2011) on the Proposal for a Regulation on Agricultural Product Quality Schemes (COM(2010)0733 – C7-0423/2010 – 2010/0353(COD)): http://www.europarl.europa.eu/oeil/popups/ficheprocedure.do?lang=en&reference=2010/0353(COD). Adopted by the EU Parliament 12.09.2012: http://www.europarl.europa.eu.

lay down 'additional rules for determining the generic status of names in order to fully protect the rights of interested parties'.

Trademark law takes the interests of competitors and consumers into account in stipulating that signs that are descriptive of the goods concerned should be available to all such traders. If a geographical name which has been registered as a certification mark, identifying certain goods, acquires principal significance as a description of those goods, it is no longer a mark but rather is a generic term and will be subject to cancellation.[100] In contrast to the GI Regulation there is no prohibition on names becoming generic once they have been registered. Trademark law considers it in the public interest that indications which may serve to designate the geographical origin of goods remain available, not least because they may be an indication of the quality and other characteristics of the type of product.[101]

The tension between the regulation of trademarks and geographical indications concerning their differing treatment of generic geographic terms is underpinned by the differing market and socio-cultural objectives they serve. The rationale underlying the EU Regulation of GIs is significantly different to trademark law in so far as it is intended to promote the 'diversification of agricultural production' and the development of the rural economy throughout the EU.[102] However the concept of rural development cannot be understood exclusively in economic terms. In addition

---

[100] §14(5), 15 USC §1064. See also Community of Roquefort v. William Fehndrich, Inc., 303 F.2d 494, 133 U.S.P.Q.633 (2d Cir. 1962) at paras. 13–14.

[101] CTM Regulation, Art. 7(1) (c). On the rationales underpinning trademark law see, William M. Landes and Richard A. Posner, *The Economic Structure of Intellectual Property Law* (2003) pp. 172–5. On the policy orientation of Regulation (EEC) No. 2081/92 and Regulation (EC) No. 510/2006, see further Dominique Barjolle and Bertil Sylvander, 'PDO and PGI Products: Market, Supply Chains and Institutions, Protected Designations of Origin and Protected Geographical Indications in Europe: Regulation or Policy?' Final Report, SRVA, Lausanne, Suisse, INRA – UREQUA, Le Mans, France, 2000, <http://www.origin-food.org/pdf/pdo-pgi.pdf>.

[102] Recital 2, Regulation 510/2006 states: The diversification of agricultural production should be encouraged so as to achieve a better balance between supply and demand on the markets. The promotion of products having certain characteristics can be of considerable benefit to the rural economy, particularly in less-favored or remote areas, by improving the incomes of farmers and by retaining the rural population in these areas. Cf. the legislative intent of the Idaho Potato Commission, Idaho Code, Title 22, 22–1201: '. . . The potato industry is one of the agricultural industries that contributes to the economic welfare of the state. It is the purpose of this chapter to promote the public health and welfare of the citizens of the state by providing means for the protection, promotion . . . and development of markets relating to the growing and promotion of Idaho potato products and by products.'

to the notion of commercial reputation that underpins trademark law, the civilian approach to the protection of GIs recognises a continuity of local skills and practices that sustain the product's reputation over generation and time.[103] Even so-called 'micro-GIs',[104] unlikely to benefit from sales beyond their immediate location, are considered potentially important to the promotion of tourism in marginal areas, in so far as they function as symbols of historical and cultural identity.

VI. ENFORCEMENT UNDER THE US TRADEMARK SYSTEM

(i) Defending Geographical Certification Marks Against Misuse

The trademark provides proprietors with exclusive rights to prevent unauthorized use of an identical or similar designation, where such use would be likely to cause consumer confusion or mislead the public as to the true origin of the product. However, the exclusive rights provided the trademark proprietor are subject to derogations that allow third parties to use in the course of trade indications of geographical origin, provided they do so in accordance with honest commercial practice.[105] For example, third party use of terms such as 'Colombian blend' or 'Colombian type' coffee, would not be actionable in trademark law as long as the true origin of the product was clearly shown on the label.

Trademark protection will not necessarily prevent third parties using such terms, without a showing of unfair advantage and damage to reputation or goodwill.[106] From the proprietors' point of view the descriptive use of the mark by third parties will involve considerably more enforcement actions, whether to oppose subsequent applicants or to cancel earlier regis-

---

103 See Dev Gangjee Relocating the Law of Geographical Indications (Cambridge University Press, 2012) at 237.

104 Tim Josling, 'The War on Terroir', Journal of Agricultural Economics Vol. 57, No. 3, 2006, 337–363 at 360–61.

105 Art. 12 of the CTM Regulation. See, e.g. Case C-100/0 *Gerolsteiner Brunnen GmbH & Co. v. Putsch GmbH*, ECJCJEU, 2004.

106 Case C-487/07 *L'Oreal SA Lancôme parfums et beauté & Cie Laboratoire Garnier & Cie v. Bellure NV*, CJEU, 2009: Art. 5(2) of First Council Directive 89/104/EEC of 1988 must be interpreted as meaning that the taking of unfair advantage of the distinctive character or the repute of a mark, within the meaning of that provision, does not require that there be a likelihood of confusion or detriment to the distinctive character or the repute of the mark or, more generally, to its proprietor.

trations of the name.[107] Perhaps as a general rule it would be more accurate to say that while geographic certification marks may protect against use with 'blend,' 'type,' or 'style', the extent to which they do is uncertain.

In so far as the Federal Trademark Dilution Act (FTDA) provides protection for any 'famous mark that is distinctive . . . through acquired distinctiveness', an anti-dilution action would be available for geographic certification or collective marks; in which case proof of distinctiveness in the relevant market would be necessary as a threshold matter.[108] As to its application of trademark dilution to geographic certification marks, there is little guidance. An indication of the way in which the distinctiveness of a geographic certification mark might be assessed by a court of appeal may be gleaned from a decision of the TTAB in Tea Board of India v. The Republic of Tea, Inc.[109] In that case the Tea Board of India,[110] proprietor of word and logo marks for Darjeeling, brought an opposition action against an application to register 'Darjeeling Nouveau' by The Republic of Tea, a California-based distributor. The TTAB began by noting that, Section 2(e)(2) of the Trademark Act which prohibits registration of a mark that is primarily geographically descriptive of an applicant's goods, provides a specific exception for marks used to certify indications of regional origin under Section 4 of the Act. The Board therefore considered that the presumption that a geographic term is 'inherently weak does not attach to geographic terms that are used to certify regional origin'. As a mark entered in the Principal Register,

---

[107] See, e.g. In re Accelerate s.a.l., 101 USPQ2d 2047 (TTAB 2012) [precedential]: refusal to register was affirmed on the ground that the applicant mark COLOMBIANO COFFEE HOUSE was merely descriptive and likely to cause confusion with COLOMBIAN for 'coffee' previously registered as a certification mark; Bureau National Interprofessionnel Du Cognac v. International Better Drinks Corp., 6 USPQ2d 1610 (TTAB 1988) (COGNAC for distilled brandy from a region in France); State of Florida, Department of Citrus v. Real Juices, Inc., 330 F. Supp. 428, 171 USPQ 66 (M.D. Fla. 1971) (SUNSHINE TREE for citrus from Florida); Community of Roquefort v. William Fehndrich, Inc., 303 F.2d 494, 133 U.S.P.Q.633 (2d Cir. 1962).

[108] Proof of distinctiveness has been a required element of a claim under the FTDA since enactment of the statute, although the precise way in which the statute incorporates that element was clarified with the enactment of the Trademark Dilution Revision Act.

[109] Tea Board of India v. The Republic of Tea, Inc., 80 USPQ2d 1881 (TTAB 2006, precedential opinion).

[110] Non-profit body established by the Government of India under the India Tea Act of 1953 for the purpose of controlling the India tea industry. Darjeeling is a district located in the state of West Bengal, India, where tea has been grown and produced in 87 'tea gardens' for 150 years.

'Darjeeling' was entitled to the presumption under Section 7(b) that the mark is distinctive for the goods and entitled to the 'greater protection' afforded such marks.[111]

Once it had established the reputation of the Darjeeling mark in the US tea market, and the priority of the opponent's right to the mark, the Board concluded that the use and registration by the applicant of 'Darjeeling Nouveau' was likely to dilute the distinctive quality of the certification mark.[112] As to the fame of the 'Darjeeling' mark, the need to consider a likelihood of dilution was obviated by the Board's finding that the mark at issue was likely to cause confusion among purchasers.[113] In *Tea Board* both marks were found to identify the same geographic source of the tea; the fact that the applicant was also a licensee of the certification mark 'Darjeeling' was only thought to increase the likelihood of consumer confusion. In the *Tea Board* decision, the mark's distinctiveness was constituted by 'the extent to which the relevant public recognizes 'Darjeeling' as a mark denoting regional origin for tea'.[114] Nevertheless, as far as protection against dilution is concerned, the degree of distinctiveness and public recognition in the US is a significant issue.

The incomplete nature and status of the decision, gives rise to uncertainty both with respect to the potential scope of an anti-dilution action and the concept of distinctiveness in relation to the definition of a GI in

---

[111] See § 7 (15 U.S.C. § 1057(b)); respecting certificates of registration; and Tea Board of India v. The Republic of Tea, Inc., 80 USPQ2d 1881 (TTAB 2006) [precedential] at p. 52.

[112] Opponent Tea Board of India alleged a violation of the TRIPS Article 22.1: the TTAB did 'not treat this allegation as a separate claim because TRIPs is not a self-executing treaty' at p. 3, Note 3. See e.g., In re Rath, 402 F.3d 1207, 74 USPQ2d 1174, 1179 n. 2 (Fed. Cir. 2005) (noting that, under 19 U.S.C. §3512(c), Congress has specifically precluded any person other than the United States from using TRIPS as a cause of action or defense.).

[113] As the TTAB stated at p. 44 (Tea Bd. of India v. Republic of Tea, Inc.: '[t]he test for determining likelihood of confusion with respect to certification marks is the same as that applied to trademarks – that is, the *du Pont* analysis'. The TTAB acknowledged at least one important difference in how that test is applied: 'because the certification mark owner does not itself use the mark, the question of whether there is a likelihood of confusion is based on a comparison of the mark as applied to the goods of the certification mark users'. DuPont factors from *E.I. DuPont DeNemours & Co.*, 476 F.2d 1357, 1361, 177 U.S.P.Q. 563, 567 (CCPA 1973). Federal Circuit-Likelihood of Confusion Test-(DuPont Factors) (applied in Champagne Louis Roederer, S.A. v. Delicato Vineyards, 148 F.3d 1373 (C.A.Fed., 1998)). See also: In re Accelerate s.a.l., 101 USPQ2d 2047 (TTAB 2012) [precedential] at p.11.

[114] Tea Bd. of India v. Republic of Tea, Inc. at p. 52.

Article 22 of the TRIPS Agreement. To all intent, Tea Board stands for the proposition that any GI that satisfies the definitional requirements of a certification trademark will be registrable, provided it is not found to be generic.[115] Thus, any designation that satisfies the definition of geographical indication in Article 22[116] would meet the *Tea Board* standard that it should identify the 'geographic source' of the goods. In addition, in a recent decision concerning the certification mark 'Colombian' for 'coffee', affirming its refusal to register 'Colombiano Coffee House', the TTAB came close to recognizing the 'natural factors' normally associated with the concept of 'terroir', when it found the mark distinctive on the basis that consumers regarded Colombian coffee 'as possessing certain distinctive qualities and characteristics due to factors associated with that region, including its flavor, aroma and body'.[117]

Nevertheless, once registered, the scope of protection is less certain than under the GI Regulation. A registered certification mark must at least be able to provide evidence of distinctiveness, if it is to defend an invalidation action. First, protection against misuse is likely to be a problem for those GIs that meet the TRIPS definition, but where consumers in the US do not perceive the sign as serving to identify a good as originating in a certain place.[118] Since geographical indications are not always known to the

---

115 Tea Bd. of India v. Republic of Tea, Inc. at p. 12; see also In re Accelerate s.a.l., 101 USPQ2d 2047 (TTAB 2012) [precedential] at p. 5.

116 In the broadest sense it only requires that the production in question should originate in a certain geographical area. Art. 1(1) of the Madrid Agreement on Indications of Source defines 'indication of source' as an indication referring to a country or to a place situated therein as being the country or place of origin of a product. Note: this definition that does not imply a particular quality, reputation or characteristic of those products, appears not to be covered under Art. 22 of the TRIPS Agreement.

117 In re Accelerate s.a.l., 101 USPQ2d 2047 (TTAB 2012) [precedential]: at p. 17. Further see Peter Brody arguing that the FTDA's protections for any 'famous mark that is distinctive, inherently or through acquired distinctiveness' should be available for geographical indications – at least those that qualify as certification or collective marks, even though such designations traditionally were not considered 'distinctive' in the trademark sense of identifying a single source of the goods: 'Geographical Indications and Dilution: Reinterpreting "Distinctiveness" Under the Lanham Act', Trademark Reporter, July-August, 2010, Vol. 100 No. 4, p. 905 at 928.

118 The issue is not whether the public is expressly aware of the certification function of the marks or the certification process underlying use of the marks, but rather is whether the public understands that goods bearing the marks come only from the region named in the marks. Institut National Des Appellations d'Origine v. Brown-Forman Corp., 47 USPQ2d 1875, 1885 (TTAB 1998).

public at large, the public is not necessarily deceived when such indications are used for products with different origin.

By the same token, such indications are often sufficiently known in the circles concerned, especially by traders, for third party use to be more than a matter of mere chance.[119] In fact, the TTAB recognizes that it would be impractical to require certifying organizations to maintain 'absolute control' over the use of a certification mark in order to prevent its becoming generic.[120] Instead, the question is whether the mark owner has made adequate efforts to control the unauthorized use of its marks. For this reason, the TTAB utilizes a test of reasonableness with respect to claims by respondents concerning the loss of distinctiveness or genericness. Recent cases indicate that provided: (a) reasonable steps have been taken by the certifying authority to protect the mark's geographical distinctiveness, and (b) there is substantial evidence that the 'primary' significance of the mark continues to denote a specific geographical region: a GI will be safe from cancellation on grounds of invalidity; or be able to pursue an opposition action against local misuse.

Despite evidence of some misuse, provided the certifier takes 'reasonable steps to prevent the public from being misled,' the trademark owner may be considered to have taken appropriate action to maintain the mark's distinctiveness.[121] For example, in *Swiss Watch International Inc. v. Federation of the Swiss Watch Industry*[122] the respondent had an extensive worldwide monitoring and enforcement system in place, including surveillance by US Customs officials. It had also brought numerous oppositions in the United States, filed letters of objection with the USPTO and negotiated the withdrawal of numerous applications. In the case of Swiss Watch, the TTAB was prepared to allow some misuse of the geographical indication. Despite evidence of twenty-two unauthorized uses of the mark, these were not found to be uses that were so extensive that 'Swiss' and 'Swiss Made' had ceased to function as certification marks because the words had become generic:[123]

---

119 GATT doc MTN.GNG/NG11/16 of Dec 4 1989 at 21.

120 Tea Board – Tea Board of India v. Republic of Tea Inc., 80 USPQ2d at 1888: at p. 17; see also Midwest Plastic Fabricators, 15 USPQ2d at 1362.

121 As stated in Midwest Plastic Fabricators, 15 USPQ2d at 1363, 'the owner must take reasonable steps, under all the circumstances of the case, to prevent the public from being misled'.

122 *Swiss Watch International Inc. v. Federation of the Swiss Watch Industry*, Cancellation No. 92046786, February 2012 (TTAB precedential opinion) at pp. 21–5.

123 The Petitioner offered evidence of 22 uncontrolled uses of trademarks that included the term SWISS: Swiss Watch Industry at 22.

> [T]he mere fact of misuse . . . is not sufficient to raise an inference that the control was not adequate or that [SWISS or SWISS MADE] has lost all significance as a mark. Even if control is not maintained and misuse occurs, it must be shown that the misuse was of such significance to permit an inference that the mark is generic.[124]

Such an approach is consistent with Art 24.6 of the TRIPS Agreement which allows Members to exclude from protection as geographical indications, signs which are 'customary in common language as the common name for such goods'. The term used in TRIPS is 'customary' which may be differentiated from the term 'generic', in so far as it is possible that use of the sign has become common but the public is nevertheless aware that it is not the correct generic name of the product.[125]

(ii) Dilution and Fame as a Measure of Recognition

Whether a geographical certification mark will be protected from dilution by blurring will depend not only on its distinctiveness, but also on its degree of recognition as a famous mark.[126] The Trademark Act defines 'famous' to mean 'widely recognized by the general consuming public of the United States or services of the mark's owner'. The definition of a 'famous' mark requires proof that a mark is 'widely recognized by the general consuming public throughout the United States as a designation of source of the goods'. Ostensibly, it would appear likely that relatively few geographical certification marks would meet such a standard, thereby restricting dilution protection to marks that are famous nationwide.[127] This definition would severely restrict the doctrine of 'niche' fame, which some courts have applied to extend dilution protection to trademarks that are well known solely in certain regions.[128]

---

124 Swiss Watch Industry at 25–6; and Tea Board of India, 80 USPQ2d at 1888: at 18.

125 Carlos M. Correa, *Trade Related Aspects of Intellectual Property Rights: a commentary on the TRIPS* Agreement, OUP (Oxford: 2007) at pp. 250–51.

126 15 USC § 1125 2(B)(iv)_ False designations of origin, false descriptions, and dilution forbidden: (B) For purposes of paragraph (1), 'dilution by blurring' is association arising from the similarity between a mark or trade name and a famous mark that impairs the distinctiveness of the famous mark.

127 Whether a mark is 'famous' under the TDRA is defined in § 43 (15 U.S.C. § 1125) (c)(2)(A): '[A] mark is famous if it is widely recognized by the general consuming public of the United States as a designation of source of the goods or services of the mark's owner.'

128 Generally, dilution claims based on niche-market proof of fame are rejected: see, Maker's Mark Distillery, Inc. v. Diageo N. Am., Inc., 703 F.

Of course, in determining whether a mark possesses the requisite degree of recognition, the court has some flexibility as it weighs in the balance all relevant factors, including the duration, extent, and geographic reach of sales and advertising.[129] Since the *Tea Board* decision did not address the opponent's dilution claim on its merits, the decision sheds little light on the kinds of marks likely to meet the requirement for proof of fame. Consequently, in respect of a geographical certification mark, it remains to be seen how strictly a court might construe the requirement that it must be widely recognized by the 'general consuming public of the United States' in order for a dilution-based claim to succeed. Moreover, since the enactment of the Trademark Dilution Revision Act of 2006, dilution claims have faced considerable uncertainty in federal courts.[130] At least, those GIs as well-known as Parma Ham or Roquefort cheese, though they are few in number, should have less difficulty in attesting to their fame. That threshold crossed, once fame is established, and assuming the marks at issue are to all intent identical, the case of V*isa International Service Association*[131] indicates that likelihood of dilution is effectively presumed.[132]

In sum, it is at least arguable that the concept of 'geographical distinctiveness' is a significant jurisprudential innovation in the evolving US law of geographical certification marks.[133] The impact of TRIPS has been such that trademark law has begun to recognize that the geographic term may constitute the dominant element in a geographic certification mark and is therefore by itself actionable as to infringing uses. In principle, the Tea Board case indicates that under the trademark system, a geographical certification trademark is entitled to the full protection of the Lanham Act, including an anti-dilution action.[134] In the case of a GI with

---

Supp. 2d 671, 699 (W.D. Ky. 2010): finding that only famous brands can sue for dilution.

129 15 USC § 1125 2(B)(i)-(iii) (Lanham Act Section 43 (c)(2)(A)).

130 *Compare, e.g.*, Louis Vuitton Malletier S.A. v. Haute Diggity Dog, LLC, 507 F.3d 252, 268–69, (4th Cir. 2007) (use of CHEWY VUITTON not likely to dilute LOUIS VUITTON and related marks).

131 Visa Int'l Serv. Ass'n v. JSL Corp., No. 08–15206 (9th Cir. Jun. 28, 2010).

132 Visa Int'l Serv. Ass'n v. JSL Corp., No. 08–15206 (9th Cir. Jun. 28, 2010) at pp. 9352–3.

133 See, Peter Brody, 'Geographical Indications and Dilution: Reinterpreting 'Distinctiveness' Under the Lanham Act', Trademark Reporter, July-August, 2010, Vol. 100 No. 4, p. 905 at 928.

134 See, Peter Brody, 'Geographical Indications and Dilution: Reinterpreting "Distinctiveness" Under the Lanham Act', Trademark Reporter, July-August, 2010, Vol. 100 No. 4, p. 905 at pp. 926–8.

a reputation, such as Darjeeling, the TTAB has shown it is willing to apply the test of reasonableness with a breadth that goes some way to match the prohibition on GIs becoming generic in EU law.[135]

Nevertheless, in scope it is relatively restrictive and considerably more uncertain, when compared with the breadth of protection offered by GI Regulation 510/2006. In accordance with Article 13(1) of the Regulation, registered names are automatically accorded dilution-like protection. It mandates protection for registered names against: 'any misuse, imitation or evocation, even if the true origin of the product is indicated or if the protected name is translated or accompanied by an expression such as style, type, method, as produced in, imitation or similar'.[136] The prohibition on unauthorized use may extend to include even dissimilar products which attempt to trade on the cachet of a PDO or PGI. For example in *Comité Interprofessionnel du Vin de Champagne v. Unilever*, the Court of 's-Gravenhage granted injunctive relief against Unilever's infringement of the PDO champagne.[137] To celebrate the 70th birthday of its Andrélon shampoos range, Unilever launched an anniversary edition of the product and accompanied the promotion with an extensive advertising campaign, which included use of the slogans 'Champagne Shampoo' and 'Champagne everyday'. The Comité Interprofessionnel du Vin de Champagne (CIVC), the body representing the interests of champagne houses and wine-growers, successfully brought summary action before the Court of The Hague based on the prohibition against 'any direct or indirect commercial use of a protected name'.[138] Similarly, it might be argued, a geographical certification mark can provide grounds to foreclose use of the term with 'blend,' 'type' or 'style', provided that the chain of distribution is well controlled.[139] Nonetheless, although analogous to the breadth

---

135 Taking a similar view see, Latha R. Nair, 'Swiss Watch International, Inc. v. Federation of the Swiss Watch Industry: The TTAB's Unwitting Message for Geographical Indications?' Trademark Reporter, May-June, 2012, Vol. 102 No. 3 at 944–5; and 955.

136 Art 13 (1)(b).

137 *Comité Interprofessionnel du Vin de Champagne v. Unilever* (2010), the Court of 's-Gravenhage ordered that Unilever cease infringement of the protected designation of origin (PDO) champagne.

138 The action was based on Article 118(m), paragraph 2(a)(ii) of Regulation 1234/2007 establishing a common organization of agricultural markets and on specific provisions for certain agricultural products, as amended by Regulation 491/2009 (an equivalent provision to Art. 13 of Regulation 510/06 in respect of agricultural products.

139 Fabio Chaddad, 'Inter-organisational Relationships in Agri-food Systems: an Integrated Transaction Cost-Network Analysis Framework' in Christian

of protection provided by the EU Regulation on GIs, the dilution provisions of the US Trademark Act, at least on a literal reading, do not offer GIs protection that is as broad or complete.[140] As the following part of the chapter explains, the European Regulation prohibits not only food products from outside the defined area using the geographical name, but also denies use of the name to products within the region that do not meet the standards set forth in the application.

VII. ENFORCEMENT UNDER THE EU *SUI GENERIS* SYSTEM

There are two tiers to the enforcement of GIs under the EU Regulation that both involve a novel mix of public and private action.[141] The first tier, which may be seen as enforcement of the product specification, will be discussed in the later part of this chapter. Instead, we will begin with the more common instances of unauthorized use, under the second tier, that is, enforcement of rights under Article 13 in regard to the misuse of GIs.

In the last part of the chapter we noted that the GI Regulation provides that registered names shall be protected against any direct or indirect commercial use of a name registered in respect of identical or comparable products; and any evocation of the name, even if the true origin of the product is indicated, or if the protected name is translated or accompanied by expressions such as 'style', 'type', 'method' or 'imitation'.[142] In the event a trademark containing an earlier GI seeks to operate in competition for the same product in the EU, the GI holder not only has the advantage of the classic priority rule as to first in time, first in right, but the absolute nature of the property rights in the GI Regulation also operate to prohibit what might otherwise be permissible under the trademark system, notably use which is descriptive of the kind, quality or intended purpose of a

---

Fischer, Monika Hartmann eds. *Agri-food Chain Relationships*, CABI Publishing (2010) at pp.46–58.

[140] Further note, on the modern scope of 'extended' passing off, *Diegeo North America & Anor v. Intercontinental Brands (ICB) Ltd and Ors* [2007] EWCA Civ 920, the Court of Appeal found that relief is not to be restricted to products of prestige. Patten LJ's view was simply that 'the concept of distinctiveness which is effective to produce the necessary goodwill provides a sufficient and comprehensive yardstick for deciding which products qualify for protection' at para. 53.

[141] See, John Henry Merryman and Rogelio Pérez-Perdomo, *The Civil Law Tradition*, 3rd ed. Stanford Univ. Press, 2007 at pp. 74–5, regarding the distinction between public and private law.

[142] Article 13(1)(b).

competing product. For example, in 1996 'Grana Padano' was registered as a PDO for Italian hard cheese. In 1998, Biraghi SpA, succeeded in registering as a CTM 'Grana Biraghi' for cheese.[143] Subsequently, the proprietor of the PDO, the *Consorzio per la Tutela del Formaggio Grana Padano*, was successful in applying for a declaration of invalidity to have the mark cancelled.[144] The Consorzio relied on Article. 14(1) of the GI Regulation, which requires the invalidation of a trademark, in circumstances where it would constitute an infringement of the PDO, in the following terms:[145]

> Where a designation of origin or a geographical indication is registered under this Regulation, the application for registration of a trademark corresponding to one of the situations referred to in Article 13 and relating to the same class of product shall be refused if the application for registration of the trademark is submitted after the date of submission of the registration application to the Commission.

The General Court held that the OHIM Board of Appeal had erred in finding that the existence of the PDO 'Grana Padano' did not prevent registration of the mark 'Grana Biraghi'.[146]

(i) Later Trademark Incorporates a Registered Geographical Indication

1. *Bureau National Interprofessionnel du Cognac v. Gust. Ranin Oy*

The term 'Cognac' has been protected as a geographical indication under EU law since 1989.[147] Under the GI system it enjoys the widest possible protection, comparable but stronger than trademark dilution, in so far as GIs are not subject to the same kinds of limitations as trademarks, notably for descriptive use. In the case of Bureau National Interprofessionnel du

---

[143] Class 29, Nice Agreement Concerning the International Classification of Goods and Services for the Purposes of the Registration of Marks, 1957, as revised.

[144] CTM Regulation, Art. 55.

[145] Art. 13 of the GI Regulation sets out that the scope of protection accorded PDOs and PGIs, and includes any direct or indirect commercial use of the registered name for comparable products and any misuse, imitation, or evocation. To the same effect see, CTM Regulation, Art.7(1)(k).

[146] Grana Case T-291/03, *Consorzio per la Tutela del Formaggio Grana Padano v. OHIM, Biraghi SpA*, Court of First Instance, 2007: at para. 89, regarding Biraghi's defense that the 'grana' is generic.

[147] Cognac is protected under Regulation No 110/2008 (Geographical indications of spirit drinks), Annex III which mentions 'Cognac' as a geographical indication identifying products in Category No 4, i.e., in the wine spirit category, having France as the country of origin.

Cognac,[148] the producer association responsible for the enforcement of the PGI, opposed two Finnish trademarks containing the name Cognac. Their success shows how under the GI system, producers of Cognac may effectively reserve the name Cognac to their exclusive use.[149] This was the case even though 'Cognac' as incorporated in the defendant's mark, did not seek to mislead consumers about the origin of the goods with respect to liqueurs containing cognac.

In 2001, defendant Finnish company Oy Gust. Ranin Gust. Ranin Oy ('GRO'), a producer of liqueurs since 1781, applied to register in Finland two figurative trademarks containing the words 'Cognac' and its Finnish translation 'Konjakki'.[150] Both were registered in 2003, for products in Class 33.[151] The Bureau National Interprofessionnel Du Cognac opposed the registration of both marks objecting to the use of the word 'Cognac' in the labels. The Finnish Patent & Registration Office rejected the opposition against the 'Hienoa Konjakkia' label, but accepted the opposition against the 'Café Cognac' label. The reason for the different result was due to the legend 'Product of France' in the 'Hienoa Konjakkia' label which was considered to remove any misconception about the origin of the product. The Bureau National du Cognac sought to annul the adverse decision.

Following a series of appeals, the Finnish Supreme Administrative Court stayed proceedings and referred a number of questions to the CJEU on the interpretation of Articles 16 and 23 of Regulation 110/2008 concerning the protection of geographical indications for spirit drinks.[152]

---

148 Bureau National Interprofessionnel du Cognac v. Gust. Ranin Oy ('GRO') (CJEU (First Chamber); Joined Cases C-4/10 and C-27/10, 2011.

149 Compare the 'Spanish Champagne' case, J Bollinger and Others v. The Costa Brava Wine Company Limited [1961] RPC 116.

150 The 'Hienoa Konjakkia' mark for 'cognac', and the 'Café Cognac' trademark for 'liqueur including cognac': Bureau National Interprofessionnel du Cognac v. Gust. Ranin Oy at para. 16.

151 In Class 33 the figurative element of the mark included the endorsement 'Cognac L & P Hienoa Konjakkia' Lignell & Piispanen Product of France 40 percent Vol 500 ml'; and a second mark for 'liqueurs containing 'konjakki'' in Class 33, the figurative element included the endorsement 'Kahvi-Konjakki Café Cognac Likööri – Likör – Liqueur 21 percent Vol Lignell & Piispanen 500 ml': Bureau National Interprofessionnel du Cognac v. Gust. Ranin Oy at para. 16.

152 Regulation No 110/2008 on the Definition, Description, Presentation, Labelling and the Protection of Geographical Indications of Spirit Drinks, came into force on 20 February 2008, replacing Regulation 1576/89 which had been in force from 15 June 1989. Both regulations protected 'Cognac' as a geographical indication ('GI') identifying a spirit drink originating from France. According to the CJEU, the regulation is applicable to trademarks registered prior to its entry

Although wine and spirit drinks are protected under separate Regulations, the main aim of the amended Regulation of 2008 was to ensure consistency of the rules for protection of geographical indications on spirit drinks with those of Regulation 510/2006 for agricultural products. The substantive question referred to the CJEU asked whether Articles 16 and 23 of Regulation 110/2008 precluded the registration of a mark containing a GI, or a term corresponding to that indication and its translation, in respect of spirit drinks which did not meet the specifications set for that GI.

With respect to Article 16(a), the CJEU found that such use constituted a direct commercial use of a GI in respect of products which are comparable to the spirit drink registered under that indication, but which are not covered by the indication. As a result, the court found that the national authorities must refuse or invalidate the registration of a mark which contains a geographical indication, or term corresponding to that indication and its translation, when it does not meet the specifications for that indication.

The CJEU therefore ruled that use of a mark which includes a geographical indication such as 'Cognac' would constitute a direct and unlawful commercial use.[153] Based on this interpretation, the Finnish national court had little choice but to hold that the use of a mark containing the GI at issue, or a term corresponding to that indication and its translation, which does not meet the relevant specifications, constitutes a direct commercial use of a GI in respect of products which are comparable, but which are not covered by the registration.

Secondly, the CJEU found that this type of use might be characterized as 'evocation'[154] under Article 16(b). The CJEU pointed out that that the concept of 'evocation'[155] covers a situation in which an identical or similar trademark incorporates part of a protected designation, so that when the consumer is confronted with the name of the product, the image triggered in his mind is that of the product whose designation is protected.[156] Equally, the court found the same principle to apply in the case of

into force, as rules for the protection of geographical indications had already been incorporated into EU law before that date: Bureau National Interprofessionnel du Cognac v. Gust. Ranin Oy at para. 32–7.

[153] Article 16(a) of Regulation No 110/2008: Bureau National Interprofessionnel du Cognac v. Gust. Ranin Oy at para. 55.

[154] For the purposes of Regulation No 110/2008, Article 16 (b).

[155] As referred to in Article 16(b) of Regulation No. 110/2008.

[156] See, Case C-87/97 Consorzio per la Tutela del Formaggio Gorgonzola [1999] ECR I-1301, para. 25, and Case C-132/05 Commission v. Germany [2008] ECR I-957, para. 44. The Court has held that that could be the position in the case of products with visual similarities and sales names which are phonetically and

the registration of a mark containing a GI, or a term corresponding to that indication and its translation, with respect to spirit drinks which do not meet the specifications required by that indication. In such a case the use of a mark containing the element 'Cognac' for spirit drinks, which do not meet the relevant specifications, may therefore be categorized as an 'evocation'.[157] Moreover, a legend indicating the French origin of the product, or the use of the geographical indication in translation or accompanied by an expression such as 'like', 'type', 'style', 'made', 'flavor', or any other similar term, would not protect the applicant trademark from cancellation.

Thirdly, consistent with Article 16(d), the court found that registration should be refused where use of the mark applied for would lead to an explicit or implicit reference to a geographic indication that is made in a way liable to mislead the public as to the origin of the product or, at the very least, to produce in the mind of the public an association regarding that origin, or to enable the trader to take unfair advantage of the reputation of the geographical indication concerned.[158]

The CJEU framed its response in relation to the situation where a mark containing a geographical indication, or a generic term and its translation, has been registered for spirit drinks, which do not meet the specifications set for that indication. In so far as the marks at issue might be said to contain a generic term corresponding to a protected geographical indication and its translation, the CJEU noted that geographical indications cannot become generic.[159] As a result, for the purposes of determining the validity of the registration of the marks at issue in the main proceedings, it was not open to the trademark applicant to argue that the indication 'Cognac' had become generic. Secondly, in accordance with the Regulation PGIs such as 'Cognac', cannot be translated either on the label or in the presentation of a spirit drink.[160] Thirdly, with respect to the unauthorized use of Cognac, the CJEU noted that the Regulation prohibits the direct or indirect commercial use of a geographical indication in respect of products which are not covered by the registration, in so far as those products are comparable to the registered spirit drink.[161]

In contrast to the trademark system, which would likely allow the

---

visually alike (Consorzio per la Tutela del Formaggio Gorgonzola, para. 27, and Commission v. Germany, para. 46).

[157] Article 16(b) of Regulation No 110/2008.

[158] Article 16(a) to (d) of Regulation 110/2008.

[159] Article 15(3)(1) of Regulation No 110/2008 in Annex III thereto.

[160] Article 15(3)(1) of Regulation No 110/2008.

[161] Article 16 of Regulation No 110/2008

applicant's descriptive use of Cognac, as permitting a legitimate differentiation in the market for Cognac and Cognac-like drinks; the CJEU, characterized defendant GRO's products as pertaining to the market in 'spirit drinks'; and was not prepared to allow that such products might be seen as constituting a separate market, comparable to the spirit drink registered under the geographical indication. Consequently, the court concluded that 'spirit drinks' covers drinks which have common objective characteristics and which are consumed, from the viewpoint of the relevant public, on occasions which are largely identical; and often distributed through the same channels.

(ii) Earlier Registered Trademarks and the Principle of Co-existence

A highly contentious issue that denotes the differing approaches to protection within civil and common law traditions, is the interrelationship of marks and GIs.[162] In cases of conflict between a trademark and later registered GI, the latter enjoys a privileged position in relation to the trademark, in so far as the principle of priority is qualified by that of the co-existence. The trademark is open to challenge from a later registered PGI or PDO, unless the mark is so well-known that consumers would be misled by use of the name as a geographical indication.[163] Although systemic conflicts between trademarks and GIs are relatively uncommon, such problems are complex, persistent and not susceptible to speedy resolution.

However, in a reversal of the priority rule, an application to register a later GI that conflicts with an earlier trademark is allowable, provided the application has been made in accordance with honest practice.[164] In other words, the derogation within trademark law in respect of geographical origin also operates inter-systemically, in the event a mark conflicts with an identical or similar geographical name for the product, even when the trademark, as the earlier right, would normally have priority. In the case of an earlier registered trademark, the CTM and GI Regulations mandate

---

[162] See, INTA letter to the Office of the United States Trade Representative (USTR) concerning Regulation 2081/92 governing geographical indications and its amendment, submitting that amended Regulation 510/2006 continues to violate the TRIPS Agreement, in that it does not fully ensure the exclusivity of prior trademarks, no matter their level of fame and degree of use: www.inta.org/Advocacy/Documents/March262004.pdf.

[163] Art. 3(4) of the GI Regulation.

[164] Some likelihood of confusion between the trade mark and the later GI may even be tolerated: see, Case C-100/02 *Gerolsteiner Brunnen*, CJEU, 2004, para. 24.

the co-existence of the two systems.[165] The term 'co-existence' refers to a legal regime under which a GI and a trademark can both be used concurrently to some extent even though the use of one or both of them would otherwise infringe the rights conferred by the other. Article 14(2) of the GI Regulation applies in respect of conflicts between earlier trademarks and a registered GI:[166]

> With due regard to Community law, a trademark the use of which corresponds to one of the situations referred to in Article 13 which has been applied for, registered, or established by use, in good faith within the territory of the Community, before either the date of protection of the designation of origin or geographical indication in the country of origin or before 1 January 1996, may continue to be used notwithstanding the registration of a designation of origin or geographical indication.[167]

The reference in Art. 14(2) to 'Community law' alludes to certain exceptions to the rights of the trademark owner. Specifically, the CTM Regulation provides an exception where an unauthorized third party is using the name in question to indicate the kind, quality, geographic origin or other characteristics of the goods or service.[168] Thus, in accordance with Art. 14, the use of an identical and later registered GI will be allowed as an exception to the trademark owner's rights, provided the use of the GI is in accordance with honest commercial practice.[169]

---

[165] Art. 164, Council Regulation (EC) No 207/2009 of 26 February 2009 on the Community Trade Mark Regulation states that the Trade Mark Regulation 'shall not affect Council Regulation (EC) No. 510/2006, and in particular Article 14 thereof'.

[166] The scope of Art. 14(2) is confined in time to those trademarks applied for, registered or established by use, either before the GI is protected in its country of origin or before the date of submission to the Commission of an application for GI registration. See further G.E. Evans (with M. Blakeney), 'The Protection of Geographical Indications after Doha: Quo Vadis?', *Journal of International Economic Law*, 2006,9(3), pp. 575–614 (2006).

[167] That is provided that no grounds for its invalidity or revocation exist as specified under the Trade Mark Directive (EEC) No. 89/104 of 21 December 1988; or the CTM Regulation (EC) No. 40/94 of 20 December 1993 on the Community trade mark (as codified in Regulation (EC) No. 207/2009 of 26 February 2009).

[168] Art. 12(b).

[169] The EC successfully argued before the WTO that GIs and trademarks constitute independent but equal forms of intellectual property in accordance with the structure of the TRIPS Agreement and in particular Art. 24.5 of that Agreement concerning their interrelationship. Their co-existence turns on the general exception as to trade mark rights in TRIPS, Art. 17, as constituting a valid defence against the exclusive rights of trademark holders: See, WTO, 'EC – Protection

1. Co-existence in *Bavaria Holland v. Bayerisches Bier*

The case of *Bavaria NV and Bavaria Italia Srl v. Bayerischer Brauerbund*[170] illustrates the principle of co-existence. The geographical name at issue was *Bavaria* for beer. The parties concerned in the dispute were the earlier trademark owner, the Dutch company Bavaria NV, and Bayerischer Brauerbund, a longstanding association of Bavarian brewers, holders of a PGI for Bavarian beer.[171] Brauerei Bavaria NV, one of the Netherlands biggest producers of beer, began to use the designation 'Bavaria' in 1925, and it became part of its company name in 1930. Bavaria NV was the proprietor and the user of several international trademarks, in force in Italy and elsewhere, which contained, together with other expressions or figurative elements, the name 'Bavaria', with registration dates as early as 1947.[172] Nevertheless, in 2001, the PGI 'Bayerisches Bier' was registered to the Bayerische Brauerbund eV (the Bavarian Brewers Association) of Munich.[173]

Subsequently, the Bavarian Brewers' Association began proceedings against Bavaria NV in Italy, seeking to prevent the Dutch company from using the name *Bavaria* in Italy and to have the company's trademark rights to the name cancelled. When the matter came before the Turin Court of Appeal, it referred to the CJEU the question as to whether the fact that the PGI had been granted protection after the registration of the trademarks meant that the Dutch company might nevertheless continue using the marks.[174] In July 2009, the CJEU affirmed the principle of co-

---

Of Trademarks And Geographical Indications For Agricultural Products And Foodstuffs', Report of the Panel, 2005, WT/DS174/R, paras 7.512–7.531.

170 Case C-343/07 *Bavaria NV and Bavaria Italia Srl v. Bayerischer Brauerbund*, CJEU, 2 July 2009.

171 The statues of the Bavarian brewers association (*Bayerischer Brauerbund*) dated back to 1917; and it had been the proprietor of the registered collective trademarks 'Bayrisch Bier' and 'Bayerisches Bier' since 1968.

172 The registration dates, the court noted, included 1947, 1971, 1982, 1991, 1992 and 1995: *Bavaria*, para. 17.

173 Art 1 of Regulation (EC) No. 1347/2001 registered the name 'Bayerisches Bier' as a PGI and recital 3 in the preamble to that Regulation stated that that PGI and the trade mark 'Bavaria' would not mislead the public as to the identity of the product, which is the standard embodied in Art. 14(3) of the original Regulation (EC) No. 2081/92.

174 The Bavarian Brewers' Association also brought suit in Germany. A second question was referred to the CJEU, and considered concurrently, in Case C-120/08 *Bavaria NV v. Bayerischer Brauerbund eV*: the referring court asked whether Art. 14(1) of Regulation (EC) No. 510/2006 applies in the case where the protected indication has been validly registered in accordance with the simplified procedure under Art. 17 of Regulation (EEC) No. 2081/92 of 14 July 1992.

existence, holding that trademarks of third parties, registered prior to the date on which the application for registration of the PGI 'Bayerisches Bier' was filed, in which the word 'Bavaria' appears could continue to exist.[175] Consequently owners of trademarks that consist of a later registered PDO or PGI run the risk of having their rights to priority and exclusivity eroded.[176]

As evidence of the threat posed by the GI to prior trademarks by the principle of co-existence, consider again the registrability of generic names. In the case of *Bavaria*, the CJEU found that the mere existence of marks in the market which incorporate the name, is no indication that the geographical name is unregistrable under the GI Regulation.[177] The PGI 'Bayerisches Bier' was considered not to have become generic even when the European market for beer contained trademarks that included the word 'Bayerisches' or translations as synonyms for the Bavarian bottom-fermentation brewing method.[178] The court concluded that registration of the PGI was justified by the need to prevent the disappearance of reputation as a result of 'popularisation through general use outside its geographical origin'.[179]

Thus, in the case of conflicts between GIs and earlier trademarks, the rules do not strictly follow the class principle of priority, first in time, first in right. A later applicant may successfully register a GI, and the trademark owner will have to accept their co-existence. The breadth of rights accorded the GI combined with its characterization as an exception to trademark rights give the GI a decided advantage in the event that the registration of geographical name is disputed.

---

[175] As the registration of the PGI was interpreted as having no adverse impact upon the validity of the 'Bavaria' trademarks, co-existence as provided for in Art. 14(2) of former Regulation 2081/92 could continue: *Bavaria*, para. 125. Similarly, see the Opinion of AG Mazek, at para. 161.

[176] Art. 14(2) of the GI Regulation privileges a later GI applicant, with the exception of marks that are held to be well known. The classic priority rule applies in respect of a later application for GI registration provided the mark is considered sufficiently well known in the relevant market sector of at least one Member State.

[177] *Bavaria*, paras 123–5.

[178] *Bavaria*, para. 105.

[179] *Bavaria*, para. 106. Also note that the geographical name that is the subject of an application for registration as a PGI or PDO cannot be regarded as generic pending the possible forwarding of the application for registration to the Commission of the European Communities by the national authorities: *Grandi Salumifici*, CJEU, 2009.

(iii) Earlier Unregistered Signs of Local Significance

1. *Anheuser-Busch Inc v. Budejovický Budvar*

In accordance with the priority rule, you might expect an earlier unregistered sign to have the advantage of a later application for registration, provided the earlier sign was in use and the application was made in good faith. In such a case, the decision as to whether to allow registration of the later sign will turn on the character and extent to which the unregistered mark has been used. In a recent decision between Anheuser-Busch Inc v. Budejovický Budvar[180] the CJEU, ruled that registration of a community trademark may be prevented only when the sign is actually used in a sufficiently significant manner in the course of trade, in a substantial part of the territory in which it is protected.

In this case between the two rival brewers, Anheuser-Busch Inc applied to register four Community trademarks (CTMs): a figurative mark containing the word 'Bud'; and a word mark BUD for beers and related services.[181] Budejovický Budvar opposed, citing several forms of prior rights that included: a figurative BUD mark for 'all types of light and dark beer', effective in Austria, Benelux and Italy; the appellation of origin 'Bud', registered under the Lisbon Agreement in respect of beer, effective in France, Italy and Portugal; and the Austrian appellation of origin 'Bud', protected in Austria under a bilateral convention with the former state of Czechoslovakia.

On most grounds, Budvar's opposition was dismissed. When both parties appealed, the Board of Appeal dismissed all Budvar's appeals, but allowed that of Anheuser-Busch. It considered that Budvar no longer appeared to refer to its international figurative mark as the basis of its opposition, but solely to the appellation of origin 'Bud'. This was in spite of the fact that it was difficult to understand how 'Bud' could be considered as an appellation of origin, or even an indirect indication of geographical origin. Secondly,the Board also held that the evidence provided by Budvar to show use of the appellation of origin 'Bud' in Austria,

---

[180] Anheuser-Busch Inc v. Budejovický Budvar (Case C 96/09 P, March 29 2011).

[181] A figurative mark featuring the word 'Bud' for goods in Classes 16, 21, 25 and 32 of the Nice Classification; and three applications in respect of the word mark BUD in Classes 32 (beers), 33 (alcoholic beverages), 35 (setting up databases, gathering data and information in databases), 38 (telecommunications, i.e. making available and supplying data and information, supplying and communicating information stored in databases), 41 (education, entertainment) and 42 (restaurant, bar and pub services; operating a database).

France, Italy and Portugal was insufficient. Thirdly, it held that Budvar had not demonstrated that the appellation of origin gave it the right to prohibit use of the word 'Bud' as a trademark in Austria or France.

Budvar appealed to the General Court, on the grounds that: (i) the sign 'Bud' could be considered to be an appellation of origin; and (ii) the conditions of Article 8(4) of the Community Trademark Regulation (40/94), in relation to an opposition based on the existence of an earlier non-registered mark of more than purely local significance, were satisfied. As to the first ground, the General Court found that 'Bud' could be considered to be an appellation of origin and that it was protected under the Lisbon Agreement, and that the validity of a national mark may not be called into question in proceedings for registration of a CTM. The General Court then upheld Budvar's appeal in relation to the use in the course of trade of a sign of more than mere local significance. On the facts, Budvar had provided proof that the signs concerned were used in the course of trade and it was unnecessary to show that the signs were used prior to the contested CTM applications.

Anheuser-Busch successfully appealed to the CJEU, which, in allowing the appeal provided guidance on the terms in Article 8(4) of Regulation No 40/94 which provides:

> Upon opposition by the proprietor of a non-registered trademark or of another sign used in the course of trade of more than mere local significance, the trademark applied for shall not be registered where and to the extent that, pursuant to the Community legislation or the law of the Member State governing that sign:
> (a) rights to that sign were acquired prior to the date of application for registration of the Community trademark, or the date of the priority claimed for the application for registration of the Community trademark;
> (b) that sign confers on its proprietor the right to prohibit the use of a subsequent trademark.[182]

The CJEU found that the General Court had misinterpreted the meaning of 'more than mere local significance'. The General Court held that Article 8(4) referred to the significance of the sign concerned and not the significance of its use, and that the significance of the sign must be understood as the geographical protection of its protection, which must not be merely local.

The CJEU found that the General Court had been incorrect in holding that it was sufficient, for the purpose of establishing that the sign 'Bud'

---

182 Council Regulation (EC) No 207/2009 of 26 February 2009 on the Community Trade Mark.

was of more than mere local significance, that the sign was protected in a number of states. The significance of the sign cannot be a function of the mere geographical extent of its protection. It followed that, in order to be capable of preventing a new CTM registration, the sign must actually be used in a sufficiently significant manner in the course of trade and its geographical extent must not merely be local. In order to ascertain whether that is the case, the CJEU said that account must be taken of the use of the sign as a distinctive element with respect not only to consumers but also to suppliers and competitors.

The CJEU further held that the General Court had erred in finding that the regulation did not require the sign 'Bud' to have been used in the territory in which it is protected and that use in a territory other than the territory of protection may be sufficient to prevent registration of a new trademark, even where there is no use at all in the territory of protection. It is only in the territory in which the sign is protected, in its entirety or in a part of it, that the exclusive rights attached to the sign may enter into conflict with a CTM. Thus, use in the course of trade must also be assessed separately for each of the territories in which the sign is protected.

Finally, the General Court had made an error of law in holding that it had to be shown only that the sign concerned was used in the course of trade before publication of the trademark application and not, at the latest, as at the date of application. In view of the considerable period of time which may elapse between the filing of an application and its publication, applying the test relating to the date of the application was considered to provide a better guarantee that the use claimed for the sign concerned is real and not an exercise whose sole aim is to prevent registration of a new trademark.

Surprisingly, in a regulatory climate that normally privileges the GI, in Anheuser-Busch Inc. v. Budejovický Budvar , the CJEU held that the purpose of Article 8(4) was to limit conflicts between signs, by preventing an earlier right which was not sufficiently significant in the course of trade, from blocking registration of a new CTM. In this finding it is possible to perceive a new preparedness in no less than the Grand Chamber of the CJEU, to recognize that the law should reflect the common economic goals shared by marks and GIs. In differentiating products both forms of industrial property serve to create market shares. However, it is the role of the law not only to ensure that they play an active role in creating market shares, but also that registration is cancelled in the event there is no actual use of the sign in the course of trade. While cancellation on grounds of non-use is well-known in trademark law, its appearance in the EU regulation of GIs is of far more recent origin, attaching to the reform of Regulation 510/2006. Consistent with the decision of the court in relation to AOs, Article 51(1)(b) of the Proposal for a Regulation on Agricultural Product Quality Scheme provides that the Commission may, on its own initiative or on request of any natural or legal person, cancel the registration where no product is placed on the market under the PDO or PGI for a period of five years.[183] The case illustrates how, in accord with the thesis of this chapter, a robust regulatory competition is incrementally transforming significant aspects of each system.

(iv) Enforcement of the Product Specification

The second tier of enforcement may be seen as pertaining to the product specification.[184] Enforcement of the specification is a mix of administrative protection and private legal action. In the first place, checks that farmers are complying with the product specification are undertaken by public authorities or by private certification bodies. Member States may also conduct administrative controls on the use of registered names on products in distribution and retail, under specific legislation, as part of the official control of EU food law. Secondly, enforcement may involve the producer association, commencing private legal action in the courts of member states.[185]

The case of *Consorzio del Prosciutto di Parma v. Asda Stores Ltd*[186]

---

[183] Article 51(1)(b), Cancellation: 'The Commission may, on its own initiative or on request of any natural or legal person having a legitimate interest, by means of implementing acts, cancel the registration . . . [where] no product is placed on the market under the traditional speciality guaranteed, the protected designation of origin or the protected geographical indication for at least five years.' Proposal for a Regulation on Agricultural Product Quality Schemes, Presidency compromise text, 23 February 2011: Committee on Agriculture and Rural Development, Report tabled for plenary sitting 12.09.2012 (first reading 12.7.2011) on the Proposal for a Regulation on Agricultural Product Quality Schemes (COM(2010)0733 – C7-0423/2010 – 2010/0353(COD)): http://www.europarl.europa.eu/oeil/popups/ficheprocedure.do?lang=en&reference=2010/0353(COD). Adopted by the EU Parliament 12.09.2012: http://www.europarl.europa.eu.

[184] Art. 4 of Reg. 510/2006.

[185] With respect to controls on the production process, according to Article 10 (3) of Regulation (EC) No 510/2006, the Commission shall make public names and addresses of the competent authorities and control bodies. These controls can result in the exclusion of producers and operators, within the defined area, who do not fulfill the requirements of the specifications.

[186] Case C-108/01Consorzio del Prosciutto di Parma & Salumificio S. Rita SpA v. Asda Stores Ltd & Hygrade Foods Ltd, CJEU, 2003 (henceforth Parma Ham v. Asda).

illustrates the breadth with which the specification may be drawn and the way in which the standards it contains may be enforced against third parties in order to maintain a premium price.[187] The action was brought by the *Consorzio di Parma*, the association responsible for the administration of the PDO 'Prosciutto di Parma', which is registered in respect of dry cured ham. The dispute concerned the sale of 'Prosciutto di Parma' by defendant Asda Stores Ltd, the operator of a chain of supermarkets in the UK. The product, bearing the description *Parma Ham*, had been purchased pre-sliced from the second defendant Hygrade Foods Ltd, in packets that bore the words 'Genuine Italian Parma Ham'. Hygrade purchased the ham from an Italian producer who was a member of the *Consorzio*, then undertook the packaging, labelling and slicing for Asda supermarkets.

The activity of Hygrade and Asda was prima facie in violation of the product specification for 'Prosciutto di Parma', which set out the terms of slicing and packaging of the product within the region of production for ham marketed in slices.[188] Accordingly, the *Consorzio* brought proceedings in the UK against the defendant companies, seeking injunctions to prohibit their activity on the ground that the slicing and packaging of the ham outside the region of Parma was contrary to the specification for 'Prosciutto di Parma'. The House of Lords stayed proceedings in order to refer the question of the enforcement of the specification in the UK to the CJEU. On reference to the CJEU, that court affirmed that under the GI Regulation the *Consorzio*, as the proprietor of the PDO, had the right to restrain the retail sale of Parma ham which had not been sliced, packaged and labelled in the region of production, provided that it was consistent with the conditions of the specification.

But for the breadth of the specification, such an arrangement might otherwise amount to a breach of European competition law. In fact, Asda argued that the effect of the slicing, packaging and labelling provisions was to confine those activities to the Parma area and to prevent firms elsewhere, in Italy or other Member States, from carrying on what should

---

[187] Similarly see the potential scope of protection conferred by a broadly drawn specification in Case C-469/00 *Ravil SARL v. Bellon Import SARL and Biraghi SpA* (*Grana* Padano cheese).

[188] In accordance with Art. 4(e) of the GI Regulation, packaging may take place in the defined geographical area provided reasons are given for doing so that relate to the quality control of the product. For example, in the case of Parma ham, slicing and packaging must take place in approved 'laboratories' within the traditional area, supervised by inspectors of the Association, who keep records of hams received: *Parma Ham v. Asda* (House of Lords) para. 6.

be legitimate slicing and packaging activities. This, it claimed, amounted to a quantitative restriction on exports from Italy or imports of unsliced hams into other Member States within the meaning of Art. 29 of the EU Treaty.[189] Notwithstanding, the CJEU concluded that if control of slicing and packaging is in furtherance of a legitimate Community objective, in this case, of guaranteeing the authenticity of sliced Parma ham purchased under the PDO, the measure could not be impugned as having a disproportionately adverse effect on trade between Member States.

In contrast, under trademark law, it would not be possible for a group of producers to prevent such activities by Asda Stores. In the absence of collective power, it would be difficult for primary producers, to enforce a licence agreement containing such terms respecting local slicing and packaging, on the basis of quality control. In a trademark licence terms of that kind would likely be unenforceable as anticompetitive. Asda would argue that in the absence of consumer confusion there is no liability, since the distinctiveness of the mark is not damaged, and the quality of the Parma ham remains unaffected irrespective of its being sliced and packaged in the UK.

VIII. CONCLUSION

This chapter set out to examine the different means by which the EU *sui generis* and the US trademark systems are adapting in response to continued pressure for the harmonization of laws protecting GIs. Its analysis rests on the hypothesis that as a result of the TRIPS Agreement, the contrasting EU and US models are engaged in a regulatory competition that is slowly transforming significant aspects of each system. It was tested by exploring the nature and extent of these differences, first in relation to signs that have allegedly become generic; and subsequently with respect to signs that, due to their identity or similarity for an identical or similar product, are in conflict over the status of their registration and use.

When it comes to recovering the intellectual capital in generic geographical names, the GI system was found to have the advantage. Producer

---

[189] Arts 34 and 35 (ex 28 and 29): 'Quantitative restrictions on exports, and all measures having equivalent effect, shall be prohibited between Member States.' Art. 29 does not preclude prohibitions or restrictions on exports justified, inter alia, on grounds of the protection of industrial and commercial property: Consolidated versions of the Treaty on European Union and the Treaty on the functioning of the European Union (OJ C115, 9.5.2008): <http://www.consilium.europa.eu/showPage.aspx?id=1296&lang=en>.

groups established within the EU, whose application is likely to meet objection based on genericness, are likely to find fewer legal obstacles and less expense in pursuing their claim under the GI Regulation. The ruling of the CJEU in *Feta* dramatically illustrates the breadth of the EU Regulation and its capacity to offer protection to terms previously considered generic. Once registered, the GI Regulation prevents any protected name from becoming generic. Although a designation may be altered, or even lost, as a result of changes in technology or processing techniques, it cannot be lost as a result of changes in understanding or usage of the protected name. Again, with respect to their comparative advantage, this analysis reveals the GI system as offering the broader protection against direct competition, going so far as to prohibit unauthorized references to registered PGIs or PDOs, such as 'Café Cognac' or 'Feta-style' cheese, that are evocative of the protected designation. In contrast, the trademark system can only offer the most famous GIs, such as 'Darjeeling' tea or 'Roquefort' cheese equivalent protection. The breadth of protection against dilution accorded the majority of geographical certification marks, having a 'normal' distinctiveness, is far less certain.

The breadth of rights accorded the GI combined with its characterization as an exception to trademark rights give the GI a decided advantage in the event that the registration of geographical name is disputed. In most instances of conflict between GIs and trademarks, the rules do not strictly follow the classic principle of priority in so far as a later name may proceed to registration as a GI, and the trademark owner will have to accept their co-existence. By comparison, trademark law considers it in the public interest that indications which may serve to designate the geographical origin of goods remain available, not least because they may be an indication of the quality and other characteristics of the type of product.[190] Thus, the trademark system takes greater account of the interests of competitors in stipulating that geographically descriptive indications or protected signs that are used descriptively, may be freely used by other traders in the absence of public confusion.

Notwithstanding the comparatively privileged position of GIs under

---

[190] On the rationales underpinning trade mark law see, William M. Landes and Richard A. Posner, *The Economic Structure of Intellectual Property Law* (2003) pp. 172–5. On the policy orientation of Regulation (EEC) No. 2081/92 and Regulation (EC) No. 510/2006, see further Dominique Barjolle and Bertil Sylvander, 'PDO and PGI Products: Market, Supply Chains and Institutions, Protected Designations of Origin and Protected Geographical Indications in Europe: Regulation or Policy?' Final Report, SRVA, Lausanne, Suisse, INRA – UREQUA, Le Mans, France, 2000, <http://www.origin-food.org/pdf/pdo-pgi.pdf>.

the *sui generis* system, this analysis has revealed some unexpected accommodation of trademark rights, notably when the Grand Chamber of the CJEU ruled that Budvar was not entitled to prohibit the use of the mark, solely on the basis that the appellation of origin 'Bud' was a sign 'used in the course of trade of more than mere local significance'.

For the most part, the differences in the two systems can be attributed to their distinct common and civil law traditions, their different values and attitudes to agriculture and the land management. The common law sees trademarks are seen as an important element of industrial policy and are instrumental in the mass production and orderly distribution of consumer goods. While civilian law considers GIs play an essential role in preserving traditional rural skills and sustaining the socio-cultural aspects of the nation's agricultural heritage.[191] It is a potent normative conflict that is likely to present a continued obstacle to the further international harmonization of GIs for some time to come.

---

[191] See, Dwijen Rangnekar, 'The Socio-Economics of Geographical Indications', UNCTAD Issue papers, No. 8. (2004) at p. 4: http://ictsd.org/downloads/2008/07/a.pdf; on 'product heritage' see, Gilles Allaire, François Casabianca and Erik Thévenod-Mottet, 'Geographical Origin: A Complex Feature of Agro-Food Products', in Elizabeth Barham, Bertil Sylvander, *Labels of Origin for Food: Local Development, Global Recognition*, CABI (2011) at pp. 4–5. Summarizing the contribution of GIs to the creation of social and cultural capital, and to the re-spatialisation and re-socialisation of food in the regions see, London Economics, 'Evaluation of the CAP policy on protected designations of origin (PDO) and protected geographical indications (PGI)', Final report, 2008, at 235; http://ec.europa.eu/agriculture/eval/reports/pdopgi/report_en.pdf;

PART V

Enforcement and Infringement Remedies

13. Extraterritorial enforcement

Marketa Trimble

For three decades international negotiations in the intellectual property area have evidenced increasing concern by countries representing major intellectual property exporters that intellectual property rights be effectively enforced.[1] This interest in enforcement was a logical step that followed the success of these countries in pursuing enhanced protection for intellectual property in international treaties and national laws; once the protection was anchored in national laws, the emphasis shifted to having the protection effectively enforced. So far, the focus has been on enforcement within individual countries; however, because infringements of intellectual property rights are transcending countries' borders with intensifying frequency and volume and are affecting rights in multiple countries,[2] the next stage in international intellectual property negotiations should address both the need to enforce rights simultaneously in multiple countries and the need to enforce rights against infringers located outside protecting countries.[3] The current extraterritorial enforcement efforts are associated with a variety of problems, which are discussed in this chapter.

---

[1] *See, e.g.*, Anti-Counterfeiting Trade Agreement, May 2011, http://www.mofa.go.jp/policy/economy/i_property/pdfs/acta1105_en.pdf (last visited 14 October 2012); U.S.–Australia Free Trade Agreement, May 18, 2004, http://www.ustr.gov/sites/default/files/uploads/agreements/fta/australia/asset_upload_file148_5168.pdf; Agreement on Trade-Related Aspects of Intellectual Property Rights, Marrakesh Agreement Establishing the World Trade Organization, Annex 1C, Apr. 15, 1994, 1869 U.N.T.S. 299 [hereinafter TRIPs]; North American Free Trade Agreement, U.S.–Can.–Mex., Dec. 17, 1992, 32 I.L.M. 289 (1993).

[2] *See, e.g.*, Marketa Trimble, *When Foreigners Infringe Patents: An Empirical Look at the Involvement of Foreign Defendants in Patent Litigation in the U.S.*, 27 Santa Clara Computer & High Tech. L. J. 499 (2011).

[3] A 'protecting country' is a country in which protection for intellectual property is sought.

I. FRAGMENTATION OF INTELLECTUAL PROPERTY RIGHTS AND THEIR ENFORCEMENT

Intellectual property rights and their enforcement are territorially fragmented; this fragmentation is inconsistent with the intangible nature of the objects of intellectual property protection, since their intangibility makes it difficult to confine them within a territory. Intellectual property travels easily, carried by information that is communicated not only through particular works or products that embed the intellectual property, such as a work of authorship or a patented device, but also through other media, such as a photograph of a work of authorship or a patent application. New information technologies continue to expand to all corners of the world and increase the speed with which, and the territorial extent to which, such information spreads. While it was relatively easy to confine information about new inventions or artwork in one country or a few countries 150 years ago, today it is difficult, if not impossible, to stop information at national borders.

Notwithstanding the fact that the intangible nature of intellectual property makes it easier to transport than movable property, its legal treatment, for some purposes, more closely resembles the legal treatment of immovable property; in fact, in England, the courts' approach to jurisdiction over foreign-registered intellectual property rights has been derived from jurisprudence concerning land.[4]

Intellectual property rights are territorially limited or 'attached' to one territory; intellectual property rights that require registration or grant are afforded only for the territory of the country where the rights are registered or granted. It is generally expected that disputes concerning the property will be resolved in the country that registered or granted the particular intellectual property right. English courts used to observe that cases concerning foreign registered rights presented local and not transitory causes of action – causes of action that could not be adjudicated outside the territory where they arose.[5]

---

[4] *See, e.g.*, *Potter v. Broken Hill Proprietary Co.* (1906) 3 CLR 479 (Austl.) (patent); Def Lepp Music v. Stuart-Brown, [1986] RPC 273 (Eng., copyright); British S. Afr. Co. v. Companhia de Moçambique, [1893] A.C. 602 (H.L.) (appeal taken from Eng.) (the original land case). The common law rule was abolished in England by the Civil Jurisdiction and Judgments Act, 1982, c. 27. *See also* Private International Law (Miscellaneous Provisions) Act, 1995, c. 42, art. 10. See the analysis of the development in England in *Lucasfilm Ltd. v. Ainsworth*, [2011] UKSC 39, [60]–[114].

[5] *Id.*

Courts' concerns over inappropriate intrusions into the sovereignty of the country that granted the intellectual property rights have made them reluctant to decide cases concerning foreign-registered rights. Because courts consider the act of granting or registering these rights an expression of a country's sovereignty that should not be subject to review by a foreign court,[6] courts refrain from deciding the validity of foreign-registered intellectual property. Courts in some countries will adjudicate infringements of the rights,[7] but courts in other countries have declined to decide either validity or infringement because of their view that questions of validity arise in most infringement cases.[8]

The result of the current universal approach to registered intellectual property rights is a fragmentation of both the acquisition and enforcement of the rights. If a patent is issued by the U.S. Patent Office, for example, the patent is granted only for the territory of the United States, where it confers exclusive rights upon the right holder and where the right holder can enforce the rights.[9] Even if identical patents are issued for the same invention in multiple countries, enforcement is fragmented by country; this is the case even when multiple parallel patents stem from a single international application under the Patent Cooperation Treaty,[10] or when

---

6 Voda v. Cordis Corp., 476 F.3d 887 (Fed. Cir. 2007); Case C-4/03, Gesellschaft für Antriebstechnik mbH & Co. KG v. Lamellen und Kupplungsbau Beteiligungs KG, 2006 E.C.R. I-06509 (Eur.) [hereinafter GAT]; Case C-539/03, Roche Nederland BV v. Primus, 2006 E.C.R. I-06535 (Eur.) [hereinafter Roche]; Rep. on the Convention on Jurisdiction and the Enforcement of Judgments in Civil and Commercial Matters Signed at Brussels, 27 September 1968, 1979 O.J. (C 59) 1, 36 (P. Jenard) (Eur.) [hereinafter Jenard Report]. See also a review of the relevant history in *Lucasfilm Ltd.*, [2011] UKSC at [60]–[114].

7 *See, e.g.*, Düsseldorf Landgericht [LG] [regional court], 4 O 128/00, 31 May 2001, 2001 GRUR INT. 983 (Ger.) (Schwungrad); Düsseldorf LG, 4 O 193/87, 1 February 1994 (Ger.) (Kettenbandförderer III); Mannheim LG, 7 O 235/01, 8 February 2002 (Ger.); Palmaz v. Boston Scientific BV, [1999] F.S.R. 352 (Neth.), reported in Bart J. Van den Broek, *Netherlands: Patents – Cross-Border Injunctions*, 20 EUR. INTELL. PROP. REV. N132 (1998).

8 *See, e.g.*, Court of First Instance, Brussels, May 12, 2000, INT'L REV. OF INTELL. PROP. AND COMPETITION LAW [IIC] 2001, 32, No. 2000/857/A, 571 (Belg.); Coin Controls Ltd. v. Suzo Int'l, [1997] 3 All E.R. 45 (Eng.) ('[O]nce the defendant raises validity the court must hand the proceedings over to the courts having exclusive jurisdiction over that issue.'). *See also* Lucasfilm Ltd., [2011] UKSC at [95]–[98]. For a discussion of the different approaches see MARKETA TRIMBLE, GLOBAL PATENTS: LIMITS OF TRANSNATIONAL ENFORCEMENT (Oxford University Press, 2012).

9 35 U.S.C. §§153, 154, 271 (2006).

10 Patent Cooperation Treaty, art. 7, June 19, 1970, 28 U.S.T. 7645 (amended Sept. 28, 1979 and modified Feb. 3, 1984 and Oct. 3, 2001). *See also* Paris Convention for the Protection of Industrial Property, art. 4bis, Mar. 20, 1883,

national patent rights are derived from a single European patent granted under the European Patent Convention.[11]

Unregistered intellectual property rights generally should not face the same obstacles that registered rights do; copyright does not require a grant or registration by a governmental agency, but vests automatically upon the creation or fixation of a work – at least in all the 166 countries that are parties to the Berne Convention.[12] Therefore, enforcement of copyright can be spared the fragmentation problem; the act of state doctrine or respect for a foreign sovereign is not at issue, and courts may extend their jurisdiction over copyright claims even if the claims arise from foreign copyright law.[13] However, copyright enforcement is challenging when multiple jurisdictions or infringers with no assets in the country of litigation are involved.

II. EXTRATERRITORIAL APPLICATION OF INTELLECTUAL PROPERTY LAWS

Enforcement of rights is often understood broadly as the process of pursuing legal interests by relying on laws that afford the rights; under this definition litigation alone is an act of 'enforcement,' regardless of its success in redressing a right holder's grievances. Under this definition

838 U.N.T.S. 305 (revised Dec. 14, 1900, June 2, 1911, Nov. 6, 1925, June 2, 1934, Oct. 31, 1958 and July 14, 1967, 'Independence of Patents Obtained for the Same Invention in Different Countries').

[11] Convention on the Grant of European Patents, art. 2(2), Oct. 5, 1973, 1065 U.N.T.S. 199 (amended in 1978, 1991, 1994, 1995, 1996, 1998, 2000 and 2005) [hereinafter European Patent Convention].

[12] Berne Convention for the Protection of Literary and Artistic Works, Sept. 9, 1896, S. Treaty Doc. No. 99–17 (1986) (as revised at Paris July 4, 1971 and amended Sept. 28, 1979). For a list of contracting parties see WIPO, Contracting Parties, Berne Convention, http://www.wipo.int/treaties/en/ShowResults.jsp?lang=en&treaty_id=15, accessed 14 October 2012.

[13] *See, e.g.*, London Film Prods. Ltd. v. Intercontinental Commc'ns, Inc., 580 F. Supp. 47 (S.D.N.Y. 1984); Lucasfilm Ltd. v. Ainsworth, [2011] UKSC 39 (appeal taken from Eng.). For an opinion contesting the conclusion that copyright is a transitory cause of action see William Patry, *Choice of Law and International Copyright*, 48 Am. J. Comp. L. 383, 468–9 (2000). For cases holding infringement of foreign copyright non-justiciable see *Lucasfilm Ltd.*, [2011] UKSC at [35]. For a general discussion on the justiciability of foreign copyright claims see, for instance, SAM RICKETSON & JANE C. GINSBURG, INTERNATIONAL COPYRIGHT AND NEIGHBOURING RIGHTS: THE BERNE CONVENTION AND BEYOND 1296–7 (2d ed. 2006).

extraterritoriality of enforcement may consist of either or both of extraterritorial application of a country's law to acts committed outside the country and extraterritorial litigation, meaning litigation under a country's substantive law conducted by a court outside of that country. Extraterritorial application occurs when a German court applies German law to conduct that occurred in the Netherlands;[14] extraterritorial litigation arises when a claim concerning conduct in Chile is filed in a U.S. court, which applies Chilean law to the conduct.[15]

The scenario illustrated by the first example – the extraterritorial application of German law to conduct in the Netherlands – may occur, for example, when a right holder encounters activities associated with his intellectual property that harm his economic interests but the cause of the harm originates in a country where he has no protection for his intellectual property. A holder of a German patent might discover that a Dutch company is supplying certain devices to another Dutch company that eventually supplies the devices to Germany where the importation and sale infringe the German patent.[16] The right holder might then want to stop the first Dutch company from aiding the second Dutch company in infringing his German patent.[17] Although it would appear to be more logical to bring an infringement suit against the first Dutch company in the Netherlands, if the right holder holds a patent only in Germany, he must rely on his German patent rights if he contests the acts of the two Dutch companies.

The necessity of applying German law extraterritorially in this scenario is a consequence of the fragmentation of protection; there is no global patent that confers rights in all countries of the world, and current practice is that most inventions, even if they are patented in multiple countries, are not patented in more than three countries.[18] However, the lack of protection in a particular country is not the only reason for which a party might want a specific country's law to be applied; a right holder might want to rely on a certain country's law because that law is more favorable to his interests than the laws of other countries, or because he wants to litigate

---

14 *See infra* note 16.

15 A U.S. court would have decided a copyright infringement case under Chilean law, for example in *London Film Productions Ltd.*, 580 F. Supp. 47.

16 Bundesgerichtshof [BGH] [Federal Court of Justice] Feb. 26, 2002, GEWERBLICHER RECHTSSCHUTZ UND URHEBERRECHT [GRUR] 599, 2002 (Ger.).

17 *Id.*

18 '[A]round 10 per cent of total patent families include filings at four or more patent offices.' 'Patent families' are defined as 'set[s] of patent applications interrelated by either priority claims or PCT national phase entries.' WORLD INTELL. PROP. ORG., WORLD INTELLECTUAL PROPERTY INDICATORS 2009 21 (2009), *available at* http://www.wipo.int/freepublications/en/intproperty/941/wipo_pub_941.pdf.

in a specific country that offers procedural advantages, and courts in that country will apply only their own intellectual property laws.

The extraterritorial reach of national laws may be established legislatively or through court interpretation.[19] In the United States the Patent Act is explicit about its extraterritorial reach in §271(f), which makes it an infringement to supply or cause to supply 'in or from the [United States]' components of an invention.[20] Even when not explicitly extraterritorial, provisions in the United States and other countries' patent laws may be interpreted by their respective courts as reaching beyond their country's borders. For example, the inducement provision of the U.S. Patent Act makes no statement about its application to acts outside the United States, but courts have interpreted it to reach those who induce from abroad the infringement in the United States of a U.S. patent.[21] In Germany, the general doctrines of aiding and abetting, although their wording in the German Civil Code is silent about their extraterritorial application, have been utilized by German courts in the patent infringement context to reach those who act abroad.[22]

Laws may also reach beyond a country's borders de facto by localization – when a country's courts localize acts within their country's prescriptive power. A Canadian company shipping goods free on board[23] to U.S. customers may be of the opinion that it operates solely in Canada, but a U.S. court will localize the company's patent infringing sale in the United States.[24] Similarly, courts may decide that even though there is an extraterritorial component in an offer to sell a patented device (when either the offer is made in a foreign country or the sale occurs or is intended to

---

[19] For a discussion of the various methods of extending U.S. intellectual property laws extraterritorially see, e.g., TRIMBLE, *supra* note 8; Curtis Bradley, *Territorial Intellectual Property Rights in an Age of Globalism*, 37 Va. J. Int'l L. 505 (1997).

[20] 35 U.S.C. §271(f) (2006).

[21] 35 U.S.C. §271(b) (2006).

[22] BÜRGERLICHES GESETZBUCH [BGB] [CIVIL CODE], Jan. 2, 2002, BUNDESGESETZBLATT, Teil I [BGBl. I] p. 42 2909, §830. *See, e.g.*, BGH Feb. 26, 2002, GRUR 599, 2002; *Sitz-Stützelement*, Düsseldorf LG, 4a O 395/02, Nov. 18, 2003. For a discussion of extraterritorial application of national patent laws see, e.g., Erhard Keller, *Patentverletzungen durch Handlungen im patentfreien Ausland*, *in* FESTSCHRIFT FÜR EIKE ULLMANN 449, 454 (Hans-Juergen Ahrens, Joachim Bornkamm and Hans Peter Kunz-Hallstein eds, 2006); TRIMBLE, *supra* note 8.

[23] For the term 'free on board' see Incoterms 2000 by the International Chamber of Commerce, *available at* http://www.iccwbo.org/incoterms/id3040/index.html, accessed 19 April 2011.

[24] Litecubes, LLC v. Northern Light Prods., Inc., 523 F.3d 1353, 1369 (Fed. Cir. 2008).

occur in a foreign country), the offer to sell falls within the territorial scope of their law. An offer made in Germany to sell a patented device would be found infringing even when the sale was supposed to occur outside Germany.[25] The U.S. Court of Appeals for the Federal Circuit opined that an offer made anywhere in the world to sell a patented device in the United States would infringe a U.S. patent.[26]

The extraterritorial application of a country's law will not present a problem as long as the law is applied by the court of the same country. For instance, in the German-Dutch example described above, there is certainly nothing to stop German courts from applying German law to its full territorial scope; indeed, as explained later, as long as the infringer is within the enforcement power of the German courts, meaning that the infringer is domiciled in Germany or has assets in Germany that can be targeted by German courts, enforcement will be successful even if it concerns a decision that resulted from the extraterritorial application of German law to acts that occurred outside Germany.

Having a foreign court apply a country's law to acts that were committed outside that country can be difficult, particularly if the application would affect parties or relationships in the country of the foreign court. Choice-of-law rules shield a country from having its courts apply foreign laws that it considers antithetical to its fundamental public policies, and foreign intellectual property laws whose extraterritorial reach is considered intrusive may be considered contrary to such public policies and denied application.[27] When a Japanese court was asked to apply the U.S. patent law provision on inducement to acts committed in Japan, the Supreme Court of Japan rejected the extraterritorial application of that provision of U.S. law, stating that '[t]o order prohibition of the act of actively inducing infringement of a U.S. patent and destruction of the infringing goods located in Japan by applying the U.S. Patent Act is contrary to the meaning of [public policy]'.[28] In these situations, conflict-of-laws rules

---

[25] *Zeitlagenmultiplexverfahren*, Düsseldorf LG, 4a O 124/05, Feb. 13, 2007.

[26] Transocean Offshore Deepwater Drilling, Inc. v. Maersk Contractors USA, Inc., 617 F.3d 1296 (Fed. Cir. 2010). 'The focus should not be on the location of the offer, but rather the location of the future sale that would occur pursuant to the offer.' *Id.* at 1309.

[27] While the extraterritorial reach of a foreign intellectual property law may indeed be considered repugnant to public policy, it is questionable whether simple differences between the substantive law that should apply based on the choice-of-law provision and the substantive law of the country in which the court sits (such as a difference in the definition of copyrightable subject matter) should warrant application of the public policy exception.

[28] Saikō Saibansho [Sup. Ct.] Sept. 26, 2002, 56 SAIKŌ SAIBANSHO MINJI

establish natural limits to the extraterritorial ambitions of foreign laws that countries may perceive as overly expansive and intrusive.

III. EXTRATERRITORIAL LITIGATION OF INTELLECTUAL PROPERTY DISPUTES

The extraterritorial effect of a foreign country's law is not the only reason for which a court may decide to refuse to apply foreign law. As explained earlier, courts are reluctant to adjudicate cases that concern foreign intellectual property rights, particularly when a case involves a decision on the validity of a registered right, such as a patent or trademark. The result is that instances of extraterritorial litigation – instances in which courts adjudicate issues concerning foreign intellectual property rights – are rare, and it appears that parties often settle their disputes once a court decides to adjudicate foreign-country intellectual property rights.[29]

Although extraterritorial litigation in general is not without problems, such as the danger of misapplication of foreign law, the fact that it is unavailable or of limited availability in intellectual property cases negatively impacts the enforceability of intellectual property rights. Without the option to litigate wherever an infringer's assets are located, right holders are forced to sue in the protecting country – the country of the grant or registration of the right – and face the additional problems of having to have the court decision subsequently recognized and enforced in a country where the infringer has assets. This makes enforcement of the rights more costly, complicated, and lengthy, and threatens the effectiveness of enforcement.

Additionally, because courts refrain from entertaining foreign intellectual property rights, a concentration of proceedings and adjudication of all related infringements of parallel rights in one court under the laws of multiple countries is impossible. This is a serious problem because the

---

HANREISHŪ [MINSHŪ], 1551 (Fujimoto v. Neuron Co. (Card Reader)), *available at* http://www.courts.go.jp/english/judgments/text/2002.9.26-2000.-Ju.-No.580.html, accessed 19 April 2011. *See also* MASATO DOGAUCHI, PRIVATE INTERNATIONAL LAW ON INTELLECTUAL PROPERTY: A CIVIL LAW OVERVIEW WIPO/PIL/01/8 10–11 (2001).

[29] *See, e.g.*, Fairchild Semiconductor Corp. v. Third Dimension (3D) Semiconductor, Inc., 589 F. Supp. 2d 84 (D. Me. 2008) (the case settled in June 2009); Baker-Bauman v. Walker, 2007 WL 1026436 (S.D. Ohio Mar. 9, 2007); London Film Prods. Ltd. v. Intercontinental Commc'ns, Inc., 580 F. Supp. 47 (S.D.N.Y. 1984). *Cf. Lucasfilm Ltd. v. Ainsworth*, [2011] UKSC 39 (appeal taken from Eng.).

current prevailing practice of fragmentation of litigation[30] exposes right holders to exorbitant litigation expense, which most right holders cannot afford, and the resulting inability of right holders to enforce their rights in multiple countries renders their rights de facto unenforceable.

IV. EXTRATERRITORIAL ENFORCEMENT OF DECISIONS CONCERNING INTELLECTUAL PROPERTY RIGHTS

Another definition of 'enforcement' focuses on the practical physical effects – acts of enforcement of rights against a party through which past infringements are remedied and future infringements possibly prevented.[31] While many parties will comply with court decisions voluntarily or agree on a settlement with the right holder, other parties must be forced to submit to court decisions. Under the practical physical effects definition, extraterritorial enforcement consists of the process of filing for recognition and enforcement of a foreign court decision in the country where the enforcement must occur; typically, this will be the country where the infringer has operations or holds assets. Therefore, this 'extraterritorial enforcement *per se*' concerns only 'extraterritorial parties' – parties without assets in the country where the decision was rendered.

Extraterritorial enforcement *per se* is a significant barrier against the extraterritorial application of a country's law. In the German-Dutch example above, the extraterritorial application of German law works only if the infringer has assets in Germany that the German court can reach to enforce its decision. If the infringer's assets are located outside the country of the court that rendered the decision, any attempt to apply national laws extraterritorially will fail unless a foreign court, meaning one in the country where the defendant is domiciled or has assets, is willing to recognize and enforce the decision, or permits the case to be re-litigated

---

30 For a mechanism that allows concentration of litigation of intellectual property cases to a certain degree in the EU/EEA see *infra* note 46. See also Marketa Trimble, *GAT, Solvay, and the Centralization of Patent Litigation in Europe*, 26 Emory Intl. L.R. (forthcoming in 2012).

31 Injunctions prohibiting prospective conduct, although quite standard in intellectual property cases, might not be issued automatically in every infringement case. See, e.g. the *eBay* case in the U.S. or the *Orange Book* case in Germany. eBay v. MercExchange, 547 U.S. 388 (S. Ct. 2006); BGH May 6, 2009, 180 ENTSCHEIDUNGEN DES BUNDESGERICHTSHOFES IN ZIVILSACHEN [BGHZ] 310, 2009 (Orange-Book-Standard, KZR 39/06).

before its own courts while applying the same law.[32] As explained earlier, re-litigation under another country's intellectual property law might not always be possible.

Recognition and enforcement rules serve a gatekeeping role by allowing courts to prevent the laws of other countries from having undesirable extraterritorial effects in their own country when the enforcement of foreign court decisions is attempted. For example, differences in standards of personal jurisdiction between the country where the decision was issued and the country where enforcement is sought can prevent recognition of a foreign decision.[33] When personal jurisdiction over a foreign defendant is based on the tortious acts of the defendant,[34] the tortious nature of those acts is measured under substantive laws, which means that the reach of personal jurisdiction in such cases coincides with the territorial reach of the applicable substantive laws. However, if the country where the resulting decision is to be enforced does not recognize the particular ground for jurisdiction on which the foreign court relied, the decision will not be recognized and enforced. Such a situation would, for example, present a hurdle to the recognition in England of a U.S. decision issued in a proceeding in which a U.S. long-arm jurisdiction was the basis for a U.S. court to exercise personal jurisdiction against an English defendant.[35] Therefore, although a U.S. court may apply substantive U.S. law to extend to particular acts by the defendant, by denying recognition of a U.S. judgment based on U.S. law, English courts will prevent the law from being enforced in England. If the case cannot be re-litigated in the U.K. under U.S. law, the non-recognition of the U.S. judgment might be fatal to the plaintiff's enforcement effort.[36]

Another reason courts deny recognition and enforcement of judgments

---

[32] In the German–Dutch example, recognition and enforcement would be secured under Regulation (EU) No. 1215/2012 of the European Parliament and of the Council of 12 December 2012 on jurisdiction and the recognition and enforcement of judgments in civil and commercial matters (recast) [hereinafter Brussels I Regulation (recast)].

[33] *See, e.g.*, ZIVILPROZESSORDNUNG [ZPO] [Code of Civil Procedure], Dec. 5, 2005, BGBl. I 3202, §328(1)(1) (Ger.); Brussels I Regulation (recast), art.45.1 (e); Uniform Foreign Country Money Judgments Recognition Act §4(b)(2) (2005).

[34] The commission of a tort is not available in all countries as a ground for personal jurisdiction.

[35] Lucasfilm Ltd. v. Ainsworth, [2009] EWCA (Civ) 1328, [191]–[195] (Eng.) (referring to DICEY, MORRIS & COLLINS ON THE CONFLICT OF LAWS 14R-048 (Lawrence Collins et al. eds, 14th ed. 2006).

[36] Although in *Lucasfilm Ltd.* the plaintiffs did not achieve recognition of the U.S. judgment, they will apparently have an opportunity to re-litigate the case in the U.K. under US copyright law.

is if the judgments are repugnant to the fundamental public policies of the enforcing country – another ground that may support the denial of recognition of a decision with an unacceptable extraterritorial effect.[37] This ground has been used when the remedy that was ordered by a foreign court would affect the party in the enforcing country in a manner that is against the public policy of that country. In a case in France, when an injunction was issued by a French court that would have affected free speech in the United States, a U.S. court refused to recognize and enforce the injunction.[38] Similarly, courts may find grounds to deny recognition to decisions by foreign courts in cases where foreign courts have decided cases regarding patents of the enforcing court's country. In the United States a court suggested that this could happen if a court in the United Arab Emirates were to decide a case involving a U.S. patent.[39]

In addition to posing a barrier to the extraterritorial effect of foreign laws, rules on recognition and enforcement of foreign decisions provide protections against other reaches that countries may view as intrusive or inappropriate.[40] For example, punitive damages will be denied recognition if the recognition of a foreign award of remedies of a criminal or punitive nature is considered against public policy.[41] Enforcements of injunctions may suffer from significant delays,[42] and if the injunctions target conduct on the internet, courts may decide that the ubiquitous nature of the medium defies any possibility for the injunctions to be enforced in a

---

37 *See, e.g.*, Brussels I Regulation (recast), *supra* note 32, at art.45.1(a); ZPO, *supra* note 33, at §328(1)(4); Uniform Foreign Country Money Judgments Recognition Act §4(c)(3).

38 Sarl Louis Feraud Int'l v. Viewfinder, Inc., 489 F.3d 474 (2d Cir. 2007). *See also* Marketa Trimble Landova, *Public Policy Exception to Recognition and Enforcement of Judgments in Cases of Copyright Infringement*, 40 IIC 642 (2009).

39 Juniper Networks, Inc. v. Abdullah Ali Bahattab, 2009 WL 6781382 (D.D.C. 2009). The court in this case 'decline[d] to defer the consideration of the issues related to the [U.S.] patent to a foreign jurisdiction'. *Id.* at *6.

40 For a discussion of the challenges that U.S. judgments face in Europe see, e.g., Samuel P. Baumgartner, *How Well Do U.S. Judgments Fare in Europe?*, 40 Geo. Wash. Int'l Rev. 173 (2008).

41 Courts may recognize the portion of damages that do not have the nature of punitive damages and comport to the courts' understanding of compensatory damages. *See, e.g.*, BGH, June 4, 1992, 118 BGHZ 312, 1993 (Ger.) (IX ZR 149/91); Saikō Saibansho [Sup. Ct.] July 11, 1997, 1993 (O) no. 1762, 51 Minshū 2537 (Japan), *translated in* http://www.courts.go.jp/english/judgments/text/1997.07.11-1993-O-No.1762.html; Cour de cassation [Cass.] [supreme court for judicial matters] 1e civ., Dec. 1, 2010, No. 1090 (Fr.) (09-13.303).

42 Marketa Trimble, *Cross-Border Injunctions in U.S. Patent Cases and Their Enforcement Abroad*, 13 Marq. Intell. Prop. L. Rev. 331, 347–9 (2009).

territorially-limited manner.[43] Pursuing contempt orders in any country other than the country that granted the patent at issue might prove challenging as well if the defendant claims a design around.[44]

It is important to note that not all decisions reaching parties outside the country of the rendering court will necessitate enforcement actions. Even if the party is not domiciled in or has no assets in the country where the decision is rendered, the party may have significant incentives to accept voluntarily the extraterritorial effects of a country's law; a party may have a strong interest in establishing future business or maintaining its current business presence in the country. Therefore, the more interconnected the global economy becomes, the more likely it is that at least some countries will be able to impose obligations extraterritorially on non-resident parties and rely on the parties' voluntary compliance. At the same time, parties with a global presence or global business interests are likely to coordinate efforts among themselves to achieve a certain uniformity in the laws of various countries, which will make the global legal environment for their businesses easier to navigate and legal compliance less complex.

V. EXISTING AND PROPOSED CONFLICT-OF-LAWS SOLUTIONS

There are three possible avenues for the future of extraterritorial enforcement. First, the current situation may continue to exist with the extraterritorial expanse of one country's law being counterbalanced by the defensive posture of another country's enforcement mechanism. Improvements to the system would rely on individual countries' unilateral actions. The recent decision of the U.K. Supreme Court in Lucasfilm v. Ainsworth[45] is an example of a unilateral action by a national court in favor of a constructive solution to some of the extraterritorial enforcement problems in intellectual property cases. Although the courts in the case refused to recognize a pre-existing U.S. judgment, the U.K. Supreme Court directed that the matter against the English defendants be re-litigated in the U.K. under U.S. law.

---

43 On the issue of territorial partitioning of the internet and the apparently increasing role of geolocation see, e.g., Marketa Trimble, *The Future of Cybertravel: Legal Implications of the Evasion of Geolocation*, 22 Fordham Intell. Prop. Media & Ent. L.J. 567 (2012).

44 For a discussion of the difficulties associated with the enforcement of a contempt order see TRIMBLE, GLOBAL PATENTS, *supra* note 8.

45 Lucasfilm Ltd. v. Ainsworth, [2011] UKSC 39 (appeal taken from Eng.).

Reliance on unilateral actions by individual countries will probably not be sufficient to address all enforcement problems. The second avenue for the future of extraterritorial enforcement would require countries to agree on a conflict-of-laws solution to extraterritorial enforcement problems and conclude an international treaty that would define uniformly applicable rules of jurisdiction, choice of law, and recognition and enforcement of foreign court decisions.

Finally, in the most coordinated avenue, countries could adopt a unitary system of protection of intellectual property rights. The creation of this type of system would eliminate the need for extraterritorial application of national laws because a single law would apply to acts of infringement in all countries, and a concentration of multiple proceedings would not be an issue, since only one proceeding would need to take place. Similarly, recognition and enforcement of foreign court decisions would be simplified under a unitary right system. A brief survey of the current initiatives in the area of conflict of laws will be useful before discussing this third possible avenue.

There are some existing mechanisms that can provide instructive lessons about the functioning of either a conflict-of-laws solution or a unitary right solution. The EU and the EEA have been testing grounds for the operation of a mechanism for enhanced cross-border enforcement of intellectual property rights through civil litigation.[46] The two jurisdiction and recognition and enforcement instruments – the Brussels Convention,[47] which was later replaced by the Brussels I Regulation,[48] and the Lugano Convention[49] – vest exclusive jurisdiction in cases that concern the validity

---

46 Concentration of litigation could also be achieved under the Hague Convention on Choice of Court Agreements, 30 June 2005 (currently not in force), which excludes a significant portion of patent-related litigation from its scope but applies to patent 'infringement proceedings [that] are brought for breach of a contract between the parties relating to such rights, or could have been brought for breach of that contract'. Hague Convention on Private International Law, Convention on Choice of Court Agreements art. 2(2) n) – o), June 30, 2005, 44 I.L.M. 1294. The Convention is limited to business-to-business scenarios. *Id.* at art. 2(1) a).

47 Convention of 27 September 1968 on Jurisdiction and the Enforcement of Judgments in Civil and Commercial Matters, Sept. 27, 1968, 1978 O.J. (L 304) 36.

48 Brussels I Regulation (recast), *supra* note 32.

49 Convention of 16 September 1988 on Jurisdiction and the Enforcement of Judgments in Civil and Commercial Matters, Sept. 16, 1988, 1988 O.J. (L319) 9 (the Lugano Convention), *revised in* Convention on Jurisdiction and the Recognition and Enforcement of Judgments in Civil and Commercial Matters, Oct. 30, 2007, 2009 O.J. (L 147) 5 (the Lugano II Convention).

of registered rights to courts in the country of registration,[50] but allow for the possibility that infringement proceedings be conducted outside the country of registration.[51] The fact that the choice-of-law Rome II Regulation[52] provides a rule for determining the law applicable to infringements of intellectual property rights[53] suggests that courts in the EU and the EEA are indeed expected to handle cases of infringement of foreign intellectual property.[54]

The functioning of the EU/EEA mechanism has exposed several problems that a conflict-of-laws solution might encounter.[55] The availability of multiple grounds for jurisdiction under the framework led to forum shopping and the practice of launching 'torpedoes' – the filing of declaratory judgment suits in slow-moving jurisdictions with the objective of delaying or defeating right holder actions. The practice of issuing cross-border injunctions that the framework allowed[56] was criticized, and the inconsistency in courts' interpretations of the exclusive jurisdiction provision was problematic. The inconsistency was not fully solved even by the two 2006 decisions of the Court of Justice of the European Union that were expected to shed light on the issue.[57]

Because it is very easy in the EU for an infringer to achieve a stay or removal of a case concerning a foreign-registered right by raising the issue

---

[50] Brussels I Regulation (recast), *supra* note 32, at art.24(4).

[51] See other grounds for jurisdiction in Brussels I Regulation (recast), *supra* note 32.

[52] Regulation (EC) No 864/2007 of the European Parliament and of the Council of 11 July 2007 on the law applicable to non-contractual obligations, 2007 O.J. (L 199) 40 (Rome II Regulation).

[53] *Id.* at art. 8.

[54] *See also Lucasfilm Ltd.*, [2011] UKSC at [91]–[92].

[55] For a discussion of the delay in the impact of the Brussels Convention on intellectual property litigation see Richard Ebbink, *A Fire-Side Chat on Cross-Border Issues (before the ECJ in GAT v. LuK)*, *in* FESTSCHRIFT FÜR JOCHEN PAGENBERG 255, 256–7 (Dietrich Beier, Laurence Brüning-Petit and Christopher Heath eds, 2006) (Ger.); Joseph Straus, *Patent Litigation in Europe – A Glimmer of Hope? Present Status and Future Perspectives*, 2 WASH. U. J.L. & POL'Y 403, 416 (2000); Volkmar Tetzner, *Die Verfolgung der Verletzung ausländischer Patente vor deutschen Gerichten unter Berücksichtigung des EWG-Gerichtsstands und Vollstreckungs-Abkommens*, 1976 GRUR 669, 669 (Ger.).

[56] For a discussion of criticism of cross-border injunctions see Marketa Trimble, *Cross-Border Injunctions*, *supra* note 42, at 355–63.

[57] GAT, *supra* note 6; Roche, *supra* note 6. See, for example, a decision by the German Federal Supreme Court to lodge a reference for a CJEU preliminary ruling on the interpretation of the Brussels I Regulation in declaratory judgment actions. BGH Feb. 1, 2011, GRUR 554, 2011 (*Trägermaterial für Kartenformulare*, KZR 8/10); *Folien Fischer AG and Fofitec AG v. RITRAMA SpA*, CJEU, C-133/11.

of validity of the right, there is probably only one scenario in the future in which courts will be able to adjudicate infringements of foreign rights – cases in which the parties do not raise the issue of validity.[58] This is the same result that seems to prevail in the United States, where a 2007 decision by the U.S. Court of Appeals for the Federal Circuit suggests that U.S. courts should refrain from deciding cases that would require them to rule on foreign patent validity.[59] Although the Court of Appeals ruled only on the question of whether jurisdiction over a foreign patent infringement exists when jurisdiction is based on one particular theory,[60] the Court's general discussion of the act of state doctrine indicates that it is opposed to extending jurisdiction based on other theories if the validity of foreign patents could be raised.[61] In fact, in one of the cases since 2007 in which a U.S. court agreed to exercise jurisdiction over foreign patents the court did so because the parties agreed not to raise the issue of patent validity in the case.[62]

Although the EU/EEA mechanism is not without problems, and experts and practitioners have called for its revision,[63] it has provided inspiration in the search for a larger-than-regional mechanism. A conflict-of-laws instrument that would resemble the Brussels Convention in scope

---

[58] But *cf.* the potential impact of the decision in Case C-616/10, Solvay v. Honeywell (Eur.), discussed in Trimble, *supra* note 30.

[59] Voda v. Cordis, *supra* note 6.

[60] The case concerned the issue of supplemental jurisdiction of U.S. federal courts.

[61] For a discussion of the impact of the decision see Eric Chan, *Asserting Foreign Patent Claims in U.S. Federal Courts: What's Left After Voda v. Cordis?*, 18 ALB. L.J. SCI. & TECH. 1, 45–6 (2007).

[62] Fairchild Semiconductor Corp. v. Third Dimension (3D) Semiconductor, Inc., 589 F. Supp. 2d 84 (D. Me. 2008). The second decision issued post-Voda v. Cordis (*supra* note 6) was Baker-Bauman v. Walker, 2007 WL 1026436 (S.D. Ohio Mar. 9, 2007).

[63] *See, e.g.*, *Proposal for a Regulation of the European Parliament and of the Council on Jurisdiction and the Recognition and Enforcement of Judgments in Civil and Commercial Matters (Recast)*, at 32, COM (2010) 748 final (Dec. 14, 2010); *An Industrial Property Rights Strategy for Europe, Communication from the Commission to the European Parliament, the Council and the European Economic and Social Committee*, at 14, COM (2008) 465 final (July 16, 2008); *Green Paper on the Review of Council Regulation (EC) No 44/2001 on Jurisdiction and the Recognition and Enforcement of Judgments in Civil and Commercial Matters*, COM (2009) 175 final (Apr. 21, 2009); Marko Schauwecker, *Europäische Union/EFTA – Revidiertes Lugano-Übereinkommen kodifiziert umstrittene EuGH-Rechtsprechung zur internationalen Zuständigkeit bei grenzüberschreitenden Patentverletzungsklagen*, 2007 GEWERBLICHER RECHTSSCHUTZ UND URHEBERRECHT, INTERNATIONALER TEIL [GRUR Int.] 552 (Ger.); Jens Adolphsen, *Renationalisierung von Patentstreitigkeiten in Europa*, 2007 PRAXIS DES INTERNATIONALEN PRIVATRECHTS [IPRAX] 15, 15 (Ger.).

but would include many more countries was proposed by the Hague Conference on Private International Law; however, the Conference's proposal for a general convention that would have covered intellectual property cases failed.[64] Consequently, the EU/EEA mechanism remains the only existing international conflict-of-laws mechanism that allows, albeit in limited circumstances, litigation of foreign intellectual property rights, including litigation of multiple countries' intellectual property rights in one national court, and that eases the process of recognition and enforcement of foreign court decisions.

The failure of the Hague proposal generated interest among intellectual property scholars in developing a conflict-of-laws proposal that would focus on cross-border enforcement of intellectual property rights. In 2002 Professors Rochelle C. Dreyfuss and Jane Ginsburg presented their proposal for a draft convention,[65] and the American Law Institute's Principles, for which they served as co-reporters, followed in 2008 as the outcome of a seven-year project.[66] Another proposal for Principles has been developed in Europe by the Group on Conflict of Laws in Intellectual Property (CLIP), which was established under the auspices of the Max Planck Institute for Intellectual Property and Competition Law,[67] and other projects sprouted in Japan and Korea.[68] The newest initiative is being taken by the International Law Association, which intends to build on the existing projects by bringing several of their participants into one committee.

A special version of the conflict-of-laws solution – an institutional solution – involves adding an institutional layer to a conflict-of-laws solution by creating a regional or international court that would adjudicate

---

64 For the limited Convention on Choice of Court Agreements that was adopted (instead of the general convention), but which has not yet entered into force see *supra* note 46.

65 Rochelle C. Dreyfuss and Jane C. Ginsburg, *Draft Convention on Jurisdiction and Recognition of Judgments in Intellectual Property Matters*, 77 CHI.-KENT L. REV. 1065 (2001–2002).

66 AM. LAW INST., INTELLECTUAL PROP.: PRINCIPLES GOVERNING JURISDICTION, CHOICE OF LAW, AND JUDGMENTS IN TRANSNATIONAL DISPUTES (2008).

67 EUROPEAN MAX-PLANCK-GROUP FOR CONFLICT OF LAWS IN INTELLECTUAL PROPERTY (CLIP), http://www.cl-ip.eu (last visited Apr. 14, 2011).

68 TRANSPARENCY OF JAPANESE LAW PROJECT, TRANSPARENCY PROPOSAL ON JURISDICTION, CHOICE OF LAW, RECOGNITION AND ENFORCEMENT OF FOREIGN JUDGMENTS IN INTELLECTUAL PROPERTY (2009), *available at* http://www.tomeika.jur.kyushu-u.ac.jp/ip/pdf/Transparency%20RULES%20%202009%20Nov1.pdf; KOREAN PRIVATE INT'L LAW ASSOC., PRINCIPLES ON INTERNATIONAL INTELLECTUAL PROPERTY LITIGATION (2010) (on file with the author).

intellectual property claims under the laws of multiple countries. Naturally, this type of solution is complex. Since 1999 the European Patent Organization has attempted to create a proposal for a European Patent Litigation Agreement that would concentrate proceedings involving multiple national patents stemming from a single European patent.[69] The project was eventually appropriated by the EU Commission, which incorporated the idea into its own proposal for an Enhanced Patent System in Europe.[70] The proposal suffered a setback in March 2011 when the Court of Justice of the European Union stated that the proposal in its then-current version was inconsistent with European Union law, and the project has faced opposition from some EU member states.[71]

Although institutional solutions are more costly than the pure conflict-of-laws solutions that rely on existing national courts, institutional solutions that create regional or international courts solve two important issues that the pure conflict-of-laws solutions do not. First, the institutional solutions allow the new courts to decide issues of validity of the registered rights at issue, thereby removing the primary obstacle to an effective concentration of proceedings of issues arising under the substantive laws of multiple countries.[72] Second, the solutions eliminate the need for a significant level of cooperation and coordination among national courts that the conflict-of-laws solutions necessarily require. The costs of establishing the new institutions are not the only downside of the institutional solutions; a concentration of proceedings in one court on a regular basis would likely lead to a gradual alignment of the substantive laws of multiple countries – an outcome that not all might consider desirable.[73]

---

69 1999 O.J. EPO 545, 548.

70 Council of the European Union, Conclusions on an Enhanced Patent System in Europe, Dec. 4, 2009, *available at* http://www.consilium.europa.eu/uedocs/cms_data/docs/pressdata/en/intm/111744.pdf.

71 In March 2011 the Court of Justice of the European Union issued an opinion that the proposed instrument was incompatible with the law of the European Union. Press Release No. 17/11, Court of Justice of the European Union, The Draft Agreement on the Creation of a European and Community Patent Court Is Not Compatible with European Union Law, (Mar. 8 2011), *available at* http://curia.europa.eu/jcms/upload/docs/application/pdf/2011-03/cp110017en.pdf.

72 The existing proposals for conflict-of-laws solutions (supra notes 66–68) would permit national courts to decide foreign registered right validity, but only with an inter partes effect.

73 For a discussion of the possible gradual alignment and related references see Trimble, GLOBAL PATENTS, *supra* note 8.

VI. UNITARY RIGHTS AS AN ANSWER TO EXTRATERRITORIAL ENFORCEMENT PROBLEMS

Existing proposals for solutions to the problems of fragmentation of enforcement of intellectual property rights have been developed often on the premise that countries wish to maintain differences among their laws and resist the creation of unitary rights for multiple countries. Both types of solutions – pure conflict-of-laws solutions, such as those based on the ALI or CLIP Principles, and institutional solutions, such as the proposed patent litigation system in the EU – require countries to compromise on their procedural rules; the conflict-of-laws solutions require countries to accept the proposition that their intellectual property rights might be adjudicated by a foreign court applying foreign rules of procedure, while the institutional solutions require countries to acquiesce to the creation of new unitary procedural rules to be applied in new courts. However, both types of solutions may be designed to allow countries to preserve the specificities of their individual substantive laws.[74]

It is understandable that the drafters of the existing proposals have focused on solutions that maintain the differences in substantive intellectual property laws, because attempts at deeper harmonization of the laws have encountered significant roadblocks at the international level. Although the effort to solve enforcement problems by avoiding contentious substantive harmonization issues is commendable, it is questionable whether countries' substantive laws will in fact be shielded from further harmonization if the interpretation of those laws is entrusted to one court – whether it be a national, regional or international court. It seems natural that any court would gravitate towards an alignment of the jurisprudence of the laws of various countries and gradually deepen the harmonization of the laws.[75]

---

[74] The current proposal for the EU patent litigation system is being combined with a proposal for a unitary EU-wide patent; the litigation system would operate for both EU-wide patents and national patents based on a single European patent. *See Proposal for a Regulation of the European Parliament and of the Council Implementing Enhanced Cooperation in the Area of Creation of Unitary Patent Protection*, at 3, COM (2011) 215 final (Apr. 13, 2011).

[75] For observations about the potential of aligning various countries' laws through interpretation in a single court see, e.g., EDUARD REIMER, EUROPÄISIERUNG DES PATENTRECHTS 259–81 (1955); Thomas Borecki, *Moving Towards Regional Patent Systems*, *in* RETHINKING INTERNATIONAL INTELLECTUAL PROPERTY: BIODIVERSITY & DEVELOPING COUNTRIES, EXTRATERRITORIAL ENFORCEMENT, THE GRACE PERIOD, AND OTHER ISSUES 58, 60 (Kraig M. Hill, Toshiko Takenaka and

Given that at least some degree of alignment would occur through judicial interpretation, it may transpire that any solution to the fragmentation of the litigation problem will have to address the fragmentation of intellectual property rights protection by providing for a fully harmonized or unitary right that will cover multiple countries. For a potential solution that would address fragmentation of both protection and enforcement, valuable lessons should be derived from the EU's experience with the two existing unitary EU intellectual property instruments – the Community trademark[76] and the Community design.[77]

With one registration, the Community trademark and the Community design confer rights that extend to all EU member states,[78] and the rights conferred are identical in every state.[79] Infringement proceedings concerning the instruments may be concentrated in a national court of the infringer's domicile, and the court may exercise jurisdiction over all related infringements of the same Community trademark or design.[80] When deciding about infringements of the instruments, national courts apply the rules as they are set by the respective EU regulations; however, because the regulations are not exhaustive, the EU legislator has permitted courts to apply national law to issues not covered by the regulations.[81]

The Community trademark and Community design situations illustrate the problems that emerge when unitary rights are created but no unified court structure is established to interpret and enforce the rights. The supplementary application of national laws to fill gaps in the EU framework for Community trademarks and Community designs is a necessary consequence of the absence of a unified court structure to adjudicate cases concerning the unitary instruments; if such a structure existed, its

---

Kevin Takeuchi eds, 2000); Remco De Ranitz, *Mr Justice Laddie in Conversation with Remco De Ranitz*, 25 Eur. Intell. Prop. Rev. 528, 535 (2003).

[76] Council Regulation (EC) No 40/94 of 20 December 1993 on the Community Trade Mark, 1994 O.J. (L 11) 1 (in effect since 1994, codified in Council Regulation (EC) No 207/2009 of 26 February 2009 on the Community Trade Mark, 2009 O.J. (L 78) 1).

[77] Council Regulation (EC) No 6/2002 of 12 December 2001 on Community Designs, 2002 O.J. (L 3) 1 (in effect since 2002).

[78] Council Regulation (EC) No 207/2009, *supra* note 76, at art. 1(2); Council Regulation (EC) No 6/2002, *supra* note 77, at art. 1(3).

[79] Council Regulation (EC) No 207/2009, *supra* note 76, at tit. II, § 2; Council Regulation (EC) No 6/2002, *supra* note 77, at tit. II, § 4.

[80] Council Regulation (EC) No 207/2009, *supra* note 76, at arts. 96–8; Council Regulation (EC) No 6/2002, *supra* note 77, at arts. 81–3.

[81] Council Regulation (EC) No 207/2009, *supra* note 76, at arts. 14, 101(2); Council Regulation (EC) No 6/2002, *supra* note 77, at art. 88(2).

courts could craft the system's own supplementary rules. The application of national laws, however minimal, creates a potential for differences in enforcement of the instruments in various member states. Since national differences depend on the place of litigation, infringers can manipulate the effects of potential infringement actions by establishing domicile in states where national laws, even though only supplementary to the EU regulations, provide the best situation for the infringer.[82] Although the differences among national laws may diminish over time,[83] with no unified court system applying a single law, differences in enforcement will persist, just as they did, for example, in the U.S. patent law before the U.S. Court of Appeals for the Federal Circuit was created in 1982, inter alia, to unify case law in patent matters.

VII. EXTRATERRITORIAL ENFORCEMENT OF INTELLECTUAL PROPERTY RIGHTS OUTSIDE THE CIVIL LITIGATION FRAMEWORK

Absent an agreement by countries on a conflict-of-laws solution or an institutional solution to extraterritorial enforcement problems, intellectual property holders continue to face significant obstacles to enforcement of their rights simultaneously in multiple countries or against infringers with no domicile or assets in the protecting country. It appears unlikely that countries other than those in the European Union or other regional structures will agree on unitary rights or a unitary litigation system; this avenue is probably the most remote option of the three possible solutions for extraterritorial enforcement. Until adequate cooperation in the area of civil cross-border enforcement is established, intellectual property holders may try to supplement civil litigation by other means of enforcement – enforcement through border measures and arbitration.[84]

---

[82] See, e.g., the CJEU holding regarding coercive measures in DHL Express France SAS v. Chronopost SA, Case C-235/09, (Ct. of Just. of the Eur. Union, Apr. 12 2011), *available at* http://eur-lex.europa.eu/LexUriServ/LexUriServ.do?uri=CELEX:62009CJ0235:EN:HTML.

[83] E.g., for provisions aimed at a partial alignment of national laws with respect to remedies that must be available in intellectual property cases see Directive 2004/48/EC of the European Parliament and of the Council of 29 April 2004 on the Enforcement of Intellectual Property Rights, 2004 O.J. (L195) 16.

[84] *See, e.g.*, TRIPS, *supra* note 1, at pt. III, §§ 4–5; Council Regulation (EC) No 1383/2003 of 22 July 2003 Concerning Customs Actions Against Goods

Practitioners have reported positive experiences with enforcement through border measures in various countries, and right holders should consider them as alternatives or supplements to civil cross-border litigation. Although border measures are an important cross-border component of cooperation among the law enforcement authorities of various countries,[85] they do not raise issues of extraterritorial enforcement because the enforcement occurs within each protecting country with regard to rights that exist under the laws of that protecting country. The only exception could be the detention of goods in transit through a protecting country when the customs authorities of that country detain the goods for infringing intellectual property rights in that protecting country. This practice has serious consequences for international trade and was recently rejected by the Court of Justice of the European Union.[86]

Arbitration may also be an avenue for resolution of intellectual property disputes that cross national borders. The fact that a well-established and widely recognized instrument for cross-border recognition and enforcement of foreign arbitration awards exists[87] enhances the potential utility of arbitration in cross-border scenarios. Cases concerning intellectual property are not foreign to arbitration; however, infringement cases are seldom arbitrated because they usually lack the necessary agreement among the parties to select arbitration as their dispute resolution mechanism.[88]

Neither border measures nor arbitration can fully replace enforcement through civil litigation. Border measures only supplement civil litigation; they do not provide damages for past infringements and can only provide a prospective remedy by preventing an importation. Arbitration only functions if arbitration awards can be enforced by courts in the enforcing country; therefore, enforcement of arbitration awards suffers

---

Suspected of Infringing Certain Intellectual Property Rights and the Measures to be Taken Against Goods Found to Have Infringed Such Rights, 2003 O.J. (L196) 7.

85 *See, e.g.*, *The WCO and the Protection of Intellectual Property Rights (IPR)*, WORLD CUSTOMS ORGANIZATION, http://www.wcoomd.org/home_cboverviewboxes_valelearningoncustomsvaluation_epipr.htm (last visited July 22 2011).

86 Case C-446/09, Koninklijke Philips Elecs. NV v. Lucheng Meijing Indus. Co., and case C-495/09, Nokia Corp. v. Her Majesty's Commissioners of Revenue and Customs (Ct. of Just. of the Eur. Union, Dec. 1, 2011).

87 Convention on the Recognition and Enforcement of Foreign Arbitral Awards, June 10, 1958, 21 U.S.T. 2517, 330 U.N.T.S. 3 (146 countries are parties to the convention).

88 Daniel Schimmel and Ila Kapoor, *Resolving International Intellectual Property Disputes in Arbitration*, INTELL. PROP. & TECH L. J., February 2009, at 5, 5.

from some of the same problems that enforcement of court decisions in civil litigation does.[89] Improving cross-border enforcement through civil litigation therefore appears to be an imperative for the next generation of international intellectual property treaties.

[89] See, e.g., the public policy exception in the Convention on the Recognition and Enforcement of Foreign Arbitral Awards, *supra* note 88, at art. V.2(b).

14. Injunctive relief in patent cases in the US, Germany and Japan: Recent developments and outlook

Christoph Rademacher

Until 2006, permanent injunctive relief was considered an obvious and – absent rare and extraordinary circumstances – quasi-automatic remedy available for patentees upon prevailing in an infringement lawsuit. Over the last decades, technological development resulted in products across many industries no longer being covered by only one patent or maybe a handful of patents. Rather, products became the result of a vast number of inventions covered by hundreds or even thousands of patents. The most notable examples are products in the semiconductors industry, which are often covered by hundreds of patents for the semiconductor chip's circuit layout, improving materials, changing packaging, etc.[1]

Major players in affected industries started to acquire large patent portfolios, often referred to as patent thickets, not only to protect their inventions, but also to accumulate a portfolio sufficiently large to exclude competitors from manufacturing, for example, semiconductors, thereby establishing a basis for complex cross-licensing of infringed patents. While cross-licensing and forming patent pools for certain standard technologies developed as a workable solution for patent thickets amongst active players with similar investments and stakes, the dynamics of the patent negotiations changed with the increasing frequency of non-manufacturing patentees seeking to enforce their patents. As non-practicing entities (NPEs) were not exposed to the risk of being forced to interrupt their own production, they could negotiate licensing arrangements with alleged patent infringers in a more aggressive and effective fashion based on a different leverage.

In 2006, the US Supreme Court handed down its opinion in *eBay vs.*

[1] DAN L. BURKE & MARK A. LEMLEY, THE PATENT CRISIS AND HOW THE COURTS CAN SOLVE IT 90 (The University of Chicago Press 2009).

MercExchange,[2] raising the bar for patentee's claims for injunctive relief. While US patent law had in principle exempted patent law from the traditional test factors imposed on equitable claims since the inauguration of the Federal Circuit in 1982,[3] the Supreme Court dismissed such exceptional treatment of patent infringement cases and ordered courts to apply the four factor test before granting injunctive relief. Specifically, the Supreme Court required a showing that (1) that the patentee has suffered an irreparable injury; (2) that remedies available at law (such as monetary damages) are inadequate to compensate for the injury; (3) that the balance of the hardships warrants a remedy in equity; and (4) that the public interest would not be harmed by a permanent injunction.[4]

In this article, the author will briefly review the standard for obtaining injunctive relief against patent infringement in the US, and will give an overview on current developments in two of the most important civil law jurisdictions: Germany, being the most important patent litigation venue in Europe, and Japan, being the jurisdiction with the most substantial and developed body of patent law in Asia.

I. UNITED STATES

(i) *ebay*

From the inauguration of the Federal Circuit to the Supreme Court's *eBay* decision in 2006, US courts denied injunctive relief after finding infringement of a valid and enforceable patent only in a few cases.[5] In such cases, the defendant showed that the patentee and plaintiff had failed to sufficiently practice the invention and thus disserved the public need.[6] Such high burden was only overcome in a few cases, usually in the medical industry where the public good relied on the availability of the infringing product.[7] In 2005, RIM, the manufacturer of the BlackBerry, was held liable for patent infringement of certain patents owned by the

---

2 eBay Inc. v. MercExchange, LLC, 547 U.S. 388 (2006).

3 *See, e.g.*, W.L. Gore & Assocs, Inc. v. Garlock, Inc., 842 F.2d 1275, 1281 (Fed. Cir. 1988).

4 *eBay*, 547 U.S. at 391.

5 *See, e.g.* Rite-Hite Corp. v. Kelley Co., 56 F.3d 1538, 1547 (Fed. Cir. 1995).

6 *Id.*

7 *See, e.g.*, Hybritech, Inc. v. Abbott Labs., 4 U.S.P.Q.2d 1001 (C.D. Cal. 1987), aff'd, 849 F.2d 1446 (Fed. Cir. 1988).

non-practicing entity NTP.[8] RIM settled, agreeing to pay damages in the amount of $612.5 million to avoid facing the enforcement of NTP's claim for injunctive relief, which would have shut down BlackBerry services in the US.[9]

While the Supreme Court denied RIM's request to grant certiorari,[10] the internet auction platform eBay convinced the Supreme Court to grant certiorari[11] in a comparable case only a few months later, in which it had been held liable for infringement of a patent owned by the NPE MercExchange.[12] eBay was facing enforcement of MercExchange's claim for injunctive relief after the Federal Circuit reversed the district court, which had in the first instance refused to grant a claim for injunctive relief despite finding infringement.[13] The Supreme Court, in one of its first major decisions in the area of patent law since the inauguration of the Federal Circuit, unanimously overruled the Federal Circuit's opinion, and ended the practice of presuming irreparable harm for infringement of a valid patent.[14] The court concluded that the four factor test had to be applied by courts in patent law cases just as in cases outside the patent world.[15] One of the concurring opinions revealed that one of the Supreme Court's reasons for re-instating the four factor test was the growing concern about the rise of NPEs and their increasingly strong bargaining position when demanding high damage claims from established market participants for infringing one or a few patents making up for only a fraction of the patents embodied in a complex product.[16]

After the Supreme Court handed down its *eBay* decision, district courts started to routinely apply the four factor test, and to reject patentee's claims for injunctive relief infringement of a valid patent. Between 2006 and 2010, courts granted claims of injunctive after finding infringement in only 72 percent of all cases, down from 95 percent before 2006.[17] Over

---

[8] NTP, Inc. v. Research in Motion, Ltd., 418 F.3d 1282, 1290 (Fed. Cir. 2005).

[9] Mark A. Lemley and Carl Shapiro, *Patent Holdup and Royalty Stacking*, 85 Tex. L. Rev. 1991, 2049 (2007).

[10] Research In Motion, Ltd. v. NTP, Inc., 546 U.S. 1157 (2006).

[11] eBay Inc. v. MercExchange, L.L.C., 547 U.S. 388 (2006).

[12] MercExchange, L.L.C. v. eBay, Inc., 275 F. Supp. 2d 695 (E.D. Va. 2003).

[13] MercExchange, L.L.C. v. eBay, Inc., 401 F.3d 1323, 1338–39 (Fed. Cir. 2005).

[14] eBay Inc. v. MercExchange, L.L.C., 547 U.S. 388, 393–4 (2006).

[15] *Id.* at 391.

[16] *Id.* at 396–7.

[17] Federal Trade Commission, The Evolving IP Marketplace: Aligning Patent Notice and Remedies with Competition, March 2011, at 256, www.ftc.gov/os/2011/03/110307patentreport.pdf (last visited Oct. 30, 2011).

the same span, the likelihood for NPEs (including universities, research institutes and independent inventors) to obtain a permanent injunction had been as high as 53 percent, which is significantly higher than statistics and studies released earlier after *eBay* had suggested.

A primary focus of the courts' analysis when determining injunctive relief was the first factor, specifically whether the patentee had suffered an irreparable injury in the course of the infringement. A showing of actual competition usually convinced the courts to grant injunctive relief, though some courts have stated that a general assertion of competition by itself would not suffice, and specific evidence of an irreparable injury (such as lost market share, lost customers or price erosion) would be required.[18]

In cases where no direct competition between the patentee and the infringer occurred, courts have still granted injunctive relief if the patentee could substantiate an irreparable injury, such as loss of reputation and tangible future sales, because of the infringement. Almost 50 percent of the NPEs receiving injunctive relief absent direct competition between patentee and defendant were universities or research institutions.[19] However, the lower likelihood of obtaining injunctive relief in cases where no direct competition occurred illustrates the tendency that NPEs have to satisfy higher requirements by a more compelling showing of irreparable harm.

(ii) International Trade Commission

The existence of a patent enforcement forum bound to different standards than the regular court system is a unique feature of the US patent landscape. The International Trade Commission (ITC) is a quasi-judicial agency authorized to enforce various laws related to international trade such as Section 337 of the Tariff Act regulating unfair practices in import

---

[18] *See, e.g.*, Verizon Servs. Corp. v. Vonage Holdings Corp., 503 F.3d 1295 (Fed. Cir. 2007) (evidence of lost customers and price erosion provided evidence of irreparable harm); Power Integrations, Inc. v. Fairchild Semiconductor Int'l, Inc., No. 04-1371, 2008 WL 5210843 (D. Del. Dec. 12, 2008) (lost market share, harm to plaintiff's reputation and goodwill); *see also* Federal Trade Commission, *supra* note 17, at 261 (with further reference cases).

[19] Emory Univ. v. Nova Biogenics, Inc., No. 1:06-CV-0141, 2008 WL 2945476 (N.D. Ga. July 25, 2008) (injunction granted); Commonwealth Scientific and Indus. Research Org. v. Buffalo Tech., Inc. ('CSIRO'), 492 F. Supp. 2d 600, 601 (E.D. Tex. 2007) (injunction granted); Johns Hopkins Univ. v. Datascope Corp., 513 F. Supp. 2d 578 (D. Md. 2007) (injunction granted), rev'd on other grounds and remanded, 543 F.3d 1342 (Fed. Cir. 2008).

trade. The vast majority of actions sought under Section 337 are actions against patent infringement being an unfair practice.

While the Supreme Court tightened the requirements for injunctive relief for patent litigation at the district courts in the *eBay* decision, patent enforcement at the ITC is not bound by such precedence. The Federal Circuit explicitly confirmed such interpretation in its December 2010 decision *Spansion Inc. v. International Trade Commission*.[20] The ITC, before issuing an exclusion order, has to consider only certain public interest factors enumerated in Section 337, specifically (1) the public health and welfare, (2) competitive conditions in the US economy, (3) the production of like or directly competitive articles in the US, and (4) US consumers, and does not have to apply the factors for equitable remedy.[21]

To prevail at the ITC, a plaintiff has to show infringement of a valid US patent by an imported product and a "domestic industry" supported by the infringed patent. Different from district courts, the ITC does not have the authority to impose damage awards. The only remedy that the ITC can grant is an exclusion order, ordering the US Customs and Border Protection to exclude importation and sale of infringing articles. Under Section 337 (d), the ITC can award two different types of exclusion orders: limited exclusion orders and general exclusion orders. Limited exclusion orders (LEOs) extend only to patent-infringing products of a specifically named respondent. General exclusion orders (GEO) extend to any infringing product irrespective of the source. To obtain a GEO, a plaintiff has to demonstrate either (1) that the source of the infringing product is not easily identifiable, or (2) that the GEO is necessary to prevent circumvention of a LEO.

The popularity of enforcing patents at the ITC has increased substantially in recent years. In the semiconductor and electronics industry, for example, virtually every final product sold in the US consists of essential parts manufactured abroad and imported into the United States, satisfying the import factor required to grant jurisdiction to the ITC. The popularity of the ITC is based not only on the availability of broad exclusion orders, but also on the comparatively high degree of technical expertise of the administrative law judges (ALJs) presiding over the enforcement procedures at the ITC as well as the tight timeframe provided for in Section 337, which limits the duration of the entire proceeding to 12 months absent extraordinary circumstances.

---

20 Spansion, Inc. v. Int'l Trade Comm'n, 629 F.3d 1331 (Fed. Cir. 2010).
21 *Id.* at 1358.

1. Limitation of limited exclusion orders

Between 1989 and 2008, it had become the practice of the ITC to extend LEOs not only to the infringing product manufactured and imported by the named respondent, but also to downstream products containing the infringing product even if such downstream products were not manufactured by the named respondent.[22] Such practice was brought to a hold, however, when the Federal Circuit released its opinion in *Kyocera v. International Trade Commission*[23] in 2008. The plaintiff, Broadcom, had obtained a LEO prohibiting the respondent Qualcomm from importing a certain type of semiconductor that infringed on Broadcom's patented technology.[24] Qualcomm was the only respondent named in the complaint. Nevertheless, the ITC – following its earlier practice – extended the LEO to downstream products manufactured by other companies than Qualcomm. While the ITC mentioned the importance of encouraging complainants to name all potential respondents in the action, it explicitly refused to determine that the failure to do so automatically precluded a remedy against downstream third parties.[25] Specifically, the ITC rejected Qualcomm's claim that Broadcom's failure to name downstream manufactures was an attempt to mislead Qualcomm and third-party manufactures as to the scope of the investigation and remedy requested.[26]

The Federal Circuit reversed the decision of the ITC on appeal[27] and found that Section 1337 (d)'s statutory language would not support the ITC's practice of extending LEOs to parties not named as respondents.[28] In essence, the court found that the ITC's practice had – contrary to the underlying statute – blurred the lines between an LEO, which is supposed to be directed to a specific person, and a GEO, which is supposed to exclude a certain product from importation.[29]

In the direct aftermath of the decision *In re Kyocera* by the Federal Circuit, complainants started to name downstream manufacturers as

---

22 Such practice had been developed in *Certain Erasable Programmable Read-Only Memories, Components Thereof, Prods. Containing Such Memories, & Processes for Making Such Memories,* USITC Pub. No. 2196, Inv. No. 337-TA-276, Comm'n Op. (Mar. 16, 1989) (EPROM Order).

23 Kyocera v. Int'l Trade Comm'n, 545 F.3d 1340 (Fed. Cir. 2008).

24 *Certain Baseband Processor Chips & Chipsets, Transmitter & Receiver (Radio) Chips, Power Control Chips, & Prods. Containing Same*, USITC Inv. No. 337-TA-543, 2007 ITC LEXIS 621 Comm'n Op. (June 19, 2007).

25 *Id.* at 50.

26 *Id.* at 50–51.

27 *Kyocera*, 545 at 1345.

28 *Id.*

29 *Id.* at 1356.

respondents and to request GEOs in addition to LEOs. For example, in its complaint against Samsung and ten other downstream manufacturers of products using Samsung's semiconductors, the complainant Spansion requested a GEO citing a pattern of unauthorized use, difficulty in identifying all sources, and ease of circumvention of an LEO.[30] In practice, however, the higher standard required for a GEO will make it more difficult for many patentees to preclude importation of the infringed product through downstream manufacturers. As mentioned above, to obtain a GEO, the complainant has to show 'exceptional circumstances,' requiring at least difficulties in identifying sources of infringing products.[31] As in *In re Kyocera*, however, it became evident that Broadcom did not have any significant difficulty naming infringing downstream manufacturers,[32] but did not want to directly sue such manufacturers as they were current or potential customers of Broadcom.[33]

2. Domestic industry requirement

Plaintiffs have to satisfy the domestic industry requirements when seeking enforcement of patents at the ITC. Specifically, they have to show existence of an industry in the United States or that such an industry is in the process of being established.[34] The domestic industry requirement necessitates satisfaction of both a technical and economic prong. The technical prong can be satisfied by showing that 'industry practices at least one claim of the patent at issue'.[35] The economic prong can be satisfied by showing a significant investment in plant and equipment, a significant employment of labour or capital, or a substantial investment in its exploitation, including engineering, research and development, or licensing.[36]

The current economic prong of the domestic industry requirement is a result of congressional action taken in 1988. Prior to 1988, Section 337 required a plaintiff to show 'systematic activity which significantly employs

---

30 Certain Flash Memory Chips & Prods. Containing the Same, USITC Pub. No. 2640, Complaint at 36–9 (Nov. 17, 2008).

31 Kyocera Wireless Corp. v. Int'l Trade Comm'n, 545 F.3d 1340, 1356 (Fed. Cir. 2008).

32 *Id.* at 1357.

33 Lily Lim and Sarah E. Craven, *Injunctions Enjoined; Remedies Restructured*, 25 SANTA CLARA COMPUTER & HIGH TECH. L.J. 787, 810 (2009).

34 19 U.S.C. § 1337(a)(1)–(2) (2000).

35 *Certain Display Controllers and Prods. Containing Same and Certain Display Controllers With Upscaling Functionality and Products Containing Same*, Comm'n Op. 52, Inv. Nos. 337-TA-491/481 (consolidated) (Feb. 4, 2005), 2005 WL 996252.

36 19 U.S.C. § 1337(a)(3).

use of American land, labor, and capital for the creation of value'.[37] Such requirements made it difficult for non-manufacturing holders of intellectual property rights such as universities and movie studios to seek enforcement of infringed intellectual property rights at the ITC. Legislative change was triggered by the decision of the ITC in *Certain Products with Gremlin Character Descriptions*,[38] in which the ITC found that the complainant, Warner Brothers Inc. Licensing Company of America, did not meet the then-existing domestic industry requirement because licensing could not form the basis of a domestic industry.[39] Believing that such interpretation of a domestic industry requirement would be too strict, Congress amended Section 337 and introduced the currently applied disjunctive three-factor test for satisfaction of the economic prong.

The detailed interpretation of the last factor, the 'substantial investment in [the patent's] exploitation, including engineering, research and development, or licensing' requirement, has been the subject of recent debate, as the interpretation of this factor determines whether the ITC can serve as a venue for non-practicing patent holders who cannot satisfy either of the first two factors.

The requirements for establishing domestic industry by substantial investment in licensing of one or multiple patents have recently been clarified by the Commission in its decision in *Certain Multimedia Display and Navigation Devices*,[40] in which it reversed the initial determination by ALJ Charneski and found that the complainant, the Japanese company Pioneer, and its US subsidiary, had failed to establish domestic industry for the asserted patents through its domestic licensing activities of its patent portfolio containing both asserted and unasserted patents. The Commission held that in order to demonstrate the required nexus between the substantial investment and the asserted patent through the licensing of a patent portfolio, a complainant has to show the relative importance of the asserted patent within the portfolio by providing evidence that the asserted patent:[41]

---

[37] H.R. Rep. No. 100-40, at 157.

[38] *Certain Products with Gremlin Character Descriptions*, Inv., Comm'n Op., No. 337-TA-201 (1986).

[39] *Certain Digital Processors and Digital Processing Systems, Components Thereof and Products Containing Same*, Inv. No. 337-TA-559, Initial Determination, at 89 (May 11, 2007) citing 132 Cong. Rec. H1782 (Apr. 10, 1986) 99th Cong., (2nd Sess. 1986).

[40] *Certain Multimedia Display and Navigation Devices and System Components Thereof and Products Containing Same*, Inv. No. 337-TA-694, Comm'n Op. (July 22, 2011) (Public Version).

[41] *Id.* at 10–11.

1) Has been explicitly discussed in the course of license negotiations,
2) Has been successfully litigated,
3) Relates to a technology industry standard,
4) Is a base patent or a pioneering patent,
5) Is infringed or practiced in the US, or
6) that the value of the asserted patent is recognized by the market in some other way.

The Commission reiterated that the complainant has the burden of proof to show the required nexus between the asserted patents and complainant's licensing activities being a substantial investment. In particular, the Commission rejected allocating funds spent in the course of licensing investments equally among patents in a portfolio and held that the nexus between asserted patents and substantial investment has to be established based on a fact-focused and case-specific basis.[42]

A different notion of the 'substantial investment through licensing activities' test was clarified in *Coaxial Cable*.[43] In *Coaxial Cable*, the ITC had to decide whether costs incurred from patent litigation activities and related to licensing could be considered a substantial investment in the patent's exploitation sufficient to show existence of domestic industry. The Commission held that litigation activities related to licensing may qualify to satisfy the economic prong, while the Commission also ruled that litigation expenses on their own and not directly related to licensing, engineering or research and development activities would not be sufficient to show a domestic industry.[44]

At the same time, the Commission held that if a complainant could show litigation costs resulting in the patentee concluding a license (in other words, deriving revenue), such litigation costs could constitute a 'substantial investment' into exploitation of the patent. A complainant would have to ensure, however, that any and all costs associated with the litigation were well documented and linked to the specific patent asserted in the ITC complaint. Also, the investments made by the patent owner by bringing the litigation would have to be substantial as required in the statute.[45] Whether an investment could be regarded as substantial would require a factual inquiry and depends on the industry in question and the

---

42 *Id.* at 13.

43 *Certain Coaxial Cable Connectors and Components Thereof and Products Containing Same*, Inv. No. 337-TA-650, Comm'n Op. (Apr. 14, 2010) (Public Version).

44 *Id.* at 43–44.

45 *Id.* at 51.

complainant's relative size.[46] On remand in *Coaxial Cable* the ITC found that 79.4 attorney work hours resulting in litigation costs of $27,506 spent on licensing and settlement efforts attributable to the specific patent were not sufficient to establish a domestic industry.[47] The reasons considered for the finding of an absence of domestic industry included the facts that the complainant had:

1) Received only one license for the technology, of which only a portion actually related to the asserted patent;
2) No established licensing program whatsoever;
3) Made no other efforts to send cease and desist letters with offers to license the asserted patent; and
4) Not engaged in other licensing offers or talks with any persons or entities other than those involved with the single license to the patent.[48]

Although finding no domestic industry for the infringement of the specific patent at question, the Commission's opinion received some criticism as it explicitly stated that litigation expenses incurred in relation with licensing could satisfy the economic prong of the domestic industry requirement test. Even in earlier cases, however, complainants had already satisfied the domestic industry test by a mere showing of licensing activities.[49]

II. GERMANY

(i) Injunctive Relief and Compulsory Licenses

Under German patent law, injunctive relief is the primary remedy awarded upon finding of infringement of a valid patent. The underlying Section 139

---

46 *Id.* (quoting *Certain Stringed Musical Instruments and Components Thereof*, Inv. No. 337-TA-586, Comm'n Op. at 25 (May 2008)).

47 *Certain Coaxial Cable Connectors*, Inv. No. 337-TA-650, *Remand Initial Determination*, at 25 (May 27, 2010) (Public Version).

48 *Id.* at 25.

49 *See, e.g.*, *Certain Semiconductor Chips with Minimized Chip Package Size and Products Containing Same*, Inv. No. 337-TA-432, Order No. 13, Initial Determination (Jan. 24, 2001); *Certain Zero-Mercury-Added Alkaline Batteries, Parts Thereof and Products Containing Same*, Inv. No. 337-TA-493, Initial Determination (June 2, 2004); *Certain 3G Mobile Handsets and Components Thereof*, Inv. No. 337-TA-613, Order No. 42, Initial Determination (Mar. 10, 2009).

(1) of the Patent Acts reads: '*Any person who exploits an invention contrary to Sections 9 to 13 may be sued by the injured party to enjoin such use.*' The section does not give the courts any discretion whether to award an injunction order or not if the patentee demonstrates infringement, and if injunctive relief is demanded. To demand injunctive relief, the patentee has to demonstrate either a risk of recurrent infringement or the risk of first infringement of a patent.[50] Unlike in the US, German civil law has no specific test for equitable relief other than the mere demonstration of infringement. Rather, equitable relief has traditionally been regarded as a direct legal consequence of the infringing conduct.

While German law does not provide for a separate test for equitable remedy, German patent law does provide the alleged patent infringer with the defense of demanding a compulsory license either pursuant to Section 24 of the Patent Act or pursuant to competition law regulations.

(ii) Compulsory License Under Patent Law

Pursuant to Section 24 of the German Patent Act, a compulsory license can in principle be granted by the federal patent court if (1) the '*applicant for a license has unsuccessfully endeavored during a reasonable period of time to obtain from the patentee consent to exploit the invention under reasonable conditions usual in trade,*' and if (2) '*public interest commands the grant of a compulsory license.*'

Case law and commentators have been trying to provide clearer definitions to what efforts have to be made by the application for a license to count as an 'unsuccessful endeavor'. Literature and case law developed certain requirements for the applicant to the license himself: accordingly, the prospective licensee has to be willing and able to technically use the invention for which a license is sought.[51] Intent to only distribute the invention does not qualify as technical use. At the same time, it is not imperative that the applicant practices the invention in his own factory. Entrustment of production to a toll manufacturer, for example, would satisfy the intent for technical use requirement. That being said, the applicant has to be directly involved in the production of the invention.[52]

---

[50] Georg Benkard, Rüdiger Rogge and Klaus Grabinski, *Patentgesetz / Gebrauchsmustergesetz* ('PatG/GebrMG', C.H. Beck, 2006), § 139, marginal note 27.

[51] RGZ 130, 360, 361.

[52] Earlier case law held that an industry association could not apply for a compulsory license for the benefit of its members due to the lack of immediate and

The applicant for a compulsory license must have made reasonable efforts to obtain a regular license before being able to obtain a compulsory license under Section 24 of the Patent Act. However, reasonable efforts in the form of a license request can even be made after a motion for a compulsory license has been filed for at the Patent Court.[53] The license request has to reflect *reasonable conditions usual in trade*. Therefore, the applicant has to indicate his willingness to pay a fair consideration for the desired use of the patent such as a reasonable license fee or a cross-license allowing use of patents owned by the applicant.[54]

Under most circumstances, the most rigorous requirement for the grant of a compulsory license under the Patent Act is to demonstrate that granting the license serves the public interest. Showing such public interest consideration is not necessary only in cases where:

1) An applicant seeks a license to practice his own and more recently issued patent, which, however, depends on the technology covered by a third party's patent (Section 24 (2) Patent Act);[55] or
2) An applicant seeks a license required to practice a dependent plant variety right (Section 24 (3) Patent Act).[56]

In other cases, the applicant has to demonstrate a public interest in the grant of the compulsory license. The term public interest is an indefinite term that must be given concrete meaning by case law based on the circumstances of the individual case.[57] Public interest would be violated if the patentee would misuse his exclusive right by concealing the invention from the general public, or if he would not be capable of sufficiently serving the reasonable demands of the domestic market. If the patentee refuses to grant a license to practice a groundbreaking invention, and if such refusal

---

direct involvement. *See* RGZ 130, 360, 362; BENKARD ET AL., *supra* note 52, §24, marginal note 10.

[53] RGZ 113, 115, 116.

[54] RGZ 171, 227, 232 f.; BPatGE 32, 184, 188/9; BGHZ 131, 247, 250 – Interferon-gamma/Polyferon.

[55] Section 24 (2) of the Patent Act reflects the consideration that patent law should promote the development of technology and should not unreasonably restrain technology; *see* Federal Patent Court, GRUR 1994, at 100/101; BENKARD ET AL., *supra* note 52, §24, marginal note 22.

[56] A grant of a compulsory license only by demonstrating the unsuccessful endeavor to obtain a regular license pursuant to Section 24 (1) No. 1 of the Patent Act is – in case of dependence on a senior right – provided for both national plant variety rights and for community plant variety rights pursuant to Regulation (EC) No 2100/94.

[57] BGHZ 131, 247 – Interferon-gamma/Polyferon.

threatens the existence of entire industries, public interest would command a grant of a compulsory license.[58]

The interests of the general public may prevail over the interests of the patentee for reasons including, but not limited to, economic relevance, the need for further development and progress of the patent technology, or in cases of an existing patent, poses a risk to the supply of a required medical treatment. The Federal Supreme Court explicitly confirmed in the *Polyferon* decision rendered in 1994 that a continued supply of a specific drug can be of public interest.[59] Such interests of the public may be particularly relevant if the patented drug features specific therapeutic characteristics, increased effectivity or a reduced risk of side effects. The high value of human health is of special virtue for the entire society. In cases of severe diseases with potentially insufficient preexisting treatments (such as cancer or polyarthritis), even small progress may be of significant value.[60] However, it shall not be sufficient to trigger public interest concerns that the new and patented technology has a new form of effectivity. The applicant for the compulsory license has to demonstrate that no treatment with comparable effectivity is available on the market.[61]

In the recent past, only very few applications for compulsory licenses under patent law have been received, and virtually no compulsory licenses have been granted.

(iii) Competition Law Compulsory License

In addition to the compulsory license issued pursuant to the Patent Act, a defendant may also raise the defense of a competition law compulsory license, which is a compulsory license granted due to a misuse of a market dominating position by the patentee pursuant to Section 20 Para. 1 of the Act against Restraints on Competition ('GWB') in conjunction with Article 82 of the EC Treaty. Section 20 (1) of the GWB provides for prohibition of discrimination and hindrance by market-dominating enterprises who 'shall not unfairly hinder, directly or indirectly, another enterprise in business activities which are usually open to similar enterprises, nor in the absence of facts justifying such differentiation, treat such enterprise directly or indirectly in a manner different from the manner of treatment accorded to similar enterprises'.

---

58 RGZ 83, 9, 14.
59 BGHZ 131, 247, 256 – Interferon-gamma/Polyferon.
60 *Id.* at 257.
61 *Id.* at 259.

While competition law compulsory licenses are most commonly rewarded in cases of patents related to industrial standards, courts may also find that a patentee misuses a market dominating position by purposefully refusing to license its technology without any reason. However, the Federal Supreme Court has confirmed that in cases where a patent does not cover a specific industry standard, the patentee's decision whether to license its technology and under what conditions is almost always at the sole discretion of the patentee, and internal reasons such as business strategy are sufficient to overcome the obligation of granting a license for competition law reasons.

The situation is quite different for patents covering industrial standards. In the recent past, the Federal Supreme Court issued two decisions on the applicability of the above provision to enterprises seeking a license in order to enter competition with market-dominating enterprises. In the decision *Standard-Spundfaß* decided in 2004, the court held that a compulsory license under competition law may be a valid defense against damage claims.[62] In *Spundfaß*, the patentee owned a patent protecting a technology for manufacturing a specific storage jar used in the chemical industry in accordance to a de facto standard promulgated by German industry guidelines and subscribed to by local industry leaders such as BASF AG, Bayer AG and Hoechst AG in the beginning of the 1990s. The applicant for the compulsory license infringed on this patent. The decision of the court was of fundamental importance as it was the first confirmation by the Federal Supreme Court that a competition law compulsory license can bind a patentee independently from the existence or absence of a compulsory license under Section 24 of the Patent Act.[63] At the same time, the court left it explicitly open whether the competition law compulsory license could also be a valid defense against a patentee's claim for injunctive relief, as injunctive relief claims were not discussed in *Spundfaß*.[64]

The question of compatibility of the competition law compulsory license with claims for injunctive relief, however, had to be addressed by the Federal Supreme Court only a few years later.[65] The plaintiff in the action, Phillips Electronics, owned several patents related to the manufacture of CD-Rs and CD-RWs. Such patents formed the basis of an industry standard summarized in the so-called Orange Book.[66] Phillips sued a

---

[62] BGHZ 160, 67 = NJW 2005, 269 – Standard-Spundfaß.

[63] *Id.*

[64] *Id.* at 274.

[65] Federal Supreme Court BGHZ 180, 312 = RCLIP-DE-91/2009 – Orange-Book-Standard.

[66] The Orange Book had been compiled in large parts by Phillips and Sony

manufacturer of CD-Rs who had not entered into the license agreement offered by Phillips. While the Federal Supreme Court granted an injunction order, a decision in line with the decisions of the lower courts, the court's opinion gave an outline of the structural requirements for obtaining a compulsory license under Section 20 of the GWB. Accordingly, a patentee has to grant a competition law compulsory license only if the defendant is acting in good faith, which, according to the court, means that the defendant must show that

- He has submitted an unconditional offer to conclude a license contract before starting to use the technology;
- He is not challenging the validity of the patent; and
- He is behaving in line with reasonable licensing conditions and has deposited a reasonable royalty fee together with submitting the offer for conclusion of a license agreement.

Such strict requirements for a 'good faith' license put the patentee in a fairly comfortable position. While the decision initially received rather favorable comments, especially from patent law practitioners,[67] a number of uncertainties remain even three years after the court handed down the decision.

One of the requirements to qualify as a good-faith licensee under the Orange Book standard is to submit a license offer before starting to use the patented technology. In order to do so, however, the applicant must be aware of the existence of the patent. In a damage claim analysis under German patent law, courts presume negligence, and thus charge market participants with the duty to keep themselves informed of ongoing patenting activities in their field of business. Some commentators have argued that binding applicants for a compulsory license to a similar standard of knowledge would be excessive, particularly in industries such as the electronics and semiconductors industry where products and standards are

---

to define optical signal characteristics, physical arrangement, writing methods and testing conditions for CD-R (Orange Book Part II) and CD-RW (Orange Book Part III); *see* Schickedanz, *Die Ermittlung von Verletzungen normbildender Patente durch indirekte Schlüsse statt durch Merkmal-für-Merkmal-Subsumtion?*, GRUR Int. 2011, 480, at 484.

[67] *See* Thomas Nägele and Sven Jacobs, loc. cit., 2009 WRP 1067; Dirk Jestaedt, *Der Lizenzerteilungsanspruch nach der BGH-Entscheidung 'Orange-Book-Standard,'* 2009 GRUR 801; Anette Gärtner and Thorsten Vormann, *Der kartellrechtliche Zwangslizenzeinwand im Patenverletzungsstreit – 'Orange Book Standard' und seine Folgen für die Praxis*, 2009 Mitteilungen, 440.

often covered by hundreds or thousands of patents. Even in cases where a defendant is put on notice by a patentee of an ongoing potential or alleged infringement, practical circumstances may require an examination period of no less than three months to enable an alleged infringer to verify whether his conduct would fall within the scope of the patent as alleged, and whether such patent would form an essential part of the specific standard in question which would make it necessary for the applicant to submit an unconditional offer to enter into a license.[68] While the standard of knowledge imposed under the presumption of negligence may be too harsh in the context of determining good faith amongst license applicants, however, it may also be – depending on the nature and the sophistication of the potential patent infringer – appropriate and reasonable to expect that the infringer is aware of relevant industry standards prior to the conduct, and that he would undertake a thorough search and analysis of whether any conduct would be in violation of the patents forming such standard.

Another issue where further guidance by case law will be required is the determination of an appropriate and reasonable royalty fee that is to be deposited by the applicant for the license. The Federal Supreme Court explicitly held that courts would be in no position to assess the adequacy of the amount offered. Here, it seems plausible to require the license applicant to demonstrate that the license fee offered reflects commercially reasonable and customary conditions. Frequently, license fees that conform to the model licensing terms disclosed by standard setting organizations committed to FRAND licensing conditions should satisfy such requirement of depositing an appropriate and reasonable fee.[69]

III. JAPAN

(i) Claim for Injunctive Relief

Japanese patent law has been modeled to a large extent on its German counterpart. In principle, this is also true for the remedies available to patentees in cases of infringement. Section 100 of the Japanese Patent

---

68 Philipp Maume and Claudia Tapia, *Der Zwangslizenzeinwand ein Jahr nach Orange Book Standard – mehr Fragen als Antworten*, GRUR Int. 2010, 923, at 924–5.

69 While in principle concluding the same, Maume / Tapia (*supra* note 72) suggest adding a safety margin of 10% to the amount calculated pursuant to FRAND to ensure that the amount deposited is sufficient.

Act provides for a claim of injunctive relief against an actual infringer as well as against a likely infringer of a patent right. Similar to its German counterpart, Japanese patent law does not provide for a separate test as a requirement for equitable relief beyond a showing infringement of a valid patent. While the necessity of incorporating requirements similar to the test derived under the *eBay* decision by the US Supreme Court has been widely discussed among Japanese academics and practitioners, no such amendments have been implemented. In light of the low success rates of Japanese patentees in Japanese patent infringement lawsuits and the difficulties defending the validity of plaintiffs' patents, the consensus in the Japanese patent community has been to refrain, at least for the time being, from introducing any measures that would result in further weakening the status of the patentee.

Japanese patent law provides defendants in patent infringement lawsuits with the defense of seeking compulsory licenses for various reasons to avoid an injunction order. In addition, defendants have attempted to assert patent misuse defenses in the past to escape injunctive relief.

(ii) Misuse Exception

The most prominent infringement case in which a defendant raised a misuse defense was the case *Canon v. Recycle Assist*,[70] which ranks as one of the most noted patent cases in Japan in the last decade. In this case, the defendant Recycle Assist recycled and redesigned printer cartridges developed by Canon for Canon's printers (for one-time only use), and imported such redesigned ink cartridges allowing for multiple uses into Japan. The essence of the litigation centred on the question of patent exhaustion (i.e. whether Canon exhausted its patent by selling the cartridges), effectively asking whether Canon's patents could extend to prohibit redesign and repair of the cartridges. Canon ultimately prevailed on this question, as the court held that Recycle Assist replaced essential parts of the device covered under Canon's patent.[71] In its defense, Recycle Assist asked the court to consider a patent misuse defense, as Canon's technology in question allowed only for one-time use of its cartridges, and thus commands customers to replace the cartridge after its ink has been used. Recycle Assist claimed that such practice constitutes patent misuse as it results in

---

[70] IP High Court, Case No. 2005(ne)10021, Grand Panel / Decided January 31, 2006.

[71] *See, e.g.*, Mizuki Sally Hashiguchi, *Recycling Efforts and Patent Rights Protection in the United States and Japan*, 33 COLUM. J. ENVTL. L. 169, 180–83 (2008).

unnecessary and unreasonable use of resources and environmental hazard. The court held, however, that a patentee would not conduct patent misuse only by protecting and adopting a technology that would be less environmentally conscious than the infringing technology.[72]

(iii) Framework of Compulsory Licenses

Under Japanese patent law, an applicant can request that a patentee grants a compulsory license for the patented technology in the following cases:

1) Where the patentee hasn't practiced the patent for at least three years (Section 83 Patent Act);
2) When the public interest commands the grant of the license (Section 93 Patent Act); or
3) When the patent covers a senior technology and blocks a dependent invention (Section 92 Patent Act).

In each of the above circumstances, the applicant for a license has to consult with the patentee regarding the grant of a regular license. Only in cases where such consultation is not successful will the respective applicant be able to seek the grant of a compulsory license.

1. Lack of practice

Pursuant to Section 83 (1) Patent Act, a license can be sought in cases where the patentee has not practiced the invention covered by the patent for the previous consecutive three years. If the patentee refuses to grant a license, the applicant can request the Japanese Patent Office resolves the dispute and determines the terms of the license. What kind of conduct by the patentee would qualify as 'practicing' the invention, however, is not entirely clear. An implementation guideline issued by the Ministry of Economics, Trade and Commerce held that 'nominal use' of the patented technology shall not be sufficient to avoid the patentee's obligation of granting a license under Section 83 Patent Act.[73] After implementation of this compulsory license system, uncertainties remained as to whether

---

[72] IP High Court, Case No. 2005(ne)10021 (English translation available at http://database.iip.or.jp/ cases/files/2005(Ne)10021.html), LEX/NEX DB # 28810330, at 21.

[73] Saitei Seido No Unyou Youryou (Implementation Outline of the Arbitration System), issued December 1, 1975 and revised April 24, 1997 (electronic copy available at http://www.jpo.go.jp/shiryou/toushin/shingikai/pdf/strategy_wg07/paper12.pdf) (last visited on Oct. 28, 2011).

importing a product covered by a patent would fall under the scope of 'nominal use,' thus exposing the patentee to the risk of having to grant a compulsory license. The prevailing view, however, continues to state that importation would be considered as nominal use only and would not constitute a sufficient practice of the invention pursuant to Article 83.[74]

The JPO would refrain from granting a compulsory license only in the cases where the patentee could demonstrate legitimate reasons for not practicing the invention.[75] A review of legitimacy has to be conducted on a case-by-case basis. The implementation guideline, however, refers to example cases such as:

- The patentee being in concise preparation of commercialization;
- A natural disaster resulting in destruction of the production facilities of the patentee; or
- The patentee having difficulty in obtaining raw material required for the production process.

Under the above criteria, it seems unlikely that a non-practicing entity that does not practice its patent through manufacturing, import and sales of technology covered by the patent, but rather commercializes its patent through licensing programs, could escape the obligation of granting a compulsory license under Section 83 of the Patent Act.

Practice requirements that a patentee has to satisfy to avoid obligations under Section 83 (1) of the Patent Act are also extended to the licensee after obtaining a compulsory license. Accordingly, if the licensee does not begin practicing the patent within a reasonable amount of time after having obtained the license, the patentee or any other interested party can request cancellation of the compulsory license. In such a cancellation proceeding, the licensee can similarly assert above 'legitimate reasons' of not having practiced the invention, which are available to the patentee under Section 85 (2) of the Patent Act.

2. License for dependent invention

Section 72 of the Patent Act prohibits practicing a patented invention if practicing such invention would infringe another party's senior patent or other registered intellectual property right. In order to be eligible to use the patented invention, the patentee has to obtain a license from the

---

[74] Nobuhide Nakayama / Naoki Koizumi, Shin Chūkai Tokkyohō (Seirinshoin, 2011), at 1294.

[75] Section 85 (2) Patent Act.

patentee holding the senior patent. In cases where both parties cannot agree on a license, Section 92 provides the holder of the patent covering the dependent invention with a claim for a compulsory license.

3. Public interest license

In cases where the exclusive effect of a patent would be in contrast to public interest rights, Section 93 of the Patent Act allows for application for a compulsory license to use the patented invention. Such showing of public interest, however, seems rather difficult. According to the Implementation Outline of the Arbitration System,[76] public interest would command the grant of a compulsory license pursuant to Article 93 of the Patent Act if:

1) There is a specific need in a field directly related to national life, such as the lives of Japanese citizens, preservation of property, or construction of a public facility; and
2) If the act of not granting a non-exclusive license of the patented invention hinders the healthy development of the entire industry, and substantial harm is found to be caused to national life as a result.

Other scenarios in which public interest would require granting a compulsory license have been mentioned in a report issued by an expert committee of the Foreign Capital Council.[77] Accordingly, a compulsory license should be granted if the exclusive effect of the patent results in confusion (e.g. corporate failures) in 1) an industry in which the patented invention is expected to be used, and is likely to result in large-scale unemployment; 2) an industry in which the patented invention is expected to be used, and extremely valuable existing facilities, which could have been used if the patented invention could be practiced, are likely to become useless as a result; or 3) a Japanese key industry, such as important export industry, or industry in the area of advanced technology, in which the patented invention is expected to be practiced, and if the lack of such practice is likely to considerably obstruct the healthy economic or technological development of these key industries.

Other than in the cases of seeking a compulsory use for the patentee's lack of practice of the invention (pursuant Section 83) or for being able

---

[76] *Supra* note 75.

[77] Published in Jurist No. 399, at 123. The key points of the report are also reprinted in a more recent report published by the Japanese Patent Office, Wagakuni ni okeru Saitei ni tsuite (*About the Japanese Arbitration System*), available at http://www.jpo.go.jp/shiryou/toushin/shingikai/pdf/strategy_wg07/ paper08.pdf (last visited Oct. 28, 2011), at 7–8.

to use a dependent and patented invention (pursuant to Section 92), a compulsory license for public interest concerns has to be granted by the Minister for Economy, Trade and Industry, as the determination and assessment of public interest concerns is considered to be beyond the responsibility of the JPO. While the above framework has been available for more than thirty years, however, there are no reported applications for a compulsory license for public interest reasons.

IV. SUMMARY

Requirements for and defenses against a patentee's claim for injunctive relief differ substantially between the US as a common law jurisdiction and Germany or Japan as traditional civil law jurisdictions. Even in the US, however, where the requirements for injunctive relief tend to be comparatively more strict, the ITC continues to present a forum where a significant portion of patentees can seek injunctive relief without satisfying the requirements for equitable relief which evolved in *eBay*. The immense surge of the ITC becoming the most frequently utilized patent litigation venue in the US witnesses the status of injunctive relief claims as the most powerful – and vice versa for the defendant, most threatening – remedy in patent lawsuits.

On the other hand, Germany and Japan continue to quasi-automatically grant injunctive relief without applying any test resembling the *eBay* test in the US. One of the reasons for the popularity of German courts as patent litigation venues has been this availability of permanent injunctive relief. Japanese courts have not enjoyed similar popularity over the last years. Such lack of popularity, however, has not been caused by the canon of remedies available, but rather by the difficulties for patentees to demonstrate the validity of their patent rights in the aftermath of the *Kilby* decision and other factors that reduce the win-rates of patentees beneath an international average. The continued availability of injunctive relief has also been considered an important factor in strengthening patentee's rights in Japan during recent discussion on the Japanese patent reform bill.

While Germany and Japan recognize plaintiffs' demands for injunctive relief from patent infringement, German and Japanese law also provide the defendant in a patent infringement lawsuit with access to a set of compulsory licenses. Though based on different legal doctrine, the grant of a compulsory license to a patent infringer in Germany or Japan would result in a constellation comparable to a US district court finding infringement of a valid patent and failing to satisfy the *eBay* test. The provision of Article 83 of the Japanese Patent Act, which allows a defendant to seek a compulsory license in cases where the patentee does not practice his patent right for more than three years, might provide even wider protection against non-practicing entities trying to enforce their patent in Japan than the test reinstituted under *eBay*.

In comparison, German patent law provides a defendant with the least possibilities to avoid issuance of an injunction order. Unlike in Japan, there is no claim for a compulsory license because of a lack of use of a patent. Also, while German courts acknowledged and granted compulsory licenses for industry standards, the procedure developed by the Federal Supreme Court makes it very difficult in practice for the applicant to come to a well-founded decision of whether to submit to a binding application for a license, or whether to deny infringement and attack the plaintiff's patent, thereby waiving the claim for a compulsory license and exposing himself to the possible effect of an injunction.

In light of such material differences, judges and legislators across patent jurisdictions have reviewed and are going to continue to review how easily and under which circumstances a patentee should be able to exclude other parties from using the patented technology. While such review has begun in the US, it is also well under way in leading civil law jurisdictions. Practical, industrial and case-specific requirements of the patent system in each jurisdiction are very likely to play a more important role for the review of injunctive relief claims than the traditional border between common law and civil law jurisdictions.

PART VI

Legal Aspects Common to all Branches of IP

15. What the treatment of covenants not to compete teaches about intellectual property and competition norms

Shubha Ghosh

I. INTRODUCTION

Intellectual property's place in the skein of competition law and policy has been a source of active scholarly and doctrinal debate. Whether intellectual property rights limit or enhance the application of competition law depends upon the nature of the market, the technology, and the business practices that are at stake. The ongoing IBM, Microsoft, and Google cases provide focal points for comparison between the US and the EU as well as between common law and civil law systems. This Chapter provides an even more compelling example for understanding intellectual property and competition law: the treatment of restrictive covenants not to compete, specifically in the employment context.

Restrictive covenants arise in both civil law and common law countries. They are generally understood as being useful in allowing employer firms to control and limit the spread of firm-specific knowledge. Furthermore, restrictive covenants allow an employer to train employees without the fear of employees later misappropriating their employer's business connections and advantages. Even more critically, restrictive covenants illustrate the role of competition in promoting innovation through the entry of new firms and products in the marketplace. The scholarly literature on the development of Silicon Valley in California points to the non-enforcement of covenants not to compete under California law for the vibrancy of the region. High velocity labor markets provide an impetus for a start-up culture that fuels innovation. Attempts to imitate Silicon Valley's success in other regions, particularly in Europe, have led reconsidering the role labor market conditions and legal regulations play in inhibiting innovation in other jurisdictions. This Chapter will examine this comparative literature, concluding that different legal regimes support different styles of innovation within a pluralistic and diverse model of capitalism.

The remainder of this Chapter consists of five sections. The first section summarizes the main findings of the comparative innovation literature. The second and third sections examine the treatment of covenants not to compete in the United States and Germany respectively. The fourth section presents a normative discussion of regional innovation in a global context. The final section offers suggestions for future research.

II. LABOR MARKETS, COMPETITION NORMS, AND INNOVATION

An economy based on innovation necessitates a business culture based on start-ups and venture capital. As Professor Gilson has pointed out, creating such a culture, one that emulates that of Silicon Valley, requires the confluence of three factors: capital, specialized financial intermediaries, and entrepreneurs (Gilson, 2003, 1069). This chapter focuses on one legal background to these three inputs: legal support for labor mobility. Such mobility is often needed for a vibrant start-up culture and for the support of entrepreneurs, who often start as employees of established firms.

The importance of labor mobility to innovation and growth in high technology sectors has been documented by Professors Saxenian, Hyde, and Gilson. Scholars have built on their insights to develop a deeper understanding of intellectual property protection within a firm and between firms. Owners of intellectual property can enjoin the use of protected information and knowledge by existing employees as well as by competitors outside the boundaries of the firm. The scope of intellectual property rules then determines the extent of competition arising from other firms, as well as from current employees and agents of an existing firm. Inter-firm and intra-firm competition, in turn, drives innovation and growth through processes of creative destruction and cumulative innovation. In this section, I summarize the conventional wisdom in order to develop the argument, in the following section, that the conventional wisdom may not apply to trade across national borders. I ultimately reject the arguments against the conventional wisdom and show how it can be modified to address the phenomenon of high velocity labor markets in international trade.

Professor Saxenian set the terms for our understanding of high technology labor markets in her comparative study of Silicon Valley and Route 128. Both labor markets functioned in the booming software industry, but Professor Saxenian noted that the California market was notably more dynamic, with greater turnover in workforce and a larger number of start-ups, than the East Coast counterpart (Saxenian, 1994,32–5; 61–3). Appropriately, since her perspective was that of a cultural anthropologist, the main explanation offered for the difference was a cultural one (Saxenian, 1994, 2–3). The West Coast labor market was defined by greater freedom and sense of innovation while the East Coast one was more conventional, tied to traditional corporate business models. Professor Saxenian's early work set the tone for much of the subsequent scholarship pursued by legal scholars, Alan Hyde and Ronald Gilson.

Particularly noticeable is the focus on regional markets. Professor Saxenian treated Silicon Valley and Route 128 as two self-contained ecosystems, each defined by unique cultural norms and history. No attention was paid to movements into or out of the two ecosystems, across either regional or national borders. Instead, the two ecosystems were painted as largely self-contained with differences in economic outcomes resulting from differences in the values based on innovation, the mentality of start-ups, and the dead hand of tradition. In recent work, Professor Saxenian has expanded her focus by incorporating international immigration into her analysis (Saxenian, 2006). Highly skilled workers, who have been granted permission to enter the US on H1-B visas, fuel much of the growth in Silicon Valley (Saxenian, 2006, 52–4). These 'global Argonauts,' as Professor Saxenian dubs them, fill a skill gap in the labor market, and the high velocity, short-term nature of their employment is defined by the terms of the entry visa (Saxenian, 2006, 10–11). These international workers arrive, Professor Saxenian argues, in response to cultural and economic pressures from the source country (Saxenian, 2006, 26–9). The short-term economic gains motivate the migration, and the skills they bring as well as the limited cultural commitments to the host country serve the needs of start-ups and other smaller firms that thrive in the dynamic ecosystem of Silicon Valley (Saxenian, 2006, 324–9). International migration of labor fits into the cultural story that Professor Saxenian tells. These new workers thrive on existing ecosystems without upsetting them.

Professor Alan Hyde draws on the same data as Professor Saxenian but uses the study of high technology labor markets to better understand the economics of the employment relationship. Professor Hyde sees the dynamics of Silicon Valley as a challenge to the traditional human capital explanation of employment, which sees labor markets as a way of acquiring and developing skills that are a critical input to the production of goods and services (Hyde, 1998, 83–5). According to human capital theory, a worker spends the early part of his career acquiring skills through education (Schwab, 12–13). Once the general skills are acquired through education, more firm specific skills are acquired through employment in a firm

(Schwab, 14). The life cycle of the worker entails the worker earning less than one's marginal product during the training phase in order to offset training costs. After training, however, the worker's wages are above productivity so that the worker can recoup the investment in training (Schwab, 15). Human capital theory would predict that labor relationships are stable and long term, and they arise from a joint investment in training between the employee and the firm (Hyde, 125–6).

As Professor Hyde emphasizes, the reality of high velocity labor markets in the technology sector belies the prediction of human capital theory. In Silicon Valley, employees often leapfrog from firm to firm and even more frequently leave existing employers to form their own start-up (Hyde, 27–8). Knowledge flows with employees, and often former employers can do little to enjoin exiting employees or share in the fruits of their success (Hyde, 32–3). What is particularly vexing for human capital theory is that this type of mobility, which seemingly contradicts the incentive structure for long-term investment and the stability of the firm, supports innovation and growth (Hyde, 15–16). Professor Hyde uses this challenge to conventional wisdom to rethink economic analyses of employment relationships. The solution to the puzzle rests in recognizing that the employment relationship entails not only the inculcation of skills through training but also the creation and propagation of knowledge (Hyde, 29–30). Labor markets are markets for people who embody human capital or expend physical effort to perform tasks, but they are also tacit markets for information. The efficient propagation of information may not occur simply through stable, long-term investments between the employer and employee. Instead, employees may see the value of information that develops in different forms of technical knowledge and know-how, and they proceed to take the information outside existing firms and into new entities and opportunities (Hyde, 38–40). The Silicon Valley model has structured employment relationships to unleash this market for information.

While Professor Saxenian adopts a cultural explanation for high-technology labor markets, Professor Hyde develops a market-based explanation, grounded in economic theory. Although the two authors differ in methodology, they share a regional focus. Professor Hyde's early work portrayed Silicon Valley as a self-contained ecosystem driven by the economic logic of information and employment markets. More recent work examines the phenomena of H1-B visa workers and places regional markets in the broader context of international migration (Hyde, 130–31). Professor Hyde concludes that economic theories of international migration that rest on wage differential or labor shortages cannot account for the phenomenon of highly skilled, short-term immigrant labor (Hyde, 136–137). As he points out, much of the benefit of the H1-B visa program can be realized through outsourcing and through filling the skill gap by hiring domestic labor (Hyde, 135). Furthermore, if the H1-B visa program is viewed as a form of political rent seeking, it is not clear whether it is the immigrants or the firms that are seeking the rents (Hyde, 135). The problem, as Professor Hyde states, is the difficulty in determining the appropriate baseline against which to measure the correct level of immigration (Hyde, 135). The deeper problem, in my opinion, is that the theory of high technology labor markets has largely focused on regional markets rather than on global markets. Both Professor Saxenian and Professor Hyde present a comparative analysis of contrasting economic and legal environments. But this comparative analysis does not readily translate to an understanding of markets that are globally integrated through the movement of people and information.

Professor Gilson extends the work of Professor Hyde to the evaluation of legal rules and institutions. Specifically, Professor Gilson builds on Professor Hyde's description of high velocity labor markets as markets for information to assess the property rights over knowledge that is generated through employment relationships (Gilson, 587). If the market for labor is a market for information, then a spillover is created when knowledge is created (Gilson, 588). Enjoining an employee from leaving a firm to use the knowledge created through the prior relationship limits the spillover effect (Gilson, 597). Therefore, the prohibition under California law against enforcing covenants not to compete, as illustrated by the 2008 California Supreme Court decision in *Edwards v. Arthur Andersen*, lends flexibility to the labor market and promotes the realization of spillovers from the creation of new firms (Gilson, 604–5). At the same time, the protection of trade secrets both across and within firms allows a firm to develop firm-specific knowledge that is proprietary in its benefits (Gilson, 599–600). As a result, the California legal regime allows the market for information to function efficiently in both the creation and dissemination of knowledge.

While Professor Gilson's analysis is more legalistic than either Professor Saxenian or Hyde in understanding the appropriate regime of property rights over information, his explanation is regional in its implications. The emphasis is on state employment rules that allow the realization of externalities within regional markets. An obvious question is to what extent are these arguments applicable nationally and globally. California's legal regime governing employment and trade secrets favors the mobility of workers and of spillover-inducing information and the creation of firm-specific knowledge. The regime is an example of what Steven Caspar describes as a Liberal Market Economy (LME), one that is conducive to the development of high technology industry.

But as Professor Caspar points out, a Coordinated Market Economy

(CME) can also support high technology innovation. He points to Germany as an example. With its stakeholder system that supports organized labor, an apprenticeship system, and greater control by shareholders in corporate bodies, Germany does not, in theory, provide the legal environment conducive to the risk-taking and business formation culture noted in Silicon Valley. Adding to the coordinated market system is an emphasis on bank finance as opposed to venture capital and extensive private capital markets, which also, in theory, would be antithetical to high technology development.

Nonetheless, Germany has developed a competitive high technology sector, especially compared to the United Kingdom, an example of an LME. Biotechnology platforms, enterprise software, and middleware are examples of products and innovations from the German high technology sector in the 1990s. As Professor Caspar describes:

> Sustained patterns of vocational training within firms, consensual decision-making, long-term employment, and patent are all linked to the systematic exploitation of particular technologies to a wide variety of niche markets in a number of medium technologies characteristic of many engineering and chemical markets (Caspar, 34).

The strategy is called 'diversified quality production' (Caspar, 34). The contemporary German high technology sector follows patterns that can be traced back to the developments of engineering and chemical sectors in the nineteenth and early twentieth centuries (Caspar, 101). Support from regional governments in the form of technology transfer offices have in part fueled these developments by permitting the licensing of university-generated technology and know-how. In addition, financial support from the federal government has supplemented the lack of venture capital finance (Caspar, 93). Despite the predictions of theory, Germany has found a niche in the high technology sector.

Comparative economic and legal studies, such as the ones in this volume, lead inevitably to the question of which system is the most desirable. Professor Casper indirectly addresses this question through a 'variety of capitalisms' approach to assessing economic performance (Caspar, 15). While it may be the case that one system provides the best results, the identification of that ideal system may be impossible and perhaps misdirected. The scholarly and policy directive may not be to identify the best, but to recognize legal and institutional strategies that support success. In this Chapter, the focus will be on covenants not to compete, admittedly only one dimension of the legal environment for a market economy. But given the scholarly focus on covenants not to compete, the experiences in LME and CME, or in the US and in Germany, provide some conditions for comparison to glean how legal institutions shape markets in a variety of ways. The next two sections describe and compare treatment of covenants not to compete in the US and Germany in order to analyze common law and civil law approaches.

III. AN OVERVIEW OF THE COMMON LAW: THE CASE OF THE UNITED STATES

The 1711 English case of *Mitchel v. Reynolds* is the first published opinion on the enforcement of a covenant not to compete. At issue was the lease of a bakery by Reynolds, a journeyman baker, who promised not to compete against the lessee during the term of the leasehold. When Reynolds breached this promise, his defended his breach on the grounds that the covenant was a restraint on trade. The court found in favor of the lessee, enforcing the covenant on the grounds that Reynolds had received valuable consideration and 'by his own consent, and for his own profit [gave] over his trade and part with it to another'. The court distinguished the enforcement of noncompetition covenants against employees. In the latter case, the court explained that noncompetition covenants against employees would not be enforceable because of

> great abuses . . . from masters, who are apt to give their apprentices much vexation on this account, and to use many indirect practices to procure such [restrictive covenants] from them, lest they should prejudice them in their custom, when they come to set up for themselves.

This criticism of guilds dates back to the 1414 decision in the *Dyer's Case*, in which the English court denied an injunction against a former apprentice sought by the guild (Fisk, 102; Thorelli, 58–9). Under the English common law, covenants not to compete that were reasonable in geographic scope and duration were enforced in the context of a sale of a business or a dissolution of partnership, but were not enforced in the employment context, unless trade secret or confidential information was involved (Fisk 262–3; Cornish & Llewelyn, 304–5). In *Yovatt v. Winyard*, an 1820 English case, the court enjoined the use and disclosure of medicinal recipes by a former veterinary trainee who had copied the recipes from his master. The court's remedy, however, applied to future uses of the recipes and not to their uses in ongoing treatment.

The treatment of covenants not to compete in the US evolved from its English common law roots to more expansive enforcement. The cases from before the Civil War follow the English precedents with covenants not to compete largely being enforced in the sale of business or dissolution of partnership contexts (Fisk, 29–30; *Keeler v. Taylor*; *Morse Twist Machine Drill Co. v. Morse*). Courts would enforce noncompetition covenants against employees only for the protection of confidences between the employer and the employee. Often, these confidences were in the household context rather than in the context of skilled or trained workers (Fisk, 99). In the latter context, the employee was free to use knowledge, even knowledge that was gleaned during the employment context. Courts were persuaded that restrictions on employees were tantamount to the guild restrictions found abusive by the English courts.

After the Civil War, with the growth of industrial employment and the movement towards a homogenous body of master-servant law that was applicable to all employees, the enforcement of covenants not to compete became stricter (Fisk, 92–4). Although some treatise writers and courts resisted the expansive enforcement of covenants not to compete, the direction of the law was towards limiting post-termination employment activities (Fisk, 105–6).

In some cases, the enforcement mirrored the rationale of *Mitchel v. Reynolds* decision. For example, in a case involving the sale of a patented invention, the court enjoined the seller from practicing and teaching the patent after the transfer because he had obtained the benefit of the invention from the sale (Fisk, 97). Protection of inventions, especially confidential information in the form of trade secrets, was an important rationale in restricting the activities of employees once they had left their employers. In *O. & W. Thum co. v. Tloczynski*, the Michigan Supreme Court upheld an injunction against an employee from using manufacturing processes and machine designs learned from the employer in the absence of a written non-disclosure agreement. In *Stone v. Goss*, a New Jersey court enjoined both the employee and the new employer who had known of the employee's duty of confidentiality from using secret methods of mixing hair-removing compounds. Also during the post-Civil War period, courts began enjoining the solicitation of customers of former employers by departed employees (Fisk, 94). Although there were cases of a court finding for terminated employees, especially if the employer acted in an anticompetitive manner, the general trend was to enforce covenants not to compete strictly against employees (Lieberstein, 61; *Post v. Merrill Lynch, Pierce, Fenner & Smith, Inc*).

Also noteworthy are the business practices that facilitated court enforcement of restrictive covenants against employees. Eastman Kodak, after learning about methods of dyeing from a German company, aggressively used noncompetitive covenants to restrict the activities of its employees (Fisk, 192). Such covenants were standard provisions in their employment contracts, and Eastman Kodak brought many cases during the early twentieth century to strictly enforce these restrictions. In some cases, Eastman Kodak was on the defensive side of such covenants, finding them as a barrier to hire away employees from competitors. In such situations, Kodak simply bought the company in order to obtain the desired employees and know-how (Fisk, 192).

Kodak's practices mirrored the expansion of corporate control of workplace knowledge within a factory system of production. The factory was replacing the craft system, and within the law, corporate control was replacing the control formerly exhibited by the guilds. But unlike the early English courts that followed the *Dyer's Case* and *Mitchel v. Reynolds* and resisted the control of the guilds over the employees, the late nineteenth century and early twentieth century courts found for the employers.

Perhaps the most striking example of this is Justice Taft's often cited 1898 decision in *United States v. Addyston Pipe & Steel Company*, in which he stated that an agreement not to compete would be valid if it was ancillary to another agreement, such as the sale of business or the dissolution of a partnership or employment contract (Fisk, 98). The inclusion of an employment contract along with the sale of business or dissolution of partnership illustrates sharply the evolution of covenants not to compete from the *Mitchel v Reynolds* decision, which expressly excluded the employment relationship from the scope of noncompetition covenants.

The contemporary treatment of covenants not to compete is to enforce them strictly if they are reasonable with respect to geographic, temporal, and industry limitations. As noted above, California as a matter of public policy has not enforced covenants not to compete against employees since 1872 when the legislature enacted what is now Section 16600 of the California Civil Code. This provision states that restrictions on employment and the practice of a profession or trade are against the public policy of the State and are void. This provision has a broad reach and has been applied against a non-California employer who sought to enforce a noncompetition covenant against a former employee who had moved to California. Interpretation of Section 16600 differs across state courts, but some general principles emerge. Section 16600 does not apply to a covenant not to compete in a sale of business or dissolution of a partnership and does not apply to the employee's fiduciary duty not to compete with an existing employer. In addition, Section 16600 does not apply to the protection of trade secrets and confidential information or to covenants restricting the solicitation of customers. Absent these limitations, which may be narrow enough to facilitate the development of goodwill and intra-firm knowledge, California law allows for post-departure employment and the free movement of labor between firms.

This section presented the evolution of the treatment of covenants not to compete within a common law jurisdiction. The next section provides some contrast with a civil law jurisdiction, specifically Germany.

IV. AN OVERVIEW OF THE CIVIL LAW: THE CASE OF GERMANY

Covenants not to compete in Germany exist against a background of long-term employment structures. As Professor Casper describes, most employees spend their careers within one firm, with promotion and advancement occurring vertically within the company as opposed to movement between companies (Caspar, 96). Although many employees may remain in middle management for their careers, there is little incentive to switch companies because prospects for advancement are the same across entities. Formation of start-ups is inhibited by the lack of venture capital and other private financial markets. Research scientists in private companies often attempt to move to management positions for the purposes of advancement.

A similar pattern arises in universities where senior chaired professors are given generous resources to develop the research of assistant professors and graduate students and to teach undergraduates. Graduate students are required to find employment as professors outside their degree-granting universities, a difficulty within Germany because of the limited number of senior positions. Professor Casper finds this pattern within universities to be a beneficial one for the development of start-ups, and he reports some evidence of academics at the start of their career moving to industry when academic prospects are uninviting (Caspar, 98). He also reports that there are collaborations between universities and industry (Caspar, 101). As a result, the German labor market thrives through network clusters as ideas flow from universities to industry and back through informal relationships.

The German labor market does not fit the model of the high velocity labor market seen in Silicon Valley. Nonetheless, technological innovation occurs through the niche markets in software and biotechnology described above. These niche markets parallel the manufacturing and chemical industries that built the Germany economy before the world wars and that were the basis for industrial development after World War Two. Professor Casper points to the stability of the labor market that comes from long-term employment protections within stable companies as consistent with this form of technological development (Caspar, 102). Furthermore, while knowledge transfers in high velocity markets occur through the movement of people, knowledge transfers in Germany occur through informal networks within industry and between universities and industry. Whether technological innovation and growth could be stronger with a Silicon Valley model is perhaps an open question. But it may also be a misleading question since the German experience shows that technological innovation can occur without high velocity labor markets.

The role of covenants not to compete in the German economic and legal environment seems inhibiting at first to the development of a start-up culture. Highly regulated since the enactment of the Commercial Code in 1900, covenants not to compete in the employment context provide the intersection of three complex legal codes: the Commercial Code, the Employment Code, and the General Civil Code. The legal regime would suggest that covenants not to compete provide extensive regulation and limitations on the movement of labor in Germany. But covenants not to compete are not that extensive within Germany. Statistics from 1990 show that among German firms, noncompetition covenants are in use for about 2.2 percent of salaried employees, 5 percent of IT staff, and 10.5 percent of management (Bauer & Diller, 2). According to one employment attorney at the Frankfurt office of Baker & McKenzie, covenants not to compete tend to be used more often by American-based companies in Germany than European-based companies. Among German companies, the more established companies with financial stability tend to use such covenants more often than newer German companies.

A closer look at the actual statutes that govern covenants not to compete and their application suggests a regime that is perhaps not that restrictive on labor mobility, at least in theory. Under the Commercial Code, restrictive covenants not to compete must be in writing and clearly state the restrictions on the employee's post employment activities. (Bauer & Diller, 5). The Code also imposes several mandatory terms on noncompetition covenants. They must be narrow with the areas of business and geographical areas restricted and must be related to the tasks actually performed by the employee in the previous employment. Furthermore, the restriction cannot last for more than two years (Bauer & Diller, 5). The Commercial Code also requires that the employer pay the employee compensation during the time the noncompetition covenant is in effect. Compensation is on a monthly basis and equal to 50 percent of the employee's salary, benefits, and variable salary last received. There is some discussion as to whether the code provisions on compensation applies only to commercial helpers, a category that excludes management, but courts have interpreted the provision as applying to managerial employees. Finally, even if the employer waives the restrictive covenant, there is a requirement that compensation be paid to the employee for up to one year as long as the conditions of the covenant are fulfilled.

Noncompetition covenants against independent contractors are governed by the General Civil Code, specifically the provisions that a term be reasonable to the restricted party under a balancing of the interests. Since the Commercial Code provisions on scope of the covenant and compensation do not apply to independent contractors, they would look to the General Civil Code requirement of reasonableness in determining the scope of the restriction and whether compensation should be paid.

Enforcement of the covenant not to compete raises some interesting challenges. The employer must show that the employee is actually in breach within the standards of the inquisitorial system. There is no discovery as understood within the US adversarial system, and so the burden is quite heavy on the employer to make the case. Preliminary injunctions are very difficult to obtain in cases involving breach of a restrictive covenant. Permanent injunctions are equally difficult. Actual damages must be proven to obtain damages although if the contract provides for a contractual penalty, it will be enforced if reasonable. Actual damages can be recovered in addition to the contractual penalty. One particularly interesting rule has to do with the treatment of solicitation of employees. Whether an employer is liable for soliciting an employee is a matter of unfair competition law, but is generally permitted. However, a restriction on a former employee soliciting employees to a new firm is void if the former employee has become an employer. This last rule is consistent with a policy of encouraging employees to move into managerial positions or to start up new firms.

Two implications arise from this analysis of noncompetition covenants under German law. First, the rules governing noncompetition covenants support limited enforcement. The compensation provisions and high burden on employers suggest that the regime may be more favorable to employee mobility than one might first presume. Second, the limitations on a start-up culture in Germany may stem from a culture of stable labor markets and long-term employment. As has been pointed out, the lack of a high velocity labor market is not inconsistent with technological innovation. As Professor Casper notes, government finance of start-ups and the existence of employment networks support an innovative economy. Covenants not to compete are not an inhibiting factor (Casper, 98). Furthermore, to the extent that non-enforcement of covenants not to compete stimulates innovation, aspects of the German law on restrictive covenants (such as the rules on solicitation of employees) are consistent with labor mobility and a start-up culture.

V. NORMATIVE FRAMEWORKS FROM THE INTERNATIONAL PERSPECTIVE

This section turns to a normative consideration of the comparison of the US and Germany in their treatment of covenants not to compete. The purpose is to locate the discussion in a broader understanding of labor mobility, knowledge diffusion, and innovation.

The historical narrative about the movement of skilled labor reveals a movement from an open system within which the movement of people was a mechanism for the communication of new ideas to a hierarchical system defined by the international rules of managed trade and the intellectual property rights. Within this hierarchical system, which culminated in the Trade Related Intellectual Property System (TRIPS) Agreement associated with the World Trade Organization in 1994, technology and information from the developed world flowed into emerging markets in developing countries, which in turn served as a source for human labor, a manufacturing base, and skilled labor (Arup 183–4). The challenge looking forward is how developing countries created new market and legal institutions to counter some of the inequities of the current hierarchical system.

Examples of the earlier open system of movement and knowledge transfer are, in part, the subject of myth. The movement of philosophers between the Hellenic peninsula and the Indian subcontinent, the role of Aristotle as tutor for a young Alexander in Macedon, the spread of Christianity through an apostolic tradition, the voyages of Marco Polo – these are each textbook cases of how movement of people facilitated the communication of knowledge and the development of syncretic knowledge systems. Needless to say, the movement of people was the sole means for communication in a world where communication technologies were nonexistent.

State institutions recognized the connection between movement of people and movement of knowledge in creative ways to manage the development of industry and the promotion of economic interests. A well-documented example of the state's role in promoting knowledge transfer through controlling the movement of people is provided by the development of the silk trade in Italy during the early Renaissance. Historian Luca Mola documents how Italian city-states attracted artisans from other regions through financial subsidies and restrictions of movements into and out of the state's borders (Mola 30–31). City-states were engaged in a competitive race to steal talent from other regions while retaining their own talent, much like contemporary start-ups and high technology companies do. Venice's enactment of what is considered the first use of patent rights to attract innovators illustrates the culmination of this race. An interesting feature of the Venetian patent system is that it granted exclusivity to innovators who introduced new inventions and products into Venice's borders. In other words, the patent was to the introducer of these inventions and products from other regions, not necessarily the inventor himself. In England, sovereign grants rewarded foreign innovators who introduced exotic spices and foods to the British Isles. These types of inducements were precedents for what were called patents of importation under US patent law.

The sovereign's role in promoting innovation internal to the region shaped much of US patent law and its role in US economic development in the nineteenth century (Ben-Atar 78–9). Alexander Hamilton, the first Secretary of the Treasury, endorsed the patent of importation (similar to the grants by Venice and the British crown) to those who went overseas, learned about inventions in other countries, and returned those innovations to the US. These importers, or introducers as described in the previous paragraph were granted patents not so much for their inventiveness, but for their ability to travel, learn, and translate knowledge within the US marketplace. The patent of importation has its vestiges in contemporary US patent law with its references to discoveries and its limitations on prior art from outside the US under 35 USC s. 102(a). Outside the patent system, industrial espionage was a profitable way to transfer knowledge from Britain and benefitted the burgeoning US textile industry. Restrictions on labor mobility in Britain were attempts to curtail such espionage, but the movement of labor across borders was a difficult mechanism for knowledge and technology transfer to prevent.

Traditional arguments in favor of high velocity labor markets implicitly assume that wealth maximization is the normative criterion for gauging policy. Rules and norms favoring labor mobility in Silicon Valley support the creation of wealth and promote economic growth. One controversy is whether this normative goal is assessed regionally or nationally. After all, if free labor mobility is desirable, the natural question is why other regions have not followed the Silicon Valley model for high technology industries. Seemingly, Professors Saxenian, Hyde, and Gilson present positive rather than normative analyses of these labor markets. But generalizing their arguments to cross-border movement of labor forces us to address the normative question of whether permitting the free movement of persons is normatively desirable. When assessing this question at the international level, one is forced to confront the question of whether the individual nation-state is the correct unit of analysis or whether the normative inquiry should adopt a global focus. Generalizing the traditional arguments in favor of high velocity labor markets to the international movement of labor may be difficult precisely because the normative foundation of international intellectual property law (and arguably immigration policy) is the maximization of the welfare of an individual nation state.

VI. SUMMARY AND CONCLUSION

Technology diffusion is important for the promotion of economic growth and development. Mobility of labor is one mechanism for technology diffusion. This chapter shows how legal rules affect the movement of labor between firms and thereby presents a hypothesis for how legal rules can affect economic growth and development through the movement of labor and ideas. The case study of Silicon Valley and the enforcement of covenants not to compete, test the relationship among restrictive covenants, labor mobility, and growth. A comparison with the treatment of covenants not to compete in Germany suggests that legal rules on the enforcement of restrictive covenants may be only one part of the legal environment determining economic growth and technology diffusion. Future research can build on the comparative points made in this chapter to further explore the connections between the diffusion of technology, the movement of labor, and legal institutions.

REFERENCES

Books and Journal Articles

Arup, Christopher (2000), *The World Trade Organization Knowledge Agreements*, Cambridge, UK: Cambridge University Press

Bauer, Jobst-Hubertus and Martin Diller (2009), *Wettbewerbsverbote: Rechtliche und taktische Hinweise für Arbeitgeber, Arbeitnehmer und vertretungsberechtige Organmitglieder*, München, DE: C.H. Beck

Ben-Atar, Doron S. (2004), *Trade Secrets: Intellectual Piracy and the Origins of American Industrial Power*, Connecticut, US: Yale University Press

Casper, Steven (2007), *Creating Silicon Valley in Europe: Public Policy Towards New Technology Industries*, Oxford, UK: Oxford University Press

Cornish, William and David Llewelyn (2003), *Intellectual Property: Patents, Copyrights, Trade Marks, and Allied Rights*, London, UK: Sweet & Maxwell

Fisk, Catherine L. (2009), *Working Knowledge: Employee Innovation and the Rise of Corporate Intellectual Property, 1800–1930*, North Carolina, US: The University of North Carolina Press

Gilson, Ronald J. (1999), 'The Legal Infrastructure of High Technology Industrial Districts: Silicon Valley, Route 128, and Covenants Not to Compete', 74 N.Y.U.L. Rev. 575–622

Gilson, Ronald J. (2003) 'Engineering a Venture Capital Market: Lessons from the American Experience', 5 Stan.L.Rev. 1067–1103 (2003).
Hyde, Alan (1998), The Wealth of Shared Information: Silicon Valley's High-Velocity Labor Market, Endogenous Economic Growth, and the Law of Trade Secrets) (1998), at http://andromeda.rutgers.edu/<diff>hyde/WEALTH.htm.
Hyde, Alan (2003), *Working in Silicon Valley: Economic and Legal Analysis of a High-Velocity Labor Market*, New York, US and London, UK: M.E. Sharpe (2003).
Lieberstein, Stanley H. (1979), *Who Owns What Is in Your Head?: A Guide for Entrepreneurs, Inventors, and Creative Employees*, Connecticut, US: Wildcat Publishing, Inc.
Mola, Luca (2000), *The Silk Industry of Renaissance Venice*, Maryland, US: The Johns Hopkins University Press (2000).
Saxenian, AnnaLee (1994), *Regional Advantage: Culture and Competition in Silicon Valley and Route 128*, Massachusetts, US: Harvard University Press (1994).
Saxenian, AnnaLee (2006), *The New Argonauts: Regional Advantage in a Global Economy*, Massachusetts, US: Harvard University Press
Schwab, Stewart (1993), 'Life-Cycle Justice: Accommodating Just Cause and Employment-at-will', 92 Mich. L. Rev. 8–56
Thorelli, Hans B. (1954), *The Federal Antitrust Policy: Originations of an American Tradition*, Baltimore, US: The Johns Hopkins Press (1954).

Cases

Edwards v. Arthur Andersen, LLP,189 P.3d 285 (Cal. 2008)
Keeler v. Taylor, 53 Pa. 467 (1866)
Mitchel v. Reynolds, [1711] 24 Eng. Rep. 347 (Q.B.)
Morse Twist Drill & Machine Co. v. Morse 103 Mass. 73 (1869)
O. & W. Thum Co. v. Tloczynski, 72 N.W. 140 (1897)
Post v. Merrill Lynch, Pierce, Fenner & Smith, Inc., 48 N.Y. 2d 84 (1979).
Stone v. Goss, 55 A. 736 (1903)
United States v. Addyston Pipe & Steel Co., 85 F. 271 (6th Cir. 1898)
Yovatt v. Winyard, [1820] 37 Eng. Rep. 425

16. Employee invention system: Comparative law perspective

Toshiko Takenaka* and Yves Reboul**

I. INTRODUCTION

Both European and East Asian countries went through major overhauls to further harmonization of patent systems and to remove obstacles for global trade since the enactment of WTO TRIPS in 1994.[1] In particular, European countries enacted the European Patent Convention ('EPC') in 1973[2] and completed harmonization in substantive and procedural aspects of patent procurement. They are enhancing their harmonization efforts in patent enforcement to create a uniform market within European Union ('EU') member states by issuing a number of EU regulations and directives. Since EU member states include both common law and civil law countries, EU regulations and directives are a unique amalgam of IP systems in both traditions.

East Asian countries' patent systems also represent another type of amalgam of IP systems in both common law and civil law traditions.

---

* Professor of Law, Washington Research Foundation/W. Hunter Simpson Professor of Technology Law, Director, Center for Advanced Study and Research on Intellectual Property (CASRIP), University of Washington School of Law. This paper is based on research that the author conducted in France at Center of Study of International Intellectual Property (CEIPI), University of Strasbourg. The author is particularly grateful for Dr. Yann Basire, who helped the author researching on employee invention system under French Law.

** Professor of Law, Director, French Department, CEIPI, University of Strasbourg.

1 World Trade Organization ('WTO'), Trade-Related Aspects of Intellectual Property Rights ('TRIPS'), Final Act Embodying the Results of the Uruguay Round of Multilateral Trade Negotiations, Apr. 15, 1994, THE LEGAL TEXTS: THE RESULTS OF THE URUGUAY ROUND OF MULTILATERAL TRADE NEGOTIATIONS 2 (1999), 1867 U.N.T.S. 14, 33 I.L.M. 1143 (1994) (http://www.wto.org/english/docs_e/legal_e/legal_e.htm)

2 Convention on the Grant of European Patents, Oct. 5, 1973, 13 I.L.M. 270 ['European Patent Convention'].

These countries originally adopted the German patent system as the model for their own patent systems. After World War II, these countries adopted many aspects from the US patent system as a result of bilateral and multilateral trade negotiations to open their markets. More recently, this US influence is further enhanced because many of these countries adopted pro-patent policies and went through overhaul reforms by using the US patent system as a model for mobilizing the patent system as a form of economic stimulus.[3] These reforms led to significant changes to key features adopted from the German patent system through patent legislation and judicial interpretation in East Asia.

In contrast, inventorship and ownership issues are left behind from these harmonization efforts both in Europe and Asia.[4] European patent scholars and professionals found that the different approaches taken in common law and civil law traditions prevent EU member states finding common ground.[5] However, inventorship is the starting point of the ownership and the ownership is a fundamental issue to give a basis to claim the right of intellectual property. In particular, allocation of the ownership of inventions resulting from the employment ('employee inventions') between the employee-inventor and the employer directly relates to a basic policy question for the patent system, promoting innovations through encouraging inventions and commercialization. Despite the necessity for harmonizing the ownership allocation rule, each jurisdiction adopts its own rule and mechanism to transfer the ownership to employers. In addition, the rule for employees' rights to compensate the transfer of ownership differs from one jurisdiction to another. Since the overwhelming majority of patent applications filed with patent offices in US, as well as EU and Asian jurisdictions are directed to employee inventions and filed by non-inventors, that is, employers of actual inventors, non-uniformity of ownership between the same employer and employee with respect to the

---

[3] An example is a reform in Japan in introducing the basic IP Law. Toshiko Takenaka, *Success or Failure? Japan's National Strategy on Intellectual Property and Evaluation of Its Impact from the Comparative Law Perspective*, 8 Wash. U. Global Study. L. Rev. 379 (2009).

[4] To promote discussions, EU has published a green paper in 1997. Promoting Innovation Through Patents: Green Paper on the Community Patent and the Patent System in Europe, COM(1997)314. However, there has been no progress in harmonization since the publication.

[5] Christopher Heath, Harmonizing *Scope and Allocation of Patent Rights in Europe – Towards a New European Patent Law*, 6 Marq. Intell. Prop. L. Rev. 11 (2002).

same invention presents a serious challenge for multinational companies to manage global patent procurements.[6]

Accordingly, this article will examine employee invention systems in major countries representing common law and civil law countries and aim to propose the best practice for allocating rights in employee inventions for harmonization. It will first examine the employee invention systems under German and US legal systems. The German patent system is a paradigm of a patent system in civil law countries. Its influence on patent jurisprudence is very significant in both European and East Asian countries because these countries revised their patent laws to harmonize with the EPC, which is in principle based on the pre-EPC German patent system. Further, Germany has a most advanced legal system providing detailed rules for balancing interests between employers and their employee-inventors through the enactment of the Employee Invention Act ('EIA').[7] Unlike many other jurisdictions, the German EIA is separate from the Patent Act.[8] Reflecting an important public policy under German Labor Law, EIA makes it clear that any agreement between an employee and employer conflicting with a provision in EIA and detrimental to employee's rights is void, and thus extensively limits the freedom of contract between employers and employee-inventors.[9]

In contrast, the freedom of contract governs ownership of employee inventions under US Patent Law,[10] which is paradigm of a patent system in common law countries.[11] There is no statutory provision to control the

---

[6] For example in Japan, 95 percent of patent applications are filed by employers. *Supra* note 5, Heath at 18–19.

[7] Arbeitnehmererfindunggesetz, ArbEG (Employees' Inventions Act). English TranslationisavailableinHelmutReitzleetal.,GesetzüberArbeitnehmererfindungen / Act of Employees' Inventions (2007). For a most comprehensive treatise in German on German EIA, see Kurt Bartenbuch and Franz-EugenVolz, Arbeitnehmerefgindergesetz (4ed, 2002) ['Bartenbach']. The ownership principle is discussed on page 254 seq. For treatises in English, see Michael Trimborn, Employees' Inventions in Germany: A Handbook for International Businesses (2009)['Trimborn']; Helmut Reitzle et al., Act on Employees' Inventions (3ed, 2007) ['Reitzle'].

[8] Patentgesetz of 1983 (Patent Act of 1983), English Translation is available at: http://www.jpo.go.jp/shiryou_e/s_sonota_e/fips_e/pdf/germany_e/e_tokkyo.pdf

[9] EIA §22.

[10] 35 U.S.C. §§ 1-376 (U.S. Patent Act)

[11] Another important common law country is United Kingdom. UK employee invention system is based on the freedom of contract and share a lot of similar features with U.S. patent systems. For discussions on U.K. employee invention system, see Jeremy Phillips and Michael J. Hoolahan, Employees' Inventions in the United Kingdom Law and Practice (1982), and *supra* note 5, Heath at 22.

ownership of invention resulting from the employment relationship except for federally funded inventions under the Bayh-Dole Act.[12] The Bayh-Dole ownership rule governs only the ownership of invention resulting from the special relationship between the Federal Government and their employees and contractors. It does not govern any other employment relationship, including the Government's contractors and their employees.[13] Instead, the terms of assignment contracts and state law govern the ownership of inventions resulting from any other employment relationship, the special relationship.[14]

On its face, US and German systems are so different that it seems impossible to reconcile their basic principles. However, some other jurisdictions in Asia and Europe have employee invention systems which are a hybrid in incorporating various features from both US and German systems. French and Japanese systems are good examples of such hybrid. Their rules of ownership and compensation for inventors share common features with the rules under US and German employee systems.

After reviewing the four systems, this article will propose a system which is based on a fine balance between interests of employers and inventors for giving inventors incentive to invent while guaranteeing their employers enough rewards for commercialization. It will take into account today's R&D environment where inventors interflow beyond the traditional notion of legal entity and propose an employee invention system, which will promote an information sharing culture and collaboration of researchers from academic and private sectors while facilitating IP professionals' patent portfolio management.

II. UNITED STATES

(i) Fundamental Rules

In the United States, only a natural person or plural natural persons can be the sole inventor or joint inventors, excluding the possibility for

---

[12] Bayh-Dole Act, Pub. L. No. 96-517, codified as 35 USC §§202-12 (Chapter 18). For detailed discussions of history and interpretation of Bayh-Dole Act, see SEAN O'CONNOR ET AL., LEGAL CONTEXT OF UNIVERSITY INTELLECTUAL PROPERTY AND TECHNOLOGY (2010) [hereinafter O'CONNOR ET AL.] *available at* http://sites.nationalacademies.org/PGA/step/PGA_058712) (last visited Aug. 21, 2011).

[13] *Bd. of Trs. of the Leland Stanford Junior Univ. v. Roche Molecular Sys.*, 131 S. Ct. 2188, 180 L. Ed. 2d 1, 98 USPQ 2d 1761 (2011).

[14] Some states enacted special legislations for employee inventions. See infra.

a non-human legal entity, such as a corporation, from inventorship. It is a fundamental rule that ownership of invention is originally vested in the inventor.[15] This rule is subjected to a narrow exception for national security related inventions under the Atomic Energy Act[16] and the National Aeronautics and Space Act[17] in the United States where the ownership is vested to the US Federal Government.[18] Thus, the examination of ownership always starts from the determination of inventorship.[19] Although the ownership issue is often intertwined with the inventorship issue, it is important to note that the inventorship issue 'who is a true and original inventor or inventors?' is a separate question from the ownership issue, 'who owns property rights in the invention made by the inventor(s)?'

The rule that the ownership of invention is assignable is another important rule. Although the patent statute applies to determine inventorship, federal law plays a very small role in the determination of ownership before filing a patent application with the US Patent and Trademark Office ('USPTO') when rights in the ownership of invention are transferred from the original inventor(s).[20] An inventor may contract to transfer rights in future inventions before completion of the inventions; nevertheless rights and obligations for the transfer under such contract is controlled by state law.[21] Such transfer may occur before or after patent filing.

A patent may be issued to an applying inventor although a patent may issue to an inventor's assignor if the inventor assigns rights in the invention to a third-party.[22] This rule is codified in patent statute that applications can be assignable by an instrument in writing.[23] The statute makes

---

15 *Stanford,* 180 L. Ed. 2d. at 12. *Gayler v. Wilder,* 51 U.S. 477, 10 How. 477, 493, 13 L. Ed. 504)(1851); *Solomons v. United States,* 137 U.S. 342, 346, 11 S. Ct. 88, 34 L. Ed. 667, 26 Ct. Cl. 620 (1980); *Beach Aircraft Corp. v. EDO Corp.,* 990 F.2d 1237, 26 USPQ2d 1572 (Fed. Cir. 1248). For a discussion of the ownership endorsed by the Supreme Court in *Stanford* in comparison with the ownership under the German EIA, see, Toshiko Takenaka, *Serious Flaw of Employee Invention Ownership under the Bayh–Dole Act in Standford v. Roche; Finding the Missing Piece of the Puzzle of the German Employee Invention Act,* 12 Texas Intellectual Property L.J. 281 (2012).

16 Atomic Energy Act (AEA) of 1954, P. L. 83-703,68 Stat. 944.

17 National Aeronautics and Space Act of 1958, P.S. 85-568, §102,72 Stat. 426 (NASA).

18 *Stanford,* 180 L. Ed. 2d. at 13.

19 Donald S. Chisum, Chisum on Patents, §22.02(1972, Supp. 2010).

20 Mary LaFrance, *Nevada's Employee Inventions Statute: Novel, Nonobvious, and Patently Wrong,* 3 Navada L. J. 88 at 90.

21 *Supra* note 19, Chisum on Patents, §22.03.

22 *Stanford,* 180 L. Ed. 2d. at 12.

23 35 U.S.C. §261.

clear that a patent application must be filed by the inventor, even if rights in the invention are transferred to a third-party. [24] This rule is unique to the US patent system.

(ii) Employer's Rights in Employee Inventions

The US Supreme Court acknowledged that it is often true that property rights in fruits of labor belong to his employer.[25] This rule does not apply to patents because the Supreme Court made it clear that mere employment is not sufficient to transfer the ownership of employee invention to the employer.[26] In general, the ownership of inventions belongs to inventors and does not transfer to their employers unless the inventors expressly agree to assign the inventions.[27] As early as 1843, the US Supreme Court has always assumed ownership of employee inventions to the inventor.[28] However, it attempted to maintain balance with interests of employers by providing a royalty-free non-exclusive license.[29] From the first patent statute in 1790, the US patent system has been granting patents only to applications filed by the first and true and inventors.[30] The same first patent statute presumes an invention made by multiple joint-inventors.[31] However, the employer of an inventor cannot be qualified for a co-inventor. Regardless of financial contribution or an instruction given by a natural person-employer, she cannot obtain any rights in the ownership of invention unless she is a joint inventor of the invention that resulted from joint labors with her inventor-employee.[32] To qualify as a joint-inventor,

---

[24] 35 U.S.C. §111. PTO Rule 41(a). Supra, note 19, Chisum §11.02[2][a]. An application should be made by the actual human inventor or inventors even if the inventor or inventors assign all rights to the invention to another person or entity. 37 C.F.R. §1.46. This rule has been modified to enable assignee-employers to file an application when the revision under American Invents Act has become effective on September 16, 2012. 35 USC §118. America Invents Act, Pub. L. No. 112-29, 125 Stat. 284, Section 4, §118 (Sept. 16, 2011).

[25] *Stanford,* 180 L. Ed. 2d. at 14.

[26] *Stanford,* 180 L. Ed. 2d. at 14.

[27] *Stanford,* 180 L. Ed. 2d. at 12.

[28] *Supra* note 19, Chisum on Patents, §22.03.

[29] Id.

[30] Patent Act of 1790, §. 6. Since patent applications were not examined under 1790 Act, patentees needed to produce evidence that he is a first and true inventor for enforcing his patent at a court.

[31] Id.§. 1.For a general discussion,*see supra* note 19, Chisum on Patents, §2.02[1].

[32] *Steams v. Barrett,* 22 F. Cas 1175 (no. 13, 337)(C.C.D. Mass. 1816) cited in *supra* note 19, Chisum on Patents, §2.02

she must make a contribution to the conception of the invention.[33] This is a stark contrast to the ownership of authorship under US Copyright Law, which gives the ownership directly to employers under the work-for-hire doctrine.[34]

An invention resulting from the performance of duty under employment does not change the fundamental rule that the ownership to inventions are exclusive to the inventor, unless there is an express agreement between the inventor and his employer to assign the rights. State contract law governs whether the agreement is valid and enforceable. Even if an employer fails to secure an express agreement from his employee, US courts developed common law rules to provide some rights; (1) if an employer is specially hired to make the particular invention (the specially hired to invent doctrine), or (2) if an employer is hired to make inventions in general (the hired to invent in general doctrine).[35] The former gives rise to a duty of assignment based on the contract to hire inventors for inventing a particular subject matter.[36] Therefore, an employer secures the ownership of employee invention under this implied license theory. The latter gives rise to a non-exclusive personal non-transferable license termed a 'shop right'.[37]

It is important to note that this 'specially hired to invent' doctrine is an exception to the ownership rule exclusive to inventors. US courts repeatedly held that an employment contract to hire an employee for inventing something in general does not give rise to a duty of assignment.[38] In a leading case involving the ownership of employee invention, *Dubilier Condenser Corp.*, the US Supreme Court emphasized the distinction between the contract of hiring an inventor for conducting research and making inventions in general, and that of hiring an inventor for making a particular invention.[39] According to the majority in *Dubilier*, hiring an employee for making an invention gives rise to an ownership assignment duty with respect to an employee invention only if the invention is the precise subject of the employment contract. This follows that a term in

---

33 *Stern v. Trustees of Columbia University*, 434 F.3d 1375, 77 USPQ2d 1702 (Fed. Cir. 2004). *See also*, *supra* note 19, Chisum on Patents, §2.02[2][a].

34 17 USC §101. *For a discussion to compare the ownership rules between copyright and patents see supra* note 20, LaFrance at 100.

35 *Supra* note 19, Chisum on Patents, §22.03[2][3].

36 *Standard Parts Co. v. Peck*, 264 U.S. 52 (1924).

37 *McClurg v. Kingslund*, 42 U.S. (1 How.) 202, 11 L. Ed. 102 (1843).

38 *Supra* note 19, Chisum on Patents, §22.03[2]. See, e.g., *Aethna-Standard Enfineering Co. v. Rowland*, 228 USPQ 292, 493 A. 2d 1375 (Pa, Super. Ct. 1985).

39 *United States v. Dubilier Condenser Corp.*, 289 U.S. 178, 17 USPQ 154 (1933).

the contract must make clear what the employer paid for and what consequently belongs to the employer. The *Dubilier* Court highlighted the distinction between rights in the ownership of inventions and other types of properties resulting from regular labor. Only the former resulted from inventive activities exercising their unique creativity beyond ordinary skill. Due to this special nature of inventions, rights in the ownership of the invention do not transfer to employers unless employees specially bargained for and agreed to the compensation for the inventions when they entered into the employment contract.

The Supreme Court also used this special nature of invention to define the scope of 'shop rights'. Employers are in equity entitled only to a license to use the invention but have no equity to demand a transfer of the ownership of invention because the invention is the original conception of the employee-inventor; it should remain as the property of the employee.[40] Since the *Dubilier* Court found the nature of the employment contract to hire the inventor for conducting research in general, it refused the employer's request to transfer patents held by its inventor-employee.

This reluctance of implying a contract to assign rights in the ownership of invention is supported by the patent policy for promoting innovations through inventions. To preserve incentives to invent, US case law prevents employers from taking away property rights in the invention and secures inventor-employees bargaining opportunities with their employers for fair value of the invention.[41] In other words, the patent policy of innovation promotion through a reward to inventors is implemented through the bargaining between inventors and their employers over a transfer of property right in the invention.

(iii) Employee's Rights in Employee Inventions

Despite the important role played by the pre-invention assignment contract in implementing a federal patent policy, US courts leave interpretation of contract terms and enforceability to the governance of state policies through the application of state contract law.[42] The US Supreme Court empowered state courts to develop their own law governing a state question such as ownership and transfer of patents.[43] However, state courts in general acknowledge the significance of federal case law and

---

40 Id., at 188.

41 *Supra* note 20, LaFrance at 93; *Supra* note 19, Chisum on Patents, §22.03[2].

42 *Supra* note 19, Chisum on Patents, §22.03[4].

43 *Erie Rr. v. Tompkins*, 304 U.S. 64 (1938).

follow the precedent of the US Supreme Court.[44] This led to a development of fairly uniform common law rules in ownership and assignment enforceability throughout state and federal courts in the United States. Under this uniform rule, an express agreement is necessary to transfer rights in the ownership of invention from an inventor to her employer.[45] The state law governs the agreement in general with some exceptions.[46]

Accordingly, different state public policies, for the ownership of an assignment agreement in employment contracts, lead to non-uniformity of the scope of inventions, which employers can secure the ownership of inventions from their employees. Unlike many civil law jurisdictions, employers are not required to pay any additional compensation as consideration for a transfer of rights in the invention.[47] This is because US courts view the payment of salary, assistance of co-employees, and right to use an employer's facility constitutes sufficient consideration.[48] Since US case law requires such a pre-invention assignment agreement, being not only expressive but also clear, by giving notice to inventors with respect to what they give up in exchange for their salary and guarantees inventors bargaining opportunity, courts find inventor salary as sufficient consideration to enforce the agreement.[49]

Although US courts favor to enforce an express assignment contract, if employees' duties of assignment are overbroad, they may decline to enforce an agreement literally.[50] Courts may reinterpret the overbroad agreement to limit the duties within a reasonable scope.[51] In some states

---

44 *See, e.g., Farmland Irrigation Co., Inc. v. Dopplmaier,* 48 Cal. 2d 208; 113 USPQ 88 (1957): *Aethna-Standard Engineering Cor. v. Rowland, 343* Pa. Supr. 64,493 A.2d 1375,228 USPQ 2d 292 (1985).

45 *Stanford,* 180 L. Ed. 2d at 12.

46 *Jim Arnold Corp. v. Hydrotech Sys.,* 109 F.3d 1567, 42 USPQ2d 1119 (Fed. Cir. 1997): *My Mail, Ltd. v. Am. On Line, Inc.,* 476 F.3d 1372, 81 USPQ2d 1832 (Fed. Cir. 2007); One of such exceptions is the question, whether a patent assignment clause creates an automatic assignment. *Stanford* 583 F.3d 832, at 841.

47 D. Parker, Note, Reform for Rights of Employed Inventors, *57 S. Cal. L. Rev. 603, 608 (1984);* Ann Bartow, Inventors of the World, Unite! A Call for Collective Action by Employee-Inventors, 37 Santa Clara L. Rev. 673 (1997).

48 *See, e.g., Goodyear Tire & Rubber Co. v. Miller,* 22 F.2d 353 (9th Cir. 1927).

49 *Aethna-Standard Engineering Cor. v. Rowland, 343* Pa. Supr. 64,493 A.2d 1375,228 USPQ 2d 292 (1985); *Dempsey v. Dobson,* 174 Pa. 122, (1896), *appeal after remand,* 184 Pa. 588 (1898).

50 Jay Dratler Jr. *Incentives for People: The Forgotten Purpose of the Patent System,* 16 HARV. J. ON LEGIS. 129 (1979).

51 *Guth v. Minnesota Mining & Manufacturing Co.,* 72 F 2d 385 (7th Cir. 1934)(discussed in *supra* note 50, Jay Dratler Jr., at 142): *Universal Winding Co. v. Clarke*, 108 F. Supp. 329 (D. Conn. 1952).

an employment contract including an overbroad assignment agreement is void and unenforceable.[52] In general, special legislations for employee inventions enacted in these states prevent employers from enforcing a contract obligating a transfer of rights in the ownership of the invention which is developed entirely on the employee's own time unless; (1) the invention relates to employers' business or to the employer's actual or 'demonstrably anticipated' research and development; or (2) results from work performed by the employee for the employer.[53] In contrast to these legislations for protecting employees' rights, only one State, Nevada, enacted an Act which allows transfer of rights in the ownership of invention automatically without any express agreement if the invention is made during the term of employment and fell within the scope of the employee's job description.[54] In other states where no special legislation is enacted, a contract to transfer rights in the ownership of any invention made during the term of employment may be valid and enforceable regardless of the inventor's duty or employer's business as long as the invention resulted from work the employee conducted for his employer.[55] In short, the freedom of contract, assuming equal bargaining powers between employers and employees, is the key principle in implementing the US employee inventions system, although some states have some limitations on the principle for protecting employees or employers. If either party fails to take advantage of the bargaining opportunity, no protection is available through a federal legislation.[56]

---

52 These states currently include California, Minnesota, North Carolina, Washington and Nevada. *Supra* note 12 ,O'Connor et al., at 85; Robert L. Gullette, *State Legislation Governing Ownership Rights in Inventions,* 62 J. Pat. & Trademark Off. Soc'y 732 (1980).

53 *Supra* note 20, LaFrance at 96.

54 *Supra* note 20, LaFrance at 88.

55 *Cubic v. Marty, 185* Cal. App. 3d 438, 1 USPQ2d 1709 (1986).

56 In the 1970s, U.S. Congress introduced a series of bills to implement a federal policy for the employee invention ownership. H.R. 15512, 91st Cong., 1st Sess. (1969), reprinted in 116 CONG.REC. 744 (1970), reintroduced as H.R. 1483, 92d Cong., 1st Sess. (1971). These bills modeled German EIA. However, these bills failed to pass Congress due to strong opposition from U.S. industry for introducing a mandatory compensation for inventors with respect to the transfer of employee invention ownership. William Hovell, *Patent Ownership: An Employer*'s *Rights to His Employee's Invention,* 58 Notre Dame L. Rev. 863 (1983); *Supra* note 12 , O'Connor et al., at 29.

III. GERMANY

(i) Fundamental Rules

The fundamental rule that ownership of invention is exclusive to the invention is common in the US and German patent systems. Under German Patent Law, a right for patent is initially vested only in the sole inventor or co-inventors who have made a creative contribution for the invention.[57] An employer cannot be an inventor or co-inventor unless he or she makes such contribution. Only a natural person can make such contribution and thus a legal entity cannot be an inventor.[58] This fundamental rule is universal to all branches of intellectual property including copyright under the German legal system. There is no exception to the rule such as the 'work for hire' doctrine under US Copyright law.[59]

Like US case law, an examination of inventorship is the starting point for deciding ownership. Patent law applies to determine who is/are the inventor(s). However, it plays a very limited role in determining the ownership of invention before filing a patent application. In general, property and contract principles under civil codes govern an assignment of property rights including those in the ownership of invention.[60] Regarding the ownership of property rights resulting from the performance of duty under an employment contract, German labor and employment law may provide a special rule governing a contract between employers and their employees reflecting public policy.[61] German courts made clear that fruits of employees' labor belong to their employer.[62] This ownership rule conflicts with the patent law rule of inventors as original owners when the invention resulted from the performance of employees' duties. To remove this

---

57 German Patent Act, § 6. BGH 2004 GRUR 50 – Verkranzungsverfaren.

58 BGH 1978 GRUR 283 – Motorkettensäge; District Court of Nürnberg-Fürth 1968 GRUR 254; Peter Mes, Patent Act (Commentary), 2005 (2nd Edition), Section 6 Patent Act, Marginal No. 8.

59 However, with respect to computer software German Copyright Law gives employers all usage rights if the software resulting from execution of employee's duty. German Copyright Law § 69b. For a general discussion of lack of work for hire doctrine under German Copyright Law, see Robert A. Jacobs, *Work-For-Hire and the Moral Right Dilemma in the European Community: A U.S. Perspective*, 16 B.C. Int'l & Comp. L. Rev. 29, 53 (1993).

60 Kraßer, Patentrecht, 2009 (6th Edition), § 40, III.

61 Kraßer, Patentrecht, 2009 (6th Edition), § 21, I a.

62 BAG (Federal Labour Court) 1961 NJW 1509; Münchener Kommentar zum BGB (Civil Code Commentary), Müller-Glöge, 2009 (5th Edition), Section 611, Marginal No. 1073.

conflict, while achieving the public policies involved in both patent law and labor and employment law, German legislators enacted a special law, the EIA, to govern an assignment of rights in the ownership of invention between employers and employees.[63]

(ii) Employers' Rights in Employee Inventions

Under the German EIA, the patent law rule that inventors are original owners prevails over that of employment law. Thus, the German EIA rule is perfectly in-line with US law in making clear that rights in the ownership of invention originally vest in inventor-employees.[64] However, it differs from the US rule in guaranteeing employers a right to claim a transfer of the ownership of employees' inventions.[65] In other words, the German EIA limits the freedom of contract and makes void with respect to any contract conflicting with a provision of the EIA and being detrimental to employees.[66]

Due to the mandatory rule reflecting strong public policies, the EIA makes clear the scope of inventions it governs. The scope covers any technical subject matter regardless of its patentability as long as it is made by an inventor-employee.[67] Under German Employment Law, an employee is a person who is bound by instructions on the grounds of an employment relationship and obliged in personal dependence on another, the employer.[68] The technical subject matter that EIA governs is classified into inventions and technical improvement proposals.[69] Inventions including utility model devices are distinguished from technical improvement proposals with respect to whether it is qualified for protection under German Patent Law or utility model registration.[70] Subject matter which is not qualified for patentability falls into the category of proposals for technical improvements and is not subject to various duties relating to patent applications.[71]

Patentable inventions are further classified into two types: service inventions and free inventions.[72] An invention made during a term of employ-

---

63 Supra note 7, Trimborn at 2; Reitzle, at 1.
64 German Patent Act § 6. *Supra* note 7, Trimborn at 1.
65 EIA § 6.
66 EIA § 22.
67 EIA § 1. *Supra* note 157, Harhoff and Hoisl.
68 *Supra* note 7, Trimborn at 13.
69 EIA § 2, §3.
70 EIA §. 2.
71 EIA §. 3.
72 EIA § 4(1).

ment is a service invention if (1) it resulted from the employee's tasks in the employer's business or public administration or (2) it is essentially based upon the experience or activities of the employer's business or public administration.[73] Any other inventions that do not fall into the definition of service invention are free inventions.[74]

With respect to a service invention, EIA guarantees employers a right to claim ownership of all property rights in the invention.[75] Before the 2009 Revision, an employer had to submit a document which met certain formality requirements under the Civil Code.[76] The assignment was not automatic and needed an additional step to consummate the right to claim transfer of ownership from the employee. This pre-2009 requirement of written instrument for executing an assignment is similar to the practice that US employers widely adopt by using the 'agree to assign' term in pre-invention assignment contracts.[77] The most significant difference from the US system is that even if employers failed to execute a pre-invention assignment contract at all, the ownership of employee invention transfers to employers in the operation of law if employers exercise their rights following the necessary procedure provided in the EIA.

A failure to exercise the claiming right may lead to a forfeiture of the employer's right in the ownership of service invention under the EIA. The German EIA has provided that inventor-employees could retain rights in the ownership if their employers did not exercise their claiming rights, within the 'four month from the receipt of proper report'.[78] It gave employees freedom to assign the ownership to a third-party including the employer's competitor. Employers who were not familiar with requirements under EIA may have failed securing the ownership of employee inventions. To remedy this problem, the German EIA was revised in 2009 to introduce a presumption to assume employers' exercise of their claiming right unless they send out a declaration to confirm that they would not exercise their rights and thereby release rights in the invention within four months from the receipt of report submitted by the employee.[79] This assumption made the German EIA's ownership transfer mechanism

---

[73] EIA §. 4(2).

[74] EIA §. 4(3).

[75] EIA §. 6(1).

[76] German Civil Code, §. 126b.

[77] *Arachnid, Inc. v. Merit Industries, Inc.*, 939 F.2d 1574, 19 U.S.P.Q.2d (BNA) 1513 (1991).

[78] EIA § 6.

[79] EIA § 6(2).

complete in protecting employers from loss of their rights in service inventions, which result from their negligent or ignorance of EIA provisions.

The EIA further protects employers' rights by making void any transactions of the ownership of service invention prior to exercise of claiming rights once an employer exercises the claiming right if the transactions negatively affect the employer's right.[80] After the 2009 revision, any prior transaction has become void when the four months for sending a declaration to release a service invention expires.[81]

(iii) Employee's Rights in Employee's Inventions

Under the German EIA, the transfer of rights through an exercise of claiming right also results in a variety of obligations on employers. These duties give rise to a variety of employees' rights for protecting their interests. The most important right for protecting employee-inventors' interests is a right for compensation, which resulted from the transfer of invention ownership to the employers. The EIA imposes a duty on employers to pay a reasonable remuneration or compensation.[82] However, an employee cannot enforce this right unless the employer begins practicing the invention.[83] The EIA requires employers to take into account multiple factors including; (1) commercial applicability of the invention; (2) duties and position of the employee; and (3) contribution by the employer for calculating the compensation.[84] Due to the complexity of taking into account the multiple factors, the EIA suggests to consult guidelines for calculating the amount of remuneration.[85]

To protect employees' rights for compensation, the EIA imposes a variety of duties on employers. The first of these duties is to file a German patent or utility model application without delay.[86] Since employees' right for compensation is based on the principle to share benefits resulting from an exclusive right in the employee invention through a patent grant (Monopoly Principle),[87] the compensation right is meaningless unless a patent application is filed to obtain an exclusive right. Employers are not

---

80 EIA § 7(2).
81 EIA § 6(2).
82 EIA §. 9(1).
83 Supra note 7, Reitzle et al., at 9.
84 EIA §. 9(2).
85 EIA §. 11.
86 EIA §. 13(1). English translation of the guidelines are included in supra note 7, Reitzle et al., 45 seq.
87 *supra* note7, Trimborn at 32.

released from this duty unless their inventor-employees agree not to file a patent application or protect the inventions as a trade secret.[88] However, employers can choose the latter option only if they inform their employee-inventors their decision of trade secret protection while acknowledging patentability of the disclosed invention under German patent or utility model law.[89] To enforce the duty of patent filing, EIA guarantees employees a right to receive a copy of the patent application when an application is filed[90] and a right to file an application under the name of the employer at the expense of the employer if the employer fails to meet the duty.[91]

The EIA further protects employees' rights for compensation during the patent prosecution in requiring employers to communicate with employee-inventors about the progress of examination and correspondence with the patent office[92] This communication is particularly critical if the employer decides to abandon the patent application or patent rights, which leads to a forfeiture of the right for compensation. To prevent employees' right for compensation from being eliminated through abandonment, the EIA guarantees employees a right to continue prosecution and maintain patents if their employers decide to abandon a patent application prior to the payment of compensation.[93]

Employees' rights include compensation for sharing the benefits of exclusive right resulting from grants of foreign patents. The EIA provides a right for employers to file foreign applications based on the ownership of the invention transferred through the claiming of their rights in employee invention.[94] The Act also gives a right to employees to file a foreign application with respect to countries in which their employers are not interested in securing patent protection by requiring their employers to release the service inventions and enable their employees to file foreign applications.[95] For equity, the EIA provides a compulsory license for the

---

88 EIA §. 13(2).

89 EIA §. 17(1).

90 EIA §. 15(1).

91 EIA §. 13(3). However, the Act does not give an option to return the ownership to employees so that they can file an application in their own name even if their employers fail to file an application. *Supra* note 7, Bartenbach at 700.

92 EIA §. 15.

93 EIA §. 16. Employees can buy out this right to transfer the patent. Employers in major German companies often offer a lump-sum payment to their employees for compensating the right for continuing domestic patent application and the right for foreign patent applications under EIA §. 14. *Supra* note 7, Trimborn at 31.

94 EIA §. 14(1)(2).

95 EIA §. 14(2). Employers must inform their release early enough so that

employer if the employee obtains a patent on a service invention in foreign countries.[96]

In short, the German EIA does not assume equal bargaining power between employees and employers. German Labor and Employment Law policy for protecting employees who have less bargaining power than employers and Patent Law policy for preserving inventors' incentive to invent, prevail in the ownership rules of employee inventions and limit the freedom of contract. These prevailing policies are in stark contrast to the strong policy of freedom of contract under the US system.

IV. FRANCE: AN EXAMPLE OF A HYBRID SYSTEM

(i) Fundamental Rules

In France, the ownership rules for inventions is provided in the French Intellectual Property Codes ('IPC').[97] The French system follows the same fundamental rule that the ownership of invention is in principle vested in the inventor.[98] However, this fundamental rule is significantly modified because the French IPC allows ownership of invention vested in employers if inventions made by an employee fall into the definition of 'mission invention'.[99] Although only a natural person or persons can be sole inventor or joint inventors and has a right to be named as the inventor, [100] employers including a legal entity can be the original owner of the invention made by their employees.[101] In vesting the original ownership of invention to a legal entity, this French ownership rule is similar to the ownership rule for national security related inventions in the United States.[102]

Unlike the US national security related inventions, where the starting point of ownership determination is the nature of invention, inventorship is the starting point for determining the ownership of French employee

employees can file a foreign application within the priority period under the Paris Convention Article 4.

96 EIA §. 14(3).

97 Intellectual Property Code (English Translation: http://www.jpo.go.jp/shiryou_e/s_sonota_e/fips_e/pdf/france_e/e_chiteki_zaisan.pdf).

98 French IPC Article L. 611-6.

99 French IPC Article L. 611-7, Paragraph 1.

100 TGI Paris, 20 mai 1988, PIBD 1988, n° 442, III, p. 444.

101 French IPC Article L. 611-9.

102 *Infra* notes 16–17.

inventions because vesting of ownership depends on the nature of the employment contract between the employer and employee. Therefore, this French ownership rule functions in a similar manner as the ownership of invention under US common law, with respect to the invention specially hired to invent rule, in that the ownership transfers to employers without any express agreement.[103]

Like the US and Germany, the ownership of invention is assignable before and after a patent application.[104] Property and contract principles under Civil Codes govern an assignment of property rights including those in the ownership of invention. Like Germany, French labor and employment law may provide a special rule to limit the freedom of contract to protect employee-inventors. French courts acknowledge a rule similar to German law to give the ownership of properties resulting from employees' labor. To remove a conflict of employee invention ownership with the labor law, French IP law provides a clear rule.

(ii) Employers' Rights in Employee Inventions

Ownership rules for employee inventions under French IP Codes (IPC) are a hybrid of the US and German systems because; (1) freedom of contract prevails with respect to mission inventions; while (2) the labor and employment law and patent law policy prevails with respect to beyond mission inventions. As discussed above, although the rules are provided as part of IP Codes, they apply only to the subject matter of inventions.[105] With respect to inventions, the rules apply only to patentable inventions.[106] The rules only control the ownership of inventions made by an inventor during the effective period of the employment contract with his employer.[107]

The French IPC classifies inventions into three categories: (1) an inventive mission invention; (2) a beyond mission invention; and (3) free inventions.[108] An invention made by an employee is an inventive mission

---

103 Infra note 35.

104 French IP Code Article L. 611-6.

105 French IPC Article L. 611-7.

106 CA Paris, 9 mars 1972, Ann. propr. ind. 1973, p. 219; Cass. com., 22 févr. 2005, Juris-Data, n° 2005–027126.

107 The employee invention ownership rules does not apply to students and trainees who are not employed by the universities and companies. Cass. com., 25 avr. 2006, RCLIP-FR-54/2006.

108 French IPC Article L. 611-7. For a discussion of the three categories, see Thomas Bouvet, Employee-Inventor Rights in France (http://www.veron.com/publications/Colloques/Employees_inventions.pdf); Asako Hatanaka, Employee Invention Compensation System in France, 53 AIPPI Japan (No. 9) 34 (2008).

invention if the invention meets one of the following two conditions: (a) the invention results from an execution of an inventive mission included in the employment contract between the inventor and his employer where the inventive mission corresponds to the employee's effective function, or (b) the invention results from studies and research the employer expressly assigned to the employee as his duty.[109]

The employee invention provision under the French IPC distinguishes a permanent mission which meets the condition '(a)' and a temporary mission which meets the condition '(b)'. A permanent mission must be supported by the terms of the employment contract between the inventor-employee and his employer. A temporary mission for assigning employees to conduct studies and research must be established by evidence other than the term of employment contract. To protect inventors, the law imposes on employers the burden for showing that an invention is qualified as a mission invention.[110] The term of contract can define the inventive mission broadly and in general.[111] However, the term should specify the mission precisely to avoid a dispute whether an invention falls into the permanent inventive mission. If the term of contract is vague and does not define the mission clearly, courts refuse to find a mission invention.[112] In addition, the inventive mission must correspond to the function of the employee, that is, within the scope of authorities and abilities of the employee.[113]

The scope of the mission invention is narrower than the scope of service invention under EIA in requiring a specific mission in the employment contract. If the scope of inventive mission invention is interpreted to include only inventions that the employee and employer had an opportunity to bargain for, the transfer of ownership through employment contract negotiation, the scope of inventive mission invention corresponds to the scope of an invention under the specially hired to invent doctrine under US case law. This follows that the freedom of contract controls the ownership rules of invention with respect to inventive mission inventions. The French IPC

---

[109] French IPC Article L. 611-7 (1).

[110] An employment contract must explicitly or implicitly support the inventive mission. Paris, 7 feb. 1991, PIBD 1991, n° 503, III, p. 394; TGI Paris, 17 feb. 2010, PIBD 2010, n° 919, III, p. 334. For a collective agreement, see Cass. com., 3 june 2008, PIBD 2008, n° 879, III, p. 460; TGI Paris, 17 feb. 2010, PIBD 2010, n° 919, III, p. 334.

[111] Cass. com., 13 oct. 1992, Juris-Data n° 1992-002229. The Court of Appeal, confirmed by the Court of Cassation on this point, retained that the functions of the employee had a general inventive mission in order to improve the technical used by the employers within the framework of the activity of the company.

[112] TGI, 3ème ch., 3ème sect., 16 oct. 2001, PIBD, 2002, n° 744, III, p. 265.

[113] *Supra* note 108, Hatanaka at 34.

endorses the outcomes of bargaining between an employer and employee and allows the employer to secure the ownership as soon as an invention is completed. The French rule should be understood that the inventor ownership belongs to the inventor is a fundamental rule and giving the ownership to employers with respect to mission inventions is an exception to the rule.[114] Accordingly, only under an exceptional circumstance where the term of contract or any other evidence expressly or implicitly indicates a bargaining over the transfer of ownership with respect to the invention in question, French courts allow employers to secure the ownership of inventions made by their employees.

However, there is a difference between US and French ownership rules. French law allows an employer including legal entities, to become an original owner of the invention. US law limits the original ownership to inventors who are natural persons and subjected the inventors to a duty of transfer to the inventor's employer. Despite this theoretical difference, in practice the mission invention and the invention under the specially hired to invent doctrine function in the same way by automatically securing the ownership of such inventions for employers.

Inventor-employees hold the original ownership of any invention that fails to meet the definition of an inventive mission invention.[115] However, such invention may be subjected to a duty of transferring the ownership of invention to the employer or a duty of granting a license to the employer if the invention falls into the definition of a 'beyond mission invention' by meeting one of the following three conditions: (a) the invention results from an execution of employee functions or duty under the employment contract; (b) the invention falls into the field of the employer's business activities; or (c) the invention is made based on the knowledge or experience of the employer, or using technologies or specific means or data of the employer.[116] With respect to beyond mission inventions, French IPC adopts an ownership transfer system similar to German EIA and

---

[114] For long time, French courts vested in employers the ownership of service inventions which resulted from the duty of employees. The Patent Act of July 13, 1978 introduced the three categories of inventions and made clear that employers obtain the ownership to inventions made by their employees only when an invention falls into the categories of inventive mission invention. See Thomas Bouvet, Employee-Inventor Rights in France, at 3–4 (http://www.veron.com/publications/Colloques/Employees_inventions.pdf).

[115] French IPC Article L. 611-7; R 611-7(2).

[116] Id. French law also guarantees employers a right to claim a grant of license. German EIA also provided a similar right for employers. A recent revision eliminated the right because employers almost always exercised a right to claim ownership if they want to practice employee inventions.

provides employers a right to claim the transfer of invention ownership.[117] It imposes on employees a duty of invention report, which must include enough information to determine which category the invention falls into.[118]

In general, the scope of the 'beyond mission inventions' is broader than the 'scope of service inventions' under the German EIA in that it includes any invention that falls into the employer's business activities regardless of the employee's task or duty. To be qualified for a service invention, the German EIA requires an invention meeting either conditions (a) or (c); conditions for 'beyond mission inventions' fall under the French IPC.[119] Inventions which meet only the condition of (b), within the scope of employer's business activities, falls into the category of free inventions under the German EIA.[120] German employers have only a right of first refusal for at least a grant of a non-exclusive license with respect to the free inventions under the German EIA.[121]

The scope of 'beyond mission inventions' is also broader than the scope of inventions under the US case law of the 'hired to invent' doctrine, which gives rise to a 'shop right.' US courts look to the totality of circumstance in determining whether an employer obtains a shop right.[122] Therefore, the scope of inventions giving rise to a shop right is uncertain. They rely on one or more of the three underlying principles for justifying a shop right: (1) implied license, (2) estoppels, and (3) equity and fairness.[123] If an employee conceived and reduced the invention to practice at home and on his own time without using any facilities of his employer, none of the principles support a shop right even if an invention falls into the employer's business. [124]

Despite the broad scope of mission inventions, employers' rights under the French IPC are not better than employers' rights under US case law because the French IPC only provides employers a right of claim to transfer ownership. Like German employers, French employers have no shop right if they fail to exercise their rights. Once the prescribed period

---

117 French IPC Article L. 611-7; R 611-1.

118 French IPC Article L. 611-7; R 611-9.

119 German EIA §4(2).

120 German EIA §4(3).

121 German EIA §19.

122 *McElmurry v. Arkansas Power & Light Co.*, 995 F.2d 1576, 27 U.S.P.Q.2d (BNA) 1129 (1993).

123 Supra note 19, Chisum, §20.03[3].

124 This scope is comparable to the scope in which U.S. state special legislations allow enforcement of pre-invention assignment contract between an employee and employer. See, *Infra* note 54.

for claiming ownership expires, a beyond mission invention becomes a free invention. French employers would then need a license from their inventor-employees if the employees obtain a patent and the employers want to use the invention.

An invention which fails to meet neither definition of an 'inventive mission invention' nor a 'beyond mission invention' is a 'free invention'. The employer of the inventor has no right or claim on the ownership of free inventions and thus the inventor is free to transfer the right to any party.

(iii) Employee's Rights in Employee's Inventions

French rules for compensating inventor-employees are also a hybrid of US case law and the German EIA. Like the German EIA, the French IPC limits freedom of contract and requires employers a payment of additional compensation for the ownership of invention with respect to mission inventions.[125] However, the French IPC respects the freedom of contract for setting the amount of compensation before invention through an individual employment contract, a company contract or a collective bargaining agreement.[126] Many such agreements adopt a method for calculating the compensation by simply multiplying a monthly salary with certain coefficients reflecting multiple factors including the significance of invention, the personal contribution by the inventor.[127] This is a stark contrast to the case-by-case analysis required by the German EIA, which require sharing the commercial profits resulting from the patent exclusivity.

French courts have long upheld the salary based calculation methods. However, the Court of Cassation made clear that the French IPC does not require a calculation to be based on a salary.[128] Thus, recent decisions

---

125 French IPC Article L. 611-7(1).

126 Id.

127 See, M.-F. Marais, *La jurisprudence de la CNIS*, *in* les droits de propriété intellectuelle sur les inventions et les créations des chercheurs salariés, Actes de colloque, Paris, 5 décembre 2000, Ed. Tec & Doc, p. 19. Mr. Marais was the president of the national commission of the employees inventions, noticed that the assessment of the amount of the additional remuneration was made in the most of cases by reference of the salary of the employee. It usually accounted two or three months of salary. He noticed also that the additional remuneration was usually weak and rarely exceeded 100 000 Francs (15 000 euros) between 1994 and 1999.

128 CA Paris, 19 déc. 1997, PIBD 1998, III, p. 157 confirmed by Cass. com., 21 nov. 2000, Rev. Lamy dr. aff. 2001, n° 34, n° 2133, obs. J. Haberer; JCPE 2001, p. 275, note J.-C. Galloux. See also, J.-P. Martin, La remuneration des inventions de salaries: un tournant? RDPI, 1998, n° 89, p. 9.

indicate an influence of the German EIA by adopting a case-by-case analysis for compensation calculation.[129] French courts make efforts for determining benefits resulting from the invention by taking into account multiple factors, particularly annual turnovers from the invention, profit margins, and R&D expenses spent for developing the invention.[130] The Court of Cassation endorsed such efforts in acknowledging the significance of turnover resulting from the invention in calculating the compensation for inventive mission inventions.[131]

With respect to 'beyond mission inventions,' the French IPC requires employers a payment of fair price if employers exercise their right of claim to transfer the ownership of invention or grant of license.[132] An inventor-employee and his employer must agree on the amount of the fair price. If they fail to reach an agreement, the fair price is determined by the joint conciliation board consisting of representatives of employers and employees, if one of the parties requests arbitration.[133] If a party is not satisfied with the arbitration decision or either party does not request arbitration, a court of the first instance sets the fair price. [134]

It is often very difficult to agree on the amount because parties need to foresee the degree of exploitation of the invention by the employer to determine the value of invention. Parties can take account an amount resulting from an average exploitation of invention by employers.[135] However, many inventions need further investment and development for commercialization. Thus, parties can agree to set a fair price amount via a two step process: (1) a payment of a preliminary lump sum amount, which the employer expects to be the profits resulting from the future exploitation of the invention when he exercises the right to claim the ownership of invention, and (2) adjustment of the preliminary amount at the end of a period that the parties agreed on to set the final amount by taking into account the exploitation of the invention during the period.[136]

---

129 See, TGI Paris, 3e ch., 3e sec., 24 sept. 2008, PIBD, n° 885, III, p. 651.

130 TGI Paris, 9 mars 2004, PIBD 2004, n° 787, III, p. 321. TGI Paris, 3e ch., 14 sept. 2005, PIBD 2005, n° 819, III, p. 690, TGI Paris, 24 sept. 2008, PIBD, n° 885, III, p. 651.

131 Cass. com. 18 déc. 2007, Comm. com. élect. 2008, n° 3, comm. n° 35, obs. C. Caron. Insofar as it does not exist any legal provision allowing to calculate the additional remuneration, this question is left to the sovereign appraisal of the judges of first and second instance.

132 French IPC Article L611-7, 2.

133 Id.

134 Id.

135 TGI Paris, 29 mai 2009, PIBD 2009, PIBD 2009, n° 903, III, p. 1340.

136 See for example, CA Paris, 10 mai 2002, Prop. ind. 2002, n° 8, comm. n°

The additional compensation as well as the fair price under the French IPC sounds similar to the compensation for service inventions under the German EIA. However, they are different from the German EIA because an employee can enforce his rights of compensation and fair price even before his employer starts practicing the invention. Moreover, the French IPC does not impose any duty on employers for filing domestic and foreign patent applications. This follows that French employees' rights for compensation and fair price do not depend on a patent grant. These rights are not based on the monopoly principle for sharing benefits from an exclusive right, which is a stark contrast to the right of reasonable compensation under the German EIA.

V. JAPAN: ANOTHER EXAMPLE OF A HYBRID SYSTEM

(i) Fundamental Rules

The rule that the ownership of invention belongs to the inventor is also fundamental to the Japanese Patent Act ('JPA').[137] Like the US and German systems, only a natural person can be the sole inventor or joint inventor, thus a legal entity cannot be the original owner of an invention.[138]

The JPA also provides a rule that the ownership of invention is assignable.[139] Such assignment may occur before and after filing of a patent application. However, when the ownership is assigned to an assignee before filing a patent application, the assignee cannot assert his ownership against a third-party unless he files a patent application with the Japan Patent Office (JPO).[140] Once an application is pending in the JPO, an assignment of ownership becomes effective only if the assignment is reported to the JPO.[141]

Like the German and French systems, Japanese labor and employment law may provide a special rule to limit the freedom of contract between

---

75, J. Raynard; Propr. int. 2002, n° 5, p. 73, obs. Warusfel. The judges decided in this case to set a price, half lump sum and half proportional in function of a future exploitation.

137 JPA Article 29, Para 1. Kosaku Yoshifuji and Kenichi Kumagaya, Tokkyoho Gaisetsu (Outlines of Patent Act) 185 (13 ed, 2000).

138 Judgment of Tokyo Dist. Ct. March 16, 1955, 6 Kakyu Minshu 479.

139 JPA Article 33, Para. 1.

140 JPA Article 34, Para. 1.

141 JPA Article 34, Para. 4.

employers and employees. Since Japanese law also adopts a rule similar to other jurisdictions, the fruits of employees' labor belong to employers,[142] a provision for ownership rules is necessary for removing a conflict between the labor and employment law and patent law with respect to inventions made by employees.

(ii) Employers' Rights in Employee Inventions

In Japan such rules regarding employee invention ownership are provided as part of the JPA.[143] Utility Model Act and Design Act cite these rules and apply to the ownership of devices (petite inventions) and designs.[144] The ownership rules for inventions made by an employee under the JPA are another form of hybrid between US and German systems. The Japanese rules are much more in line with US case law than with the German EIA, because they are based on the freedom of contract and the transfer of ownership between employees and employers exclusively relies on an express assignment contract. The rule that employment alone is not sufficient to transfer the ownership of employee invention to the employer but may give rise to a royalty free nonexclusive license is common to the JPA and US case law.[145] The JPA adopts an aspect of the German EIA for limiting the freedom of contract in guaranteeing reasonable compensation for inventor-employees.[146] The JPA further limits the freedom of contract by preventing employers from executing a pre-invention assignment contract with respect to free inventions.[147]

Like the German EIA, the JPA classifies employee inventions into two categories: (1) *Shokumu* (service or duty) invention, and (2) free invention. An invention by an employee is a service invention if the invention (a) falls into the field of employer's business activities, AND (b) resulted from an act which is included in the employee's duty.[148] Any invention, which fails to meet both or either conditions, falls into the category of free invention.

Without an express assignment contract, the JPA does not provide an employer any right in the ownership of invention made by an employee except for a shop right, a royalty free non-exclusive license.[149] In contrast,

---

142 Takashi Araki, Labor Law, 243 (2009).
143 JPA Article 35.
144 Japanese Utility Model Act, Article 11, Japanese Design Act, Article 15.
145 JPA Article 35, Para. 1.
146 JPA Article 35, Para. 3.
147 JPA Article 35, Para. 2.
148 JPA Article 35, Para. 1.
149 JPA Article 35, Para. 1.

the JPA expressly prevents employers from executing a pre-invention assignment with their employees with respect to free inventions.[150] In other words, Japanese employers are prevented from securing the ownership of inventions made by their employee as soon as the inventions are complete, unless the invention falls into the category of service invention. This restriction on pre-invention assignment does not apply to a contract between an inventor and a party who has no employment contract with the inventor because an unbalanced bargaining power between inventors and their employees justifies an exception to the freedom of contract for protecting inventors.

Japanese scholars interpret the employee invention ownership rules to put emphasis on a rule that employers have no right except for shop rights unless there is an express assignment contract with their employees.[151] Due to this strong policy for protecting inventor's interests and incentive to invent, Japanese courts are very reluctant to find an implied contract and impose a duty on the inventor to transfer the ownership.[152] There is no established case law comparable to the specially hired to invent doctrine under US case law, which gives rise to an implied assignment contract. Courts may find an implied assignment contract without an express agreement only when an estoppel doctrine prevents an employee from asserting their ownership for failing to object to his employer's filing multiple applications on his inventions over a reasonable period, which gives rise to acquiescence of the employer's ownership of the employee's inventions.[153]

Moreover, the scope of service invention under the JPA is much narrower than the scope of service inventions under the German EIA or the scope of 'beyond mission inventions' under the French IPC. Both the German EIA and French IPC guarantee employers a right to claim the ownership of invention, if an employee made an invention using tangible and intangible assets of the employer.[154] The scope of inventions giving rise to a right to claim ownership under the French IPC is broader

---

[150] JPA Article 35, Para. 2.

[151] Tatsuki Shibuya, 1 Chiteki Zaisanho Kogi (Intellectual Property Law Lectures) 131 (2d, 2006); Nobuhiro Nakayama, 1 Chukai Tokkyo Ho (Detailed Explanation of Patent Law) 352 (3d, 2000).

[152] *Supra* note 151, Nakayama at 352. A leading Japanese scholar criticizes a case in which Tokyo District Court found an implied contract to assign the ownership of an invention made by an employee. The employee filed a patent application in contrary to his employer's decision to keep the invention as a trade secret. Judgment of Tokyo Dist. Ct., July 14, 1959 10 Rodo Kankei Minji Saiban Reishu 645.

[153] Judgment of Tokyo Dist. Ct. Sept. 19, 2002; Hanrei Jiho No. 1802, 30.

[154] German EIA §4(2); French IPC Article L-117 (2).

than that of the German EIA by allowing employers claiming ownership of employee invention as long as the invention falls within the field of employers' business activities. In contrast, the JPA provides no basis for Japanese employers from preventing their employees from executing a pre-invention assignment contract and assigning the ownership of invention even if their employees used their assets to develop the invention as long as the invention does not relate to the employees' tasks.[155] The German EIA guarantees a right of first refusal for at least a grant of a non-exclusive license with respect to inventions related to the employer's business activities even if the inventions fall into the category of free invention as long as the inventor is employed by the employer.[156]

Japanese employers have more protection in service inventions than German and French employers only with respect to a shop right. US employers are also protected by a shop right. Unfortunately, the scope of service invention under the JPA is narrower than the scope of inventions under the hired to invent in general doctrine, which gives rise to a shop right. Japanese employers are not entitled to any right for license or a right of first refusal with respect to inventions made by their employees unless the invention relates to the employees' tasks. In short, the JPA provides employers the least protection among the four jurisdictions.

(iii) Employee's Rights in Employee's Inventions

The JPA is in line with the German EIA in limiting the freedom of contract for guaranteeing a right of compensation for inventors. Once the ownership of invention is transferred or an exclusive license is granted to employers, employees are entitled to rights of a *taika* (fair price) for the transfer or a grant of an exclusive license.[157] Like the French IPC, employers can adopt a method of calculating this fair price through an individual contract or collective bargaining contract.[158] However, the JPA makes clear that the process of adopting a calculation method must be fair and

---

155 *Supra* note 153, Judgment of Tokyo Dist. Ct. Sept. 19, 2002. Tokyo District Court interpreted the scope of employee's duty broadly and found that an invention falls into the category of service invention when an employee who worked in his employer's R&D department and made the invention in violating his employer's order with respect to his assignment of duty as long as the employee completed the invention by using the employer's facilities and assistance provided by other employees. However, if an employee is not hired to invent at all, it is unlikely that the court found that the invention resulted from the employee's duty.

156 German EIA §19(1).

157 JPA Article 35, Para. 3.

158 JPA Article 35, Para 4.

reasonable and gives courts power to examine the process by taking into account, a) the appropriateness of negotiation between employers and employees for adopting the calculation method, b) the degree of disclosure to employees with respect to factors to be used in the calculation, and c) feedback from employees to support the calculation method.[159] If a court finds the payment according to the calculation method unreasonable, it can set a fair price on a case-by-case basis by taking account of profits that the employer expects to receive, expenses and contribution that the employer has made, the employee's employment condition and other factors.[160] Courts can also set a fair price if there is no agreement for the fair price between employers and employees.[161]

Since the rule giving employers power to negotiate with their employees for adopting a method to calculate a fair price is introduced in a recent revision, Japanese courts have not found any calculation method unreasonable.[162] It is not clear from the text of the JPA whether courts can find a fair price resulting from a calculation method unreasonable even if it finds the process for adopting the method is reasonable and fair. Legal commentators support a view that courts can find the price unreasonable regardless of a reasonable process.[163] This view is contrary to the Japanese industry's view that courts should uphold the fair price paid by an employer as long as the process adopting the method resulting in the fair price is reasonable.[164]

Due to the fact that the JPA does not impose on employers duties of domestic and foreign patent applications, the fair price is distinguished from the compensation under the German EIA because it is not based on the monopoly principle to share profits resulting from an exclusive right. Instead, the fair price under the JPA is comparable to the fair price for 'beyond mission inventions' under the French IPC, and thus should be decided at the time of transfer of the ownership by foreseeing the value of invention. If an invention provides turnovers and profits that an ordinary employer or employee would not have been able to expect, courts should

---

159 *Id.*

160 JPA Article 35, Para. 5.

161 Id.

162 This new rule was introduced in 2004. The new rules under the 2004 Revision apply to a transfer of employee invention ownership which is executed on and after April 1, 2005.

163 Japanese scholars support that an employee can request adjustment if his invention brings unexpected profits.

164 Project Team on Employee Invention System, Analysis of Cases on Employee Invention Disputes, 59 Chizai Kanri 701 (2009) [' Analysis of Cases on Employee Invention Disputes'].

not grant a request of additional adjustment for employees. In short, courts should uphold the amount of fair price resulting from the calculation method which is adopted by a fair process through: a) negotiations with employees; b) disclosures of a calculation method adopted through the negations; and c) feedbacks from employees to support the calculation method as long as the amount resulting from the calculation reflects the fair value of invention at the time of ownership transfer.

VI. ANALYSIS: THE BEST PRACTICE

(i) Fair Bargaining v. Mandatory Compensation

The four jurisdictions adopt different approaches in transfer of ownership and compensation for the transfer. The German system is clearly distinguished from the US system because it assumes a lack of equal bargaining power between employers and their employees. A serious flaw of the German approach is ignoring today's research and development environment and employment arrangements in Germany. Unlike employees who were strongly controlled by labor unions at the time the German EIA was enacted, some German employees negotiate their employment contracts freely and move from one employer to another if they are unhappy with their employment conditions.[165] Although the size of the group which moves to improve their employment class may vary, one jurisdiction to another, depending on the welfare structure, employment protection legislation and the transfer-oriented labor market policies and the high degree of occupational specificity of the schooling system in each jurisdiction,[166] employees who made inventions that have significant value to employers have enough bargaining power to negotiate for their employment conditions and compensation. Applying the same compensation rule for these employees and other employees is unfair for not only employers but also employees who do not have bargaining power, and thus did not negotiate an employment contract. Although the practice under the German EIA takes into account the status of employees, and thus the salary and

---

[165] A report indicates that approximately 50 percent of German employees changed their employers and secured a new job which requires more or different skills than the previous job, assuming that the higher skills requirement are reflected in higher pay and extended responsibilities. Danish Technical Institute, Job Mobility in the European Union: Optimising its Social and Economic Benefits – Final Report, 35 (http://ec.europa.eu/social/images/icons/lang/en.gif).

[166] *Id*, at 75.

benefits paid through the employment contract,[167] it is unfair and a waste of time for German employers because the German EIA requires a case-by-case analysis to compensate each employee for each invention regardless of an employee's salary, which already included compensation for the entire project.[168]

The US system, assuming equal bargaining power between employers and employees, also has a serious flaw because many employees do not have equal bargaining power with their employers, particularly those who are fresh from their schools and immediately begin working for their employers. Despite obvious disparity in bargaining power, US courts modify or rescind a pre-invention assignment contract only in the most egregious situations where the employers' bad faith is obvious.[169] However, many US employers provide intra-firm reward plans including promotions and privileges to bonus' employees who provide great value to the employers.[170] If employees are unhappy with the plans, employees with a good record of performance have ample opportunities to move to another employer with a better plan or start their own business by taking a high risk in R&D.[171] In short, the US system encourages innovations through a high mobility of bright employees[172] by letting employers compete with each other through a variety of reward options for such employees instead of government operated compensation.[173] The system does not protect employees who prefer to take a relatively low risk reward for their inventions from their current employers instead of high risk rewards from new employers or their own entrepreneurship.

This great social mobility is considered unique to the United States.[174]

---

167 *Supra* note 7, Trimborn at 53.

168 *Supra* note 5, Heath at 21. A study indicates German employers spend twice as much administrating employee inventions than the economic gain resulting from these inventions.

169 Robert Merges, *The Law and Economics of Employee Inventions,* 13 Harv. J. Law & Tec 1(1999).

170 *Id.*,at 38.

171 *Id.*,at 30.

172 David Cooper, Innovation and Reciprocal externalities: Information Transmission via Job Mobility, 45 Journal of Economic Behavior & Organization 403 (2001).

173 *Supra* note 169, Merges at 37.

174 Joseph Ferrie, History Lessons: The End of American Exceptionalism? Mobility in the United States since 1850, 19 Journal of Economic Perspectives, 199 (2005). U.S. has a high mobility country with large share of workers in short-term jobs, and small share in long-term jobs. Hiroshi Ono, *Life Time Employment in Japan, Concept and Measurement,* SSE/EFI Working Paper Series in Economics

Thus, the US system may not work in other jurisdictions, particularly those with low job mobility and limited opportunities to voluntarily job transition to a better position.[175] For such a jurisdiction, the French system works more effectively than the German and US systems because it reflects today's employment arrangement in distinguishing some employees who have bargaining power from others. The former group can engage a fair negotiation based on equal bargaining power when their employers hired them to engage a specific project or assign them to engage a special project. Inventions resulting from these projects give rise to inventive mission inventions. In such a circumstance, salary and other benefits reflect a compensation for the entire project including inventions resulting from the project. Therefore, the compensation for inventive mission inventions under the French IPC should be viewed comparable to employee reward plans provided by US employers instead of a compensation for the ownership of mission inventions. Recent French IPC revision limits employers' freedom to select reward options by making an additional compensation mandate.[176] Recent case law emphasizes efforts to share value of inventions between employers and employees for calculation of compensation.[177] Instead, the best practice should encourage job mobility of bright employees who have bargaining power by letting their employers, who are familiar with the industry, the technology and employees, choose the best reward option and compete to attract them.[178]

With respect to those who do not have a bargaining power and are hired to engage research and development in general, the French system protects their interests and preserves their incentive to invent by guaranteeing a right of compensation for the fair value of invention. The French system also protects employers from a risk of unexpected additional payment for compensation, and thus encourages investment for commercialization by requiring determination of the compensation amount at the time of own-

---

and Finance No 624, 24 (2007) (http://swopec.hhs.se/hastef/papers/hastef0624.pdf)

[175] *Supra* note 165, EU Job Mobility Report, at 118. Germany is listed as one of out of balance job mobility countries where voluntary job transitions are scarce compared to the Anglo-Saxons, the Scandinavians and the Baltic countries and Slovak Republic.

[176] French IPC was revised in 1990 to make the payment of compensation for mission inventions mandatory. Thus, an agreement is not enforceable if a compensation for mission invention depends on exploitation of such invention. TGI Paris, 3e ch., 1re sect., 15 déc. 2009; CA Paris, 8 déc. 2010, Juris-Data n° 2010-027274.

[177] *Supra* notes 128-131.

[178] *Supra* note 169, Merges at 44.

ership transfer.[179] Moreover, in the age of the patent thicket, a calculation of such compensation must be simple to minimize transactional costs to employers. The French system allows a lump-sum payment based on the expected annual turnovers and profits. In contrast, the transaction cost of the German system is tremendous because it requires a case-by-case analysis and annual payment based on turnover and profits for compensating service inventions.[180] A survey indicates that many German employers face serious challenges to provide the compensation under the German EIA.[181] Therefore, in practice many German employers adopt lump-sum payments for compensation, although such payments may be in conflict with the German EIA.[182]

In contrast to US, German and French systems, which are explained in the context of bargaining, the Japanese system is very confusing if it relies on a fair bargaining between employers and employee. The US influence is clear from its requirement of express assignment contract for the transfer of ownership and a grant of shop right to employers. The new rule for encouraging negotiation and adopting a calculation method supports that the system presupposes a bargaining between employers and employees. However, the JPA also makes clear the strong policy of inventor protection in restricting pre-invention assignment contracts with respect to free inventions. Japanese courts interpreted the ownership rules under the Pre-2004 Revision JPA more in line with the German EIA than the US system in awarding the amount of fair price to share the profit resulting from the exclusivity of the patent.[183] This interpretation subjects Japanese employers who have already paid compensation to a risk of litigation for additional payment from their employees, which led to the adoption of new rules under the 2004 Revision based on a fair bargaining between employers and employees.[184] Despite the new rules, Japanese courts are keenly

---

[179] *Supra* notes 136–6.

[180] *Supra* note 169, Merges at 43. Christopher Leptien, *Incentives for Employed Inventors: An Empirical Analysis with Special Emphasis on the German Law for Employees' Inventions*, 25 R&D MGMT. 213, 214–15 (1995).

[181] *Supra* note 180, Leptien at 213

[182] Erich R. Franke and Lothar Steiling, *Novellierung des ArbEG – Kein Ende in Sischt Die Industrie reagiert mit Inventive-Systemen* (Revision of German EIA – No End of the Industry Reacts with Inventive System), Einsele and Franke ed, VPP 50th Anniversary Festschrift 281 (2005).

[183] See, e.g., Judgment of Tokyo District Court, June 8, 2008. For a general discussion of Japanese courts' calculation of fair price, see supra note 164, Analysis of Cases on Employee Invention Disputes, at 707.

[184] Yukiyoshi Takayama, Employee Invention System, Tokugikon No. 238, 23 (2005).

aware of a lack of employee bargaining power due to low job mobility in the Japanese industry[185] and may not change the practice based on the German monopoly principle. Such a clear conflict between the rules in the JPA based on fair bargaining and the reality of Japanese society, which lacks fair bargaining, may introduce a lot of uncertainty with respect to what extent courts give value to the agreement for calculating a fair price.

(ii) Ownership Transfer Mechanism

Among the four jurisdictions, the German and French systems adopt a mechanism for employers to secure the ownership of employee invention through a right of claim to transfer the ownership with respect to service inventions and beyond mission inventions. Such mechanisms effectively prevent holdup problems in employer–employee transactions.[186] Employers should secure ownership of inventions made by their employees through such mechanisms as long as the invention falls within the scope of the employers' business activities, which effectively promotes innovation by taking advantage of employers' facilities that are very likely complementary to such inventions.[187] It is useful to resolve the ownership dispute early and well address the challenge for managing intellectual property in today's research and development environment where researchers and innovations inter-flow beyond the boundaries of firms.[188] Interaction of researchers from multiple-firms and the high mobility of such researchers enhance information diffusions and inter-firm relation among firms in regions where research universities and their spin-offs concentrate, such as Silicon Valley.[189]

In such a region, a variety of arrangements are made between researchers and firms where the researchers engage R&D. Many such arrange-

---

[185] Japan has the lowest job mobility among the OECD states. *Supra* note 174, Hiroshi Ono at 24.

[186] *Supra* note 169, Merges at 12.

[187] *Supra* note 169, Merges at 16. A shop right, a non-exclusive license also prevents holdups in employer-employee transactions. Therefore, it makes sense that German EIA provides employers a right of refusal for free inventions which fall within the scope of employers' business activities.

[188] Reder, Margo E.K., *Board of Trustees v. Roche Molecular Systems Inc.: Negotiating the Web of Competing Ownership Claims to Inventions Arising from Government-Funded Academic-Industry Collaboration* (November 2, 2010). Business Law Review, Vol. 44, at 16, 2011. Available at SSRN: http://ssrn.com/abstract=1701706e

[189] Walter W. Powell, Trust-Based Forms of Governance, in Trust Organization: Frontiers of Theory and Research, 51.

ments are informal and may not fall into the traditional notion of employment. Relying on a private contract for transfer of ownership will subject employers to a risk of falling into a technical contract drafting trap. This is particularly true in the case of SMEs and non-profit organizations such as universities because of their limited resources to hire legal professionals.[190] Since researchers may execute inconsistent assignment contracts without bad faith, sophisticated legal professional teams at large firms may face due diligence problems.[191]

The mechanism under the German EIA can effectively protect employers' rights in ownership with respect to an invention made by an inventor under a contract, which falls into a traditional notion of employment. An obligation is imposed on employees to report their inventions to employers by operation of law. An expiration of a prescribed period after the reception of report automatically transfers the ownership to his employer. The French system uses a pre-2009 revision German EIA mechanism and requires an employer to exercise his right for transfer of ownership. It may not fully protect employers who are unfamiliar with the mechanism. German employers, particularly SMEs, failed to secure ownership by failing to exercise their rights within the prescribed period, which led to the current system that adopts a presumption of exercising a right to claim transfer of ownership unless the employer notifies his employee to release the service invention within the prescribed period.

However, even the current system may not fully address the challenge in intellectual property management in today's R&D environment. It is possible to expand the notion of employment to include innovative and informal relationships between inventors and firms. Expansion of the notion of employment may result in multiple employment relationships with different firms for the same inventor. Setting up an ownership transfer mechanism will at least help inventors and firms who associate with the inventors in determining at an early stage to which firm the ownership is entitled.

(iii) Shop Right

Only US and Japanese employers are entitled to a shop right. This is because employers need a shop right for protection as a defense against an infringement claim of a patent issued to their employees or assignors

---

190 Even a university as sophisticated as Stanford fell into a trap. *Stanford*, 180 L.Ed. 2d 1.

191 Supra note 188, Reder at 16.

in case they failed to secure ownership of the employee invention through an express assignment contract. It is not necessary for the German and French systems to give a shop right to employers because employers were given an opportunity to secure the ownership through a right of claiming ownership transfer. German experience indicates that employers want a full ownership or at least exclusive license if they are interested in inventions. Thus, German employers seldom selected an option for claiming limited right such as non-exclusive license. Thus, a recent revision eliminated the option. The French IPC still offers an option to claim a limited right, such as a non-exclusive license. Unlike a shop right under US and Japanese Systems, French employers may pay a royalty if they select the option and secure a grant of non-exclusive license.

It is likely that US and Japanese employers may not need a shop right once they can secure ownership through a right to claim the ownership by adopting an ownership transfer mechanism. They should be estopped from asserting a shop right once they indicated their disinterest in practicing an invention and releasing service inventions. Otherwise, employees are not able to find a party who is willing to commercialize their inventions.

In contrast, firms who are associated with the inventor by providing knowledge and/or facilities etc., but were not qualified for the entitlement of ownership should receive a shop right. As discussed above, multiple firms may contribute in different ways for inventions. Through an ownership transfer mechanism, these firms may negotiate an ownership arrangement such as sharing the ownership among them or choosing one firm for the ownership while granting exclusive licenses to other firms. A shop right not only protects these law firms but also encourages them to reach an agreement for the ownership.[192]

(iv) Employers' Rights on Inventions in Scope of Employers' Business Activities

A review of four jurisdictions revealed that systems, other than the Japanese system, guarantee employers an access to use an invention made by employees if the invention falls into the scope of the employer's business. The US system allows such access through a pre-invention assignment contract, the German system provides a right of refusal for a license

---

[192] As a split entitlement in the form of the shop right also prevents holdups in employer–employee transactions for inventions related to employer's business, it will also address holdups in transactions among different firms who contributed to the invention made by an employee. *Supra* note 169, Merges at 18.

and the French system provides a right to claim transfer of ownership. It is unlikely that an employee can transfer ownership of his invention to a third-party for commercialization or start his own business by securing a patent on his own without violating a company rule. Such transfer or business creates a conflict of interest with his employer if the invention is within the scope of employer's business. Giving employers the opportunity to take the ownership or license makes sense because it effectively prevents the possible conflict of interest.

In contrast, the Japanese system expressly prevents employers from executing a pre-invention assignment contract with an employee with respect to an invention within the scope of business activities unless the invention results from the employee's current and past duties through pre-invention assignment contract, and thus falls into the category of service invention. Although this restriction aims to protect employees, the JPA encourages possible conflict of interests by allowing a pre-invention assignment contract with a party other than employers. This restriction does not apply to an assignment from an employee to his employer after completion of invention. It may be too late for an employer to secure the ownership if its employee transfers the ownership to a competitor through a pre-invention assignment contract or starts his own business based on the invention. To encourage commercialization of inventions by employers, the JPA should guarantee employers a right of refusal or at least a grant of a non-exclusive license.

VII. CONCLUSION

A review of ownership rules for inventions made by employees under the US, German, French and Japanese systems revealed that the French system adopts the best practice in maintaining a fine balance between the interests of employers and employees by preserving an employees' incentive to invent while minimizing employers' transactional cost for intellectual property management. The French system also properly reflects the reality of today's R&D environment, where employees with different bargaining powers work for employers under a variety of employment arrangements. The US system is based on an employees' bargaining power supported by job mobility. It works well in the US but may not work well in other jurisdictions where job mobility is limited. It may be improved by adopting an ownership transfer system from the German and French systems for early resolution of ownership disputes resulting from interflow and collaboration of researchers from multiple firms. Through the scope of inventions the Japanese system allows employers secure ownership is much more limited than any scope of inventions employers in other jurisdictions can secure. Japanese courts have interpreted the ownership rule under the JPA with an emphasis of employees' rights. A recent revision introduced a new rule based on a fair bargaining position between employers and employees. Because the bargaining power and job mobility of employees in Japan are much less than those in the US, it is unclear how Japanese courts will interpret the new rules. Therefore, a further revision may be necessary to clarify if the JPA relies on fair bargaining between employers and employees.

Interflow and collaboration of researchers expand beyond boarders. Conflicting employee invention ownership rules present a serious challenge in managing intellectual sproperty to multinational firms and public research institutions. To try to cope with this challenge, legal professionals use a choice of law provisions in employment contracts. Courts may not enforce the choice of law provisions because of the public nature of the intellectual property. Only a global harmonization of ownership rules can effectively address the challenge of intellectual property management.

17. Exhaustion of intellectual property rights in the European Union

Theo Bodewig[1]

I. THE PRINCIPLE OF EXHAUSTION AS DEVELOPED BY THE EUROPEAN COURT OF JUSTICE

The exhaustion of IP Rights under the Law of the European Union (EU) is a well-established doctrine. It was developed by the European Court of Justice (ECJ) as a compromise between the principle of the freedom of movement of goods in the whole territory of the EU on the one hand and the necessity of effective protection of intellectual property rights under the laws of the member states and the EU itself on the other.

One of the main tasks of the EU is to create an internal market between its member states.[2] The idea is that goods, services, persons and capital can move freely from one member state to another. This idea is codified in the four basic freedoms of the Treaty on the Functioning of the European Union (TFEU): The freedom of movement of goods,[3] services,[4] persons (legal and natural)[5] and capital.[6] The exhaustion doctrine is chiefly concerned with the freedom of movement of goods (though there can be some overlap with the freedom of services).

The conflict between the freedom of movement of goods under EU law and the national laws for the protection of intellectual property rights

---

1 University Professor, Dr. jur., Humboldt University Berlin.

2 *See* TEU art. 3(3) ('The Union shall establish an internal market. It shall work for the sustainable development of Europe based on balanced economic growth and price stability, a highly competitive social market economy, aiming at full employment and social progress and a high level of protection and improvement of the quality of the environment. It shall promote scientific and technological advance.').

3 TFEU art. 28.

4 TFEU art. 56.

5 TFEU art. 45.

6 TFEU art. 63.

like patents, copyrights, designs, trademarks, etc. is grounded in the territoriality principle of IP laws. Since national IP protection only has effect in the respective territory, national laws traditionally protect national rights holders by granting exclusive rights including an importation right. This means that the holder of a national IP right can block unconsented importation of goods incorporating his right no matter if these are goods produced in the other country by an infringer or if they are genuine goods produced by the rights holder himself or with his consent. He is protected against importation of infringing imports as well as against parallel imports.

Since in modern economies many products are protected by patents, copyrights and design rights and practically all products are protected by trademarks, it is immediately obvious that national importation rights at the will of the rights holder could re-erect the national borders that the principle of freedom of movement of goods tries to eliminate.

This conflict has not gone unnoticed by the drafters of the TFEU. While Art. 34 TFEU places quantitative restrictions on imports and all 'measures having equivalent effect' are forbidden, Art. 36 TFEU gives the member states the right to deviate from this principle and via national law to restrict the freedom of movement of goods for the protection of 'industrial and commercial property'.[7] Furthermore Art. 345 states that the TFEU will not interfere with the national property rights systems.[8] IP rights are considered to be industrial and commercial property as well as part of the national property rights system. Taking this language literally could lead to the impression that the national importation right (as well as the other exclusive rights granted under national IP laws) will be covered by the exemption in Art. 36 and guaranteed under Art. 345. As explained above, such interpretation would, however, make the freedom of movement of goods a hollow promise.

The ECJ, therefore, has tried to find a compromise which secures to the freedom of movement of goods a meaningful field of application while at

[7] TFEU art. 36 ('The provisions of Articles 34 and 35 shall not preclude prohibitions or restrictions on imports, exports or goods in transit justified on grounds of public morality, public policy or public security; the protection of health and life of humans, animals or plants; the protection of national treasures possessing artistic, historic or archaeological value; or the protection of industrial and commercial property. Such prohibitions or restrictions shall not, however, constitute a means of arbitrary discrimination or a disguised restriction on trade between Member States.').

[8] TFEU art. 345 ('This Treaty shall in no way prejudice the rules in Member States governing the system of property ownership.').

the same time does not sacrifice effective protection of IP rights. This compromise is the exhaustion doctrine as developed and applied by the ECJ.[9]

Analyzing the respective provisions of the TFEU, the Court found that the national exclusive importation rights are 'measures having equivalent effect[10]' to quantitative restrictions. According to Art. 34 TFEU, they interfere with the freedom of movement of goods. Therefore, they can only be justified if they fall under the exemption of Art. 36 TFEU as necessary for effective protection of IP rights. The court denies undifferentiated justification for national importation rights. It states that the exclusive importation right against parallel imports from EU member states of genuine goods does not belong to the core, the essence, the specific subject matter of IP rights. For the same reason, this denial is not a forbidden interference with national property rights systems under Art. 345 TFEU.[11] The specific subject matter certainly covers the possibility to enforce the IP rights against infringers. It is a misuse of these rights, however, to try to block the freedom of movement of goods legally marketed in one member state by using the IP rights against the importation of such genuine goods. Therefore, the rules of the TFEU can be invoked to protect the principle of the freedom of movement of goods against the enforcement of national importation rights in such limited cases.

Applying this interpretation of the Treaty, the Court found that the first sale of the protected product by the rights holder or with his consent, not only exhausted his IP right in this member state but also his parallel IP

---

[9] The Court did not invent the exhaustion doctrine (or the first sale doctrine, as the principle is known in the US). The exhaustion doctrine is a standard part of the national laws of most countries including the member states of the EU in the form of national exhaustion. Accordingly the rights holder cannot control further the distribution of his goods in the national territory once he has put them into commerce there. In a way this is to secure freedom of movement of goods on the national level. It is, therefore, not surprising that the ECJ transferred this well known and accepted principle of national law to the EU level to safeguard EU-wide freedom of movement of goods.

[10] TFEU art. 34.

[11] The ECJ first distinguished between the existence of an IP right which the Treaty could not interfere with and its exercise which the Treaty rules could be applied against, *see, e.g.,* Case 119/75, Terrapin Ltd. v. Terranova Industrie CA Kapferer & Co.,1976 E.C.R. 1039, 1061. This distinction is peculiar since the essence of an IP right is the right to exclude. Restricting the right to exclude (regulating its exercise), therefore, at the same time interferes with the content of the right, its existence. The court later changed its language that the Treaty does not interfere with the specific subject, the essence of IP rights. Therefore, the specific subject matter of each kind of IP rights like patents, trademarks, copyrights, design etc. has to be clarified.

rights in all other member states. Consequently the Court established the following general rule for European exhaustion of IP rights: The holder of a national or EU IP right may not invoke a national importation right against imports of goods into the country of protection, if the goods have been put into commerce in another member state of the European Economic Area by the rights holder himself or with his consent.[12]

To understand the extent of this doctrine and the range of interference with the national rights, it is instructive to explore the imports a rights holder can still block:

- He can block the imports of goods which have been put into commerce outside the EEA[13] (e.g. in the US, Japan or Mexico) even if they are genuine goods marketed by the rights holder himself or his licensee.
- He can block the imports of goods which have not been put into commerce yet. For example, these are goods the rights holder was still warehousing or which have been distributed only to an affiliate company.
- He can block the imports of goods which have not been put into commerce by the rights holder or with his consent (regularly by a licensee). This includes all infringing goods produced and sold into commerce by third parties. It may also include products by the licensee which are produced and marketed in violation of the contract or are put into commerce under a compulsory license.

In other words, the IP right is not exhausted as such. The rights holder also has not completely lost his importation right. However, the rights holder may not control the redistribution of such objects which he himself or someone else with his consent has put into commerce in the EEA.

---

[12] This principle has in the meantime been codified in several EU regulations and directives, *see, e.g.*, Community Trademark Regulation 40/94 art. 13, First Trademark Harmonization Directive 89/104 EEC art. 7, Community Design Regulation 06/2002 art. 21, Design Directive 98/71/EC art. 15. It has also been incorporated in many national IP laws of the member states. Even if it is not implemented expressly it nevertheless will be applied on the national level due to the superiority of EU law.

[13] The European Economic Area was created by a treaty between the EU and the member states of the European Free Trade Association (EFTA) Iceland, Norway and Liechtenstein (Switzerland in a referendum voted against joining the EEA). According to this treaty most rules of the EU including the exhaustion doctrine also apply to these three countries.

(i) The Exhaustion Principle as Applied to Different IP Rights

The application of the exhaustion doctrine to the main kinds of IP rights by the ECJ will be illustrated by selected cases in the following sections.

1. Exhaustion of Patent Rights in Europe

The classic case and basic setting of facts relate to patented pharmaceuticals marketed by the rights holder at lower prices in the UK than in other EU member states.[14] A wholesale company bought those pharmaceuticals and wanted to sell them in the Netherlands where prices were considerably higher. Based on the patent law of the Netherlands, the rights holder wanted to block these imports. The ECJ found the rights exhausted and allowed importation. The reason for the price differences (maximum price regulation in the country of export, differences in buying power, different tax rates, etc.) are not taken into account by the Court.

In a slightly different setting of facts, the pharmaceuticals had been marketed in the UK by the holder of a statutory license.[15] Here the Court let the patent owner block the imports into another member state with the argument that the rights owner did not consent to the first entry into commerce.

In still another case, a German pharmaceutical company and holder of a German patent had sold its products in Italy.[16] The prices in Italy were lower than in Germany because Italy, at that time, did not allow patent protection for pharmaceuticals. The ECJ was unimpressed. Since the products were put on the Italian market by the rights holder, re-importation into Germany could not be stopped. It should, however, be mentioned that the pharmaceuticals produced and marketed in Italy by third companies could be blocked from entering the German market.

Finally, an Italian company wanted to import portable toilets into the UK. A British company held a patent on the toilets and wanted to stop the imports. This seems to be the classic situation. The Italian company argued, however, that not only did the British company have a patent only in the UK, the invention could not have received patent protection anywhere else in the EU. The reason was that according to then UK law (now changed) prior art older than 50 years could not destroy novelty while in all other member states it could. The court ruled that absent harmonizing EU rules each member state could decide for which inventions patent

---

14 Case 15/74, Centragfarm BV v. Sterlin Drug Inc., 1974 E.C.R. 1147.

15 Case 19/84, Pharmon BV v. Hoechst AG, 1985 E.C.R. 2281.

16 Case 187/80, Merck & Co. Inc. v. Stephar BV, 1981 E.C.R. 2963.

protection should be available.[17] Therefore, the normal rules of exhaustion should apply.[18]

II. EXHAUSTION OF TRADEMARK RIGHTS IN EUROPE

In the same manner as patent owners, the owners of trademarks tried to block the re-importation or parallel importation of genuine goods. The ECJ applied the same rules developed for patent rights. Goods bearing the rights holders trademark can move freely in the EEA, if put on the market in one of the member states by him or with his consent.[19]

(i) Worldwide or European-wide Exhaustion

Trademarks, however, pose some special problems that patents do not. The first is the question of EU-wide or worldwide exhaustion. Before the First Harmonization Directive of the EU, Germany, Austria and the Scandinavian countries applied the principle of worldwide exhaustion to trademarks. German courts had ruled that the re-importation of genuine goods from any country in the world could not infringe on the trademark owners' rights and could not deceive the public about their origin since they were original goods the owner had rightfully put his mark on. This position came into doubt when the First Harmonization Directive required all member states of the EU to introduce EU-wide exhaustion of trademarks.[20] The question was whether worldwide exhaustion could be kept since it included EU-wide exhaustion or if it had to be reduced to only EU-wide exhaustion. The ECJ decided for the latter.[21] Therefore, all member states now apply only EU-wide exhaustion of trademarks.

---

17 This follows from TFEU art. 345.

18 Case 35/87, Thetford Corp. v. Fiamma SpA, 1988 E.C.R. 3585.

19 Joint cases 15/74, 16/ 74, Centrafarm BV v. Sterling Drug Inc., 1974 E.C.R. 1147.

20 First Harmonization Directive art. 7 provides: '1. The trademark shall not entitle the proprietor to prohibit its use in relation to goods which have been put on the market in the Community under that trademark by the proprietor or with his consent. 2. Paragraph 1 shall not apply where there exist legitimate reasons for the proprietor to oppose further commercialization of the goods, especially where the condition of the goods is changed or impaired after they have been put on the market.'

21 Case C-355/96, Silhouette Int'l Schmied GmbH & Co. KG v. Hartlauer Handelsgesellschaft mbH, 1998 E.C.R. I-4799.

(ii) The Problem of Repackaging

A second problem relates to when goods are imported from a different member state where they have been marketed by the trademark owner and it is not possible or feasible to sell them in the country of importation in an unchanged condition. Packaging sizes may differ from country to country. For example, larger sizes cannot be marketed in all countries and some repackaging may be necessary. National law may require that use instructions, warnings, list of ingredients, etc. must be written in the respective official language. There are several reasons why repackaging is necessary to bring the imported products successfully to the market.

The term 'repackaging' is applied broadly by the ECJ.[22] It means the change of content or look of the original outer or inner packaging by:

- bundling together of smaller packages with or without affixing trademark;
- adding new labels (naming importer or generic name);
- including new labels or new text on inner packaging;
- exchanging package inserts;
- changing the quantity of original package;
- scratching off batch or tracking numbers.

Repackaging, however, may cause problems and interfere with legitimate interests of the trademark owner or the public. The integrity of the products could be endangered during the process; the new packaging could be shoddy and, therefore, damage the reputation of the trademark owner when the trademark of the owner is re-affixed to the new packaging. The affixation of the trademark to a product is, however, the exclusive right of the trademark owner.

It does not come as a surprise, therefore, that many cases before the ECJ circle around the problem of when, how, to what extent and under what conditions repackaging by the importer is allowed. Case by case the Court has developed several criteria which must be fulfilled and now consistently applies them.[23]

---

[22] Case C-348/04 Boehringer Ingelheim KG v. Swingward Ltd. 2007 E.C.R. I-3391 (Boehringer Ingelheim II, Grounds 28).

[23] *See, e.g.*, Case 102/77, Hoffmann-La Roche & Co. v. Centrafarm Vertriebsgesellschaft Pharmazeutischer Erzeugnisse mbH, 1978 E.C.R. 1139; joint cases C-427/93, C-429/93, C-436/93, Bristol-Myers Squibb v. Paranova A/S, 1996 E.C.R. I-3457 and more recently, Case C-143/00, Boehringer Ingelheim KG v. Swingward Ltd. 2002 E.C.R. I-3759 (Boehringer Ingelheim I).

Importation and distribution of repackaged genuine products is allowed if:

- reliance on trademark rights by the proprietor, in order to oppose the marketing of repackaged products under that trademark, would contribute to the artificial partitioning of the markets between Member States;
- the repackaging cannot affect the original condition of the product inside the packaging;
- the new packaging clearly states who repackaged the product and the name of the manufacturer;
- the presentation of the repackaged product will not damage the reputation of the trademark and of its proprietor; thus, the repackaging must not be defective, of poor quality, or untidy; and
- the importer gives notice to the trademark proprietor before the repackaged product is put on sale and, on demand, supplies him with a specimen of the repackaged product.

These conditions must be proven by the parallel importer.[24]

Regarding the proportionality principle to be observed when repackaging, the ECJ applied the principle only to the necessity of repackaging not to the style or manner. The Court held:

> The condition that the repackaging of the pharmaceutical product, either by reboxing the product and re-applying the trademark or by applying a label to the packaging containing the product, be necessary for its further commercialization in the importing Member State, as one of the conditions which, if fulfilled, prevent the proprietor under Article 7(2) of Directive 89/104, as amended by the Agreement on the European Economic Area, from opposing such commercialization, is directed solely at the fact of repackaging and not at the manner and style of the repackaging.[25]

(iii) Different Trademarks in Different Countries

Sometimes identical products are sold under different trademarks in different countries. The trademark used in the export country may be unknown in the import country. Identical marketing may consequently prove to be unsuccessful. The importer may plan to replace the trademark

---

[24] Case C-348/04, Boehringer Ingelheim KG v. Swingward Ltd., 2007 E.C.R. I-3391 (Boehringer Ingelheim II, Operative part 1).

[25] *Id., see also* Case C-276/05, Wellcome Foundation Ltd. v. Paranova Pharmazeutika Handels GmbH, 2008 E.C.R. I-10479.

from the export country with the trademark used and known in the import country. Doing this, however, interferes with the exclusive right of the owner to affix his trademark to the products he chooses.

If the trademark owner deliberately chooses different trademarks in different member states to separate the national markets, the ECJ will see this as misuse to maintain different price levels, making the free flow of goods and marketing in the import country practically impossible or extremely difficult. In such cases the invocation of the exclusive right to affix the trademark would be deemed a misuse.[26] However, the use of different trademarks is not automatically considered against EU law.

Normally in a common market, companies would try to use identical marketing methods and trademarks in the different parts of the market. There are, however, many completely legitimate reasons why such a practice may not be chosen. The different trademarks (e.g. a different spelling) may be required by the law of the import country; older conflicting marks may exist in the import country; the trademark used in the export country may be descriptive, deceptive or offensive in the language of the import country; the trademark of the export country may have negative connotations in the import country; the owner may have bought a successful and well regarded mark in the import country and lose its reputation if required to use the lesser known mark of the export country; etc.

Since affixing a different trademark to the product than the owner had chosen is the most severe interference with his rights, this can only be allowed if it is objectively necessary to market the product in the import state. The ECJ has held that the importer is not allowed to do this only for the economic reason to better penetrate the market.[27] If, however, legal

---

[26] *See* Case 3/78, Centrafarm BV v. American Home Products Corp., 1978 E.C.R. 1823 (Grounds 19–22).

[27] Case C-379/97, Pharmacia & Upjohn SA v. Paranova A/S, 1999 E.C.R. I-6927 (Grounds 43: 'It follows that it is for the national courts to examine whether the circumstances prevailing at the time of marketing made it objectively necessary to replace the original trademark by that of the importing Member State in order that the product in question could be placed on the market in that State by the parallel importer. This condition of necessity is satisfied if, in a specific case, the prohibition imposed on the importer against replacing the trademark hinders effective access to the markets of the importing Member State. That would be the case if the rules or practices in the importing Member State prevent the product in question from being marketed in that State under its trademark in the exporting Member State. This is so where a rule for the protection of consumers prohibits the use, in the importing Member State, of the trademark used in the exporting Member State on the ground that it is liable to mislead consumers. Grounds 44: 'In contrast, the condition of necessity will not be satisfied if replacement of the trademark is explicable solely by the parallel importer's attempt to secure a commercial advantage.')

rules forbid the use of the trademark of the export country and require a change, the importer may affix the legally uncontroversial mark of the import country.

(iv) Different Owners in Different Countries

Sometimes an identical mark is protected in different countries for different owners. This can happen because the owner of the mark in one country did not bother to protect it in the other country but a third party did, or the trademarks were originally owned by the same company but later expropriated as alien property[28] or simply sold to another company.[29] The question then arises whether the placement into commerce by one owner can be considered to be with the consent of the other.

Apart from the *Café Hag I* decision which the ECJ expressly admitted to be wrong in *Cafe Hag II*, the Court has held that actions by independently operating businesses owning identical trademarks in different countries cannot be mutually attributed to the other respective business. It follows that if the trademarks in the different countries are owned by truly independent businesses, their actions cannot be interpreted as resulting from the consent of the owner of the mark in the other country. Importation can be blocked.[30]

(v) Announcement Right

The announcement right is the right of a dealer or service provider to announce to the public which brands he sells or provides services under. To do this he also has the right to use protected trademarks.[31]

---

[28] Case 192/73, Van Zuylen Frères v. Hag AG, 1974 E.C.R. 731 (Hag I) and Case 10/89, SA CNL-Sucal N.V. v. Hag AG, 1990 E.C.R. I-3711 (Hag II). The trademarks in Germany and the Benelux countries originally belonged to Hag AG, Germany. The Benelux mark following WWI was confiscated and assigned to Van Zuylen. Though the trademark owners in both cases were totally independent companies the ECJ in Hag I decided that because of the common origin of the trademark import of German coffee into Benelux could not be stopped. In Hag II the Court expressly admitted that this was wrong and ruled that in the opposite situation because there was no consent the German trademark owner could stop Belgian coffee from being brought on the German market.

[29] Case C-9/93, IHT Internationale Heiztechnik GmbH v. Ideal-Standard GmbH, 1994 E.C.R. I-2789.

[30] *Id.*

[31] Case C-63/97, BMW Nederland BV v. Ronald Karel Deenik, 1999 E.C.R. I-905. There may be some dispute about the extent and form of the use. Does the

A question arose in the *Evora* case[32] whether an announcement by a discount store selling Dior perfumes could be forbidden as detrimental to the luxury image of the 'Dior' mark. The ECJ disagreed as long as Evora kept its advertisements and announcements to the style, format, etc. of the usual advertising practices of this kind of business.

(vi) Sale Without Strings Attached

Another question relating to consent was referred to the ECJ by the English High Court. Davidoff perfumes had been sold by the British owner of the trademark into a Southeast Asian country. From there they were to be re-imported into the EU. Since the sales contract did not forbid such re-imports, the English court explained that under English law this could be interpreted as tacitly allowing such re-imports. The ECJ was asked if such an interpretation would violate European law. The ECJ said it would.[33] Interpreting the contract to permit re-imports without any indication of intent to do so from the contract, would interfere with the rights of the European trademark owner by endangering his ability to stop imports of goods from countries outside the EEA. The principle of European-wide exhaustion to protect against third country imports would be undermined.

III. EXHAUSTION OF COPYRIGHTS IN EUROPE

Again, the same general rule of exhaustion for patents or trademarks also applies to goods incorporating copyrights. If those goods have been put into commerce by the copyright owner or with his consent in a member state of the EEA, importation into another member state cannot be stopped. There are, however, certain special aspects of copyright law which require mentioning.

---

retailer only have the right to use the mark in standard writing or can he also use logos and picture marks? The criterion is what is necessary to make an announcement work. This probably requires also the use of logos and picture marks but not for example, the copying of whole advertisements.

[32] Case C-337/95, Parfums Christian Dior SA v. Evora BV, 1997 E.C.R. I-6013.

[33] Joint cases C-414/99, C-415/99, C-416/99, Zino Davidoff SA v. A & G Imports Ltd., 2001 E.C.R. I-8691.

(i) Rental of Products

EU law provides (and requires national laws to similarly provide) that the rental right is not exhausted by putting a product incorporating a copyright, such as books, CDs, DVDs, on the market. The copyright owners, therefore, can extract a rental fee from commercial rental companies for such material.[34]

(ii) Goods or Services

It is well established that books, sound recordings and DVDs which have been put into commerce by the copyright owner or his licensee in one member state of the EEA can be freely imported into another member state.[35]

In the *Coditel I* case a similar but different question was posed.[36] A German TV station had aired the movie 'Le Boucher' under a German broadcasting license. A Belgian cable company received the signals of the German broadcast and distributed them to its Belgian customers. The Belgium broadcasting license was held by another company which brought suit against the Belgium cable company. The cable company argued that the signals had been distributed from Germany legally (with the consent of the copyright owner) and, therefore, under the exhaustion principle could be freely redistributed in Belgium. The ECJ disagreed. The case did not touch the freedom of movement of goods. Providing TV programs is a service and the exhaustion principle does not apply to services. Territorially restricted licenses of the copyright owner will hold. The cable company was at fault.

Recently this system of territorial licenses has been put under pressure by the ECJ in the *Premier League* decision.[37] It concerned the territorially

---

[34] Directive 2006/115/EC of the European Parliament and of the Council of 12 December 2006 on rental right and lending right and on certain rights related to copyright in the field of intellectual property.

[35] Case 78/70, Deutsche Grammophon Gesellschaft mbH v. Metro-SB-Großmärkte GmbH, 1971 E.C.R. 487.

[36] Case 62/79, Coditel v. Cine Vog Films, 1982 E.C.R. 881.

[37] Joint cases C-403/08, C-429/08, Football Association Premier League Ltd. v. QC Leisure, *see* http://curia.europa.eu/juris/fiche.jsf?id=C%3B403%3B8%3BRP%3B1%3BP%3B1%3BC2008%2F0403%2FJ&pro=&lgrec=en&nat=&oqp=&dates=&lg=&language=en&jur=C%2CT%2CF&cit=none%252CC%252CCJ%252CR%252C2008E%252C%252C%252C%252C%252C%252C%252C%252C%252C%252Ctrue%252Cfalse%252Cfalse&num=C-403%252F08&td=ALL&pcs=O&avg=&mat=or&jge=&for=&cid=2761232#.

restricted licenses for broadcasting soccer games. The Court, however, did not apply the exhaustion doctrine but based the decision on competition law which prohibits an absolute territorial protection for exclusive licensees.

(iii) Collecting Societies

Copyright law in Europe is still national law though it is widely but not completely harmonized by European Directives. A German copyright is valid in Germany, a French copyright in France, etc. There still is no EU-wide copyright.

Individual creators and authors of literary works, music, movies, pictures, etc. normally will not have the capacity to collect the license fees due to them by the thousands of users of their works. This is done by collecting societies to whom the authors have assigned their rights. In Europe these collecting societies work on a national basis and grant licenses for their respective territories. They are only beginning to form cooperation agreements with their foreign sister organizations to collect fees for the use of their members' works in other countries.

If a French collecting society grants a license to produce a sound recording, the license covers the French copyright. If this sound recording is legally placed on the French market, can it then be freely imported into Germany where the French producer has not bothered to buy a license to the German copyright from the German collecting society? The German collecting society for musical rights, GEMA, argued that since a license to the German copyright had not been acquired importation could be stopped. The German license fee would have to be paid. At the least, GEMA requested that the difference between the (lower) fee in France and the (higher) fee in Germany should be paid.

The ECJ decided against GEMA.[38] The right to distribute the tangible object incorporating the copyrighted works – the LP, CD or other sound recording – had been exhausted.[39]

---

[38] Joint cases 55/80, 57/80, Musik-Vertrieb membran GmbH v. GEMA, 1981 E.C.R. 147.

[39] The European Commission is suspicious about the current system of national collecting societies. Since most of them have a monopoly in their national market the Commission sees problems under EU competition law. For some time now the European Commission has been working on a new licensing system. Ideally it would enable the national collecting societies not only to grant licenses for their own territory but also for the territory of other member states thereby forcing them to compete for rights holders and licensees. For the activities of

(iv) Digital Distribution

Digital distribution of software, music, movies, etc. protected by copyright law poses another as yet unsolved problem for the exhaustion doctrine. The exhaustion doctrine was developed in a world where IP rights were incorporated in tangible objects like books, LPs, CDs, etc. Traditional distribution methods of selling those tangible objects led to the seller losing access to the work and at the same time the buyer gaining it. At any time there was but one owner of the object and one user. Exhaustion only applied to the right of further distribution of this tangible object, not the right to copy it and create a second tangible object.[40] This did not change even when simple methods of analog copying were introduced and used, such as photocopying and copying of cassette tapes, LPs and even video tapes.

The invention of digital copying and the possibility of distribution via the Internet, together with worldwide access by millions and millions of people, nearly unlimited storage space and negligible costs, have lifted copying of copyrighted works to a totally unforeseen level. At the same time, distribution methods change from analog exchange of tangible products to digital uploading and downloading. While it is still true that a tangible object such as a hard drive or a CD/DVD (and a computer) is needed to make the work stored in digital form perceptible to the human senses, digital distribution inevitably requires copying even if only on the hard drive of the receiving party and only temporarily. This means that a second copy is created for the buyer on his hard drive while the seller keeps his copy on his computer. Third and more copies can easily be produced at minimal costs.

How does the classic principle of exhaustion fit into this digital world? How must it be adjusted? These questions are even more complicated by the fact that digital distribution occurs in very different forms which may require different legal treatment. With the permission of the copyright owner, software may be downloaded by the buyer or it may be uploaded (automatically in the case of updates) by the seller; movies may be made available via streaming whereby at no time is the whole work (temporarily) stored on the computer or they may be downloaded entirely for repeated viewing; sound recordings may also be streamed or transferred

the Commission, *see* http://ec.europa.eu/internal_market/copyright/management/management_en.htm.

40 A limited right to make copies may be allowed under fair use principles but it is not the consequence of exhaustion.

completely with or without a license to make (a limited number of) copies, to play on one or more computers and on CD-players.

Many questions are open and hardly any are resolved under European law:

- Does streaming lead to exhaustion of distribution rights? Probably not since the work is stored on the hard drive only temporarily and never in its entirety. Creating a lasting copy would violate the contract. Streaming seems to be more akin to a rental than to a sale.
- Does the permission to download a work lead to the exhaustion of the re-distribution right? In strict application of the classical exhaustion doctrine, only if the tangible medium of the first copy (the hard drive) is sold and the seller does not keep a copy in his possession. Some may argue that the buyer can also make a copy on a CD for redistribution as long as he deletes the copy from his computer (which would create problems of control).
- Can software be legally bought and installed on a computer only be resold with the computer or the hard drive? After installing the software, may a CD with the software be sold freely even if the program is not deleted from the computer?

Only the future will show how the ECJ and the national courts will finally answer these questions. A first decision has been handed down by the ECJ on July 3, 2012[41] declaring that an author of a software cannot oppose the resale of his 'used' licences allowing the use of his programs downloaded from the internet. In effect this means that the copyright in the software distributed digitally under certain conditions has been exhausted.

---

41 UsedSoft GmbH v. Oracle International Corp. (Case 128/11), http://curia.europa.eu/juris/document/document.jsf?text=&docid=124564&doclang=en&mode=req

PART VII

Appendix

18. The patent laws of old

Mario Franzosi

The creation of a patent system was not a conception of modern cultures that were developing an industrial structure. Instead, it was a natural creation of societies interested in something new. Here the oldest documents are reproduced.

The laws are herein collected, but not the privileges. Privileges were granted in ancient times for new inventions, on an individual basis. They were numerous, especially in the Middle Age. A law, instead, assures a protection to everybody who satisfies certain conditions (in this case, one that has made an invention).

The first patent law was enacted in Sybaris, a city in the South of Italy, before the Roman domination; this area was called Magna Graecia. The law was mentioned by Atheneus, an ancient writer of various expressions on the culture of this area of the world. It is not clear when the law was enacted: surely before (and probably, shortly before) 506 B.C., when Sybaris was defeated and destroyed by the rival city Croton.

As it may be expected, the law fully harmonizes with the spirit of Sybaris, a city of luxury and research of pleasure, less interested (as the common opinion goes) in moral values. Thus, the law granted an exclusive right for a limited time to creators of new culinary recipes (or, as the translation goes, of 'original and elaborate dishes'). The purpose of the law was to promote the progress of culinary art science by securing, for a limited time, an exclusive right to the creators. A monopoly was a mean to encourage the research of new solutions in the area, such encouragement deriving from the exclusive right to exploit a creation and derive profits therefrom. We find these principles in modern systems.

This is the text of the passage of Atheneus, from the work *Depnosophistai* (the banquet of the savants); the document is derived from the text in the Biblioteca Marciana of Venice (Figure 18.1):

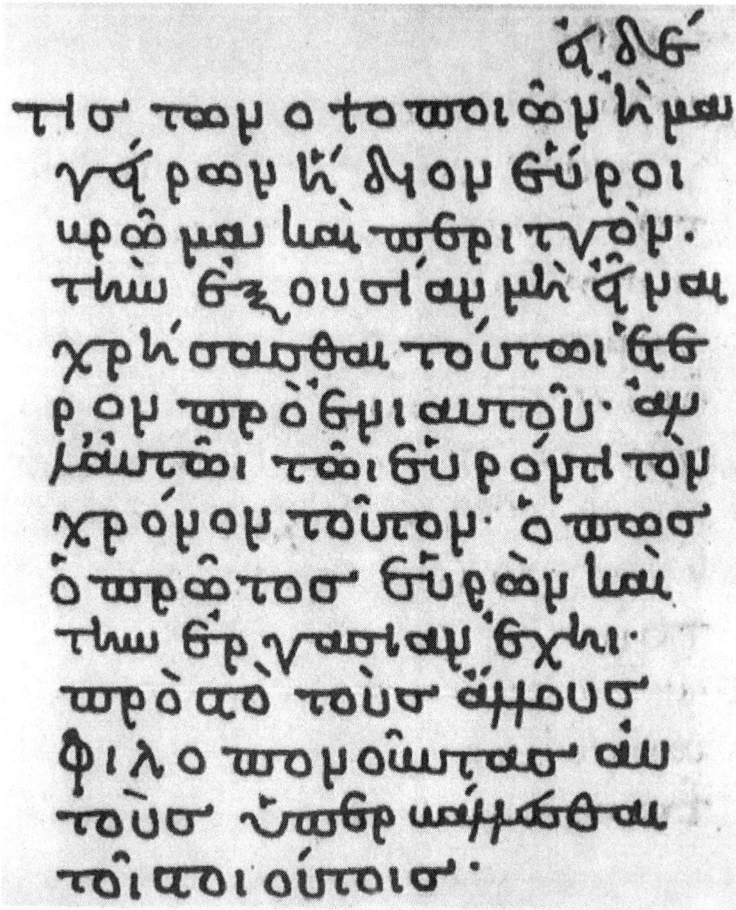
ἀ.δε
τις τῶν ὀψοποιῶν ἢ μα
γείρων ἴδιον εὕροι
βρῶμα καὶ περιττόν.
τὴν ἐξουσίαν μὴ ἄλλῳ
χρήσασθαι τούτῳ ἕτε
ρον πρὸ ἐνιαυτοῦ· ἀλ
λ' αὐτῷ τῷ εὑρόντι τὸν
χρόνον τοῦτον· ὅπως
ὁ πρῶτος εὑρὼν καὶ
τὴν ἐργασίαν ἔχῃ·
πρὸς τὸ τοὺς ἄλλους
φιλοπονοῦντας αὖ
τοὺς ὑπερβάλλεσθαι
τοῖς τοιούτοις·

Figure 18.1 The law of Sybaris, circa 510 B.C.

This is the translation:[1]

> *Where one of either the caterers or the cooks invents an original and elaborate dish, no one other than the inventor is allowed to use the recipe therefore, before a year has passed, such that the inventor has the exclusive right to derive a profit therefrom within the aforesaid period, and this in order for the others to make an effort and stand out for inventions in the same field.*

---

1 Gulick,Deipnosophistai of Atheneus, in Loeb Classical Library, London-Cambridge (Mass.) 1955, p. 348.

The passage of Atheneus was known to historians.[2] Among the jurists, probably the first to mention the law were Frunkin and Gomme; the present writer is simply a discoverer of discoverers.[3]

Some scholars have doubted that the passage of Atheneus corresponds to reality, and believe it may have been an invention of Atheneus.[4] There seems to be no reason to have any doubts.

For two thousand years, there has been no trace of any law for the protection of invention. Privileges were granted (on an individual basis) to new technology, new at least for the country where that title was granted. There are numerous traces of privileges granted, mostly from the 13th century on, in Venice, England, Florence, and France.[5]

---

2 Probably the first scholars that mention the law were **Casaubon**, *Ad Athenae*, I, XII, ch. 4, Lugduni 1621; **Leopardi** (1798–1837), *Zibaldone di Pensieri*, 4455; **Charles Anton**, *A Classical Dictionary, etc.*, 1841, 1273. See also **Cichorius**, in Jahrbuch fuer Nationaloekonomie, 1922, 46; **C. Faraggiana**, *Ateneo XII 521 C-D: Una antica legge sibaritica*, Aevum, 1987, 76.

3 **Frunkin**, *The Origin of Patents*, 27 JPOS 143 (1945); **Gomme**, *Patents for Invention*, London 1946, p. 4 ff; **Franzosi**, in Riv. Dir. Ind. 1965, I, 155; **Id.**, Studi Parmensi 1967, 329.

4 See **Chisum**, *Principles of Patent Law*, New York (NY), 2001, p.6; **Prager**, *Early Growth and Influence of Intellectual Property,* 34 JPOS 106 (1952).

5 Most frequently quoted are:

1100 (circa): The King of Jerusalem granted clothiers skilled in the art of dyeing the right to exclude others in exchange for an annual fee.

1323: privilege granted by Venice to Johannes Teuthonicus for a grain mill.

1324: privilege granted by Edward II (England) to skilled German miners.

1331: privilege granted to John Kempe of Flanders for building a clothing industry in England.

1332: privilege granted by Venice to constructors of windmills. It included a favorable loan for 12 years.

1409: privilege granted by Florence to Guerinus de Mera, to produce wool with the technology of Milan.

1416: privilege granted by Venice to Franciscus Petri for building and maintaining waterworks. It included a prohibition to all others to build waterworks within a 10 miles radius.

1421: privilege granted (for 3 years) by Florence to Filippo Brunelleschi for some type of machine or kind of transportation.

1449: privilege in England to John of Utynam for 20 years for glass manufacture. Possibly, the Venice state granted a similar privilege in 1450.

1460: privilege granted by Venice to Jacobus for a machine for raising water.

The first privilege mentioned in France is a 10 year exclusive monopoly granted in 1551 by the King Henry the Second to Abel Foullon. It is probably the first privilege that required a full description. The title was '*Usaige et Description de l' Holometre pour Scavoir Mesurer Toutes Choses qui sont soubs l' Estendue de l' Oeil.*'

The first American privilege was granted by the Colony of Massachusetts in 1641 to Samuel Winslow for a method of making salt.

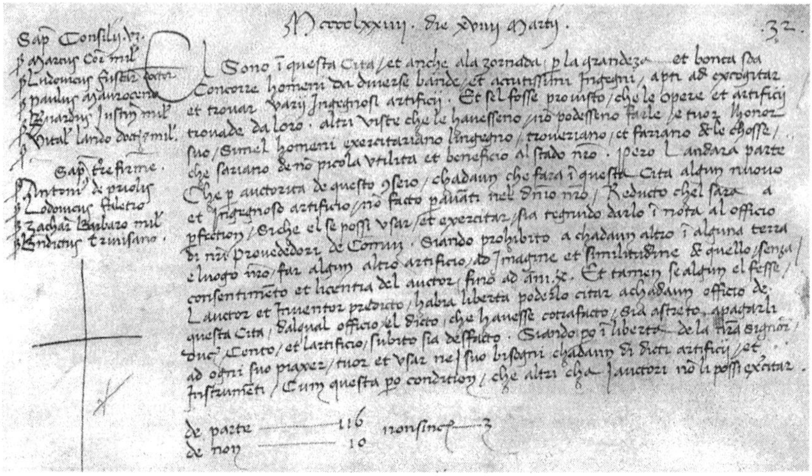

Figure 18.2 The law of Venice, 1474 A.D.

Those individual privileges were so numerous that the Byzantine emperor (with a seemingly anticipation of the English Statute of Monopolies) deemed it necessary to prohibit further granting of monopolies, and abolished the old.[6]

The first law that granted a monopoly for a long period of time (10 years) for improvements in all areas was the Venetian statute of 1474. Here is the original text (Figure 18.2):

In modern character it says:

MCCCCLXXIIII die XVIII Martij.

El Sono in questa cita, et anche ala zornada per la grandeza et bonta soa concorre homeni da diverse bande, et accutissimi Ingegni, apti ad excogitar et trouar varij Ingegnosi artificij. Et sel fosse prouisto, che le opere et artificij trouade da loro, altri viste che le hauesseno non podesseno farle, e tuor lhonor suo, simel homeni exercitariano lingegno, troueriano, et fariano dele chosse, che sariano de non picola vtilita et beneficio al stado nostro. Pero L andara parte Che per auctorita de questo Conseio, chadaun che fara in questa cita algun nuovo et ingegnoso artificio, non facto paruanti nel dominio nostro, Reducto chel sara a perfection, Siche el se possi vsar, et exercitar, sia tegnundo darlo in nota al officio di nostri Proueededori de Comun. Siando prohibito a chadaun altro in alguna terra e luogo nostro, far algun altro artificio, ad Imagine et similitudine de quello, senza consentimento et

[6] Emperor Zeno, 483 A.D. Only privileges already granted for clothing or foods were maintained.

licentia del auctor, fino ad anni X. Et tamen se algun el fesse, L auctor et Inventor predicto, habia liberta poderlo citar achadaun officio de questa Cita, dal qual officio, el dicto, che hauesse cotrafacto, sia astreto apagarli ducati Cento, et artificio, subito sia desfacto. Siando pero in liberta de la nostra Signoria, ad ogni suo piaxer, tuor et vsar ne i suo bisogni chadaun di dicti artificij, et Instrumenti, Cum questa pero condition, che altri cha i auctori non li possi exercitar.

And the translation into English:

MCCCCLXXIIII the 19th day of March.

There are in this city, and also there come temporarily by reason of its greatness and goodness, men from different places and most clever minds, capable of devising and inventing all manner of ingenious contrivances. And should it provided, that the works and contrivances invented by them, others having seen them could not make them and take their honor, men of such kind would exert their minds, invent and make things which would be of no small utility and benefit to our State. Therefore, decision will be passed that, by authority of this Council, each person who will make in this city any new and ingenious contrivance, not made heretofore in our dominion, as soon as it is reduced to perfection, so that it can be used and exercised, shall give notice of the same to the office of our Provisioners of Common. It being forbidden to any other in any territory and place of ours to make any contrivance in the form and resemblance thereof, without the consent and license of the author, and this for ten years. And if somebody does this, the said author and inventor will have the liberty to cite him before any office of this city, by which office the foresaid who shall infringe be forced to pay him the sum of one hundred ducates and the contrivance be immediately destroyed. Being then in liberty of our Government at his will to take and use in his need of said contrivances and instruments, with this condition, however, that no others than the authors shall exercise them.

The law was applied to a significant extent. More than 100 patents were granted in the following 80 years.

In 1623 a bill was presented to the English Parliament (the bill was passed and became a law on May 25, 1624). It declared that all monopolies, dispensations, and grants to compound penalties were void, with the exception of '*any manner of new manufacture,*' for which a right was given to the '*true and first inventor*'.

Here is (in part) the text of the Statute (21 Jac. 1, c. 3):

An Act concerning Monopolies and Dispensations with Penal Laws, and the Forfeitures thereof (z). [A.D. 1623]
Forasmuch as your most excellent majesty in your royal judgment, and of your blessed disposition to the zeal and quiet of your subjects, did in the year of our Lord God 1610 publish in print to the whole realm, and to all posterity, that all grants of monopolies, and of the benefit of any penal laws, or of power to dispense with the law, or to compound for the forfeiture, are contrary to your majesty's laws, which your majesty's declaration is truly consonant, and agreeable to the

ancient and fundamental laws of this your realm: and whereas your majesty was further graciously pleased expressly to command that no suitor should presume to move your majesty for matters of that nature; yet, nevertheless, upon misinformation and untrue pretences of public good many such grants have been unduly obtained and unlawfully put in execution, to the great grievance and inconvenience of your majesty's subjects, contrary to the laws of this your realm, and contrary to your majesty's royal and blessed intention, so published as aforesaid:" for avoiding whereof and preventing of the like in time to come, BE IT ENACTED, that all monopolies and all commissions, grants, licenses, charters, and letters patents heretofore made or granted, or hereafter to be made or granted to any person or persons, bodies politic or corporate whatsoever, of or for the sole buying, selling, making, working, or using of anything within this realm or the dominion of Wales, or of any other monopolies, or of power, liberty, or faculty, to dispense with and others, or to give licence or toleration to do, use, or exercise anything against the tenor or purport of any law or statute; or to give or make any warrant for any such dispensation, licence, or toleration to be had or made; or to agree or compound with any others for any penalty or forfeitures limited by any statute; or of any grant or promise of the benefit, profit, or commodity of any forfeiture, penalty, or sum of money that is or shall be due by any statute before judgment thereupon had; and all proclamations, inhibitions, restraints, warrants of assistance, and all other matters and things whatsoever, any way tending to the instituting, erecting, strengthening, furthering, or countenancing of the same, or any of them, are altogether contrary to the laws of this realm, and so are and shall be utterly void and of none effect, and in no wise to be put in ure or execution. 2. And all monopolies, and all such commissions, grants, licences, charters, letters patents, proclamations, inhibitions, restraints, warrants of assistance, and all other matters and things tending as aforesaid, and the force and validity of them, and every of them, ought to be, and shall be for ever hereafter examined, heard, tried, and determined, by and according to the common laws of this realm, and not otherwise. (omissis)[7]

---

7 . Here are the 3rd, 4th and 5th provisions:

'*3. And all person and persons, bodies politic and corporate whatsoever, which now are or hereafter shall be, shall stand and be disabled, and uncapable to have, use, exercise, or put in ure any monopoly, or any such commission, grant, license, charter, letters patents, proclamation, inhibition, restraint, warrant of assistance, or other matter or thing tending as aforesaid, or any liberty, power, or faculty grounded or pretended to be grounded upon them, or any of them. 4. And if any person or persons at any time after the end of forty days next after the end of this present session of parliament shall be hindered, grieved, disturbed, or disquieted, or his or their goods or chattels any way seized, attached, distrained, taken, carried away, or detained by occasion or pretext of any monopoly, or of any such commission, grant, license, power, liberty, faculty, letters patents, proclamation, inhibition, restraint, warrant of assistance, or other matter or thing tending as aforesaid, and will sue to be relieved in or for any of the premises, that then and in every such case the same person and persons shall and may have his and their remedy for the same at the common law by any action or actions to be grounded upon this statute; the same action and actions to be heard and determined in the courts of king's bench, common pleas, and exchequer, or in any of them, against him or them by whom he or they shall be so hindered,*

6 (a). Provided also, that any declaration before mentioned shall not extend to any letters patents (b) and grants of privilege for the term of fourteen years or under, hereafter to be made, of the sole working or making of any manner of new manufactures within this realm (c) to the true and first inventor (d) and inventors of such manufactures, which others at the time of making such letters patents and grants shall not use (e), so as also they be not contrary to the law nor mischievous to the state by raising prices of commodities at home, or hurt of trade, or generally inconvenient (f):the same fourteen years to be accounted from the date of the first letters patents or grant of such privilege hereafter to be made, but that the same shall be of such force as they should be if this act had never been made, and of none other (g).(omissis)[8]

---

grieved, disturbed, or disquieted, or against him or them by whom his or their goods or chattels shall be so seized, attached, distrained, taken, carried away, or detained; wherein all and every such person and persons which shall be so hindered, grieved, disturbed, or disquieted, or whose goods or chattels shall be so seized, attached, distrained, taken, or carried away, or detained, shall recover three times so much as the damages which he or they sustained by means or occasion of being so hindered, grieved, disturbed, or disquieted, or by means of having his or their goods or chattels seized, attached, distrained, taken, carried away, or detained, and double costs: and in such suits or for the staying or delaying thereof, no essoign, protection, wager of law, aid, prayer, privilege, injunction, or order of restraint, shall be in any wise prayed, granted, admitted, or allowed, nor any more than one imparlance: and if any person or persons shall after notice given that the action depending is grounded upon this statute, cause or procure any action at the common law grounded upon this statute to be stayed or delayed before judgment by colour or means of any order, warrant, power, or authority, save only of the court wherein such action as aforesaid shall be brought and depending, or after judgment had upon such action shall cause or procure the execution of or upon any such judgment to be stayed or delayed by colour or means of any order, warrant, power, or authority, save only by writ of error or attaint, then the said person and persons so offending shall incur and sustain the pains, penalties, and forfeitures ordained and provided by the statute of provision and praemunire made in the sixteenth year of the reign of king Richard the second.'

8 Here are the other provisions:

'7. Provided also, that this act or anything therein contained shall not in any wise extend or be prejudicial to any grant or privilege, power, or authority whatsoever heretofore made, granted, allowed, or confirmed by any act of parliament now in force, so long as the same shall so continue in force. 8. Provided also, that this act shall not extend to any warrant or privy seal made or directed, or to be made or directed by his majesty, his heirs or successors, to the justices of the courts of the king's bench or common pleas, and barons of the exchequor, justices of assize, justices of oyer and terminer and gaol delivery, justices of the peace, and other justices for the time being, having power to hear and determine offences done against any penal statute, to compound for the forfeitures of any penal statute depending in suit and question before them, or any of them respectively, after plea pleaded by the party defendant. 9. Provided also, that this act or anything therein contained shall not in any wise extend or be prejudicial unto the city of London, or to any city, borough, or town corporate within this realm, for or concerning any grants, charters, or letters patent to them, or any of them made or granted,

Figure 18.3 The first American patent

No other law was issued for more than 160 years. Then the United States issued the law of April 10, 1790. A copy of the original document is not included here; the text of the law can be found on the First Congress, Sess. II. Ch. 7, 1790.

The first patent was granted on July 31, 1790 to Samuel Hopkins, for '*Making Pot ash and Pearl ash*'. This is the original document (Figure 18.3):

Also France adopted a law shortly after the French Revolution. It was a law issued in the name of Louis XVI: *Loi du 7 janvier 1791, sur la propriété des Auteurs d' inventions et découvertes en tout genre d' industrie.*[9] The law follows (Figure 18.4):

---

or for or concerning any custom or customs used by or within them or any of them; or unto any corporations, companies, or fellowships of any art, trade, occupation, or mystery, or to any companies, or societies of merchants within this realm erected for the maintenance, enlargement, or ordering of any trade or merchandise; but that the same charters, customs, corporations, companies, fellowships, and societies, and their liberties, privileges, powers, and immunities, shall be and continue of such force and effect as they were before the making of this act, and of none other; anything before in this act not contained to the contrary in any wise notwithstanding.'

9 One of the last acts of the king, who was later suspended and then executed.

L O I

Relative aux Découvertes utiles, & aux moyens d'en aſſurer la propriété à ceux qui ſeront reconnus en être les Auteurs.

Donnée à Paris, le 7 Janvier 1791.

LOUIS, par la grâce de Dieu, & par la Loi conſtitutionnelle de l'État, ROI DES FRANÇOIS: A tous préſens & à venir; SALUT.

L'ASSEMBLÉE NATIONALE a décrété, & Nous voulons & ordonnons ce qui ſuit:

DÉCRET DE L'ASSEMBLÉE NATIONALE, du 31 Décembre 1790.

L'ASSEMBLÉE NATIONALE, conſidérant que toute idée nouvelle, dont la manifeſtation ou le développement peut devenir utile à la ſociété, appartient primitivement à celui qui l'a conçue, & que ce ſeroit attaquer les *droits de l'homme* dans leur eſſence, que de ne pas regarder *une découverte induſtrielle* comme la propriété de ſon auteur; conſidérant en même temps combien le défaut d'une déclaration poſitive & authentique de cette vérité, peut avoir contribué, juſqu'à préſent, à décourager l'induſtrie françoiſe,

Figure 18.4 The French law of 1791

en occasionnant l'émigration de plusieurs artistes distingués, & en faisant passer à l'étranger un grand nombre d'inventions nouvelles, dont cet Empire auroit dû tirer les premiers avantages; considérant enfin que tous les principes de justice, d'ordre public & d'intérêt national, lui commandent impérieusement de fixer désormais l'opinion des Citoyens françois sur ce genre de propriété, par une Loi qui la consacre & qui la protège, décrète ce qui suit:

ARTICLE PREMIER.

Toute découverte ou nouvelle invention, dans tous les genres d'industrie, est la propriété de son auteur; en conséquence, la Loi lui en garantit la pleine & entière jouissance, suivant le mode & pour le temps qui seront ci-après déterminés.

II.

Tout moyen d'ajouter à quelque fabrication que ce puisse être, un nouveau genre de perfection, sera regardé comme une invention.

III.

Quiconque apportera le premier en France une découverte étrangère, jouira des mêmes avantages que s'il en étoit l'inventeur.

IV.

Celui qui voudra conserver ou s'assurer une propriété industrielle du genre de celles énoncées aux précédens articles, sera tenu:

1.° De s'adresser au secrétariat du Directoire de son

Figure 18.4 (continued)

Département, & d'y déclarer par écrit ſi l'objet qu'il préſente eſt d'invention, de perfection ou ſeulement d'importation.

2.° De dépoſer ſous cachet une deſcription exacte des principes, moyens & procédés qui conſtituent la découverte, ainſi que les plans, coupes, deſſins & modèles qui pourroient y être relatifs, pour, ledit paquet, être ouvert au moment où l'inventeur recevra ſon titre de propriété.

V.

Quant aux objets d'une utilité générale, mais d'une exécution trop ſimple & d'une imitation trop facile, pour établir aucune ſpéculation commerciale, & dans tous les cas, lorſque l'Inventeur aimera mieux traiter directement avec le Gouvernement, il lui ſera libre de s'adreſſer, ſoit aux Aſſemblées adminiſtratives, ſoit au Corps légiſlatif, s'il y a lieu, pour confier ſa découverte, en démontrer les avantages & ſolliciter une récompenſe.

V I.

Lorſqu'un inventeur aura préféré aux avantages perſonnels aſſurés par la Loi, l'honneur de faire jouir ſur le champ la Nation des fruits de ſa découverte ou invention, & lorſqu'il prouvera par la notoriété publique, & par des atteſtations légales que cette découverte ou invention eſt d'une véritable utilité, il pourra lui être accordé une récompenſe ſur les fonds deſtinés aux encouragemens de l'induſtrie.

V I I.

Afin d'aſſurer à tout inventeur la propriété & la jouiſſance temporaire de ſon invention, il lui ſera délivré un *titre* ou *patente*, ſelon la forme indiquée dans le règlement qui ſera dreſſé pour l'exécution du préſent Décret.

Figure 18.4 (continued)

The last law, the most recent, the most needed, the most aspired to, at least in Europe, would be a European Regulation or Treaty, establishing a truly European cross-border jurisdiction. However said law, though badly needed, is still missing. The European legislators are hesitant. There is a lot of criticism for this lack of action, but from a human point of view, the prudence of the rulers is well understandable. Shortly after the enactment of the law of Sybaris, the city was destroyed; and shortly after the enactment of the French law, King Louis XVI lost his head (in a literal, real sense). Perhaps the European legislators are afraid that by issuing the law they would also lose their heads (or perhaps they had lost them already?).

Index